Global Law

The Library of Essays in Global Governance

Titles in the Series:

Global Health
John J. Kirton

Global Law
John J. Kirton with Jelena Madunic

Global Trade
John J. Kirton

International Finance
John J. Kirton

International Organization
John J. Kirton

Global Law

Edited by

John J. Kirton with Jelena Madunic

University of Toronto, Canada

Routledge
Taylor & Francis Group
LONDON AND NEW YORK

First published 2009 by Ashgate Publishing

2 Park Square, Milton Park, Abingdon, Oxfordshire OX14 4RN
711 Third Avenue, New York, NY 10017

Routledge is an imprint of the Taylor & Francis Group, an informa business

First issued in paperback 2018

British Library Cataloguing in Publication Data
Global law. – (The library of essays in
global governance)
1. International Law
I. Kirton, John J. II. Madunic, Jelena
341

Library of Congress Control Number: 2008924495

ISBN 978-0-7546-2662-6 (hbk)
ISBN 978-1-138-37842-1 (pbk)

Contents

Acknowledgements vii
Editor's Preface ix
Introduction xi

PART I THE SOURCES AND DEVELOPMENT OF INTERNATIONAL LAW

1 Hans J. Morgenthau (1940), 'Positivism, Functionalism, and International Law', *American Journal of International Law*, **34**, pp. 260–84. 3
2 Philip C. Jessup (1947), 'The Subjects of a Modern Law of Nations', *Michigan Law Review*, **45**, pp. 383–408. 29
3 H. Lauterpacht (1955), 'Codification and Development of International Law', *American Journal of International Law*, **49**, pp. 16–43. 55
4 Richard A. Falk (1967), 'New Approaches to the Study of International Law', *American Journal of International Law*, **61**, pp. 477–95. 83
5 Myres S. McDougal and W. Michael Reisman (1980), 'The Prescribing Function in World Constitutive Process: How International Law is Made', *Yale Studies in World Public Order*, **6**, pp. 249–84. 103
6 Ian Brownlie (1981), 'The Reality and Efficacy of International Law', *British Yearbook of International Law*, **52**, pp. 1–8. 139
7 John H. Jackson (1998), 'Global Economics and International Economic Law', *Journal of International Economic Law*, **1**, pp. 1–23. 147

PART II COMPETING THEORIES OF INTERNATIONAL LAW

8 William D. Coplin (1965), 'International Law and Assumptions about the State System', *World Politics*, **17**, pp. 615–34. 173
9 Robert O. Keohane (1997), 'International Relations and International Law: Two Optics', *Harvard International Law Journal*, **38**, pp. 487–502. 193
10 Christoph Schreuer (1993), 'The Waning of the Sovereign State: Towards a New Paradigm for International Law?', *European Journal of International Law*, **4**, pp. 447–71. 209
11 Kenneth W. Abbott, Robert O. Keohane, Andrew Moravcsik, Anne-Marie Slaughter and Duncan Snidal (2000), 'The Concept of Legalization', *International Organization*, **54**, pp. 401–19. 235

PART III HARD LAW, SOFT LAW, LEGALIZATION AND NORMS

12 Kenneth W. Abbott and Duncan Snidal (2000), 'Hard and Soft Law in International Governance', *International Organization*, **54**, pp. 421–56. 257

13 Martha Finnemore and Stephen J. Toope (2001), 'Alternatives to "Legalization": Richer Views of Law and Politics', *International Organization*, **55**, pp. 743–58. 293
14 Judith Goldstein and Lisa L. Martin (2000), 'Legalization, Trade Liberalization, and Domestic Politics: A Cautionary Note', *International Organization*, **54**, pp. 603–32. 309
15 Benedict Kingsbury (1998), 'Sovereignty and Inequality', *European Journal of International Law*, **9**, pp. 599–625. 339
16 Walter Mattli (2001), 'Private Justice in a Global Economy: From Litigation to Arbitration', *International Organization*, **55**, pp. 919– 47. 367

PART IV DOES INTERNATIONAL LAW MATTER? COMPLIANCE, LEGITIMACY AND ACCOUNTABILITY

17 Abram Chayes and Antonia Handler Chayes (1993), 'On Compliance', *International Organization*, **47**, pp. 175–205. 399
18 Andrew P. Cortell and James W. Davis, Jr (1996) 'How do International Institutions Matter? The Domestic Impact of International Rules and Norms', *International Studies Quarterly*, **40**, pp. 451–78. 431
19 Thomas M. Franck (2006) 'The Power of Legitimacy and the Legitimacy of Power: International Law in an Age of Power Disequilibrium', *American Journal of International Law*, **100**, pp. 88–106. 459

PART V THE LAWS OF WAR AND FORCE

20 Richard Falk (1996), 'The Complexities of Humanitarian Intervention: A New World Order Challenge', *Michigan Journal of International Law*, **17**, pp. 491–513. 481
21 Thomas M. Franck (2003), 'The Use of Force in International Law', *Tulane Journal of International and Comparative Law*, **11**, pp. 7–19. 505

Name Index 519

Acknowledgements

The editors and publishers wish to thank the following for permission to use copyright material.

Ian Brownlie (1981), 'The Reality and Efficacy of International Law', *British Yearbook of International Law*, **52**, pp. 1–8. Copyright © 1981 Ian Brownlie.

Copyright Clearance Center for the essays: Hans J. Morgenthau (1940), 'Positivism, Functionalism, and International Law', *American Journal of International Law*, **34**, pp. 260–84; H. Lauterpacht (1955), 'Codification and Development of International Law', *American Journal of International Law*, **49**, pp. 16–43; Richard A. Falk (1967), 'New Approaches to the Study of International Law', *American Journal of International Law*, **61**, pp. 477–95; Thomas M. Franck (2006) 'The Power of Legitimacy and the Legitimacy of Power: International Law in an Age of Power Disequilibrium', *American Journal of International Law*, **100**, pp. 88–106.

European Journal of International Law for the essay: Benedict Kingsbury (1998), 'Sovereignty and Inequality', *European Journal of International Law*, **9**, pp. 599–625.

Harvard International Law Journal for the essay: Robert O. Keohane (1997), 'International Relations and International Law: Two Optics', *Harvard International Law Journal*, **38**, pp. 487–502. Copyright © 1997 The President and Fellows of Harvard College and the Harvard International Law Journal.

Johns Hopkins University Press for the essay: William D. Coplin (1965), 'International Law and Assumptions about the State System', *World Politics*, **17**, pp. 615–34. Copyright © 1965 The Johns Hopkins University Press.

Michigan Journal of International Law for the essay: Richard Falk (1996), 'The Complexities of Humanitarian Intervention: A New World Order Challenge', *Michigan Journal of International Law*, **17**, pp. 491–513

MIT Press for the essays: Kenneth W. Abbott, Robert O. Keohane, Andrew Moravcsik, Anne-Marie Slaughter and Duncan Snidal (2000), 'The Concept of Legalization', *International Organization*, **54**, pp. 401–19. Copyright © 2000 The IO Foundation and the Massachusetts Institute of Technology; Kenneth W. Abbott and Duncan Snidal (2000), 'Hard and Soft Law in International Governance', *International Organization*, **54**, pp. 421–56. Copyright © 2000 The IO Foundation and the Massachusetts Institute of Technology; Martha Finnemore and Stephen J. Toope (2001), 'Alternatives to "Legalization": Richer Views of Law and Politics', *International Organization*, **55**, pp. 743–58. Copyright © 2001 The IO Foundation and the Massachusetts Institute of Technology; Judith Goldstein and Lisa L. Martin (2000), 'Legalization, Trade Liberalization, and Domestic Politics: A Cautionary Note', *International*

Organization, **54**, pp. 603–32. Copyright © 2000 The IO Foundation and the Massachusetts Institute of Technology; Walter Mattli (2001), 'Private Justice in a Global Economy: From Litigation to Arbitration', *International Organization*, **55**, pp. 919–47. Copyright © 2001 The IO Foundation and the Massachusetts Institute of Technology; Abram Chayes and Antonia Handler Chayes (1993), 'On Compliance', *International Organization*, **47**, pp. 175–205. Copyright © 1993 World Peace Foundation and the Massachusetts Institute of Technology.

Oxford University Press for the essays: John H. Jackson (1998), 'Global Economics and International Economic Law', *Journal of International Economic Law*, **1**, pp. 1–23; Christoph Schreuer (1993), 'The Waning of the Sovereign State: Towards a New Paradigm for International Law?', *European Journal of International Law*, **4**, pp. 447–71.

Yale Journal of International Law for the essay: Myres S. McDougal and W. Michael Reisman (1980), 'The Prescribing Function in World Constitutive Process: How International Law is Made', *Yale Studies in World Public Order*, **6**, pp. 249–84.

Every effort has been made to trace all the copyright holders, but if any have been inadvertently overlooked the publishers will be pleased to make the necessary arrangement at the first opportunity.

Editor's Preface

This volume on global law is one of five works prepared for the International Library series on global governance in the major fields of international relations today. As with the other volumes, it assembles in one easily accessible collection the most important essays that have shaped scholarship in the field in the post-Second World War years.

Scholarship in global law has been significantly driven by theory, research, reviews, commentaries and summaries of case practice published in books, edited volumes, research reports, working papers from research institutions, reports from national governments and international organizations, court records and, increasingly, from pieces made available directly on the Internet. However this collection contains only those works published in scholarly journals, above all in those peer-reviewed, English-language journals that stand at the centre of the respective disciplines that make up the field. The focal point is those essays that have defined and driven the debates, theories and research in political science, while recognizing that there is a great diversity of important scholarship within this discipline and the many subfields and approaches which now make it up. Moreover, this collection, as with the field of international law in political science and international relations, also draws from a rich interdisciplinary inheritance, starting with works from international law and economics. Indeed, many political science courses in international law are taught by colleagues from law schools, and taken by students envisaging further study in law schools. Moreover, important political science research projects are undertaken in collaboration with colleagues in law. Hence this collection relies substantially on essays produced by international legal scholars for international legal scholars and practitioners, which have also been of central value to political scientists teaching, studying and researching global law.

Selecting the most important pieces of enduring value from this rich inheritance required a systematic review comprising several stages. The first was to compile a list of the classic essays most used in reading lists in relevant courses as I encountered them from my undergraduate through graduate school years, to my own courses taught over a period of 30 years at the University of Toronto from the sophomore to the Ph.D. level in international relations and global governance. The second step was to check this list against the essays most cited and used in the major textbooks and monographs on international law and international organization and relations. The third step was to undertake a thorough review of the major journals in the field and in the discipline and field more generally to ensure that key works were not overlooked and to see which had endured as the most referenced and referred to over many years. The fourth step was to check several composite indexes and databases to identify the works most cited by scholars today. The fifth and final step was to send the resulting list out to several trusted colleagues who are experts in the international law field, asking them to confirm the selections or adjust them with additions or deletions they might propose.

Even with these procedures, I was left with far too many attractive, indeed compelling, candidates than the 500-page limit for this book allowed. A little relief came from sending pieces that deserved inclusion here for inclusion in the parallel volumes I was producing on

Global Trade, International Finance, International Organization and Global Health, and for companion volumes others were producing for Ashgate's International Library series. Another was to set aside those essays that reviewed together several key books in the field, despite their value as an overview of the state of the field at a given time. Further exclusions arose at the margins as I adjusted the table of contents to provide as comprehensive and balanced a treatment of the overall field as I could. Finally, many strong candidates had to be excluded due to the need to focus on the works of most value to political scientists, especially those written by political scientists and published in political science journals, even while fully cognisant of the enormous contribution made by international lawyers from many traditions since the very start of the field. The excluded pieces with the strongest claim have been noted, and where possible highlighted, in the Introduction to this volume.

In preparing this volume, I have been assisted by several individuals whose contribution I gratefully acknowledge here. I am indebted to Kirstin Howgate at Ashgate, who first proposed this project, and to Dymphna Evans for her support in my decision to go ahead. I acknowledge the important role of Madeline Koch, Managing Director of the G8 Research Group, in securing essays and providing editorial assistance, and of Laura Sunderland, Senior Researcher of the G8 Research Group, in scanning journals and books, obtaining the candidate essays and otherwise helping me assess and select them. I was most fortunate to have, from the start, the help of Jelena Madunic, an outstanding individual from the University of Toronto's Law School, whose immense contribution makes it proper, and me proud, to include her as my collaborator in this work.

I acknowledge with particular pleasure the intellectual contribution of Professors Harriet Friedmann and Rima Berns-McGown, with whom I have taught a graduate seminar on 'International Governance' at the University of Toronto for many years, and our many exceptional students in that class, particularly those from our joint programme in international relations and law who forced us to forge the link between the two communities every week. I thank my scholarly colleagues from law schools on the 'EnviReform' project that I recently directed: Julie Soloway, Chris Tollefson and Michael Trebilcock. I appreciate the inspiration of two leading international lawyers turned policy practitioners, Alan Gotlieb and William Graham. I am above all particularly grateful to my career-long colleague and friend Alan Alexandroff for his responding to my request to review my preliminary list with many thoughtful and valuable suggestions, which I have done my best to incorporate in this final version of the work. Any shortcomings in this book remain, of course, entirely my own.

In conclusion, I owe more than I can express to two individual lawyers who have guided me over the past two decades into and through the challenges of putting one's scholarly discipline as a political scientist to work in the policy and political world. Pierre Marc Johnson and Sarah Richardson have been my close and cherished companions as we worked together to identify how trade could be linked with the environment to mutual advantage in North America and elsewhere, and how global law, soft and hard, could be used to generate more ecologically sustainable global governance everywhere. It is to Pierre Marc and Sarah that I dedicate this book.

JOHN J. KIRTON
University of Toronto, Canada

Introduction

Scholars of international relations exploring cooperation among states often focus their work on international regimes, commonly defined as 'sets of implicit or explicit principles, norms, rules and decision-making procedures around which actors' expectations converge in a given issue area of international politics' (Krasner, 1982, p. 186; also 1983; see also Ruggie, 1983; Young, 1991). Global law, and the customs and treaties of which it is composed, are thus central to this work. For international law addresses the implicit and explicit character of international regimes, the principles, norms and rules at their heart, and the question of whether they make a difference in adjusting the expectations, and thus behaviour, of those party or subject to them.

Since its inception, these elements have served as the subjects and structure of the defining debates in the field of global law. Does international law arise, exist and take effect principally as implicit assumptions and practices that are retroactively recognized and recorded by all observers? Does it flow from principles deduced from a higher religious or 'natural' order? Does it emerge primarily as explicit, written agreements negotiated *ex ante* and accepted as legitimate by those states that created them and whose behaviour they are designed to bind? Does international law primarily consist of, and exert its effects from general principles identifying fact, causation and rectitude, from norms prescribing and proscribing behaviour, or, as in a country's domestic setting of authority, from specific rules presented with considerable precision, obligation and delegation, including procedures and penalties for non-compliance? Does it apply directly only to those states party to it, or to their intergovernmental organizations, sub-federal governments, or civil society actors and individual citizens inside? And how much and how does international law make a difference to state, non-state and individual actors' assumptions, expectations, calculations and behaviour? Does it bring these various actors in global governance towards a single standard or practice, producing cooperation, dampening and preventing conflict and promoting the well-being of the global community as a whole? Most broadly, what are international law's sources, subjects and future in a rapidly changing world?

Over the decades, scholars of international politics from competing theoretical traditions have offered dramatically different answers to these core questions, even as virtually all acknowledged the importance of international law to their field. As that field developed during the Second World War, the pioneering international legal scholar turned realist political scientist Hans Morgenthau, following a tradition dating back to E.H. Carr (1939) and Niccolò Machiavelli (1988 [1515]), warned in his classic *Politics Among Nations* (1948) against the idealist illusion of a reliance on an international law that would largely prove to be ineffective in practice and thus dangerous for those who trusted it. Subsequently, the eminent American legal scholars Grenville Clark and Louis Sohn responded in *World Peace through World Law* (1958) by designing a more robust United Nations Charter to bring peace to otherwise war-prone states. In doing so they followed an 'idealist tradition' stretching back to philosopher Immanuel Kant (1970, 1996 [1795]) and scholar-turned statesman Woodrow Wilson (1984

[1918]). In his classic work *Toward Perpetual Peace* Kant had argued in 1795 that world peace was only possible through the formation of an international legal order, in which states, internally organized around republican principles, would create an explicit regime of cosmopolitan law and institutionalize it in a voluntary 'league of nations' without coercive powers, which would respect the human rights of individuals as 'citizens of the earth' at home and abroad (Kant, 1996 [1975]). From the English school, the legendary Hedley Bull argued in *The Anarchical Society* (1977) that while sovereign states existed in a world of anarchy without an overarching centre of authority, they also lived in a society with common institutions and rules, where international law and its principles played an important role (see also Bull, 1966). Since then this debate has flourished, as has the scholarship behind it in both its theoretical and empirical domains (O'Neal and Russett, 1999; Doyle, 1983).

This debate and its development form the focus of this volume. This work is based on a careful selection of the classic and contemporary journal essays of enduring value that are and will be central to the scholarship on global law now and in the years ahead. The selections are those essential to the work of political scientists specializing in the discipline's subfield of international law. They are also important for scholars and practitioners from the disciplines of law, economics, human rights and environmental studies, and all seeking to understand and use the instrument of international law to advance their policy and normative concerns. This volume provides a conveniently accessible collection of those essays that constitute the core of the field, define its classic and contemporary debates, and guide today's scholarly research and policy debates. It places the selected essays in the context of evolving debates and real-world developments, and highlights their distinctive contributions to the field. Beyond that, it lets them speak for themselves, without adding any independent critique of their content. The selection has been guided not by any particular philosophy or approach to the field, but by a desire for comprehensiveness and balance across successive generations of scholars from the post-Second World War era and from liberal institutionalists, constructivists, realists, political economy theorists and proponents of newer theoretical traditions. An emphasis has been placed on contributions dealing with core concepts of comprehensive application and of cumulative, continuing relevance in defining the research and debates of today, together with essays that have helped pioneer new areas of study of the richly textured, complex and constantly evolving field of global law.

The Sources and Development of International Law

This collection starts with the foundational questions of what international law is, where it came from and how it has developed over time. International legal scholars and practitioners trace the concept of international law back over many millennia, to the historical and juristic writing of ancient Greece and ancient Rome. However, they commonly consider Hugo Grotius's 1625 treatise *De Jure Belli ac Pacis* to mark the birth of international law as understood and practised today (Grotius, 1970). This treatise, along with the works of other eminent scholars of the seventeenth and eighteenth centuries such as Francisco Suarez (1612), Samuel Pufendorf (1729 [1672]) and Emerich de Vattel (1916 [1758]), served as the foundation for the development of international law (Bull, 1966). These legal scholars were the first to articulate a comprehensive vision of international law by identifying its sources, detailing its content and articulating its normative framework. In particular, the Grotian tradition, resting on natural law foundations, human rationality and the principle of *pacta sunt servanda* (agreements must be respected), gave way to the development of legal positivism which moved from the deduced, implicit, spontaneous and customary to more explicit, negotiated and codified international law (Murphy, 1982; Charney, 1993).

Scholars of international politics also start around the time of Grotius with the 1648 Treaties of Westphalia that gave rise to the modern state system in which political units claim exclusive sovereign authority over a defined territory and its people, while interacting with other such states in a world where no higher, common, single centre of legitimate authority exists. The Treaties of Westphalia codified an end to the European wars of religion and established the fundamental principles which underpin international law to this day: the sovereign equality of states, external recognition, non-intervention in internal affairs, the right to self-determination and of self-defence when attacked. The ensuing centuries saw the cumulative codification of customary international law, negotiated treaties and intergovernmental institutions to embed them (Oppenheim, 1912). The world wars of the twentieth century highlighted the need to establish international political and juridical forums to develop, legitimize, arbitrate and apply international law. This led to the establishment of the League of Nations and the Permanent Court of International Justice. The latter became the International Court of Justice (ICJ) in 1945 when the United Nations (UN) was born. The UN, its specialized agencies and its sister Bretton Woods bodies – the International Monetary Fund and World Bank formed in 1944 – produced the twentieth century's most significant international legal documents (Higgins, 1963). These include the UN Charter itself, the Universal Declaration of Human Rights, the Economic and Social Covenant, the Geneva Conventions, the Convention on the Law of the Sea and, in 2005, the principle of the international responsibility to protect. The growth of such instruments continued throughout the unpromising years of the long Cold War (McWhinney, 1963).

Part I begins at the very dawn of this post-war order, when scholars started seriously to consider whether the pre-war edifice was a sound foundation on which international law could and should be built in the years ahead. In Chapter 1, 'Positivism, Functionalism, and International Law' (1940), Hans Morgenthau himself boldly claims: 'All the schemes and devices by which great humanitarians and shrewd politicians endeavored to reorganize the relations between states on the basis of law, have not stood the trial of history' (p. 3). He proceeds to offer a critique of the prevailing positivist approach to international law and to develop an alternative functional theory to fulfil the basic scientific task of knowing what is and why it is so, rather than normatively and idealistically inquiring about what ought to be. He concludes that this scientific, functional approach 'will also prepare the ground for satisfying the greater ethical and political desire to improve international relations by means of the law' (p. 27).

Phillip Jessup, inspired by Kant's normative and prescriptive insights, in Chapter 2, 'The Subjects of a Modern Law of Nations' (1947), argues in contrast that individuals as well as states have now become the subjects of international laws and treaties. He does, however, acknowledge that their rights and duties are unequal in a still state-centred world. He concludes that an international government will be necessary to ensure the ultimate function of law – the elimination of force.

In Chapter 3, 'Codification and Development of International Law' (1955), Hersch Lauterpacht surveys the problems, products and prospects of the codification of international law based on the first five years of the work of the UN's International Law Commission, unfolding amid the chill of the Cold War. He acknowledges that the political climate has not been conducive to realizing the Charter's charge to study, recommend and encourage 'the progressive development of international law and its codification'. But he affirms the imperative importance of the task, and argues that it involves bringing about an agreed set of rules to develop and improve the law, rather than just imparting systematic precision to existing rules. It extends to inducing governments to accept new law. It is thus inherently a political process, to be undertaken through the UN, independent of governments, but assisted by private efforts. Above all, it must be driven by the international interest as an end in itself. It cannot be held hostage to governments' existing legislation, as some governments have started to recognize. While aimed at universal acceptance, the existing political divisions in the world mean universality should require only that all countries be given an equal opportunity to participate in the process, which should proceed within a limited circle of states to produce real results. National governments should devote more resources to the task, for the current political problems lie not within but outside the Commission and may pass at some future time.

Richard Falk, in Chapter 4, 'New Approaches to the Study of International Law' (1967), explores the role of international law, international lawyers and their differing approaches at a time when the US was approaching the peak of its long war in Vietnam. He notes that since the Second World War legal scholars have properly been examining the role of law in the context of international politics, thus bringing their field closer to those of social scientists. Scholars of international law should not seek to justify current government policies but should search for the functional equivalents of legislatures, court and executives, by examining how international law is woven into the bureaucracy of modern states, helping private citizens use international law to oppose their government's policies and adopting an extra-national or transnational view focused on the common law of mankind. Falk reviews the four methodological approaches then used to study law in the US – policy science, functionalism, systems theory and the phenomenological focus on individual cases – concluding that all have their value in moving the field ahead in the desired ways.

Myres McDougal and Michael Reisman go further. In Chapter 5, 'The Prescribing Function in World Constitutive Process: How International Law is Made' (1980), they criticize the naturalist, sociological and historical approaches to international law in the customary tradition, seeing the making of law as a decisional prescription, communicating to, and creating in, a target audience expectations about policy content, authority and control. Therefore, both the content of the codified norm and the process of creating it constitute international law. Its components of control and authority will vary with the type of prescription being communicated, the level of crisis and the nature of the community.

In Chapter 6, 'The Reality and Efficacy of International Law' (1981), Ian Brownlie challenges the dismissal of international law by many thinkers. Brownlie argues that governments demonstrably use the rules of international law in their own decision-making and international behaviour for purposes other than propaganda. International law is required, and respected, for international travel and commerce. Indeed, it may well be more efficacious and internally consistent among states than the public law within them. Because international law is essentially that among states, it is conditioned by reciprocity more than internal legality. Internationally it acts much as administrative law in national systems, serving as 'internal, logically necessary and familiar' rather than 'external, coercive and alien' (p. 143) to states. It is thus the 'best tool available' (p. 146) for states. Scholars should thus focus on the vast evidence of how it is actually used.

In Chapter 7, 'Global Economics and International Economic Law' (1998), John Jackson examines the role of law and institutions in the face of economic globalization, and the contribution of scholars of law and other disciplines to the theories and policies regarding those affairs. Noting that 90 per cent of international law covers economic matters, he identifies how the internationalization of once domestic economic activities has increased the need for and role of international law, and the institutions in which it is entrenched. He points to the development of constitutional law at the international level, grounded in the interconnected governmental institutions and practices that comprise the world trading system, centred on the new World Trade Organization (WTO). As a 'normative realist' he identifies several ways in which these developments should guide future scholarly research.

Competing Theories of International Law

As highlighted by the first three essays, the modern field of international law has developed through the defining debates among scholars with distinctive and competing conceptions and theories of the content, origins and impact of international law. Early theories of international law, largely grounded in natural law positing universal norms and rules derived from the very nature of human beings, stood in stark contrast to a legal positivism seeing international law as simply the rules articulated and agreed upon by sovereign states, with no morality involved.

Post-war international legal scholars such as Jessup (Chapter 2), Schwarzenberger (1947), Brierly (1958), Gross (1965), McDougal (1960), Henkin (1970, 1979) and Corbett (1971) developed more nuanced frameworks. Increasingly following in their and Morgenthau's footsteps were leading scholars of international politics such as Fisher (1961), Hoffman (1960, 1961), Wright (1963), Keohane (Chapter 9, 1989), Finnemore and Sikkink (1998) and Simmons (2000). They created sophisticated models which explain the development of international law and provide an account of why and how states comply with international norms, rules, treaties or customs. The scholarship of both communities extended into ethical dimensions (Donnelly, 1986), environmental concerns (Palmer, 1992) and gender dynamics at work (Charlesworth, Chinkin and Wright, 1991). Their work has served to crystallize the theoretical distinctions which animate the most vibrant debates in the field of international law. Part II focuses on the more important of these theories and the great debates among them.

In the first essay, Chapter 8, 'International Law and Assumptions about the State System' (1965), William Coplin rejects the prevailing realist assumption of the Cold War era that the sole function of international law is to restrain state action, and is thus ineffective. He argues that it also serves as an effective institutional means of developing, reflecting and communicating a general consensus on the nature of the international system, as is evident in the development of supranational powers and the United Nations. He concedes that international law remains a 'quasi-authoritative' device (p. 175) because its norms represent only an imperfect consensus of member states, given the decentralized nature of law-creation and law-application in the international community.

In Chapter 9, 'International Relations and International Law: Two Optics' (1997), American political scientist Robert Keohane considers and combines the normative approach, which is focused on how norms and their processes of interpretation affect states, and the positive 'instrumental' theories, which emphasize how law is used by states to attain their interests. He argues that while norms do matter for interests and for reputation, normative and instrumental prescriptions are reliably reconciled within highly valued international institutions which align material and non-material incentives. Institutions thus need to be consistent with both broad patterns of power and interests and the basic normative commitments of their members, while creating interests and incentives to develop reputations which support these institutions.

Christoph Schreuer, in Chapter 10, 'The Waning of the Sovereign State: Towards a New Paradigm for International Law?' (1993), challenges the long dominant view that international law is that which exists and operates only between sovereign territorial states. While the classic model remains relevant, he argues that it has serious shortcomings in both the empirical and the policy-relevant normative domains. International law has long accepted non-state actors such as the Holy See, the International Committee of the Red Cross, international organizations, corporations and individuals. Now the decentralized nature of the system and the assignment of various functions to different levels of organization make the classic model increasingly inaccurate, both within the EU and throughout the globe. A more inclusive approach that captures and fosters this modified legal order will bring more inherent stability to the system, fewer abuses, more rationality and a more optimum allocation of tasks.

In Chapter 11, Kenneth Abbott, Robert Keohane, Andrew Moravcsik, Anne-Marie Slaughter and Duncan Snidal suggest that 'The Concept of Legalization' (2000) in international relations is a form of institutionalization characterized by the three dimensions: obligation, precision and delegation. Each dimension is logically independent, differing empirically in degree. The authors produce a great variety of combinations between high precision, obligation and delegation ('high' legalization) and its low equivalents ('soft' legalization). Most empirical combinations lie in the middle where rich mixes of politics and law unfold.

Hard Law, Soft Law, Legalization and Norms

Of the many debates that have defined the evolving field of international law, none has been more continuously central than that between 'hard' and 'soft' law in their various forms (Kirton and Trebilcock, 2004). While these labels mean different things to different scholars they do capture enduring and essential features of a great divide. On the one hand stand those who see international law among states as having the 'hard' properties of contractual negotiation and acceptance, explicitness, precision, obligation, delegation, institutionalization and authoritative compliance and enforcement just as its domestic equivalents do within the sovereign jurisdiction of a single state. On the other stand those who conceive of international law, in a world of anarchy rather than hierarchy, as more implicit, spontaneous, informal and dependent on the ongoing, voluntary processes of communication, consensus, contestation and change among those who create and are affected by it. The debate between the two unfolds in the realm of what empirically is international law, what its effects are and what normatively it should be (Weil, 1983).

Whether the emphasis be placed on hard rules or soft principles and norms, the concept of international regimes in which international law is embedded extends to decision-making procedures, commonly conceived to be those within formally constituted intergovernmental organizations or informal international institutions among states and non-state actors (Duffield, 2007). Within the hard law realm, legalized liberal institutionalism places a premium on such intergovernmental organizations and their domestically ratified charters and treaties. Scholars have thus focused on how international law is developed, applied and enforced through international organizations such as the United Nations (Gross, 1965), the Bretton Woods (Simmons, 2000) and functional bodies, the European Union (Garrett, 1995; Mattli and Slaughter, 1998), the North American Free Trade Agreement, and in newer fields such as human rights (Donnelly, 1986) and the environment (Kennan, 1970; Palmer, 1992; Biermann and Bauer, 2005). In the twenty-first century the field has expanded still further to embrace 'private authorities' that create and enforce soft law of often considerable importance, outside the formal state-to-state realm (Mattli, Chapter 16).

There is a natural tendency among international lawyers in both the scholarly and the practitioner community to conceive of law as being as inherently 'hard' as it is in the domestic domain, and thus viewing its international equivalent to be, in practice but not in normative aspiration, very 'soft' in degree and even in kind. Scholars of international politics, in contrast, have a broader set of instincts. Realists assume hard law to be irrelevant or dangerous to the creation of international cooperation. Liberal-institutionalists consider it to be desirable if still imperfectly realized. Constructivists conceive of a soft process of communication and consensus that can and should progressively compel state behaviour and the conceptions of interest and identities of states and other legitimate actors onthe world stage.

In the field of contemporary international politics, centre stage is occupied by liberal institutionalists with a decidedly hard conception of international law. Its very label of 'legalization' suggests that it increasingly resembles the more familiar form of domestic law. The conception and categorization of the legalized liberal institutionalists was put forward in a special thematic issue of the leading journal *International Organization* in the summer of 2000.

In the piece drawn from it that constitutes the first essay in Part III, 'Hard and Soft Law in International Governance' (Chapter 12), Kenneth Abbott and Duncan Snidal offer a realist's response to legalization's core claims. They suggest that international actors choose to solve specific substantive and political problems through the soft or hard forms of legalized governance that promise superior institutional solutions. Actors often prefer softer forms, because they are easier to obtain, better cope with uncertainty, better respect sovereignty and facilitate compromise among different types of actors. Using an interest-based approach, but one that includes norms and non-state actors, Abbott and Snidal illustrate, with empirical cases, the advantages of various forms of international legal arrangements.

In Chapter 13, 'Alternatives to "Legalization": Richer Views of Law and Politics' (2001), Martha Finnemore and Stephen J. Toope argue from a constructivist perspective for a broader conception of international law and legalization. They see them as social phenomena deeply embedded in the practices, beliefs and traditions of different societies and show how such a conception's sensitivity to law's legitimacy, congruence with social practice, rationality, adherence to due process and participation in its construction produces more robust intellectual and empirical research.

Judith Goldstein and Lisa Martin, in Chapter 14, 'Legalization, Trade Liberalization and Domestic Politics: A Cautionary Note' (2000), argue that domestic politics affect how international law is developed, interpreted and applied. An increasingly legalized global trade regime, which has sought to liberalize trade, has changed the global information environment and the nature of government obligations, and has thus spurred the mobilization of domestic interest groups on trade. While more explicit institutionalized international law with high degrees of precision, obligation and delegation may increase national compliance, protectionist domestic interest groups may also be inspired to produce less trade openness and international co-operation as a result.

In Chapter 15, 'Sovereignty and Inequality' (1998), Benedict Kingsbury similarly argues, from a political economy perspective focused on distributional effects, that the soft law tendency to erode the hard law sovereignty norm increases inequalities among and within states in an age of globalization and democratization. The current theory of international law and the classic concept of sovereignty neglect such inequalities. Globalization and democratization mean international rules and institutions become more intrusive, transnational civil society becomes more active and unitary state control diminishes. The normative concept of state sovereignty is increasingly challenged by a functional view in which the state now competes with supranational, private and local actors in regulatory authority. This increases inequality among states, weakens restraints on coercive intervention, diminishes the critical role of the state as a locus of identity and an autonomous zone of politics, and redivides the world into zones.

In Chapter 16, 'Private Justice in a Global Economy: From Litigation to Arbitration' (2001), Walter Mattli observes that private commercial parties employ diverse dispute resolution mechanisms, especially private international courts, ad hoc arbitration and other dispute-resolution techniques such as conciliation and mediation. These mechanisms vary in their procedural and adaptive flexibility, and in the centralization of procedural safeguards and information collection. Rational parties select the most effective and appropriate one, a choice that will depend upon the available enforcement mechanisms, uncertainty regarding the behaviour and interest of contractual partners, and other externalities.

Does International Law Matter? Compliance, Legitimacy and Accountability

Whatever the sources, causes, dominant dimensions and content of international law, the ultimate question for scholars and practitioners of international politics and law is what difference international law makes. Above all, how does it affect the expectations, behaviour, incentives, interests and the very identities of the states and non-states actors enmeshed in it? Here the central questions are how much and why states comply with the international commitments that they make in both the highly legalized hard law and the more informal soft law domains (Chayes and Chayes, 1995). Students of international politics from the realist tradition have argued that states comply with international law only when they have created it and for as long as and insofar as it serves their interests, and do not comply when these conditions change. In contrast, the eminent scholar of international law, Louis Henkin, has famously claimed that, 'almost all nations observe almost all principles of international law and almost all of their obligations almost all of the time' (1979, p. 47). Realists respond that while this may be empirically correct, it is those instances in which nations do not observe their obligations under international law that are most significant. Even when countries comply with international law in important cases where it does not seem to be in their interest, there remains the important question of why they obey.

These questions of how much and why states comply have given rise to a wealth of theoretical and empirical scholarship. This focuses on topics ranging from the impact of highly legalized bodies such as the World Trade Organization and its dispute settlement mechanism to the more informal institutions among major powers such as the Group of Eight (Von Furstenberg and Daniels, 1991; Kokotsis, 1999). It embraces the domestic entrenchment and effects of international law in government decision-making and among domestic publics. And it extends to broader issues of legitimacy, accountability, transparency and participation (Franck, 1988; Reinisch, 2001). Thus Part IV begins with the concepts and record of compliance, moves to the domestic impact of international law and ends by emphasizing the importance of, and need, for legitimacy in international organization.

In the first contribution, Chapter 17, 'On Compliance' (1993), Abram Chayes and Antonia Handler Chayes frame the new dialogue between scholars of international law and international relations on compliance with international agreements by advancing three propositions. First, it is plausible and useful to assume a propensity by states to comply with their international legal obligations. Second, states deviate from treaty obligations not out of a deliberate desire for national advantage, but for other reasons such as ambiguity and indeterminacy of treaty language and limitations on the capacity of parties to carry out their undertakings, which make the deviations justifiable to other states. Third, the treaty regime should be held to a level of compliance that is 'acceptable' given the interests which the treaty is designed to protect, and not to a stricter standard of absolute compliance. As non-compliance is a deviant, rather than an expected, behaviour, the international community ought to de-emphasize coercive enforcement mechanisms, and address the sources of non-compliance that can be mitigated.

In Chapter 18, 'How do International Institutions Matter? The Domestic Impact of International Rules and Norms' (1996), Andrew Cortell and James Davis, Jr turn to domestic politics to explain compliance. They argue that government officials and social interest groups invoke international rules and norms to advance their domestic interests. In doing so, they incorporate them into domestic debates and use them to influence national policy decisions. Depending on the domestic structural context and the domestic salience of the particular international rule or norm, these groups can thus affect state choice and behaviour.

Thomas Franck, in Chapter 19, 'The Power of Legitimacy and the Legitimacy of Power: International Law in an Age of Power Disequilibrium' (2006), challenges the new view among some American international lawyers and their government soulmates that states do not abide by international law where the use of force is concerned, just as realist and rational choice theory predicts. Franck argues that such a view can become a self-fulfilling prophecy in a world where the perception of law's compliance pull is what largely gives it force. He proceeds to demonstrate that the claim of the rational choice realists is empirically untrue. Recalling his earlier argument that law's legitimacy flows from its compliance created by symbolic validation, coherence, adherence and, above all, determinacy, Franck shows that most states comply with international law most of the time. Moreover, states claim they are doing so when they are not, try to hide their illegal activities and expect even the most powerful states to abide by the law as well. He shows that these dynamics operated in the UN-unapproved invasions of Kuwait in 1999 and Iraq in 2003. The first secured approval from the community of nations that an adaptation of the old law was necessary. The latter one did not – to the detriment not of international law, but of the US and Britain as violators of that law. Noting that the major threat to international law comes from obsolescence rather than desuetude, Franck concludes that the UN has done well in adapting the law, substantively and procedurally, to an ever-changing world.

The Laws of War and Force

Franck's focus on the use of force in recent cases highlights the classic, core concern of international law and international politics. It is the area where the impact of international law has long thought to be the weakest and the most difficult to improve. This longstanding view acquired new dimensions in the post-Cold War years over the growing challenges of humanitarian intervention to prevent genocide in a world now free to act across the old Iron Curtain confines. It received even more in the post-9/11 period which brought terrorism of global reach from non-state actors who might have and might use weapons of mass destruction of various kinds.

In Chapter 20, 'The Complexities of Humanitarian Intervention: A New World Order Challenge' (1996), Richard Falk observes that the post-Cold War years saw interventionary diplomacy by the great powers shift from purely geopolitical to more humanitarian forms focused on alleviating human suffering. This was especially so for the US, acting directly or through the United Nations or NATO. While this shift was normatively welcome from the standpoint of morality and law, the shallowness of governments' ability and will to succeed led largely to failure. Interveners should thus focus on conflict prevention, balancing national self-determinations with human rights, fostering peace settlements among exhausted combatants, supporting transnational, grassroots initiatives and getting the powerful states to agree that such measures foster global stability and prosperity. Without this emphasis, the early post-Cold War period has seen an early enthusiasm for intervention replaced by disillusionment. Given the failure of humanitarian intervention in the past and prospective future, and the limited beneficial role international law has to play here, an ethos of non-intervention likely and understandably lies ahead.

Thomas Franck, in Chapter 21, 'The Use of Force in International Law' (2003), argues that the UN Charter is both a repository of time-tested principles and a foundation for extending international law to solve the practical problems of a changing world. Because the UN's individual political organs rather than an overarching legal ICJ interpret their own charters, in the UN 'the Charter *is* what the principal organs *do*' (p. 506). The result is not a judicial process formally focused on impartiality and principled consistency, but a political one that proceeds importantly through legal discourse and a great awareness of the precedents that individual actions and decisions will create. Since 1945 this process has extended the UN's willingness legally to allow the use of force in seven ways, including the ones most relevant to today. But in all cases it has done so cautiously, gradually and pragmatically, with critical regard for the extreme necessity, motives, proportionality, reasonableness and, above all, evidence at hand. As the US faced its decision to use force against Iraq without fresh UN Security Council approval in the spring of 2003, Franck insisted that it meet these criteria, as judged by an international jury of its peers. Because the US was not the world's single superpower able to get what it wanted by acting alone, it needed to secure the consent of the global community on matters important to it and to reciprocally support other countries when they acted on matters important to them. In words that appear both poignant and prescient, Franck concluded, as an American, 'If we act to destroy the U.N. system because we have decided that its faults outweigh its merits, what else will take its place except lonely American imperium?' (p. 517).

JOHN J. KIRTON WITH JELENA MADUNIC

References

Biermann, Frank and Bauer, Stephan (eds) (2005), *A World Environment Organization: Solution or Threat for Effective International Environmental Governance?*, Aldershot: Ashgate.

Brierly, James L. (1958), *The Basis of Obligation in International Law and Other Papers*, Oxford: Clarendon Press.

Bull, Hedley (1966), 'The Grotian Conception of International Society', in Herbert Butterfield and Martin Wight (eds), *Diplomatic Investigations*, Cambridge, MA: Harvard University Press, pp. 51–73.

Bull, Hedley (1977), *The Anarchical Society*, London: Macmillan.

Carr, E.H. (1939), *The Twenty Years' Crisis, 1919–1939: An Introduction to the Study of International Relations*, London: Macmillan.

Charlesworth, Hilary, Chinkin, Christine and Wright, Shelley (1991), 'Feminist Approaches to International Law', *American Journal of International Law*, **85**, no. 4 (October), pp. 613–45.

Charney, Jonathan I. (1993), 'Universal International Law', *American Journal of International Law*, **87**, no. 4 (October), pp. 529–51.

Chayes, Abram and Chayes, Antonia Handler (1995), *The New Sovereignty: Compliance with International Regulatory Agreements*, Cambridge, MA: Harvard University Press.

Clark, Grenville and Sohn, Louis (1958), *World Peace through World Law*, Cambridge, MA: Harvard University Press.

Corbett, Percy (1971), *The Growth of World Law*, Princeton, NJ: Princeton University Press.

Donnelly, Jack (1986), 'International Human Rights: A Regime Analysis', *International Organization*, **40**, no. 3 (Summer), pp. 599–642.

Doyle, Michael (1983), 'Kant, Liberal Legacies and Foreign Affairs', *Philosophy and Public Affairs*, **12** (Summer and Fall), pp. 205–35 and 323–53.

Duffield, John (2007), 'What are International Institutions?', *International Studies Review*, **9** (Spring), pp. 1–22.

Finnemore, Martha and Sikkink, Kathryn (1998), 'International Norm Dynamics and Political Change', *International Organization*, **52** (Autumn), pp. 887–917.

Fisher, Roger (1961), 'Bringing Law to Bear on Governments', *Harvard Law Review*, **74**, pp. 1180–40.

Franck, Thomas M. (1988), 'Legitimacy in the International System', *American Journal of International Law*, **82**, no. 4 (October), pp. 705–59.

Garrett, Geoffrey (1995), 'The Politics of Legal Integration in the European Union', *International Organization*, **49**, no. 1 (Winter), pp. 171–82.

Gross, Leo (1965), 'The United Nations and the Role of Law', *International Organization*, **19**, no. 3 (Summer), pp. 537–61.

Grotius, Hugo (1970), 'Prolegomena to the Law of War and Peace', in M.G. Forsyth, H.M.A. Keens-Soper and P. Savigear (eds), *The Theory of International Relations: Selected Texts From Gentili to Treitschke*, London: Allen & Unwin (reprinted Piscataway, NJ: Transaction, 2008).

Henkin, Louis (1970), *How Nations Behave: Law and Foreign Policy*, Praeger: New York.

Henkin, Louis (1979), *How Nations Behave* (2nd edn), New York: Columbia University Press.
Higgins, Rosalyn (1963), *The Development of International Law through International Organization*, London: Oxford University Press.
Hoffman, Stanley (ed.) (1960), *Contemporary Theory in International Relations*, Englewood Cliffs, NJ: Prentice-Hall.
Hoffman, Stanley (1961), 'International Systems and International Law', in Klaus Knorr and Sidney Verba (eds), *The International System: Theoretical Essays*, Princeton, NJ: Princeton University Press, pp. 205–37.
Kant, Immanuel (1970), 'Idea for a Universal History from a Cosmo-Political Point of View', 'On the Commonplace: That may be Correct in Theory but is Useless in Practice', 'The Metaphysical Elements of Justice' and 'Perpetual Peace: A Philosophical Essay', all in M.G. Forsyth, H.M.A. Keens-Soper and P. Savigear (eds), *The Theory of International Relations: Selected Texts From Gentili to Treitschke*, London: Allen & Unwin (reprinted Piscataway, NJ: Transaction, 2008).
Kant, Immanuel (1996 [1795]), *Toward Perpetual Peace*, in the *Cambridge Edition of the Works of Immanuel Kant*, ed. and trans. Mary J. Gregor, Cambridge: Cambridge University Press, pp. 311–52.
Kennan, George (1970), 'To Prevent a World Wasteland: A Proposal', *Foreign Affairs*, **48** (April), pp. 401–13.
Keohane, Robert O. (1989), *International Institutions and State Power: Essays in International Relations Theory*, Boulder, CO: Westview.
Kirton, John and Trebilcock, Michael (eds) (2004), *Hard Choices, Soft Law: Voluntary Standards in Global Trade, Environment and Social Governance*, Aldershot: Ashgate.
Kokotsis, Eleonore (1999), *Keeping International Commitments: Compliance, Credibility and the G7, 1988–1995*, New York: Garland.
Krasner, Stephen (1982), 'Structural Causes and Regime Consequences: Regimes as Intervening Variables', *International Organization*, **36**, no. 2 (Spring), pp. 185–205.
Krasner, Stephen (ed.) (1983), *International Regimes*, Ithaca, NY: Cornell University Press.
McDougal, Myres (1960), 'Some Basic Theoretical Concepts About International Law: A Policy-Oriented Framework of Inquiry', *Journal of Conflict Resolution*, **4**, pp. 337–54.
Machiavelli, Niccolò (1988 [1515]), *The Prince*, ed. Quentin Skinner and R. Price, Cambridge Texts in the History of Political Thought, Cambridge: Cambridge University Press.
McWhinnney, Edward (1963), 'Soviet and Western International Law and the Cold War in the Era of Bipolarity', *Canadian Yearbook of International Law*, **1**, pp. 40–81.
Mattli, Walter and Slaughter, Anne-Marie (1998), 'Revisiting the European Court of Justice', *International Organization*, **52**, no.1 (Winter), pp. 177–209.
Morgenthau, Hans (1948), *Politics Among Nations: The Struggle for Power and Peace*, New York: Alfred A. Knopf.
Murphy, Cornelius F. (1982), 'The Grotian Vision of World Order', *American Journal of International Law*, **76**, no. 3 (July), pp. 447–98.
O'Neal, John R. and Russett, Bruce M. (1999), 'The Kantian Peace: The Pacific Benefits of Democracy, Interdependence, and International Organizations, 1885–1992', *World Politics*, **52**, no. 1 (October), pp. 1–37.
Oppenheim, L. (1912), *International Law* (2nd edn), London: Longmans, Green.
Palmer, Geoffrey (1992), 'New Ways to Make International Environmental Law', *American Journal of International Law*, **86**, no. 2 (April), pp. 259–83.
Pufendorf, Samuel (1729 [1672]), *Of the Law of Nature and Nations* (4th English edn), trans. B. Kennet, London: J. Walthoe, R. Wilkin *et al.*
Reinisch, August (2001), 'Securing the Accountability of International Organizations', *Global Governance*, **7**, no. 2 (April–June), pp. 131–50.

Ruggie, John G. (1983), 'International Regimes, Transactions, and Change: Embedded Liberalism in the Postwar Economic Order', in Stephen D. Krasner (ed.), *International Regimes*, Ithaca, NY: Cornell University Press, pp. 195–232.

Schwarzenberger, Georg (1947), 'The Inductive Approach to International Law', *Harvard Law Review*, **60**, no. 4 (April), pp. 539–70.

Simmons, Beth A. (2000), 'The Legalization of International Monetary Affairs', *International Organization*, **54**, no. 3 (Summer), pp. 573–602.

Suarez, Francisco (1612) *Tractatus de legibus ac deo legislatore*, Coimbria.

Vattel, Emerich de (1916 [1758]), *The Law of Nations or the Principles of Natural Law*, trans. Charles G. Fenwick, Washington, DC: Carnegie Institution.

Von Furstenberg, George and Daniels, Joseph (1991), 'Policy Undertakings by the Seven "Summit" Countries: Ascertaining the Degree of Compliance', *Carnegie-Rochester Conference Series of Public Policy*, **35**, pp. 267–308.

Weil, Prosper (1983), 'Towards Relative Normativity in International Law', *American Journal of International Law*, **77**, no. 3 (July), pp. 413–42.

Wilson, Woodrow (1984 [1918]), 'Fourteen Points', in *The Papers of Woodrow Wilson*, vol. 45, ed. Arthur S. Link *et al.*, Princeton, NJ: Princeton University Press, p. 536.

Wright, Quincy (1963), 'Toward a Universal Law of Mankind', *Columbia Law Review*, **63**, pp. 440–60.

Young, Oran R. (1991), 'Political Leadership and Regime Formation: On the Development of Institutions in International Society', *International Organization*, **45**, pp. 281–308.

Part I
The Sources and Development of International Law

[1]

POSITIVISM, FUNCTIONALISM, AND INTERNATIONAL LAW

By Hans J. Morgenthau

Assistant Professor of Law and Political Science, University of Kansas City

If an event in the physical world contradicts all scientific forecasts, and thus challenges the assumptions on which the forecasts have been based, it is the natural reaction of scientific inquiry to reëxamine the foundations of the specific science and attempt to reconcile scientific findings and empirical facts. The social sciences do not react in the same way. They have an inveterate tendency to stick to their assumptions and to suffer constant defeat from experience rather than to change their assumptions in the light of contradicting facts.[1] This resistance to change is uppermost in the history of international law. All the schemes and devices by which great humanitarians and shrewd politicians endeavored to reorganize the relations between states on the basis of law, have not stood the trial of history. Instead of asking whether the devices were adequate to the problems which they were supposed to solve, it was the general attitude of the internationalists to take the appropriateness of the devices for granted and to blame the facts for the failure.[2] When the facts behave otherwise than we have predicted, they seem to say, too bad for the facts. Not unlike the sorcerers of primitive ages, they attempt to exorcise social evils by the indefatigable repetition of magic formulae. As the League of Nations was a failure, let us have another League. As the first and second Peace Conferences of the Hague did not succeed, let us have a third one. As arbitration never settled a political conflict which otherwise would have led to war, let us have more arbitration for the prevention of war. As the Disarmament Conference was a senseless waste of intellect and time, why not convoke another Disarmament Conference?

It is a strange paradox that the lay public has observed a much more sceptical and realistic, therefore scientific, attitude toward international law than the science of international law itself. The laymen were much quicker to recognize the gap between the rules of international law as represented by science, and the rules of international law as they exist in actual experience. The breakdown of the main bulk of post-World War international law has altogether destroyed public confidence in a science which, unmoved by what

[1]As to this tendency, see Lancelot Hogben, The Retreat from Reason (Conway Memorial Lecture, London, 1936); Lynd, Knowledge for What? (Princeton, 1939).

[2] See Wild, "What Is the Trouble with International Law?" Am. Pol. Sci. Rev., Vol. XXXII (1938), p. 479: "Too often in the past he has assumed the attitude that the world is out of step with his law, and too seldom has he considered the point that perhaps his science is partly to blame."

experience may show, invariably follows its preconceived pattern.[3] This breakdown implies the practical refutation of the ideas which have determined the development of international law in the last half-century. Hence, the science of international law is now confronted with the alternative of maintaining the traditional pattern of assumptions, concepts and devices in spite of the teachings of history, or of revising this pattern and trying to reconcile the science of international law and its subject-matter, that is, the rules of international law as they are actually applied.[4] The present writer has always held that only the latter way leads to theoretically correct and practically useful results. In the following paper the attempt will be made to reëxamine the methodological assumptions with which the traditional science of international law starts. These assumptions are embodied in the positivist doctrine of law.

THE LEGAL PHILOSOPHY OF POSITIVISM

Positivist philosophy restricts the object of scientific knowledge to matters that can be verified by observation, and thus excludes from its domain all matters of an *a priori*, metaphysical nature.[5] Juridic positivism transfers this delimitation into the legal sphere. The juridic positivist delimits the subject-matter of his research in a dual way. On the one hand, he proposes to deal exclusively with matters legal, and for this purpose strictly separates the legal sphere from ethics and *mores* as well as psychology and sociology. Hence, his legalism. On the other hand, he restricts his attention within the legal sphere to the legal rules enacted by the state, and excludes all law whose existence cannot be traced to the statute books or the decisions of the courts. Hence, his *étatist* monism. This "positive" law the positivist accepts as it is, without passing judgment upon its ethical value or questioning its practical appropriateness. Hence, his agnosticism. The positivist

[3] Professor Quincy Wright could report in 1930 (Research in International Law since the War, p. 25): "Of the twenty jurists with whom the writer has corresponded, only two betrayed a note of pessimism at the prospects, and that in both cases was qualified."

[4] Such reëxamination is called for by many writers; see, for instance, Philip Marshall Brown, this JOURNAL, Vol. 33 (1939), p. 149; Djuvara, *Recueil des Cours de l'Académie de Droit International* (cited hereafter as Hague *Recueil*), Vol. 64 (1938), p. 485; Hudson, Proceedings of the 2nd, 3rd, and 5th Conferences of Teachers of International Law (Washington, 1925, 1928, 1933), pp. 86 *et seq.*, 72, 94, 95, respectively; MacKenzie, Proceedings of the 6th Conference of Teachers of International Law (Washington, 1938), p. 109; Friedman, "The Disintegration of European Civilization and the Future of International Law," Modern Law Review, Vol. 2 (1938), p. 213.

[5] For the characteristics of positivist philosophy, see Comte, *Discours sur l'esprit positif* (Paris, 1844), p. 41 *et seq.;* Mill, Auguste Comte and Positivism (London, 1866), p. 6 *et seq.;* see especially, the excellent article, "Positivism," by Ruggiero in Encyclopedia of the Social Sciences, Vol. 12, p. 260.

The most penetrating contemporaneous criticism of positivist science is to be found in Mortimer J. Adler, What Man Has Made of Man (New York, 1937), especially pp. 28, 87, 97, 131, 132, 158 *et seq.*, 192, 233, 238 *et seq.*

cherishes the belief that the "positive" law is a logically coherent system which virtually contains, and through a mere process of logical deduction will actually produce, all rules necessary for the decision of all possible cases. Hence, his system worship and dogmatic conceptualism.[6]

The historic importance of the positivist school of jurisprudence for the science of law was fourfold. First, positivism accepted the breakdown of the great metaphysical systems of the eighteenth and the early nineteenth centuries and the resulting decadence of metaphysical jurisprudence as an established fact. It endeavored to save the scientific character of jurisprudence by eliminating from it all metaphysical elements, thus separating it from the discredited doctrines of natural law. In the second place, positivism recognized that the subject-matter of jurisprudence was the law and nothing but the law, and that neither non-legal subjects nor non-legal considerations could have any place in it. Furthermore, legal positivism learned from the positivist movement in philosophy and the natural sciences that scientific objectivity is dependent upon an object intelligible in experience, and a method aimed at knowledge, not at evaluation. Finally, the great legal codifications of the European continental countries and the Anglo-American statutory law found in positivism a technique of interpretation and representation. This technique fulfilled its purpose satisfactorily as long as the social and political philosophy of the statutes, either directly expressed by them or indirectly derived from them by way of logical deduction, was sufficient to meet the economic and social needs as well as the political demands and ethical requirements of a given society at a given historical moment.

To be sure, this correspondence between the statutes and the standards of society has never existed completely; even under stationary conditions there will always be a marginal sphere which does not allow the mere logical subsumption of a given case under statutory law without violating the standards of society. In order to satisfy the positivist assumptions of the logical completeness of the legal order and at the same time meet the standards of society, these standards were first to be read into the statutes from

[6] For the characteristics of juridic positivism, see Finch, Hague *Recueil*, Vol. 53 (1935), p. 557, and The Sources of Modern International Law (Washington, 1937), p. 20; Oppenheim, "The Science of International Law: Its Task and Methods," this JOURNAL, Vol. 2 (1908), p. 333 *et seq.;* Bergbohm, *Staatsvertraege und Gesetze als Quellen des Voelkerrechts* (Dorpat, 1876), p. 40 *et seq.;* and *Jurisprudenz und Voelkerrecht* (Leipzig, 1892), pp. 51, 52; Kelsen, *Die philosophischen Grundlagen der Naturrechtslehre und des Rechtspositivismus* (Berlin, 1928); Pound, "Mechanical Jurisprudence," Columbia Law Rev., Vol. 8 (1908), p. 605; Morris Cohen, "The Concepts of Juridical and Scientific Law," *Politica*, Vol. 4 (1939), p. 8 *et seq.;* Ripert, "*Droit naturel et positivisme juridique,*" *Annales de la Faculté de Droit d'Aix*, nouvelle série, No. 1 (Marseilles, 1918), pp. 19, 20, 32 *et seq.;* Anzilotti, *Cours de Droit International*, Vol. 1 (Paris, 1929), p. 18 *et seq.;* Waline, "*Positivisme philosophique, juridique et sociologique,*" *Mélanges Carré de Malberg* (Paris, 1936), p. 519; Gény, *Science et Technique en Droit privé positif* (Paris, 1915), Vol. 2, pp. 15 *et seq.*, 31, 37, 38. A good survey is to be found in Erim, *Le Positivisme juridique et le Droit International* (Paris, 1939).

which they then appeared to have been derived by a mere logical process. Through the back door of pseudo-logical interpretation the outlawed company of natural law and extra-legal value judgments reëntered the legal system. This kind of pseudo-logical legerdemain became the predominating interpretative technique of legal positivism in the period of its decadence. In the last decades of the nineteenth century the standards of society went far away from the economic, social, political, and ethical assumptions from which the systems of statutory law had started.[7] Hence, the positivists were compelled to resort to a series of pseudo-logical makeshifts in order to maintain the fiction of "legal self-sufficiency," [8] on which positivist jurisprudence had founded its theoretical system.

From three sides this fiction was, and still is, under attack. From the one side, sociological and realist jurisprudence, inspired partly and indirectly by the original sociological positivism of Comte, does away with the artificial barriers by which positivism has separated the legal sphere from the whole domain of the social sciences to which it actually belongs. Thus it destroys the positivist assumptions together with the positivist conclusions. From the other side, the neo-positivism of Kelsen's pure theory of law maintains the basic assumptions of positivism but undertakes to achieve the positivist ends by purifying the legal science from all material, non-legal elements, thus eliminating the subject-matter of positivist crypto-metaphysics.

Several schools of revived natural law, as well as the politico-ideological power of totalitarianism, have joined in this dual scientific attack. Totalitarianism has ostracized positivist jurisprudence as a manifestation of liberalistic decadence in Germany and Italy, where the domination of juridic thought by positivism has been at times almost undisputed, and where positivism has exerted its most far-reaching and fertile influence on the development of the legal science. Deprived of its traditional strongholds by political suppression and undermined by scientific criticism, positivism is no longer a guiding influence in modern legal thought.

POSITIVISM AND INTERNATIONAL LAW

In international law, unlike the other branches of legal science, positivism is still a determining influence. Ever since the turn of the century, internationalists have started with positivist assumptions, have followed the positivist method, and have professed adherence to the principles of positivism.[9]

[7] An excellent analysis of this development is to be found in Bonnecase's history of the French "*École de l'Exégèse.*" *La Pensée juridique française de 1804 à l'heure présente*, Vol. 1 (Bordeaux, 1933).

[8] Roscoe Pound, An Introduction to the Philosophy of Law (New Haven, 1937), p. 57.

[9] Cavaglieri could write in 1911 ("*La Conception positive de la société internationale,*" *Revue gén. dr. pub.*, Vol. 18 (1911), p. 260): "Parmi ceux qui s'adonnent aux études de droit international, il n'est aujourd'hui personne qui ne fasse pas solennellement profession d'adhérer à la nouvelle conception positive du droit. . . ." Some years later Ripert could say (*Annales, loc. cit.*, p. 18): ". . . cette génération professe un positivisme juridique absolu."

Neither the opposition of natural law,[10] nor Kelsen's neo-positivist criticism,[11] nor, finally, the rather implicit criticism of legal sociologists,[12] has been able to affect the predominance of positivist thought over the science of international law. The Permanent Court of International Justice still follows the time-honored pseudo-logical method of traditional positivism which prevailed in the jurisdiction of the domestic supreme courts at the turn of the century. The annals of this highest international tribunal record no instance where an advocate, like Brandeis in Muller *v.* Oregon,[13] dared to break through the network of positivist formulae, nor of any majority opinion which would not have clung, on a very high level of technical perfection, to the traditional pattern of positivist argumentation. When Judge Hudson looks for a realistic decision with respect to international law he has to turn to the Court of Appeals of the State of New York.[14] Compared to municipal law, international law is in a retarded stage of scientific development. As represented by its sanest elements, the science of international law still stands where the science of municipal law stood in 1910; in terms of its post-World War development, its most spectacular branches, invaded by the political ideology of Geneva, have gone back at least to the point from which positivism started in the last decades of the nineteenth century.

The collapse of the international law of Geneva, when for the first time its fictions were confronted with the full reality, meant of necessity the breakdown of the science which had been only its ideological reflection. The

[10] Professor Lauterpacht (Private Law Sources and Analogies of International Law (London, 1927), p. 27, note 5; p. 58, note 7; Oppenheim-Lauterpacht, International Law, Vol. 1 (1937, p. 100) defends the opinion that positivism no longer dominates the science of international law, but has been replaced by a new doctrine of moderate natural law. It is difficult to share this opinion. Natural law and the post-war science of international law have only this in common, that they overstep the limits of experience. However, one would do injustice to the great metaphysical systems of natural law by identifying them with the post-war science of international law. Whereas Suarez and Grotius were fully aware of the aprioristic, metaphysical character of their propositions and had good philosophical reasons for adhering to them, post-war positivism helplessly confuses reality and imagination, wish and fact, because no longer does it possess the scientific means of distinguishing between both. *Cf.*, also, Laski, The State in Theory and Practice (New York, 1935), p. 198; Wild, *loc. cit.*, p. 483 *et seq.*

[11] See, especially, *Das Problem der Souveraenitaet und die Theorie des Voelkerrechts* (1928).

[12] See, especially, Max Huber, *Die soziologischen Grundlagen des Voelkerrechts* (Berlin, 1928); Ray, Hague *Recueil*, Vol. 48 (1934), p. 631 *et seq.;* Schindler, *ibid.*, Vol. 46 (1933), p. 229 *et seq.;* Morgenthau, *La Notion du "politique" et la théorie des différends internationaux* (Paris, 1933), pp. 37 *et seq.*, 65 *et seq.*, and *La Réalité des normes, en particulier des normes du droit international* (Paris, 1934), pp. 139, 140, 215.

[13] 208 U. S. 412 (1908). An excellent appraisal of the theoretical importance of this case is to be found in Frankfurter, "Hours of Labor and Realism in Constitutional Law," Harvard Law Rev., Vol. 29 (1916), p. 353.

[14] See the reference to Cardozo's opinion in Techt *v.* Hughes, 229 N. Y. 222, 241 (1920), in Hudson, "International Law in the Twentieth Century," Cornell Law Quarterly, Vol. 10 (1925), p. 435, note 75.

post-World War science of international law shared the short-lived and delusive splendor of its political master, and now shares with him the final detection of their common sham existence as well as the resulting disrepute. The helplessness of the science of international law in the face of those dangers, its very unawareness of them, its sincere self-deception as to its scientific character, are perhaps the gravest indictments which can be brought against the scientific value of the positivist doctrine of international law.[15] The failure of the post-World War science of international law is not due to personal or accidental circumstances; it grows out of the very assumptions and methods which have led juridic positivism to defeat in the domestic field. Yet, in the international field the disastrous consequences of the genuine weakness of the positivist doctrine are doubled by the absence of the conditions which in the domestic domain made juridic positivism at least a temporary and apparent success.

Juridic positivism starts with the assumption that its subject-matter is to be found exclusively in the written law of the state. Only the rules of law, and all the rules of law which statutes and court decisions present as such, are the material with which the positivist doctrine has to deal. The criterion of the existence, that is, the validity of a legal rule, is, then, its incorporation into the written law of the state. We do not repeat here what we have said elsewhere of the scientific value of this juridic monism,[16] and consider only the results of its being applied to the rules of international law. This criterion for the validity of legal rules means, if transferred to the international field, that the only valid rules of international law are those which are revealed by the decisions of courts and international treaties duly ratified and not formally revoked. Yet this concept is at once confronted with two problems for which the positivist doctrine of international law has no solution. On the one hand, all rules embodied in written documents are not valid international law, and, on the other hand, there are valid rules of international law other than the rules embodied in written documents. The positivist formula as applied to international law is at once too narrow and too broad.[17]

[15] For criticism of post-war international law, see especially, Beckett, "International Law in England," Law Quarterly Rev., Vol. 55 (1939), pp. 261, 262, 266; Borchard, this JOURNAL, Vol. 27 (1933), p. 518, Vol. 28 (1934), p. 108; Hill, *ibid.*, Vol. 23 (1929), p. 617; John Bassett Moore, *ibid.*, Vol. 27 (1933), p. 607; the same, International Law and Some Current Illusions (New York, 1924); the same, "An Appeal to Reason," Foreign Affairs, Vol. 11 (1933), see especially pp. 548, 585; the same, "Post-War International Law," Columbia Law Rev., Vol. 27 (1927), see especially p. 412.

[16] See Morgenthau, *La Réalité des Normes*, p. 106 *et seq.; cf.* also, the rather analytical than critical remarks by Edwin D. Dickinson, Hague *Recueil*, Vol. 40 (1932), pp. 337, 344; Siotto-Pintor, *ibid.*, Vol. 41 (1932), pp. 265, 266; Verdross, *ibid.*, Vol. 30 (1929), p. 276.

[17] To the following discussion, see Morgenthau, "*Positivisme mal compris et théorie réaliste du Droit international,*" *Mélanges Altamira* (Madrid, 1936), p. 3 *et seq.;* see also, Affolter, "*Der Rechtspositivismus in der Rechtswissenschaft,*" *Archiv fuer oeffentliches Recht*, Vol. 12 (1896/97), pp. 40, 41.

The science of international law has not developed a criterion to distinguish, in an objective way, between *seemingly* and *actually* valid rules of international law. "One can assert that nine-tenths of the traditional doctrines of international law are not actual international law," said Professor George Jellinek as far back as 1905.[18] Declared Professor Oppenheim a few years later:

> It is also indispensable that the science should free itself from the tyranny of phrases. As things are, there is scarcely a doctrine of the law of nations which is wholly free from the tyranny of phrases. . . . Any one who is in touch with the application of international law in diplomatic practice hears from statesmen every day the complaint that books put forth fanciful doctrines instead of the actual rules of law. Now it is often not difficult to push the irrelevant to one side and to extract what is legally essential from the waste of phrase-ridden discourse. But there are entire areas in which the tyranny of phrases so turns the head that rules which absolutely never were rules of law are represented as such.[19]

"On no subject of human interest, except theology," said John Chipman Gray at about the same time, "has there been so much loose writing and nebulous speculations as on international law." [20]

If these statements were true in the first decade of the century, the development of the post-World War science of international law has only added to their significance. The Covenant of the League of Nations, for instance, is a duly ratified document which has never been repealed. But has it ever been valid international law as a whole? If not, which provisions never had the quality of valid legal rules, and which ones lost this quality in the course of the gradual collapse of the institution of Geneva? No treatise of the law of nations offers any general criterion to answer these questions, nor do the concrete answers given with reference to the actual validity of Article 16 of the Covenant reveal any such underlying objective criterion. The absolute denial of any validity, the assertion of a so-called "de facto revision," and the defense of full validity, are advanced side by side.[21] Similar problems arise with respect to the Briand-Kellogg Pact and the Peace Treaties of 1919, as well as to other political treaties, such as the Pact of the Little Entente, alliance treaties, the concepts of aggression, independence, intervention, government, and so forth.[22] They are em-

[18] *System der subjektiven oeffentlichen Rechte* (Tuebingen, 1905), p. 321; see also the even stronger criticism by Bergbohm, *Staatsvertraege*, p. 8.

[19] The Future of International Law (Oxford, 1921; first in German, 1911), pp. 58, 59; see also, The Science of International Law, pp. 315, 334.

[20] Nature and Sources of the Law (New York, 1927; first edition, 1909), p. 127.

[21] *Cf.*, for instance, Schwarzenberger, in The New Commonwealth Quarterly, Vol. 3 (1937/38), pp. 263, 360 *et seq.*; *ibid.*, Vol. 4 (1938/39), p. 60 *et seq.*; for an excellent statement of the problem, see Kunz, *id.*, p. 131, and this JOURNAL, Vol. 33 (1939), p. 33.

[22] An excellent contribution to the understanding of this problem is to be found in Baty, "The Trend of International Law," this JOURNAL, Vol. 33 (1939), p. 653 *et seq.*, and "The Abuse of Terms," *ibid.*, Vol. 30 (1936), p. 377.

bodied in written documents which were duly ratified and never invalidated. Have they ever been valid law from the beginning, and what has become of them in the years of their violation? Are they still valid? If they are not, what destroyed their validity? These are questions which the interpreter of domestic statutes, subject to a rational process of validation and invalidation, is not likely to be asked, and hence the positivist doctrine of international law, following the pattern of domestic positivism, has nothing with which to answer them.[23]

The basic assumption of juridic positivism, that its exclusive subject-matter is the written law of the state, leads legal science not only to the inclusion of alleged legal rules which no longer have or never have had legal validity, but also to the exclusion of undoubtedly valid rules of law. Positivist jurisprudence, starting with the axiom of "legal self-sufficiency," separates the law from the other normative spheres, that is, ethics and *mores*, on the one hand, and from the social sphere, comprehending the psychological, political, and economic fields, on the other hand. By doing so, positivism severs the actual relations between the law and the other branches of the normative and social sphere. It proceeds on the assumption that the law, as it really is, can be understood without the normative and social context in which it actually stands.[24] From the application of this assumption to international law there results a threefold delimitation of legal research, contrary to the exigencies of the reality, and hence a threefold misconception of what international law really is.

1. The normative sphere, comprehending the totality of rules governing a given society, is one whole with regard to the basic precepts it contains.[25]

[23] This absence of any scientific test for the validity of the rules of international law is responsible for the perplexity into which some of the foremost representatives of the international law of Geneva have fallen in recent years. Professor Scelle, who had founded a whole system of "positive" international law upon "international solidarity," "international federalism," and like "social facts," in 1937 arrives at the conclusion that there is no such thing as international law at all. "Il n'y a plus en Europe de droit des gens," he writes in the *Journal des Nations* (No. 1665, Feb. 28 and March 1, 1937). "Il n'y a plus des traités." "The conclusion seems unescapable," says Professor Zimmern ("The Decline of International Standards," International Affairs, Vol. 17 (1938), p. 12), "that positive international law, so called, has no claim to the name of law." (See also the same, The League of Nations and the Rule of Law 1918–1935 (London, 1936), p. 94.) These scholars, who never cared for such "abstract" problems as the criterion of the validity of a rule of law, now fall from one error into the other. First, they accepted the assumed validity of post-war international law without question; now, since it is obvious that the main bulk of this so-called international law never has been valid law at all, they identify this product of their imagination with the main bulk of pre-war international law, which today is as valid as it has ever been, and declare that international law simply does not exist!

[24] "Can we even understand English law without going beyond the actual rules themselves?" asks Paton in his interesting paper, "Whither Jurisprudence," *Politica*, Vol. 4 (1939), p. 16.

[25] To the following discussion, see Pound, "The Part of Philosophy in International Law," Proceedings of the 6th International Congresss of Philosophy (New York, 1927), p. 374 *et*

Although there may be in a given society particular legal rules which contradict particular ethical rules or *mores*, and *vice versa*, the main bulk of basic ideals to be realized, of ends to be achieved, and of interests to be protected, is generally the same in the different branches of a given normative order. Law, ethics, and *mores* support each other in the pursuit of these aims. Legal rules refer to ethics and *mores* for the determination of their meaning and *vice versa*.[26] The guiding influence, however, as to the ideals, ends, and interests to be pursued by the norms under which a given society lives, emanates from the ethical sphere. From it law and *mores* receive the fundamental distinctions between the good and the bad, the ends to be advanced and the ends to be opposed, the interests to be protected and the interests to be repudiated. At the base of any legal system there lies a body of principles which incorporate the guiding ideas of justice and order to be expounded by the rules of law. The intelligibility of any legal system depends upon the recognition of such a set of fundamental principles which constitute the ethical substance of the legal system, and shed their illuminating light upon each particular rule of law.

This recognition is relatively easy to perform in the domestic field, where the constitution codifies the main bulk of those fundamental principles, and a highly integrated public opinion provides supplementary moral guidance. The task is much more difficult with respect to international law. Here there is no body of such principles separate from the ordinary rules of law. Some of those principles may be only partly expressed in these rules; others may not be expressed at all, and hence have to be detected, in a dangerously uncertain procedure, in the general moral ideas underlying the international law of a certain time, a certain civilization, or even a certain nation. Yet the successful search for these principles is as essential for the scientific understanding of international law as of any legal system.

Legal positivism is unable to grant this recognition; for at its basis there is the hostility to all matters metaphysical, that is, those which cannot be ascertained by actual observation. Since non-legal rules have generally entered the horizon of the positivist jurist as metaphysical rules of natural law, the positivist is inclined to identify natural law and ethics as such, and to repudiate both as metaphysics. However, to exclude *a priori* a certain subject-matter from scientific research by calling it metaphysical, instead of impartially examining actual experience, is to blind oneself to a preconceived idea originating, not in experience, but in mere reasoning, and thus to do violence to the facts. Hence, the positivist concept of the normative sphere

seq.; Bentwich, The Religious Foundations of Internationalism (London, 1933), especially p. 262 *et seq.;* Zimmern, "International Law and Social Consciousness," Transactions of the Grotius Society, Vol. 20 (1934), p. 25 *et seq.; cf.*, particularly, the brilliant paper by Schwarzenberger, "The Rule of Law and the Disintegration of the International Society," this JOURNAL, Vol. 33 (1939), p. 56.

[26] We have dealt with this problem in *La Réalité des Normes*, p. 155.

itself reveals a metaphysical attitude, a kind of negative metaphysics which plainly contradicts the very assumptions of a positive science.[27]

Yet positivism has never been quite able to live up to its legalistic and anti-metaphysical assumptions. The very nature of its subject-matter has compelled it time and again to violate its own assumptions and make use of fundamental principles not revealed by "positive" law. In order to give at least apparent satisfaction to these assumptions, positivism dares to make use of such principles only under the disguise of positivist concepts, and therefore develops a fictitious method which tries by pseudo-logical arguments to derive from "positive," that is, written, rules of international law something that those rules do not contain. The interminable and quite sterile discussions on the foundation of the binding force of international law are evidence of this word-juggling, since this is a problem which, as defined in the positivist terms of mutual consent and the like, is contradictory in itself, and hence insoluble within the framework of positivism. The foundation of the binding force of "positive" law can logically be found, not in this "positive" law itself, but only outside it.[28] Another example is the problem of sovereignty as defined and solved by positivism. Here again a fundamental principle which, by its very nature, cannot be derived from "positive" law, but from which "positive" law itself rather derives its meaning, is to be dealt with as if it were a rule of "positive" international law. It is for these helpless attempts to conciliate its legalistic assumptions with actual juridic experience that the positivist doctrine of international law is bound to misrepresent the reality of international law and to fail to do justice to its actual content.[29]

2. The precepts of international law need not only to be interpreted in the light of the ideals and ethico-legal principles which are at their basis. They need also to be seen within the sociological context of economic interests, social tensions, and aspirations for power, which are the motivating forces in the international field, and which give rise to the factual situations forming the raw material for regulation by international law.[30] The correctness of

[27] For this point, see Liard, *La Science positive et la métaphysique* (4th ed., Paris, 1898), pp. 38, 57, 72. See also Ruggiero, *loc. cit.*, p. 261: "Not only the extreme difficulty of maintaining itself on a level strictly positive and not exceeding the limits of experience but also the tendency . . . to identify objectivity with materiality, have often caused positivism to range over into materialism, that is, into metaphysics, in contradiction to its own premises." As to the specific legal phenomenon of "positivism ending in disregard of positive law," see Lauterpacht, in Modern Theories of Law (London, 1933), pp. 132, 133; and Morgenthau, *Positivisme mal Compris*, pp. 3, 4.

[28] Strupp, Hague *Recueil*, Vol. 47 (1934), p. 298; Brierly, The Law of Nations (London, 1936), p. 45.

[29] Brierly, The Shortcomings of International Law, p. 4 *et seq.;* Morgenthau, "The Problem of Neutrality," University of Kansas City Law Rev., Vol. VII (1939), p. 110; Wild, *loc. cit.*, p. 478 *et seq.*

[30] For this point, see Brierly, *op. cit.*, pp. 5, 16; Kenneth Colegrove, Proceedings of the 5th Conference of Teachers of International Law, p. 97; Ray, *Annales Sociologiques*, série C,

this postulate for the interpretation of municipal law is today self-evident. Nobody would ever try to interpret social legislation without reference to the conflicting social interests to be evaluated and the social relations to be settled. Nobody would ever endeavor to grasp the legal meaning of economic legislation without making economic interests and conflicts part of the reasoning. Even where the reference to the underlying economic and social forces and relations is not always explicit, as in the field of contracts, the sociological context is nevertheless always referred to by implication. It is only because of the highly typical character of the factual situations and their social and economic significance, with which everybody is familiar, and which are completely and adequately expressed in the legal rules, that the mere reference to those legal rules implies the consideration of the social and economic factors which are at their basis.

It was, historically, the most disastrous error of positivism to misunderstand completely this implicit reference to the sociological context which every legal rule contains. This error can be traced back to the tradition of the pandectists, who had in the Roman law the classical model of a highly typified legal system which expressed with perfect appropriateness the fundamental interests and relationships which can arise from the social activities of men. So perfectly was this sociological context represented in the abstractions of the Roman law, that the pandectists were only too prone to forget its very existence and to deal with those abstractions as with independent logical entities. So did the positivists, both in the municipal and international fields.[31] This methodological error was of minor importance where the legal concepts were true abstractions from the interests and relations which they were supposed to regulate. When, however, those legal rules were applied to interests and relations to which some of them referred only partly, others not at all, that methodological error was bound to have a disastrous influence upon the scientific value of positivist jurisprudence. In the domestic field, it became instrumental in distorting the legal reality and originating that positivist conceptualism with which a decadent legal science attempted to adapt the old legal rules to new economic and social needs, but at the same time maintained the fictitious assumption that the written law already contained, logically, all the rules necessary for the solution of those new problems. Thus the juridical pseudo-logic became the artificial makeshift by which a stationary law could be reconciled with a moving social reality.

In the international field, the methodological error of neglecting the socio-

No. 3, p. 14 *et seq.; cf.* especially, the excellent remarks by Friedman, Modern Law Review, Vol. 2 (1938), p. 194; and review, *ibid.*, p. 81.

[31] For the influence of Roman law upon international law, see Pound, *loc. cit.*, pp. 376, 377; Lauterpacht, Private Law Sources, p. 23 *et seq.;* Alvarez, *Nouvelle Conception des Études juridiques*, p. 47 *et seq.*

logical context of international law led to even worse consequences.[32] In the domestic field, the correspondence between legal concepts and sociological context was at least a temporary fact, and within this limit the negligence of the sociological context and the assumption of the "self-sufficiency" of the written law could be justified. In the most important branches of international law this correspondence has never, and could never, have existed. The sociological relationships underlying those branches of international law are characterized by their individual, non-typical nature.[33] A political situatiòn in the international field is not likely to repeat itself, since the variety of factors of which it is composed makes for an indefinite number of possible combinations. Hence only a strictly individualized rule of law will be adequate to it. International law provides partly for such individualized rules by restricting the application of a rule to one individual case and leaving the regulation of similar future cases to new legislative efforts. Peace treaties are instances of such individualized rules of international law. In part, however, international law does maintain the form of the general, typical rule of law and depends on the interpretation of the rule to provide the flexible meaning which the ever-changing sociological context requires. All political treaties which are intent upon establishing permanent rights and duties between the contracting parties are of this kind. The same generally and typically worded text may imply quite different rules, according to the political function which it is supposed to fulfill.[34] Thus one is able, for instance, to distinguish three different periods in the history of the Treaties of Locarno.[35] Those three periods are characterized by three significant changes in the normative content of the rules, resulting from changes in the political context, although the wording of the rules remained unchanged. The Covenant of the League of Nations, as a whole, as well as particular provisions, for instance, Article 16, have been submitted to similar modifications as a result of factual sociological developments and not of legislative changes.[36]

The same phenomenon occurs not only in temporary succession, but also

[32] Reeves, Proceedings of the 2nd Conference of Teachers of International Law, pp. 72, 73.

[33] This high degree of individualization is clearly recognized by Brierly, Hague *Recueil*, Vol. 58, p. 16; Ray, *ibid.*, Vol. 48, p. 699; Schindler, *ibid.*, Vol. 46, p. 265.

[34] The same phenomenon with regard to municipal social legislation has been excellently described by Frankfurter, *loc. cit.*, pp. 369, 370: "It is now clearly enough recognized that each case presents a distinct issue; that each case must be determined by the facts relevant to it; that we are dealing, in truth, not with a question of law but the application of an undisputed formula to a constantly changing and growing variety of economic and social facts. Each case, therefore, calls for a new and distinct consideration, not only of the general facts of industry but the specific facts in regard to the employment in question and the specific exigencies which called for the specific statute."

[35] See Morgenthau, "*Théorie des Sanctions internationales,*" *Revue de Droit Int. et de Lég. Comp.*, Vol. 16 (1935), p. 832.

[36] See Morgenthau, "The Resurrection of Neutrality in Europe," Am. Pol. Sci. Rev., Vol. 33 (1939), p. 473.

under contemporaneous yet different sociological conditions. The identical text of an arbitration treaty or non-aggression pact may have quite different legal meanings, according to the political situation existing between different contracting parties.[37] Even one and the same legal rule, as, for instance, Article 16 of the Covenant, lends itself to different interpretations with respect to states living under different political conditions.[38]

The positivist doctrine of international law has completely ignored this particular relationship between the rules of international law and their sociological context. Positivism transplanted schematically the highly refined positivist method of formalist and conceptualist interpretation into the domain of international law. This method developed under, and was justified by, the specific domestic conditions of a temporarily stabilized society where there was approximately no tension between law and sociological context but almost complete rationalization and representation of the sociological context within the concepts of positive law. Schematically applied to a law and a society of a distinctly different nature, this method was bound to produce entirely inadequate results. Where the experience of international law showed that an individual situation required an individual interpretation of the legal rule, the positivist method could not fail to disregard all individual aspects of the factual situation and concentrate upon the general wording of the legal rule which, by virtue of its logical self-sufficiency, was supposed to contain all elements necessary for its understanding; and to this the reference to the sociological context could contribute nothing. An arbitration treaty which submitted all conflicts between the contracting parties to international tribunals was a legal document that revealed its legal significance through its text, *i.e.*, another step towards the establishment of an international order based upon respect for law. Whether the treaty was concluded between Switzerland and Uruguay, or Denmark, Sweden, and Norway, or Great Britain and France, or Germany and Poland in 1925, 1935, or 1939—these were "political" considerations irrelevantly lying beyond the scope of positivist interpretation.[39]

3. The positivist doctrine, by recognizing as international law only the rules enforced by states, excludes from the domain of international law all rules whose validity cannot be traced to the written documents of states. On the other hand, the positivist doctrine cannot deny that such rules, like most rules of general international law, actually exist. Confronted with the embarrassing dilemma of violating its own *étatist* assumptions or of dis-

[37] Leresche, "*La Crise du Droit des Gens,*" *Rev. int. Française du Droit des Gens,* Vol. 6 (1938), p. 303.

[38] See the excellent criticism by Barandon, *Das System der politischen Staatsvertraege seit 1918* (Handbuch des Voelkerrechts, Vol. 4), p. 1.

[39] See author's analysis of arbitration treaties concluded under different political circumstances, in International Jurisdiction, its Nature and its Limits (in German, 1929), p. 131 *et seq.*

regarding an obvious part of legal experience, the positivist doctrine has taken refuge in a concept which has become a veritable panacea for its theoretical troubles. We are referring to the concept of customary law, which has served for the traditional doctrine of international law as a kind of collective designation for all the rules of international law the origin of which cannot directly be traced to written sources. The insurmountable theoretical difficulties of explaining the existence of a so-called customary law have been pointed out elsewhere,[40] and this is no place to resume the discussion. It is sufficient to state that the reconciliation which the positivist doctrine is able to establish between its monist, legalistic assumptions and the existence of a so-called customary law, is merely apparent. In order to save these assumptions as well as those facts, it resorts to a series of fictions, like tacit consent, recognition, judicial admission, and so forth, which indirectly endeavor to attribute the existence of the so-called customary rules of international law to the legislative will of states.

PREFACE TO A FUNCTIONAL THEORY OF INTERNATIONAL LAW

The fundamental weakness of the positivist doctrine of international law lies in its inadequacy to international law as it really is. Unfaithful to its own assumptions, it contains at the same time more and less than the actual rules of international law, which it furthermore submits to subjective evaluation in the light of ethical and political principles of assumedly universal, yet doubtful, validity. A truly scientific theory of international law must avoid these mistakes in order to come closer to the reality. It seems to be a logical choice to call such a theory by the name of realist. There are, however, two objections to this choice. On the one hand, the increasing disrepute of the traditional doctrine of international law has led no few practitioners of this doctrine to demonstrate their closeness to the reality of international law by calling themselves "realists."[41] This misuse has deprived the term of its distinctive character in the international field. On the other hand, realism has become a collective designation for several tendencies in modern jurisprudence, all aiming at replacing, by different means, the fictitious legalism of traditional jurisprudence with a conception nearer to the realities of the law. All these tendencies have this in common: They do not regard the legal rules as definitely determined by their legislative or judicial formulation, but search for the psychological, social, political and economic forces which determine the actual content and working of legal rules and

[40] *La Réalité des Normes*, p. 89 *et seq.;* for criticism of the doctrine of customary international law, see also, Brierly, Hague *Recueil*, Vol. 58, p. 29; Ray, *ibid.*, Vol. 48, pp. 697, 698.

[41] See, for instance, Kaufmann, Hague *Recueil*, Vol. 54 (1935), pp. 319, 320; Scelle, *ibid.*, Vol. 46 (1933), p. 691; Verdross, *ibid.*, Vol. 30 (1929), p. 277; Le Fur, in *Revue de Droit International*, Vol. 17 (1936), p. 7—authors who have certainly not very much in common besides the claim of being "realists." *Cf.* also, Lundstedt who, according to Pound, *loc. cit.*, p. 145, qualifies Pound, Kelsen, and Duguit as "realists"!

which, in turn, are determined by them. In other words, their scientific goal is to formulate uniform functional relationships between those forces and the legal rules. Hence, "realist" jurisprudence is, in truth, "functional" jurisprudence.[42]

The legacy which positivism has left to the science of international law consists in the task of comprehending the international law of a given time as standing in a dual functional relationship with the social forces of this time. On the one hand, international law is the function of the civilization in which it originates, that is, of the regulative ideas laid down in the ethics and *mores* of this civilization, of the political, economic and general social forces prevailing in it, and, finally, of the specific psychological factors manifesting themselves in the individuals determining it. On the other hand, international law is a social mechanism working towards certain ends within this same civilization which, in turn, as far as determined by it, becomes a function of this same international law. By systematizing the rules of a given international law under the viewpoint of this dual functional relationship between rules and social forces, the functional theory will arrive at a real scientific understanding of the material element of the legal rules which positivism even at its best was able to describe and systematize only according to superficial legalistic viewpoints.[43]

Six important consequences for a functional theory of international law

[42] Although the doctrine developed in the text is undoubtedly of a sociological nature, we would rather prefer to avoid the term; for sociological jurisprudence, through the influence of Professor Pound's writings, is associated with the idea of "social engineering," which is, from the standpoint of the contemporaneous legal science, a very premature proposition; see, *infra* VI under.

[43] The principles of functional jurisprudence, as understood in this paper, have been admirably formulated by Llewellyn, "Legal Tradition and Social Science Method—a Realist's Critic," Essays on Research in the Social Sciences (Brookings Institution, 1931); and "Some Realism about Realism," Harvard Law Rev., Vol. 44 (1930/31), p. 1236 *et seq.* The transition from positivism to functionalism is excellently described by Pound, "Fifty Years of Jurisprudence," *ibid.*, Vol. 51 (1937/38), pp. 446, 447: "The determining impetus came from positivism and the direction was sociology, leading to functional study of legal institutions in the light of all the social sciences, and tends to consideration of the legal order as a social institution rather than exclusive consideration of the legal materials with which tribunals work in upholding that order." See also, Hudson, Cornell Law Rev., Vol. 10, p. 434. The functional viewpoint is excellently developed also by P. Alex, *Du Droit et du Positivisme* (Paris, 1876), see especially pp. 12 *et seq.*, 26 *et seq.*, 39, 118. This work, completely forgotten today, endeavors to apply the principles of a well-understood positivism to jurisprudence, and thus puts by implication the subsequent aberrations of juridic positivism in the right light. See also, the penetrating article by Felix S. Cohen, "The Problems of Functional Jurisprudence," Modern Law Review, Vol. 1 (1937/38), p. 5; and Malinowski, "The Group and the Individual in Functional Analysis," Am. Jour. of Sociology, Vol. 44 (1938/39), p. 951: "I would like to add that the science of modern jurisprudence could become inspired by anthropology in treating legal phenomena within the context of social life and in conjunction with other norms of conduct." For the philosophical background, see Kallen, "Functionalism," Encyclopedia of the Social Sciences, Vol. 6, p. 523.

can be drawn from this recognition of the functional relationship between social forces and international law.[44]

I. A functional theory of international law has to start with the recognition of the particularly intimate nature of this relationship.[45] In the domestic field, legal rules can be imposed by the group which holds the monopoly of organized physical force, that is, the officials of the state. The international sphere is characterized by the absence of such a group. International law owes its existence to identical or complementary interests of states, backed by power as a last resort, or, where such identical interests do not exist, to a mere balance of power which prevents a state from breaking these rules of international law. Where there is neither community of interests nor balance of power, there is no international law. Whereas domestic law may originate in the arbitrary will of the rule-making agencies of the state, international law is usually the result of objective social forces. When, in the international field, an arbitrary rule-making power tries to impose rules supported neither by common interests nor by a balance of power, these rules never become valid law, or gain only ephemeral existence and scant efficacy; the history of the rules embodied in the Treaty of Versailles and the Covenant of the League of Nations is a striking example of this.

It is also due to this intimate relationship between social forces and legal rules that in the international field fundamental changes of the social forces and, hence, of the legal rules, follow each other at frequent intervals and in an abrupt, often violent, manner. In the domestic field the regulative social force dominating all others is the state. It has developed not only an overwhelming power apparatus, but also highly refined mechanisms of legislative and judicial readjustment, which lead the social forces into certain channels without disrupting the legal and social continuity. Here, the state selects in authoritative decisions the social forces to be recognized by the law. It decides to what extent the existing legal rules shall yield to changing conditions, to what extent they shall resist them, and in what ways they shall try to transform them. In the international field the authoritative decision is replaced by the free interplay of political and military forces. This makes a gradual readjustment of the law to changing social conditions extremely difficult. Any fundamental change of the social forces underlying a system of international law of necessity induces the prospective beneficiaries of the change to try to bring about a corresponding change of the legal rules, whereas the beneficiaries of the legal *status quo* will resist any change of the old order. Here a competitive contest for power will determine the

[44] These consequences can be stated within the limits of this paper only in very general terms, and other consequences may be revealed through application of the principles developed in the text to special problems; see the enumeration of possible further consequences, in *Positivisme mal compris*, p. 20.

[45] This relationship is clearly recognized by Huber, *op. cit.*, p. 9 *et seq.;* Schindler, *loc. cit.*, p. 237 *et seq.;* see also, *La Réalité des Normes*, pp. 139, 140, 215.

victorious social forces, and the change of the existing legal order will be decided, not through a legal procedure provided for by this same legal order, but through a conflagration of conflicting social forces which challenge the legal order as a whole.[46]

Where such a conflict between social forces and the rules of law exists, the character and function of the whole legal order undergo a transformation. We have proposed to call this relationship by the name of "tension," and have dealt with its legal consequences elsewhere.[47]

II. This recognition of the peculiar relationship between social forces and rules of international law provides the clue for restating, in functional terms, the doctrine of the validity of international law.[48] A rule of international law does not, as positivism was prone to believe, receive its validity from its enactment into a legal instrument, as, for instance, an international treaty. There are rules of international law which are valid, although not enacted in such legal instruments, and there are rules of international law which are not valid, although enacted in such instruments. Enactment, therefore, is no objective criterion for the alleged validity of a rule of international law. A rule, be it legal, moral, or conventional, is valid when its violation is likely to be followed by an unfavorable reaction, that is, a sanction against its violator. An alleged rule, the violation of which is not followed by such a sanction, is a mere idea, a wish, a suggestion, but not a valid rule. An alleged rule of international law, against the violation of which no state reacts, and is likely to react, is proved, by this very absence of probable reaction, not to be a valid rule of international law. The gradual invalidation of the territorial provisions of the Treaty of Versailles, and of most articles of the Covenant of the League of Nations, by violation and non-intervention of sanctions against these violations, are experimental proof of the correctness of this concept of validity.[49]

How, then, are we to know beforehand when such sanctions are likely to intervene in behalf of a violated norm, and when not, and, hence, how are we

[46] This problem, which refers to the validity of international law and its dynamic aspects, should be clearly distinguished from the problem discussed *supra*, under par. 2. There we had to do with the question as to how in the international field the particular characteristics of the social context are represented in the material concepts of the legal rules.

[47] On the theory of international "tensions," see Morgenthau, International Jurisdiction, p. 59 *et seq.;* and *La Notion du "Politique,"* p. 37 *et seq.* This theory has been thoroughly discussed by Ray, *Annales sociologiques, série C*, No. 1 (1935), p. 163 *et seq.*

[48] As to the problem of the validity of international law, see Morgenthau, *La Réalité des Normes*, pp. 28 *et seq.*, 212 *et seq.* Professor Timasheff, An Introduction to the Sociology of Law (Cambridge, 1939), p. 271, calls the theory developed there an "artificial construction." However, it seems to us that the artificiality of this theory is only the reflex of the artificial character of international law itself; as to this theory of validity in general, see his remarks, *ibid.*, pp. 142, 166, 299, 300. The psychological mechanism underlying the validity of international law is well described by Baty in this JOURNAL, Vol. 33 (1939), p. 653.

[49] For the relationship between sanctions and validity, see also, "*Théorie des Sanctions Internationales*," *loc. cit.*, pp. 474 *et seq.*, 809 *et seq.*

to say, in an objective, scientific way, which norms are valid and which are not? The consideration of the functional factor will give the answer.

1. The commonest and simplest test for the validity of an alleged rule of international law is this: State A has, in the past, requested State B to perform certain actions corresponding to the rule, whereas State B, in turn, has requested State A to perform certain actions corresponding to the same or another rule. Where these identical or complementary interests in the mutual observance of these rules did not suffice to guarantee the actual observance, both states were willing to enforce compliance with the rule by protest, reprisal, or military action. Where there was, in the past, a recognized identical or complementary interest in a certain action on the part of two or more states, together with the willingness to enforce this action, there exists the likelihood that the same sanctions for the sake of the same interests will also be performed in the future. Respect for the status of diplomatic representatives has been, in the past, an interest recognized and guaranteed with sanctions by all states; therefore, the forecast is justified that the states will follow the same course of action in the future.

The enactment of rules corresponding to such interests in international treaties may indicate the permanent nature of those interests, but this is an assumption which needs support from the facts and which can be disproved by them. Another indication of the permanence of such interests is their sublimation into moral principles, which pretend universal validity and endeavor to give certain interests of exceptional importance a justification superior to that which they could derive from the law.

2. The situation, however, is not always so simple. Three possible situations present themselves for examination. It can be that:

(a) Identical or complementary interests survive the willingness to enforce the actions corresponding to them. The provisions of the Treaties of Locarno were the function of identical and complementary interests of the contracting parties. When Germany violated these treaties by remilitarizing the Rhineland, the interests of the signatories in the demilitarization survived their willingness to enforce an attitude corresponding to their interests, and thus the respective rules of international law lost their validity.

(b) The willingness to enforce certain actions corresponding to identical or complementary interests survives the interests themselves. The provisions of the Treaty of Versailles establishing the German-Polish frontier from the outset did not correspond to the interest of both states. These provisions were observed for a period of twenty years because there existed a balance of power between both nations and their respective allies, which prevented either of them from violating the law.

(c) The interests and the willingness to enforce the actions corresponding to them disappear altogether. In this category belong the French-Russian and German-Italian military alliances, the Pact of the Little Entente, the political provisions of the Covenant of the League of Nations, and numerous provisions of the Peace Treaties of 1919.

What does the analysis of these cases show with regard to the validity of international law? In the cases (a) and (c) the rules of international law become invalid according to the functional concept of validity because no longer does there exist a likelihood of sanctions being performed, should those rules be violated. In case (b) the validity of the rules depends upon a balance of power, which may be stable for a certain time, and then suddenly become unstable, but which in our time is of a rather permanently unstable and precarious nature. All cases have this in common, that they make forecasts as to the likelihood of sanctions extremely uncertain. The enactment of the rules in international treaties is here of no avail, and, as contemporaneous examples have amply shown, is rather misleading. Their conformity with moral principles is scarcely more illuminating because of the aforesaid difficulty of ascertaining the exact moral nature of such principles.

Where the functional relationships between sociological forces and international law is in a state of transition from (1) to one of the situations under (2) the development may as well stop at an intermediate point between (1), on the one hand, and (2 a) and (c), on the other; proceed to (2 b); or, finally, come to an end at (2 a) or (c). Here, the validity of the respective rules of international law is, so to speak, in suspense, and may be as well maintained or destroyed. With respect to such rules the science of international law becomes a system of guesses, enjoying a greater or lesser chance of being proved true according to the factual development of the functional relationship between the social forces and the rules of international law.[50]

III. It follows from this analysis that there exist two obviously different types of international law, one founded upon the permanent and stable interests, the other based upon the temporary and fluctuating interests of states.[51] This differentiation is not only of fundamental importance for the understanding of the validity of international law; it leads to yet more far-reaching consequences as to the subject-matter, the methods, and the scientific character of the science of international law. One might even say that it leads to the recognition of two different sciences of international law which deal with different subject-matters, and apply, or rather ought to apply, different methods of research and systematization.

The main bulk of the concepts and principles of international law has been derived from municipal civil law. These concepts and principles have been

[50] Wharton, International Law Digest, Vol. 2 (Washington, 1881), p. 34, makes, in connection with Jones *v.* Walker, 2 Paine 688, a very interesting distinction between necessary, that is, juridic, and voluntary, that is, political validity.

[51] The classical concept of *jus necessarium* (see Morgenthau, *Positivisme mal compris*, pp. 16, 17) and Huber's distinction between territorial and extraterritorial rules (*loc. cit.*, p. 45 *et seq.*) refer to related but not identical differentiations. See also, Starke, "Monism and Dualism in the Theory of International Law," British Year Book of International Law, Vol. 17 (1936), p. 78 *et seq.*

developed within a legal system characterized by the extraordinary stability of the interests underlying it. Hence its application is, of necessity, restricted to legal systems based upon equally stable interests. In the international field such stable interests exist, for instance, with respect to diplomatic privileges, territorial jurisdiction, extradition, wide fields of maritime law, arbitral procedure, and so forth. This is the classical field of traditional international law as it has gradually developed in the practice of states since the sixteenth century. We propose to call these rules non-political international law, originating in the permanent interests of states to put their normal relations upon a stable basis by providing for predictable and enforceable conduct with respect to these relations.

But there is another type of international law which expresses, in terms of rights and duties, temporary interests ever given to change. In this category belong political agreements, especially treaties of alliance and their modern substitutes, which, under the legalistic disguise of treaties of general arbitration, consultation, or friendship, frequently pursue aims at least preparatory to close political ties. The traditional science of international law treats both types of international law alike, applying to both the concepts and methods developed in municipal civil law.[52] By doing so, it cannot but draw a completely distorted picture of those rules which belong in the category of political international law. Under such treatment, their validity appears to be firmly established, whereas it is actually always precarious; the interests which they are supposed to serve appear to be permanent and definite, whereas they are actually exposed to continuous change and are more or less uncertain; and consequently, the rights and duties established by them appear to be clearly determined, whereas they are subject actually to the most contradictory interpretations.

This writer knows of only one monograph dealing with political international law as an independent subject-matter requiring concepts and methods of its own: Rafael Erich's *Alliances and Alliance Treaties*.[53] He is aware of only a few references clearly stating the functional relationship between the political rules of international law and the underlying social factors: Judge Manley O. Hudson remarks that "if international law is to be built on solid foundations, it is no more possible to ignore the political and social phases of the prevailing international order than it is possible to ignore similar phases of the prevailing national order in the building of municipal law";[54]

[52] This problem is clearly seen by Whitehead, "An Appeal to Reason," Atlantic Monthly (March, 1939), p. 311: "Obligation, in European foreign policy, arises from the immediate situation and from duty to the future. Formal law can refer only to situations sufficiently stable." See also, Hudson, *loc. cit.*, p. 435: "Where the nineteenth century sought the vindication of natural rights, it must be our task to ascertain and evaluate interests."

[53] In German, Helsingfors, 1907.

[54] The Permanent Court of International Justice (New York, 1934), p. 567; see also p. 552 *et seq.*, and Proceedings of the 2nd Conference of Teachers of International Law, p. 40, with Fenwick, *ibid.*, p. 69, and this JOURNAL, Vol. 33 (1939), p. 107, agreeing. In the same

a similar remark in the Harvard Research in International Law reveals the same author;[55] and, finally, Professors Jessup[56] and Wild[57] urge the functional approach. There seems to be only one judicial opinion clearly pointing to the practical consequences of this relationship: Judge Anzilotti's dissenting opinion in the Austro-German Customs Union Case.[58] It remains for a functional theory of international law to develop systematically concepts and methods capable of conveying the legal characteristics, as well as the functional dependence on political factors, of political international law.

IV. As we have seen, there exist functional relationships not only between the law and the non-normative social forces, but also between the law and the other branches of the normative sphere, that is, ethics and *mores*. The latter are threefold with regard to the validity and the content of the rules of law.

As has been shown elsewhere,[59] the validity of any legal system reposes upon a fundamental norm which itself cannot be of a legal nature, but belongs of necessity to the domain of ethics and *mores*. Thus, the validity of the legal system of the United States reposes, on the one hand, upon an ethical rule enjoining upon the President, the members of Congress and of the Supreme Court to obey the Constitution, and, on the other hand, upon the *mores* keeping alive among the citizens the respect for the Constitution. When one or the other of these ethical foundations is lacking, the validity of the Constitution and of the legal system founded upon it is in a precarious state. When all are lacking, the Constitution, and with it the whole legal system, have ceased to exist as a living legal order even though they may not have been formally invalidated.

Not only does the validity of the legal system as a whole repose upon ethics and *mores*, but the validity of individual legal rules also stands frequently in a particular functional relationship with ethics and *mores*. It can be that the validity of one and the same precept, for instance, "Thou shall not kill,"

direction points the remark by McNair, Hague *Recueil*, Vol. 43 (1933), pp. 251 and 252: "Nous appartenons à l'école de ces juristes qui pensent que la science du droit international a besoin aujourd'hui des matériaux à mettre en oeuvre plus que des thèses et des monographies."

[55] Research in International Law under the Auspices of the Faculty of the Harvard Law School, this JOURNAL, Supp., Vol. 29 (1935), p. 953; see also pp. 937, 938, 947.

[56] Proceedings of the 3rd Conference of Teachers of International Law, p. 134 *et seq.*

[57] Am. Pol. Sci. Rev., *loc. cit.*

[58] As to the defectiveness of the majority decision from the functional standpoint, see Hudson, "The World Court and the Austro-German Customs Régime," American Bar Association Journal, Vol. 17 (1931), p. 793: "In our national courts, a refusal to take account of the social and political conditions to which law must be applied, has produced some of the sharpest criticism of our legal systems. . . . An international court might similarly build a law in disregard of the political factors which condition its application, but it would almost certainly lack both the appearance and the substance of reality."

[59] *La Réalité des Normes*, pp. 76 *et seq.*, 174 *et seq.*, 216 *et seq.*

reposes upon the likelihood that against its violation there will be performed sanctions pertaining to the domains of ethics and *mores*, as well as to the realm of the law. Many provisions of the Constitution, of civil and criminal law, belong to this category, and, therefore, are at the same time legal rules, ethical rules, and rules of the *mores*. It is obvious that this double or triple guaranty has an important bearing upon the observance and validity of a given precept. When such a multiple guaranty exists, that is, when ethics, *mores* and law coöperate to realize a certain order of things, there is a much greater likelihood that this order will be realized than when the law alone strives for this goal.[60]

It has already been pointed out that legal rules receive their precepts partly from ethics and *mores*. The meaning of these precepts requires explanation in the light of these other rules from which it is derived. The Constitution itself, for instance, does not reveal what "due process of law" or "freedom of contract" is; it is only by reference to the ethics and *mores* of a certain period of constitutional history that the meaning of these constitutional concepts can be determined.

The recognition, with regard to international law, of these three fundamental relationships, here hinted at rather than actually explained, calls for the discussion of a series of problems which the traditional science of international law does not even care to pose. What is, for instance, the empirical nature of the dual relationship between international law, on the one hand, and ethics and *mores* on the other? Are there ethics and *mores* of a truly international nature, or do we call by the name of "international," ethics and *mores* the precepts of which have been developed under the determining influence of the individual states and are applied to international affairs in the interest of these states? Which rules of international law belong, at the same time, to ethics and *mores*, and so have a greater chance of being observed? The meaning of which rules of international law can be only determined by reference to ethics and *mores*, and to what kind of ethics and *mores* do these rules refer? [61]

V. It follows from the preceding discussions that no branch of the traditional science of international law is more in need of reform than the doctrine of interpretation. The traditional doctrine has limited its efforts to transferring schematically the time-honored common and Roman law principles of interpretation to the international field. It has discussed the problem whether the wording of a treaty or the intentions of the parties shall be the main source of interpretation; it has gone deeply into the question whether preparatory materials may be used for purposes of interpretation; and it

[60] To this "cumulative" relationship, see *ibid.*, p. 185 *et seq.* To the following discussion see the general theoretical explanations, *ibid.*, p. 155 *et seq.;* and the remarks referring to them by Timasheff, *op. cit.*, pp. 62, 83, 84, 272, 324.

[61] The aforementioned papers by Friedman and Schwarzenberger (*supra*, notes 4, 25) are a promising beginning in this direction.

has advanced a great variety of so-called "rules of construction." Yet it has completely overlooked the fact that, due to the peculiar relationship between social forces and rules of international law, the problem of interpretation in the international field shows unique aspects for which the traditional civil law technique of interpretation is utterly inadequate.

When in the domestic field the meaning of a contract is ascertained by the usual means of interpretation, the interpretative job is done. It is generally not too difficult to perform the same task with regard to an international treaty; but then the real problem of interpretation just begins. A contract of civil law generally uses standardized language whose legal meaning is definite, or at least can be ascertained according to objective, universally recognized characteristics. An international treaty is not necessarily of the same nature. Its real meaning may be disguised with diplomatic language so that its wording is indicative only of what it does not mean. Under such circumstances, it is only from the social context that this treaty will receive its meaning. The political situation of the parties, and their intentions with respect to this situation, have to be ascertained from the viewpoint of the subject-matter of the treaty in question, for the time of the conclusion of the treaty as well as for the time of the interpretation; for, as we have seen, the legal meaning of an international treaty is ever subject to change. From this analysis one may then conclude, in a laborious and always highly uncertain manner, what might be the probable objective of the treaty and the legal meaning of the particular stipulations serving this purpose.

What, for instance, does the term "independence" in an international treaty mean? Its meaning may coincide with the accepted meaning of the term, it may be somewhat different, it may be the exact opposite, or it may have no legal meaning at all. The rules of construction will be of no avail with respect to this problem. It is only from the background of the social context and of the function the treaty is supposed to fulfill within it, that a scientific interpretation can hope, at least within certain limits, to receive a satisfactory answer. The answer will, for instance, vary according to whether the state to which the term applies is a colonial, semi-colonial, or non-colonial country; whether the treaty is concluded between two states of equal or different political power; whether or not in the last alternative, the more powerful state has imperialistic intentions with respect to the other party; whether the treaty is of a bilateral nature, pursuing a specific political aim, or is supported by the consensus of a great number of states for the sake of a general purpose common to all of them.

VI. To fulfill its task, the functional theory of international law has to take another step beyond positivism. It was the assumption of the positivist concept of science to be more scientific than any previous approach to an understanding of things. Positivist science was supposed to be free from all metaphysical elements, not asking how things ought to be and what their "real" essence might be, but seeking only uniform relations between things verifiable in experience. "*Je ne propose rien, je ne suppose rien, j'expose,*" was Comte's device. But just as Comte ended in the metaphysics of his "religion of humanity," so juridic positivism was not satisfied with knowing what the law actually was and how it worked. It was only too eager to remodel the world of the law after idealistic assumptions whose universal validity the respective authors took for granted. This tendency, variously strong in the different branches of municipal law, is uppermost in the positivist doctrine of international law. The science of international law, completely absorbed by practical problems as to what the rules of international law should be, is paying almost no attention to the psychological and sociological laws governing the actions of men in the international sphere, nor to the possible legal rules growing out of such actions. Who would dare embark upon such research would be called "impractical," and the results of his studies, if ever mentioned at all, would be qualified as "worthless." Grandiose legalistic schemes purporting to solve the ills of the world have replaced the less spectacular, painstaking search for the actual laws and the facts underlying them. This presumptuous enterprise has contributed nothing to the betterment of international relations, let alone the knowledge of what these international relations actually are. It has only shown the utter futility of all attempts to reform human conditions on the basis of idealistic assumptions without knowing the laws under which these conditions stand. As William Graham Sumner put it:

> In this view, the worst vice in political discussions is that dogmatism which takes its stand on "great principles" or assumptions, instead of standing on an exact examination of things as they are and human nature as it is. . . . The social sciences are, as yet, the stronghold of all this pernicious dogmatism; and nowhere does it do more harm than in politics. The whole method of abstract speculation on political topics is vicious. It is popular because it is easy; it is easier to imagine a new world than to learn to know this one; it is easier to embark on speculations based on a few broad assumptions than it is to study the history of states and institutions; it is easier to catch up a popular dogma than it is to analyze it to see whether it is true or not. All this leads to confusion, to the admission of phrases and platitudes, to much disputing but little gain in the prosperity of nations.[62]

"The eagerness for premature practical application . . . ," to express the same thought in the words of Vilfredo Pareto, "is ever obstructing the progress of science, along with a mania for preaching to people as to what they ought to do—an exceedingly bootless occupation—instead of finding out what they actually do." [63]

Why, then, is it that the field where the social sciences are able to work successfully is much narrower than the corresponding field of the natural

[62] "Democracy and Responsible Government," in The Challenge of Facts and Other Essays (New Haven, 1914), pp. 245, 246.

[63] The Mind and Society, Vol. 1 (New York, 1935), p. 185.

sciences? It is again Sumner who knows an answer to this question. "The reason is because the elements of any sort of problem which we do not know so far surpass in number and importance those which we do know that our solutions have far greater chance to be wrong than to be right." [64] Thus, the problem which the science of international law has to solve is clearly set. The natural sciences had to discover the laws governing nature before they could hope to dominate the natural forces, to prevent the dangers emanating from them, and to use them for human aims. In the same way, the social sciences cannot hope to master the social forces unless they know the laws which govern the social relations of men. In the natural sciences, the discovery of the infinitesimal calculus by Newton and Leibniz was bound to precede many modern technical inventions. The millennial attempts at constructing the airplane could not succeed as long as Carnot had not established his purely theoretical propositions on thermodynamics. Were it not for the theoretical efforts of Faraday, who himself did not invent anything of practical value, there would not be today any of the multiple uses of electricity for practical purposes. Had not Maxwell and Hertz, without any practical objective, carried out certain "abstruse and remote" calculations in the field of magnetism and electricity, Marconi could never have invented wireless and the radio.[65]

The science of international law, as well as the social sciences in general, are still awaiting their Newton, their Leibniz, their Faraday, their Carnot, their Maxwell, and their Hertz. To expect the contemporaneous lawyer to be an "engineer" or "technician" of the law means to expect Edison before Faraday, Wright before Carnot, Marconi before Maxwell and Hertz. And this is certainly a futile expectation. The great task which lies before the social sciences is to prepare the work of the latter so that the former can build upon it. By joining them in this endeavor the functional theory of international law will not only fulfill the task of any scientific doctrine, that is, to know what is and why it is; it will also prepare the ground for satisfying the greater ethical and political desire to improve international relations by means of the law.[66]

[64] "Speculative Legislation," *op. cit.*, p. 219.

[65] For the relationship between theory and practice in the natural sciences, see Meyerson, *La Déduction relativiste* (Paris, 1925), p. 333 *et seq.; Identité et Réalité* (Paris, 1926), pp. 36, 37; *Du Cheminement de la Pensée*, Vol. 1 (Paris, 1931), p. 3 *et seq.;* Flexner, "The Usefulness of Useless Knowledge," Harpers (October, 1939), p. 544.

[66] A highly illuminating discussion of the problem, only hinted at in the text, is to be found in Professor Hankin's paper, "Social Science and Social Action," American Sociological Rev., Vol. 4 (1939), p. 1; see also, Professor Lundberg, "Contemporary Positivism in Sociology," *ibid.*, p. 52 *et seq.* The problem is stated with intuitive insight by Lincoln Steffens in his letter of June 18, 1919, to Laura Suggett (The Letters of Lincoln Steffens (New York, 1938), Vol. 1, p. 472), picturing Wilson in Paris: "He is righteous. If only he were intelligent, scientific! But the unmoral, scientific, intellectual type is for the next generation to produce. Our part is to use the transition period to raise the questions, point away from all persons and individual guilt to the physical and economic enemies of Man."

[2]

THE SUBJECTS OF A MODERN LAW OF NATIONS

Philip C. Jessup *

INTERNATIONAL law is generally defined or described as law applicable to relations between states. States are said to be the subjects of international law and individuals only its "objects." Treatises on international law accordingly usually proceed at the very outset to examine the nature and essential characteristics of the fictitious jural person known as the state.

But there has welled up through the years a growing opposition to this traditional concept. Numerous writers have attacked the dogma from a variety of approaches. Duguit, Krabbe, and Kelsen and others have impugned the philosophical and juridical basis of the concept.[1] Georges Scelle has called the traditional view "une vue fausse, une abstraction anthropomorphique, historiquement responsable du caractère fictif et de la paralysie de la science traditionnelle du droit des gens."[2] The record of progress toward the goal of acknowledging the international legal position of the individual has been traced by many jurists.[3] Politis has graphically said: "Formerly the sovereign State was an iron

* Hamilton Fish Professor of International Law and Diplomacy, Columbia University.

[1] 1 DUGUIT, TRAITÉ DE DROIT CONSTITUTIONNEL, 3d ed., 713 (1927); Krabbe, "L'Idée Moderne de l'État," 13 HAGUE RECUEIL 1926.III.514; KRABBE, THE MODERN IDEA OF THE STATE (1922); KELSEN, GENERAL THEORY OF LAW AND THE STATE (1945).

[2] "Règles Générales du Droit de la Paix," 46 HAGUE RECUEIL 1933.IV.331 at 343. Cf. Dunn, "The International Rights of Individuals," PROC. AM. SOC. INT. L. 14, 16 (1941).

[3] Cf. e.g., SEGAL, L'INDIVIDU EN DROIT INTERNATIONAL POSITIF (1932); POLITIS, THE NEW ASPECTS OF INTERNATIONAL LAW (1928); Le Fur, "Le Développement Historique du Droit International," 41 HAGUE RECUEIL 1932.III.505; TÉNÉKIDÈS, L'INDIVIDU DANS L'ORDRE JURIDIQUE INTERNATIONAL (1933); cf. LAUTERPACHT, PRIVATE LAW SOURCES AND ANALOGIES OF INTERNATIONAL LAW 73 ff. and 305 (1927). See also Garner, "Le Développement et les Tendances Récentes du Droit International," 35 HAGUE RECUEIL 1931.I.609 esp. p. 695, note 1; Aufricht, "Personality in International Law," 37 AM. POL. SCI. REV. 217 ff. (1943); Pintor, "Les Subjects du Droit International autres que les États," 41 HAGUE RECUEIL 1932. III.251.

cage for its citizens from which they were obliged to communicate with the outside world, in a legal sense, through very close-set bars. Yielding to the logic of events, the bars are beginning to open. The cage is becoming shaky and will finally collapse. Men will then be able to hold free and untrammeled communication with each other across their respective frontiers."[4]

This discussion starts with the hypothesis that a change in the old fundamental doctrine has been accepted, and proceeds from that point to consider certain modifications in the traditional body of international law which would be desirable or necessary if individuals as well as states were considered subjects of the law of nations. There is therefore no occasion here to continue the debate as to whether under existing international law individuals are subjects of the law or only its "destinataires."[5] Those who will may consider some of the observations here as *lex lata*, while others will deal with them as made *de lege ferenda*. It remains true, as Sir John Fischer Williams has said, that it "is obvious that international relations are not limited to relations between states."[6] The function of international law is to provide a legal basis for the orderly management of international relations. The traditional nature of that law was keyed to the actualities of past centuries in which international relations were inter-state relations. The actualities have changed; the law is changing.[7] The conclusion may be that states remain the organs for conducting even those international relations which involve individuals and it may also be true, as the same able writer has said, that when "the world is more fully organized politically . . . the disappearance of the State as we know it will mean that international law will either be wholly absorbed into a general body of law or will preserve a separate existence only as a branch of a general system."[8] But one may also agree with him that de Madari-

[4] POLITIS, id. 30, 31.

[5] Cf. SPIROPOULOS, TRAITÉ THÉORIQUE ET PRATIQUE DE DROIT INTERNATIONAL PUBLIC 42 ff. (1933).

[6] WILLIAMS, ASPECTS OF MODERN INTERNATIONAL LAW 18 (1939) .

[7] "The existence of rules of international law governing relations between states and foreign individuals is not inconceivable, but their existence has not been proved, and, if it should be proved, the contents of the rules will necessarily differ from those rules which concern relations between sovereigns." FEILCHENFELD, PUBLIC DEBTS AND STATE SUCCESSION 582 (1931). As indicated above, this discussion assumes the proof by way of hypothesis and proceeds to consider the content of the international law of the future.

[8] WILLIAMS, CHAPTERS ON CURRENT INTERNATIONAL LAW AND THE LEAGUE OF NATIONS 19, 20 (1929). Cf. SCHÜCKING, THE INTERNATIONAL UNION OF THE HAGUE CONFERENCES 147, 150 (1918).

aga's insistence that we want to supplant *inter-national* law by "world law, or to use a fine Roman expression, *jus gentium, le droit des gens,* the law of the World Commonwealth," involves merely a superficial change of name.[9] The term "Modern Law of Nations" has been used here nevertheless to suggest the point that the acceptance of the hypothesis on which this discussion proceeds involves a break with the past.[10]

For the purposes of this writing, therefore, international law or the law of nations, must be defined as law applicable to states in their mutual relations and to individuals in their relations with states.[11] International law may also, under this hypothesis, be applicable to certain interrelationships of individuals themselves, where such interrelationships involve matters of international concern. So long, however, as the international community is composed of states, it is only through an exercise of their will, as expressed through treaty or agreement, or as laid down by an international authority deriving its power from states, that a rule of law becomes binding upon an individual.[12] When there is created some kind of international constituent assembly or world parliament, representative of the people of the world, and having authority to legislate, it will then be possible to assert that international law derives authority from a source external to the states. This would be true even though in origin it might well be states which agreed to the creation of such a representative legislature. The inescapable fact is that the world is today organized upon the basis of the coexistence of states and fundamental changes will take place only through state action whether affirmative or negative.[13] The only possible alternative would be revolution on a world scale which would circumvent the existing system of states as national revolutions have cir-

[9] ASPECTS OF MODERN INTERNATIONAL LAW 18 and 20 (1939), and cf. his CHAPTERS ON CURRENT INTERNATIONAL LAW AND THE LEAGUE OF NATIONS 7, note 2 (1929).

[10] Other problems which will need to be considered in connection with a modernization of the law of nations can not be covered here, but will be treated by the author in a book to be published in 1947 by the Macmillan Company.

[11] Cf. SPIROPOULOS, TRAITÉ THEORIQUE ET PRATIQUE DE DROIT INTERNATIONAL 43 (1935).

[12] Cf. Borchard, "The Access of Individuals to International Courts," 24 AM. J. INT. L. 359 (1930). Many writers distinguish the individual as a subject of international law from the individual as a creator of norms; cf. e.g., Rundstein, "L'Arbitrage International en Maitière Privée," 23 HAGUE RECUEIL 1928.III.331; Strupp, "Les Régles Générales du Droit de la Paix," 47 id. 1934.I.263; AKZIN, PROBLÈMES FONDAMENTAUX DU DROIT INTERNATIONAL PUBLIC 125 ff. (1929).

[13] 1 HYDE, INTERNATIONAL LAW, 2d ed., §§11A-C, pp. 38 ff. (1945).

cumvented preexisting constitutional or governmental law and procedure. It is true to say that states themselves operate by virtue of the will of individuals and that the individual is thus the ultimate source of authority. Yet so firmly rooted is the international state system that we are accustomed to think in terms of the state itself as the ultimate authority and sole actor.

There is no novelty in the suggestion that states may delegate the exercise of some of their customary attributes. The classic case is that of the European Commission of the Danube established under the Treaty of Paris of March 30, 1856. The commission was given legislative, administrative and judicial powers.[14] The Central Commission for the Navigation of the Rhine established under Article 109 of the Final Act of Vienna of 1815 had comparable powers.[15] The regulations of these commissions were directly applicable to individuals and individual infractions of the rules were directly cognizable by the commissions. Thus the international bodies dealt directly with individuals in the same manner in which national bodies customarily deal with them. The same remark may be made in regard to those exceptional cases in which individuals have been given by treaty the right to appear before international tribunals.[16] The notable cases are those of the Central American Court of Justice established in 1907, the Mixed Arbitral Tribunals established by the peace treaties at the end of World War I, and the Arbitral Tribunal for dealing with the rights of minorities in Upper Silesia under the Geneva Convention of 1922 between Poland and Germany. In such cases the international tribunal acted directly upon the claim of an individual and the judgment ran in favor of the individual. In the case of the United Nations, it is not yet clear to what extent the powers delegated to its organs will be exercised directly upon the individual. The measures of enforcement ordered by the Security Council may be directly applicable to individuals.[17] The de-

[14] See TÉNÉKIDÈS, L'INDIVIDU DANS L'ORDRE JURIDIQUE INTERNATIONAL 84 (1933); Hostie, "Examen de Quelques Régles du Droit International dans le Domaine des Communications et du Transit," 40 HAGUE RECUEIL 1932.II.403 at 488 ff.; CHAMBERLAIN, THE REGIME OF INTERNATIONAL RIVERS: DANUBE AND RHINE, c. 3, p. 47 (1923). See also P.C.I.J. Ser. B., No. 14, Adv. Op. on Jurisdiction of European Commission.

[15] Hostie, ibid.

[16] The question of individuals as beneficiaries of treaty provisions is reserved for discussion elsewhere.

[17] But the national state may be the intermediary through which measures are brought home to the individual; cf. Eagleton, "The Individual and International Law," PROC. AM. SOC. INT. L. 22 and 24 (1946), citing Pub. L. 264, 79th Cong.,

velopment of the Trusteeship Council and the Commission on Human Rights may produce similar situations. Current proposals for the establishment of a United Nations Atomic Energy Commission may well lead to the creation, by special treaty to which states will be parties, of a rule-making authority which will enact rules directly binding upon individuals. Thus it may become a rule of international law that no state shall use atomic bombs; it may also become a rule of international law that no state *or individual* shall, without international license, manufacture, possess or traffic in atomic bombs or fissionable materials.[18]

States may agree to separate the legislative function from the law-enforcing function so far as international agencies are concerned. Enforcement may be left to national authorities as is customary under treaties for the protection of fisheries, the control of the slave trade and the traffic in narcotics. The degree of delegation does not affect the principle. Just as a national legislature may delegate certain regulatory authority and powers to an administrative commission or officer, so the community of states may delegate to an international authority. Although one may in both cases trace the authority back to its original source, the individual will deal with the immediate and not the remote source and will regard the former as the origin of his rights and duties.[19]

In using the term "individual" in connection with the hypothesis here under discussion, it should be understood that various types of groups or associations of individuals are included. International law, particularly in claims cases, is accustomed to dealing with corporations as "citizens" or "nationals" of states in the same way in which it deals with natural persons. So long as national law creates these juristic persons, international law must deal with them as individuals.[20] Accordingly, under the hypothesis, corporations or partnerships may also be subjects of international law. In this instance, however, the fiction

1st sess. [59 Stat. L. 619 (1945)] on enforcement of United Nations Measures by the President.

[18] See the recommendations of the report of the Atomic Energy commission to the Security Council contemplating the definition of international crimes in connection with the use of atomic weapons and the punishment of both persons and nations, 15 DEPT. ST. BULL. 1090 (1946).

[19] Cf. BALLADORE PALLIERE, DIRITTO INTERNAZIONALE PUBLICO 286 (1937).

[20] "Every system of law that has attained a certain stage in its development seems compelled by the ever-increasing complexity of human affairs to add to the number of persons provided for it by the natural world, to create persons who are not men." 1 POLLOCK and MAITLAND, HISTORY OF ENGLISH LAW, 1st ed., 469 (1895), quoted by Fischer Williams in "The Legal Character of the Bank for International Settlements," 24 AM. J. INT. L. 665 at 666 (1930).

of the juristic person introduces new complications in the international field, since a corporation may be created under the law of State *A*, may have its principal place of business in State *B*, may have directors who are nationals of State *C* and stockholders who are nationals of State *D*.[21]

Special mention should be made of the problem created by the growing tendency of the state to assume and to discharge functions which in the formative period of international law were normally considered to be the function of private interests.[22] Where the state, for example, sets up a government corporation to manage a fleet of merchant vessels or to operate a government monopoly in matches or tobacco, international law has tended toward the acceptance of a rule which would distinguish the corporation from the state. The development has taken place especially in connection with the law of sovereign immunity before the courts of another state; such immunity is denied to government corporations in the jurisprudence of many countries.[23] Even where no governmental corporation is interposed, the sovereign character of the state has not been recognized by some courts when the state acts as a private trader.[24] In a socialized state it would seem to be distinctly to the advantage of the state to separate its political character from its business functions in order that economic relations may be carried on without the frictions and prestige considerations which may be involved if the business is handled on a political level. Perhaps the Soviet corporation fulfill this function.[25] It has been found useful, for example, for European railway administrations, both public and private, to arrange their affairs through the Union of International Transport by Rail before whose arbitral tribunal no distinction is made between the governmental and the private administration.[26] The for-

[21] See Timberg, "Corporate Fictions: Logical, Social and International Implications," 46 COL. L. REV. 533 at 572 (1946).

[22] See Friedmann, "The Growth of State Control over the Individual, and Its Effect upon the Rules of International State Responsibility," 19 B.Y.B. INT. L. 118 (1938).

[23] Harvard Research in International Law, Draft Convention on Competence of Courts in Regard to Foreign States, Article 12 and Comment, 26 AM. J. INT. L. SUPP. 641 (1932).

[24] See Art. 11 and Comment, id. 597 ff. and cf. the changing view of the Supreme Court of the United States as reflected in Republic of Mexico v. Hoffman, 324 U.S. 30, 65 S. Ct. 530 (1945).

[25] See Hazard, "Soviet Government Corporations," 41 MICH. L. REV. 850 (1943).

[26] See Hudson and Sohn, "Fifty Years of Arbitration in the Union of International Transport by Rail," 37 AM. J. INT. L. 597 at 600 (1943).

mation of international corporate bodies in finance such as the International Bank for Reconstruction and Development, and The International Monetary Fund, in the development of atomic energy as in the proposed United Nations Atomic Energy Commission, and in other fields may serve in international economic relations to reduce the number of instances in which private individual and public governmental interests have clashed on the international level.[27] There is a corresponding possibility that all clashes of interest would be raised at once to the level of national interests with ensuing complications in international relations. The recognition of the international legal personality of corporate or other bodies, whether private, governmental or intergovernmental, would tend to bring their interrelationships under normal international legal controls, exercised by appropriate international organizations and procedures which would need to be established.

Since statehood is not here an essential criterion for a subject of international law, there ceases to be any difficulty about the legal personality of various other entities. In traditional international law there has been debate about the status of the Holy See, the great chartered companies of an earlier period, various "semi-independent" political entities and international organizations. The Dutch East India Company and the British East India Company had the power to make war and peace and to conclude treaties on which their states relied as the basis of rights. Because of the traditional concept that only states were international persons, Judge Huber as sole Arbitrator in the *Palmas Island* case between the United States and the Netherlands, felt compelled to hold that the agreements made by these companies were not "in the international law sense, treaties or conventions capable of creating rights and obligations such as may, in international law, arise out of treaties." But at the same time he felt impelled to attribute to them certain legal significance which is hardly distinguishable in fact from that which they would have had if he had called them international law treaties[28] Under traditional international law, third states did not

[27] See Timberg, "Corporate Fictions: Logical, Social, and International," 46 COL. L. REV. 533 at 556 (1946); Communication of the Delegation of the United States to the Secretary-General of the United Nations, Sept. 24, 1946, 15 DEPT. ST. BULL. 659 (1946); Finer, "The T.V.A.: Lessons for International Application," I.L.O., Studies and Reports, Ser. B, No. 37 (1944); Schmitthoff, "The International Corporation," 30 GROT. SOC. TRANS. 165 (1945). It is interesting to note that fifteen governments have agreed to organize a "Caribbean Tourist Development Association" which is to be a Delaware corporation, 15 DEPT. ST. BULL. 735 (1946).

[28] SCOTT, HAGUE COURT REPORTS, 2d Ser., 115 ff. (1932); cf. LAWRENCE, THE PRINCIPLES OF INTERNATIONAL LAW, 4th ed., 73 ff. (1911); WHEATON, ELEMENTS OF INTERNATIONAL LAW, 8th ed., 26 (1936).

attribute the quality of statehood to the native princes of India although, perhaps as a matter of domestic policy, the British courts treated them as such.[29] In the United States, although the Supreme Court has applied the international law rules concerning treaties to agreements with the Indian tribes, their status was early determined by Chief Justice Marshall to be that of "domestic dependent nations."[30] An international tribunal has held that the Cayuga Indians had no standing before it save as represented by a state.[31] Under the hypothesis here taken, these entities may also be subjects of international law as may other national minority groups which may come under the protection of special provisions in treaties.

Colonies and other political subdivisions have long been admitted as members of various international unions such as the Universal Postal Union, and the International Institute of Refrigeration. Under Article I of the Covenant of the League of Nations they could also become members of the League if they were "fully self-governing"; the provision was designed to provide for the membership of the British dominions and India. This situation has necessitated fine legal distinctions since the entities were not states and yet had a certain international position.[32] According to Schwarzenberger, "The attempts which have been made to decide in the abstract whether entities which are not States are subjects or objects of international law do not lead beyond mutually contradictory assertions. The only premise which it is safe to state, is that the existing subjects of international law are free to extend the application of international law to any entity whom they see fit to admit to the realm of the international legal system."[33] All such entities are here recognized as subjects of international law.

There has been debate also about the status of various international organizations.[34] Whether or not the League of Nations should be considered an international person was hotly debated, the juridical argu-

[29] Mighell v. Sultan of Johore, [1894] 1 Q.B. 149; Duff Development Co. v. Kelantan, [1924] A.C. 797. A parallel situation is presented by the recognition of the status of the Philippine Commonwealth in courts of the United States: Bradford v. Chase National Bank, (D.C. N.Y. 1938) 24 F. Supp. 28; Hooven & Allison Co. v. Evatt, 324 U.S. 652, 65 S. Ct. 870 (1945).

[30] Cherokee Nation v. Georgia, 5 Pet. (30 U.S.) 1 at 17 (1831).

[31] Great Britain (The Cayuga Indians Claim) v. United States, United States-Great Britain Arbitration, NIELSEN'S REPORT, pp. 307 and 272 (1926).

[32] Cf. the solution of STRUPP, ELÉMENTS DU DROIT INTERNATIONAL PUBLIC UNIVERSEL, EUROPÉEN, ET AMÉRICAIN 22-23 (1927).

[33] 1 SCHWARZENBERGER, INTERNATIONAL LAW 62 (1945).

[34] Cf. Brierly, "Le Fondement du Caractère Obligatoire du Droit International, 23 HAGUE RECUEIL 1928.III.526.

ments reflecting the political controversy over the question whether the League was to be considered a "super-state."[85] Sir John Fischer Williams calls attention to the striking case of the international personality of the Reparations Commission established under the Treaty of Versailles. Once created by states, the commission enjoyed a large degree of independence. It could not be ordered by the Allied Governments "not to give Germany 'a just opportunity to be heard.'" A delegate to the commission was not in legal contemplation the agent of his government and was not paid by his government; he could be recalled by his government, but his acts were not subject to governmental ratification. The judicial decisions of the commission bound the states, and majority rule applied in reaching decisions.[86]

In the formation of the various United Nations organizations, it has become customary to insert in their constitutions or charters some reference to their legal status. Thus, for example, Article XV of the Constitution of the Food and Agriculture Organization provides: "The Organization shall have the capacity of a legal person to perform any legal act appropriate to its purpose which is not beyond the powers granted to it by this Constitution."[87] In general, the history of the drafting of these provisions suggests that the drafters were concerned chiefly with the legal status of such organizations under national law; could they take title to real and personal property, make contracts, and sue in national courts? In regard to the United Nations Organization itself, there was evident a distinct reluctance to include in the Charter

[85] "The League of Nations appeared before the Court of Appeal of Geneva as an 'international organism' enjoying privileges and immunities exempting it from the jurisdiction of local courts." ALLEN, THE POSITION OF FOREIGN STATES BEFORE NATIONAL COURTS 6 (1933). See also PFANKUCHEN, A DOCUMENTARY TEXTBOOK OF INTERNATIONAL LAW 52 (1940).

[86] "A Legal Footnote to the Story of German Reparations," 13 B.Y.B. INT. L. 9 at 34 (1932). See also the same author's article, "The Legal Character of the Bank for International Settlements," 24 AM. J. INT. L. 665 (1930), and HUDSON, INTERNATIONAL TRIBUNALS, PAST AND FUTURE 67 (1944), where the Bank for International Settlements is also mentioned in the same connection as having the right under treaties to appear as a party before international tribunals.

[87] Food and Agriculture Organization of the United Nations, Report of the First Session of the Conference, 1945, p. 87. Cf. Art. 47 of the Convention of the International Civil Aviation, 1944, Dept. of State Pub. 2282, p. 72; Art. 66 of the Constitution of the World Health Organization, Final Acts of the International Health Conference, 1946, U. N. Doc. E/155; Art. IX of the Articles of Agreement of the International Monetary Fund and Article VII of the Articles of Agreement of the International Bank for Reconstruction and Development, Dept. of State Pub. 2187, pp. 42 and 88; Article XII of the Constitution of UNESCO, Dept. of State Pub. 2457, p. 21, Article 73 of the suggested Charter for an international Trade Organization of the United Nations, Dept. of State Pub. 2598, p. 44.

any provision relative to the international status of the organization. Thus Article 104 merely provides: "The Organization shall enjoy in the territory of each of its members such legal capacity as may be necessary for the exercise of its functions and the fulfillment of its purpose." The subcommittee of Committee IV/2 of the San Francisco Conference in reporting this text, stated: "As regards the question of international juridical personality, the Subcommittee has considered it superfluous to make this the subject of a text. In effect, it will be determined implicitly from the provisions of the Charter taken as a whole."[38]

Yet under Article 43 it is clear that the organization may make agreements with states and there is no reason to believe that the agreement-making power will not be exercised also in other connections as, for example, the current proposals for an agreement between the United Nations and the state in which its headquarters are to be located.[39]

As Borchard has suggested, we now have "autonomous corporations formed under a constitution which assures their perpetuity, grants them immunities from taxation and other local burdens, and yet subjects them to judicial responsibility for their business activities. . . . These are no longer mere agencies of the constituent states, hampered by the unanimity rule of sovereignty. . . ."[40]

The reasons why international organizations do not have a *locus standi* before the International Court of Justice are more political than juridical. The Statute of the Court retains the provision in Article 34 of the Statute of the Permanent Court of International Justice that only states may be parties in cases before the Court. A determined effort was made in the United Nations Committee of Jurists which drafted the Statute in Washington, and later in Committee IV/1 of the San Francisco Conference, to amend this article so as to permit intergovernmental organizations to have direct access to the Court as parties.[41] The International Labor Organization was the body which

[38] See Reiff, "Work of the United Nations 'Legal Committees,'" 15 DEPT. ST. BULL. 3 at 12 (1946); Preuss, "The International Organization Immunities Act," 40 AM. J. INT. L. 332, 341 (1946).

[39] See U. N. Doc. A/67, September 1, 1946, p. 23.

[40] Borchard, "Relation of Bretton Woods Agreements to Other Types of International Organization," INSTITUTE ON MONEY AND THE LAW, N.Y. Univ. L. Q. Rev. Supp., 99 at 110 (1945). Cf Sumberg, "Financing International Institutions," 13 SOCIAL RESEARCH 276, 278 (1946).

[41] 14 Doc. of U. N. Conf. on Int. Org., San Francisco, 133 ff. (1945); 13 id. 233, 270 (1945).

naturally came first to mind in this connection and the relations between it and the Soviet Union had not then been brought into adjustment. Under the Statute of the Permanent Court, the ILO was to be at liberty to furnish information in contentious labor cases but no such case arose. In advisory proceedings, international organizations were permitted to furnish information "and even to take part in the oral proceedings which were almost invariably held."[42] The committee vote in both Washington and San Francisco was against the proposals for amending Article 34 but the door was left open for international organizations, if authorized by the General Assembly, to request advisory opinions.[43] Under Articles 34 and 66 of the new statute, international organizations may furnish information to the Court in appropriate cases. The United Nations itself, represented by its Security Council or General Assembly[44] may request advisory opinions as could the Council and Assembly of the League of Nations under the old statute, but the United Nations could not be a party to a contested case before the Court. The result has no significance in law or logic relating to the legal personality of international organizations. The consequence of the reluctance to accord them standing before the International Court of Justice is revealed by a provision in the Working Draft of the proposed "Convention/Agreement between the United Nations and the United States of America" relative to the location of the United Nations headquarters in the United States. Under Article 38 of the Draft, disputes concerning interpretation or application are to be referred to a special tribunal of three arbitrators, the third member in case of deadlock to be selected by the President of the International Court of Justice.[45]

THE DOCTRINE OF EQUALITY

The fact that such individuals, groups or bodies have legal personality and are subjects of international law does not necessarily imply that they have equal rights and duties. A fundamental document such as the Charter of the United Nations may confine membership in that

[42] HUDSON, INTERNATIONAL TRIBUNALS, PAST AND FUTURE 68-69 (1944).

[43] Article 96 of the Charter, 15 Doc. of U. N. Conf. on Int. Org. 352 (1945).

[44] The Economic and Social Council was given the right to request advisory opinions by a resolution of the General Assembly adopted on December 11, 1946 under the authority of Article 96 of the Charter. U. N. Doc. A/201.

[45] U. N. Doc. A/67, September 1, 1946, p. 23. See also Domke, "The Settlement of Disputes in International Agencies," 1 THE ARBITRATION JOURNAL (N.S.) 145.

organization to states, thus excluding from membership individuals, corporations, and various types of dependencies.[46] But another instrument of like origin may create an international organization composed of states, dependencies and corporations or individuals. A treaty would thus no longer be properly defined as an agreement between states; it may be an agreement between a state and an individual. The criterion distinguishing a treaty from what has usually heretofore been called a contract, is whether the agreement imposes obligations and confers rights under international or under municipal law. There have been examples of agreements between states which were municipal law contracts as, for instance, the usual type of contract of State *A* to purchase land from State *B* for the erection of an embassy and some loan contracts such as the Inter-Allied loans of World War I which are couched in terms of municipal law and not of international law.[47] A concession contract from a state to a national (individual or corporation) of another state or to a stateless person may also, under our hypothesis be an international law agreement, thus eliminating the type of controversy revealed in certain decisions of Mixed Claims Commissions.[48] Special international tribunals may be established for the adjudication of controversies arising out of such contracts between a state and an individual and other international tribunals may be open only to states as is prescribed by Article 34 of the Statute of the International Court of Justice.

It is thus apparent that much of the existing law concerning the nature and qualifications of states as international persons is still pertinent, regardless of the acceptance of the hypothesis that individuals are also subjects of the same law. But certain concepts stand in need of clarification. The principle of the equality of states is among the principles which need to be reappraised. In saying that states are equal, the assumption is implicit that all the subjects of international law enjoy equality, one with the other. As Dickinson has pointed out, this statement is true of equality in the sense of "equality before the law" or "equal protection of the law" which is a matter of status, but not necessarily true of equality used in the sense of "equality of capac-

[46] But see Kelsen, "Membership in the United Nations," 46 COL. L. REV. 391 at 392 (1946), on the question whether the original members of the United Nations are all states.

[47] See Mann, "The Law Governing State Contracts," 1944 B.Y.B. INT. L. 11 (1944).

[48] See Judge Nielsen's dissent in United States of America on behalf of International Fisheries Company v. United Mexican States, NIELSEN, INTERNATIONAL LAW APPLIED TO RECLAMATIONS 520 (1933).

ity for rights," which he notes is not essential to the reign of law.[49] In Dickinson's sense, equality would still appertain to all subjects of international law, whether individuals or states; both would enjoy the equal protection of the law. But the actual existing inequalities of capacity for rights which is apparent in the present international state system, would continue and be sharpened with reference to the differences between states and individuals.

As is also true in the case of other parts of international law, the writings on the subject of equality often fail to distinguish between the legal principle and the political maxim. There was an historical period in which the doctrine of equality of states had to make its way as the national state emerged in Europe out of the collapse of the empire, but for a century at least, statesmen and international politicians have been able to assert the existence of the principle without fear of verbal contradiction but with some certainty that while equality is preached, inequality will be practiced. The international problem of equality is the result of the coexistence of two facts:

1. States are not factually equal; their power differs;
2. States have "feelings" and the psychological factor can not be ignored in international politics.

Power may be overcome by superior power or checked by an equivalence of power. From this principle there has evolved in the interest of maintaining the peace, the plan of the balance of power. Power may be surrendered and from this principle stem plans for disarmament, for an international police force, and for a world state. Power may be utilized by those who have it for the general advantage of the international community as a result of a conviction of self-interest in such utilization. This is the theoretical basis of the United Nations Charter which recognizes the existence of power and entrusts its exercise, under agreed limitations, to those who possess it.

Just as within states the last hundred years reveals a growth of social consciousness and of a public conscience, so has it been, in lesser degree, in the international community. Contrasting the Congress of Vienna of 1815 and its aftermath with the Paris Peace Conference of 1919 and its aftermath, one finds in both situations the original domi-

[49] DICKINSON, THE EQUALITY OF STATES IN INTERNATIONAL LAW 4 (1920). As Kelsen, "Membership in the United Nations," 46 COL. L. REV. 391 at 398 (1946), points out, Article 35 of the Statute of the International Court of Justice recognizes the principle of equality between members of the United Nations and non-members by requiring that conditions on which the court is to be open to "other states" shall not "place the parties in a position of inequality before the Court."

nance of the Great Powers, but in the latter period, as the League of Nations developed, there is a growing participation, and, comparatively, a growing influence of the middle and small powers commanding a world audience through the Geneva forum. Moving on to the San Francisco Conference of 1945 and the early stages of the United Nations, one observes that the voice of the middle and small powers is louder, more insistent and, again comparatively, more productive of results.

The psychological factor may properly be called the prestige factor. This is not universally true, as for example when the small riparian states on the Danube have demanded representation on a river commission with a view to exercising at least some influence over decisions which vitally affect them. Here a legal interest may be involved and appeal made to the legal principle of equality before the law. But the insistence of certain diminutive states at the Hague Peace Conference of 1907 for permanent and equal representation on the bench of the proposed International Court of Arbitral Justice, was much less genuinely a reflection of legal interest than of prestige considerations.

As one examines the manifestations of the doctrine of equality of states in international relations, one seems to detect the emergence of a notion that it does no violence to the doctrine if unequal rights or privileges are accorded on the basis of a formula which fairly reflects a recognizable degree of interest. One may compare the United States constitutional doctrine that a reasonable classification of persons affected saves a statute from doing violence to the constitutional guarantee of the equal protection of the laws. Examples of this emergent notion are abundant in connection with various international organizations. For instance, in the International Institute of Agriculture, voting was determined by membership in one of five classes, members of Class I having five votes and members of Class V having one vote. Equality was admitted in the sense that each state was free to choose the class to which it wished to belong, but membership in Class I involved an assessment of 16 units of the budgetary base, and membership in Class V involved the assessment of only one unit.[50] A comparable plan in the Bretton Woods agreement led states to seek a larger allotment of shares in the Fund in order to be entitled to larger credit facilities, and to avoid larger allotments of shares in the Bank with resulting larger obligations to subscribe capital.

It is relatively easy to find formulae for inequalities in voting

[50] A similar plan had been utilized in the agreement of December, 1907 creating the International Office of Public Health.

power and in representation in technical international organizations where interest can be measured by statistics or factual criteria. It is supremely difficult to find acceptable formulae in political organizations where the prestige factor and problems of political existence may be at stake. Great powers have power because they are great and not because a skilful draftsman has invented an ingenious formula. The platform of the League to Enforce Peace in 1918 suggested that "The representation of the different nations in the organs of the League should be in proportion to the responsibilities and obligations they assume." This suggestion is not dissimilar to the actual basis of five-great-power control of the Security Council of the United Nations. The provisions of the Charter on regional arrangements reflect in large part the wide concessions which the United States in pursuance of the Good Neighbor Policy has actually made to the principle of political equality in the Americas. The United Nations organization is affirmed by the Charter to be "based upon the principle of the sovereign equality of all its Members" but no one can deny that unequal rights, privileges and responsibilities are also recognized throughout the Charter.[51] Some of the factual inequalities are based on the more readily measurable types of interest as in the composition of the Trusteeship Council. Some, as in the voting formula for the Security Council, are based upon the inescapable fact of power differentials. It is true, as Woodrow Wilson said, that "all nations are equally interested in the peace of the world"; it is not true that all can make equal contribution to its maintenance.[52]

The doctrine of equality of states has been championed by small states and their spokesmen. It is they who see in it a safeguard against encroachments by the greater powers. The great powers have their divisions among themselves within their small circle, but in a major sense the conflict of interest in terms of designing international organization or world government, has been between the great powers on the one side and the small and middle powers on the other. When the

[51] In his fable, ANIMAL FARM (1946), George Orwell describes the amendment of the animals' principle "All Animals are Equal" by the addition of the words "But Some Animals are More Equal than Others." The Charter might realistically be amended in the same way.

[52] The above discussion of equality is based largely upon the writer's introduction to a series of studies on the subject prepared in the graduate seminar in International Law at Columbia University; Peterson, "The Equality of States as Dogma and Reality," 60 POL. SCI. Q. 527 (1945). Herrera, "Evolution of Equality of States in the Inter-American System," 61 id. 90 (1946). The writer has also had the benefit of other unpublished studies of the seminar, especially Lande, "Revindication of the Principle of Legal Equality of States in the Period between the Franco-Prussian War and the First World War."

international community lacked any form of internationally democratic organization, there was no other safeguard to which the smaller powers could appeal.[58] With the development of international organization, even in the still relatively primitive form which the United Nations takes, there is a possibility that the function of equality as a legal and political principle may be fulfilled by a doctrine of community interest, the acceptance of which is taken as a second hypothesis in this discussion. Given the forum of the General Assembly and also of the Security Council to which any state may appeal, and given the extension of the acceptance of the compulsory jurisdiction of the International Court of Justice, all operating on the basis of the acceptance of the principle of community interest in the maintenance of a developed law of nations, the safeguards of the international organization may suffice to protect the legal interests of all subjects of international law, whether states or individuals. Thus all subjects of the law would be guaranteed equal protection of the law although equal capacity for rights would still differ with factual criteria. The prestige factor would still need to be taken into account as a matter of international politics as is true in any social relationships, but it would tend to become more clearly recognized in its true light, stripped of confusion with the sound legal principle of equality. States would still seek the prestige of representation on various international commissions and other bodies but progress could be made along the lines of the development of an international civil service in which individuals would be selected on the basis of their competence rather than on the basis of state representation. The formula already in use in UNRRA and in the Charter (Article 101)—"Due regard shall be paid to the importance of recruiting the staff on as wide a geographical basis as possible"—would still represent a sound principle of administrative organization.

The acceptance of the adaptation of the legal principle of equality of states to the principle of equality of subjects of the law, whether states or individuals, is necessary to the development of new doctrines of human rights under the Charter of the United Nations, a subject which cannot be treated within the scope of this article.

It is not impossible to accord equal protection of the law to states and to individuals when these two different subjects of international law appear before an international forum. The experiment has been tried with some success in the special regime for the protection of the minori-

[58] As Lande, ibid., points out, the small states have at times been the beneficiaries of the rivalries among the great powers.

ties in Upper Silesia. Kaeckenbeeck, in his excellent analysis of this regime says: "Even when, as a result of what is almost a fiction, a State and a private person stand side by side as parties before an international tribunal—a new and still quite exceptional departure—it is essential that the impartiality of the judge should not be affected by the difference in the importance of the parties, if I may put it in this way, and in this connection it is essential that the judge should treat the parties as equals. But from another standpoint, if we are not to lose touch with reality, it must be admitted that the interests of a State and the interests of an individual are not on the same level, and further, that the feelings of a nation, with their consequences, both national and international, are not commensurate with the psychological and material satisfaction which an individual receives when his strict rights are recognized."[54] He notes that in the matter of costs of the judicial or arbitral procedure, for example, the state is in a very different position from the individual and that "costly justice . . . would upset the balance very strongly in favour of the State." Similarly in the matter of language, which is always a difficulty for any international body, states are in a position to hire skillful attorneys to plead in any required language, while the individual would be at a complete loss unless his own language could be used.[55] Kaeckenbeeck's observations are directed to a pioneering experiment in the field of international recognition of individual rights and it was essential to the success of that experiment that compromise and adjustment should play a large part. Similarly in connection with the Mixed Arbitral Tribunals established under the Peace Treaties at the end of World War I, it has been noted that while the individual could appear in his own right before the tribunal, there was no procedure open to him for the collection of a judgment rendered in his favor save through the assistance of his government.[56] As the law develops and the world community becomes more familiar with the problem and its possible solutions, the difficulties will tend to minimize themselves although they may never be wholly obliterated. One difficulty inherent in the minority regimes was that they were imposed only on certain countries and did not represent a principle accepted by the whole world and notably by the great states.

[54] KAECKENBEECK, THE INTERNATIONAL EXPERIMENT OF UPPER SILESIA 78 (1942). Cf. in the same sense TÉNÉKIDÈS, L'INDIVIDU DANS L'ORDRE JURIDIQUE INTERNATIONAL 35 (1933).

[55] KAECKENBEECK, id. 500.

[56] Blühdorn, "Le Fonctionnement et la Jurisprudence des Tribunaux Arbitraux Mixtes Créés par les Traités de Paris," 41 HAGUE RECUEIL 1932.III.141.

When the position of the individual is internationally recognized and the rights of man are placed under international protection against both the small and the great states, equality before the law may be insisted upon with respect both to states and to individuals.

It has been said that "big commercial and industrial enterprises increasingly often deal with States on a footing of complete equality" and the arbitration between the Lena Goldfields Company Ltd. and the Soviet Union has been cited in this connection.[57] In some instances the private corporation may even be factually in a more advantageous position than the government with which it deals.[58] The necessity for considering the problem of equality in such international commercial relationships would take a different form but would not be eliminated if there should be "international incorporation of private business firms conducting operations on an international or world scale.[59]

If the foregoing be now factually true regarding the relations between private corporations and states, there is no reason why a modern law of nations should not embody the result in an appropriately qualified rule of law. *A fortiori*, equality between states and international organizations presents no legal difficulty if both are considered subjects of the law of nations.

A modern law of nations must also take account of the principle of equality as applied to relations between and among individuals who are nationals of different states whether those states be "sovereign" equals or political subdivisions of a world government. Some aspects of traditional international law are illuminating in this connection even though they have been conceived in terms of inter-state rights and duties with respect to individuals characterized as citizens and aliens.

In the history of the law of responsibility of states for injuries to aliens it has been urged, notably by Latin-American jurists, that the standard of treatment of aliens should be equality with nationals. This standard has been accepted by some other states, such as the United States, only as a minimum. This latter point of view is supported by invoking the doctrine of the international standard. Thus it is maintained that if the treatment of nationals in Country *X* falls below the

[57] 1 SCHWARZENBERGER, INTERNATIONAL LAW 215 (1945). The Arbitral award in this case is summarized in Ann. Dig. of Pub. Int. L. Cases, Case No. 1 (1929-1930).

[58] The United Fruit Company might be suggested as an example; see KEPNER, SOCIAL ASPECTS OF THE BANANA INDUSTRY (1936) and sources there cited; also American Banana Co. v. United Fruit Co., 213 U. S. 347, 29 S. Ct. 511 (1909).

[59] Studies of the need for and methods of such incorporation were suggested by the delegation of the United States to the Secretary-General of the United Nations on September 24, 1946, 15 DEPT. ST. BULL. 659 (1946).

minimum standard, equality of treatment is no defense to a claim on behalf of an injured alien.[60]

In commercial treaties there is a standard clause known as the national treatment clause, much used especially in connection with shipping, which assures to the nationals of one contracting party equality with the nationals of the other in specified matters.[61] Such national treatment clauses are to be contrasted with most-favored-nation clauses which use as a standard equality with the most favorable treatment accorded to nationals of another state.[62]

The same principle of legal equality is to be found in the law restraining states from certain types of discrimination. This is a subject upon which adequate monographic studies are lacking but certain examples may be noted.[63] Thus the United States Immigration Act of 1924 was questioned by various foreign governments on the ground that it contained improper discrimination against their nationals. The Japanese objection was specifically based on the ground that the proposed law was "obviously aimed against Japanese as a nation."[64]

By no means are all examples of discriminatory treatment illegal under international law; states have wide latitude to accord or withhold special privileges and this latitude may be used for bargaining purposes. The British-American Claims Commission under the Treaty of August 18, 1910, properly refused to award compensation even under its equity powers when the United States had compensated some but not all cable companies damaged by its cutting submarine cables during the Spanish-American war—the original destruction having

[60] See Jessup, "Responsibility of States for Injuries to Individuals," 46 COL. L. REV. 903 (1946). But the Montevideo Convention of 1933 on Rights and Duties of States declares in Article 9: "Nationals and foreigners are under the same protection of the law and the national authorities and the foreigners may not claim rights other or more extensive than those of nationals." U. S. TR. SER., No. 881.

[61] See MCCLURE, A NEW AMERICAN COMMERCIAL POLICY 62 (1924); Cutler, "The Treatment of Foreigners," 27 AM. J. INT. L. 225 at 226 (1933). Cf. Art. 15 of the Chicago Convention on International Civil Aviation, International Civil Aviation Conference, Dept. of State Pub. 2282, p. 59 (1944).

[62] "The most favored nation clause embodies the principle of equality of treatment in international economic relations." Snyder, "The Most Favored Nation Clause and Recent Trade Practices," 55 POL. SCI. Q. 77 (1940). Cf. Article 8, Suggested Charter for an International Trade Organization of the United Nations, Dept. of State Pub. 2598 (1946).

[63] See id., Articles 21 and 22.

[64] The Japanese Ambassador to the Secretary of State, April 10, 1924, [1924] 2 U. S. FOR. REL. 369 at 372; The Secretary of State to President Coolidge, May 23, 1924, ibid. 39. Cf. GARIS, IMMIGRATION RESTRICTION 263 ff., 349 (1927); FENWICK, INTERNATIONAL LAW 177 (1924).

been a lawful exercise of belligerent rights.[65] A tribunal of the Permanent Court of Arbitration in 1904 held in the *Venezuelan Preferential Claims* case that the three countries, Germany, Great Britain and Italy, which had resorted to force to compel Venezuela to pay the claims of their nationals, were entitled to priority over other creditor states in the distribution of ear-marked Venezuelan assets.[66]

Inequality or discrimination as between local and foreign creditors particularly in bankruptcy proceedings has been so widely recognized as an injurious trade barrier that numerous bipartite and multipartite treaties have dealt with the matter. The fact that in many of these instances the distinctions are based on residence rather than on nationality is illustrative of the point that the merging of the sovereign state system into a world government would not be a panacea and would not eliminate the need for international law. There is a sufficient unanimity in the views expressed by various international bodies, business and legal, governmental and private, to warrant the devotion of early attention to this problem when the proposed International Trade Organization is established. As has been suggested, such an effort might well proceed on the principle stated by Mr. Justice Jackson that "we cannot successfully cooperate with the rest of the world in establishing a reign of law unless we are prepared to have that law sometimes operate against what would be our national advantage." [67]

INDEPENDENCE AND INTERDEPENDENCE

Independence is another quality or characteristic which states are commonly said to possess under international law. Historically this concept has been convenient because it helped to differentiate those po-

[65] Great Britain (Eastern Extension, Australasia & China Telegraph Co. Claim) v. United States, NIELSEN'S REPORT, 73 (1923).

In his argument before the tribunal, Wayne McVeagh as counsel for the United States said: "It is not enough that the conduct of the allies in making war upon Venezuela was equally meritorious with the policy pursued by the other creditor nations in abstaining from war and in seeking to collect the claims presented by them by peaceful methods. Before you can award preferential treatment to their claims, you must declare their conduct to be more meritorious than the conduct of those nations which abstained from making war; for equality of treatment is the rule and preferential treatment can only be accorded as an award of merit." The Venezuelan Arbitration before The Hague Tribunal, 1903, S. Doc. 119, 58th Cong., 3d sess., p. 1133.

[66] SCOTT, THE HAGUE COURT REPORTS 55 (1916).

[67] Nadelmann, "Legal Treatment of Foreign and Domestic Creditors," 11 L. AND CONTEM. PROB. 696 at 709 (1946), quoted from Jackson, "The Rule of Law Among Nations," PROC. AM. SOC. INT. L. 18 (1945). Nadelmann's article is an excellent discussion of the whole subject and contains ample citations on the points which have been noted here.

litical groupings which determined their own policies, especially in international relations, from those which acknowledged a certain subordination to other groups. Only fully independent groups were considered to be "states" although the terms "semi-independent state" and even "sovereign dependency" have had currency. The doctrine had additional importance, however, as a basis for those rules of international law which sought to restrict interferences by one state in the affairs of another. An interference in the affairs of a vassal, a protectorate, a colony, or other unit which was in a position of political subordination to a state, might be justified by that relationship whereas it would not be justified if the other unit were also an independent state. The doctrine of independence of states is thus also linked to the development of a legal system for the protection of the weak against the strong and in this respect it is akin to the doctrine of equality. To that extent, the acceptance of the principle of community interest and the perfection of forms of international organization will tend to diminish the importance of the concept of independence although it will remain one of the criteria for identifying a state in cases where that classification retains its importance. In this connection Chapter XI of the Charter of the United Nations with its "Declaration Regarding Non-Self-Governing Territories" and Chapters XII and XIII on the Trusteeship System and the Trusteeship Council are significant indications of the acceptance which has already been accorded to the community interest in non-independent groups.

It may be suggested that it would be more conformable both to the realities and to the desiderata of the international community, if instead of emphasizing that each state is independent of every other, it were frankly asserted that each state is *dependent* on all other states, linked together in the society of nations or in a world government. But the terms "dependent" and "dependence" have connotations which would clearly make them inacceptable in this connection. The same thought is conveyed by the acceptance of the hypothesis of community interest. The thought might be expressed concisely by saying that every state has the quality of "interdependence" with every other state. Interdependence would connote both rights and duties. The rights would include respect for its territorial integrity and its safety and observance toward it by all other states of the rules of international law designed for mutual well-being. The duties would include the obligation to accord to other states reciprocal respect and observance.

The acceptance of a general concept of community interest, or interdependence, has been referred to as a second hypothesis upon which this discussion proceeds. Briefly, the new concept would imply an abandonment of the traditional theory as stated by Judge Story that if a state violates international law, this is a wrong of which only the state directly injured may complain.[68] In a sense this change would be comparable to substituting for the present "tort" basis of international law, a basis more comparable to that of criminal law in which the community takes cognizance of law violations. In other instances, however, the change would be a shift in the direction of more-extended governmental functions of an organized international community as in case processes of collective recognition should be substituted for the present unilateral action.[69]

Limited interdependence, through cosignature of multipartite treaties is a familiar aspect of traditional international law. For example, Paragraph I of Article 386 of the Treaty of Versailles provided that "In the event of violation of any of the conditions of Articles 380 to 386, or of disputes as to the interpretation of these articles, any interested Power can appeal to the jurisdiction instituted for the purpose by the League of Nations." This provision was quoted by the Permanent Court of International Justice in its first Judgment in the case of the *S.S. Wimbledon*, involving the right of free passage provided by the treaty as the regime for the Kiel Canal. A refusal of passage to a French vessel was the subject of proceedings against Germany before the Court. The proceedings were instituted jointly by France, Great Britain, Japan and Italy, and Germany raised the question as to whether such joint application was proper inasmuch as only France could "adduce a prejudice to any pecuniary interest." The Court held that the joint application was proper since "each of the four Applicant Powers has a clear interest in the execution of the provisions relating to the Kiel Canal, since they all possess fleets and merchant vessels flying their respective flags."[70] If the legal quality of interdependence were recognized, the same reasoning could be applied to the interest of any maritime state in a question involving the freedom of the seas or the navigation of an international river and it would not be necessary to show that the state asserting the interest was a party to any treaty which might be involved. This would mark a clear change from the traditional position which has been well stated by Verdross in saying that the "merely ideal interest of the other states in maintaining the inter-

[68] United States v. La Jeune Eugenie, (C. C. Mass. 1822) Fed. Cas. No. 15,551.

[69] Cf. Postulate 4 of THE INTERNATIONAL LAW OF THE FUTURE, A.B.A.J. Pub., 32 (1944).

[70] P.C.I.J., Ser. A, No. 1, p. 20 (1931).

national legal order is . . . insufficient" to support a claim to act. But he admits there may be exceptional cases where the general interest is involved as when some state embarks on a career of lawlessness.[71] Upon the acceptance of the concept of interdependence, the exception would become the rule.[72]

Tentative assertion of such a right in connection with the common interest of all neutral states in the upholding of the law of neutral rights is to be found in the views expressed by several European governments in connection with Trent Affair in 1861.[73] The same thought was utilized in various proposals for armed neutralities or leagues of neutrals.[74]

The history of the Concert of Europe throughout much of the nineteenth century is illustrative of the acceptance of a concept of interdependence as a legal norm in international relations at least so far as the affairs of the European continent were concerned. It is true that this instrument was wielded by the Great Powers, often for selfish ends and that they tended to ignore the rights of the small powers. But as the action of the Concert was frequently rationalized and defended, there was an invocation of a concept of community interest, of interdependence. Procedurally, the Great Powers asserted their right to act as the instruments of the public law of Europe. Thus Lord Salisbury defended the action of the Concert in respect of Greece by referring to "the federated action of Europe" enacting rules as a "legislature" in the interests of European peace.[75] Numerous discussions and agreements concerning the neutralization of Switzerland, and other areas reflect the acceptance of the concept of interdependence.[76] The famous

[71] VÖLKERRECHT 165 (1937), citing Vattel and Hefter in accord on these exceptional cases.

[72] Garner in 1925 argued that states should have "an admitted legal right to protest against violation of the law" even where no immediate injury could be shown; RECENT DEVELOPMENTS IN INTERNATIONAL LAW 814.

[73] Harvard Research in International Law, Draft Convention on Rights and Duties of Neutral States in Naval and Aerial War, Art. 114, commentary, 33 AM. J. INT. L. SUPP. 788 ff. (1939); French Statement in 55 BR. & FOR. S. P. 610-612, and [1862] U. S. FOR. REL. 307; Austrian position in 55 BR. & FOR. S. P. 618 and German statement, id. 624; also British summary of these views, id. 641 ff.

[74] See 4 JESSUP, NEUTRALITY, ITS HISTORY, ECONOMICS AND LAW, TODAY AND TOMORROW 160 ff. (1936); Bülow to Lord Granville, Aug. 31, 1870, FONTES JURIS GENTIUM, Ser. B, Sectio I, Tom. I. Pars 1, 2.

[75] Address in the House of Lords quoted in I WESTLAKE, INTERNATIONAL LAW, 2d ed., 322 (1910); cf. LAWRENCE, THE PRINCIPLES OF INTERNATIONAL LAW, 7th ed., 250 (1923).

[76] See General Act of the Congress of Vienna, June 9, 1815, Articles IX, LXXXIV, XCII, 2 BR. & FOR. S. P. 3 (1915); cf. Peterson, "The Equality of States as Dogma and Reality," 60 POL. SCI. Q. 527 at 547 (1945).

declaration in the treaty of Paris of March 30, 1856 is comparable in its pronouncement that the Sublime Porte was admitted to participate in the advantages of the public law and Concert of Europe. The signatory powers accordingly agreed to respect the independence and territorial integrity of the Ottoman Empire and said that they would consider any act tending to violate this engagement as a question of general interest.[77] The joint interest of the powers in the "open door" for China and respect for Chinese territorial integrity may also be noted. The concept of interdependence is clearly recognized in the Covenant of the League of Nations and in the Charter of the United Nations.[78]

An interesting assertion of the right of a state to secure satisfaction because of the injury it sustains through the weakening of the international legal system through any breach of a rule of international law was made by the French Government in its case against Italy before a tribunal of the Permanent Court of Arbitration in the cases of the *Carthage* and the *Manouba*. These two French ships had been captured by the Italians during their war with Turkey; the French claims for indemnity were submitted to arbitration. In addition to material compensation for the damage to the vessels, the French Government asked for the "sum of one hundred thousand francs as reparation for the moral and political injury resulting from the failure to observe international common law and conventions binding both Italy and France." The Tribunal, correctly under the existing law, refused to make such an award, holding that the establishment by an arbitral tribunal of the fact of a breach of international legal obligations "constitutes in itself a serious penalty."[79]

SOVEREIGNTY

Sovereignty, in its meaning of an absolute, uncontrolled state will, ultimately free to resort to the final arbitrament of war, is the quicksand upon which the foundations of traditional international law are built. Until the world achieves some form of international government in which a collective will takes precedence over the individual will of the sovereign state, the ultimate function of law which is the elimination of force for the solution of human conflicts, will not be fulfilled.

[77] 46 BR. & FOR. S. P. 8 (1856).

[78] See Commentary on the League of Nations Covenant by the British Government, reprinted in BUTLER, A HANDBOOK TO THE LEAGUE OF NATIONS, 2d. ed., 172 (1925).

[79] SCOTT, HAGUE COURT REPORTS 332 and 335 (1916).

There must eventually be organs empowered to lay down rules—a legislature; there must be judicial organs to interpret and apply those rules—a judiciary; and there must be organs with power to compel compliance with the rules so interpreted and applied—a police force. It is not within the scope of this article to deal with these organizational and procedural developments, but their importance is not minimized. As in regard to the legal attribute of equality, the function of sovereignty as a legal concept was to protect the state in a world devoid of any alternative to self-protection. The gradual development of adequate modernized law and organization should provide such an alternative.

Because the international system has so far failed to meet the central problem of war, it is often inaccurately assumed that no progress has been made in the direction of limiting the free exercise of state will.[80] Once it is agreed that sovereignty is divisible[81] and that it therefore is not absolute, various restrictions on and relinquishments of sovereignty may be regarded as normal and not stigmatizing. The slow but steady development of majority rule in international organizations[82] bears witness to the change which is taking place. Of great significance is the contrast between the Covenant of the League of Nations which left to each member freedom to decide whether it would participate in sanctions recommended by the Council, and Chapter VII of the Charter of the United Nations whereby the members relinquish the power of decision to the Security Council and are bound to take action upon the basis of that decision. Notable also are those numerous provisions in the Charter which recognize that the treatment of the individual citizen is no longer a matter solely of domestic concern and that the denial of fundamental human rights to a citizen can no longer be shrouded behind the impenetrable cloak of national sovereignty.[83] Sovereignty in the sense of exclusiveness of jurisdiction, in certain domains, and subject to overriding precepts of constitutional force, will remain a usable and useful concept just as in the constitutional system of the United States the forty-eight states are considered sovereign. But sovereignty in its old connotations of ultimate freedom of national

[80] Cf. Postulate 3, INTERNATIONAL LAW OF THE FUTURE, A.B.A.J. Pub., 29 (1944); Jessup, "Force under a Modern Law of Nations," 25 FOR. AFF. 90 (1946).

[81] See the practical argument to this effect in I OPPENHEIM, INTERNATIONAL LAW, 5th ed., by Lauterpacht, § 69, p. 116 (1937).

[82] See RICHES, MAJORITY RULE IN INTERNATIONAL ORGANIZATION (1940).

[83] See Norman Wait Harris Memorial Foundation, Proceedings 21st Institute, The United Nations and The Organization of Peace and Security, 99, 126 (1945).

will unrestricted by law, is not consistent with the principles of community interest and of the status of the individual as a subject of international law. With the development of international law regulating the state's use of force and the implementation of the spirit of those provisions of the Charter which should make any resort to war clearly illegal, sovereignty would no longer constitute a major obstacle to the development of a genuine international community. Theoretical difficulties confronting the acceptance of the supremacy of international law would then disappear.

[3]

CODIFICATION AND DEVELOPMENT OF INTERNATIONAL LAW *

BY H. LAUTERPACHT

One of Her Majesty's Counsel; Fellow of the British Academy

The object of the present article is to survey the problems and to assess the achievements and prospects of the codification of international law within the United Nations in the light of the experience of the first five years of the activity of the International Law Commission. The Charter, in Article 13, imposes upon the General Assembly the obligation to "initiate studies and to make recommendations . . . for the purpose of encouraging the progressive development of international law and its codification." In pursuance of that article the General Assembly set up the International Law Commission and adopted a Statute regulating its functions and organization. The first session of the Commission took place in 1949. Since then, it has been meeting in yearly sessions lasting between eight and eleven weeks. In the intervals of the sessions, some of its members, acting as *Rapporteurs,* have studied and submitted reports on selected topics. The Commission itself has adopted and laid before the General Assembly a number of draft declarations, conventions and articles.[1]

Normally the results of an effort extending for five years would warrant an attempt to review the achievements of an organ of the United Nations in what was hoped would become an important field of its activity. This is so, although, from one point of view, it might appear doubtful whether the time has arrived for any such assessment. As in the case of many other aspects of the Charter, the political climate has not been propitious for revealing the full potentialities of the objects of the United Nations. However, such endeavor as has been possible in the conditions prevailing in the first decade of the existence of the United Nations has helped to draw attention to some more general features of codification. Accordingly, alongside of the discussion concerned with the general revision of the Charter of the United Nations, it may be desirable to consider any necessary improvements in the methods and the constitution of its organ entrusted with the codification and progressive development of international law. That there is room for a very substantial difference of opinion on the subject of the prospects and importance of codification may be seen from a comparison of the following views expressed, respectively, prior to the commencement of the activity of the International Law Commission and after what may be regarded as the initial experimental period of its

* This article was written before Professor Lauterpacht's election as one of the Judges of the International Court of Justice. It is intended to embody some of the results of his experience as a member of the International Law Commission. [ED.]

1 See below, note 39.

work: In 1947, the author of a penetrating analysis of the problem of codification of international law and of the task of the Commission in the light of its Statute, expressed his considered view that "it is surely evident that the implementing of Article 13 of the Charter is a task the urgency and importance of which yield place to none of the other problems that face the international lawyer to-day." [2] In 1953, a former Judge of the International Court of Justice committed himself to the opinion that attempts to codify international law within the larger community of the United Nations constitute a clear menace to the development of international law and that "the prospects of codification of international law on a universal plane are nil." [3] As will be suggested later,[4] this drastic estimate on the part of a lawyer not usually given to extreme statements does not necessarily bear the pessimistic interpretation which appears on the face of it. However, it is a statement which calls for reflection.

I. The Absence of Agreed Law and the Meaning of Codification

In the first instance, the experience of codification under the United Nations fully confirms the lesson of past attempts to the effect that there is very little to codify if by that term is meant no more than giving, in the language of Article 15 of the Statute of the International Law Commission, precision and systematic order to rules of international law in fields "where there already has been extensive State practice, precedent and doctrine." For, once we approach at close quarters practically any branch of international law, we are driven, amidst some feeling of incredulity, to the conclusion that although there is as a rule a consensus of opinion on broad principle—even this may be an overestimate in some cases—there is no semblance of agreement in relation to specific rules and problems. Thus, for instance, with regard to the law of treaties, perhaps the only principle of wider import as to which there is no dissent is that treaties ought to be fulfilled in good faith. Even that statement is accurate only if we reduce the emanations of the so-called *rebus sic stantibus* doctrine to the manageable confines of a general principle of law applied by an international tribunal at the instance of the state which claims to be released from the treaty on account of a change in vital circumstances. Apart from that general and unavoidable acceptance of the basic principle, *Pacta sunt servanda,* there is little agreement and there is much discord at almost every point.

By way of example, reference may be made to one portion of the law of treaties which the writer of this article had recent occasion to investigate in some detail, namely, their conclusion and validity. There is a difference of opinion on the very notion of the treaty in relation to the question of who may be parties thereto. Can public international organizations, *i.e.* organizations of states, be parties to treaties? They seem to

[2] Jennings in British Year Book of International Law, Vol. 24 (1947), p. 329.

[3] Charles de Visscher, *Théories et realités en droit international public* (1953), pp. 177, 181.

[4] See below, p. 38.

have concluded a great many of them—between themselves, with the United Nations (which is itself a public international organization) and with states (both Members of the United Nations and others). But the International Law Commission adopted in 1951 a provisional article in which the definition of a treaty covered states only as distinguished from organizations of states. About one-third of international agreements are at present concluded by way of exchanges of notes. However, in the course of its initial consideration of the subject, the Commission decided provisionally, by a bare majority, that exchanges of notes do not come within the purview of the law of treaties. On both these questions the Report on Treaties which the Special *Rapporteur* submitted in 1953 to the Commission reached contrary conclusions.[5] The legal meaning of the signature of the treaty is contested. Is it no more than a clerical act of authentication which implies no legal rights and obligations and which the signatory states are entitled to ignore at will? Or is it an act which connotes some, if imperfect, obligations such as abstention, in the period between signature and ratification, from conduct aimed at impairing the effectiveness of the substantive provisions of the treaty; a measure of obligation to submit the treaty to national authorities for confirmation or rejection; and perhaps the duty to ratify the treaty confirmed by the competent legislative authority? There is an even sharper controversy as to the necessity of ratification of treaties which are silent on the question whether they require such action or not. Is it a condition of the validity of treaties that they must be ratified unless they contain a specific provision exempting them from the requirement of ratification? Or is such exemption to be implied from the nature of the compact in the sense, for instance, that some types of agreement do not require ratification? Or is it the rule that no ratification is required unless the treaty expressly provides for it? There is a wide and unresolved divergence of views and practice as to the effect of the disregard of constitutional limitations on the part of the organ which ratifies or otherwise accepts a final treaty obligation on behalf of the state. Is that state bound by the treaty; or is it free to repudiate it; or is it bound in certain circumstances, for instance, if it has acted upon it or derived benefits from it; or, while not bound, is it in some contingencies under a duty to pay compensation to the other contracting party? Varying answers have been given to these questions.[6] With regard to accession to treaties, there are conflicting views and practices on the question whether accession can take place prior to the treaty entering into force or only subsequent to that event—with the result that treaties which might enter into force if the first alternative is adopted, may never materialize if the

[5] Report on Treaties, by H. Lauterpacht, U.N. Doc. A/CN.4/63, Arts. 1 and 3.

[6] The position is illustrated, in the sense suggested above, by the fact that although Mr. Fitzmaurice (as he then was), writing in the British Year Book of International Law (Vol. 15 (1934), p. 113), adopted, in a searching analysis, a more definite attitude in respect to some of them and although he adhered to the same view in 1948 in his lectures at the Hague Academy, after stating what he considered to be the law, he added the following words of caution: "these excellent precepts are unfortunately only too often honoured in the breach" (*Recueil*, Vol. 73 (1948), Tome II, p. 357, note 1).

second view is allowed to prevail. If the treaty provides, as do the Hague Conventions of 1907, that accession may be effected only by agreement of the contracting parties, does that mean all contracting parties or merely the majority of them? Are the "Contracting Parties" in this connection the original signatories or also those who have subsequently validly acceded to the treaty? On the important subject of reservations to multilateral treaties [7] it has become doubtful whether there is now any generally agreed law at all.

The same lack of certainty or agreement envelops the law relating to the validity of treaties from the point of view of reality of consent, legality of subject-matter, and compliance with requirements of form. Has the prohibition or limitation of the right to have recourse to war or force rendered obsolete the rule of traditional international law which disregards the vitiating effect of duress? Is the vitiating effect, if any, of duress absolute or only in relation to the guilty state in the sense that a treaty imposed by that state is invalid? Conflicting answers have been given to these questions. The same uncertainty prevails as to the limits of the principle that a treaty is void if its performance involves an act which is illegal under customary international law. There is an even more pronounced difference of view as to the illegality of treaties inconsistent with previous treaty obligations binding upon one or both of the parties—a problem which raises a host of questions, including that of the validity of the Charter of the United Nations itself. There is conflicting or ambiguous judicial and arbitral authority as to the requirement of written form as a condition of validity of treaties. The exact meaning of the provisions of the Charter of the United Nations in the matter of enforceability of non-registered treaties in relation to Members and non-Members is far from commanding a uniform answer.

It would be possible to continue that sorry tale in relation to the entirety of the law of treaties and, indeed, of most of international law.[8] The fact, which is both disquieting and chastening, speaks for itself. There is, upon reflection, nothing astonishing about it. How could it be otherwise in a society in which judicial settlement is sporadic, in which there is no legislative activity in the accepted sense and in which custom is slow of growth and controversial in interpretation and application? It is probably a fact that the absence of agreed rules partaking of a reasonable degree of certainty is a serious challenge to the legal nature of what goes by the name of international law. That circumstance alone supplies cogent proof of the justification, nay, of the urgency of the task of codification of international law. The matter is not merely one of *elegantia juris* and of a "better expression of international law" in the sense that it evokes "a somewhat vague and distant interest of States." [9] Clarity and certainty are not mere embellishments of the law. They are, particularly in the

[7] See below, p. 21.

[8] See Survey of International Law in Relation to the Work of Codification of the International Law Commission (Memorandum by the Secretary General, 1949), p. 7.

[9] Charles de Visscher, *op. cit.*, p. 180.

international sphere, of its essence. Within the state obscurity and uncertainty of the law are a drawback, but it is a drawback which is provisional inasmuch as the uncertainty can be removed with regard to a particular controversy by the decision of a court endowed with compulsory jurisdiction. This is not the position among states. The jurisdiction of international tribunals is still voluntary. The compulsory jurisdiction of the International Court of Justice under the Optional Clause of its Statute is not universally accepted. Even in relation to those states which have accepted it, it has been weakened in many cases by reservations to the point of being nominal. There have been instances, among enlightened states bound by the Optional Clause, of differences as to clearly legal rights and obligations being settled by recourse not to the International Court of Justice but to reprisals.[10] As the result, the uncertainties, gaps, and obscurities of the law are not merely perpetuated. They feed and grow on their own evil inasmuch as they are kept alive and magnified by the conflicting and extreme assertions of the parties to disputes. The call for codification is therefore not the product of legal perfectionism. It is an imperative need of international society, and it is only on account of more pressing problems assailing its very existence that the consciousness of the urgency of codification has been relegated into the background.

It may, of course, be said that the seriousness of the challenge can be exaggerated; that, after all, tribunals applying international law have not felt themselves frustrated by the absence of agreed rules of law; that there is in the background that vast reservoir of creative judicial decision applying general principles of law now elevated to the status of one of the main sources of international law; and that there is therefore no danger that, even if such contingency were admissible (or, indeed, conceivable), an international tribunal might be compelled to decline to render a decision on account of the absence of a rule of law directly bearing upon the issue before it. The comfort to be derived from these and similar considerations is deceptive. This is so not only for the reason of the absence, in principle, of compulsory jurisdiction of international tribunals. Even apart from that fact, the anomaly of international tribunals having to resort to judicial legislation, under the respectable guise of the application of general principles of law, instead of applying existing legal rule, is obvious and needs no elaboration. (It is significant that one of the principal recommendations of the Committee of Jurists who in 1920 framed the Statute of the Permanent Court of International Justice was that the Council of the League of Nations should proceed with the task of codification of international law. They assumed that the absence of clear and agreed rules of law and the corresponding latitude or discretion of international tribunals are not likely to assist in inducing governments to undertake the commitments of obligatory judicial settlement.)

10 It was reported in 1953 that the French Parliament enacted, apparently as a measure of reprisals against the United States, legislation compelling certain categories of foreign nationals resident in France to perform military service there. It was alleged that the United States was acting on legislation identical in substance.

Moreover, experience has shown that on occasions decisions of international tribunals themselves, far from supplying the missing element of completeness, may infuse an element of doubt and uncertainty where hitherto there existed relative clarity and agreement. Two examples will illustrate that point: Prior to the Advisory Opinion of the International Court of Justice on the *Reservations to the Genocide Convention* [11] it was thought that the principle of unanimous consent is the generally accepted rule of international law on the subject; namely, the principle that ratification or any other method of accepting a multilateral treaty is void if accompanied by reservations not agreed to by all other parties to the treaty. The Court declined to hold that the principle of unanimous consent constituted, as matter both of existing practice and of the reason of the thing, the rule of international law. It laid down novel principles of its own to which, if it may be said so with respect, it is difficult to deny qualities of statesmanship and reasonableness. These principles are based on the test of compatibility of the reservations with the object and the purpose of the treaty. However, in the absence of legal rules and procedures ensuring the application of these principles, that test is no more than a subjective and necessarily abstract standard which in itself can provide no working solution of the difficulty. It is probable that the traditional rule of unanimity affords no such solution of the problem and that alternative procedures must be envisaged. That such modifications of the rule of unanimity are feasible is shown by the attitude adopted in 1953 at the General Assembly by the United Kingdom, notwithstanding the fact that it considered the unanimity rule to be the established rule of international law.[12] However, as stated, the opinion of the Court on *Reservations to the Genocide Convention,* while denying the existence of a binding rule on the subject and while formulating a new general test of admissibility of reservations, left in abeyance the question of its practical application. Thus on occasions judicial activity, far from supplying the missing link of certainty and clarity, may achieve the opposite effect. It may do so in two directions: it may disturb or do away with the conviction, hitherto operative, of the existence of an agreed rule of law; after having done that, it may accentuate the anomaly by laying down a principle which is incomplete and which requires further elaboration if it is to be of practical value. Such absence of complete solution may be due to the legitimate disinclination to strain the processes of judicial legislation. However, while considerations of that order explain the resulting gap, they do not fill it.

Another example in the same category was provided by the judgment of

[11] I.C.J. Reports, 1951, p. 15; digested in this JOURNAL, Vol. 45 (1951), p. 579.

[12] An attitude which Sir Gerald Fitzmaurice subsequently elaborated in constructive detail in an article in the International and Comparative Law Quarterly, Vol. 2 (1953), pp. 1–26, and which was given practical application by the representative of the United Kingdom in the Human Rights Commission in 1954 in connection with the Final Clauses of the proposed Covenant of Human Rights (Doc. E/CN.4/L.345 and Add. 1). The British proposals substituted for the principle of unanimity the requirement of consent by a substantial majority of the parties.

the International Court of Justice in the *Anglo-Norwegian Fisheries Case.*[13] Prior to that judgment the rule that the base line of territorial waters runs parallel to the sinuosities of the coast and that the ten-mile line across the mouth of the bay is the base line in regard to bays had not been universally accepted. But it had been generally accepted. The Court declined to view it in that light. It considered that there was no such agreed practice on the subject as to warrant its recognition as a rule of law. After having held that, it proceeded to lay down principles of a general and subjective nature, which need more detailed formulation before they can become a working rule of law.

Enough has been said to draw attention to what probably is a fact, namely, that the task of codifying international law, if it is to mean anything, must be primarily one of bringing about an agreed body of rules rather than introducing systematic order and precision into legal rules already covered by customary or conventional agreement of states. At present the area of such agreement is small in the extreme. To put it into different words: There is little substantive meaning or practical purpose in the definition, already referred to, of codification given in Article 15 of the Statute of the International Law Commission, namely, "precise formulation and systematization of [existing] rules of international law in fields where there already has been extensive State practice, precedent and doctrine." For the existence of a rule of international law does not necessarily follow, as that definition seems to assume, from the existence of "extensive State practice, precedent and doctrine." These may demonstrate the non-existence of an agreed rule of international law. The fact that, because of the absence of agreed law, codification in the sense of making the law precise and systematic has little or no actual application in relation to international law, has been recognized by practically all writers and, generally, by those who have become actively engaged in the work of codification at international conferences and otherwise.[14] It is

[13] I.C.J. Reports, 1951, p. 116; digested in this JOURNAL, Vol. 46 (1952), p. 348.

[14] See, *e.g.* Professor Brierly's statement as *Rapporteur,* in 1947, of the Committee on the Progressive Development of International Law to the effect that any work of codification reveals gaps and uncertainties, and that "if you were to disregard these uncertainties and these gaps and simply include in your code rules of existing law which are absolutely certain and clear, the work would have little value" (A/AC.10/30, pp. 2, 3); Survey of International Law in Relation to the Work of Codification (Memorandum by the Secretary General, 1949): "It is clear that if the task of the International Law Commission were confined to fields with regard to which there is a full measure of agreement among States, the scope of its task would be reduced to a bare minimum"; Flournoy, in this JOURNAL, Vol. 24 (1930), p. 468: "Early in the discussions at the recent Hague conference it was realized that there was little international law on the subject of nationality which could be codified, if 'codification' is to be limited to the reduction to writing of rules of law already generally agreed upon by states"; as to the London Conference of 1909, see Jennings, *op. cit.,* p. 307. In its reply to the inquiry of the League of Nations subsequent to the Hague Conference of 1930, the British Government expressed the view that the work of that conference would have been more useful if it had been recognized from the outset that its function was one of legislative codification, and it expressed doubts as to "the likelihood of important branches of international law being found to which the application of consolidating methods would be

inconvenient and it is a cause of confusion that that fact has been ignored in the Statute of the International Law Commission and that the task of making the—non-existent—agreed law precise and systematic was there made to constitute one of the two principal features of the work of the Commission.

II. Reasons of Absence of Agreed Law

There would normally be little object in a pedantic analysis of a definition of codification in the Statute of the International Law Commission —a definition which may have been arrived at rather hastily amidst the pressure of business of the General Assembly. However, the matter is more than one of definition. For, as stated, Article 15 of the Statute of the Commission, especially when taken in conjunction with the definition of "development of international law" as contained there, would seem, unless explained to the point of being disregarded, to exclude from the purview of the activity of the Commission practically the entire field of codification in its larger sense. For the area of international law in which no more is needed than "precise formulation and systematization," *i.e.*, codification in the apparent sense of Article 15, is insignificant. For that reason a more accurate definition of the work of the Commission must concentrate not on the task of giving precision to, or systematic formulation of, existing agreed law, but on bringing about agreement where so far there exists only conflict of views and practice. However, if that is so, it is essential for the better understanding of the task of codification thus conceived to realize that it, in turn, has two aspects.

There are, in the first instance, situations where there exists a divergence of views and practice but where the reasons for the absence of agreement are intrinsically of little moment and where one group of states can afford, or can reasonably be held to be able to afford, a change in their views or practice for the ostensible reason that no substantial interest of their own is involved. Let us consider, for instance, from this point of view the question, already referred to, of the requirement of ratification in cases in which the treaty is silent on the matter. There are impressive arguments in favor of either of the two solutions as summarized above. The discussion on the subject has been learned and vigorous. However, on reflection, it does not really matter much, in terms of actual interests of states, which solution is adopted. This is so particularly if it is borne in mind that the

useful" (League of Nations Doc. A. 12. 1931). The same view was expressed with all requisite clarity by Senator Elihu Root as far back as 1911. He said: "To codify municipal law is to state in systematic form the results of the law-making process already carried on by a nation through its established institutional forms. To codify international law is primarily to set in motion and promote the law-making process itself in the community of nations in which the institutional forms appropriate for the carrying on of such a process have been so vague, indistinct, uncertain and irregular that they could hardly be said to exist at all." This Journal, Vol. 5 (1911), p. 579. He gave expression to the same view, in almost identical terms, in 1925, *ibid.*, Vol. 19 (1925), p. 681. It is of interest to note that this generally acknowledged and most conspicuous feature of international codification finds no expression in the language of the Statute of the International Law Commission.

difference between the two points of view on this question is a matter of emphasis. Thus those who urge that in the absence of provisions to the contrary a treaty is not binding unless ratified, admit of broad exceptions not only in case of the wide range of exchanges of notes and intergovernmental agreements, but also by reference to the previous practice of the parties and other attendant circumstances. Moreover, the importance of the subject appears in the proper perspective if it is recalled that in fact practically all treaties regulate the matter one way or another: they either lay down that the treaty shall be ratified or they provide that it shall enter into force upon signature, that is to say, that it need not be ratified. This being so, the proper task of the work of codification (and of the work connected therewith) is to bring authoritatively to light the modest dimensions of the issue involved and the absence of any important national interest militating against the adoption of an agreed uniform solution. These factors do not diminish the necessity for codification. For the justification of a legal rule does not depend upon the frequency of the situations which give rise to its application or the weight of the interest involved.

The same considerations apply to other questions, jurisprudentially more complicated, such as the relevance of the disregard of constitutional limitations or of inconsistency with previous treaty obligations, questions in which the doctrinal and juridical issue is real and in which there is no obvious preponderance of argument in favor of one solution. It is perhaps unimportant, in this connection, whether the solution in one sense is juridically obvious or whether it can be reached only after a laborious balancing of relevant considerations. What *is* important is that such solution—whatever it may be—does not affect any weighty or vital national interest. From that point of view it is, for instance, of little consequence whether the law as eventually codified will prescribe that a treaty must be in the form of a written document or whether it will endow with valid effect obligations assumed by way of an oral undertaking. Undoubtedly, it is preferable that a rule should be adopted which is juridically sound and workable. But no one—no person and no government—ought to be so sure of his position, in matters not affecting interests of significance, as to permit disagreement on the merits of a rule of that category to perpetuate a situation in which there is no agreed rule at all. The absence of an agreed rule is a greater evil than the adoption of a rule which is perhaps not as good as the one which could have been adopted.

We have been concerned so far with that wide—by far the widest—area of divergence in which agreement and uniformity could be achieved by a mutual process of accommodation in a sphere which is predominantly not one of conflicting interests but of doctrine and juridical controversy. However, this is not the most important aspect of the problem which confronts the task of codification. For there is, secondly, that source of disagreement which *is* due to conflicting interests and claims in the political, economic and strategic spheres. Of this, the present position of the law relating to the limits of territorial waters provides an instructive example. It may, of course, be contended, not altogether inaccurately, that notwithstanding the various claims to a wider limit, the traditional rule of customary international law on the subject is still law; that it is so regarded by the principal maritime Powers whose aggregate tonnage comprises by far the largest part of the tonnage of the world's shipping; that there has been no agreement to displace that rule; and that claims, whether exorbitant or not, going outside it have, in general, met with protests. However, although this may be so, it cannot be denied that the traditional rule has been widely and actively challenged in practice. What can the work of codification by lawyers do in this field? Or can it be said that the problem here is political in nature? It is so, though not exclusively so. Whenever the absence of an agreed rule is due to a divergence of interests, the function of codification is, in a distinct sense, no less political that that of legislation generally. However, it is clear at the same time that in this context political, economic, and cognate factors are also factors of legal relevance. It is the business of codification, after revealing fully the extent of the divergence in all its implications, to use these factors as legitimate components of an eventual legal rule.

The manner in which the International Law Commission has approached this subject illustrates the potentialities of this method of approach. The Commission has refrained from proposing solutions by way of a mechanical compromise in the nature of an average of the various figures of mileage claimed by various states. It has attempted, in the first instance, to take the rough edges off the problem by formulating, in 1953 and in preceding years, in precise language the widely adopted practice of contiguous zones, not exceeding twelve miles, in connection with customs, immigration, fiscal or sanitary regulations.[15] There have been, so far, no indications that the principal maritime nations will feel bound to resist such indirect approach to the problem. On the direct issue of the limit of territorial waters a proposal was laid by the *Rapporteur* before the Commission in 1953, startling and extreme at first sight, but on closer scrutiny deserving of consideration as showing one of the possible methods of codification in relation to a subject of this character. The proposal was in substitution for that submitted in 1952 in which it was laid down, by way of an attempt at a compromise, that the breadth of the territorial waters should be fixed by the coastal state but that it may not exceed six marine miles. In 1953 it was proposed that the maximum breadth of the territorial waters to be fixed by the coastal state may not exceed twelve miles, subject, in addition to the guarantees of the right of innocent passage, to the limitation that the coastal state may only claim exclusive fishing rights for its nationals up to three miles.[16] No expression of opinion is here called for as to the propriety or wisdom of the proposal for a twelve-mile limit as a basis of future discussions, even if the sting has been taken out of it by excluding fisheries from the operation of the sovereignty of the coastal state in the zone outside three miles. But the proposal is indicative of the

[15] Report by M. François on the Regime of the Territorial Sea (U.N. Doc. A/CN.4/53), p. 11.

[16] Second Report by M. François on the Regime of the Territorial Sea (U.N. Doc. A/CN.4/61), p. 10.

possibilities of meeting the difficulty by way of a combination of the claims of the coastal state to an extended limit with the essential features of the freedom of the seas, of which unimpeded freedom of navigation, not referred to in the proposal, must be regarded as fundamental. Some such combination may, upon analysis, prove identical with the notion of contiguous zones and thus provide a solution of a problem which otherwise may become a source of serious weakness to the authority of international law. For its authority is bound to be impaired by the fact that, while the principal maritime states uphold the traditional rule as a fully valid principle of international law, a considerable number of states have legislated and acted in defiance of that principle. In a further report, submitted in 1954, the Special *Rapporteur* outlined yet another possible solution. He proposed (1) that the breadth of the territorial sea shall be three nautical miles measured from the base line of the territorial sea, but (2) that the coastal state may extend the territorial sea up to a limit of twelve nautical miles from the base line, subject to the following conditions: (a) that there shall be guarantee of free passage in the territorial sea as provided in the draft; (b) that the coastal state may claim exclusive fishery rights for its nationals only up to a distance of three nautical miles measured from the base line of the territorial sea; that beyond this limit fishing in the territorial sea may be regulated by the coastal state solely for the purpose of protecting the resources of the sea and without any discrimination against foreign nationals;[17] and that the validity of the measures adopted for these purposes by the coastal state must be submitted to conciliation or, if no agreement is reached, to arbitration.[18] These successive hesitating and apparently contradictory reports and alternative proposals reveal the intricacy of the problem involved and the nature of the task required for its solution. In this and similar cases the task of codification, confronted with an acute divergence of practice in a matter affecting important interests of states, calls for a combination of legislative activity with measured adherence to a legal rule sanctioned by tradition and by considerations of unimpaired validity. For the validity of the principle of the freedom of the sea is far from spent. However, that principle can be preserved only by dint of its being adjusted to the reasonably conceived interests of the coastal state and, in relation to the high seas proper, through the adoption of rules which will prevent the freedom of the seas from becoming a regime of anarchy and waste. It is in this light that the articles finally drafted by the International Law Commission in 1953 in the matter of fisheries and the continental shelf[19] must be viewed.

[17] An apparently liberal provision which may hide pitfalls of substantive discrimination inasmuch as measures of conservation may affect exclusively methods employed by aliens for catching fish (for instance, trawl-fishing) but not against methods used by inshore fishermen (*e.g.*, line fishing).

[18] Third Report by M. François on the Regime of the Territorial Sea (U.N. Doc. A/CN.4/77), p. 5.

[19] Report of the Fifth Session (1953), General Assembly, 8th Sess., Official Records, Supp. No. 9 (A/2456), pp. 12–19; this JOURNAL, Supp., Vol. 48 (1954), pp. 27–43.

These, then, are the two aspects of codification in relation to matters on which there has either never been agreed law or on which there is no longer agreed law. In relation to one aspect, the business of codification is to bring about uniformity by persuasion and instruction pointing to the absence of any substantial reason for continued disagreement. In relation to the other aspect, its task is more exacting; it is to bring about an agreed rule of law where the source of divergence *is* due to a substantial conflict of interests and claims and where no less persuasion and instruction, coupled with attempts at a practical and statesmanlike reconciliation of opposing principles and considerations, are required as a condition of the emergence of an agreed rule. In neither case is the task one of purely academic order. Governments do not take well to intimations, when coming from outsiders, that no substantial interest of their own is involved. Thus, in connection with the preparation of draft conventions on elimination or reduction of statelessness, they have shown impatience with the argument that deprivation of nationality by way of punishment serves either no national interest at all or an interest of a sentimental nature so questionable as hardly to outweigh the more general objections against deprivation of nationality resulting in statelessness. Neither, in cases of a genuine conflict of claims and interests, are they easily amenable to counsel of moderation and accommodation emanating from scholars and external agencies. Yet it is a fact that such evaluation of national interests and their reduction to a common denominator of national and international interest is of the essence of codification. These considerations have a distinct bearing on the character of the work of codification and of the organs engaged on it.[20] To this subject we will return presently.

III. Change and Development of Existing Law

We may now turn from codification in cases where there is no agreed rule of law to those in which the existing law is agreed, undisputed, and amply covered by precedent and doctrine, but in which a change—a development—is felt to be called for by considerations of progress, of mutuality of enlightened economic interest, of international interdependence, of good faith, of morality, of the rights of man. There is no question here of "progressive development of international law" as meaning the preparation of draft conventions on subjects which, in the somewhat unhelpful language of Article 15 of the Statute of the Commission, "have not yet been regulated by international law or in regard to which the law has not yet been sufficiently developed in the practice of States." Two subjects on which the International Law Commission produced drafts in 1953, namely, those on elimination and reduction of statelessness and on arbitral procedure, provide an instructive example of this aspect of its activity. Thus there is, so far as the existing law is concerned, general agreement on the subject of statelessness. According to international law, states are fully at liberty to adopt legislation resulting in statelessness; for instance,

[20] See below, p. 40.

by not conferring nationality at birth or by depriving persons of their nationality by way of penalty or otherwise. The matter is regulated, and abundant though often melancholy practice has grown around it. But, to paraphrase the language of the Preamble of the Draft Convention on Elimination of Statelessness, that practice is productive of much hardship offensive to the dignity of man; it provides a cause of international friction; and it is inconsistent with the more general principles of international law acording to which nationality is an essential link between the individual and the law of nations. It is a change in the existing agreed law and practice that is here the proper object of codification.

The same applies to the main aspect of the Code of Arbitral Procedure as drafted by the Commission. Its purpose is to do away with an existing feature of the law of arbitral procedure which often renders somewhat nominal the obligation to settle a dispute by arbitration. Thus, according to existing law, if the parties cannot agree on the choice of arbitrators or if the arbitrators are unable to agree on the selection of the umpire, then, in the absence of provisions on the subject in the treaty of arbitration, the entire procedure collapses and with it the obligation to settle the dispute by arbitration. Similarly, if one of the parties maintains that the award is null and void on account of excess of jurisdiction on the part of the tribunal, there is, as the law stands at present, no obligatory judicial or other machinery for resolving the dilemma. By asserting that there has taken place excess of jurisdiction a party to the dispute may, in effect, avoid the fulfillment of its principal obligation. Here again, in a field covered by the practice of states, change and development are felt to be desirable having regard to the requirements of good faith and to the effectiveness of international obligations.

The states participating in the Hague Codification Conference of 1930 fully realized that codification could not be confined to a registration or systematization of existing law. The Assembly of the League of Nations, in laying down in 1927 the broad principles which were to govern the work of the conference to be convened, adopted a recommendation that "the Governments which might be invited to the Conference should be informed that the codification effort to be undertaken by the first Codification Conference must aim at adapting existing rules to contemporary conditions."[21] The drawbacks and dangers resulting from any deliberate limitation of the task of codification to a mere restatement of the existing law were illustrated in a revealing manner in the report submitted in 1951 by the International Law Commission on the question of reservations to multilateral treaties. That report was, apart from certain suggestions of procedural innovations, confined to a restatement of the traditional rule based on the principle of the unanimous consent of all contracting parties to reservations appended by states. This was so, although the Commission was invited by the General Assembly to study the question "both from the point of view of codification and from that of the progres-

[21] League of Nations Official Journal, 1927, Spec. Supp. No. 55. And see above, note 14.

sive development of international law." The International Court of Justice, when called upon to give an advisory opinion on substantially the same question, made in effect a pronouncement which was in the nature of a progressive development of this aspect of international law.[22] The result, somewhat strange, was that, while the organ called upon to *apply* international law made a contribution to its *development* on the subject in question, the International Law Commission, whose competence is less narrowly drawn, confined itself to restating the existing position as it saw it. It is equally significant that it was the view of the Court rather than that of the Commission which commended itself to the large majority of the states represented at the General Assembly. The feature of the situation thus created, which calls for comment, is that the Commission in its desire to confine itself to a restatement of the existing law was inclined in its report to regard that law as satisfactory. No such virtue can reasonably be attributed to the rule of unanimity in the sphere of reservations—and elsewhere. It is probable that that approval of what was considered the traditional doctrine stemmed from the conviction that where there exists a clear and easily ascertainable rule of law, its alteration is outside the province of the codifying body. Any such view misrepresents the true task of codification. Even within that very limited field where there is both agreement and considerable practice, the work of codification cannot discard *a limine* the legislative function of developing and improving the law.

IV. The Distinction Between Codification and Development in the Statute of the International Law Commission

It follows from the preceding observations that, unlike codification in other fields, codification of international law must be substantially legislative in nature. It must consist essentially in inducing governments (or some governments) to accept new law. This is so primarily in all cases in which their practices and views are in articulate conflict, both where the conflict does not correspond to an actual divergence of interests and where it does so correspond. This is so, secondly, where views and practices agree, but where a progressive change in the law is considered desirable. Somewhat strangely, these by far the widest and typical areas of codification are not in fact covered by the Statute of the International Law Commission. For, as mentioned, the Statute provides only (a) for codification (in the sense of introducing precision and systematization) in cases in which there exists essential agreement evidenced by long practice, precedent and doctrine, and (b) for "development" where there is as yet no regulation of international law and no sufficient practice, precedent or doctrine. It does not provide for codification where there exists practice but no agreement; neither does it provide for development where existing practice calls for a change. It is probable that the result thus achieved is due to an oversight in drafting; it is so drastically out of keeping with

22 See above, p. 21.

experience and with the views persistently expressed on the subject [23] that it cannot be regarded as intentional. It is not surprising that the relevant Article 15 of the Statute of the Commission has been disregarded in practice. It must be so left out of account in the future unless the work both of codification and development is to be reduced to nominal dimensions.

For these and other reasons it has proved impracticable to pay attention to the emanations, formulated in various articles of the Statute of the Commission, of the distinction thus conceived between codification and development of international law—articles which bear both on the methods of preparing drafts and on action to be taken upon them by the General Assembly. There is no good reason for deploring this departure from the letter of the Statute. In most cases the work of the Commission on a given topic partakes of the nature both of codification and development. The Draft Code of Arbitral Procedure constitutes a conspicuous procedural innovation—a development—in providing machinery of a binding character intended to prevent the frustration of the original undertaking to arbitrate. At the same time, in the words of the report of the Commission on the subject, the Draft Code "must be considered as being primarily in the nature of codification of existing international law" inasmuch as it is based on the autonomy of the parties (which is the basis of the traditional law on the subject) with regard to the composition of the tribunal, the determination of its competence as well as of its law and procedure, and, above all, the respect for the sovereignty of both parties as expressed in their agreement, voluntarily undertaken, to settle the dispute by arbitration. The purpose of the Draft Code is to give effect to the sovereignty of both parties and to protect it against being rendered nugatory by the unilateral will of one of them.

The Draft Convention on Statelessness constitutes "development"—a change in the law—in the sense that it limits the freedom of states, hitherto forming part of the law, to create and augment causes of statelessness. At the same time it constitutes codification in a double sense: (a) the proposed change in the law gives expression to the policy of many states, as already expressed in their legislation, to reduce or eliminate causes of statelessness; (b) the very change as proposed is in accordance with the wider principle of existing international law according to which nationality is the link between the individual and international law. The Draft Articles on the Continental Shelf seem naturally to fall within the orbit of "development" inasmuch as they cover a situation of obvious novelty and formulate new rules calculated to shape that situation by reference to the existing principle of the freedom of the sea. From a different point of view they may be said to codify and consolidate that existing principle by reference to the problems created by the claims to the continental shelf put forward by various states and not challenged by others, with the result that these claims may now be fairly held to constitute part of international practice. The Draft Articles on Fisheries,

[23] See above, note 14.

providing as they do for obligatory regulation by an international authority, clearly went outside the existing law. But the Commission, while stating that the articles fall generally within the category of development of international law, attached importance to noting that they are not altogether in the nature of a drastic departure from the principles of international law. This was so on account of their admitted connection with the prohibition of abuse of rights, a doctrine which the Commission considered to provide a satisfactory legal basis for the rules formulated by it.[24] Undoubtedly, it is useful and desirable that in its drafts the Commission should state in what respects and in what parts its work constitutes essentially a re-affirmation, a codification, of existing law and how far it amounts to development. As the report adopted in 1953 shows, the Commission has attempted in most cases to perform that task. There is all the difference between doing that and treating a topic as a whole as being exclusively in the nature of codification or exclusively in the nature of development and adopting different procedures for the elaboration of its drafts and bringing it to fruition by way of governmental action. In this respect, too, it is to be hoped that an early opportunity may be taken to eliminate the shortcomings of an experimental Statute.

In the light of the preceding observations and of the experience of codification under the League of Nations and the United Nations, the following submissions in relation to some main general problems of codification seem to be appropriate.

V. Private and Official Codification

In the first instance, the codification of international law can have but little justification and but slender chances of success, in terms of eventual acceptance by states, if it is confined to purely private effort, however scholarly and thorough. Mere academic restatement of the law, however competent and impartial, cannot hope to answer the real need. For, as already suggested, the field of agreed law to be restated is severely limited. The main need is for agreeing on the law and, in some cases, for changing it. From this point of view it is probable that the work of codification, if it is to achieve its primary purpose, must take place under the auspices of governments, acting, if possible, through and within the United Nations; that there must be constant co-operation with governments, and that the eventual, though not immediate, result of codification must be envisaged in the form either of conventions ratified by states or drafts and pronouncements enlisting the support of governments, not necessarily of all governments, in diverse other ways falling short of conventions envisaged in Article 23 of the Statute of the International Law Commission. That article enumerates the various courses open to the Commission in respect of drafts finally submitted by it to the General Assembly.[25] The Com-

[24] Sec. 100 of the Report of the Commission of 1953. This report, which, like other reports of the Commission, is published also in this Journal, Supp., Vol. 48 (1954), pp. 1–70, provides an instructive illustration of the submissions in the text.

[25] Although that article refers to "codification," it is clear—and this has been the practice of the International Law Commission—that it applies also to "development."

mission may recommend to the General Assembly that it in turn recommend the report to the Members with a view to the conclusion of a convention or that it convene a conference to conclude a convention. But, according to that article, the Commission may consider that it will be sufficient to recommend that the General Assembly take note of the report or adopt it by resolution, or even that no action be taken, the report having already been published. Whatever the proposal of the Commission, the General Assembly may adopt any of these courses. These provisions, envisaging as they do diverse stages of official codification, are capable of elastic application.

Codification thus conceived, as distinguished from restatement of the law by private scientific effort, has been exposed to much trenchant and weighty criticism.[26] Thus it has been said that codification under governmental auspices undertaken with the view to concluding conventions, far from achieving its object, tends to retard progress by revealing divergencies where none had been expressed or anticipated before; that it imparts a political character to what might otherwise be a purely scientific process; and that, by giving to any actual or assumed discrepancy a rigid complexion of finality, it impairs such prospects of success as may otherwise exist. These objections are perhaps less persuasive than they appear at first sight. They seem to leave out of account the view that, unless the work of codification is thought of in terms of eventual acceptance by governments, it has little meaning;[27] that the making of the law—and codification of international law is to a large extent within that category—is necessarily a political process; that the disclosure of disagreement must constitute the first step towards agreement; that little is gained by nursing the illusion that all is well; that governments have been able in the past to reach agreement on many matters; that such agreement need not be unanimous; that even if reached between a number of states, not necessarily the majority of them, it may still, in proportion to its intrinsic merits, constitute an achievement and provide a legal standard of regulation available for acceptance by others in the light of the experience of its actual working; and that it does not therefore necessarily follow that the result of official codification will be to reduce its content to a level determined by the most obstructive and least progressive governments. Such result might be inevitable if codification were conceived only as *universal* codification whose *raison d'être* lies in acceptance by all governments. This, as will be sub-

26 See, in particular, the paper contributed in 1946 by Sir Cecil Hurst in Transactions of the Grotius Society, Vol. 32 (1946), pp. 135–153, and the report of a committee under the chairmanship of Sir Arnold McNair, in International Law Association Report, Vol. 42 (1947), pp. 64–121.

27 "It does not require great perception to see that a mere restatement of existing law, however elegantly and liberally accomplished, would be ludicrously inadequate to meet the needs of contemporary international society, and it would be tragic if the comparative ease with which this process could be set in motion were to blind us to the need of something much more radical in the way of law-making. Radical law-making can only be done in time by the vehicle of the multipartite treaty." Jennings, *op. cit.*, p. 309.

mitted presently, is by no means the case. There is an element of oversimplification in the apprehension that attempts at codification may leave things in a condition worse than they were before by casting doubt upon principles hitherto generally accepted and by enabling some governments to cloak political claims for a change of the law in the garb of existing legal rules as they purport to see them.[28]

Some caution, it may be stated in this connection, may usefully be shown in describing the Hague Codification Conference of 1930 as a failure. There is room for the view, which cannot be elaborated here in detail, that the conference and the preparatory work which preceded it were a success, even if they were not immediately successful. Its main Convention on the Conflict of Nationality Laws entered into force and gave the impetus, in particular with regard to nationality of married women, to radical legislative changes on matters previously described as forming unalterable and fundamental features of national systems of law.[29] Its preparatory work and the deliberations concerning territorial waters must provide, as shown in the reports and discussions of the International Law Commission, the starting point of any future attempts in this direction. It is often forgotten that the results of the Conference of 1930 would have been more spectacular if its conveners had chosen the easy path of selecting for codification technical and other subjects unlikely to raise controversy rather than three topics fraught with conflict already both latent and apparent prior to the conference.[30]

Undoubtedly, the international composition of the official organs engaged in the work of codification must, because of the unavoidable infusion of the political element implicit in the consideration of national interest, tend to blur the element of scientific detachment. However, this is not a drawback limited to official efforts at codification. As experience shows, there is no assurance that that element can be entirely eliminated from the deliberations of scientific bodies which, although of a private character, are international in their composition. Neither can the political element be ruled out if the task of the codifying body acting under the auspices of governments or of the United Nations is limited to a mere "restatement" as distinguished from an effort aiming at producing conventions. For its work is bound

[28] Judge de Visscher, after apparently associating himself with such apprehension, admits that the divergencies revealed at the Hague Conference of 1930 were due less to the desire of governments to resume their liberty of action at the expense of existing law than to disagreements of substance due to the various not sufficiently clarified aspects of the problems involved and that "*ce rappel à certaines réalités de la réglementation internationale . . . a rapproché le droit de la vie internationale envisagée dans sa diversité et sa croisssante complexité.*" *Op. cit.*, p. 181.

[29] See, *e.g.*, the statement of the Commissioner in the *Elise Lebret* case, decided by the French-American Commission under the treaty of 1880, to the effect that the rule of automatic change of the nationality of a wife in consequence of a change in the nationality of the husband was part of the "public law of the world." Reported in Wilson, The International Law Standard in Treaties of the United States (1953), p. 57.

[30] Professor Brierly, writing in 1931, observed that "the results of the Hague Conference, such as they are, are greater than we were entitled to expect." British Year Book of International Law, Vol. 12 (1931), p. 6.

to be influenced by the belief that somehow such restatement is likely to be of practical application and corresponding political importance. Rigid detachment from political and economic factors underlying divergent legal conceptions when practiced by bodies which, unlike judicial tribunals, are called upon to shape the law of the future, may often be achieved only at the price of the diminished practical value of the solutions formulated by them. Above all, it is difficult to disregard what is probably the paramount factor in the situation, namely, that the ultimate need is not for a collective treatise or encyclopedia restating the existing agreed law, but a legislative process of codification improving, completing and developing international law.

Once this has been realized, so-called private codification assumes its proper place as a desirable aid and stimulus to official activity in this field. The work of the Harvard Research, the most important and successful in the sphere of private codification, has shown the wide possibilities of such effort in which the devotion and the competence of individuals, unhampered by claims of geographical representation, can achieve results with an economy of expense and time which cannot be expected from official bodies of international composition. There is room for the resumption, on an enlarged scale and on a broader basis, of the endeavor thus begun in order, after a quarter of a century, to bring up to date the topics already covered, to complete the prodigious undertaking of the Harvard Research by the inclusion of subjects which it had left on one side, and to keep alive, as a permanent effort, the task of continuous and encyclopedic presentation and periodic scrutiny and revision of the entire body of international law. As in the past, such activity cannot be in the nature of a mere restatement of the existing law. The Drafts of the Harvard Research, while giving an exhaustive account of existing practice, at the same time indicated what, in the absence of an agreed or satisfactory practice, ought to be the law of the future. This they did with regard to practically every subject which they covered. Unlike in the case of the Harvard Research, while discarding the hampering artificialities of rigidly conceived geographical representation, such efforts need not be limited to groups of scholars from one country. There are compelling reasons in support of the view not only that "there is room" for the resumption of the constructive and creative work of private codification thus conceived, but that there may be a measure of urgency in picking up the threads of an imposing endeavor interrupted by the cataclysm of the second World War. So long as the official work of codification under the aegis of the United Nations is of nominal dimensions, owing to the limited resources at the disposal of the codifying agency and to the rudimentary character of the machinery provided by the General Assembly for examining and for bringing to legislative fruition the drafts and reports prepared by the International Law Commission, codification by non-official bodies must be deemed to be an urgent task worthy of general support. In the sphere of constructive and farsighted promotion of ideas of international peace and the rule of law, it is not easy to think of objects of enlightened private munificence more worthy of assistance than non-official codification as here described. Pending realization of the desirable developments in the field of official codification, this may be the main instrument for furthering and keeping effectively in being a prominent object of the Charter of the United Nations.[31]

VI. The Independence of the Codifying Agency

While it is imperative that the task of codification should be attempted, alongside of any other methods, under the auspices of governments and that the body entrusted with that task should be an organ of the United Nations, it is of equal importance that it should be independent of governments not only in its composition but also in other relevant aspects. Thus it is essential for the success of codification that the reports and drafts as finally put before governments and the General Assembly should express, with all requisite and, if need be, uncompromising clarity, the views of the codifying agency as to the solution which is accurate *de lege lata* and desirable *de lege ferenda.* This is so, although, as stated, the task of codification must be approached with the view to its eventual adoption within the framework of positive international law as distinguished from its value as a scientific exposition, however full and informative. Although account must be taken of the attitude of governments, there is little or no merit in proposals of codification which anticipate, to the extent of regarding it as decisive, the possible opposition of governments and which are couched in terms of the lowest common denominator of probable general acceptance. Governments are composed of human beings and they must be credited with the capacity for being influenced by the intrinsic merits of drafts as finally elaborated. Experience has shown that governments are often less "realistic" than pessimism or lassitude makes them out to be. Undoubtedly, the proposals put before them must take into account the not unnatural reluctance of governments to consent to changes which may amount to a modification or an abandonment of their law and practice and necessitate complicated amendments in their legislation. Admittedly, codification must be the result of a laborious process of adjustment of, and compromise between, conflicting interests of states. But once the codifying agency, which is not composed of representatives of governments, has reached the conclusion that a draft is desirable and dictated by the interests of the international community, by the rationally conceived interest of states and the requirements of a progressive development of international law as an instrument of international co-operation and as the protector of the rights of the individual conceived as the ultimate subject and beneficiary of all law, then it must take the risk that the General Assembly will do no more for the time being than take note of the report which has been published. A report, adopted after mature consideration and after taking into account the views expressed by governments, is bound to exercise an influence and to rally around it the support of enlightened states.

[31] Sir Arnold McNair, in two lectures delivered at the Law Center of New York University and published in 1954 under the title, "The Development of International Justice," has given the weight of his authority in support of this aspect of codification of international law (see, in particular, pp. 24–31).

Of such possibilities the Draft Convention on the Elimination of Statelessness, tentatively formulated in 1953, provides an instructive example. Some states, such as the United Kingdom, could subscribe to that convention practically without a change, or any significant change, in their legislation.[32] Some countries may see in it no more than an embodiment—startling at first sight because of its completeness—of their own deliberately pursued legislative policy on the subject. On the other hand, states, such as the United States of America with its Nationality and Immigration Law enacted in 1952, would have to be prepared, at an appropriate time, to abandon provisions of municipal law which, enacted in what was considered to be a period of acutely felt danger and crisis, disregard the avowed general tendency not to augment causes of statelessness. It is not improper for a codifying body not composed of representatives of governments to urge that no vital national interest is involved in such renunciation of a national practice, however emphatic and however recently adopted. There can be no question of the dignity and sovereignty of states being involved in the expression, on the part of the codifying body, of the view that deprivation of nationality by way of punishment is, upon impartial examination, unrelated to any national interest of importance; that it has been abandoned, either formally or in practice, by many states without obvious detriment to their safety and well-being; and that the absence of national interest in its retention is coupled with a clear international interest in its abandonment. In particular, no impropriety can reasonably attach to any insistence, on the part of the codifying agency, on the essential irrelevance of the consideration, conceived as an exclusive consideration, that a specific product of codification necessitates changes in the national law. For clearly any codification, unless in the exceptional case of a restatement of the law agreed by all states, must necessitate changes in the law of some states. The same applies, more obviously, to codification which consists in a development of the law. In fact, the task of legislative codification of international law must remain sterile and lacking in moral authority unless it becomes axiomatic that the international interest—the interest of international society as such—is a legitimate factor in the situation not only as a means of reconciling divergent national interest but also as an end in itself. This may not be the view of some of the states intent upon perpetuating any particular practice. The time may therefore be distant when the Draft Convention on the Elimination of Statelessness will be adopted generally or even by the majority of states. This circumstance does not affect its intrinsic justification and eventual influence. It is not only of interest to note that the first great Power—the United Kingdom—which formulated its attitude toward the far-reaching proposals of the Commission on the subject, expressed its approval of the principal article of the more drastic Convention on the Elimination of Statelessness in preference to that on the Reduction of Statelessness.[33] What is of equal significance is the preparedness of some states to adopt an attitude toward

[32] See below.

[33] U.N. Doc. A/CN.4/82, p. 11.

proposals for a change in international law on this subject, not by reference to the fact that such changes are inconsistent with their existing legislation, but in the light of the intrinsic merits of the proposals in question. Thus the Norwegian Government, after drawing attention to the fact that the adoption of the Conventions on Reduction or Elimination of Statelessness would necessitate drastic changes in Norwegian law, continued as follows:

> Considering the important humanitarian aspects of the matter and the importance of demonstrating some liberality in the international co-operation aimed at relieving statelessness, the Norwegian Government will not be adverse to the idea of seeking to effect the necessary changes in the law provided there is some prospect of general adherence to one of the draft conventions on the part of Governments.[34]

Undoubtedly, it is useful for the codifying body to be informed of the state of the law in the countries concerned, but there is a distinct element of unhelpfulness in a reply which views the existing legislation of the state as the exclusive relevant factor in the situation. There is little object in creating an agency for codification and then confronting it with the existing anomalies and divergencies in the law as the factor of decisive relevance.

While it is of the essence of the successful accomplishment of the task of the codifying agency that governments should respect its independence by not treating it as a body confined to a registration of the existing municipal legislation and other practices of states, it is of equal importance that the International Law Commission should preserve its independence of governments not only, in the manner as here indicated, with regard to the character of its proposals, but also with regard to its own methods and procedure. The Commission is an organ of the United Nations. But it is an organ *sui generis.* It is not a political body and there may be a measure of incongruity in its procedure and deliberations being governed by technical and rigid rules appropriate to committees of the General Assembly, for instance, that a majority of two-thirds shall be required for a reconsideration of any decision taken during any session of the Commission. These considerations apply generally to the wider aspects of the activity of the Commission. The influence of its work must in a large measure depend upon the product having the support of the substantial majority of its members. Unlike in the case of other bodies where the necessity for action calls for decisions by a majority, however slender, the authority and effectiveness of drafts prepared by a codifying agency must be decisively impaired if formulated under the impact of the hazards and alignments of voting. For similar reasons it is desirable, contrary to the existing practice, that the reports of the Commission should give as full a publicity as is practicable to opposing or supplementary views of the minority or of individual members. The reasons which have prompted the recognition of the right of the judges of the International Court of Justice to append

[34] U.N. Doc. A/CN.4/82/Add. 1. See also the reply of the Dutch Government conceived in the same spirit (Doc. A/CN.4/82/Add. 6).

dissenting or separate judgments or opinions apply with no less cogency to the work of the International Law Commission.[35]

VII. The Problem of the Universality of Codification

Codification constitutes a need of international society at large and it is in accordance with its purpose that it should be undertaken within the orbit of the general organization of states represented within the United Nations and that it should aim at universal acceptance. While this appears to be the ultimate objective, the universal character of codification cannot, in the light of experience, mean more than that all states should be given an equal opportunity of participating in the work of codification and of associating themselves with its results. In particular, it cannot mean that the values of codification ought to be judged by the degree of generality of its acceptance or that its content should be allowed to be influenced decisively by any desire to approximate universality. From this point of view, so long as there exists no international legislature able to impose upon all members of the international community the law as formulated by a majority of states after due consideration of the national and international interests involved, the scope of codification in the international sphere must differ from that within the state. As a rule, universal acceptance of the results of codification can be achieved in the international sphere only at the risk of making it nominal and retrogressive. This is so in particular in periods when political divisions in the world and the conflict of some fundamental notions of law as between groups of states render impracticable, in most matters, any attempt to achieve generally agreed statement or development of the law. International law, whether codified or not, implies essentially a restriction of the sovereignty of states whose relations it governs. It is in the nature of things that states wedded to an uncompromising maintenance of their sovereignty cannot view with favor attempts at effective codification. The deliberations of the International Law Commission on the subject of nationality and statelessness provided an instructive example of that difficulty arising from the fact that some of the members of the Commission were opposed to the codification of that subject on the ground that regulation of nationality is a matter which is exclusively within the domestic jurisdiction of states. There can therefore be no objection to accepting as accurate the statement, referred to above,[36] of Judge Charles de Visscher to the effect that the prospects of a codification of international law on *a universal plane* are at present non-

[35] Any diminution of that right, for reasons of possible abuse, is not in keeping with the scientific character of the Commission and is, on more general grounds, indefensible. The authority of the decisions and drafts of the majority of the Commission is grounded in their intrinsic merit as distinguished from the formal fact of their being the result of a majority vote. As a rule, it cannot be impaired—it stands to gain—by an accompanying expression of the view of the minority. Where the persuasive force of a report of the majority is in fact in danger of being impaired by an accompanying expression of dissent, it may perhaps be desirable that it should thus be impaired.

[36] See p. 17.

existent. It is not necessary to impart to that view a degree of pessimism going beyond the apparent intention of its author.

For the fact that universal codification is not practicable or perhaps, in the existing circumstances, desirable, does not warrant sweeping conclusions in relation to codification as such. On the contrary, the reality of codification, its effectiveness, and its ultimate beneficence must be enhanced if it is envisaged, in the first instance, as extending to a limited circle of states. Drafts and conventions, formulated as part of the systematic codification of international law and approved by the General Assembly or subsequently adopted at a conference by a limited number of states, must be regarded as amply fulfilling, in the first instance, the purposes of codification as generally understood and as contemplated by the Charter. When formulated after prolonged and mature study and when supplemented by scientific comment and accompanying materials giving an exhaustive account of governmental and judicial practice, they are bound to constitute, even when they enter into force only between a restricted number of states, all that can be legitimately expected and all that is objectively required in the first stages of codification of international law. The fact that the Hague Convention on the Conflict of Nationality Laws has entered into force only among a small number of states, has not impaired its authority and its influence. Products of codification, even if initially approved or accepted only by a limited number of governments, constitute a positive and tangible achievement and a starting point for a gradual extension of their operation. The very fact that their authors, having discarded the spurious inducements of immediate universal participation and the resulting artificialities or retrogression of diplomatic compromise, have framed them so as not to sacrifice the reality of the context to appearance of universality, must add to their value.

Undoubtedly, as stated, in the work of codification under the aegis of the United Nations all states must be given the opportunity of participating in the preparatory work of codification even if there is doubt as to the genuineness of their attachment to that task and the prospects of their ultimate association with its results. Their views must be listened to with the respect to which they are entitled. Patience, tolerance and statesmanship will find means of reducing the danger of the stature and results of codification being impaired in the course of preparation by those who in any case are unlikely to subscribe to it. For there may be little object in meeting the views and interests of states which are in any event likely to keep aloof. On the other hand, in view of the potential general character of codification, means ought to be considered for associating with it states which are not at present Members of the United Nations. Some such association has proved practicable in the case of the International Court of Justice.

VIII. The Part of Governments

As experience has shown, the task of codification is impossible of achievement unless aided by the co-operation on the part of governments at every stage. Such collaboration entails heavy commitments of more than administrative nature. In the first instance, it involves the discharge of the delicate and often difficult task of securing an adequate composition of the codifying body. While the Statute of the International Law Commission provides in Article 2 that "the Commission shall consist of fifteen members who shall be persons of recognized competence in international law," it also lays down in Article 8, as a consideration to be borne in mind by the electors, that although the members of the Commission should individually possess the qualifications required, "in the Commission as a whole the representation of the main forms of civilization and of the principal legal systems of the world should be assured." It may be possible to take account of these two sets of considerations without doing violence to the letter and spirit of the Statute, but this may not be feasible in all cases. Apart from the undeniable necessity of making the codifying body as representative as possible, the nature of the task to be fulfilled by it is not without relevance in this connection. In an organ which is concerned not only with the restatement of existing law but also with its change and development, qualities of statesmanship and experience may legitimately count for no less than expert knowledge. In this respect the requirement of expert composition of the Commission need not necessarily follow the exacting conditions laid down in the constitutions of some other international bodies.[87] At the same time it is clear that an adequate proportion of membership fulfilling the requirements of Article 2 of the Statute of the Commission is an indispensable condition of the proper fulfillment of its task. The care and conscientiousness with which governments discharge that function, in this and similar spheres, is a touchstone of their sense of responsibility to the international community. Obviously, it is also an essential factor in the adequate fulfillment of the objects entrusted to any particular organ. A government which proclaims its devotion to an object of international endeavor and co-operation and which at the same time fails in its duty to make the best contribution, insofar as it lies with it, to the membership of the organ concerned, lays itself open to a charge of contradictory conduct inimical to international interest. It is probable that this aspect of governmental action or omission constitutes, as a matter of moral duty and international trust, one of the crucial problems of international organization in general.

Secondly, the collaboration of governments involves, as an important condition of the success of the work of codification, the furnishing of information as to the existing law and practices of the state concerned, a burdensome task for an already overburdened department of government. Such information is not a mere product of research. Insofar as it expresses the official view of a state as to its understanding of the law, it may be relied against it in the future to some extent. As such, the supply of information is a task of some complexity. It is a task which, unless performed perfunctorily and unhelpfully, constitutes a considerable addition

[87] Such as the Universal Postal Convention or the International Telecommunications Convention.

to the responsibilities, on a high level, of governments. The provision of such information cannot be delegated exclusively to subordinate officials. The same applies, more conspicuously, to comments on drafts prepared by the codifying organ. Such comments may require interdepartmental consultation and decisions on a high level of governmental responsibility in a manner often approaching decisions preliminary to the assumption of international obligations. For, as already noted, this is not only a question of supplying information as to legislation and other practice in the past; it may be a question of a state agreeing in advance to a change in its law. Yet it is clear that without such collaboration the work of codification, operating in a vacuum, must remain unreal. This being so, codification, conceived as a systematic long-range effort and as distinguished from attempts of limited scope, may require the creation of something in the nature of a special section in legal departments of foreign offices. It is bound to add to the responsibilities of the foreign offices as such. In the absence of some special machinery created for that purpose, no sustained collaboration on an adequate scale can reasonably be expected from them. For their normal concern is with matters of immediate practical concern and urgency.[38] It follows that, unless within the foreign offices of the Members of the United Nations machinery is devised on a larger scale than exists at present for assisting the work of codification and shaping effectively a constructive attitude towards the drafts and proposals put forward by the International Law Commission, its activity must continue to remain within a restricted orbit. For, severely circumscribed as that activity has been, owing to its constitution and the resources available to it, its output has probably been as great as governments have been able to cope with. There can be no appreciable advance in the sphere of official codification unless governments are in the position to make it part of their own effort. Similar considerations apply to the machinery established within the General Assembly—at present through its Legal Committee—for assessing and acting upon the drafts and reports of the International Law Commission.

[38] This aspect of the situation was cogently commented upon by Senator Elihu Root as far back as 1911. See this JOURNAL, Vol. 5 (1911), p. 580.

In answer to the request of the Commission to be supplied, in accordance with Art. 19(2) of its Statute, with "texts of laws, decrees, judicial decisions, treaties, diplomatic correspondence and other documents relevant to: (1) treaties; (2) arbitral procedure, and (3) the regime of the high seas," the French Government replied that it "unfortunately cannot consider communicating all the documentary material which has appeared on these three classic topics, representing as it does several tons of its archives," but that it was "prepared to supply the Commission with such of these texts as it possesses and as are requested in conformity with Article 19, paragraph 2" (U.N. Doc. A/CN.4/19, p. 27). Art. 19(2) refers to a "detailed request." The request could have been made "detailed," without undue effort, by compiling, within the three topics mentioned, an exhaustive catalogue of subjects. Yet it is clear that governments may be unable to comply with a request of this nature, essential to the scientific fulfillment of the task of the Commission, without considerable research conducted by staff deputed for that purpose. There also arises the question whether the Commission, with the resources available to it, is in the position to make full use of the material thus supplied.

It is not surprising that there may be a reluctance on the part of governments to undertake extended responsibilities in the sphere of codification at a time when the state of international relations claims their urgent attention in other directions and when the very task of codification appears, by comparison, to partake of a measure of unreality. However, these conditions are not inevitably permanent. If and when international relations enter, or revert to, channels of legality and orderliness, codification of international law in the wider sense as here described will claim more persuasively than it can do at present that it is an urgent function of organized international society; that it is of importance for the authority and effectiveness of international law and international judicial and arbitral settlement; and that organs entrusted with the task of codification must be endowed with a constitution and resources commensurate with its place in the scheme of the Charter. For it is only by way of exception that ideas are stronger than men and agencies charged with their translation into reality. Thus viewed, the progress and the fortunes of codification under the auspices of the United Nations must to a large extent be determined by the following considerations:

In the first instance, in time of stress—and international society has been living through times of stress in the first decade of the existence of the United Nations—it may be provident, for the sake of continuity and preservation of future possibilities, to maintain what is no more than a token force in this and other spheres. Such token forces and their limited achievements need not be regarded as fully expressive of the potentialities of the major purpose of their being. If this is so, then there is no reason to view with dismay the fact that in the initial period of its existence the organization of the Commission has been rudimentary and its achievements correspondingly limited.[39] Thus it may be held that any development in

39 The Survey of International Law in Relation to the Work of Codification of the International Law Commission, prepared in 1948 and published as Memorandum submitted by the Secretary General, expressed, on p. 17, the optimistic view that "in two decades or so" the work of the Commission may "cover practically the entire field of international law." It seems, in the light of the first five years of the activity of the Commission, that having regard to the resources open to it by virtue of its Statute and the time available for its periodic meetings, the completion of that task may require several generations. By that time the first products of its labors would necessarily become obsolete. A general survey of the results of the first five years of the activity of the Commission illustrates this aspect of the situation. In 1949 the Commission adopted a Draft Declaration of Rights and Duties of States. In 1950 it drafted its "formulation of the Nürnberg Principles." In 1951 it adopted a tentative "Draft Code of Offences against the Peace and Security of Mankind" and a Report on Reservations to Multilateral Treaties. It finally adopted the Draft Code in 1954. In 1953 it submitted a final draft code on certain aspects of arbitral procedure. Of the three major topics—treaties, régime of the high seas, and nationality—of its systematic program of codification none was within sight of completion at the end of the first five years' period of its activity except for isolated subjects, namely, the Articles on the Continental Shelf and the Draft Conventions on Elimination and on Reduction of Future Statelessness and the incomplete Draft Articles on the Régime of the Territorial Sea. The Commission also submitted, in 1954, proposals for the reduction of existing statelessness.

the direction of transforming the Commission into a continuously functioning body may not be practicable in the absence of conditions enabling governments to provide it with membership of unchallenged efficacy in conformity with Article 2 of its Statute,[40] and unless appropriate machinery, as indicated above, is devised within the framework both of the foreign offices and the General Assembly for taking action on the reports and drafts prepared by the Commission. These considerations may, for a time, be decisive. On the other hand, it is arguable that the evolution of the Commission as an effective instrument of acknowledged competence may in itself pave the way for the changes, deemed desirable, with regard both to the character of its membership and the attitude of governments and the General Assembly towards the work of the Commission and its products. The difficulties surrounding the realization of the aspect of the Charter are not inherent in it; they lie outside it. The rational assumption, which admittedly is an assumption of faith, is that these difficulties may be of a transient character.

Secondly, while some of the objects of the Charter of the United Nations are such that their realization in a particular period must be impeded or halted by the unfavorable realities of the political situation or constitutional limitations such as the requirement of unanimity, these factors are not necessarily relevant to all spheres of activity of the United Nations. They are not decisive in connection with codification, which is outside the purview of the rule of unanimity. There may be wisdom and foresight in the resolve to use to the full the opportunities already available with respect to some needs of the international community without waiting until it is practicable to bring nearer fruition all the purposes proclaimed in its constitution.

Thirdly, there are disadvantages in permitting an important and, in a wider perspective, urgent object of the United Nations and of the international community in general to be fulfilled, for an indefinite or prolonged period, by "token forces." For once the scope and the stature of the task of codifying and developing international law have been reduced to dimensions out of keeping with its true significance, it may be difficult to alter the initial pace and character of the endeavor thus begun and to restore to it the momentum and the dignity commensurate with the true merits of its original purpose.

[40] There is room for considering to what extent the requisite expert element in the composition of the Commission may be effectively secured by a method of election—or appointment—differing from that adopted in its Statute as formulated in 1948. Such method might consist in appointment by separate or joint action, possibly with or without association with the General Assembly, of other organs of the United Nations, such as the Secretary General or the International Court of Justice.

[4]

NEW APPROACHES TO THE STUDY OF INTERNATIONAL LAW *

By Richard A. Falk

Of the Board of Editors

I. New Trends in Observation and Assessment in International Legal Studies

International law is both a contemplative academic subject and an active ingredient of diplomatic process in world affairs.[1] The failure to maintain the clarity of this distinction accounts for considerable confusion about the nature and function of international law in the world today. An international lawyer is also a citizen of a nation-state who often holds strong views as to preferred courses of foreign policy. One way for him to vindicate these views is to demonstrate their compatibility or incompatibility with governing rules of international law. Confusion arises in scholarly settings whenever the adversary presentation of views is not distinguished from the scholarly assessment of opposing lines of adversary presentation.

The use of military force by the United States in Viet-Nam offers an example of this sort of problem. The United States Department of State has issued a memorandum defending American use of force as legal on the principal ground that it amounts to legitimate collective self-defense against aggression by North Viet-Nam.[2] This memorandum is obviously an adversary document stating "our side" in the legal controversy and making very little effort to assess impartially the facts or the law in support of the other side. Hanoi could issue its own memorandum that could construe the facts and present the law in a manner favorable to its actions. In domestic society we have no problem distinguishing the argument of counsel from the judgment of the court; the former is understood as adversary, the latter as impartial. In international society the absence

* I should like to acknowledge with gratitude the support given by the Center of International Studies of Princeton University enabling me to prepare this essay. A somewhat longer version will appear as a chapter in a book entitled *New Approaches to International Relations*, under the editorship of Morton A. Kaplan, and scheduled for publication by St. Martin's Press in 1967. The volume, in turn, arose from a series of papers given at the Harris Conference at the University of Chicago, June 1–4, 1966.

1 Myres S. McDougal has made the useful distinction between "theories *of*" and "theories *about*" international law to call attention to this dual rôle. McDougal, "Some Basic Theoretical Concepts About International Law: A Policy-Oriented Framework of Inquiry," 4 Journal of Conflict Resolution 337–354 (1960).

2 "The Legality of U. S. Participation in the Defense of Vietnam," Department of State, Office of Legal Adviser, March 4, 1966, reprinted in 60 A.J.I.L. 565 (1966); see also Congressional Record, March 10, 1966, pp. 5274–5279, and 54 Dept. of State Bulletin 474 (1966).

of generally competent adjudicating institutions makes it very difficult to move beyond the adversary level of discourse.

The academic international lawyer has a potential contribution to make to the extent that he is capable of substituting an adjudicatory for an adversary orientation. If the academic international lawyer succeeds in establishing for his legal analysis a reputation of impartiality, then the perception of the relationship between challenged national conduct and rules of international law can be elevated to a higher level of discourse. To revert to the legal controversy in the United States regarding the use of force in Viet-Nam, it seems unfortunate that five of the most distinguished American international lawyers should have chosen to write an open letter to President Johnson in which they confirm the legality of the United States position as "defensible" under international law.[3] Of course, the position is defensible in legal terms, but would an impartial tribunal of experts find it more defensible than the counter-arguments—and, if so, with respect to which issues?[4]

The international lawyers of the period after World War I, dominated by approaches associated with legal positivism or natural law, achieved a different sort of policy irrelevance from the policy justifications of recent years. These earlier international lawyers detached law from the political context of world affairs and made very rigid analyses of the regulation of state conduct by invoking supposedly fixed and unambiguous rules of restraint. They relied for a new system of world order upon agreed legal rules, but they failed to develop an adequate appreciation of the social and political difficulties of making these rules into effective behavioral norms.[5] The Covenant of the League, the Kellogg-Briand Pact, and the general seriousness with which prohibitions upon the use of aggressive force were taken by international lawyers are indicative of this general failure to understand the limited effect of rules of restraint upon the central activities of the nation-state in a social system as decentralized in its distribution of power and as horizontal in its institutional structure as is international society.

In the 1940's and 1950's, new critiques of international law as legalistic and moralistic were salutory efforts to persuade well-intentioned governments away from any general reliance upon such rules in the pursuit of

[3] The letter to President Johnson, dated Feb. 14, 1966, was signed by Professors William W. Bishop, Jr., Richard R. Baxter, Myres S. McDougal, Louis B. Sohn, and Neill H. Alford, Jr.; it may be found in the Congressional Record, Feb. 23, 1966, pp. 3694–3695. An earlier letter supporting the legality of U. S. action was sent to the President after it had been circulated by Professor E. Ernest Goldstein and signed by thirty-one professors of international law; see Congressional Record, Appendix, Jan. 27, 1966.

[4] These counter-arguments concern the charges of breaking faith with the Geneva Agreements of 1954, the degree and nature of North Vietnamese infiltration, the relationship between the Viet-Cong and Hanoi, the claims of American intervention in South Viet-Nam, and so on; legal issues include allegations of violations of the laws of war, disproportionate use of force in self-defense, and armed attack against North Viet-Nam.

[5] *Cf.* Walter C. Schiffer, The Legal Community of Mankind (1954).

their interests and the defense of their values.[6] A modicum of realism suggests that rules governing recourse to violence can be manipulated; the complementarity of a system of legal rules assures that a legal pretext, at least, will always be available to a government.[7]

And given the absence of impartial procedures to review contradictory legal claims put forward by nation-states in a dispute, there is no very persuasive means to appraise the relative merits of the legal argument. The understanding of a legal order, then, must be expanded to include an awareness of the prospects for upholding a fairly stable set of expectations about what is permissible and what is impermissible conduct, an awareness that shifts inquiry from the rules to the social and institutional means available for their effective implementation. The leading international lawyers in the period following World War II have been increasingly sensitive to this need to examine the rôle of law in light of the over-all setting of international politics. Some of the most impressive work along these lines has been done by Myres McDougal, C. Wilfred Jenks, Morton Kaplan, Nicholas deB. Katzenbach, Eric Stein, Julius Stone, and Wolfgang Friedmann. These scholars give great attention to the definition of realistic goals for international law in light of the decentralized character of international society. There is almost a consensus present among contemporary international lawyers that such an intellectual orientation is essential to the fruitful study of international law. The result of this orientation is to bring the study of international law into ever closer association with the outlook, method, and concerns of the social scientist.

In his analyses, the international lawyer cannot afford to hold constant the context within which law is created and applied or within which legal controversy takes place. For the student of domestic law the institutional social context is fairly clearly established and can more easily be taken for granted, although the bearing of changing pressures and values upon the development of all phases of law is not widely accepted. For international lawyers the first task, in a sense, is to find functional equivalents for the legislature, court, and executive and then to measure the degree to which these equivalents produce law-conditioned behavior in international affairs. So long as international lawyers conceived of the search for functional equivalence in terms of mechanical identity, the results of their labors produced either artificial enthusiasm or premature despair. Such a mechanical approach tends to give exaggerated prominence to the central institutions that do exist in international society—especially to the International Court of Justice—and produces either an attitude that such

6 Among the most influential critics of a legalistic-moralistic approach to foreign policy have been George F. Kennan and Hans J. Morgenthau. See Kennan, American Diplomacy 1900–1950, pp. 95–96 (1951); Morgenthau, In Defense of the National Interest 101, 102, 144 (1951).

7 For an extreme articulation of the notion that legal order is constituted by complementary norms, see Myres S. McDougal, "The Ethics of Applying Systems of Authority: The Balanced Opposites of a Legal System," in Harold D. Lasswell and Harlan Cleveland (eds.), The Ethic of Power 221–240 (1962).

institutions as do exist constitute the international legal system or the conclusion that, despite the formal existence of equivalent institutions, their impact on international behavior is so marginal and sporadic as to deprive of legal quality the ordering of relations among states.

The development of a more sophisticated approach to the notion of functional equivalence makes it possible to achieve a richer sense of the character of international law. In particular, increasing stress is now being put upon the distinctive ordering characteristics of an international society conceived of in predominantly horizontal and decentralized terms.[8] The most pronounced consequence of this stress is to shift the focus of inquiry from the activities of primitive international institutions to the activities of national legal institutions in generating, enforcing and repudiating the rules and expectations associated with international law. It is a commonplace hypothesis that it is necessary to correlate patterns of authority with patterns of power in an effective social order. One can thus infer, in a manner relevant to the study of international law, that the effective locus of authority will be on the national level. Systematic attention is now being given for the first time to the rôle of national institutions and decision-makers in upholding and developing international law, but it has yet to proceed very far on a comparative basis.[9]

Roger Fisher has done some notable work that points out very forcefully the extent to which international law attains a certain effectiveness merely because it is woven into the complex bureaucratic structure of the modern state.[10] Bureaucratic decision-making is by its nature rule-governed. A bureaucrat called upon to act on behalf of the state would not normally even consider that the commission of a violation to promote national policy was an option open to him. Of course, there exist both a wide range of discretion to interpret rules and many areas within which rules (which are, after all, only crystallized expectations about permissible behavior) are not established, but the whole impulse of a bureaucratized response is to find a consistent formula that can deal with recurrent situations and that will be acceptable to as many of the relevant actors as possible. Thus accommodation and reciprocity operate to structure a legal response and thereby tend to minimize friction arising from conduct and to maximize the prospects for regularizing the conduct in question. One form of "technical assistance" that may promote the effective implementation of international law among the new states consists of helping these states to build into their developing bureaucracies a place for legal advice in foreign affairs, through the provision of a trained

[8] See, *e.g.*, Myres S. McDougal, "International Law, Power, and Policy: A Contemporary Conception," 82 Hague Academy Recueil des Cours 132–260 (1953); also Falk, The Role of Domestic Courts in the International Legal Order 21–52 (1964).

[9] Some interesting material on the rôle of national decision-makers is to be found in H. C. L. Merillat (ed.), Legal Advisers and Foreign Affairs (1964); *cf.* also Richard B. Bilder, "The Office of the Legal Adviser: The State Department Lawyer and Foreign Affairs," 56 A.J.I.L. 633 (1962).

[10] Fisher, "Bringing Law to Bear on Governments," 74 Harvard Law Review, 1130–1140 (1961).

cadre of bureaucratic specialists in international law whose dignity and influence depend on the acceptance of this advice. Similarly, in the developed countries one way to enhance greatly the rôle of law in world affairs would be to raise to cabinet level the status of the legal adviser and to appoint to the post a prominent man of influence, ambition, and competence.

We need to complement the work on bureaucratic decision-making with more searching forms of inquiry into the relevance of law to political decision-making. There are certain international situations of conflict and crisis in which the overriding goals of national policy are chosen almost independently of what the law, impartially assessed, might be supposed to require. Consequently there exists a rather misleading and destructive tendency to conclude that international law has nothing whatever to do with the behavior of states or with the maintenance of international stability in this sort of political setting. Government lawyers are called in, if at all, to provide legal arguments for a decision taken on other grounds, so that official action will seem legally defensible, especially in the eyes of domestic public opinion. Certainly this rationalizing function of international law seems dominant with respect to U. S. military participation in Viet-Nam or to the armed intervention of 1965 in the Dominican Republic.[11] And in Soviet international practice there is almost no indication that international lawyers, in their rôle as experts on international law, advise on policy or are permitted to comment objectively on the relationship between Soviet practice and relevant rules of international law. The rôle of international law has in these situations been restricted to one of rationalization, and there is little indication that the existence of international law has had much bearing on the execution of the various phases of foreign policy. Such an exclusion of law from the procedures of political decision-making does suggest a willingness to conceive of national interest as exclusively defined by national will and by the relative capabilities of interested parties to assert control over the event in question.

But political decision-making need not require the exclusion of international law. By the formulation of the political position in terms of a distinct legal claim, the nature of an international controversy may be clarified and the rival actor made somewhat less likely to over-react. International law can operate as an assured medium of diplomatic communication, allowing for processes of claim and counterclaim to delimit the area of dispute and clarify the stakes of a particular conflict. The degree to which international law facilitates international communication is a new subject for scholarly investigation.[12] An informed awareness of

[11] For a general analysis, see Wolfgang Friedmann, "United States Policy and the Crisis of International Law," 59 A.J.I.L. 857–871 (1965). It is generally true that Communist states have not even bothered to put forth serious legal arguments to support their positions in international disputes.

[12] A perceptive stress on communication as a function of international law is found in the recent work of William D. Coplin. See his "International Law and Assumptions About the State System," 17 World Politics 617–634, and his book: The Functions of

legal expectations in a situation of crisis may also strengthen inclinations to exercise maximum self-restraint in achieving the political end in view. One way to command support for, or to minimize opposition to, political claims, especially those involving the use of force, is to show a high regard for relevant rules of international law. The interdiction by the United States of Soviet "offensive" missiles bound for Cuba in 1962 is a prominent example of structuring a political claim to reinforce rather than to detract from the relevance of international law to the conduct of foreign policy.

A characteristic of a decentralized social system is that the political claims of the powerful nation-states serve as legal precedents for other, less powerful, members of international society. Nuclear testing by the United States and the Soviet Union created permissive precedents that are very difficult to repudiate. Relative power plays a much greater rôle in creating precedents than in repudiating them. There is a kind of reciprocity and symmetry operative in international society, as in all social systems, that makes the assertion by one state of a legal claim to act in a specified way available to other states similarly situated. Such symmetry owes much to the external aspects of the ideology associated with national sovereignty, an ideology that has contributed so centrally to the constitutive structure of traditional international law through ideas of the equality of states, the absoluteness of territorial jurisdiction, and the doctrine of non-intervention.[13]

One implication of such symmetry is that the capacity of a powerful state to assert unilaterally a claim on behalf of its own immediate interests may have a rather detrimental system-wide impact upon the satisfaction of its intermediate-term interests. That is, the characteristic processes of political action in world affairs are shaped in part by rationales designed to legitimize the claims issued by powerful states pursuing unilateral and partisan aims. The Soviet Union's endorsement of support for wars of national liberation—a departure from the Charter conception of permissible use of force—provides a complex example of unintended consequences flowing from an original departure in doctrine and practice from legal expectations. Among the consequences of such a departure is that it weakens the impact of Soviet objections to the more militant posture of the Chinese and to the interventionary anti-Communist policies and practices of the United States. Likewise the unilateral nature and the scale of the United States rôle in support of the Saigon Government in Viet-Nam are generating precedents (with regard to outside participation in civil wars) that seem to impair existing precedents of neutrality and limited intervention that might have been strengthened had the United States chosen an alternative course of action.

International Law: An Introduction to the Role of International Law in the Contemporary World (1966).

[13] *Cf.* Leo Gross, "The Peace of Westphalia, 1648–1948," 42 A.J.I.L. 20–40 (1948). See also Richard N. Rosecrance, Action and Reaction in World Politics 17–191 (1963).

It is, of course, important to distinguish legal doctrine from political behavior. Despite a doctrinal insistence upon territorial sovereignty, frequent examples exist of intervention by the powerful in the affairs of the weak.

Part of the inquiry directed at the rôle of international law on the domestic level is to take note of the increasing use of international law by private citizens, at least in democratic societies, as a way to restrain, or dramatize opposition to, the undertakings of their own national governments. This development is attributable, in part, to a withering of nationalist sentiment in the developed countries, reflecting both a universal humanistic ethic popular among intellectuals of all countries and a widespread fear that even the most powerful nations must act with caution in the nuclear age. The existence of this trend is some indication that international lawyers are adopting an outlook based on an extranationalistic view of international law, which can serve as a transnational source of judgment on issues of disputed legality. Dramatic evidence of this outlook is the effort to present cases in domestic courts to test the willingness of these courts to question the legality under international law of government conduct. Notions of sovereign immunity are giving way as barriers to such challenges on behalf of international law. The idea that international law is of concern only in state-to-state relations is also giving way, undermined, in part, by the imposition after World War II of criminal responsibility on the leaders of Germany and Japan because of their alleged violation of international law. The precedent of the Nuremberg Judgment is now being invoked against those who helped to create it, the argument being that if individuals have a duty to avoid violating rules of international law, then this duty of the individual must be protected by the domestic system, and thus that a domestic court must not decline to determine whether or not its own government is violating international law (just as it determines whether or not its own government is violating domestic law).[14]

By and large these attempts to make use of domestic courts in this fashion have failed, the court refusing to regard the plaintiff as competent to raise the issue or itself as competent to decide it. Typical reasoning of this sort was used in the *Pauling* cases, instituted to prevent further contamination of the atmosphere by continued nuclear testing.[15] Another example is the *Eminente* proceeding brought by a French national in 1965 against President Johnson, Robert McNamara, and Dean Rusk to collect $1,000,000 in damages to plaintiff's property allegedly sustained in United States bombing of North Viet-Nam in violation of international law.[16] However, the mere presence of these cases on court dockets is significant to the extent that it can dramatize a shift in the locus of loyalty from the national scene to the common law of mankind. To the extent that domestic courts dismiss such claims because the conduct of foreign policy is a non-reviewable exercise of executive discretion, these cases serve to highlight

[14] For a relevant argument on this issue see the Steel Seizure Case: Youngstown Sheet and Tube Company *v.* Sawyer, 343 U. S. 579 (1952).

[15] Linus C. Pauling and others *v.* McNamara, 331 F. 2d 796 (1964); Pauling *v.* McElroy, 278 F. 2d 252 (1960).

[16] Emilio Eminente *v.* Lyndon Baines Johnson, McNamara, Rusk, No. 19,802, U. S. Court of Appeals for the District of Columbia (1966). Briefs for both sides have been submitted to the court, but no decision has been rendered as yet.

prerogatives claimed by a state in its foreign affairs that it would not dare claim for domestic affairs. Further, these cases call attention to the discrepancy between the appeals of statesmen for the rule of law in world affairs and their insistence upon the non-reviewability of their own conduct within their own domestic courts. Surely if the conduct of foreign policy is not subject to review in a forum as sympathetic with national perspectives as a domestic court is normally inclined to be, then the outlook for entrusting vital legal disputes to international tribunals is indeed dim.

The relevant point here is that the study of international law can benefit greatly by more systematic and comparative attention to the extent to which, and manner by which, domestic institutions apply international law. The *Sabbatino* controversy is an excellent example of the use and abuse of international law by the main branches of government in the domestic system; it has led to a legislative formulation of a rule binding upon domestic courts because it is posited as the "authoritative" domestic interpretation of international law.[17]

A Japanese domestic court in the *Shimoda* case provides the only example of an attempt by a legal tribunal to assess the legality of the atomic attacks upon Hiroshima and Nagasaki.[18] The court's decision is particularly significant; first, because it involves a review under international law of belligerent action carried out in the course of a major war by the victorious Powers; and, second, because the review was undertaken at the instance of individuals, five survivors of the attacks. The conclusion reached by the Tokyo court that the atomic raids violated international law has an impact, the ultimate strength of which is at yet immeasurable, upon the status of nuclear weapons as legitimate military weapons. To the extent that such an impact exists, it illustrates how the growth of international legal standards may be the result of determinations of law reached at the domestic level. The case illustrates as well that individuals may be beginning to make a legislative input to the international system, thereby complicating further the notion that rules of international law can be formed only by the consent of sovereign states.

Contemporary approaches to international law are searching for ways to encompass the rôle of actors other than nation-states, ways that are descriptive of the relevance of law to international behavior.[19] Wolfgang Friedmann has called attention to the relevance of regional actors to the growth of effective international law in a world divided on such funda-

[17] For full documentation see Lyman M. Tondel, Jr. (ed.), Hammarskjöld Forums, No. 7: The Aftermath of Sabbatino (1965), which includes texts of the judicial opinions.

[18] See Falk, "The Shimoda Case: A Legal Appraisal of the Atomic Attacks upon Hiroshima and Nagasaki," 59 A.J.I.L. 759–793 (1965); for the complete text of the court's decision, see Falk and Saul H. Mendlovitz (eds.), The Strategy of World Order: Toward a Theory of War Prevention, Vol. I, pp. 314–353 (1966).

[19] For one attempt to redefine the scope of law in world affairs to include actors other than nation-states, see Quincy Wright, "Toward a Universal Law of Mankind," 63 Columbia Law Review 440–460 (1963).

mental matters as human rights and the ownership of private property.[20] As yet no adequate work has been done on the degree to which regional actors are bound either by the rules governing nation-states in their relations with other regional actors or by some nascent interregional law of a distinctive sort. In addition, only very primitive speculation has taken place on the relations between the United Nations, regional organizations, and nation-states. There are important issues involving the danger of regional aggression against a state that opposes the regional consensus in some fundamental way, as Israel opposes the Arab League, Cuba, the Organization of American States, and South Africa the Organization of African Unity.[21] International lawyers are growing sensitive to the need to adapt their framework of inquiry to take account of the contemporary structure of international society, especially the relevance of regional actors and international institutions to the regulation of all sorts of behavior with transnational implications.

A different source of regulatory authority arises from the efforts of bloc actors to moderate the limits of conflict by establishing rules of the game in their relations *inter se*.[22] The significance of these rules depends upon the degrees to which certain relations are perceived in bipolar terms and upon the acceptance of, and reliance upon, processes of communication to establish commonly perceived limits of conflict. The Soviet Union and the United States are both competing for political influence in the new states of Asia and Africa. One consequence of this competition is the manipulation of civil strife so as to produce desired outcomes; another, in special cases, is intervention with overt military power. At the same time, these two pre-eminent world Powers seek to avoid an escalation of small wars above certain thresholds. Therefore, rules of the game that limit the extent and nature of participation in civil wars would seem to serve the common interest of both Powers without unduly interfering with their freedom of political action. Among the most significant of these rules is a prohibition upon the use of nuclear weapons to support one's proxy faction. Another calls for the confinement of the geographical scope of violence to the territorial limits of the state that is the scene of the violence. The decision in February of 1965 to extend the war in Viet-Nam by bombing north of the Seventeenth Parallel is a very significant challenge to this rule unless the civil war is viewed as a struggle between North Viet-Nam and the Saigon élite in South Viet-Nam.[23] Given the inability of the

20 Friedmann, The Changing Structure of International Law 60–71 (1964).

21 For some very preliminary considerations, see Falk, "Operation Stanleyville: A Lesson in Third World Politics," The Correspondent 63–73 (Winter, 1965).

22 See Edward McWhinney, "Soviet and Western International Law and the Cold War in the Era of Bipolarity," 1 Canadian Yearbook of International Law 40–81 (1963).

23 The official U. S. justification claims collective self-defense against an armed attack by North Viet-Nam. One difficulty with this argument is that the pattern and stakes of conflict resemble more closely a civil war. If the conflict is treated as a civil war, then there is no legal basis for bombing North Viet-Nam, even if the factual basis is prior intervention on behalf of the Viet-Cong. Counter-intervention may be permis-

United Nations to interpose itself effectively in situations of Cold-War violence, these informal rules of the game are an important ingredient of contemporary world order, and their importance is to some extent dependent upon their character as norms being perceived and understood by relevant decision-makers.[24] If law is identified with community expectations and a violation of law consists of the disappointment of these expectations, then there is no real problem presented by assimilating this kind of "rule" into the analysis used to deal with rules created by the more traditional procedures associated with treaty-making and customary international law.[25]

In fact, one of the major issues challenging time-honored approaches to international law is the development of a more adequate theory of the basis of legal obligation in international society.[26] C. Wilfred Jenks has been particularly articulate in suggesting the need to supplant a sovereignty-oriented notion of consent with a community-oriented notion of consensus.[27] Considerable recent attention has been given to the law-creating potential of various sorts of resolutions passed by the General Assembly.[28] Considerable work needs to be done to formulate the conditions under which and the extent to which various categories of resolutions do have a law-creating impact. It is also necessary to investigate the interaction between resolutions and attitudes toward permissible and impermissible behavior and thereby to achieve some understanding of when and how the General Assembly can exert an effective influence, as well as to identify some of the occasions upon which its actions are likely to be futile.

Some authoritative insight into the juridical status of these issues has been given in several of the dissenting opinions in the *South West Africa Cases* decided by the International Court of Justice in July of 1966. In the course of this complex litigation the argument was made that the practice of *apartheid* is "illegal" because of the law-creating effect of formal acts of the General Assembly supported by an overwhelming majority of the membership.[29] It is also relevant to take note of the use by the

sible, but not when it takes place outside the territorial limits of the political entity enduring the civil war.

24 Relevant patterns of strategic thinking can be adapted to the analysis of the operation of international law in crisis situations; see especially Thomas C. Schelling, The Strategy of Conflict (1960).

25 For a clear account of traditional processes of law-creation, with some attention to recent developments, see Clive Parry, The Sources and Evidences of International Law (1965).

26 For the background of traditional thinking, see the title essay in James L. Brierly, The Basis of Obligation in International Law (1958).

27 *E.g.*, Jenks, Law, Welfare and Freedom 83–100 (1963).

28 *E.g.*, Oscar Schachter, "The Relation of Law, Politics and Action in the United Nations," 109 Hague Academy Recueil des Cours 171–200 (1963); Rosalyn Higgins, The Development of International Law Through the Political Organs of the United Nations 1–10 (1963; Asamoah, The Legal Significance of the Declarations of the General Assembly of the United Nations (1966).

29 The relevant portion of the argument is reprinted and commented upon in Falk and Mendlovitz, The Strategy of World Order, Vol. III, pp. 75–90 (1966); for text of the judgment and a digest of the dissenting opinions, see 61 A.J.I.L. 116 *et seq.* (1967).

Shimoda decision of "declaratory" rules of air warfare to draw and support inferences about obligatory standards of behavior. The main point is that the traditional dichotomy between what is obligatory and what is permissive is crumbling and that therefore international lawyers need a more adequate and comprehensive theory of legal obligation than that developed to serve an international society consisting only of states, in which the existence of law subserves the ideology of national sovereignty.

II. From Impressionism to Scientific Inquiry: A Focus on Developing Methodologies

The new methodologies available for the study of international law are seeking, above all, to move beyond the impressionism of earlier approaches. In each area of international law there are a body of practice and a set of attitudes associated with the interesting legal questions. These data need to be collected and organized in a systematic fashion to permit the formulation of well-evidenced generalizations. In turn, these generalizations can then be formulated as propositions about the relation of law and behavior which are subject to validation and refutation. Only in this manner can international legal studies begin to acquire a scientific character, a character that assures that the expansion of knowledge is cumulative and not just accumulative.

The term "impressionism" is used to characterize approaches, still accepted by some, in which legal analysis is based upon a partial selection of relevant material and in which the criteria for selection are arbitrary reflections of the researcher's values, national locus, and imperfect factual knowledge. To move legal research techniques beyond impressionism there is a need for a fuller investigation of the extent to which the advances in the technology of knowledge can be put to work by international lawyers. However, although admirable efforts have been made in the field, there is considerable reason to suppose that the data of international legal studies are not generally susceptible to quantification in any form that will not trivialize or even distort inquiry. International practice is not sufficiently iterative to permit the aggregation of instances of recurrence. What seems primarily needed to advance inquiry, at present, are (1) a systematic framework of inquiry adapted to various relatively specialized subject matters, and (2) co-ordinated efforts by scholars willing to conduct inquiry within a suitable framework. I have outlined elsewhere the nature of such an enterprise directed toward assessing the participation of the recently independent states of Asia and Africa in the international legal system.[30] If implemented, even by a less-than-global program of study, it would produce a body of knowledge, organized on a comparative basis, which is considerably "harder" than the speculative interpretations upon which international lawyers have, by necessity, previously relied. On the

30 Falk, "The New States and International Legal Order," a series of lectures delivered at the Hague Academy of International Law in 1966, to be published in its Recueil des Cours. The fifth lecture sets forth the tentative sketch of such a framework.

basis of this knowledge, generalizations could be advanced with more confidence and their validity could be confirmed or challenged by direct observation of behavior. Such a reorientation of international legal studies is more likely to come about in a social science setting than in the law schools, whose principal educational function remains one of vocational training, a function best served by teaching students to think about legal problems in ways sensitive to their resolution through counseling, diplomacy, and adjudication.

The study of international law has been heretofore dominated by lawyers mainly concerned with developing these particular skills. Research has concentrated on the analysis of legal issues in problem areas or on the presentation of more or less exhaustive informational surveys that collect the experience of the past. This is a beneficial tradition of continuing validity. It merely needs to be complemented by the approaches to knowledge that are developing within the social sciences for the observation and assessment of human behavior.

In the United States today there seem to be present three main methodological orientations used in the study of international law: policy science, functionalism and systems theory; a fourth methodological orientation, less well-established than the other three, can be identified under the label of "phenomenological perspectives." These approaches are not mutually exclusive; each accords attention to the social and political setting of law and each takes seriously the bearing of the interests, goals, and values of the participants in international society upon the character and nature of international law and its prospects for effective growth. This evidence of agreement on a common point of methodological departure is a remarkable achievement, reversing as it does a long tradition of legal studies devoted only to a detached observation of "legal data" (that is, treaties, judicial decisions, formal diplomatic correspondence, and the like). Attentiveness to the international context of international law has also produced a far livelier awareness of the relations between law and power in world affairs, thereby introducing realism and avoiding the inclinations toward wishful thinking, legalism, and moralism evident in earlier generations of international lawyers. Among the evils inflicted by strict adherence to the precepts of legal positivism, and now being overcome by the newer approaches, is a tendency to create an artificial distance between the "is" of international politics and the "ought" of international law.

As Myres McDougal has so ably demonstrated, one rôle of law is to help a social system move toward the attainment of its goals.[31] An acceptance of this rôle does lead the international lawyer into prescriptive as well as descriptive postures and makes necessary a sharp discrimination among the different legal tasks undertaken by the scholar. But this emphasis upon prescription is not legalism or moralism; it is an articulation

[31] McDougal has recently stated his conception in an "unpublished address" (available in mimeographed form under the title "Jurisprudence for a Free Society") delivered at the University of Georgia Law School in 1965.

of the contribution that can be made in legal contexts to the goals of those actors possessing power and endowed with certain values.

In matters of approach, some disagreement arises about the extent to which policy alternatives can be prescribed in "scientific" terms in concrete instances.[82] Some jurists contend that an analysis of international law can only clarify the nature of choice, whereas others allege that it can indicate the proper decision as well. In the former instance, the legal authority supporting and opposing various policy options is presented without any claim that lawful action can be identified; in the latter instance, not only are the legal implications of the choice set forth but the legal argument is accorded priority according to its relative capacity to promote the policies at stake in the decision-making situation.

Further disagreement centers upon the way in which the political context is to be made relevant to legal appraisal. The discussion of the problem of distinguishing the national from the cosmopolitan perspective is important here. Does one analyze the policy content of legal choice in terms of national policy, of world-wide policy, or of some combination of policy outlooks? International lawyers have not yet taken clear or successful account of what J. David Singer has so usefully identified as the "level-of-analysis" problem.[83]

Policy Science. This approach is associated with the work of Myres S. McDougal, supported by the influence and collaboration of Harold D. Lasswell and emanating from the atmosphere in American legal thought established by the legal realist movement.[84] Inquiry is organized in terms both of factual events in community process and of the decision-maker authorized to make legal decisions. McDougal, with the help of a series of distinguished collaborators, has tried to take systematic account of all the variables that a fully rational decision-maker would want to take account of. These variables include all the factors bearing upon common interest and arising from what has happened in the past, what is expected in the present, and what is desired in the future. Thus the decision "required" by law is not determined exclusively by applying the past legal rules and precedents governing the situation.

The control asserted by the legal past is further diminished by McDougal's emphasis on the complementary norms relevant to any legal controversy. Viewed from the perspective of the decision-maker, then, there

82 *E.g.*, Leo Gross, "Problems of International Adjudication and Compliance with International Law: Some Simple Solutions," 59 A.J.I.L. 48–59 (1965).

83 Singer, "The Level-of-Analysis Problem in International Relations," in Klaus Knorr and Sidney Verba (eds.), The International System 77–92 (1961); see also McDougal's analysis in "The Impact of International Law upon National Law: A Policy-Oriented Perspective," in McDougal and Associates, Studies in World Public Order 157–236 (1960).

84 McDougal's principal writings to date, mostly in collaboration, have been (in addition to the collection of essays cited in the previous note and the Hague lectures cited in note 8): Law and Minimum World Public Order (with Florentino P. Feliciano, 1962); The Public Order of the Oceans (with William T. Burke, 1963); Law and Public Order in Space (with Harold D. Lasswell and Ivan A. Vlasic, 1964).

is available a plausible legal argument for almost any line of decision that seems to maximize the desired policy outcome. Assuming a national decision-maker, the content of desired policy should be an accommodation of the global (inclusive) interests of the world community and of the more exclusive interests of the nation-state on whose behalf he acts. McDougal relies heavily on Scelle's notion of *dédoublement fonctionnel* to conclude that the national decision-maker, since he is alternatively claimant and judge, can serve simultaneously both national and world policies.

The stress on the national decision-maker follows from McDougal's emphasis on the international legal order as relatively decentralized. Therefore, the most important authority functions are performed by the decision-makers attached to the actors with the predominance of effective control over behavior. As a result, national decision-making is the basic focus for legal inquiry, and rather subordinate attention is accorded the central institutions of international affairs.[35]

McDougal has given a generalized description of the decision-making process, one that is free from conventional predispositions about the location and nature of the decision-maker. Thus it is not biased, as legal inquiry so often is in favor of judicial decision-makers. Given McDougal's stress on the conjunction of power and authority, the focus of inquiry is upon the political official called upon to assert claims on behalf of the national system to act in world affairs or to react to foreign claims that affect its interests. It is participation in this claiming process that gives rise to the most typical situation in which international law is applied and shaped to conform to preferred policy. Such a dynamic orientation contrasts with the static conception of the relation between rules of law and behavior that normally dominates the legal imagination.[36] The notion of a legal decision as a claim, with promise of reciprocity, to act in a specified way authorized or challenged by a given decision-maker is very well adapted to the patterns of interaction in a decentralized political system. Such an approach also makes it possible to encompass different sorts of decision-makers with varying rôles in the national or international systems.

The test of legality (or of whether an action is in accordance with law) is the degree of an action's conformity to relevant community expectations. This test of legality upsets traditional notions because, as contrasted with rule-orientation, it appears indefinite and subject to manipulation and results in conclusions that need to be expressed as degrees of illegality. Its great advantage is that it reflects realistically both the decisiveness and the limits of decision-making in construing the requirements of law. In the first instance the content of law is determined by examining conclusions reached by those entrusted with the authority to make decisions.

The ultimate vindication of law for McDougal is its secularly based

[35] See McDougal, Harold D. Lasswell, and W. Michael Reisman, "The World Constitutive Process of Authoritative Decision," scheduled to appear as a chapter in The Future of the International Legal Order, edited by C. E. Black and Falk.

[36] For an extreme example, see Hans Kelsen, The Principles of International Law (1944).

capacity to promote the fulfillment of social values specified in terms of human dignity, together with the realism with which it reflects the genuine shared demands and expectations of people. The content given to human dignity is rather clearly derived from the individualistic ethics of a progressive democratic society in the West. Each decision-maker, according to McDougal, is supposed to use the authority at his disposal to promote human dignity. Decision-makers are not encouraged to use a free-wheeling discretion, as the content of human dignity is to be objectively specified in terms of community preferences as understood through the social sciences and other contemporary knowledge. McDougal is fully sensitive to the fact that one of the important community preferences is that authority be used in a predictable fashion and that this requires a high degree of deference to precedent.

This comprehensive framework of inquiry has served McDougal and his associates well in their efforts to restate major portions of the substance of international law. A series of significant volumes has given a new insight into the traditional materials of international law in such areas as the law of outer space, the law of the oceans, and the law governing the use of violence. The quality of this scholarly achievement certainly places it among the great milestones in the history of international legal thought and assures it a permanent place in the study of the subject matter of international law.

Functionalism. There is a widespread acceptance by a group of influential international lawyers of the belief that the way to improve upon a positivist, rule-oriented approach is to correlate the development and study of international law with the satisfaction of certain social functions in the international system. The functionalist approach is represented, to varying degrees, by Percy Corbett, C. Wilfred Jenks, Wolfgang Friedmann and Julius Stone. The functionalist point of departure is the sharp separation between interests *perceived* by nation-states as vital or as non-vital. So far as interests perceived as vital are concerned, it is realistic to conclude that states are not yet disposed to entrust their realization to the rules and procedures of international law. So far as interests perceived as non-vital are concerned, states are willing to entrust their realization to "the rule of law" and to support specialized international institutions dedicated to upholding it. These non-vital interests include such matters as postal service, telecommunications, health, conservation, safety, and cultural exchange. In such areas important policies are at stake, and international institutions can work effectively to bring satisfaction without in any way appearing to challenge the prerogatives of the sovereign state. Such an image of international legal order is especially appealing to those jurists who are rather skeptical about the capacity of international law to regulate the use of force by nation-states.

Recent functionalist work has thrown into useful focus the inventive capacity of legal technique to fashion solutions for social problems. Wolfgang Friedmann has demonstrated, for instance, the manner in which the idea of the international corporation and the joint venture has arisen to meet the needs of the developing countries for investment capital without at the same time arousing their suspicion of and hostility to the foreign investor.

Functionalism is really not a coherent framework of inquiry in the manner of McDougal. It is instead only a jurisprudential orientation that generates a certain style of inquiry and concentrates upon certain sorts of legal developments. Its basic outlook emphasizes only those activities not regarded by national governments as politically significant. Therefore, functionalists concentrate on the rôle of law at the margins of international conflict. Friedmann sums up the functionalist claim rather well:

> The functionalist approach is thus no miracle solution, but it affords an important means of by-passing the propagandist atmosphere of political international assemblies, and of bringing the nations together in practical tasks of mutual interest and benefit.[37]

The approach closely parallels the efforts of David Mitrany in relying upon a functionalist dynamic that is operative in international specialized agencies as the most promising arena within which to promote political integration at the international level and to erode through time the pre-eminence of the sovereign state. It was Mitrany's central presupposition that, if nations would co-operate in the satisfaction of the common needs, then an international ethos would emerge among the civil servants working in these international institutions. These activities could begin modestly with such uncontroversial subject matter as the provision of an international postal service and the development of techniques to halt the international spread of disease. Gradually more sensitive subjects could be dealt with, such as labor standards and capital loans. As states gained confidence in the capacity of international institutions to perform services, and as the institutions gained confidence and independence, there would take place, according to the Mitrany view, a gradual expansion of activities and a slow withering away of state power. However, as Stanley Hoffmann, among others, has shown, the dynamics of functionalist growth do not assure a spill-over into areas in which the vital interests of states are engaged.

Ernst Haas has recently reformulated Mitrany's conception of functionalism in a stimulating manner, taking particularly interesting account of the degree to which political conflict can contribute to, rather than hamper (as Mitrany supposed), the growth of international institutions.[38] Using the experience of the International Labor Office as a principal example, Haas shows that the use of the I.L.O. by Western states to embarrass the Soviet Union for failures to allow trade unions requisite freedom created institutional precedents that were subsequently invoked by Afro-Asian states to bring pressure on Portugal and South Africa. Haas argues that, without the political background's having generated the original precedent, it would have been impossible to organize the later

[37] Friedmann, An Introduction to World Politics 57 (5th ed., 1965).

[38] Haas, Beyond the Nation-State (1964).

action. A principal conclusion of Haas's study is that the avoidance of "politics" is not necessarily conducive to the growth of international institutions. This line of analysis can also lead to a parallel reformulation of the functionalist approach to international law, and especially it can lead to examinations of the law-creating potential of international crisis and conflict. Such a re-examination of the prospects for the growth of law could combat the literalism usually found in the functionalist approach, a literalism that assumes that the growth of law is dependent upon convergent interests and values and upon the voluntary acceptance of the benefits of international law in areas where co-operation seems possible without political friendship. The Haas variation on traditional functionalism suggests that out of a political clash there may arise a precedent that can be used for unintended future purposes.

Systems Theory. A third major approach evident in international legal studies arises from a reliance upon "the international system" as a basic concept by which to organize the contextual data relevant to the rôle of law. System theorists tend to specify historical or analytical models of the way in which power is distributed and conflict conducted as a basis upon which to assess the rôle of law. The rationale for this approach is that (1) context is relevant and (2) the relevance of context can be established through the specification of a small number of strategic variables. The distribution of power among the units in a system and the stakes of conflict are especially significant variables in identifying the system and distinguishing it from another.

Morton Kaplan has done the most fundamental work to vindicate the use of the systems theory as the basis for the study of international law.[39] Kaplan's analytic models of plausible international systems suggest rather clearly the usefulness of investigating the extent to which the character and rôle of international law are conditioned by the character of the international system. In collaboration with Nicholas deB. Katzenbach, Kaplan has taken a further step in this direction in *The Political Foundations of International Law* (1961). The Kaplan-Katzenbach book demonstrates the value of the systems approach by its very incisive analysis of norms of non-intervention in the balance-of-power and loose bipolar international systems. Kaplan and Katzenbach effectively disclose the relevance of political factors to the operation of law in world affairs. Their approach interestingly appraises the strengths and weaknesses of international law by reference to the kind of international system that is posited.

Stanley Hoffmann has tried to orient the systems approach to international law in the tradition of historical sociology.[40] Thus Hoffmann endeavors to construct a system by observing the patterns of conflict in a past period of international relations and by correlating these patterns with prevailing social structures operative in international society. This effort is in contrast, one would suppose in view of Hoffmann's earlier critique

39 Kaplan, System and Process in International Politics (1958).

40 "International Systems and International Law," in Knorr and Verba, *op. cit.* note 33 above, at 205–237.

of Kaplan's approach,[41] to the more analytic models of the international system. The difference may be mainly one of intellectual style, Kaplan preferring an analytical mode of rhetoric and Hoffmann a more historico-sociological mode. Further, Kaplan derives many of his models from the history of the main currents of international politics, whereas Hoffman seems responsive to the conceptualization of the main systemic alternatives that have been derived by Kaplan. The analytic mode does permit a somewhat greater freedom of inquiry, as it encourages the projection of trends in world affairs and the positing of possible future international systems. This orientation toward the future is compatible with those features of McDougal's approach that call upon the international lawyer to engineer a new international order that more clearly fulfills the values of human dignity.[42]

The work of Kaplan has stimulated a more programmatic use of models of the future of the international legal order by Saul Mendlovitz and this writer.[43] We posit a future international system in the form of the Clark-Sohn plan for a vastly strengthened United Nations operating in a totally disarmed world.[44] The Clark-Sohn model gives more specific content to an international system than does the analytic style of Kaplan. Our efforts might be regarded as using the rather Utopian proposals of Clark and Sohn to write one possible history of the future and thereby to achieve the same kind of empirical grounding in the actuality of social structure and political conflict that Hoffmann derives from his scanning of the history of the past.

We use the distance between the present international system and the Clark-Sohn model posited as a preferred future international system as the real center of inquiry. We organize the data of international law to emphasize the prospects for and obstacles to transition from one international system to another. This emphasis on transition brings analysis to grips with the hard problems of assessing the limits of political attainability, whereas at the same time the approach accepts the commandment issued by McDougal and Lasswell that the international lawyer employ his professional training to invent, appraise, and create a better international legal order.

Phenomenological Perspectives. There is, finally, an approach to the study of the international legal order that emphasizes depth analyses of single "cases." The objective of these analyses is both to clarify the particular set of issues involved in a dispute and to illuminate the general

[41] See Hoffmann's excerpt from his own essay in Hoffmann (ed.), Contemporary Theory in International Relations 40–50 (1960).

[42] I have undertaken with Cyril E. Black of Princeton a multi-volume study along these lines under the general title: The Future of the International Legal Order (cited in note 35 above).

[43] The Strategy of World Order. Vol. I: Toward a Theory of War Prevention; Vol. II: International Law; Vol. III: The United Nations; Vol. IV: Disarmament and Economic Development (1966).

[44] Grenville Clark and Louis B. Sohn, World Peace Through World Law, 3rd ed. (1966).

structure of the legal order. Brainerd Currie has used this approach to cast great light upon fundamental problems in the field of the conflict of laws.[45] In my judgment, cases such as *Sabbatino, Shimoda,* or *South West Africa* all offer the international lawyer excellent material for the development of general theory from a phenomenological perspective, that is, from a perspective that emphasizes the concrete phenomena of legal experience and finds support in the philosophical tradition associated with phenomenology.[46]

The extension of phenomenology to international legal studies should be made in explicit terms. There is a need for a jurisprudential rationale. It is important to distinguish between the penetration of a particular case to discover the general attributes of the legal system and the traditional analysis of a line of cases to discern the evolution of legal doctrine. The phenomenologist is interested in the case as a useful example only when it both typifies and enacts fundamental legal controversies of the sort that go on in a variety of distinct substantive settings.

"The case" as the unit of analysis requires some explanation. A judicial decision is a convenient example of a case, but is only one example. A particular civil war might serve as a case for the study of the international law of civil wars,[47] or a debate in the Security Council might serve to provide a phenomenological basis for the analysis of the international protection of human rights, the scope of domestic jurisdiction, or the legal character of peacekeeping operations.[48]

In conclusion, then, the phenomenological approach is a technique useful for combining concrete analysis of legal problems that are intrinsically interesting with the formulation of more general ideas about the relationship between international law and international behavior.

45 Currie, Selected Essays on the Conflict of Laws (1963).

46 For attempts to carry out this procedure, see Falk, The Role of Domestic Courts in the International Legal Order (1964); *idem,* "The Shimoda Case: A Legal Appraisal of the Atomic Attacks upon Hiroshima and Nagasaki," 59 A.J.I.L. 759–793 (1965). I am in the process of making such an analysis of the South West Africa Cases.

For the character of phenomenology, see Q. Lauer, Phenomenology: Its Genesis and Prospect (1958); A.-T. Tymieniecka, Phenomenology and Science in Contemporary European Thought (1962). For background, see E. Husserl, Ideen zu einer reinen Phänomenologie und phänomenologischen philosophie (1913); English trans. pub. under title: Ideas: General Introduction to Pure Phenomenology (Collier ed., 1962).

47 In 1966 the Carnegie Corporation awarded the American Society of International Law a grant to support the study of a series of specific civil wars as "cases" to create empirical support for generalizing about the international law of civil war in the contemporary world.

48 This type of analysis is used in the fourth lecture of the series cited in note 30 above. The cases used are the Security Council debates concerning Goa (1961), the U.N.'s Stanleyville Operation (1964), and Indonesia's guerrilla activity in Malaysia (1964).

[5]

The Prescribing Function in World Constitutive Process: How International Law is Made*

Myres S. McDougal†
W. Michael Reisman††

No problem has proved more refractory to lawyers and scholars than understanding and explaining how international law is made. Domestic analogues, whose explanatory power may be inadequate even in their own contexts, have so little relevance to the complexities of international politics that those who invoke them finish either by throwing up their hands and conceding that the model is inappropriate for the task[1] or by painting themselves into the palpably absurd position that there is no international law.[2] But, of course, there are many effective international norms. To gainsay such norms because of a theory is a grotesque caricature of understanding and scholarship. As the world becomes more pervasively transnational and interdependent, an understanding of how international law is

* This article is the first chapter of a book in progress entitled Prescription and World Public Order. Research has been supported in part by a grant from the National Science Foundation, administered by Policy Sciences Foundation, Incorporated. We note, with sadness, the death of our colleague and collaborator on the early stages of this project, Harold D. Lasswell.
† Sterling Professor Emeritus, Yale Law School; Distinguished Visiting Professor of Law, New York Law School.
†† Professor, Yale Law School.
1. H. Hart, The Concept of Law 208-31 (1961).
2. J. Austin, The Province of Jurisprudence Determined 12, 127, 142, 201 (1954).

made and, even more to the point, of how to make it, becomes a matter of greatest practical urgency. In any community how law is made immensely affects the shaping and sharing of all values.

The making of law is a decision function[3] which may be conveniently described as prescription. By prescription, we refer to a process of communication which creates, in a target audience, a complex set of expectations comprising three distinctive components: expectations about a policy content; expectations about authority; and expectations about control.[4] Schematically, these indispensable, coaxial expectations may be indicated as follows:

Communicators { *policy content* / *authority signal* / *control intention* } → Target Audience

Each of these expectation components may itself be complex. In a heterogeneous community of varying

---

3. Prescription is one of seven component functions which comprise the various types of decision: intelligence, promotion, prescription, invocation, application, termination and appraisal. A functional approach to decision-making offers the student of authoritative decision an alternative to the traditional more limiting organic approach (popularized by Montesquieu) which focuses on the institutional divisions of formal government: the executive, legislature, judiciary and administration. The major shortcoming of an organic analysis is that it does not discriminate clearly among the many different types of authoritative decision; the same organ characteristically engages in a multiplicity of types of decision. *See* McDougal, Lasswell & Reisman, *The World Constitutive Process of Authoritative Decision* (pt. 2), 19 J. Leg. Educ. 403, 415-37 (1967) [hereinafter cited as *World Constitutive Process* II].

4. With the exception of historicalists and certain cults of naturalism, virtually all jurisprudential schools have recognized a distinctive policy component in prescription and, with varying degrees of clarity, have appraised that content in terms of its contribution to the achievement of minimum and/or optimum public order. It was the positivism of John Austin, curiously, which underlined the control element as one of the distinctive indicators (in Austin's view exclusive) of prescription. J. Austin, *supra* note 2, at 16-18, 24, 26. But Austin had little conception of the authoritative component in the sense of community expectations.

levels of interaction, the authority signal may have to incorporate, either simultaneously or sequentially, many different authority systems. Similarly, control intention communications may involve complex packages of promised indulgences and threatened deprivations directed to different audiences. The point of emphasis is that all three components must be copresent if we are to speak meaningfully of law.

The relative importance, within the prescribing function, of the control and authority components may vary with, among other things, the type of prescription being communicated, the level of crisis, and the nature of the community. In an integrated community in which authority is relatively stable and internalized in participants, authority may be the major sustaining and characterizing factor in prescription; behavior not conforming to authoritative communication is likely to cause dysphoria in the deviating actor and may trigger autopunitive responses. In a less integrated community, control may be the primary characterizing and sustaining element of prescription. The interplay between the authority and control elements of prescription is complex and variable.[5] Anticipation of the probable means of application of power does not necessarily lead to expectations of authority; on the other hand, stabilized patterns of control may tend to shape authoritative expectations.[6] In certain marginal situations, authority may constitute the sole base value for a particular process of prescription. This may be treated as prescription only if the requisite element of control is subsequently brought into play, thus creating in the audience the expectation that certain behavior not only should be followed but will indeed be required.

---

5. This interplay, furthermore, is frequently overlooked. To be sure, many theorists are aware that a prescriptive theory cannot rest on authority alone. Rather than recognizing a control component, however, they will often fill the lacuna by turning to further authority. *See, e.g.*, Parsons & Shils, *The Social System*, in Toward a General Theory of Action 202-03 (T. Parsons & E. Shils ed. 1951)(social integration depends upon the internalization of common values and the enunciation of "role expectations by occupants of responsible roles").

6. *See* H. Lasswell & A. Kaplan, Power and Society 133-34 (1921)(analysis of role of control and authority in structure and practice of political processes).

The concept of prescription is broader, and more precise, than the commonly used term, legislation. Legislation rests on an organic and structural conception, deriving from the assumption that law is made solely or primarily by centralized legislatures. This orientation is patently inadequate for the study of international law with its dearth of centralized legislative bodies. Even within a more highly organized community, legislation is often no more than a procedural label, with little or no relevance to the creation of expectations of authority and control in the rank and file audience to which it is directed. A significant amount of legislation is not prescription: it is no secret that the legislatures of certain states are notorious for producing voluminous legislation but no prescription. Nor does all prescription, properly so called, derive from legislative bodies. As Maine observed, to limit law to the legislature is to exclude from scholarly focus many of the most vigorous sources of authority; systems that do not have institutionalized legislatures have law, but not legislation.[7] Even in systems in which there are legislatures, the abundance of prescriptive creativity far outruns any specific institution. The mongrel term "judicial legislation," for example, is so common that it no longer astonishes our lexical sensibilities.[8] Observers and participants accept the fact that many governmental agencies which are not legislative make law. The point of emphasis is that the concept of prescription allows scholarly examination of all the processes of creating expectations about authority and control, whereas a focus on "legislation" tends to restrict the observer to the specific actions of a legislature.

In the global community, as in its lesser component communities, the processes of communication by which prescriptions are generated range from the most formal, organized, and specialized through many gradations to the most informal, unorganized, and nonspecialized.[9] When prescriptive processes are most

7. H. Maine, Ancient Law 20-42 (1875).

8. *See* B. Cardozo, The Nature of the Judicial Process 98-142 (1921)(legislative rules derived from judicial decision-making).

9. *See, e.g.*, W. Sumner, Folkways (1906)(discussing the informal, non-specific ways in which laws can be made). Contemporary sociology and social psychology, particularly role theory, are permeated with the suggestion of informal, unorganized and non-specialized normative systems. A writer such as Goffman has developed extraordinary sensitivity to the most subtle codes of normative

formal, organized, and specialized, they may be conveniently analyzed in terms of a sequence of four distinctive steps or phases: the initiation of the process; the exploration of relevant facts and potential policies; the choice and formulation of the policy to be projected as authoritative for the community; and the communication of the prescriptive content and expectations about authority and control to the target audi-

9. (continued)
behavior. *See* E. Goffman, Relations in Public (1971). *See also* Gibbs, *Norms: The Problem of Definition and Classification*, 70 Am. J. Soc. 586 (1965). Significantly, in virtually all of this literature, though the existence of norms is taken for granted, there appears to be no concern with how they are made, or more important, how power is used to sustain them through time. *But see* M. Sherif, The Psychology of Social Norms (1936)(study of the psychological factors affecting the formation of social norms).

In earlier studies we sought to generalize the process by which vaguely formulated customary law is made in terms of the reciprocal claims and mutual tolerances of states in the course of cooperative activity. *See* McDougal, *The Hydrogen Bomb Tests and the International Law of the Sea*, 49 Am. J. Int'l L. 356 (1955) (continuous interaction of nation-state decision-making is critical to formation of law of the sea)[hereinafter cited as *Hydrogren Bomb Tests*]; McDougal & Schlei, *The Hydrogen Bomb Tests in Perspective: Lawful Measures for Security*, 64 Yale L.J. 648 (1955)(discussing process of claim assertion and adjustment in development of law relating to nuclear testing). In emphasizing the importance of the expectations of the communicatees of a prescriptive message, we indicated that it was not so much the initial claims as the combination of such claims and reciprocal tolerances which created the "expectations of pattern and uniformity in decision, or practice in accordance with rule, commonly regarded as law." *Hydrogen Bomb Tests*, *supra*, at 358 n.7.

This "process of communication" description of the development of customary law has been adopted and elaborated by a number of subsequent writers. *See* K. Wolfke, Custom in Present International Law 63 (1964)(on development of law through continuous process of claim assertion, appraisal, and acceptance); MacGibbon, *Customary Law and Acquiescence*, 33 Brit. Y. B. Int'l L. 115 (1957) (on role of acquiescence in development of customary rights and obligations).

We seek here to extend this mode of description to all types of international lawmaking. It would seem facilitative of the rational performance of the various intellectual tasks which both decision-makers and observers must perform to think of prescription as a continual process, in which both formulated and non-formulated components are merged, each affecting the other.

ience.[10] Even when a prescriptive process is highly informal in procedure and implicit in its communication, some rough approximation to these phases may be observed. The most realistic description of the prescribing function requires, however, its relation to other decision functions in the global community's more comprehensive process of authoritative decision.

I

Focusing on the various component functions of authoritative decision should not obscure the fact that each function contributes to the performance of every other and that, at a microscopic level of analysis, all decision functions are, in fact, replicated in the performance of any single one. Thus, the intelligence function delivers to the prescriber's attention the aggregate of community goals likely to be affected or approximated in a proposed prescription, appropriate trend and condition data on how past efforts to secure such goals have succeeded or failed, and possible alternatives in prescriptive programs, including information about the possible social effects of such alternatives. In its shaping of expectations about the future, emphasizing or de-emphasizing possible choices, intelligence affects both demands and identities. Insofar as a prescriber has the structural and temporal capacity to digest and relate intelligence to the prescriptive tasks before him, the rationality of prescription will be enhanced. Conversely, through prescription, intelligence pathologies will, in the long run, be inflicted on the larger social process.[11]

The promotion function is particularly critical to the overall performance of prescription. By facilitating both formal enactment and the development of informal expectations about authority and control, promotion contributes the intensities in demand and, properly

10. A sequential analysis is often useful in analyzing all decision functions. *See, e.g.*, Lasswell, McDougal & Reisman, *The Intelligence Function and World Public Order*, 46 Temple L.Q. 365, 368-70 (1973)(any given intelligence task can be broken down into three sequential stages).

11. For a detailed treatment of the intelligence function, see *id.*

regulated, adds new sources of information about goals, trends, and conditions. Where promotion misfunctions, the predominance of one or more power groups may serve to attenuate the flow of information to prescribers and, in extreme circumstances, may reduce the prescriber's role to the mere formality of endorsing with tokens of legitimacy the demands of those with naked power.

Every decision function is subject to a complex set of authoritative expectations. Compliance with these expectations determines, in part, the lawfulness of the performance of that decision function within the larger constitutive process. The prescribing function prescribes for the other functions; that is, it is constantly engaged in establishing authoritative principles of content and procedure for the performance of all other decision functions. Thus, for example, procedures and substantive priorities are prescribed for the intelligence function, and every phase of the promotional process is sustained by a network of authoritative prescriptions. Prescription also prescribes for itself, that is, the prescribing function itself is subject to detailed regulation. This ongoing internal procedure involves a continuous feedback and reappraisal of the conformity of actual prescriptive effects with prescriptive goals.

Both invocation and application involve the implementation of prescribed policies in social process. The efficacy of these decision functions will thus determine whether prescription is a controlling or merely verbal operation. Repeated invocations and applications, whether formal or informal, may reinforce diffuse expectations and, by creating expectations of future uniformities in decision, add certainty to other indices of expectation. In particular, the way appliers ascertain, supplement, and integrate past prescriptions very directly affects the course of future expectations about authority and control. The prescriber's image of the degree of the probable effectiveness of his own function will obviously influence his efforts, including the social sectors which he chooses to prescribe for, the content of prescriptions, and the sanctions provided. A prescriber's sense of futility and meaninglessness need not manifest itself in inactivity; it may also express itself in wildly unrealistic prescriptions which have no chance of implementation and which further erode community expectations about the effectiveness of the prescribing function.

The quality of the termination function may have subtle but important impacts on prescription. Even proposals for termination or failure in efforts to terminate may reinforce other indices of expectation. The realistic prescriber, oriented in a social process of continuous change, expects a continual redefinition of prescription. Hence he realizes that the contribution of his function to the aggregate goal realization of the entire decision process depends upon the subsequent termination of many of the prescriptions to which he now attaches high symbols of authority. In the absence of such termination, prescriptions that were rational at some point in the past but that are no longer so become obstacles to goal realization and, as the power process shifts, may engender nonauthoritative change. Such change erodes prospectively the authority of the prescriptive process.

The appraisal function, examining past successes and failures, tests the aggregate performance of prescription and affects predispositions about future acceptability. Where there is persistent goal deviation, personal or structural responsibility is imputed. The self-regulation of prescribers for effectiveness will, hence, depend upon appropriate appraisal.

II

It should be no cause for surprise that the major jurisprudential theories have made little contribution to realistic description of transnational prescribing processes.[12] The "natural law" emphasis has been more concerned with search for the "bases of obligation" or "validity" of law in general than with inquiry about the empirical paternity of particular prescriptions.[13] Even when it has concerned itself with particular prescriptions, this emphasis has encouraged the illusion

12. For a more detailed critique of the contributions of the major jurisprudential theories of international law, see McDougal, Lasswell & Reisman, *Theories About International Law: Prologue to a Configurative Jurisprudence*, 8 Va. J. Int'l L. 188 (1968) (outlining suggestions for a more viable theory of international law) [hereinafter cited as *Theories About International Law*].

13. The quest for "source of obligation" or "binding character" or legitimacy, or any of the multitude of equivalents, can quickly take on aspects of mysticism or of "infinite regress" when not accompanied by the specification of operational *referents* in terms of the empirical expectations of community members about

that the appropriate quest is not for the means by which law is in fact created, but rather for the "sources" of a law somehow mysteriously preexisting, which the naturalist commonly locates in inaccessible transempirical realms.[14] Plainly the word "source" can be no more than the vaguest reference to certain social processes. In tautological fashion, the naturalist assumes and then discovers a source, but never describes nor explores its social dynamics.[15]

Despite its emphasis upon uniformities in behavior, the historical approach, with its distinctive disdain for conscious law-creating processes and concern for mythical, national groups with inbred *volksgeisten*, does not appear to have formulated a comprehensive theory

13. (Continued)
authority and control. *See* Fitzmaurice, *The Foundations of the Authority of International Law and the Problem of Enforcement*, 19 Mod. L. Rev. 1, 8-13 (1956)(search for source of obligation akin to search for "a sort of will-o'-the-wisp, an *ignis fatuus* that only recedes further into the distance as one approaches it, and that can never actually be reached"). *See also* Fitzmaurice, *The Law and Procedure of the International Court of Justice, 1951-54: General Principles and Sources of Law*, 30 Brit. Y.B. Int'l L. 1, 8-18 (1953) (discussing valid regulatory power of international law)[hereinafter cited as *Law and Procedure of the International Court of Justice*].

14. The word "sources" has multiple and ambiguous uses. Briggs for example identifies (1) the "*basis* of international law," which includes derivational exercises from assumed theories; (2) the *causes* of international law, including factors such as "reason, convenience, tradition, policy, necessity, and concepts of justice or of social solidarity" which influence "the development of international law" but which are said, curiously, to be irrelevant to providing "working criteria by which to distinguish law from practice or from opinions of what the law should be"; (3) the "evidences of international law," sometimes referring to "substantive rules" and sometimes to the "documentary sources" in which such rules find expression; and (4) the "methods or procedures by which international law is created," which the author prefers. The Law of Nations 43-52 (2d ed. H. Briggs 1952).

15. Grotius contributed to secularizing the notion of authority with his reference to state practice and his theory that the "impelling desire for society" constituted the source of law. Grotius, De Jure Belli Ac Pacis §6 at 11-12 (1925). *Quoted in Theories About International Law*, *supra* note 12, at 223. However, Grotius failed to distinguish the components of authority and control implicit in his conception and did not use them when performing relevant juristic tasks. Some later naturalists recognized the significance of effective power, but failed to identify a workable model linking it with their notion of authority. *See id.*

about how such uniformities create transnational expectations about policy, authority, and control.[16] The analytical or positivistic emphasis has had understandable difficulty in organizing and conducting inquiry about the creation of a kind of law whose existence it frequently denies.[17] Ignoring the realities of contemporary transnational prescription, this emphasis has tremendously exaggerated the image and importance of the autonomous nation-state, often confining law creation to the activity of state officials and stipulating the consent of every affected state to the making of law.[18] Moreover, the positivists have commonly confused function with structure, in insisting upon the indispensability of centralized legislative bodies to the creation of "genuine" law.

Despite its concern with the causes and consequences of decision, the sociological emphasis would appear to have taken its technical concepts largely from the analytical school and, hence, often to have succumb-

---

16. The historicalists offered an empirical approach in their analysis of community, which they found to consist of "individuals interacting in a given geographical area at a minimum level of intensity and sharing a number of critical perspectives." *Theories About International Law*, *supra* note 12, at 234. However, the historicalists failed to apply their factor analysis to an exploration of the "manifold of social events conditioning behavior." *Id.* at 240. Rather,

> [t]rend projection for the historicalist is simply the elusive assumption that the mechanisms of development characteristic of the group spirit will continue to be refined, and that prescriptive efforts that diverge from group spirit will be rejected in the course of time.
>
> Given this orientation, historicalism was not concerned with strategies of invention. In the historicalist frame of reference, the human actor is subservient to his group and physical environment; hence any activity aimed at realizing preferences not in conformity with the group spirit is an exercise in futility.

Id.

17. *See* Austin, *supra* note 2, at 140-42, 200-01 (international "law" not truly law because lacks determinate author).

18. *See* Tunkin, *Remarks on the Juridical Nature of Customary Norms of International Law*, 49 Calif. L. Rev. 418, 427-28 (1961)(concept of customary norms contradicts generally recognized principles of international law) [hereinafter cited as *Customary Norms*].

ed to the same parochial cultural presuppositions.[19] Some of the proponents of the "realistic" emphasis have, unhappily, carried their notions that law is only what courts or officials do to the extreme of completely fusing the functions of prescription and application: there can be no authoritative community expectations about a matter, they contend, until some judge or other official applies them in a particular instance.[20]

III

The more detailed contemporary description of the transnational prescribing process is something of a mélange of these various inherited confusions. It has become almost ritual presentation among commentators to make Article 38 of the Statute of the International

---

19. Strictly speaking, there is not so much a sociological school of international law, as a sociologistic fashion or style of communication. The common feature of sociologistic jurisprudence is concern with the identification of conditioning factors and a consensus, at least on the verbal level, that these factors are to be found in the predispositions of the human being and various environmental factors. The majority of sociological jurists has sought to understand how law comes about, with little regard for the ends and consequences of that process. In this latter respect, the sociological perspective adds little to that of the analytic school. *Theories About International Law, supra* note 12, at 260-61.

20. *See* J. Gray, The Nature and Sources of Law 82-83, 85-86, 90-93, 101 (1909). For an application of this view, see Justice Cardozo's opinion in New Jersey v. Delaware, 291 U.S. 363, 383 (1933) ("International law ... has at times, like the common law within states, a twilight existence during which it is hardly distinguishable from morality or justice, until at length the *imprimateur* of a court attests its jural quality.")

The legal realist school was in many ways a flamboyant expression of sociological jurisprudence, but it was more concerned with ends and more polemical and iconoclastic than its parent movement. Current international realists such as Carlston and Ross, *see, e.g.,* K. Carlston, Law and Organization in World Society (1962) and A. Ross, Constitution of the United Nations: Analysis of Structure and Function (1950), are distinguished by the strong behavioralist strands in their work, by their emphasis on operations and control, and by their continuing gnawing doubt about the existence of international law.

Court of Justice, a specification of the competence of the court, the central focus of exposition. This Article is commonly regarded as of the "highest authority" and as expressing "the duty of any tribunal which is called upon to administer international law."21 It may be recalled that the Article reads:

> 1. The Court, whose function is to decide in accordance with international law such disputes as are submitted to it, shall apply:
>
> a. international conventions, whether general or particular, establishing rules expressly recognized by the contesting states;
>
> b. international custom, as evidence of a general practice accepted as law;
>
> c. the general principles of law recognized by civilized nations;
>
> d. subject to the provisions of Article 59, judicial decisions and the teachings of the most highly qualified publicists of the various nations, as subsidiary means for the determination of rules of law.
>
> 2. This provision shall not prejudice the power of the Court to decide a case *ex aequo et bono*, if the parties agree thereto.22

Once, however, this focus is established, all agreement among commentators ends. It is furiously debated whether the itemization of "sources" is comprehensive; what the priorities, if any, are among the different sources; whether different sources are "formal" or "material"; what the precise wording in the different itemizations of the Article means; and how the significance of each itemized source is to be determined and assessed in particular instances of controversy.23 Unhappily, amidst all this debate, little attention is given to the difficult intellectual tasks confronting decisionmakers or observers in the common case in which

---

21. J. Brierly, The Law of Nations 56 (6th ed. 1963).

22. United Nations, Statute of the International Court of Justice art. 38.

23. For discussion of this debate, see K. Raman, Prescription of International Law By Customary Practice 697 n.29 (1967) (unpublished thesis in Yale Law School Library).

the sources are ambiguous, incomplete, or contradictory or in which they create expectations inimical to basic community policy.

The initial itemization of "international conventions" prompts some commentators to champion agreements as an important "direct, conscious, and purposive"[24] modality for law creation, offering the closest approach to the deliberate and explicit formulations of legislative processes in national societies. From this perspective, agreements may be both "formal" for the parties and others, and "material" or "evidentiary" sources of the expectations about authority and control which comprise customary law. Other commentators, however, find it difficult to understand how agreements, which in some versions of inherited international myth are supposed to "bind" only the immediate parties, can create "obligation" for third parties. Posing the problem as a quest for "consent" rather than for empirical expectations about the probable course of future decision, such commentators distinguish between the creation of "law" and the creation of "obligations," and insist that even agreements can derive their "binding" quality only from "a rule of customary law to that effect."[25] This would appear greatly to subordinate agreements to custom as an exclusive law creating modality.

The infelicities in expression of Article 38's reference to "international custom" are paralleled entirely by the imprecision of the conception which it seeks to communicate. The greatest difficulty for both decision makers and scholars is distinguishing the usage or practice that is mere extra-legal habit from the custom that carries expectations of general community authority and control. The comprehensive process of co-operative behavior through which expectations about authority and control are engendered is commonly truncated into two relatively exclusive "elements": a "material"

24. L. Oppenheim, The Future of International Law 24 (1921). *See* J. Brierly, *supra* note 21, at 51 (positivism teaches that international law is sum of rules to which states have consented); M. Hudson, International Legislation xv-xvi (1931)(international law stems, *inter alia*, from agreements).

25. C. Parry, The Sources and Evidences of International Law 53 (1968). *See Law and Procedure of the International Court of Justice*, *supra* note 13, at 68.

element in a flow of behavior and a "subjective" element in a variously conceived *opinio juris*. There is, however, unending debate about 1) the degree of generality and uniformity a practice must have attained, including its geographical and temporal dimensions, 2) the content of the subjectivities (whether of preexisting law, mere ethics, unlawfulness, etc.) which must be established and 3) whether these subjectivities are required to be established by evidence independent of the behavior of the participants.[26] There is increasing argument about the relevance of resolutions of the United Nations General Assembly for establishing *opinio juris*, and both proposals and rejections of "instant" custom abound.[27] It is sometimes suggested, in complete contradiction of the flow of decision and expectation, that the only relevant practice is the practice of states and that the other important participants in transnational processes of effective power do not share in the creation of customary law.[28] Finally, it is occasionally insisted, conversely to the argument noted above about agreement,[29] that custom is not an independent mode of law creation, but rather requires a unanimous consent which makes it tantamount to explicit agreement.[30]

The provision for recourse to "the general principles of law recognized by civilized nations" has been no

---

26. For an extensive discussion of the contours of the debate and each of the enumerated points, see Raman, *supra* note 23, at 275-371, 433-36, 482-545, 667-86.

27. *See, e.g.*, J. Castaneda, Legal Effects of United Nations Resolutions 168-77 (1969)(organs as broadly representative as General Assembly are particularly well qualified to determine when practices have become principles of international law); H. Bokor-Szego, The Role of the United Nations in International Legislation 49-67 (1978)(despite fact that resolutions of international organizations have no binding force, they are significant in effecting changes in process of custom formation and in establishing new norms through custom).

28. *See Customary Norms*, *supra* note 18, at 421, 423-26 ("*Opinio juris* signifies that the states treat this or that customary norm as juridically binding"); Restatement of Foreign Relations §1, Comment d, (1965)(where U.N. organs exercise lawmaking functions, such exercise constitutes concerted action of member states and not of an international entity).

29. *See* p. 261 *supra*.

30. *See* Tunkin, Theory of International Law 118-23, 126-28 (1974)(recognition by states is essential to legal status of custom).

less variously interpreted. Sometimes these principles are presented as natural law absolutes "having such inherent validity that they cannot be either contested or dispensed with" in any legal system,[31] sometimes as mere distillates of the more essential notions found in national law systems, and sometimes, overlapping with custom, as generalizations derived from the repetitive behavior of international and national officials.[32] It is simultaneously doubted whether there are any such principles, or whether any such principles as may be asserted are "law," or whether they constitute a distinctive source of law.[33] Sometimes it is insisted that the adjective "civilized" is invidious and unnecessary and that reference may be made to the practice of all states;[34] at other times it is suggested that only the practice of the more mature and developed states is relevant.[35] In this day of contending systems of world public order it is occasionally urged that shared principles are not likely to be found in the practice of states belonging to "two opposing social systems," and that "in consequence of the emergence of the socialist countries and the new states of Africa and Asia, the developmental base of general international law has contracted."[36] More positively, it is sometimes recognized that one function of the authorization of recourse to "general principles" is to afford a decision maker or other evaluator some latitude of creativity in supplementing or modifying "positive law"[37]: the decision maker

31. Fitzmaurice, *Some Problems Regarding the Formal Sources of Law*, in Symbolae Verzijl 154 (1958).

32. *See Customary Norms*, *supra* note 18, at 419 ("Historically a customary norm of international law appears as a result of reiterated actions of states"); Raman, *supra* note 23, at 149-245 (detailed treatment of participation of nation-states in formation of international law).

33. G. Herczegh, General Principles of Law and the International Legal Order 24 (1969)(noted Western authors question the existence of "general principles of law recognized by civilized nations"); Parry, *supra* note 25, at 84 (questioning whether "general principles" are a distinct source of law "at all").

34. Herczegh, *supra* note 33, at 11 n.2.

35. B. Cheng, General Principles of Law 25 (1953).

36. Tunkin, *supra* note 30, at 34.

37. *See* Herczegh, *supra* note 33, at 34 (general legal principles affect the interpretation and application of law and may be used to fill-in gaps in positive law).

is to be "permitted to reason, though not to legislate" by the "application of analogies."[38]

The traditional interpretations of the authorizations for recourse to "judicial decisions" as "subsidiary means for the determination of rules of law"[39] would appear to undercut the importance in fact of the role of uniformities in adjudicative decisions, whether international or national, in creating parallel uniformities in expectations about authority and control which transcend national boundaries. It is commonly agreed that such decisions are "material" sources of law, but frequently questioned "whether they constitute formal sources of law."[40] In conventional myth, as Sir Gerald Fitzmaurice writes, "Judges . . . declare or formulate or clarify or interpret or apply, or possibly develop the law; but they do not create, change or repeal it: that is for the legislature."[41] The illusion is sometimes entertained, even by the highest authorities, that if a national court, in a case properly before it, declares what it thinks international law is or ought to be, it is engaging in unwarranted, unilateral lawmaking for the whole globe.[42] Additional confusion is caused by the stipulation in Article 59 of the Statute of the International Court of Justice that "[t]he decision of the Court has no binding force except between the parties and in respect of that particular case." Such an attempt to limit the impact of judicial decisions ignores the fact that even in the absence of a technical doctrine of precedent or *stare decisis*, judges, like other rational beings, commonly make reference to the lessons of past experience, and that the members of the communities they represent expect this of them. In light of these confusions, it is understandable that little has been done to develop appropriate principles of content and procedure for appreciating the genuine contribution of adjudicative decisions to the creation of transnational expectations about authority and control.

---

38. Parry, *supra* note 25, at 83.

39. Art. 38, para. 1(d). *See* p. 260 *supra*.

40. Fitzmaurice, *Some Problems Regarding the Formal Sources of Law* in Symbolae Verzijl 168-69 (1958)(where decisions of domestic tribunals are binding, they are formal sources of law, but where, as with international tribunals, decisions have no precedential force they are merely material sources of law).

41. *Id.* at 169.

42. This illusion permeates Mr. Justice Harlan's opinion for the Court in Banco Nacional de Cuba v. Sabbatino, 376 U.S. 398 (1964). *Cf.* Tunkin, *supra* note 30, at 184.

The teachings of "the most highly qualified publicists of the various nations" cause less difficulty; it appears generally agreed that these are indeed "subsidiary means for the determination of rules of law."[43] Despite the flow of great books through the centuries and their repeated invocation and employment in instances of controversy, the writings of publicists are uniformly relegated to such categories as "material sources" or "mere evidences." It is also sometimes noted that the doctors often disagree.

The provision for decision "*ex aequo et bono*, if the parties agree thereto," seldom explicitly invoked in practice, has caused commentators some difficulty in effecting its reconciliation with an evaluator's creativity and more general freedom to appreciate other sources.[44] Thus, one writer has insisted that because of the stipulation for agreement of the parties, the International Court of Justice is not otherwise authorized to invoke the test of "reasonableness" in its comprehensive evaluation of the options in decision before it: only "intermediate decision makers" may have recourse to reasonableness.[45] Another scholar has suggested that decision *ex aequo et bono* in this context may refer to the possibility of some kind of political or compromise determination, beyond the considerable equitable discretion that the Court has in its application of the law to almost any conceivable case.[46] The author of a recent monograph suggests that "in opposition to the strict explication of legal rules equity means a balance and compensation of the interests of the litigants and has a function in mitigating the rigour of legal provisions rather than in filling the gaps of law."[47]

In light of the developments of recent decades, the most striking omission from the itemization in Article 38 is, of course, that of reference to the role of international governmental organizations in the

---

43. Art. 38, para. 1(d). *See* p. 260 *supra*.

44. *Cf.* M. Habicht, The Power of the International Judge to Give a Decision "Ex Aequo et Bono" 67-69 (1935)(*ex aequo et bono* is extraordinary procedure that allows judge to base his decision exclusively on considerations of equity).

45. MacGibbon, *supra* note 9, at 134.

46. Ascribed by senior author to R. Y. Jennings and confirmed by Prof. Jennings in telephone conversation, Cambridge, England, Dec. 20, 1980 (on file with *Yale Studies in World Public Order*).

47. Herczegh, *supra* note 33, at 101.

creation of both explicitly formulated law and customary expectations. It is increasingly recognized that these organizations, and especially the United Nations, contribute to the creation of international law in many different ways and that any realistic description of transnational prescribing processes must take this contribution into account.[48] The contribution of such organizations, through the performance of the intelligence and recommending functions, the maintenance of established structures of authority, and the making of law through explicit agreement is of long standing knowledge. More recently, awareness has grown that the General Assembly of the United Nations, though explicitly endowed with only a recommending function, has, in augmentation of traditional processes of customary creation, come to provide a relatively universal parliamentary forum in which the peoples of the world can deliberately, with whatever comprehensiveness and precision they desire, proclaim what they think the law to be. Whether any particular resolution embodies the expectations about future decision necessary to constitute prescription must of course depend upon many variables, including the number and effective power of the states voting for and against the resolution, the compatibility of the policy content of the resolution with prior customary and conventional expectations and other contemporary communications, and the measures subsequently taken or not taken to put the resolutions into effective practice.

As indicated in the references above to "general principles" and "*ex aequo et bono*," some contemporary descriptions offer at least modest recognition that a decision-maker or observer, confronted with opposing claims about the content and authority of relevant prescription, must commonly consider and assess not merely some single source or tidbit of prescription, but the whole range or flow of sources and outcomes in prescription, and that these multiple sources and outcomes are often incomplete, ambiguous, and contradictory in their messages. Thus, Professor Brierly, in an eloquent discussion of "The place of 'reason' in the modern system,"

48. *See* Falk, *On the Quasi-Legislative Competence of the General Assembly*, 60 Am. J. Int'l L. 782 (1966)(General Assembly is endowed with and actually exercises a limited international legislative power); *Cf*. A. D'Amato, The Concept of Custom in International Law 3-4 (1971)(United Nations resolutions not usually recognized as binding by states that cast dissenting votes).

observes:

> [N]o system of law consists only of formulated rules, for these can never be sufficiently detailed or sufficiently foreseeing to provide for every situation that may call for a legal decision; those who administer law must meet new situations not precisely covered by a formulated rule by resorting to the principle which medieval writers would have called natural law, and which we generally call reason. Reason in this context does not mean the unassisted reasoning powers of any intelligent man, but a 'judicial' reason, which means that a principle to cover the new situation is discovered by applying methods of reasoning which lawyers everywhere accept as valid, for example, the consideration of precedents, the finding of analogies, the disengagement from accidental circumstances of the principles underlying rules of law already established.[49]

Similarly, Bin Cheng writes: "In place of the theory of the logical plenitude or self-sufficiency of the positive law, the modern theory maintains that the positive law has always been and always should be guided, supplemented and perhaps even corrected by an unformulated law."[50] Kopelmanas appropriately emphasizes the high creativity in a finding of "custom": "We have already seen that the formation and existence of a custom depend on its conformity with the social needs of a legal order."[51] He adds, "Sometimes it is merely the satisfactory and reasonable character of the custom which allows a decision whether a particular rule has or has not the character of a legal rule."[52] More recently, Sir Gerald Fitzmaurice has queried whether "*exceptional circumstances justify a departure from the normal rules*"[53] and pointed to the fact that the International Court of Justice in the *Norwegian Fisheries*

49. J. Brierly, Law of Nations 66 (6th ed. 1963).

50. B. Cheng, *supra* note 35, at 16-17.

51. Kopelmanas, *Custom as a Means of Creation of International Law*, 18 Brit. Y.B. Int'l L. 127, 148 (1937).

52. *Id.* at 151.

53. *Law and Procedure of the International Court of Justice*, *supra* note 13, at 18.

case,[54] in its finding and application of customary law "based its Judgment very largely on such factors as the exceptional character of Norway's coast, the marked dependence of the population of northern Norway on fishing, and so on."[55] Unfortunately, however, this frank, if inconclusive and undeveloped, discussion of the different tasks confronting an applier or other evaluator of alleged prescription is still too often beclouded by abstruse infusions of a mystifying doctrine of *non liquet* and by fears that too explicit recognition of the creative necessities in decision would, in the contemporary decentralized world arena, impose too great a burden upon judges.[56]

Moreover, these commentators fail to recognize that the formulas of Article 38 are misleading not only because they direct the inquirer to an ambiguous and capriciously limited array of sources from which international law is alleged to derive, but even more seriously because they suggest to the inquirer that he or she may regard whatever emanates from these sources as, in fact, law. But this assurance may, in particular contexts, be belied by other communications or signals about authority and control. The product of a particular source may well be syntactic illusion, bearing little relation to genuine community expectations.

IV

One possible route of escape from our inherited confusions about prescription and its application lies both in the more explicit recognition and contextual description of the contemporary comprehensive process of transnational prescription, and in a more careful discrimination and specification of the several different intellectual tasks which must be performed by any applier or other evaluator who is confronted with an alleged prescription.

The diversity and abundance of the processes of communication by which prescriptions, that is, the projections of policy attended by expectations of authority

---

54. Fisheries Case (United Kingdom v. Norway) [1951] I.C.J. 116.

55. *Law and Procedure of the International Court of Justice*, *supra* note 13, at 18–19.

56. *See* J. Stone, *Non Liquet and the Function of Law in the International Community*, 35 Brit. Y.B. Int'l L. 124, 152 (1959).

and control, are created in the contemporary world arena are staggering. The peoples of the world communicate to each other expectations about policy, authority, and control, not merely through state or intergovernmental organs, but through reciprocal claims and mutual tolerances in all their interactions. The participants in the relevant processes of communication, the communicators and the communicatees, range from the most specialized to the least specialized in prescription, and include not merely the officials of states and intergovernmental organizations but also the representatives of political parties, pressure groups, private associations, and the individual human being *qua* individual, with all his or her identifications.

The perspectives of participants include those both most deliberately and least deliberately related to prescriptive purposes, and exhibit demands, identifications, and expectations with every degree of compatibility or incompatibility with common interests and basic general community policies. The situations of interaction and communication are both official and non-official, organized and unorganized. The organized situations include the familiar diplomatic, parliamentary-diplomatic, parliamentary, adjudicative, and executive arenas and all situations are characerized by differing degrees of institutionalization, temporal duration, geographic range, and expectations of crisis. The different participants bring many varying base values,[57] in terms of authority and controlling power, to bear upon particular interactions. The strategies employed by participants in the management of their base values display every possible degree of explicitness or implicitness in relation to prescription, range along the whole spectrum of coercion and persuasion, and include, not merely the modalities suggested in Article 38 of the Statute of the International Court of Justice, but the entire complex of procedures employed in the varying types of power arenas and all the strategies characteristic of the different value processes. The culminating outcomes of all this communication represent a very great range both in the facts about shared perspectives in relation to policy, authority, and control and in the

57. Any value cherished in a community may, of course, serve as a base of power, as well as be a demanded value. *See* McDougal, Lasswell & Reisman, *The World Constitutive Process of Authoritative Decision* (pt. 1), 19 J. Leg. Educ. 253, 289-300 (1967). For an illumination of the concept of base value, see H. Lasswell & A. Kaplan, *supra* note 6, at 83-84.

evidences of such perspectives in the shape of explicit formulations and unarticulated assumptions. The most important point is that the outcomes in shared expectations, in whatever degree they approach prescription and however they may be evidenced, are a function of the total configuration of factors that affect and produce them.

From this perspective of the process by which international law is made, it is now possible to identify in a more discriminating and precise fashion the inescapable intellectual operations performed by any evaluator, including members of a target audience and especially official appliers of alleged prescription. It may be emphasized that the subjectivities of communicatees are an indispensable component of prescription and that authoritative appliers are important members of the target audience of prescription. It is impossible to describe prescription comprehensively without making reference to application, since the subjectivities of appliers are a necessary component of prescription. Any realistic description of a process of prescriptive communication requires reference, beyond the strategies and subjectivities of communicators, to the subjectivities of the communicatees and the intellectual operations incumbent upon them. It is suggested that these operations may be conveniently categorized in three-fold fashion.[58]

(1) *Ascertaining expectations about content, authority and control*

This task requires a genuine effort to achieve the closest possible approximation to the effective aggregate general community expectation about the content, authority, and control of alleged prescriptive communications. The adequate performance of this task demands a disciplined systematic survey and assessment of all features of the process of communication and its context that may affect expectation. The task and procedures are substantially comparable whether the expectations sought are those of the general community, of some lesser regional community, of simply a number of participants, or even of the immediate parties to a controversy.

---

58. These operations are, of course, integral goals of the application function. *See* McDougal, *Human Rights and World Public Order: Principles of Content and Procedure for Clarifying General Community Policies*, 14 Va. J. Int'l L. 387, 394-96 (1974).

(2) *Supplementing incomplete and ambiguous communications*

This task requires the remedying of the inevitable gaps and ambiguities in prescriptive expectation by reference to more general, basic community policies about the shaping and sharing of values. In conventional presentations this task is sometimes described as the exercise of "reason" or the invocation of analogies. Its adequate performance demands, however, the disciplined employment of a comprehensive set of procedures, including: specifying each of the opposing claims about prescription in terms of the interests sought to be protected and the particular demands for authoritative decision; formulating the different options open to the relevant decision-maker or other evaluator (which may be more extensive than the decisions demanded by the opposing parties); estimating the consequences of alternative choices upon the aggregate inclusive interests of the general community and the exclusive interests of the particular parties; and choosing the option which promises to promote the largest aggregate long-term common interest, inclusive and exclusive.

(3) *Integrating expectations with basic community policies*

This task requires decision-makers or other evaluators, recognizing that they are responsible for the total policy of the community which they represent or of which they are members, to reject even the most explicit, precisely formulated expectations when such expectations are inimical to basic, more intensely demanded community policies. This task is made authoritative with respect to international agreements both by the newly formulated constitutive prescription about *jus cogens* and by the rapidly emerging global Bill of Human Rights. The considerations that prompted the making of the prescription for international agreements apply, however, no less cogently to the less deliberately formulated prescriptions of customary law. The adequate performance of this task demands procedures comparable to those recommended for supplementing expectations, with explicit specification of the more intensely demanded general community policies and deliberate rejection of any prescriptive intimations that contravene these policies.

Effective performance of these three operations, and indeed of any decision component, requires the application of a series of interrelated intellectual tasks, including: suggesting the broad policies appropriate for a global prescribing process, examining the degrees of approximation to the policies in past trends in practice, identifying the factors that appear to have affected past practice, projecting possible future patterns in practice, and recommending possible improvements in constitutive prescribing structures and procedures.[59] Part V of this Article focuses on the first of these tasks; it offers a provisional specification of appropriate policies for the global prescribing function.[60]

V

Students of the prescribing function frequently ask of a particular norm if it is "good law," that is, they seek to appraise a prescription for its consonance with the common interests of the relevant community. But there is an anterior question, which is larger and more enduring than the question of the quality of a particular norm. It is the clarification of basic community policy for the making of prescriptions at the constitutive level. This anterior question recognizes that the prescribing function in any community is part of its more comprehensive constitutive process, and thus focuses not on the content of particular norms, but on the process by which such norms are made.

The focus upon constitutive process is not a theoretical exercise. From time to time, international lawyers have the opportunity to participate in a major and explicit "constitutional" case in which basic policies about lawmaking itself are considered and perhaps changed. Key issues in the *Certain Expenses* case[61] and in the *Namibia* case,[62] for example, were whether participation in international lawmaking within the United Nations should be extended from the restricted membership club of the Security Council to the more inclusive

59. A more detailed exposition of these intellectual tasks is offered in *Theories About International Law*, *supra* note 12, at 204-06.

60. What we seek is the specification, rather than the derivation, of relevant policies. *See Theories About International Law*, *supra* note 12, at 207.

61. Advisory Opinion on Certain Expenses of the United Nations, [1962] I.C.J. 151.

62. Advisory Opinion on Legal Consequences for States of the Continued Presence of South Africa in Namibia (South West Africa) Notwithstanding Security Council Resolution 276 (1970), [1971] I.C.J. 16.

General Assembly. In addition to these dramatic cases, virtually every controversy and all practice has a constitutive dimension in which the question of prescription and its structuring is inherent. The lawyer cannot effectively perceive and exploit these opportunities and the scholar cannot appraise the choices made without a clarification and specification of the basic community policies pertinent to the prescribing function. The most general question is what basic policies would we wish to see implemented if it were possible to design an optimum prescriptive process.

The securing of appropriate world public order, minimum and optimum, requires the establishment and maintenance of a prescriptive process whose outcomes--norms prescribed and potential norms rejected--are effective, rational, and inclusive. Effectiveness does not require the absolute application of every norm. Rather, it imports the maintenance of a contextually appropriate level of uniformity and stability in interaction which is substantially consistent with and popularly attributed to expectations of control as well as of authority. Rationality demands that prescriptions express common rather than special interests, with an appropriate balancing of protection for both inclusive and exclusive interests.[63] Inclusivity requires that prescriptions extend to all interactions, whoever the participants and whatever the geographical locus of activity, insofar as the interactions affect common interests. The achievement of effective, rational, and inclusive prescriptions depends upon an aggregate process, each feature of which is structured so that it contributes to the preferred outcomes. Hence, we consider *seriatim* the policies for each feature which may be instrumental to achieving prescriptive outcomes facilitative of a world order of human dignity.

A. *Participants*

The policy stipulating a wide sharing of power for each decision function in the constitutive process applies equally to the prescribing process. Every participant affected by the outcomes of decision processes should have the opportunity to influence their content, while no participant or small group of participants should be allowed to prevent others from prescribing in the common interest. We reject the seductively simple doctrine of a unanimity requirement which, under the guise of the

63. *See* p. 275 *infra*.

maximum sharing of power, vouchsafes a veto to an entrenched minority and enfranchises a single participant or a small group with the power to paralyze both the formal and informal prescriptive processes of an entire community. Such a veto in fact involves a concentration rather than a wide sharing of power and should be eschewed in all but the most exceptional circumstances.

A commitment to a representative prescriptive process cannot be translated into a general and unswerving loyalty to a particular set of political institutions or practices. The test of any institution or practice is the degree to which it provides maximum possible participation within the specific context, having due regard for the shifting complex of policies necessary to the maintenance of the desired public order. Hence, preferences for such specialized institutions as referendum, proportional representation, varying formulas of weighted voting, and direct and indirect democracy must always turn upon a contemporary and particular correlation of basic policy and context.

The informality of many parts of the transnational prescriptive process, in which expectations about policies, authority, and control are created by both official and non-official cooperative behavior, often yields an appropriate inclusivity. When this inclusivity is achieved, such processes present a preferred democracy and representativeness in that they involve a constant accommodation of the interests and behavior of all participants who are affected by the prescriptions being created. But neither in procedure nor substance does custom assure prescriptions in conformity with minimum or maximum order needs of human dignity; there are, unfortunately, no rational, invisible hands that automatically guide social interaction toward desired values. Hence, the application of a customary prescriptive process may require the same supplementation and policing as does the application of more formal prescriptions. Customary processes do, nevertheless, often provide a higher degree of democracy and representativeness than do many more formal prescribing processes.

B. *Perspectives*

The perspectives appropriate to the rich diversity of potential lawmaking activities in the contemporary global arena range between two extremes in consciousness of lawmaking. On the one hand, prescription refers to those activities deliberately and manifestly designed to make law, such as attend participation in multilateral agreements or formal bilateral agreements. Yet, it also includes those activities least deliberately so designed, indeed even those manifestly purporting to flout the products of past prescribing processes, no less than those accompanied by *ex gratia* disclaimers.

The perspectives of community members, that is, the objectives for which they establish and maintain the constitutive process, have been appropriately considered a crucial element in prescription. Indeed, a certain constellation of perspectives about policy, authority, and control is what is commonly meant by prescription. Even traditional theories about the making of international law have seldom pushed to the extreme of behavioralism, with emphasis exclusively upon externally observable operations. But the uncontrovertible statement that subjectivities are important in both process and outcomes of lawmaking is not enough. What is required beyond this explicit recognition of the relevance of perspectives is a more detailed specification of the demands, identifications, and expectations appropriate to a preferred prescribing process.

1. *Demands*

An observer may characterize the claims of states and other participants--however they justify themselves --in terms of common or special interests. The former serve the interests of the entire world community; the latter do not, but are asserted irrespective of the interests of others. Where demands for comparatively high or complete national control serve the interests of the world community, we term them common exclusive interests to distinguish them from both special interests and claims for more inclusive or shared control. In a public order aspiring toward human dignity, the demands of participants in transnational prescriptive processes must achieve, above all, a commitment to common interests and a rejection of special interests. It is within this broad commitment that an accommodation must be sought between the inclusive interests of many participants and the exclusive interests of particular participants.

Demands for particular policies--even about common interests--may vary in their intensity; intense recognition of common interests in certain standards, such as those relating to minimum order, is a prerequisite to community. This category of most intense demands includes the emerging legal formula of *jus cogens*, with its insistence upon the overriding necessities of controlling unauthorized violence and coercion and the very recent conventions concerning the basic human rights of the individual. We urge explicit recognition and continuous appraisal of such preemptory demands, testing them through time for their instrumentality and utility in the achievement of minimum and optimum order in particular contexts.

2. *Identifications*

Social interaction is not discrete; it is physically continuous and psychically integrated. Hence, individual performance in the most nuclear of exclusive groups may significantly determine perceptions and performance in other groups of increasing inclusivity. Because the conception of human dignity that we recommend involves, perforce, the widest participation in the shaping and sharing of all values, it is often arenas of primary and direct rather than secondary and representative interaction that determine the level of human dignity an individual can achieve. For this reason, policies about appropriate identifications for prescriptive functions should avoid emphasizing either inclusive or exclusive identifications at the expense of the other. What is required is an appropriate balance, permitting the individual to recognize that the realization of the common interests of the most comprehensive community of which he is a part is a function of his routine operations in diverse groups of varying inclusivity or exclusivity, and vice versa. Identification with the most comprehensive inclusive community thus does not import repudiation of membership and loyalty in the many less inclusive groups in which the individual's life transpires; it may, however, require revisions in the priority and intensity of the diverse loyalties of the self-system.

3. *Expectations*

At every level of social interaction, the policy content people seek to prescribe and the techniques they employ to assemble and communicate the authority and control components of prescription are deeply affected by the matter-of-fact expectations they entertain. As in the performance of every other decision function, we urge that matter-of-fact expectations about social process, effective power and authoritative decision be made realistic and contextual. Such realism and contextuality can avoid the Scylla of cynical despair over possibilities of prescribing changes in the world arena and the Charybdis of giddy utopianism which assumes that every necessary change can be effected by prescription. Realistic expectations can aid in the identification of proper targets and the setting of appropriate timetables. Prescribers who do not orient themselves realistically and contextually in the manifold of events of which they are part and which they seek to effect, sacrifice not only the potential effectiveness of their own purposive behavior but, in the aggregate, enlarge the gap between authority and control, enervating and ultimately extinguishing the process of authoritative decision within which they operate. An effective intelligence function is indispensable to an effective prescribing function.

C. *Arenas*

Prescription is an interactive communicative process; the features of the situations in which it takes place--structural, temporal, geographical, or spatial--have subtle but pervasive and important impacts on outcomes as well as pre-outcome phases. Hence, it is important to project a complex of preferred policies for prescriptive arenas so that advantage may be taken of every potential in the management of situational features.

1. *Organized and Unorganized Arenas*

The assumption that organized institutions always perform tasks more efficiently than the non-organized is incorrect. Any rational effort toward improving the global prescribing process must appropriately balance both organized and unorganized arenas. The tremendous potentialities of the United Nations bodies, the specialized agencies, the regional organizations, and specially organized multilateral conferences for the clarification and articulation of common interests have scarcely begun to be exploited. At the same time, both scholars and general community decision makers must take fuller and more positive account of the generation of customary law in the many unorganized arenas of the global process.

Every interaction of even the most minimal duration generates, reinforces, and changes one's expectations and demands on oneself and others regarding the full range of values being shaped and shared. Accordingly, a comprehensive theory of prescription cannot limit its focus to those organized situations which are specialized to lawmaking and dismiss the vast range of unorganized interactions in which customary expectations are created and sustained. Indeed, unorganized prescriptive arenas have, as already emphasized, often played an important function in democratizing the lawmaking function. It is important that the authority of unorganized as well as organized prescriptive situations be recognized in order that assessments of law for both scholarly and decision-making purposes take full account of all situations in which authoritative expectations are shaped.

We recommend, further, clear recognition of the distinction between public order and civic order, the latter being a domain which is consciously demarked and reserved for relatively autonomous private decision.[64] Contextual investigation has shown that the maximum policy dividend in human dignity is gained by permitting participants themselves to regulate a large sector of their lives. This maximum realization of human dignity is assured only if delimitations of public and civic order are made after the full range of actual prescriptive situations is examined.

2. *Specialized and Non-Specialized Prescriptive Arenas*

Analytical positivistic categories of jurisprudential thought have often attempted to restrict attention to a limited number of specialized prescriptive arenas as the exclusive sources from which "law" comes. As Eugen Ehrlich emphatically showed, however, any scholar who has limited his attention to certain ritualized activities of a legislature has covered only a minuscule segment of the creative processes by which expectations about policy, authority, and control are generated in social interaction.[65] Jurisprudential dogmatics aside, no serious observer limits attention to a single specialized prescriptive organ. "Judicial lawmaking" and such open-ended terms as custom, "general principles," and precedent force attention to a number of other prescriptive processes. As indicated above,[66] prescription need not be a specialized or purposive process. Because the creation of expectations is a consequence ancillary to almost all relatively stable interaction, a plenary conception of prescription cannot limit itself to so-called specialized prescriptive arenas. We therefore recommend that attention be directed to all interactive

---

64. For development of the concept of civic order (the areas of life in which the individual is subjected to the least public or private coercion), see M. McDougal, H. Lasswell & L. Chen, Human Rights and World Public Order 801 (1980); *see also* R. Arens & H. Lasswell, In Defense of Public Order 204-05 (1961).

65. E. Ehrlich, Fundamental Principles of the Sociology of Law 20-22 (1962).

66. *See* p. 252 *supra*.

situations in which expectations about value allocation are prescribed.

3. *Centralized and Decentralized Arenas*

Policies of representativeness, if they are to achieve their maximum realization without jeopardizing minimum world order, must accommodate prescriptive processes of varying degrees of organization transpiring in a broad range of geographical arenas, from the most centralized to the most decentralized. The social tendency of interacting individuals to generate reciprocal expectations relating to all the value exchanges involved in their specific interactions should receive authoritative encouragement in direct proportion to the degree of exclusivity of impact of their relations. The maximum direct and representative participation of all actors will be realized only if the prescriptive competence of the most decentralized arenas is fully employed. As the inclusivity of a flow of interactions increases, however, either in terms of direct participation or the diffusion of value effects, the competence of a more centralized prescriptive process should be recognized.

Recognition of the prescriptive creativity of all social interactions of minimum duration does not mean that the observer or decision-maker must accept the authority of all. The determination of an arena of authoritative prescription, whatever its degree of centralization or decentralization, is a function of constitutive decision and is taken with full regard for the unique features of the context as well as for the plenary range or policies of the community in question. The flexibility of both observers and constitutive decision-makers will be enhanced, however, by cognizance of the full range of arenas which are available.

4. *The Integration of Universal and Regional Arenas*

Intimately related to the policy of balancing centralized and decentralized arenas is the crucial constitutive policy of integrating universal and regional arenas into a coherent aggregate global process of prescription that promotes an ongoing dynamic responsiveness to the changing requirements of common interest. Overlapping and intersecting arenas, conveniently described as universal and regional, but often involving a richer geographical and interest variation, are constantly creating expectations; the challenge is to determine the sectors in which prescriptive authority should be accorded to varying geographic and interest levels and constantly to appraise allocations of prescriptive competence in terms of the extent to which they realize inclusive goals and are productively integrated within the most comprehensive global community process. Fundamental policy recommendations are, then, the recognition of the prescriptive competence of diverse geographical arenas, the determination of such allocations on the basis of common interests, and the integration of prescriptive competence for value and spatial sectors in a manner most consonant with the interests of the world community.

5. *Continuous and Intermittent Institutions*

In the world community, as in any lesser community, the aggregate flow of prescriptions must be continuous if it is to respond effectively to the challenges of an ever-changing social and environmental context. Hence, we recommend the institutionalization of continuous prescriptive processes. A preference for continuity does not exclude allowance for and recognition of an authoritative prescriptive competence for intermittent processes which arise because of specific stimuli and, under certain circumstances, present the optimum form for procedural and substantial policy realization. Past practice has sought to meet this policy requirement within the limitations of its formal theory by indirect and often *sub rosa* recognition of the prescriptive competence of decision-makers who are not formally authorized to prescribe. Hence, the praetor was permitted his periodic edicts; in contemporary practice, the inevitable "legislative" role of the judge is recognized. These partial and informal recognitions of an intermittent prescriptive competence, however, do not fulfill the requirements of a rational and maximally effective process of authoritative decision because their very covertness prevents an ongoing appraisal of the conditions under which an intermittent prescriptive authority, deviating from established institutional patterns, should be recognized and the criteria by which its operation should be evaluated.

6. *Institutional Responsiveness to Crisis*

It is commonplace that institutionalized decision must be able to deal with extraordinary as well as with ordinary problems. Unfortunately, institutionalized processes frequently develop a rigidity, if not *rigor mortis*, paralleled on the psychological level by a resistance to change on the part of entrenched elites. Ego involvement in a certain set of procedures may lead the individual to view any suggested change as a repudiation of the self and to regard every retention of established practice as a vindication of the self. Such inflexibility on both the personal and aggregate institutional levels handicaps optimal response to those situations of major crisis, in which the imminent loss of crucial values is perceived. The net result of this handicap may be to increase or accelerate the crisis while paralyzing institutional decision processes from rational and effective response. Constitutive processes of prescription should, by appropriate personnel and structural adjustment, be made sensitive to potential crises, anticipating them where possible and responding at the earliest appearance. This sensitivity should characterize both the most comprehensive global constitutive process and the comparable internal processes of its lesser constituent communities.

D. *Bases of Power*

A prescription is distinguished from other preferential statements in that it is viewed as authoritative by those to whom it is addressed and in that its audience concludes that the prescriber, or a surrogate official, intends to and, indeed, can make it controlling. The expectations of the target audience are of course inferred from the total context, including various features of the function of application. The putative prescriber must, therefore, seek authority and control upon which to base his acts. From the standpoint of public order, an appropriate prescriptive process requires both explicit and implicit authority and the optimal marshaling of bases in such manner as to create the necessary expectations of control in the promulgative sequences of prescription and its application. We consider each of these requirements *seriatim*.

1. *Explicit Bases of Authority*

The 19th century historicalist school of jurisprudence drew particular attention to the ongoing, indigenous process of prescription which attends any flow of interaction and which generates expectations of authority in the minds of participants without reference to official, organized arenas of prescription. From a policy oriented perspective, however, the fact that interacting participants ineluctably prescribe in no way discharges observers and decision-makers from the necessity of rationalizing and optimalizing processes of prescription which fulfill the basic requirements of adequate world public order: effectiveness, rationality, and inclusivity. Consequently, in sharp distinction to the historicalist, we have emphatically recommended the establishment and maintenance of a wide and varied range of organized prescriptive processes, capable of considering prospectively, and by systematic application of the intellectual tasks of decision, the prescriptive requirements of a world public order of human dignity. Such processes patently require explicit bases of authority coextensive with the scope of their prescriptive aspirations. Explicit bases of authority, it may be added, are not identical with textual affirmations of authority. Although a text may be a tentative indicator of a base of authority, it is not sufficient unless it corresponds to shared expectations of elites relevant to the prescriptive aspirations of the process in question.

2. *Implicit Bases of Authority*

The demand for adequate explicit bases of prescriptive authority is balanced by a coordinate demand for full recognition of the fact of, and continuing potential for, the generation of implicit expectations of authority in the myriad patterns of social interaction. Policies of economy and representativeness are served not by a totalitarian incorporation of all sectors of life into the public order, but rather by reserving areas of social life for the prescriptive and applicative regulation of the participants directly concerned. Hence, the notion of implicit and regenerating authority in all social interaction must be recognized. Because authority, in its empirically referential sense, is simply expectations shared by individuals as to how decisions will be made, any attempt to inventory authority in the global or less inclusive arenas of the world will perforce be obliged to examine both explicit and implicit authority expectations.

3. *Effective Control*

We distinguish authoritative decision from pretended decision because the communications of the former in regard to policies for value allocation include sufficiently credible indications of an intention to render authoritative policy into controlling fact to create expectations of effectiveness in a target audience. There is, as we have emphasized, scant utility in speaking of law in any community unless expectations of authority and control are copresent. If prescriptive processes in the world community are to be effective, rational, and inclusive, they must be buttressed by processes of effective control. Since control is never an arithmetical computation discrete from context, it is obvious that the components of effectiveness will vary from context to context and will be decisively shaped not merely by the allocation of base values, but also by the content of the prescription and in particular the groups it alternately indulges and deprives. Therefore, our recommendation is that inclusive prescriptive processes be girded with a control base in the relevant values adequate to secure common interests.

E. *Strategies*

The optimum policies for the strategic procedures involved in the characteristic sequences of prescription can be most economically considered in terms of exploration, characterization, and communication, the more important sequences which must be adequately performed for effective prescription.[67] We consider each briefly.

1. *Exploration*

The process of prescription is initially concerned with an examination of the facts, including the features of present and projected contexts relevant to future policy. It is also concerned with an inventory of the alternative policy choices which are available for prescription. Policies for this phase of exploration, as for any intelligence function, involve comprehensiveness, selectivity, dependability, and creativity. The achievement of these policies depends both upon the economy of institutional processes or unorganized routines and upon the base values made available.

2. *Characterization*

The median prescribing sequence entails a process of characterization of the products of systematic exploration in decision about what facts are to be regarded as relevant and what policies are to be projected into the future; this characterization moves, in its appraisal of the probable value consequences of different policies, steadily from provisionality to comparative finality. The policies relevant to rational characterization

---

67. *See* pp. 252-54 *supra* for a sequential analysis of prescription.

are those of deliberation and reasoned assessment in terms of common interest.

3. *Communication*

The final strategic sequence of prescription, often overlooked in jurisprudential models, involves communication to the target community of the policy content of the prescription, activation of authority signals, and the modulation of credible control intentions. The sequence of communication involves more than the legal concept of promulgation. Promulgation refers to a ritualized act without which an authoritative applier is not supposed to give effect to a putative prescription. Communication, by contrast, involves a set of techniques, varying with context, aimed at creating shared common subjectivities in the target audience. On the constitutive level, communication involves an ongoing mobilization of community attention for continuing interest in the prescriptive response to significant problems. Insofar as this general mobilization is successful, individuals will be constantly involved in participating in and monitoring prescriptive processes, demanding contextually and temporally appropriate prescription, accepting common and rejecting special interests, and testing inherited prescription for its contemporary contribution to community goals.

Conclusion

The examination of past trends in the global prescribing process for ascertaining the degree of approximation to recommended policies must, of course, require a systematic survey of the functioning of the different features of that process in relation to the outcomes in prescription achieved concerning all the important problems of constitutive process and public order. Effective inquiry about the factors conditioning past practice and possible projections into the future, with estimate of potential losses and benefits to policy, will depend upon the delicate, contextual assessment of a whole array of predispositional and environmental variables. The recommendation of more detailed, rational improvements in the global prescribing function, in the light of knowledge acquired through appropriate trend and scientific study, will require exploration of every facet, for identification of possible changes, both of the most comprehensive constitutive process of authoritative decision and the effective power processes which establish and maintain authoritative decision.

[6]

THE REALITY AND EFFICACY OF INTERNATIONAL LAW*

By IAN BROWNLIE[1]

THE writer's contact with international law dates back to 1954 when he began work on a doctoral thesis under the supervision of Judge Sir Humphrey Waldock, as he later became. Since then he has been engaged with the subject more or less continuously and this in both academic and practical contexts. It follows that the approach must be somewhat *ex parte*. As Justice Powell is reported to have said, on taking the oath of office, when asked if he supported the American constitution: 'certainly I support the constitution; after all, it has always supported me.'

Of course, even the best-formed and well-tested body of principles, whether in the social or natural sciences, may acquire a penumbra of doubt. Doubting is fashionable, and in the context of international relations doubting often takes some unhealthy forms. Doubts based upon ignorance and strong suppositions about the conduct of States lead not to healthy inquiry but to a neurotic nihilism. A much-paraded desire for order and justice is transformed into glib assertions of anarchy and into luddite attacks on international institutions, and this on the excuse that the international order is imperfect. In any case, it must be accepted that the quality and performance of international law has been given a low rating by some very reputable thinkers. The object of the present paper must therefore be this penumbra of respectable doubt.

First of all, the reality of international law, that is to say, the actual use of rules described as rules of international law by governments, is not to be questioned. All normal governments employ experts to provide routine and other advice on matters of international law and constantly define their relations with other States in terms of international law. Governments and their officials routinely use rules which they have for a very long time called the 'law of nations' or 'international law'. It is not the case that the resort to law is propagandist—though it sometimes is. The evidence is that reference to international law has been a part of the normal process of decision-making. Some of the evidence is to be seen in the volumes of the *British Digest of International Law* which relate to the period 1860–1914. There are to be seen the confidential opinions of the Law Officers of the Crown.

The law delimits the competence of States. No journey by air could take place in reasonable conditions if it were not for a network of legal structures involving the jurisdiction of States, the agreements of States and various I.C.A.O. procedures and standards. The law also provides the tools for constructing institutions. Typically, what is, in effect, the *loi-cadre* of the E.E.C. is a multilateral treaty.

At any time international society contains a certain number of dangerous eccentrics. In the recent past one head of State has been probably a cannibal, another a murderous psychopath and in a third example the prime minister and foreign minister are former members of well-known terrorist organizations. Moreover, the regime in Tehran has gone in for the taking of hostages as an instrument of policy and has produced a system of self-righteous anarchy which is isolated from other Muslim States. The existence of these depressing memorials of the abnormal proves no more about the general role of law and the habit of legality than the existence within *national* communities of criminal individuals and groups, alienated and violent minorities and forms of racialism, the last often reinforced by the internal law and administrative practices.

Given the reality of international law, its actual role in the business of States, the more interesting and necessary inquiry is into the performance or efficacy of the law.

As a first line of approach it may be said that international law confronts certain objective and inescapable features of the political landscape. In the first place, the addressees of the rules are normally and primarily the governments themselves. It is too often forgotten that this feature is shared by public law within States. Like the law of the constitution, international law addresses the very agents who should apply the rules: the rules are essentially principles of self-limitation and, for governments, they are immanent and not external.

A connected proposition would be this: on empirical grounds, given the number of civil wars, wars of secession and *coups d'état* since—let us say—1945, a good case can be made out for saying that public international law is *more* efficacious than *public* law within States. At any rate, whether or not such a judgment is sustainable, those who would judge international law would do well, on grounds of logical consistency, to start out by taking a hard look at the performance of *national* legal systems. It is a striking fact that in discussion of the efficacy of sanctions directed at the Smith regime in Rhodesia after U.D.I. it was common for reference to be made to the 'ineffectiveness' of United Nations resolutions. In this context it was unusual to hear reference to the efficacy of the Southern Rhodesia Act of 1965 and the law of treason as applicable in Rhodesia. Logically the Westminster *grundnorm* was as much in issue as the New York *grundnorm*.

Indeed, within States a fair degree of common sense prevails in assessing the performance of law. It does not seem sensible to say, for example, that because the rule of law is weak in Northern Ireland, and murders occur continuously, we can conclude that the law of the United Kingdom is not a reality. That kind of logic involves saying that if an ideal score of one hundred is not achieved any other lesser score is not to be counted.

There is a second inescapable feature of the political landscape. International law is essentially a law *between* States and this remains true in spite of the appearance of various international organizations and the significance of human rights standards. There is no world State. Thus even if the assumption be made that a world federal State or whatever is a desirable goal, since State law will be more effective, then the whole question of the efficacy of international law would become moot if such a global State were formed. In other words, the Austinian 'command theorist' can only be satisfied on the terms that the experiment is set aside. In passing it may be asked whether public order in a world federal State would be necessarily enhanced. At least it would as a matter of terminology: a 'war' between India and Pakistan would be described as 'provincial civil strife' in the region of South Asia, which is as good as describing 'the poor' as 'the less well off'.

The general problem has other facets. Perhaps the key to the whole discussion is the proposition that legality is indivisible. The bizarre goings-on which we usually describe as serious breaches of international law'—genocide, hostage-taking, various other breaches of human rights—are the product of government policies as such. The Watergate affair involved a decision to use methods, previously employed against foreign political targets, against political groups at home. At the less dramatic level the dumping of oil at sea in breach of treaty standards is the consequence of the relative inefficacy of domestic law in enforcing those treaty standards. The protection of the environment and much of the protection of human rights depend upon the application of standards *within the national legal and administrative systems*. Probably the biggest single obstacle to treaty enforcement is the inability of national administrations in many countries to cope with even a minimal burden. Once again it is perhaps the case that international legality is more readily primed than internal legality simply because international relations are for the most part conditioned by reciprocity. Thus it appears that the growth of legality in China, such as it is, has been quicker in respect of those matters relating to commercial law, foreign trade and treatment of foreigners generally.

Both legal systems, international and domestic, exhibit cases of what may be called the discretion not to prosecute. Within the United Kingdom the more striking examples include the non-prosecution of the Ulster conspiracy in 1912–13, the readiness to negotiate with Ian Smith and his fellow conspirators and the aftermath of the revelations of breaches of Rhodesian sanctions contained in the Bingham Report. It is a delicate matter to provide parallel cases in international relations. The failure to condemn the Indian intervention at the independence of Bangladesh or the Tanzanian intervention to overthrow Idi Amin may be appropriate as examples, and some would instance the attitude of most governments to the Entebbe operation by Israeli forces.

The fact is that legal and political systems from time to time face situations in which the positive way forward involves amnesty and a healing of social wounds rather than the inflexible application of the law. The example of the policy of the Nigerian Government after the defeat of the Biafrans deserves notice as a model of peaceful reconciliation and the avoidance of revenge.

In national life the law is not expected to cover all events; by a paradox in international relations almost every event, including large areas of administrative activity, is considered to be classifiable as lawful or unlawful. Much of what is considered to be a 'part of international law'—the constitutions of international organizations, the standards and recommendations of such organizations—is in reality to an extent the functional counterpart of administration in national systems. Many treaties are concerned with the statement of agreed policies and programmes or constitute promises of particular performances: they are part of a process of dealing and not much more. A major source of confusion in international law lies in the overlap between the concept of State responsibility (or the concept of delict) and the notion of the *ultra vires* act. In other words, many cases of illegal behaviour on the part of States are really the equivalent of the *ultra vires* act by a public body or minister which is not also a tort. The constant outcome is an inflation of the concept and incidence of illegality in international life.

This apparent inflation of illegality on the plane of international relations has a further dimension. Reference to international law, not only by laymen but also by lawyers, has become a sloppy and shorthand way of stating the need for effective regulation of major problems such as the control and reduction of armaments, the protection of the environment, the conservation and allocation of resources and so forth. The crude truth is that the law is not a substitute for the political will of States in facing problems on a basis of co-operation. The constant reference to the alleged inadequacies of the law, as though it were an unsuccessful and isolated totem, is unhelpful and ensures that the fire of criticism is directed to the wrong quarter.

Against this background, what may be called the question of the effectiveness of international law can be addressed. At some risk of stating the obvious it is worth creating a realistic perspective. A government seeks the advice of a lawyer outside its own legal staff. Governments may be assumed to know their own business and they frequently decide that they need advice on international law matters. The issue of effectiveness *tout court* of the law simply does not come up. A high proportion of officials have not heard of Austin, Salmond, Kelsen, Hart or Dworkin. Whilst this may be an intellectual loss to those officials, the conduct of State business goes forward in the absence of conceptual or jurisprudential doubt. There is no reason to think that even those who have heard of the legal philosophers allow their knowledge to impede the progress of business.

There is another aspect of the subject which lies completely outside the framework of thinking within the category of effectiveness. In certain important areas of international affairs the terms and categories of international law provide the syntax, the very fabric, of the subjects concerned. This is true particularly of the law of the sea. In practical terms a marine biologist acting as general watchdog for his firm's interests must understand the law of the sea. The law has similarly become stitched into the subject of human rights, the question of sovereignty (or title) in respect of territory and international monetary transactions. Moreover, certain important aspects of planning by naval staffs are informed by legal considerations, more especially in the context of low-level coercion and the drafting of the rules of engagement for naval commanders. In all these contexts the law, so to speak, sets the scene and provides the contours of the landscape of decision-making. The law is thus not external, coercive and alien but internal, logically necessary and familiar.

So far, apart from an apparently philistine reference to the fact that many officials do not know much about jurisprudence, at least as it is known in Anglo-American law schools, the question of how we define 'law' has been avoided. In a sense this question is supernumerary. If States use international law, and they do, then it seems impertinent to question the classification of the rules, since even if governments have made some error (according to *academic* categories) the rules still exist and have to be examined. However, by way of concession, an excursion into jurisprudence, a tactical strike, will be carried out.

The usual approach to law as a phenomenon is to seek a definition of law or something called 'positive law'. Thus Holland[1] proposes the following: 'A law, in the proper sense of the term, is therefore a general rule of human action, taking cognisance only of external acts, enforced by a determinate authority, which authority is human, and, among human authorities, is that which is paramount in a political society.' This resembles the Austinian view of law as a coercive order.

Fashions and the methods of legal science change. Today, against the background of a literature offering a variety of definitions, writers are more cautious and do not try to offer a 'definition of *a* law' or of 'law'.

Thus Hart in *The Concept of Law*, published in 1961, is concerned to isolate a *concept* and not to offer a *definition*. Hart gives two specific qualities of the concept:

(i) the existence of both primary and secondary rules; the former type are laws concerning human actions and accidents of the usual kind, the latter are concerned with conferring powers and helping to identify those competent to make, and change, the primary rules;

[1] *The Elements of Jurisprudence* (1st edn., 1880), p. 41.

(ii) The existence of an ultimate *rule of recognition* which provides the particular system of rules with its criteria of validity, in other words, a rule which specifies the sources of valid rules.

This approach is more empirical and more fruitful than the search for a 'definition' and yet the methodology is not dramatically different. The basic assumption is that *the* concept of law awaits identification if only the incorrect views of the Austinians are discarded. Law is presented as a concept which has some special qualities and its own integrity.

This assumption seems to me to be in its own way as restrictive as the prescribing of some neat definition. It tends to inhibit examination of the enormous number of social roles which quantities called 'law' have in fact played. The study of law as a phenomenon is presented as a search for a species of butterfly which, it is believed, has certain characteristics, though it has not yet been found. Butterflies noticed during the search are ignored as not corresponding to the model searched for. When a butterfly is found which for a while is thought to correspond to the model then others noticed are *ex hypothesi* of no account.

In other words, the Hart approach is an example of *a priorism* and over-simplification, all the more influential because it refers to a *concept* of law and proceeds from a writer of authority and sophistication. So in his opening chapter Hart is already referring to the 'clear standard cases' constituted by the legal systems of 'modern states',[1] which are contrasted with the 'doubtful cases' exemplified by 'primitive law' and international law. In this way he partitions his material at the outset of his study and, it would seem, decides to rely on a certain type of political framework as offering the evidence for conclusions on law in general.

Like Austin, Hart offers views related primarily to the way things are ordered in the more developed modern States. In adopting this type of presentation, and in coming to the conclusions about law referred to earlier, Hart relies on conceptions which do not derive from an empirical study of the evidence. In a university setting the highly generalized study of law within a jurisprudence syllabus leads easily to the assumption that one is dealing with a concept, a logical whole, a system of norms and so on. Moreover, the analyst and philosopher, eager to make law respectable in terms of other disciplines, and to make it fit into his particular intellectual system, is inevitably drawn to the abstract presentation. But, socially and politically, it is difficult to believe that those in charge of even the more organized societies of recent times have been very conscious of law as a unitary concept or system, and as a system consisting of primary and secondary rules.

The elements of the abstract model of law offered by Hart are inextricably bound up with political and social quantities which have to be caricatured by him and others in order to be accommodated to the abstract model. Thus in a system in which rules by convention stand with other

[1] *The Concept of Law* (1961), p. 3.

kinds of rules, both common law and statute, as in the British Constitution, there is no neat 'ultimate rule of recognition' which provides an intellectual basis for a system of rules, but a complex state of political fact referred to compendiously as the law and custom of the constitution. Moreover, in many societies there is nothing which approximates to a single rule of recognition as a guide to the law-determining agencies. The rules of recognition may vary. Thus in Turkey and Iran modern city-based code law has at times marched with adherence to local custom and Koranic law by the peasant peoples of the provinces and the nomadic groups. Lack of social cohesion cuts across any notion of a unity of legal rules based on a system both known and accepted throughout the country concerned.

The highly political provenance of the secondary rules in the Hart model, i.e. the basic principles of the constitution detailing the competent law makers, means that to describe them as 'secondary rules' is to adopt a level of abstraction which is unhelpful. Thus some secondary rules, for example, the principle of parliamentary sovereignty in the United Kingdom, may be much more significant than others similarly classified.

Of especial importance is the fact that the operation of the secondary rules may break down without affecting the operation of the primary rules to any great extent, or at all. Civil strife may place the secondary rules in jeopardy and possibly change them, yet during the time when the political foundations are being remade there is generally no legal vacuum—acts in the law of the ordinary sort are valid; there is no moratorium for crime and even after a change of sovereignty there is no moratorium on ordinary crime as opposed to political crime committed in the territory prior to the change.

The work of Hart and others avoids the cruder aspects of the notion that legal rules operate as coercive orders from particular human beings received and obeyed by the population at large. However, the intellectual conception of law with its emphasis on rules of recognition shares some of the mechanical oddities of the notion of coercive orders, since it assumes that law operates in a community of well-tutored individuals receptive to a particular system of norms. Yet it is obvious that populations do not see law in this way and it is a fact that a large section of a population may take note of secondary rules, and thus primary rules as well, laid down by rival authorities, for example, a separatist movement, a militant church at odds with the civil authority or tribal custom which runs contrary to the code of law of the central administration. Law is relative to the social order of things, and the reasons for its effectiveness are not to be referred to a single notion of obedience or of appreciation of the validity of norms according to a central principle.

The general emphasis on secondary rules and reference to compulsory jurisdiction of courts and a legislature as the normal marks of a legal system lead Hart to give a low, or at any rate abnormal, status to public international law among other systems.[1] The lack of a compulsory jurisdiction and a legislature is regarded by Hart not as the special feature of a system which operates in conditions of a certain kind, but as the marks of an outcast, of a butterfly which is not wanted for the pre-determined collection. Yet as we have already said, the stability of international relations compares quite well with internal law, given the grand total of municipal systems ruptured by civil strife since 1945. And whilst it may be said that international law lacks secondary rules, this matters less if one accepts the view that secondary rules do not play such a decisive role in maintaining the more basic forms of legality in municipal systems.

With all its faults, international law is the best tool available for dealing with the affairs of States. On the evidence the law provides a more practical basis for approaching international problems and the settlement of disputes than, for example, natural law in its various forms, Islamic jurisprudence, the principles of socialist internationalism, or so-called 'equity'.

A persistent feature of the debate about the effectiveness of international law is the tendency to pursue the argument in terms of jurisprudence, or otherwise in more or less abstract terms. The legal theorists have to an extent dictated the terms of the debate and this is unfortunate for a number of reasons. The legal philosophers, with few exceptions, are unacquainted with international law. Certainly they lack knowledge of its practical applications. Thus there is much theorizing, usually on the basis of testing the law of nations against criteria which are thought to be characteristic of domestic legal systems, and not enough examination of the vast array of evidence of the actual role of international law, both in the routine stewardship of State affairs and also in more strenuous political circumstances. As it has been suggested above, if a government official considers that the legal aspects must be carefully taken into account in the process of decision-making, then to an important extent, the law has a significant role and is thus 'effective'. Whether in a given situation the law is ultimately 'effective' is a question of taste, in other words it is a matter of political and moral evaluation. When the law is seen to be 'ineffective', the cause is not 'the law' but the absence of organization, political will, sufficient personnel or funding, and so forth. Law, whether national or international, is not a source of alibis for politicians and administrators.

[1] See *The Concept of Law*, chapter X.

[7]

GLOBAL ECONOMICS AND INTERNATIONAL ECONOMIC LAW

*by John H. Jackson**

INTRODUCTION

It is commonplace to comment on the extraordinary evolution of international economic activities towards linkages and interdependence, and the stress which these developments are putting upon existing economic and governmental institutions, both national and international. This article tentatively explores these circumstances in the context of some of the fundamental theoretical and policy thinking about international economic affairs today, reflecting on the role of law and institutions in those affairs, and in turn on the potential contribution of legal and multidisciplinary scholarship to those affairs and the theories and policies which shape them.

1. THE GLOBAL ECONOMIC LANDSCAPE AND IMPLICATIONS OF INTERDEPENDENCE: OF STOCK MARKETS, BANANAS, AND PUMPKINS

It surprises few people today to see comments about the profound and growing extent of international economic interdependence and linkages. The causes of these developments are numerous: incredible advances in efficiency of communication, extraordinary reductions in transport costs, growing prevalence of instant tele and cyber transactions, treaty and other norms causing reduction of governmental barriers to trade, an economic climate more favourable to principles of markets economics, cross-border influences of competition which have driven increases in production and service efficiencies, and last but not least: the blessing of relative peace in the world.

Manifestations of this 'globalization' abound: stock market trends that flow quickly around the world; impacts of national government monetary and fiscal decisions; effects of fraud within certain banking or other financial enterprises; worries about health and safety of products moving across borders such as foodstuffs, pharmaceuticals, machinery, appliances; effects of

* John H. Jackson is University Professor of Law of Georgetown University Law Center, and Hessel E. Yntema Professor of Law Emeritus, University of Michigan Law School, Ann Arbor, Michigan. Consistent with the policy of the journal, indicated in the journal's preliminary pages, this article represents only the views of its author, and these views are not to be taken as representing the views of the Board of Editors of the *Journal of International and Economic Law* or of Oxford University Press.

governmental mismanagement and sometimes corruption; worries about the power of non-government and private enterprises and their capacity in some cases to operate on the global economy while largely ignoring particular national governmental regulatory protections; and flows of 'cultural' influences involving various media often moving swiftly with new communication techniques to transmit music or drama across borders (with substantial economic implications and other effects, even to cause a new taste in Paris for halloween pumpkins!). A road-map of the various links and cause-effects of a multitude of economic actions becomes an impenetrable maze of pathways, commonly without clear guidebooks to assist their understanding.

Almost every conceivable type of government economic regulation now must take account of the international and competitive implications of its activity, and often national government officials feel frustrated at their relative inability to control economic forces that vitally affect their constituents and prevent fulfilment of official goals and promises on behalf of their constituents. Sometimes governments are tempted to utilize their power to influence economic forces to benefit better their own constituents at the expense of other societies (a beggar-thy-neighbour approach). In some of these cases competition among governments to capture such benefits can result in damaging the welfare of all participants – a phenomenon suggesting a 'prisoner's dilemma' analysis. One astute experienced political leader has said, 'All politics is local'.[1] But another astute economic writer has noted, 'All economics is international'.[2] When juxtaposed, these pithy comments reflect some of the policy dilemmas with which political leaders must grapple.

In recent years, particularly, as the cold war and its threat of major disaster seems to have receded, there has been much discussion and speech-making about the shifting emphasis from 'geo-politics' to 'geo-economics' (or some would say to the game of 'geo-monopoly'). News media attention has begun to refocus on economic matters, with front page attention given to international trade, legislative initiatives relating to trade, problems of food safety, World Trade Organization (WTO) cases about bananas, the activity of financial institutions such as the World Bank or the International Monetary Fund (IMF), and many other economic subjects relating to investment, competition policy, etc. Scholarly efforts and governmental policy studies have also been giving increased attention to the problems mentioned above. Nevertheless, the careful observer is struck by how much we do not know, and how often scholarship and studies seem only to repeat the obvious or emphasize advocacy of preconceived positions or struggle without adequate

[1] See Tip O'Neill and Gary Hymel, All Politics is Local (1994).

[2] Peter F. Drucker, Trade Lessons from the World Economy, Foreign Affairs, January/February 1994, page 99.

empirical data on which to make judgments.[3] Very high government officials have been known to disparage solidly accepted economic wisdom or make statements about legal norms that are misleading or plain wrong. It seems clear to this observer that there is great need and opportunity for reflective scholarly attention to many different systemic and 'constitutional' issues about our globalized economy.

The degree to which treaties and international law now appear to 'intrude' on national and subfederal government decision-making seems to support the statements made above. Governments sometimes feel hemmed in, and sometimes object that they cannot take action sought even by their democratic constituencies. The North American Free Trade Agreement (NAFTA) in some respects went very far in its measures seeking national government changes arguably necessary to fulfil the NAFTA international obligations. This was true for the NAFTA investor protection rules, and also in relation to environment and labour standards.[4] World Trade Organization provisions, perhaps particularly those in the intellectual property agreement[5] which require governments to fulfil certain standards regarding their court systems, and also some of the detailed agreements relating to services (especially financial services or telecommunications),[6] appear to insert their rules quite deeply into national legal systems. Of course, one answer to at least some of the criticisms of international rules which operate to constrain governments, is that the global market forces already constrain governments, and sometimes in ways which are not as healthy as the negotiated treaty text.

The remaining parts of this article will explore some particular facets of the problems outlined above. Part 2 will note the importance which significant thinkers and theorists attach to human institutions and the role of legal rules associated with such institutions.

Part 3 will look at the meaning of the phrase 'international economic law', noting some of the dimensions of such a subject title, and some of the difficulties for policy, theoretical, and scholarly work focusing on this subject. Part 4 will then look at some traditional market economic concepts regarding the role of government action (presumably to enhance the effective working of markets) and suggest how these concepts are affected by globalization and the legal rules of international institutions.

Part 5 will briefly reflect on some attributes and activities of existing international economic institutions, with a focus on the newest and arguably the most important of these, namely the WTO (although most of the discussion

3 See, for example, papers delivered at a conference at Harvard University Center for Business and Government, October 1995 on 'World Trade and Services', which discuss the lack of accurate empirical information concerning trade in services.

4 North American Free Trade Agreement, entered into force 1 January 1994. See especially chapters 11 and 18, as well as the NAFTA Side Agreements on Labour and Environment.

5 See WTO Annex 1C: Agreement on Trade-Related Aspects of Intellectual Property Rights.

6 World Trade Organization (note 8) Annex 1C (TRIPS) and 1B (Services).

could easily apply to other international economic organizations). Finally, Part 6 will examine some of the thinking about future directions of the world trading system and its constitution, and reflect on the implications of those for scholarship on subjects embraced within the broad topic of 'international economic law'.

Throughout these parts, however, there is at least one common focus for the discussions found in this article. This is the notion that we are dealing with a form of 'constitutional law', involving in this area the broad concept of 'constitution' going considerably beyond a written document, and embracing a variety of interconnected governmental institutions as well as evolving practice of many such institutions. The focus is truly the 'world trading system', and its legal framework – that which we can here call the 'constitution'.

2. MARKETS AND GOVERNMENTS AND THE ROLE OF LAW

Whether economic policies which are based on market principles[7] are the best approach for maximizing human satisfaction is, of course, controversial. Various alternatives have been much debated, and many of those largely rejected, but substantial arguments are made in favour of some sort of mixture of policies, perhaps to temper the perceived negative effects of 'too pure market approaches'. Whatever mixture may appeal to certain societies, however, it seems reasonably clear that markets can be very beneficial,[8] and even when not beneficial, market forces demand respect and can cause great difficulties when not respected.[9]

Yet even when stressing the benefits of market economics, important thinkers note the importance of human institutions which guide and shape markets. Two Nobel Prize winning economists stress this proposition. Ronald Coase has stated:[10]

> It is evident that, for their operation, markets . . . require the establishment of legal rules governing the rights and duties of those carrying out transactions . . . To realize all the gains from trade, . . . there has to be a legal system and political order . . . Economic policy consists of choosing those legal rules, procedures and administrative structures which will maximize the value of production. . . .

More recently Douglas North said:[11]

[7] See Richard Lipsey, Paul Courant, Douglas Purvis, and Peter Steiner, Microeconomics (10th edn, 1993); Avinash K. Dixit and Barry J. Nalebuff, Thinking Strategically (1991); Max Corden, Trade Policy and Economic Welfare (1974); Peter B. Kenen, The International Economy (1994); Paul Krugman, International Economics: Theory and Policy (1994).

[8] For an overview of the economic principles which support policies of liberal international trade rules, see in this issue the article by Alan Sykes.

[9] See, e.g., James Flanigan, Turmoil is Free Market Watershed, Los Angeles Times, 29 October 1997, page 1 Home Edition.

[10] Ronald Coase, The Firm, the Market and the Law (reprint of 1960 article) ch. 5. Note, see also C.A.E. Goodhart, Economics and the Law: Too Much One-Way Traffic? (1997) 60 MLR 1.

[11] Douglas C. North, Institutions, Institutional Change and Economic Performance (1990).

> That institutions affect the performance of economics is hardly controversial. . . . Institutions reduce uncertainty by providing a structure to everyday life. . . . Institutions affect the performance of the economy by their effect on the costs of exchange and production.

Human institutions embrace many structures and take many forms, but it is very clear that law and legal norms play the most important part of the institutions which are essential to make markets work. The notion that 'rule of law' (ambiguous as that phrase is) or a rule-based or rule-oriented system of human institutions is essential to a beneficial operation of markets, is a constantly recurring theme in many writings.

With respect to international economics, the world is fortunate to have the advantage of institutions such as the Bretton Woods system (including the General Agreement on Tariffs and Trade, GATT) established through the vision of statesmen, scholars and diplomats at the end of World War II. At least some of the credit for relative peace and economic growth of the past half century goes to those institutions and their rules.[12] And now, of course, we have a major new organization established on 1 January 1995 in our landscape of economic institutions, namely, the WTO, with an extraordinarily elaborate set of rules.

A critical question almost always asked by anyone confronted with an international law rule is 'Why do they matter?' Put another way, there exists much cynicism about the importance or effectiveness of international law rules. Frequently the public can read news of violations of such rules by major and minor nations. In some cases such violations, even when admitted to be such (often there is bitter and inconclusive argument on this question), are rationalized or declared 'just' by national leaders. Thus the cynicism about international rules cannot be surprising.

A more careful examination of the role and effectiveness of international rules is necessary, however. First, it should be observed that not all domestic rules are always obeyed either. Yet there are many international rules which are remarkably well observed. Why this is so has been the subject of much speculation[13] which will not be repeated here. Notions of reciprocity and a desire to depend on other nations' observance of rules lead many nations to observe rules even when they do not want to.

At least in the context of economic behaviour, however, and particularly when that behaviour is set in circumstances of decentralized decision-making, as in a market economy, rules can have important operational functions. They may provide the only predictability or stability to a potential

[12] John H. Jackson, World Trade and the Law of GATT (1969) ch. 2. At least some credit for over 50 years of relative peace (avoiding a World War III) can be attributed to reasonably successful activities of the International Monetary Fund and the World Bank.

[13] See Louis Henkin, How Nations Behave (2nd edn 1979); Roger Fisher, Improving Compliance With International Law (1981) at 12–16; Abram Chayes, The New Sovereignty: Compliance with International Regulatory Agreements (1995).

investment or trade–development situation. Without such predictability or stability, trade or investment flows might be even more risky and therefore more inhibited than otherwise. If such 'liberal trade' goals contribute to world welfare, then it follows that rules which assist such goals should also contribute to world welfare. To put it another way, the policies which tend to reduce some risks, lower the 'risk premium' required by entrepreneurs to enter into international transactions. This should result in a general increase in the efficiency of various economic activities, contributing to greater welfare for everyone.

Assuming then that institutions are important, and that law plays a significant role in those institutions, what legal principles can we identify that play such a role? Obviously this can be a vast subject, certainly ripe for scholarly and policy attention of various kinds for years to come. But perhaps one particular principle can here be mentioned, namely the value of a 'rule oriented' approach to design of international institutions relating to economic activity.[14]

The 'rule oriented approach' focuses the disputing parties' attention on the *rule*, and on predicting what an impartial tribunal is likely to conclude about the application of a rule. This in turn, will lead parties to pay closer attention to the rules of the treaty system, and this can lead to greater certainty and predictability which is essential in international affairs, particularly *economic* affairs driven by market oriented principles of decentralized decision making, with participation by millions of entrepreneurs. As noted above, such entrepreneurs need a certain amount of predictability and guidance so that they can make the appropriate efficient investment and market development decisions.[15]

The phrase 'rule orientation' is used here to contrast with phrases such as 'rule of law', and 'rule-based system'. Rule orientation implies a less rigid adherence to 'rule' and connotes some fluidity in rule approaches which seems to accord with reality (especially since it accommodates some bargaining or negotiation). Phrases that emphasize too strongly the strict application of rules sometimes scare policy-makers, although in reality they may amount to the same thing. Any legal system must accommodate the inherent ambiguities of rules and the constant changes of the practical needs of human society. The key point is that the procedures of rule application, which often centre on a dispute settlement procedure, should be designed so as to promote as much as possible the stability and predictability of the rule system. For this purpose the procedure must be creditable, 'legitimate', and reasonably efficient (not easy criteria).

For example, suppose countries A and B have a trade dispute regarding

[14] See, e.g., John H. Jackson, The World Trading System (1997) at 109; John H. Jackson, The WTO Constitution and Jurisprudence (forthcoming in 1998) ch 4.

[15] See e.g., Douglas North, above n. 12.

B's treatment of imports from A to B of widgets. One technique would involve a negotiation between A and B by which the most powerful of the two would have the advantage. Foreign aid, military manoeuvres, or import restrictions on other key goods by way of retaliation would figure in the negotiation. A small country would hesitate to challenge a large one on whom its trade depends. Implicit or explicit threats (e.g., to impose quantitative restrictions on some other product) would be a major part of the technique employed. Domestic political influences would probably play a greater part in the approach of the respective negotiators in this system, particularly on the negotiator for the more powerful party.

On the other hand, a second technique suggested – reference to agreed rules – would see the negotiators arguing about the application of the rule (e.g., was B obligated under a treaty to allow free entry of A's goods in question?). During the process of negotiating a settlement it would be necessary for the parties to understand that an unsettled dispute would ultimately be resolved by impartial third-party judgments based on the rules so that the negotiators would be negotiating with reference to their respective predictions as to the outcome of those judgments and not with reference to potential retaliation or actions by the exercising of the power of one or more of the parties to the dispute.

In both techniques negotiation and settlement of disputes is the dominant mechanism for resolving differences; but the key is the perception of the participants as to what are the 'bargaining chips'. Insofar as agreed rules for governing the economic relations between the parties exist, a system which predicates negotiation on the implementation of those rules would seem, for a number of reasons, to be preferred. The mere existence of the rules, however, is not enough. When the issue is the application or interpretation of those rules (rather than the formulation of new rules), it is necessary for the parties to believe that if their negotiations reach an impasse the settlement mechanisms which take over for the parties will be designed to fairly apply or interpret the rules. If no such system exists, then the parties are left basically to rely upon their respective 'power positions', tempered (it is hoped) by the good will and good faith of the more powerful party (cognizant of its long-range interests).

As the world becomes more economically interdependent, more and more private citizens find their jobs, their businesses, and their quality of life affected, if not controlled, by forces from outside their own country's boundaries. Thus they are more affected by the economic policy pursued by their own country on their behalf. In addition, the relationships become increasingly complex – to the point of being incomprehensible to even the brilliant human mind. As a result, citizens assert themselves, at least within a democracy, and require their representatives and government officials to respond to their needs and their perceived complaints. The result of this is increasing citizen participation, and more parliamentary or congressional participation

8 *Journal of International Economic Law 1 (1998) 1–23*

in the processes of international economic policy, thus restricting the degree of power and discretion which the executive possesses.

This makes international negotiations and bargaining increasingly difficult. However, if citizens are going to make their demands heard and influential, a 'power-oriented' negotiating process (often requiring secrecy, and executive discretion so as to be able to formulate and implement the necessary compromises) becomes more difficult, if not impossible. Consequently, the only appropriate way to turn seems to be toward a rule-oriented system, whereby the various citizens, Parliaments, executives and international organizations will all have their inputs, arriving tortuously at a rule which, however, when established will enable business and other decentralized decision-makers to rely upon the stability and predictability of governmental activity in relation to the rule.[16]

The degree of desired flexibility for rules is a subject discussed by important writers, sometimes with a suggestion that certain rules be raised to 'constitutional status' and embedded in national legal systems.[17]

With these 'policy building blocks' in mind, we can now turn to several other dimensions of the subject of international economic law.

3. UNDERSTANDING INTERNATIONAL ECONOMIC LAW

It is appropriate to ask what we mean by 'international economic law'. This phrase can cover a very broad inventory of subjects: embracing the law of economic transactions; government regulation of economic matters; and related legal relations including litigation and international institutions for economic relations. Indeed, it is plausible to suggest that 90 per cent of international law work is in reality international economic law in some form or another. Much of this, of course, does not have the glamour or visibility of nation-state relations (use of force, human rights, intervention etc.), but does indeed involve many questions of international law and particularly treaty law. Increasingly, today's international economic law (IEL) issues are found on the front pages of the daily newspapers.[18]

To some extent IEL can be divided into two broad approaches which cut across most of the subjects embraced by IEL. These approaches can roughly

[16] Adapted from John H. Jackson, 'Governmental Disputes in International Trade Relations: A Proposal in the Context of GATT', 13 J World Trade Law 3–4 (1979) and John H. Jackson, 'The Crumbling Institutions of the Liberal Trade System', 12 J World Trade Law 98–101 (1978); John H. Jackson, The World Trading System (2nd edn 1997).

[17] See, e.g., Ernst-Ulrich Petersmann, Constitutional Functions and Constitutional Problems of International Economic Law (1991). Professor Petersmann has also written profoundly on this theme in some of his other numerous writings. See also articles in this issue by Petersmann and Cottier.

[18] A more elaborate version of some of these thoughts are expressed in the following article: John H. Jackson, 'International Economic Law: Reflections on the "Boilerroom" of International Relations', 10 Am U J Int'l Law Policy 595–606 (1995).

be termed 'transactional' or 'regulatory'. Both have their place, but activities of research and policy formulation can be substantially different, and should be understood.

Transactional IEL refers to transactions carried out in the context of international trade or other economic activities, and focuses on the way mostly private entrepreneurs or other parties carry out their activity. Much of the literature, for example, is descriptive. It can be valuable as instruction for potential players, to show 'how to do it', and warn against pitfalls. It can also go further and make suggestions for change.

Regulatory IEL, however, emphasizes the role of government institutions (national, local or international). Although it can be argued that the international trade transaction is the most government regulated of all private economic transactions (usually requiring at least a report for each transaction, e.g., a customs declaration), nevertheless, most traditional attention to IEL has been focused, perhaps for practical and pragmatic reasons, on transactions. Yet arguably in today's world the real challenges for understanding IEL and its impact on governments and private citizens' lives, suggest a focus on IEL as 'regulatory law', similar to domestic subjects such as tax, labour, anti-trust, and other regulatory topics.

But apart from its breadth, what are some of the characteristics of IEL which, for example, might affect the approach to it of scholars or policymakers? The following are some tentative ventures to explore these characteristics, but they are obviously by no means complete.

(1) International economic law can not be separated or compartmentalized from general or 'public' international law. The activities and cases relating to IEL contain much practice which is relevant to general principles of international law, especially concerning treaty law and practice. Conversely, general international law has considerable relevance to economic relations and transactions. It is interesting, for example, to compare the number of cases handled by the GATT dispute settlement system (approximately 250)[19] to those handled by the World Court (approaching 100). Numbers do not tell the whole tale, but there certainly are some GATT cases that have had as profound consequences on national governments and world affairs as have International Court of Justice (ICJ) cases. The GATT cases are rich with practice relating to the general question of international dispute resolution, and some of this practice has broader implications than simply for the GATT (and now WTO) system itself.

(2) The relationship of international economic law to national or 'municipal' law is particularly important. It is an important part of understanding international law generally, but this 'link', and the interconnections between IEL and municipal law are particularly significant to the operation and

[19] See Robert Hudec, Enforcing International Trade Law: The Evolution of the Modern GATT Legal System (1993) at 417–585 (indexing 207 GATT complaints from July 1948 to November 1989).

effectiveness of IEL rules. For example, an important question is the relationship of treaty norms to municipal law, expressed by such phrases as 'self executing' or 'direct application'.[20]

(3) As the title phrase 'international economic law' suggests, there is necessarily a strong component of multidisciplinary research and thinking required for those who work on IEL projects. Of course, 'economics' is important and useful, especially for understanding the policy motivations of many of the international and national rules on the subject. Obviously, it is just as important to understand some of the criticisms of economic analysis, and to treat with scepticism some of the economic 'models'. Likewise, there are alternative value structures which should balance some economic notions of 'efficiency'. Thus, various lifestyle choices and certain long-range value objectives can at least appear, and perhaps be contradictory to some economic objectives, as some of those economic objectives are phrased by certain writers.

In addition to economics, of course, other subjects are highly relevant. Political science (and its intersection with economics found generally in the 'public choice' literature) is very important, as are many other disciplines, such as cultural history and anthropology, geography etc.

(4) Work on IEL matters often seems to necessitate more empirical study than some other international law subjects. Empirical research, however, does not necessarily mean statistical research, in the sense used in many policy explorations. For some key issues of international law there are too few 'cases' on which to base statistical conclusions (such as correlations), so we are constrained to use a more 'anecdotal' or case study approach. This type of empiricism, however, is nevertheless very important, and a good check on theory or on sweeping generalizations of any kind. Since this often requires a study of particular cases, or at least of certain groups of cases, with considerable quantitative elements, it is frequently necessary to master a considerable amount of detail to understand some of the interplay of forces affecting international economic relations and the law concerning those relations.

(5) Another characteristic of IEL, or at least of the problems of research and producing scholarship about IEL, is that, like many subjects of international relations, there is often a substantial problem with obtaining information. Diplomatic habits and sometimes legitimate needs of governments for confidentiality can impose special burdens on scholars, although in recent years a variety of special information sources, such as focused newsletters and internet sites, have ameliorated some of these burdens.

[20] See John H. Jackson, 'Status of Treaties in Domestic Legal Systems: A Policy Analysis', 86 Am J Int'l Law 310 (1993) (examining policy issues concerning the relationship between international treaties and domestic law); see also Thomas Cottier, 'The Relationship of WTO Law, National and Regional Law' in this issue.

(6) As the subjects of international economics became more central to government policy decisions and studies, these subjects also became more prominent in the news media and more deeply interconnected with political groups and agenda. Of course, historically there have been periods of intense public debate about international economic policies such as tariffs, or 'anti-dumping' and unfair trade arguments.[21] But with a post-cold war shift to 'geo-economics' and with developing fears among certain citizen groups about the influence of globalization on their personal and family well being[22] the 'politization' of international economic policy issues, and therefore of legal issues related to them, has led to various studies by different groups on IEL issues (such as those involved in the debate about the 'fast track' procedure with respect to the USA's treaty-making rules involving the US Congress).[23] These competing studies, sometimes with vastly different conclusions, obviously pose risks to the careful scholar.

What does all this imply for research? Clearly it influences the selection of priorities for research and successfully carrying out IEL research. Empiricism, multidisciplinary approaches, and the breadth of legal understanding to relate not only general international law principles with IEL, but also both with national constitutional and other law, create quite a burden.

In some cases (maybe most) it would seem preferable to shape research so as to be useful for the 'active users', the legal professionals (government or private) who must regularly cope with international law concepts and legal rules. This is a 'policy research' preference rather than a 'theory' preference, although obviously there are many situations in which theory has important relevance to policy. But such theory needs to be 'good theory', and normally good theory must be tested, usually by empirical observation.

4. REGULATING CROSS-BORDER ECONOMIC ACTIVITY

Earlier sections of this article noted the very broad range of subjects related to IEL, and hinted at the problems facing governments who wish to regulate economic activity to achieve a wide variety of government objectives. Almost daily the news media suggest new or recurring problems of this type. The recent case of an airline merger involving Boeing and MacDonald Douglas is an example of potential problems for nation-states attempting to regulate anti-trust and competition policy.[24] Tainted foodstuff imports is

[21] For example, discussion about the Smoot-Hawley Tariff Act of 1930, and debate in 1948–51 about an International Trade Organization (ITO).

[22] Debates during the May 1997 French Elections, and the 1994 debate in the USA on WTO acceptance come to mind.

[23] See, e.g., numerous news articles in the USA during October and November 1997.

[24] See, e.g., Teresa Wyszomierski and Christopher Lingle, 'Lessons of the Boeing Merger', *The Journal of Commerce* 29 July 1997 at 8.

another example.[25] The international 'breakthrough' in early 1997 regarding a telecommunications international agreement is yet another example[26] as is the banking crisis in Asia and various response attempts (often focusing on IMF activity).

In the financial services area, we also have to worry much more about problems of fiduciary relationships, prudential protections of consumers, fraud, reminding us of the BCCI case. Other subjects include environment regulation, continuing work on agricultural trade, product standards, consumer protection in its broader ramifications, securities regulation as we move into a 24-hour market. If you begin to push the frontier of the subject, you have to think also of such things as labour regulations, labour standards, and even human rights.

Indeed, almost every conceivable area of economic activity which for one reason or another attracted governmental concern and often regulation, is now impacted by actual or potential international regulation of one kind or another. Thus we need to step back and ask what are the common elements of these many specific topics and often ad hoc government responses? The fundamental subject appears to be the question of 'regulation of economic behaviour which crosses national borders'. How should policy-makers (and scholars) approach this broad question? Are there some general principles of government regulatory activity which could be applied in most or all situations involving cross-border economic behaviour? Can we develop some sort of general framework for policy analysis of this type? Here is a preliminary and tentative ('work in progress') attempt to do that.[27] These and many more questions can appropriately engage scholarly and policy-makers' attention for years to come.

Look first at typical economic analysis of regulation.[28] Generally speaking market-oriented economists talk about avoiding governmental interference, except when there is something called 'market failure'.

As to market failure, the most familiar and the most commonly reiterated in the economics literature are the problems of monopoly (competition policy); the problems of asymmetry of information (for instance, the consumer versus the expert sellers); the problems of government distortions for a

[25] See, e.g., Stephanie Nall, 'Meat Dispute Threatens to Spoil US–Europe Trade', *The Journal of Commerce* 27 March 1997 at 1; Stephanie Nall, 'EU, US Sling Charges, Threats at One Another', *The Journal of Commerce* 3 April 1997 at 1.

[26] See, e.g., John Zarocostas, 'US Urged to Back Telecom Accord' *The Journal of Commerce* 14 February 1997 at 1a.

[27] These thoughts are drawn partly from this author's following publications which may also interest the reader: John H. Jackson, Hyman Soloway Lecture: The Uruguay Round, World Trade Organization, and the Problem of Regulating International Economic Behaviour (1994) (published in 1995); John H. Jackson, 'Reflections on Constitutional Changes to the Global Trading System', 70 Chi Kent L Rev (1996) at 511.

[28] See, e.g., Richard Lipsey, Paul Courant, Douglas Purvis and Peter Steiner, Microeconomics (10th edn, 1993) especially Part 4.

variety of reasons (and those get very, very troublesome because there are many different valid policy reasons why governments step in that do not have to do with the functioning of the market, and yet they cause distortions in the market). There is also the public goods problem, where the market cannot adequately give incentive for the creation of things that the public needs, because there is the opportunity for the whole public to use it, or capture it, i.e., to 'free ride'. This is a subject, of course, that is very close to intellectual property questions. And there are questions which are related to some of the others just mentioned, such as the question of distributive justice, or other alternative policies of governments.

One of the interesting features of this fairly traditional economic analysis is that it is almost always developed in the context of a single domestic economy. We must now ask, 'What difference does it make that we are in the kind of international-linked world that we are in?'. Look first at monopoly, or competition policy. In some cases, you are really talking about a world economy; you are not talking about a national economy. And, so, that may change entirely your first judgment as to whether government intervention is necessary. For example, maybe there is a national monopoly, but, over time, borders have been thrown open to the product in such a way that the national monopoly really is no longer a market failure, because it has to struggle against the rest of the world. But, you can also see that the opposite conclusion is possible. It may be that things that do not look like they are a market failure domestically, when you look at or hypothesize a closed economy. However, when you move to the international system, because of various formal or informal linkages of various kinds, you may indeed find that there is market failure. And so, the international dimension of this creates the potential for different judgments on the question of whether we have the particular market failure or monopoly or competition policy questions.

Asymmetries of information is another case very ripe for difficulties enhanced by the international market. First of all, we have language differences worldwide, which makes it much harder for many persons to understand information. We have deep cultural differences where a 'yes' means 'no', a 'no' means 'maybe', and vice versa. We have a whole variety of factors: distance, different legal systems, the ability to enforce contracts in different ways, and so on. So, the asymmetries of information can give rise to many different conclusions, based on international activities.

Government distortions, of course, provide many possibilities. Are we beginning to face *international* government distortions? Are we beginning to face the regulations, for instance, of GATT, such as its textile system, as an illustration of how the international regulatory system begins to create distortions?

Public goods provide yet another set of market failure possibilities. There are many public goods in the worldwide *international* landscape. One is peace and security; peacekeeping in the United Nations, for instance. Another is human rights. There are certain broader values than just economic market-oriented values. Thus again the international landscape would lead us to a conclusion that the market is not able to cope in the way that we think that it ought to.

Distributive justice suggests a variety of policies within the scope of a domestic market progressive taxation, welfare, safety nets, a social market economy etc. But, internationally, of course, we have this problem also the developing countries argue for certain preferences. They argue for an international financial safety net, almost the equivalent of international bankruptcy.

So the next question is what should be the government response to market failure? In the economic literature, there are generally several kinds of responses that have been suggested – ways that governments can intervene. The government can tax. The government can subsidize. The government can regulate, create penalties for deviant behaviour of various kinds. The government can try to alter various market incentives, such as by creating a system of permits, for instance, that are purchased or bid for, to allow certain environmental degradation under certain systems.

However, some of the governmental responses suggested in the event of national market failure cannot easily be used in a globalized situation. How is a government going to tax foreign people? Suppose a domestic government tries to regulate but a foreign government sees an opportunity to assist its own business participants by lax regulations, a so-called 'race to the bottom' idea or 'regulatory competition'? Thus many of the tools for government responses will not work in the same way in a globalized situation. And that forces us to consider the problems of regulatory competition, 'race to the bottom' and downward harmonization, something that the environmentalists have warned about during the last few years. When one begins to analyse these situations, sometimes with the aid of game theory (particularly the so-called 'prisoners dilemma')[29], one is pushed towards *international* co-operation as a necessary ingredient for handling these issues.

However, there are arguments for and against such internationalization. Governments may or may not be acting in the best interests of their society because of the distortions of governmental policy that are sometimes described by public choice theories. For example, a government leader wants to be re-elected this autumn and therefore will not vote for a trade treaty. There is also a reverse side. An international institution can provide an additional buffer for national policy officials to make arguments in favour of the goals of an international institution. They can say that their nation is constrained by the international law and must obey these obligations.

[29] Avinash K. Dixit and Barry J. Nalebuff, Thinking Strategically (1991).

However, there are risks in international co-operative activity or international 'governance'. Some of those risks are in the institutional details, such as the danger of decision rules like 'consensus' that lead to the lowest common denominator approach that inhibits some countries from embracing higher standards concerning product safety or environmental considerations. There are situations where it is going to be very hard or impossible to achieve agreement because of the cultural differences and the economic diversities in the world. And we have to worry that some institutions can be abused, that when we yield 'sovereignty' to some institutions, we could find that down the road (as has been alleged in some of the existing international organizations) there is corruption or misallocation of resources, or a distortion of the voting patterns.

Economists teach us that trade liberalization creates more goods or more welfare for everyone overall, but you can not say that every particular person will be better off. There will be some winners and some losers. What do you do about the losers, particularly if they are disadvantaged? Who should bear adjustment costs? Beyond that clearly there are goals that are not so oriented towards economics, such as keeping the peace, which is an important element of international relations theory and international economic theory.[30] So we have to construct the institutions that will follow or mediate among these and other goals such as human rights, crime abatement, drug traffic reduction etc. These considerations thus pose various questions about whether the relevant international institutions are the appropriate place to resolve these issues.

Furthermore, even though globalization may affect a nation's decision as to 'market failure' and the need for government intervention, that does not necessarily lead to the desirability of international intervention. It could be that the market failure consequences are confined to the domestic economy, even though they have been partly caused or influenced by globalization effects. Or, it could be that national government action could effectively 'correct' the problem.

In a number of cases, the optimum approach could be some kind of international, or global, response, but the institution concerned may be weak, or so fraught with the potential abuse that on a cost–benefit analysis you decide that you really cannot choose that institution for certain decisions. You may have to fall back on national governments for intervention, because of the dangers, or risks, of the international system. Sometimes the international system is so rigid because it is difficult to renegotiate a treaty, for example, that once a measure is in place it is virtually impossible to amend it. We have seen elements of that in the GATT, and maybe now in the WTO.

[30] See Alan Sykes 'Comparative Advantage and the Normative Economics of International Trade Policy' in this issue.

When we look at the international intervention, there are a series of different possibilities. There are also regional or unilateral possibilities, such as the nation-state acting through extraterritorial measures, or US section 301-type measures, of threatened sanctions, or threatened retaliation.

Thus we must turn to the question of institution building, i.e., 'constitution-making', at the international level. There are goals for the institutions that we might need and some of these goals are addressed, for example, in the WTO. It is not clear that the WTO is going to be able to succeed with respect to all these goals, however, but they deserve some thought.

One important goal is the concept of a rule-oriented system that provides the predictability and stability for the system for which many see a need for a variety of reasons, as we have already discussed.

However, there are other things to consider, such as whether an institutional structure recognizes and gives some deference to the real power configurations, so as to lead powerful governments to accept and implement the rules and decisions of the institution.

Other institutional goals include participation of citizenry. We are clearly moving beyond elites in the conduct of international policy. The environmentalists again have begun to teach us about the necessity of having more open and more accessible procedures.[31]

In addition, there is the need for checks and balances. We have to be cautious about what we do institutionally and internationally in the regulatory area because we do not want the system to get out of hand. Often there is some confidence in national governments, and thus some worry about the delegation of 'sovereignty'. Perhaps there is a vestige of usefulness in the concept of 'sovereignty' when it is used to express the concept of checks and balances against too much concentration of power in an international institution.

In Part 6 of this article, this analysis is built on and certain alternative institutional approaches to designing the 'International Economic Constitution' explored.

5. EXISTING INTERNATIONAL ECONOMIC INSTITUTIONS: THE WORLD TRADE ORGANIZATION AND RULE ORIENTATION

The Bretton Woods Conference of 1944 established the charters for the World Bank (IBRD)[32] and the IMF. Participants at the 1944 conference recognized the need for a third institution for the subject of international trade, although they did not feel able at Bretton Woods to undertake a draft of that institution, partly because that conference was oriented toward monetary problems and was convened by and for the monetary authorities of the

[31] See, e.g., in this issue the article by Daniel Esty, NGO's at the World Trade Organization.

[32] International Bank for Reconstruction and Development (IBRD).

participating states rather than the trade authorities. Consequently one of the first tasks of the new United Nations and its Economic and Social Council (ECOSOC) in 1946 was to launch preparations for an International Trade Organization (ITO). But, as is well known, the ITO Charter (of Havana 1948) never came into force, because the United States Congress would not approve it.[33] Instead, the GATT, which for reasons partly relating to the constitutional structure of the USA[34] had come into 'provisional force', filled the gap left by the ITO failure, and became *de facto* the major trade treaty and institution for international trade relations and diplomacy.

Despite this uneasy history and the 'birth defects' of the GATT,[35] these institutions played a remarkably successful role for almost 50 years. Yet during the eighth major trade negotiating round of the GATT, it became apparent that a new institutional structure would be necessary, and thus the WTO was born, coming into effect 1 January 1995.[36] In the short span of its new life, the WTO appears to be the prodigal child of the international trading system, already achieving a membership of more than 130 countries (with over 30 more negotiating for membership)[37] and over 105 dispute settlement procedures initiated under the new WTO rules for those procedures.

Significantly, it now seems clear that the WTO represents a further enhancement (compared to the GATT whose evolution was in this direction anyway)[38] in the direction of rule orientation. This is particularly demonstrated by the new WTO dispute settlement procedures.[39]

The full implications of the Uraquay Round (UR) Agreement and its new institutions are undoubtedly not fully understood yet by any government

[33] Susan A. Aaronson, Trade and the American Dream: A Social History of Postwar Trade Policy (1996).

[34] John H. Jackson, 'The General Agreement on Tariffs and Trade in United States Domestic Law', 66 Michigan L Rev 249 (1967); see generally, John H. Jackson, World Trade and the Law of GATT (1969); John H. Jackson, William Davey and Alan O. Sykes, International Economic Relations (3rd edn, 1995).

[35] John H. Jackson, The Uruguay Round and the Launch of the WTO – Significance and Challenges, Chapter 1 of American Bar Association Book on the Uruguay Round (1996) reprinted from *World Trade Organization.*

[36] 'Final Act Embodying the Results of the Uruguay Round of Multilateral Trade Negotiations, opened for signature 15 April 1994, Marrakesh, Morocco', 33 ILM 1140–272 (1994). See also H.R. Doc. No. 316, 103d Cong., 2d Sess., 1994).

[37] See WTO website at: http://www.unicc.org/wto.
As of 22 October 1997, the WTO lists 132 members. Its 'State of Play' document on disputes lists 105 disputes.

[38] John H. Jackson, The WTO Constitution and Jurisprudence (forthcoming in 1998), see especially, section 4.2 on 'The GATT Dispute Settlement Procedure and its Evolution'.

[39] These are principally set forth in the Dispute Settlement Understanding (DSU), which is Annex 2 to the WTO 'Charter' in the Final Act of the Uruguay Round, above n. 37.

which has accepted them. In the USA during 1994 there was considerable discussion about the impact of the UR treaty and the WTO on 'US Sovereignty'.[40] While the term 'sovereignty' has been much criticized as out of date and archaic, nevertheless, some of the issues in this 'great debate' are vital and contemporary. To a great extent these issues concern 'allocation of power' as between a nation-state and an international regulatory system. To name a few examples, there are questions whether a product safety standard should be controlled by an international body, or a nation-state government, or even by subfederal government units. There are also questions about how to apply certain well-established international policies such as 'most favoured nation' treatment (non-discrimination as between different nations) or 'national treatment' (non-discrimination as between domestic products or services and imported products or services). In addition there are questions about whether disputes about these and other issues should be resolved by an international body or not. In fact, a close analysis of sovereignty turns out to be very complex, and the subject can be 'decomposed' into dozens of more specific issues.

Clearly acceptance of any treaty in some sense reduces the freedom of scope of national government actions. At the very least, certain types of actions inconsistent with the treaty norms would give rise to an international law obligation, and the amount of constraint might then vary with the institutional mechanisms for enforcement, but also the national domestic government structure or political attitude towards international norms. Some sceptics might dismiss an international norm as ineffective and thus not constraining. But if a treaty norm were 'self-executing' or 'directly applicable' in a domestic legal system, it could have a greater constraining effect. Even without those effects, a treaty can have important domestic legal effects, such as influencing how domestic courts interpret domestic legislation. Beyond that, a treaty norm even without domestic legal effect can have weight in some domestic policy debates where some advocates will stress that positions contrary to their views would raise 'serious international or treaty concerns'. Thus the 'sovereignty objection' can be seen to be directed more to the question where should a decision be made, and what influences on that decision should be permitted?

Related both to the 'sovereignty' question and to the promise of greater 'rule orientation', the new dispute settlement procedures (and now practice and developing jurisprudence) seem demonstrably tilted towards rule orientation. Indeed speeches by international and national leaders indicate this and point to it with pride and satisfaction. Although the text of the DSU

[40] John H. Jackson, 'The Great 1994 Sovereignty Debate: United States Acceptance and Implementation of the Uruguay Round Results' in Jonathan Charney, Donald K. Anton and Mary Ellen O'Connell (eds), *Essays in Honor of Louis Henkin* (forthcoming in 1998), also in 36 Colum J Transnational L 15788 (1997).

has clauses that arguably go both ways, if you read the DSU through carefully and inventory the clauses that are relevant, you can easily come to the conclusion that the DSU opts for the rule-oriented procedure.[41]

The issue of a nation-state's participation in an international dispute settlement procedure poses sovereignty questions of a different sort from those of institutional structure. If a nation has consented to a treaty and the norms it contains, why should it object to an external process which could rule on the consistency of that nation's actions with the treaty norms? It might be argued that such objections manifest a lack of intent to follow the norms, sort of accepting the treaty with fingers crossed behind the back. Indeed, there may be some elements of this thinking in this context. However, it could also be suggested that a nervousness about international dispute procedures reflects a government's desire to have some flexibility to resist future strict conformity to norms in certain special circumstances, particularly circumstances that could pose great danger to the essential national objectives. This is sort of an 'escape clause' idea where a nation could accept norms with sincere intent to follow them except in the most severe and egregious cases of danger to the nation or to its political system. (Candidly though, it may also be noted that danger to the political fortunes of the ruling party in such a nation may take on great weight in these considerations.)

Apart from these 'escape clause' notions, however, there is an institutional concern that the dispute procedures may not be objective, may be subject to procedural irregularities, overreaching or may have other important defects that even other nations would recognize, but which are not redressed by the treaty or its institutional structure. This danger, either at the outset or developing at some later time, could legitimately constrain a nation's willingness to enter into stringent commitments to a dispute settlement procedure.

The major change in the DSU is the elimination of 'blocking' when the Dispute Settlement Body (DSB) considers the report. Since the report is deemed adopted unless there is a 'consensus' against adoption (the 'reverse consensus') and since the 'winning party' could always object, the adoption is considered to be virtually automatic. The *quid pro quo* for this automaticity, however, is the appeal which is now for the first time allowed. If an appeal is taken, then the report is not 'adopted'; instead an appellate

[41] See, e.g., DSU article 3, para. 2, which in part reads:

> 3.2 The dispute settlement system of the WTO is a central element in providing security and predictability to the multilateral trading system.

Also see the speech of King Hassan II for the host government of the April 1994 Marrakesh ministerial meeting to conclude the Uruguay Round, where he said:

> By bringing into being the World Trade Organization today, we are enshrining the rule of law in international economic and trade relations, thus setting universal rules and disciplines over the temptations of unilateralism and the law of the jungle.

division of three individuals drawn from a permanent roster of seven individuals (with renewable four-year staggered terms)[42] considers the first level report, receives arguments from the parties, and writes its own report. This report is also sent to the DSB where the same 'reverse consensus' rule applies to adoption, again making it virtually certain to be adopted. It is this 'automaticity' that scares some diplomats and critics of the WTO system, although in many other international tribunals 'automaticity' in the sense of no opportunity to block a report, also exists.

How does all this fit the 'sovereignty objections'? Again, it is abundantly clear that 'sovereignty' is not a unitary concept, but rather a series of particular considerations centred around the problem of allocation of power. Thus when objection is made to the USA accepting the WTO because of the WTO dispute settlement procedures, the specific ('decomposed') issues of that objection are substantially different from those regarding the problem of treaty norm application, or the institutional structure of decision-making. In addition, the sovereignty objection really could be a series of specific objections about the nature or details of the dispute procedure. These in turn must be considered in the aggregate (unless there were options which allowed a nation to accept some details but not others), and that aggregate weighed against the policy advantages of belonging. 'Sovereignty' thus is not a magical wand that one waives to ward off any 'entanglement' in the international system, but rather is a policy-weighing process.

6. FUTURE POLICY AND FUTURE SCHOLARSHIP

Where may all this discussion lead? Obviously the previous sections suggest many implications for future directions of the international institutions. While the explicit focus has been on the new WTO, many of the matters discussed can and often should apply to other international economic regulatory and institutional entities and subject matter, whether monetary organizations or environmental treaties, or numerous other contexts. And these matters obviously have implications for policy and scholarly attention.

To attempt a complete inventory or a complete landscape of the potential directions and problems for the future would be folly besides being inappropriate or unfeasible for this article. But a number of further matters can be mentioned for both policy consideration and scholarly attention. Among these would be attention to subjects logically building on the analyses developed in previous sections. One can, for example, mention some of the institutional questions and alternative possibilities needing exploration, partly summarizing matters discussed earlier in this article.

Assuming for the moment that a policy analysis of the various questions raised about appropriateness and difficulty of government market interven-

[42] Article 17 DSU.

tion suggests the necessity of taking international action or establishing some form of international co-operation, then it becomes necessary to explore a series of questions relating to the modalities of such international action or co-operation, including the possibility of designing institutions for that purpose.[43]

Clearly there are a number of different ways to approach the question of international effects on national markets. We can roughly inventory them under the subtopics of 'unilateral', 'bilateral', 'regional', and 'multilateral'. Running through all of these levels ('vertical analysis') are several general questions, such as:

(1) Should co-operative approaches be basically voluntary, or should they be binding (under international law)? If binding, should there be sanctions?

(2) Should the emphasis on co-operation be procedural, or relate more substantively to the rules being applied?

(3) With respect to substantive rules, should the approach be that of national treatment (non-discrimination between domestic and imported goods), most favoured nation (non-discrimination among imported goods and exporting countries), or should there be some sort of minimum standards as the basis of a rule to apply?

In addition, one can explore several different 'principles of managing interdependence' that would influence the techniques of co-operation:

(1) Harmonization, a system that gradually induces nations towards uniform approaches to a variety of economic regulations and structures. An example would be standardization of certain product specifications. Another example would be uniformity of procedures for applying countervailing duties or escape clause measures.

(2) Reciprocity, a system of continuous 'trades' or 'swaps' of measures to liberalize (or restrict) trade. The GATT negotiations are in this mold.

(3) Interface, which recognizes that different economic systems will always exist in the world and tries to create the institutional means to ameliorate international tensions caused by those differences, perhaps through buffering or escape clause mechanisms.

Obviously a mixture of all these techniques is the most likely to be acceptable, but that still leaves open the question of what is the appropriate mixture. For example, how much should the 'trade constitution' pressure nations to conform to some uniform 'harmonized' approaches, or is it better simply to establish buffering mechanisms that allow nations to preserve diversity but

[43] See John H. Jackson, 'Alternative Approaches for Implementing Competition Rules In International Economic Relations', Aussenwirtschaft – Swiss Rev Int'l Econ Rel No. 2/94, St Gallen, Switzerland 225 (1994).

try to avoid situations where one nation imposes burdens (economic or political) on other nations?

Closely connected to this previous point is an issue that may be loosely characterized as being similar to 'federalism'. This is the issue of the appropriate allocation of decision-making authority at different levels of government which are discussed in Part 4.

In order to regulate international economies today, there is a very high probability that the international community will turn toward the formation and designing of a treaty-based multilateral institution which could enable it appropriately and efficiently to respond to the problems of such regulation. Thus it is particularly important to begin thinking about some of the key questions that should be considered in designing international institutions. A series of 'lawyer-type questions' then emerge, such as:

(1) Questions of rule-making at the international level, and whether procedures adequately consider some of the scientific and moral concerns involved in the subjects that are linked to trade.

(2) Questions of international dispute settlement procedures and to what extent they adequately consider opposing policy goals, or provide for appropriate advocacy from interested authorities and citizen groups.

(3) Questions of whether the international procedures incorporate adequate democratic processes including transparency, and right to be heard.

(4) Questions of the relation of international rules to domestic constitutional and other laws.

(5) Questions about the operation and procedures of national constitutional bodies and how these promote or inhibit international co-operation.

(6) Questions about the activity of interest groups, both those broadly oriented and those more oriented to specific interests or single issues, and how this activity relates to international institutions and procedures.

(7) Questions concerning the problems of regulatory competition: governments seeking lower standards of regulation in order to attract economic activity to their societies (the 'race to the bottom', or 'race to the top', or in the USA the 'Delaware Corporation' problem).

These questions, which have perhaps become most apparent in the context of environment and competition policy, also relate to a long list of other potential policy areas that can cause clashes with international trade and other international economic policy goals. Such policy areas could certainly include:

- Labour standards
- Commodity agreements and regulation
- Product standards (food, pharmaceutical, safety of goods etc.)
- Insurance

- Banking and fiduciary institutions
- Investment protection
- Securities regulation and institutions
- Government procurement procedures and preferences
- Shipping and transport (including air transport)
- Intellectual property protection and regulation
- Taxation

To close, the reader can probably see that the reflections in this article are consistent with ideas of a 'pragmatist school' of international law scholarship.[44] The phrase 'normative realist' has also been used, suggesting that scholars should feel some responsibility for moving the subject forward despite the difficulty and limitation of resources, and despite the sometimes pessimistic viewpoint that mere 'realism' can engender.

Let us hope that this will be the case, and take comfort in the observable fact that many fine scholars, young and older, are now embarked on some of these endeavours as well as other endeavours reflecting other appropriate priorities, as a burgeoning literature relevant to the subject of this article bears witness. There is reason to be optimistic that the combination of such scholarship and sensible policy-maker attention to it, will assist in repeating and continuing the relative success of the achievements of international economic institutions during the last 50 years.

[44] See, e.g., David Kennedy, 'The International Style in Postwar Law and Policy: John Jackson and the Field of International Economic Law', 10 Am U J Int'l L Policy 671 (1995).

Part II
Competing Theories of International Law

[8]

INTERNATIONAL LAW AND ASSUMPTIONS ABOUT THE STATE SYSTEM

By WILLIAM D. COPLIN*

MOST writers on international relations and international law still examine the relationship between international law and politics in terms of the assumption that law either should or does function only as a coercive restraint on political action. Textbook writers on general international politics like Morgenthau,[1] and Lerche and Said,[2] as well as those scholars who have specialized in international law like J. L. Brierly[3] and Charles De Visscher,[4] make the common assumption that international law should be examined as a system of coercive norms controlling the actions of states. Even two of the newer works, *The Political Foundations of International Law* by Morton A. Kaplan and Nicholas deB. Katzenbach[5] and *Law and Minimum World Public Order* by Myres S. McDougal and Florentino P. Feliciano,[6] in spite of an occasional reference to the non-coercive as-

* I want to thank Dr. Robert W. Tucker of the Johns Hopkins University and Richard Miller of Wayne State University Law School for their constructive criticism of the first draft of this article.

[1] Hans J. Morgenthau, *Politics Among Nations* (New York 1961), 275-311. The entire evaluation of the "main problems" of international law is focused on the question of what rules are violated and what rules are not.

[2] Charles O. Lerche, Jr., and Abdul A. Said, *Concepts of International Politics* (Englewood Cliffs, N.J., 1963), 167-87. That the authors have employed the assumption that international law functions as a system of restraint is evident from the title of their chapter which examines international law, "Limitations on State Actions."

[3] J. L. Brierly, *The Law of Nations* (New York 1963), 1. Brierly defines international law as "the body of rules and principles of action which are binding upon civilized states in their relations. . . ."

[4] Charles De Visscher, *Theory and Reality in Public International Law* (Princeton 1957), 99-100.

[5] Morton A. Kaplan and Nicholas deB. Katzenbach, *The Political Foundations of International Law* (New York 1961), 5. In a discussion of how the student should observe international law and politics, the authors write: "To understand the substance and limits of such constraining rules (international law), it is necessary to examine the interests which support them in the international system, the means by which they are made effective, and the functions they perform. Only in this way is it possible to predict the areas in which rules operate, the limits of rules as effective constraints, and the factors which underlie normative change." Although the authors are asking an important question—"Why has international law been binding in some cases?"—they still assume that international law functions primarily as a direct restraint on state action. For an excellent review of this book, see Robert W. Tucker, "Resolution," *Journal of Conflict Resolution*, VII (March 1963), 69-75.

[6] Myres S. McDougal and Florentino P. Feliciano, *Law and Minimum World Public*

pects of international law, are developed primarily from the model of international law as a system of restraint. Deriving their conception of the relationship between international law and political action from their ideas on the way law functions in domestic communities, most modern writers look at international law as an instrument of direct control. The assumption that international law is or should be a coercive restraint on state action structures almost every analysis, no matter what the school of thought or the degree of optimism or pessimism about the effectiveness of the international legal system.[7] With an intellectual framework that measures international law primarily in terms of constraint on political action, there is little wonder that skepticism about international law continues to increase while creative work on the level of theory seems to be diminishing.[8]

Therefore, it is desirable to approach the relationship between international law and politics at a different functional level, not because international law does not function at the level of coercive restraint,

Order (New Haven 1961), 10. The authors suggest that if any progress in conceptualizing the role of international law is to be made, it is necessary to distinguish between the "factual process of international coercion and the process of authoritative decision by which the public order of the world community endeavors to regulate such process of coercion." This suggestion is based on the assumption that international law promotes order primarily through the establishment of restraints on state actions.

[7] There are a few writers who have tried to approach international law from a different vantage point. For a survey of some of the other approaches to international law and politics, see Michael Barkun, "International Norms: An Interdisciplinary Approach," *Background*, VIII (August 1964), 121-29. The survey shows that few "new" approaches to international law have developed beyond the preliminary stages, save perhaps for the writings of F. S. C. Northrop. Northrop's works (e.g., *Philosophical Anthropology and Practical Politics* [New York 1960], 326-30) are particularly significant in their attempt to relate psychological, philosophical, and cultural approaches to the study of law in general, although he has not usually been concerned with the overall relationship of international law to international political action. Not mentioned in Barkun's survey but important in the discussion of international law and politics is Stanley Hoffmann, "International Systems and International Law," in Klaus Knorr and Sidney Verba, eds., *The International System* (Princeton 1961), 205-38. However, Hoffmann's essay is closer in approach to the work by Kaplan and Katzenbach than to the approach developed in this article. Finally, it is also necessary to point to an article by Edward McWhinney, "Soviet and Western International Law and the Cold War in a Nuclear Era of Bipolarity: Inter-Bloc Law in a Nuclear Age," *Canadian Yearbook of International Law*, I (1963), 40-81. Professor McWhinney discusses the relationship between American and Russian structures of action, on the one hand, and their interpretations of international law, on the other. While McWhinney's approach is basically similar to the one proposed in this article in its attempt to relate international law to politics on a conceptual level, his article is focused on a different set of problems, the role of national attitudes in the contemporary era on ideas of international law. Nevertheless, it is a significant contribution to the task of analyzing more clearly the relationship between international law and politics.

[8] See Richard A. Falk, "The Adequacy of Contemporary International Law: Gaps in Legal Thinking," *Virginia Law Review*, L (March 1964), 231-65, for a valuable but highly critical analysis of contemporary international legal theory.

but because it also functions at another level. In order to illustrate a second functional level in the relationship between international law and politics, it is necessary to examine the operation of domestic law. In a domestic society, the legal system as a series of interrelated normative statements does more than direct or control the actions of its members through explicit rules backed by a promise of coercion. Systems of law also act on a more generic and pervasive level by serving as authoritative (i.e., accepted as such by the community) modes of communicating or reflecting the ideals and purposes, the acceptable roles and actions, as well as the very processes of the societies. The legal system functions on the level of the individual's perceptions and attitudes by presenting to him an image of the social system—an image which has both factual and normative aspects and which contributes to social order by building a consensus on procedural as well as on substantive matters. In this sense, law in the domestic situation is a primary tool in the "socialization"[9] of the individual.

International law functions in a similar manner: namely, as an institutional device for communicating to the policy-makers of various states a consensus on the nature of the international system. The purpose of this article is to approach the relationship between international law and politics not as a system of direct restraints on state action, but rather as a system of quasi-authoritative communications to the policy-makers concerning the reasons for state actions and the requisites for international order. It is a "quasi-authoritative" device because the norms of international law represent only an imperfect consensus of the community of states, a consensus which rarely commands complete acceptance but which usually expresses generally held ideas. Given the decentralized nature of law-creation and law-application in the international community, there is no official voice of the states as a collectivity. However, international law taken as a body of generally related norms is the closest thing to such a voice. Therefore, in spite of the degree of uncertainty about the authority of international law, it may still be meaningful to examine international law as a means for expressing the commonly held assumptions about the state system.

The approach advocated in this article has its intellectual antecedents in the sociological school, since it seeks to study international law in relation to international politics. Furthermore, it is similar to that of the sociological school in its assumption that there is or should be a significant degree of symmetry between international law and politics

[9] See Gabriel A. Almond and James S. Coleman, eds., *The Politics of the Developing Areas* (Princeton 1960), 26-31, for an explanation of the concept of socialization.

on the level of intellectual constructs—that is, in the way in which international law has expressed and even shaped ideas about relations between states. It is hoped that this approach will contribute to a greater awareness of the interdependence of international law and conceptions of international politics.

Before analyzing the way in which international law has in the past and continues today to reflect common attitudes about the nature of the state system, let us discuss briefly the three basic assumptions which have generally structured those attitudes.[10] First, it has been assumed that the state is an absolute institutional value and that its security is the one immutable imperative for state action. If there has been one thing of which policy-makers could always be certain, it is that their actions must be designed to preserve their state. Second, it has been assumed that international politics is a struggle for power, and that all states seek to increase their power. Although the forms of power have altered during the evolution of the state system, it has been generally thought that states are motivated by a drive for power, no matter what the stakes. The third basic assumption permeating ideas about the international system has to do with maintaining a minimal system of order among the states. This assumption, symbolized generally by the maxim "Preserve the balance of power," affirms the necessity of forming coalitions to counter any threat to hegemony and of moderating actions in order to avoid an excess of violence that could disrupt the system.

It is necessary at this point to note that an unavoidable tension has existed between the aim of maintaining the state and maximizing power, on the one hand, and of preserving the international system, on the other. The logical extension of either aim would threaten the other, since complete freedom of action by the state would not allow for the limitation imposed by requirements to maintain the system, and a strict regularization of state action inherent in the idea of the system would curtail the state's drive for power. However, the tension

[10] The following discussion of the assumptions of the state system is brief, since students of international politics generally agree that the three assumptions listed have structured most of the actions of states. This agreement is most complete concerning the nature of the "classical" state system. The author is also of the opinion that these assumptions continue to operate today in a somewhat mutated form. (See his unpublished manuscript "The Image of Power Politics: A Cognitive Approach to the Study of International Politics," chaps. 2, 4, 8.) Note also the agreement on the nature of classical ideas about international politics in the following: Ernst B. Haas, "The Balance of Power as a Guide to Policy-Making," *Journal of Politics*, xv (August 1953), 370-97; Morton A. Kaplan, *System and Process in International Politics* (New York 1957), 22-36; and Edward Vose Gulick, *Europe's Classical Balance of Power* (Ithaca, N.Y., 1955).

has remained constant, with neither norm precluding the other except when a given state was in immediate danger of destruction. At those times, the interests of the system have been subordinated to the drive for state survival, but with no apparent long-range effect on the acceptance by policy-makers of either set of interests, despite their possible incompatibility. The prescriptions that states should be moderate, flexible, and vigilant[11] have been a manifestation of the operation of the system. Together, the three basic assumptions about the state system have constituted the conceptual basis from which the policy-makers have planned the actions of their state.

I. Classical International Law and the Image of the State System

Almost every legal aspect of international relations from 1648 to 1914 reinforced and expressed the assumptions of the state system. State practices in regard to treaties, boundaries, neutrality, the occupation of new lands, freedom of the seas, and diplomacy, as well as classical legal doctrines, provide ample illustration of the extent to which the basic assumptions of the state were mirrored in international law.

The essential role of treaties in international law reflected the three assumptions of the state system. First, treaty practices helped to define the nature of statehood. Emanating from the free and unfettered will of states, treaties were the expression of their sovereign prerogatives. Statehood itself was defined in part as the ability to make treaties, and that ability presupposed the equality and independence usually associated with the idea of the state. Moreover, certain definitive treaties, like those written at the Peace of Augsburg (1515) and the Peace of Westphalia (1648), actually made explicit the attributes of statehood. The former treaty affirmed the idea that the Prince had complete control over the internal affairs of the state, while the latter emphasized that states were legally free and equal in their international relationships.[12] Even the actual wording of treaties expressed the classical assumption about the sanctity of the state. Whether in the formal references to the "high contracting parties" or in the more vital statements about the agreement of sovereigns not to interfere with

[11] See Gulick, 34; and for a discussion of the principles of moderation, flexibility, and vigilance, *ibid.*, 11-16.

[12] For the effects of the two treaties, see Charles Petrie, *Diplomatic History, 1713-1939* (London 1949), 111; David Jayne Hill, *A History of Diplomacy in the International Development of Europe* (New York 1924), 603-6; and Arthur Nussbaum, *A Concise History of the Law of Nations* (New York 1961), 116.

the actions of other sovereigns, treaties were clear expressions of the classical idea of the state.[13]

Treaty law also contributed to the evolution of the classical assumption regarding the maintenance of the international system. Both explicitly and implicitly, treaties affirmed the necessity of an international system. Whether or not they contained such phrases as "balance of power," "just equilibrium," "universal and perpetual peace,"[14] "common and public safety and tranquillity,"[15] "public tranquillity on a lasting foundation,"[16] or "safety and interest of Europe,"[17] the most important treaties during the classical period affirmed the desirability of maintaining the international system.[18] Also, many treaties reaffirmed earlier treaty agreements, contributing to the idea that the international system was a continuing, operative unity.[19] Therefore, treaties usually reminded the policy-maker that the maintenance of the international system was a legitimate and necessary objective of state policy.

Finally, treaties affirmed the necessity and, in part, the legality of the drive for power. The constant juggling of territory, alliances, and other aspects of capability was a frequent and rightful subject of treaty law. Treaties implicitly confirmed that power was the dynamic force in relations between states by defining the legal criteria of power and, more important, by providing an institutional means, subscribed to by most of the members of the system, which legalized certain political transactions, such as territorial acquisition and dynastic exchange.

A second state practice which contributed to the classical assumptions about the state system was the legal concept of boundaries. Inherent in the very idea of the boundary were all three assumptions of the classical system. First, the boundary marked off that most discernible of all criteria of a state's existence—territory.[20] A state was sovereign within its territory, and the boundary was essential to the demarcation and protection of that sovereignty. Freedom and

[13] E.g., *The Treaty of Ryswick, 1697* in Andrew Browning, ed., *English History Documents*, VIII (New York 1963), 881-83.

[14] *Treaty of Ryswick*, Article I, in *ibid.*

[15] *Barrier Treaty of 1715*, Article I, in *ibid.*, Vol. X.

[16] *Treaty of Vienna, 1713*, in *ibid.*, Vol. VIII.

[17] *Treaty of Quadruple Alliance, 1815*, in *ibid.*, Vol. XI.

[18] Leo Gross, "The Peace of Westphalia, 1648-1948," *American Journal of International Law*, XLII (January 1948), 20-40.

[19] For a treaty which expressed the necessity of keeping prior obligations, see *Treaty of Aix-la-Chapelle, 1748*, in Browning, ed., Vol. X.

[20] See John H. Herz, *International Politics in the Atomic Age* (New York 1962), 53, for a discussion of the role of territory in the classical state system and the international legal system.

equality necessitated the delineation of a certain area of complete control; the boundary as conceptualized in international law was the institutional means through which that necessity was fulfilled. Second, the boundary was essential for the preservation of the international system.[21] After every war the winning powers set up a new or revised set of boundaries which aided them in maintaining order by redistributing territory. More important, the boundary also provided a criterion by which to assess the intentions of other states. Change of certain essential boundaries signified a mortal threat to the whole system, and signaled the need for a collective response.[22] Finally, the legal concept of boundaries provided a means through which the expansion and contraction of power in the form of territory could be measured. Since the boundary was a legal means of measuring territorial changes, international law in effect reinforced the idea that the struggle for power was an essential and accepted part of international politics. All three assumptions of the state system, therefore, were mirrored in the classical legal concept of boundaries.

Another international legal concept which reflected the assumptions about the state system was the idea of neutrality. The primary importance of neutrality law lay in its relation to the classical emphasis on the preservation of the international system. The practice of neutrality was an essential element in the mitigation of international conflict because it provided a legitimate means of lessening the degree of violence in any given war (by reducing the number of belligerents) and also made those involved in a war aware of the possibility of hostile actions from outside should the conflict weaken the participants too greatly. In short, the legal concept of neutrality implied that the actions of states must remain moderate and flexible in order to preserve the state system.[23]

There were other aspects of international legal practice which substantiated the assumptions of the state system. For instance, since the sixteenth century the law pertaining to the occupation of new lands and to freedom of the high seas constituted a vital aspect of international law, and provided "legitimate" areas in which the struggle for power could take place.

From the outset, most of the non-European areas of the world were

[21] See Hoffmann, 212, 215, for a discussion of the way in which territorial settlements in treaties aided stability within the system. He calls this function part of the law of political framework.

[22] E.g., the English and French attitude toward Belgium.

[23] For a discussion of the role of neutrality in the balance of power system, see McDougal and Feliciano, 391-413.

considered by the great powers to be acceptable arenas for the struggle for power. International legal practice made it easy for states to gain control of land overseas by distinguishing between the laws of occupation and the laws of subjugation. This distinction made it easier for powers to extend control over non-European territorial expanses because it enabled states to "occupy" territory legally without actually controlling it.[24] Through the laws of occupation, international law confirmed the assumption that colonial expansion was part of the struggle for power.

The law of the high seas also contributed to the idea of the struggle for power. The expansion of trade, military power, and territorial domain was, throughout almost the entire history of the state system, greatly dependent upon the free use of the high seas. The laws of the sea were designed so that maximum use could be made of this relatively cheap mode of transportation. Like the laws of occupation of non-European territory, sea law helped to keep the distribution of power among European states in continuous flux.[25]

Therefore, both the laws of the seas and the laws governing the occupation of new lands were instrumental in "legalizing" areas for conflict. Given the assumption that states always maximize their power, a free sea and the easy acquisition of non-European lands provided the fluidity needed for the states to struggle for power. Moreover, both sets of laws removed the area of conflict from the home territory, thus enabling states to increase the scope of their struggle without proportionately increasing its intensity.[26]

A final category of international law which reinforced the assumptions about the state system was the law of diplomacy. The legal rationalization behind the rights and duties of diplomats (i.e., since diplomats represent sovereign states, they owe no allegiance to the receiving state) emphasized the inviolability of the state which was an essential aspect of the classical assumptions.[27] At the same time, the very fact that

[24] L. Oppenheim, in H. Lauterpacht, ed., *International Law* (New York 1948), I, 507.

[25] The attempt to control a "closed sea" was sometimes a bid by a powerful state to freeze the *status quo*—e.g., Portugal's control of the Indian Ocean in the sixteenth and seventeenth centuries (Nussbaum, 111).

[26] Analysts have argued over whether colonialism reduced or exacerbated international antagonism. Without settling the argument, it seems safe to say that the struggle for colonies was a more spectacular and relatively less dangerous system of conflict than was competition for European land.

[27] For the relationship of the assumption of statehood and the functioning of diplomatic immunities, see a discussion of the theoretical underpinnings of diplomatic immunities in Ernest L. Kelsey, "Some Aspects of the Vienna Conference on Diplomatic Intercourse and Immunities," *American Journal of International Law*, LXXXVIII (January 1962), 92-94.

even semi-hostile states could exchange and maintain ambassadors emphasized that all states were part of a common international system.[28] Finally, the classical functions of a diplomat—to make sure that conditions are not changing to the disadvantage of his state and, if they are, to suggest and even implement policies to rectify the situation—exemplified the rule of constant vigilance necessary in a group of states struggling for power. Therefore, in their own way, the laws of diplomacy expressed all three of the assumptions of the state systems.

The assumptions of the state system were reinforced not only by the legal practices of states but also by the major international legal theories of the classical period. Three general schools of thought developed: the naturalists, the eclectics or Grotians, and the positivists.[29] In each school, there was a major emphasis on both the state and the state system as essential institutional values. Whether it was Pufendorf's insistence on the "natural equality of state,"[30] the Grotians' concept of the sovereign power of state,[31] or Bynkershoek and the nineteenth-century positivists' point that treaties were the prime, if not the only, source of international law,[32] the state was considered by most classical theorists to be the essential institution protected by the legal system. At the same time, almost every classical writer on international law either assumed or argued for the existence of an international system of some kind.[33] Along with Grotians, the naturalists maintained that a system of states existed, since man was a social animal. Vattel, probably the most famous international lawyer in the classical period, asserted that a balance of power and a state system existed.[34] Even the positivists of the nineteenth century assumed that there was an international system of some kind. This is apparent from their emphasis on the balance of power,[35] as well as from their assumption

28 Morgenthau, 547.

29 For a discussion of the precise meaning of these classifications, see Nussbaum.

30 *Ibid.*, 149.

31 Hugo Grotius, *The Rights of War and Peace*, ed. with notes by A. C. Campbell (Washington 1901), 62.

32 Cornelius Van Bynkershoek, *De dominio maris dissertatio*, trans. by Ralph Van Deman Mogoffin (New York 1923), 35.

33 De Visscher, 88. For similar interpretations of classical and pre-twentieth-century theorists, see Walter Schiffer, *The Legal Community of Mankind* (New York 1951), chap. 1; or Percy E. Corbett, *Law and Society in the Relations of States* (New York 1951).

34 Emeric de Vattel, *The Laws of Nations* (Philadelphia 1867), 412-14.

35 G. F. Von Martens, *The Law of Nations: Being the Science of National Law, Covenants, Power & Founded upon the Treaties and Custom of Modern Nations in Europe*, trans. by William Cobbett (4th ed., London 1829), 123-24.

that relations between nations could be defined in terms of legal rights and duties.[36]

Therefore, there was a consensus among the classical theorists of international law that international politics had two structural elements: the state, with its rights of freedom and self-preservation; and the system, with its partial effectiveness in maintaining a minimal international order. That the theorists never solved the conflict between the idea of the unfettered sovereign state, on the one hand, and a regulating system of law, on the other, is indicative of a conflict within the assumptions of the state system,[37] but a conflict which neither prevented international lawyers from writing about an international legal order nor kept policy-makers from pursuing each state's objectives without destroying the state system.

Although the norms of classical international law sometimes went unheeded, the body of theory and of state practice which constituted "international law as an institution" nonetheless expressed in a quasi-authoritative manner the three assumptions about international politics. It legalized the existence of states and helped to define the actions necessary for the preservation of each state and of the system as a whole. It reinforced the ideas that vigilance, moderation, and flexibility are necessary for the protection of a system of competing states. And finally, international law established a legalized system of political payoffs by providing a means to register gains and losses without creating a static system. In fact, this last aspect was essential to the classical state system. With international law defining certain relationships (territorial expansion, empire-building, etc.) as legitimate areas for political competition, other areas seemed, at least generally in the classical period, to be removed from the center of the political struggle. By legitimizing the struggle as a form of political competition rather than as universal conflict, international law sanctioned a form of international system that was more than just an anarchic drive for survival.

[36] Almost all of the nineteenth-century positivists assumed that relations between nations were systematized enough to allow for a system of rights and duties. E.g., William Edward Hall, *A Treatise on International Law* (Oxford 1904), 43-59; Henry Wheaton, *Elements of International Law* (Oxford 1936), 75. Wheaton does not discuss duties as such, but when he talks about legal rights he distinguishes between "absolute" and "conditional" rights. According to Wheaton, the "conditional" rights are those resulting from membership in the international legal system. This formulation implies the existence of corresponding duties.

[37] See Von Martens, 123-34, for the intellectual and legal problems growing out of the assumption that states may legally maximize power but that they also have a responsibility "to oppose by alliances and even by force of arms" a series of aggrandizements which threaten the community.

II. Contemporary International Law and the Assumptions of the State System

As a quasi-authoritative system of communicating the assumptions of the state system to policy-makers, contemporary international law no longer presents a clear idea of the nature of international politics. This is in part a result of the tension, within the structure of contemporary international law itself, between the traditional legal concepts and the current practices of states. International law today is in a state of arrested ambiguity—in a condition of unstable equilibrium between the old and the new. As a result, it no longer contributes as it once did to a consensus on the nature of the state system. In fact, it adds to the growing uncertainty and disagreement as to how the international political system itself is evolving. The following discussion will attempt to assess the current developments in international law in terms of the challenges those developments make to the three assumptions of the state system. It is realized that the three assumptions themselves have already undergone change, but our purpose is to show where contemporary international legal practice and theory stand in relation to that change.

THE CHALLENGE TO THE STATE AND THE SYSTEM

The current legal concept of the state is a perfect example of the arrested ambiguity of contemporary international law and of the threat that this condition represents to the assumptions of the state system. On the one hand, most of the traditional forms used to express the idea of statehood are still employed. Treaty-makers and statesmen still write about "respect for territorial integrity," the "right of domestic jurisdiction," and the "sovereign will of the high contracting parties." Moreover, most of the current substantive rights and duties, such as self-defense, legal equality, and territorial jurisdiction, that are based on the assumption that states as units of territory are the irreducible institutional values of the system continue to be central to international legal practice.[38] On the other hand, certain contemporary developments contrast sharply with the traditional territory-oriented conceptions of international law.[39] With the growth of international entities possessing

[38] E.g., Charles G. Fenwick, *International Law* (New York 1952), chap. 11.

[39] For a survey of current challenges to traditional international law, see Wolfgang Friedmann, "The Changing Dimensions of International Law," *Columbia Law Review*, LXII (November 1962), 1147-65. Also, see Richard A. Falk, *The Role of the Domestic Courts in the International Legal Order* (Syracuse 1964), 14-19, for a discussion of the fact that while there is a growing "functional obsolescence" of the state system, the

supranational powers (e.g., ECSC), the legal idea of self-contained units based on territorial control lacks the clear basis in fact that it once enjoyed. Many of the traditional prerogatives of the sovereign state, such as control over fiscal policy,[40] have been transferred in some respects to transnational units. While the development of supranational powers is most pronounced in Europe, there is reason to believe, especially concerning international cooperation on technical matters, that organizations patterned on the European experience might occur elsewhere.

Another significant manifestation of ambiguity in the territorial basis of international law is found in the post-World War II practice of questioning the validity of the laws of other states. The "act of state doctrine" no longer serves as the guideline it once did in directing the national courts of one state to respect the acts promulgated in another.[41] Once based on the assumption of the "inviolability of the sovereign," the "act of state doctrine" today is the source of widespread controversy. The conflicting views of the doctrine are symptomatic of the now ambiguous role of territoriality in questions of jurisdictional and legal power. Although these developments in current legal practice are only now emerging, they nonetheless can be interpreted as a movement away from the strictly and clearly defined legal concept of the state that appeared in classical international law.

---

assumptions of the state system continue to operate for psychological and political reasons.

[40] E.g., Articles 3 and 4 of the *Treaty Establishing the European Coal and Steel Community* (April 18, 1951).

[41] For an excellent discussion of the legal and political problems related to the question of the "act of state doctrine" in particular, and of territorial supremacy as a concept in general, see Kenneth S. Carlston, *Law and Organization in World Society* (Urbana, Ill., 1962), 191-93, 266-69. Also, for a discussion of the problem in a larger framework, see Falk, *Role of the Domestic Courts.* Since World War II, states, especially on the European continent, have found increasingly broader bases to invalidate the effect of foreign laws. Traditionally, states have refused to give validity to the laws of other lands for a small number of narrowly constructed reasons (e.g., refusal to enforce penal or revenue laws). Today many states have declared foreign laws invalid for a variety of reasons, the most important being the formulation that the national court cannot give validity to a foreign law that is illegal in terms of international law (see "*The Rose Mary Case*," *International Law Report* [1953], 316ff.), and the most frequent being a broad interpretation of "sense of public order" (see Martin Domke, "Indonesian Nationalization Measures Before Foreign Courts," *American Journal of International Law*, LIV [April 1960], 305-23). The most recent case in American practice, the *Sabbatino* decision (Supplement, *International Legal Materials*, III, No. 2 [March 1964], 391), appears to reaffirm the traditional emphasis on the territorial supremacy of the national legal order in these matters, but is actually ambiguous. On the one hand, the Opinion of the Court applied the "act of state doctrine" in declaring the Cuban law valid, but on the other hand, the Court stated that "international law does not require application of the doctrine."

Other developments in contemporary international law represent, theoretically at least, a challenge to the assumption that the state and its freedom of action are an absolute necessity for the state system. Most noticeable has been the attempt to develop an international organization which would preserve a minimal degree of order. Prior to the League of Nations, there had been attempts to institutionalize certain aspects of international relations, but such attempts either did not apply to the political behavior of states (e.g., the Universal Postal Union) or did not challenge the basic assumptions of the state system (as the very loosely defined Concert of Europe failed to do). As it was formulated in the Covenant and defined by the intellectuals, the League represented a threat to the assumptions of the state system because it sought to settle once and for all the tension between the policy-maker's commitment to preserve his state and his desire to maintain the state system by subordinating his state to it through a formal institution.

Proponents of the League saw it as a means to formalize a system of maintaining international order by committing states in advance to a coalition against any state that resorted to war without fulfilling the requirements of the Covenant. If it had been operative, such a commitment would have represented a total revolution in the legal concept of the state as an independent entity, since it would have abolished the most essential of all sovereign prerogatives, the freedom to employ coercion. However, the ideal purpose of the League, on the one hand, and the aims of politicians and the actual constitutional and operational aspects of the League, on the other, proved to be quite different. Owing to certain legal formulations within the Covenant (Articles 10, 15, 21) and the subsequent application of the principles (e.g., in Manchuria and Ethiopia), the hoped-for subordination of the state to the system was not realized.[42]

Like the League, the United Nations was to replace the state as the paramount institutional value by establishing a constitutional concert of powers. However, it has succeeded only in underscoring the existing tension between the drive to maintain the state and the goal of maintaining the system. In the Charter itself, the tension between the state and the system remains unresolved.[43] Nor does the actual

[42] For a useful discussion of the relationship between the idea of collective security and the assumption of the balance of power system, see Inis L. Claude, *Swords into Plowshares* (New York 1962), 255-60; and Herz, chap. 5. It is necessary to make a distinction between the theory of collective security, which certainly would challenge the basic assumptions of the state system, and its operation, which would not.

[43] Compare Articles 25-51, or paragraphs 2-7 in Article 2, for the contrast between system-oriented and state-oriented norms.

operation of the United Nations provide a very optimistic basis for the hope that tension will be lessened in the future.

In terms of international law, regional organizations constitute a mixed challenge to the traditional relationship between the state and the system. Although certain organizations represent an attempt to transcend the traditional bounds of their constituent members on functional grounds, this does not necessarily mean that those members have rejected the state as a political form. In reality, if regional organizations represent any transformation at all in the structural relationship between the state and the system, they constitute an attempt to create a bigger and better state, an attempt which is not contrary to the traditional assumptions of the state system. In spite of the fact that some organizations are given supranational power and present a challenge in that sense, most of the organizations are as protective of the sovereign rights of the state as is the United Nations Charter (e.g., the OAS Charter) or are not regional organizations at all, but military alliances.[44]

A more serious challenge, but one somewhat related to the challenge by regional organizations, is the changing relation of the individual to the international legal order. In the classical system, international law clearly relegated the individual to the position of an object of the law. Not the individual, but the state had the rights and duties of the international legal order.[45] This legal formulation was in keeping with the classical emphasis on the sanctity of the state. Today, however, the development of the concepts of human rights, international and regional organizations, and the personal responsibility of policy-makers to a higher law not only limit the scope of legally permissible international action but, more important, limit the traditional autonomy of the leaders of the state over internal matters.[46] The idea that the individual rather than the state is the unit of responsibility in the formulation of policy has a long

[44] This is not to say that regional organizations do not represent a challenge to the concept of the state on psychological or social grounds. Obviously, the type of allegiance to a United Europe would be different in kind and degree from the traditional allegiance to a European state. However, in terms of the challenge to the legal concept of the state, regional organizations still adhere to the idea that the constituent members are sovereign in their relationship with states outside the organization.

[45] See Corbett, 53-56, for a discussion of the place of the individual in classical international law.

[46] Most modern writers have noted that the individual no longer stands in relation to international law solely as the object (e.g., Corbett, 133-35, or Friedmann, 1160-62), though they are agreed that, to use Friedmann's words, "the rights of the individual in international law are as yet fragmentary and uncertain."

intellectual tradition;[47] however, it is only recently that the norms associated with that idea have become a part of international law.

Although the role of the individual in international law is small and the chances for its rapid development in the near future slight, it represents a more vital challenge to traditional international law and to the assumptions of the state system than either international or regional organizations. Since the principle of collective responsibility (of the state) rather than individual responsibility has traditionally served as the infrastructure for the rights and duties of states,[48] the development of a place for the individual in the international legal system that would make him personally responsible would completely revolutionize international law. At the same time, by making the individual a higher point of policy reference than the state, the development of the role of the individual represents a challenge to the assumption once reflected in classical international law that the preservation and maximization of state power is an absolute guideline for policy-makers. The evolving place of the individual in the contemporary international legal system, then, is contrary to the traditional tendency of international law to reaffirm the absolute value of the state.

THE CHALLENGE TO THE CONCEPT OF POWER

One of the most significant developments in international law today relates to the assumption that states do and should compete for power. In the classical period, international law, through the legal concepts of neutrality, rules of warfare, occupation of new lands, rules of the high seas, and laws of diplomacy, reinforced the idea that a struggle for power among states was normal and necessary. Today, many of these specific legal norms still apply, but the overall permissible range of the struggle for military power[49] has been limited by the concept of the just war.

The idea of the just war is not new to international law. Most of the classical writers discussed it, but they refused to define the concept in strict legal terms and usually relegated it to the moral or

[47] According to Guido de Ruggiero, *The History of European Liberalism* (Boston 1959), 363-70, the liberal conception of the state has always assumed that the individual was the absolute value, though this idea has not always been operative.

[48] For an excellent discussion of the role of collective responsibility in international law, see Hans Kelsen, *Principles of International Law* (New York 1959), 9-13, 114-48.

[49] Although the military struggle today is considered to be only one aspect of the struggle for power, it is the one most closely related to the problem of order in both the classical and the contemporary system, and therefore the most crucial in the relationship between law and politics.

ethical realm.[50] The nineteenth-century positivists completely abandoned the doctrine with the formulation that "wars between nations must be considered as just on both sides with respect to treatment of enemies, military arrangements, and peace."[51] However, with the increased capability of states to destroy each other, a movement has grown to regulate force by legal means.

This movement developed through the Hague Conventions and the League of Nations and, in some respects, culminated in the Kellogg-Briand Pact of 1928. Today, the just war is a more or less accepted concept in international law. Most authors write, and most policy-makers state, that aggression is illegal and must be met with the sanction of the international community. The portent of this formulation of the assumption regarding power is great since, theoretically at least, it deprives the states of the range of action which they once freely enjoyed in maximizing their power and in protecting themselves. If the only legal justification for war is self-defense, or authorization of action in accordance with the Charter of the United Nations,[52] then a war to preserve the balance of power or to expand in a limited fashion is outlawed. While the traditional formulation of international law provided a broad field upon which the game of power politics could be played, the new formulations concerning the legal use of force significantly limit and, one could argue, make illegal the military aspects of the game of power politics.[53] The freedom to use military power, once an essential characteristic of sovereignty and an integral part of international law, is no longer an accepted international legal norm.

The concept of the just war directly challenges the assumptions of the state system, because it implies that the military struggle for

[50] See D. W. Bowett, *Self-Defense in International Law* (Manchester 1958), 156-57; and Nussbaum, 137, 153-55, 171.

[51] See Nussbaum, 182-83. Also see Ian Brownlie, *International Law and the Use of Force by States* (Oxford 1963), 15-18.

[52] Actually, the range of action provided by the contemporary formulation, especially regarding the authorization in accordance with the United Nations Charter, could be broad and could conceivably take in "balancing" action if the deadlock in the Security Council were broken. The reason for this is the very ambiguous mandate for Security Council action spelled out in the Charter. It is possible under this mandate to call the limited "balancing" action, typical of the eighteenth century, an action taken to counter a "threat to the peace." Nonetheless, given the current stalemate within the Security Council, and the nature of the General Assembly actions to date, it is safe to conclude that contemporary international law has greatly limited the wide-ranging legal capacity that states once had in deciding on the use of force.

[53] See Brownlie, 251-80, for a discussion of the contemporary legal restrictions on the use of force. Also see Kaplan and Katzenbach, 205, for a discussion of the just-war doctrine and its compatibility with the balance of power system.

power is no longer a normal process of international politics. No longer does international law legitimize the gains of war, and no longer do policy-makers look upon war as a rightful tool of national power.[54] This is not to say that states do not use force in their current struggles or that the doctrine of the just war would deter them in a particular case. However, the doctrine does operate on the conceptual level by expressing to the policy-makers the idea that the use of force is no longer an everyday tool of international power politics. In terms of the traditional assumption about the state's natural inclination to maximize power, the contemporary legal commitment to the just-war doctrine represents a profound and historic shift.

III. International Law and the Reality of Contemporary International Politics

Contemporary international legal practice, then, is developing along lines which represent a threat not only to traditional concepts of international law but also to the assumptions of the state system. The sporadic developments in international and regional organizations, the evolving place of the individual in the international legal system, and the doctrine of the just war are manifestations of the transformation occurring today both in the structure of international law and in attitudes about the state system. Actually, of course, the traditional conceptions of international law and the classical assumptions about international politics are not extinct.[55] Rather, there is in both international law and politics a perplexing mixture of past ideas and current developments. The only thing one can be sure of is that behind the traditional legal and political symbols which exist today in a somewhat mutated form, a subtle transformation of some kind is taking place.

It is not possible to evaluate the line of future development of the assumptions about the state system or the international legal expression of those assumptions from the work of contemporary theorists of international law. The most apparent new expressions are those that propose increased formalizations of world legal and political

[54] Certainly, technological developments have been primarily responsible for the rejection of war as a typical tool of international power. In this case, as in most, international legal doctrine mirrors the existing attitudes and helps to reinforce them.

[55] As in the past, international lawyers are still concerned with definitions and applications of concepts of territorial integrity, self-defense, and domestic jurisdiction, and policy-makers are still motivated by the traditional ideas of state security and power. However, the traditional political and legal symbols have been "stretched" to apply to current conditions. For a development of this position see Coplin, chaps. 4 and 8.

processes.[56] On the other hand, much international legal theory today seems to be dedicated to an affirmation of the traditional assumptions of international politics. Political analysts like Hans Morgenthau,[57] E. H. Carr,[58] and George F. Kennan,[59] and legal theorists like Julius Stone,[60] P. E. Corbett,[61] and Charles De Visscher,[62] are predisposed to "bring international law back to reality."

This trend toward being "realistic" occupies the mainstream of current international legal theory,[63] and to identify its exact nature is therefore crucial. Many writers who express this viewpoint seem to fear being labeled as overly "idealistic." They utter frequent warnings that international law cannot restore international politics to order, but, on the contrary, can exist and flourish only after there is a political agreement among states to maintain order. In short, it is assumed

[56] E.g., Arthur Larson, *When Nations Disagree* (Baton Rouge, La., 1961); or Grenville Clark and Louis B. Sohn, *World Peace Through World Law* (Cambridge, Mass., 1960). These theorists and others who fall under this classification are "radical" in the sense that what they suggest is antithetical to the assumptions of the state system as traditionally developed. These writers are not necessarily utopian in their radicalism. This is especially true since adherence today to the traditional assumptions might itself be considered a form of (reactionary) radicalism. However, the radical scholars, in the sense used here, are very scarce, especially among American students of international law. Today there is a very thin line separating the few radical scholars from the more numerous radical polemicists of world government.

[57] Morgenthau writes (277): "To recognize that international law exists is, however, not tantamount to assessing that . . . it is effective in regulating and restraining the struggle for power on the international scene."

[58] E. H. Carr, in *The Twenty Years' Crisis, 1919-1939* (London 1958), 170, writes: "We are exhorted to establish 'the rule of law' . . . and the assumption is made that, by so doing, we shall transfer our differences from the turbulent political atmosphere of self-interest to the purer, serener air of impartial justice." His subsequent analysis is designed to disprove this assumption.

[59] George F. Kennan, *Realities of American Foreign Policy* (Princeton 1954), 16.

[60] Julius Stone, *Legal Control of International Conflict* (New York 1954), introduction.

[61] Corbett, 68-79, 291-92.

[62] De Visscher writes (xiv): "International law cannot gather strength by isolating itself from the political realities with which international relations are everywhere impregnated. It can only do so by taking full account of the place that these realities occupy and measuring the obstacle which they present."

[63] The programs of the last two annual meetings of the American Society of International Law exemplify the way in which the concern for reality (as power) has come to dominate international legal theory. In the 1963 program, the relationship between international law and the use of force was not discussed by international legal theorists but by two well-known writers on the role of conflict in international politics. The 1964 program manifested the same tendency. It centered on the question of compliance with transnational law, a topic treated in a socio-political framework by most panelists. This point is not to be taken as a criticism of the two programs, both of which were excellent and very relevant, but as proof of the assertion that the mainstream of contemporary theory of international law is significantly oriented to the role of power.

that international law cannot shape international political reality, but can merely adjust to it. Although there are complaints of too much pessimism in current legal theory,[64] most writers, given the initial predisposition to avoid "idealism," do not heed them.

The desire of contemporary theorists to be "realistic" has been crucial to the relationship between contemporary international law and the assumptions of the state system. In their effort to achieve realism, current theorists have not examined their traditional assumptions about international politics. When they talk about adjusting international law to the realities of power, they usually have in mind the traditional reality of international politics. Today, a large share of the theoretical writing on international law that is designed to adapt law to political reality is in effect applying it to an image of international politics which itself is rapidly becoming outmoded. Much contemporary international legal theory, then, has not contributed to the development of a new consensus on the nature of international politics but instead has reinforced many of the traditional ideas.

In order to understand more fully the relation of international law to world politics, it is necessary to do more than examine law merely as a direct constraint on political action. The changes in the conceptual basis of international law that are manifested in current practice and, to a lesser extent, in current legal theory are symptomatic of a series of social and institutional revolutions that are transforming all of international politics. To conclude that international law must adjust to political reality, therefore, is to miss the point, since international law is part of political reality and serves as an institutional means of developing and reflecting a general consensus on the nature of international reality. In the contemporary period, where the international legal system is relatively decentralized, and international politics is subject to rapid and profound development, it is necessary to avoid a conceptual framework of international law which breeds

[64] Many writers, even realists like Morgenthau (*op.cit.*, 275) and others like McDougal and Feliciano (*op.cit.*, 2-4), decry the modern tendency toward "cynical disenchantment with law," but it is obvious from their subsequent remarks that they are reacting more against the "utopianism" of the past than the cynicism of the present. There have been a few who have attacked the "realist" position on international law (e.g., A. H. Feller, "In Defense of International Law and Morality," *Annals of the Academy of Political and Social Science*, vol. 282 [July 1951], 77-84). However, these attacks have been infrequent and generally ineffective in starting a concerted action to develop more constructive theory. For another evaluation of the "realist" trend, see Covey T. Oliver, "Thoughts on Two Recent Events Affecting the Function of Law in the International Community," in George A. Lipsky, ed., *Law and Politics in the World Community* (Berkeley 1953).

undue pessimism because it demands too much. If international law does not contribute directly and effectively to world order by forcing states to be peaceful, it does prepare the conceptual ground on which that order could be built by shaping attitudes about the nature and promise of international political reality.

[9]

International Relations and International Law: Two Optics*

Robert O. Keohane**

> The surprising thing about international law is that nations ever obey its strictures or carry out its mandates.[1]

> Public international law appears to be quite a well articulated and complete legal order even though it is difficult to locate the authoritative origin or substantive voice of the system in any particular area. Each doctrine seems to free ride somewhat on this overall systemic image . . . . Thus the variety of references among these discursive areas always shrewdly locate the moment of authority and the application in practice elsewhere—perhaps behind us in process or before us in the institutions of dispute resolution.[2]

These quotations from international lawyers encapsulate some of the puzzlement that faces a political scientist trying to understand the political underpinnings of international law. Governments make a very large number of legal agreements, and, on the whole, their compliance with these agreements seems quite high.[3] Yet what this level of compliance implies about the causal impact of commitments remains a mystery.

If states' respect for international law is surprising or puzzling to eminent professors of the subject, it is probably more so to many political scientists. Traditionally, political scientists have styled themselves as "realistic" rather than "idealistic." They are utilitarians of one form or another. According to this view, elite states seek to maintain position, wealth, and power in an uncertain world by acquiring, re-

---

* Originally given as a Sherrill Lecture at Yale University Law School on February 22, 1996.

** James B. Duke Professor of Political Science, Duke University. President, International Studies Association, 1988–1989. B.A., Shimer College, 1961; Ph.D., Harvard University, 1966. This Comment was written while the author was a Fellow at the National Humanities Center, Research Triangle Park, North Carolina; he wishes to express his gratitude to the Center for intellectual stimulation and financial support.

1. Thomas M. Franck, *Legitimacy in the International System*, 82 AM. J. INT'L. L. 705, 705 (1988).

2. DAVID KENNEDY, INTERNATIONAL LEGAL STRUCTURES 293 (1987).

3. LOUIS HENKIN, HOW NATIONS BEHAVE: LAW AND FOREIGN POLICY (2d ed. 1979).

taining, and wielding power—resources that enable them to achieve multiple purposes. States use the rules of international law as instruments to attain their interests. International law can thus be interpreted through such an "instrumentalist optic." In political science, work on international regimes—the rules guiding cooperative practices in international relations—has focused on many issues familiar to international lawyers, using a more or less nuanced version of this optic. Indeed, one eminent international lawyer—conversant with and sympathetic to political scientists' work on regimes—has characterized such work on regimes as "reinventing international law in rational-choice language."[4] That is to say, political scientists have "discovered" what to lawyers seems obvious: rules structure politics. However, as Professor Slaughter herself was generous enough to observe, political scientists have attempted more rigorously to explain phenomena with which international lawyers regularly deal. The result has been a greater convergence of research agendas than we observed two decades ago. In Professor Slaughter's words, "regime theorists" and international lawyers agree that "legal rules and decision-making procedures can be used to structure international politics,"[5] and the functions they ascribe to international regimes are remarkably similar.

Therefore, research in both law and political science has recently focused on the effects of rules in international affairs. However, there remain great differences in how observers interpret what they see. The "instrumentalist optic" puts little weight on a major theme of students of international law, namely the impact that shared norms, and the processes by which those norms are interpreted, have on state policies. Hence the "instrumentalist optic" is challenged by a "normative" one.[6] Contrasting these two optics helps to identify a key issue: How important is persuasion on the basis of norms in contemporary world politics?

I recognize that some authors, notably Friedrich Kratochwil, have viewed this causal way of looking at the problem as questionable.[7] Such an analysis indeed separates causal explanation from the function of

4. Anne-Marie Slaughter Burley, *International Law and International Relations Theory: A Dual Agenda*, 87 AM. J. INT'L L. 205, 220 (1993)

5. *Id.* at 221.

6. My discussion of instrumentalist and normative optics parallels my analysis of "rationalistic" and "reflective" approaches to international relations some years ago. Robert O. Keohane, *International Institutions: Two Approaches*, 32 INT'L. STUD. Q. 379 (1988), *reprinted in* ROBERT O. KEOHANE, INTERNATIONAL INSTITUTIONS AND STATE POWER 158 (1989). Here I am focusing less on abstract arguments, and more on attempts to understand the impact of norms on specific patterns of state behavior. Work on international law during the past few years has done quite a bit to bridge the gap between the abstraction of reflectivist theorizing, on the one hand, and observed state behavior, on the other.

7. *See* FRIEDRICH V. KRATOCHWIL, RULES, NORMS AND DECISIONS: ON THE CONDITIONS OF

moral judgment to which norms are fundamental.[8] By doing so, however, it hardly denies that such judgments are made. And the causal issue is surely central to the debate about the role of rules, even though causal inferences, especially in complex situations such as these, are always flawed. Not to confront the causal impact of rules is to evade the central issue of the role of international regimes and international law in world politics. Hence, I regard the distinction between my two optics as revolving around the problem of causality.

Both optics suffer from poorly articulated causal mechanisms or pathways. That is, it is often unclear how predicted results follow from the theory's assumptions. After discussing each optic, I will seek to sketch three concepts which seem intrinsic to the causal pathways on which both optics rely—interests, reputation, and international institutions. The role of norms could be better understood if we can construct a synthesis of the two optics that is more explicit about the role of these concepts in linking norms to actions. This Comment will attempt to integrate the best elements of the two optics into a more coherent and convincing image of how rules are used by states and how they affect state behavior.

I. THE "INSTRUMENTALIST" OPTIC

The "instrumentalist optic" focuses on interests and argues that rules and norms will matter only if they affect the calculations of interests by agents. International institutions exist because they perform valuable functions for states. They can make a difference, but only when their rules create specific opportunities and impose constraints which affect state interests. A crude version of instrumentalism discounts the observation that states often conform to rules. In this view, states only accede to rules that they favor, and comply because such conformity is convenient. According to this optic, when their interests diverge from the rules, the latter will be modified, reinterpreted, or broken to suit the convenience of powerful states. Loopholes and exceptions may be found. States will attempt to "free-ride." Even if a state benefits from other states' compliance with rules, it may benefit more if others continue to comply while it pursues its short-term self-interest. The more compelling the interest to a state in behaving contrary to the rule, the more modification, reinterpretation, and breach there will be. Compliance will be explained more by interests and power than by legitimacy.

PRACTICAL AND LEGAL REASONING IN INTERNATIONAL RELATIONS AND DOMESTIC AFFAIRS (1989).

8. *See id.* at 100.

Subtler instrumentalist arguments recognize that rules, as part of the environment faced by a state, exert an impact on state behavior. They do so, in this view, not because the norms they reflect persuade people that they should behave differently. Rather, they alter incentives, not merely for states conceived of as units, but for interest groups, organizations, members of professional associations, and individual policymakers within governments.

This optic is by no means exclusively the province of political scientists. The revised Restatement of American Foreign Relations Law emphasizes state interests: "international law generally is largely observed because violations directly affect the interests of states, which are alert to deter, prevent, or respond to violations."[9] Another compliance-inducing interest is the desire to maintain a pattern of beneficial cooperation. A state "may decide to forgo the short-term advantages derived from violating rules because it has an overriding interest in maintaining the overall system."[10]

Law professors, however, tend to extend their analysis beyond interests. From their standpoint, a significant drawback of relying on interests is that the impact of law itself in such a conceptualization is small. Abram and Antonia Chayes view the instrumental approach as too passive. "In our view, what is left out of this institutionalist account is the active role of the regime in modifying preferences, generating new options, persuading the parties to move toward increasing compliance with regime norms, and guiding the evolution of the normative structure in the direction of the overall objectives of the regime."[11]

For many political scientists, interest-based propositions are more congenial. However, even those who are attracted to instrumentalism and its functional logic should recognize that it handles poorly that which makes politics interesting; that is, the unanticipated consequences of human action. Instrumentalism, especially its most powerful tool, game theory, does quite well as long as we can assume that actors can anticipate the conditions of future strategic choice. However, instrumentalism cannot deal very well with situations in which choices today affect what people will believe tomorrow when the interests can be reinterpreted.

Instrumentalist arguments are too often taken as obvious, not requiring testing. State "interests" may be inferred from their behavior, which is then "explained" by the very same interests. When states

9. *In* LOUIS HENKIN ET AL., INTERNATIONAL LAW: CASES AND MATERIALS 1007 (1987) [hereinafter ILC].

10. Phillip R. Trimble, *International Law, World Order and Critical Legal Studies*, 42 STAN. L. REV. 811, 833 (1990).

11. ABRAM CHAYES & ANTONIA HANDLER CHAYES, THE NEW SOVEREIGNTY: COMPLIANCE WITH INTERNATIONAL REGULATORY AGREEMENTS 229 (1995).

violate rules, they must have had interests in doing so; when they refrain from reneging, their interests determined that as well. Like Viola in the first act of *Twelfth Night*, such an argument is "fortified against all denial."[12] We do not yet have a well-specified or empirically tested instrumentalist theory of compliance with international commitments.

II. INTERNATIONAL LAW AND THE "NORMATIVE OPTIC"

International lawyers often argue that the legitimacy of norms and rules has causal effect. Phillip Trimble declares that international law is a form of "rhetoric," whose persuasiveness is largely a function of its legitimacy. Legitimacy, in turn, is related to the process by which it is created, its consistency with accepted general norms, and its perceived fairness or specificity.[13] Legitimacy, says Thomas M. Franck, exerts a "compliance pull," which competes with the pull exerted by interests in reneging. Rules that are determinate and coherent—important components of legitimacy—are associated with greater compliance than those that are not, at least in part because their clarity makes it possible "to dismiss bogus, self-serving interpretations."[14] Officials may routinely keep many commitments because they have respect for law.[15] "Because of the requirements of law or of some prior agreement, nations modify their conduct in significant respect and in substantial degrees."[16]

Several international lawyers emphasize that the normative power of treaty rules, whether one calls it "legitimacy" or something else, is "derive[d] from a complicated dialogic process of interpretation and application, extending over time."[17] In this view, law operates through the activities of "interpretive communities," which operate largely through international institutions. The International Monetary Fund, the Standing Consultative Commission in the SALT agreements, the International Labor Organization, and the International Whaling Commission constitute examples of institutions within which challenges and defenses of state behavior, relative to rules, take place. Interpretive communities, in this view, constrain subjective interpretations, promote habitual compliance, and impose reputational costs on violators of norms, as interpreted by these communities.[18]

---

12. William Shakespeare, Twelfth Night act 1, sc. 5.
13. *See* Trimble, *supra* note 10, at 839–40.
14. Franck, *supra* note 1, at 738.
15. *See* Thomas M. Franck, The Power of Legitimacy Among Nations (1990); Trimble, *supra* note 10.
16. ILC, *supra* note 9 at 9; *see also* Louis Henkin, How Nations Behave: Law and Foreign Policy 42 (2d ed. 1979).
17. Chayes & Chayes, *supra* note 11, at 134.
18. *See* Ian Johnstone, *Treaty Interpretation: The Authority of Interpretive Communities*, 12 Mich.

According to this "normative optic," norms have causal impact. The impact of interests and power is by no means denied, but such explanations are not sufficient. Norms and rules do not operate mechanically; they are always subject to contestation, interpretation, and reinterpretation. But the norms and rules themselves set the terms of the interpretive discourse. They exert a profound impact on how people think about state roles and obligations, and therefore on state behavior. This "normative optic" shows respect for the discourse that takes place when commitments are contested. It is also consistent with the attention that policymakers pay to norms and ideas about what makes norms legitimate. How else can one account for the enormous amount of argument over rule interpretation? The assumption on which this activity relies is that states are obliged to follow rules to which they have consented.

When one looks for strong motivations for governments to take the discourse seriously, however, the arguments become vague. The "central proposition" of *The New Sovereignty* is that "the interpretation, elaboration, application, and ultimately, enforcement of international rules is accomplished through a process of (mostly verbal) interchange among the interested parties."[19] But why should such verbal interchange exert such an impact? Compliance is said to preserve "connection to the real world" and prevent "isolation,"[20] but it is not clear that noncompliance leads to isolation. Much of this discourse can be explained as facilitating the solution of problems of coordination or assurance, through generally understood and precise language, by specifying focal points, and by linking issues together through the use of precedent. However, the literature promoting the normative optic says little about the boundaries of effectiveness of such discourse; it is not always effective. What conditions facilitate or inhibit its operation? In the end, the claim that discourse leads to compliance rests largely on a reputational argument. In this view, an important motive of state leaders is to maintain their reputation, which exerts a substantial pull toward compliance. "In an interdependent and interconnected world, a reputation for reliability matters."[21] But as Heymann and Kratochwil have perceptively argued, reputation is a tricky concept, and may provide a weak basis for confidence in the impact of rules, unless the conditions under which such confidence is justified are carefully spe-

J. INT'L. L. 371 (1991), *excerpted in* ANTHONY D'AMATO, INTERNATIONAL LAW ANTHOLOGY 121–24 (1994).

19. CHAYES & CHAYES, *supra* note 11, at 118.

20. *Id.* at 27.

21. *Id.* at 230.

cific.[22] I will discuss reputation, and its implications for the two optics, below.

Empirically, it is hard to validate causal arguments about the impact of norms or discourse. It is often pointed out that norms can exist even if human behavior sometimes contradicts them.[23] This is a fair point, but as I have noted, it begs the causal questions in which I am most interested. "Legitimacy" is difficult to measure independent from the compliance that it is supposed to explain. For instance, Franck describes a rule's compliance "pull power" as "its index of legitimacy."[24] Yet legitimacy is said to explain "compliance pull," making the argument circular. Phillip Trimble admits that his claim that compliance may depend on legitimacy "may be difficult to prove empirically."[25]

In addition, there are some serious methodological issues not fully addressed by writers in this tradition. Assume arguendo that the crude instrumentalists were right: states only comply with rules that are in their material interests to obey or that are enforced by the threats of powerful states. We could then assume in this hypothetical illustration that norms carry little weight. Now let us make some other assumptions about the particular situation that we observe.

1) Agents are quite good at assessing their interests and anticipating the actions of others.

2) A few powerful states made most of the rules and seek to enforce them, and

3) Coordination and assurance situations—in which everyone has an interest in following the rules provided that others do so as well—are common.

Under these conditions, we would expect to see many international legal agreements, and a high level of compliance, even if norms played no role whatsoever. We would only be observing a "selection effect;" that is, agreements that were neither self-enforcing nor enforceable by the powerful states' threats, would normally not be made in the first place. Observing that states follow international law most of the time does not, therefore, yield a valid causal inference. Certainly legal rules provide "focal points" for coordinating state behavior.[26] Do they also exert a significant causal impact on the behavior of states? Or more properly, under what conditions do they exert such an impact? The

22. *See* Philip B. Heymann, *The Problem of Coordination: Bargaining and Rules*, 86 HARV. L. REV. 797 (1973); KRATOCHWIL, *supra* note 7.

23. *See id.*

24. Franck, *supra* note 1, at 712.

25. Trimble, *supra* note 10, at 842.

26. Geoffrey Garrett & Barry Weingast, *Ideas, Interests, and Institutions: Constructing the European Community's Common Market*, *in* IDEAS AND FOREIGN POLICY 173 (Judith Goldstein & Robert O. Keohane eds., 1993).

normative optic presents us with intriguing observations that seem anomalous for the mainstream political science view. However, when we seek to establish causality, we are left with an incomplete argument and empirical ambiguity.

III. EVALUATION

Both of these optics seem necessary, yet neither is sufficient. It is as if each observer only has one eye, and is wearing blinders. What each one sees, emerges with great clarity, but it is not the whole picture, and neither viewer has any depth perception. It can hardly be disputed that some states follow the instrumentalist optic some of the time. Most of the time, however, the policies of all states are affected by their material interests, as perceived by their elites; and the relative power capabilities of states are relevant to the degree to which they can achieve their purposes. The literature on international institutions has demonstrated, over the last twenty years, that states do modify their behavior in light of rules, although the extent to which they do so is contested.

What is at issue, however, is not the relevance of the instrumentalist optic, but its sufficiency. Is persuasion on the basis of norms also important in world politics? Are interests redefined in light of principled beliefs, rather than only instrumentally in terms of power, wealth, and position? At this point, my rhetorical dichotomy between the instrumentalist and normative optics begins to break down. Instrumental arguments play a key role in the claims of analysts who attribute persuasive weight to rules. In particular, as discussed above, concern for reputation—a classically instrumentalist concept—plays a major role in arguments about why states obey rules. We will now have to move from outlining the differences between the two optics, to analyzing how the normative optic depends on, but goes beyond, the instrumental one. The fundamental question can be stated simply: Do discourse and persuasion matter, or are calculations of interest and power all that really count?

To answer this question, we need somehow to trace out the causal pathways on which these two optics rely and to generate testable propositions from them. Although not attempted in the present Comment, researchers should eventually test these hypotheses against evidence chosen to minimize bias, rather than merely to illustrate arguments. My approach here is to focus on three concepts that seem essential to any coherent account of how rules relate to state action: interests, reputation, and institutions. They are nodes on causal pathways; one could not make a coherent argument about the impact of rules without passing through these nodes. Both optics recognize the role of interests and reputation. The normative optic, and the most persuasive versions of instrumentalism, also acknowledge the role of institutions—discounted only by crude self-styled "realists," to their peril.

IV. THE OPTICS' CAUSAL PATHWAYS AND THEIR COMMON NODES

The persuasiveness of either optic relies on a narrative account that traces a causal pathway from its favored explanatory variables to compliance. Such a pathway has to pass through the elites within countries, and in both optics, these elites are viewed as making calculations about the consequences of their actions. That is, they are rational in the limited sense that they seek to relate means to ends in such a way as to achieve their ends most reliably. These rational elites do not have full information, either about alternatives or about their consequences. On the contrary, they operate under considerable uncertainty.[27] Making decisions under uncertainty, they need to calculate interests and assess the reputations of others, within the context of institutional procedures and rules.

A. *Interests*

Both optics focus on the "interests" of policy elites. For instrumentalists, these interests are usually taken to be power, wealth, and position (position in the international system with regard to states and offices for individuals). The basic instrumentalist heuristic is to attribute observed behavior to the rational pursuit of self-interest. The ideal instrumentalist "explanation" identifies a causal pathway linking behavior to underlying interests. Other causal processes, such as those involving misinformation or cognitive failure, may be appealed to. However, they usually gain their heuristic force from the failure of rational-interest explanations to provide a compelling account of the behavior in question.

An implication sometimes drawn from instrumentalist argument is that more demanding international rules are likely to be more vulnerable than rules requiring less extensive cooperation. For instance, George Downs and Stephen Rocke calculate how vulnerable different tariff reductions would be in GATT based on various assumptions about transparency and the required time for retaliation. They assume that states, being instrumentalists, will break rules when it is advantageous to do so. They wish to understand what level of cooperation can be

27. Charles E. Lindblom, The Intelligence of Democracy (1965).

sustained by reciprocity-based strategies.[28] They fail to consider the possibility that demanding rules, involving liberalization of tariffs, would alter participants' conceptions of their interests. Yet it is the fixity or plasticity of interests that is precisely at issue in many contemporary international relations debates. International institutions may affect states' formulations of their own interests. If interests become "endogenous" in this sense, institutions with demanding rules could be less, rather than more, vulnerable to reneging, as the increasing authority of the European Union would appear to suggest.

International lawyers also discuss interests, but they are inclined to point out, along with many political scientists, that "the concept of self-interest is itself problematic."[29] Whose self? Which interest? High-level governmental actors play multiple roles, ranging from tough negotiator with foreign governments to official sworn to uphold the law. It is not obvious which role will define the individual's view on a given issue. Even if the role is clear, there are likely to be competing interests. For instance, the President may need to choose between the immediate benefits of reneging on a commitment and the uncertain, longer-term costs of doing so. Over time, as the examples of trade politics and the European Union illustrate, policies will alter the structure of the political economy—including existing firms and groups and their own preferences. Hence policies may alter the interests of states.[30] Often, as historical institutionalists have argued, these changes are not anticipated by the agents who initiated the policy change.

Furthermore, constructivist lawyers and political scientists have made a strong case that the roles that representatives of states assume, and even their conceptions of self-interest, depend significantly on the rules and practices of international institutions.[31] Consequently, how actors' interests are constructed remains an open question. The instrumentalist optic has interests more sharply in focus than the normative optic: it is clearer what those interests are, and that the arguments being made are not circular. But the fact that institutions can structure interests means that interests are not the instrumentalists' trump cards after all.

B. Reputation

Both optics recognize that policymakers are concerned about their reputations. Hence their immediate interests are not necessarily con-

28. *See* George Downs & Stephen A. Rocke, Optimal Imperfection ch. 4 (1995).

29. Trimble, *supra* note 10, at 842 n.115.

30. Ronald Rogowski, Commerce and Coalitions (1989).

31. Kratochwil, *supra* note 7; Alexander Wendt, *Anarchy Is What States Make of It: The Social Construction of Power Politics*, 46 Int'l Org. 39 (1992).

trolling. They may be concerned about what Robert Axelrod has called "the shadow of the future"—that is, the effects of their present actions on others' future behavior.[32] To many international lawyers, reputation is a bulwark for the maintenance of commitments: "Considerations of 'honor,' 'prestige,' 'leadership,' 'influence,' 'reputation,' which figure prominently in governmental decisions, often weigh in favor of observing law."[33] However, it may be desirable to have a reputation not only for keeping agreements, but for vigorously pursuing one's interests, helping one's friends, and punishing one's enemies.[34] Clearly, these reputational incentives may be in conflict; and the latter incentives do not necessarily counsel compliance with commitments. Reputations come in many forms. Our joint optic must take into account the potential value of a reputation for keeping agreements; but it must also consider the less savory forms of reputation.

As Philip Heymann observed, reneging on commitments has consequences for reputation only when a limiting set of conditions is met. "[A]ny violation must be known; it must be known by a party whose reactions to the violation are important to the violator; and the expected costs of violation to the violator must exceed the benefits of giving in to the conflicting temptation."[35] Furthermore, for the expected costs of reneging to be substantial, some party other than the violator must have both the ability and the incentive to react to the violation. Unfortunately for those who rely on reputation, these conditions are often not met in the world of politics.

There is a second problem with reputation as a guarantor of compliance. Governments may value reputations for toughness or even for being willing to bully weaker states, more than they value reputations for compliance with commitments. United States intervention in the Caribbean helped it maintain a reputation for toughness, whether against pro-communist rulers or detested dictators, while foregoing an opportunity to forge a reputation for fidelity with commitments. Reneging on its financial commitments to the United Nation seems to have conferred additional leverage on the United States, rather than reducing its influence as a result of a weakened reputation.

A third difficulty with reliance on reputation is that strong governments are sometimes monopolists in the sense that they can compel others to interact with them.[36] For example, once the United States

32. Robert Axelrod, The Evolution of Cooperation (1984).

33. Henkin, *supra* note 16, at 52, *cited with approval in* Johnstone, *supra* note 18, at 390.

34. Thomas Schelling, The Strategy of Conflict (1980); *see also* David Kreps & Robert Wilson, *Reputation and Imperfect Information*, 27 J. Econ. Theory 253 (1982).

35. Heymann, *supra* note 22, at 822–23.

36. *But see* Robert Keohane, After Hegemony: Cooperation and Discord in the World Political Economy 129–30 (1984). In this previous work, I relied on an analogy

became a great power, and particularly after it became hegemonic in the West, other countries could not avoid dealing with it. The United States was "the only game in town," and even if its reputation suffered, other governments had little choice as to with whom to transact.

Finally, even if governments are concerned about their reputations for compliance with agreements, they may be able to devise strategies, or legal arguments, to veil their noncompliance. If concealing noncompliance is impossible, they may still seek to differentiate the situations in which they failed to comply, from ongoing relationships on which they want to continue to make agreements.

A dramatic instance of such differentiation occurred at the peace conference at Ghent in 1814 between the United States and Great Britain. Britain, which had been allied with various Indian tribes, sought a definite and permanent boundary between the United States and Indian territories, a request that the United States negotiators refused on the grounds that the population of the United States must have room to expand. The American negotiators worked to differentiate this aim (which entailed frequent breaking of commitments) from reneging on boundary agreements with European countries.

> If this be a spirit of aggrandizement, the undersigned are prepared to admit, in that sense, its existence; but they must deny that it affords the slightest proof of an intention not to respect the boundaries between them and European nations, or of a desire to encroach upon the territories of Great Britain . . . . They will not suppose that [Great Britain] will avow, as the basis of their policy towards the United States, the system of arresting their natural growth within their own territories, for the sake of preserving a perpetual desert for savages.[37]

In other words, reneging on commitments to "savages" was not to affect the United States reputation for keeping commitments to "civilized" powers.

Before discussing the third "node" in our decision-making process—institutions—let us assess briefly the two nodes analyzed above. Interests are indeed important. However, actors can redefine their own interests, in light of policies followed by others and the practices of international institutions. Hence, interests are neither fixed nor firm; they are not a solid platform on which to build a theory of rational

---

between reputation and the credit ratings of borrowers, as discussed by Walter Bagehot. Unfortunately, this analogy is fallacious. Lenders have many borrowers to lend to. If one borrower's reputation suffers, creditors can lend to others at only a slight cost, representing the reduction in interest rates resulting from a decline in demand.

37. 9 AMERICAN STATE PAPERS 407 (2d. ed., T.B. Wait and Sons, 1817).

self-interest. Both optics see reputation as important, but reputations can be instrumental for a variety of purposes, depending on the context. The normative optic seems to make reputation both more one-dimensional than it is, and larger than life—like a cardboard cutout figure in the normative telescope. Concerns about reputation sometimes lead to the fulfillment of commitments, but they do not always do so. Thinking creatively about institutions could derive clues to a better understanding of both interests and reputation, and how norms could affect state decisions through their effects on interests and reputation.

C. *Institutions*

Lawyers and political scientists both recognize that institutions matter. In modern states, calculations about the consequences of different courses of action, in response to changes in the external world, depend on the authority of legislatures, executives, and courts, and on the rules that govern the access to power of nongovernmental actors. International lawyers have had a lot to say about the role of domestic governments, domestic courts, and the European Court of Justice, in the implementation and interpretation of law.[38]

Sophisticated instrumentalists recognize that the rational, self-interested actions of the political actors they study are contingent on institutions. Agenda-setting and delegation have become important topics in political science.[39] Two of the most important functions of institutions are to provide information to participants and to link issues to one another in the context of a larger set of valued activities.[40] By looking more closely at the role of information, we can see how a coherent instrumentalism is dependent on beliefs and, therefore, on norms.[41] Indeed, we could understand the mutual relationship between beliefs and interests in a more sophisticated way by sketching missing

38. BENEDETTO CONFORTI, INTERNATIONAL LAW AND THE ROLE OF DOMESTIC LEGAL SYSTEMS (1993); Burley, *supra* note 4; Anne-Marie Burley & Walter Mattli, *Europe Before the Court: A Political Theory of Legal Integration*, 47 INT'L ORG. 41 (1993).

39. ANDREW MORAVCSIK, WHY THE EUROPEAN COMMUNITY STRENGTHENS THE STATE: DOMESTIC POLITICS AND INTERNATIONAL COOPERATION (Center for European Studies Working Paper Series No. 52, 1994); J. MARK RAMSAYER & FRANCES MCCALL ROSENBLUTH, JAPAN'S POLITICAL MARKETPLACE (1993); Kenneth Shepsle & Barry Weingast, *The Institutional Foundations of Committee Power*, 81 AM. POL. SCI. REV. 85(1987); Lisa L. Martin, Democratic Commitments: Legislatures and International Cooperation (Oct. 1995) (unpublished manuscript, on file with Harvard University Center for International Affairs).

40. *See* KEOHANE, *supra* note 36, at 244–45; Lisa L. Martin, *Interests, Power and Multilateralism*, 46 INT'L ORG. 765 (1992).

41. *Cf.* David Kreps, *Corporate Culture and Economic Theory*, *in* PERSPECTIVES ON POSITIVE POLITICAL ECONOMY 90 (James E. Alt & Kenneth A. Shepsle eds., 1990) (analyzing the proposition in the area of corporate culture); Paul Milgrom et al., *The Role of Institutions in the Revival of Trade: The Law Merchant, Private Judges, and the Champagne Fairs*, 2 ECON. & POL. 1 (1990).

links that involve institutions and reputation. There are three components.

First, we could begin with the instrumentalist premise that institutions depend on interests. But as game theory shows, behavior also depends on the information one has. In Prisoners' Dilemma and Assurance games, strategy is contingent upon expectations about others' behavior. Indeed, the major lesson of modern game theory is how behavior is sensitive to different information conditions. Since world politics involves strategic interaction, any good theory of world politics needs to treat information as a variable.

Second, it follows that interests as interpreted by actors (even when the motivational base is entirely material self-interest) depend on information as well as on underlying payoffs. Therefore, interests depend on reputations.

Finally, reputations depend on institutions. States cultivate reputations because of what good reputations will enable them to achieve. In the normative optic, their purpose is to realize their principles; in the instrumentalist one, to achieve self-interested objectives. Institutions that lengthen the shadow of the future or link otherwise separate issues together may create incentives to cooperate now for the sake of promoting cooperation by others later.[42] Hence institutions matter even if they cannot enforce rules from above because they affect reputations which are useful to cultivate. But concern about reputation is not a magic elixir that aligns self-interests with benign norms such as promise-keeping.

Thinking clearly about reputation and institutions helps us to see how the insights of the instrumentalist and normative optics may jointly contribute to our understanding of international regimes and international law. Interests shape institutions, which affect beliefs, including reputations, which in turn affect interests. In particular, institutions can affect what kind of reputation it is most useful for governments to acquire. Institutions that states strongly value can promote cooperation by linking normatively prescribed behavior, such as fulfilling commitments, to the continued receipt of material or normative benefits from the institutions.

The benefits of fulfilling one's own commitments may be material, such as the rewards of most-favored nation treatment in the World Trade Organization. They may also be instrumental to other self-interested objectives. For instance, not being a notable violator of GATT or WTO rules is important if a state seeks to bring cases against other

42. Axelrod, *supra* note 32; Lisa L. Martin, *Heterogeneity, Linkage, and Commons Problems*, *in* Local Commons and Global Interdependence: Heterogeneity and Cooperation in Two Domains 71 (Robert O. Keohane & Elinor Ostrom eds., 1994).

states that arguably are breaking or bending the rules. Blocking a consensus in the European Union on issues of importance to others may be costly to the success of one's own initiatives. Conversely, reneging on commitments to the United Nations, as the withholding of United States dues has shown, may carry few costs, and may even enhance the reneger's leverage in institutional bargaining.

The benefits of fulfilling commitments may also be normative. The reward may be acceptance as a "member in good standing" of the international trading community, or even the knowledge that one is helping to uphold valued institutions. But it is hardly of great normative value to have a reputation for supporting institutions that one despises. There are few rewards for blindly acquiescing in attempts by a majority in the United Nations to create law that is inconsistent both with one's principles and interests.

Within the context of valued institutions, instrumental and normative incentives work in tandem with each other, not at cross-purposes. In instrumentalist language, what is essential to an institution for it to function well is that it helps to align these various types of incentives in ways that support the mission of the institution. In normative language, well-functioning institutions are those that facilitate persuasion and cooperation on the basis of widely held values. In practice, these two descriptions may amount to the same thing.

CONCLUSION

The two optics that I have constructed here are stylizations, perhaps even stereotypes. Few experienced or perceptive observers of international relations would exclusively adopt one or the other. I share the aspirations of many commentators to find a productive synthesis between them. Let me briefly review the keys to my proposed synthesis. Interests are changeable, responding to changes in descriptive information, causal beliefs, and principled beliefs. Hence norms matter for interests. So do beliefs about others' beliefs; that is, reputation. Concern for reputation can be a means of reconciling instrumentalist prescriptions with normative ones. However, this reconciliation only takes place reliably within the context of highly valued institutions, which align material and extra-material incentives. Institutions are especially important for the way in which they can alter beliefs, can sometimes influence what we want or do, and can always affect how others will behave if they have any impact at all.

If I am right, much depends in world politics not only on material interests and on normative views but on how institutions are designed. Institutions need to be consistent with both broad patterns of power and interests. But they also need to create interests and incentives to develop reputations which support the institutions. Institutions also need to be consistent with the basic normative commitments of their members, so that having a reputation for supporting the institution has intrinsic, as well as instrumental, value.

My analysis, if true, has implications for our work as citizens, advocates, and policy advisors.

Since institutions tend to persist, democratic governments should be alert to ensure that their principles and rules reflect the values of democratic societies, while being sufficiently flexible to adapt to the changing demands of international society. We need to align our interests with the norms we value, as we adjust these practices to the demands of others. Such alignments of interests with values require institutions. Showing the necessity for such institutions, and helping to craft them, constitute intellectual and policy challenges for international lawyers and political scientists. Designing effective international institutions is a worthy vocation that international lawyers and political scientists can embrace together, with enthusiasm and a sense of purpose.

[10]

The Waning of the Sovereign State: Towards a New Paradigm for International Law? *

Christoph Schreuer **

I. Introduction: The Dominant Role of the Sovereign State

The concept of an international community made up of sovereign States is the basis of our intellectual framework for international law. A look at history, however, tells us that conceptions of world order have by no means always been shaped by the model of sovereign co-equal actors with a territorial basis. Although there are old historical precedents for relations between territorial communities on an equal footing, the imperial conceptions of Roman times and of the Middle Ages were based on entirely different ideas. They were strongly hierarchical and paralleled religious or secular concepts of subordination and dependence. Sixteen forty-eight, the year of the Peace of Westphalia, is usually given as the decisive date for the transition from the vertical imperial to the horizontal inter-State model.[1] Needless to say, in historical terms this is an oversimplification. The Empire existed until 1806 and the process towards sovereign equality was gradual. It culminated with the collapse in the early twentieth century of the Austro-Hungarian and Ottoman Empires, and the displacement of the Concert of Europe as the most important international arena by an open global community of States.

Colonialism was not really a deviation from this movement. The existence of different forms of social organization in other parts of the world was a welcome excuse for European powers with colonial ambitions to deny statehood to these communities and to annex the territory inhabited by them.[2] Decolonization consisted basically of the extension of European political structures to these

* This article is a revised version of a paper presented at the Paul H. Nitze School of Advanced International Studies (SAIS) in Washington, D.C. on 21 February 1992.

** Edward B. Burling Professor of International Law and Organization, Paul H. Nitze School of Advanced International Studies.

1 See Falk, 'The Interplay of Westphalia and Charter Conceptions of International Legal Order', in R. Falk & C. Black (eds), *The Future of the International Legal Order*, Vol. 1 (1969) 32, 43.

2 Cf. Ginther, 'Systemwandel und Theoriendynamik im Völkerrecht', in P. Feuerstein, C. Parry, *Multum non Multa, Festschrift Lipstein* (1980) 31, 36.

communities.[3] The sovereign State as the prototype of international actor has become the universal standard.

Contemporary international law presupposes this structure of co-equal sovereign States. The international community's constitutive set-up is dominated by it. The classical sources of international law depend on the interaction of States in the form of treaties and customary law. Diplomatic relations are conducted between States. Official arenas, like international organizations and international courts, are largely reserved to States. The protection of individual rights still depends mostly on diplomatic protection through State representatives. Central concepts of international law, like sovereignty, territorial integrity, non-intervention, self-defence or permanent sovereignty over natural resources all rely on the exclusive or dominant role of the State.[4]

Interestingly enough, the advent of participants with new ideological orientations, like the socialist States or the developing countries, has not detracted from this State-centred perspective. Despite their claims for a more progressive world order, statehood and the exclusive prerogatives attached to it have been very prominent in their programmes.

This classical model of international law as the law to be applied among sovereign States has undoubtedly served useful purposes, but it also has serious shortcomings. The concentration of authority at the level of national governments has facilitated the abuse of power. The internal exercise of power has largely been insulated from the scrutiny of the larger community by such concepts as sovereign prerogative and internal affairs. The need to protect the national community from external danger frequently serves as a justification for internal repression.[5]

The convergence of formal authority in the hands of a small central ruling elite, the government, has also contributed to an inherent instability in the international system. This concentration of official transnational contacts has created dangerous breaking points in international relations. The highly personalized nature of inter-State relations conducted by a small number of individuals creates situations where disagreements on specific issues can lead to disproportionate consequences for the respective national communities, or the international community at large.

International law has responded to these and many other problems with a rapidly growing body of substantive rules ranging from human rights issues to control over the use of military force. These prescriptions have limited the freedom of lawful action by States in detail but have left the basic structure of international law unchanged. The States have retained control over their obligations. International law has increased in volume, but has mostly remained a law that is applicable among States. Sovereignty is no longer absolute. It has been harnessed to some extent, but its core has remained

3 A good example for the clash between the classical concept of statehood and other cultural concepts of control of a society over territory is provided by the International Court of Justice's analysis in the *Western Sahara* case, ICJ Reports (1975) 10.

4 See Koskenniemi, 'The Future of Statehood', 32 *Harv. Int'l L.J.* (1991) 397, 406.

5 Koskenniemi, ibid., at 397-400.

intact. The volume of international regulation has not changed the basic power structures.

The obvious weakness of the traditional system has prompted a search for alternatives. A recurrent theme in this search is the projection of the State's internal organization onto the international level. However, the structures of the modern State and its legal system are not necessarily a useful model for international organization.[6] World State or super State institutions are not the answer.[7] They are unrealistic because they do not reflect the decentralized nature of the international community, a feature which is likely to persist in the foreseeable future. They are inadequate because centralism is not a promising recipe for social stability or a better world order. A civil war is no improvement over an international conflict. These models are also undesirable because they tend to stifle pluralism and cultural diversity. This applies not only to global systems but to regional ones as well. For instance, it is unhelpful and misleading to judge progress in the European Community by its approximation to a United States of Europe, which is usually modelled after the United States of America.

The traditional image of the international community composed of sovereign and equal States has not only displayed practical shortcomings, but has also shown weaknesses as a theoretical model. In particular, the concept of equality among States is to a large extent based on fiction. The enormous differences between participants in terms of power and wealth have created a constant tension between basic conceptions of international law and reality.

In addition, the monolithic picture of an international legal community consisting of States was never entirely accurate. International law has always accepted certain actors in addition to States, at least for certain purposes. They include the Holy See, international organizations, the International Committee of the Red Cross, Amnesty International, corporations and individuals. However, the dominant role of States has never really been questioned by these additional actors. They were either established and controlled or at least tolerated by the States.

II. Towards a Greater Diversity of Participants

More important than a description of present realities are certain trends perceptible in the role of actors in the international system and in authoritative power structures. States are delegating or relinquishing some of their functions to other actors on the sub-State level as well as on the inter-State level.

6 Falk, *supra* note 1, at 42.
7 See also Bleckmann, 'Zur Strukturanalyse im Völkerrecht', 9 *Rechtstheorie* (1978) 143, 155.

A. Sub-State Entities

In federal States official functions are divided between the federal government and the component units (states, regions, cantons, provinces). International law has a tendency to turn a blind eye to federal structures and regards their distribution of functions as an internal matter. This attitude has reinforced a unitary conception of the sovereign State and of international law as a horizontal system of co-equal participants.

A number of national constitutions concede limited authority to sub-State entities to regulate certain matters across national boundaries with other States or sub-State entities.[8] Countries with provisions or practice to this effect include Germany,[9] Switzerland,[10] Canada,[11] the United States,[12] most recently Austria,[13] and the now defunct constitutions of Yugoslavia[14] and the USSR.[15] The practical importance of these competences varies considerably. In the United States it is very limited and of little or no political relevance.[16] In all these constitutions, the foreign relations power of sub-State entities is limited to matters assigned to them for internal regulation and is subject to strict federal control.

Not infrequently, sub-State entities enter into local transboundary arrangements to regulate matters such as environmental protection, utilization of lakes and rivers and regional planning.[17] The classification of these arrangements as extra-legal and not properly belonging to the sphere of international law[18] is probably more the expression of an inability to come to terms with this phenomenon than an adequate description of reality.

8 Generally see L. Wildhaber, *Treaty-Making Power and Constitution* (1971) 254-343; L. di Marzo, *Component Units of Federal States and International Agreements* (1980); H.J. Michelmann, P. Soldatos (eds), *Federalism and International Relations, the Role of Subnational Units* (1990).

9 Article 32 para. 3 of the German Basic Law (Constitution); W. Rudolf, 'Bundesstaat und Völkerrecht', 27 *Archiv des Völkerrechts* (1989) 1.

10 Article 9 of the Swiss Constitution; Wildhaber, 'External Relations of the Swiss Cantons', 12 *Can. Y.B. Int'l L.* (1974) 211.

11 L. di Marzo, *supra* note 8 at 42-48, 60-61, 70-74, 84, 91-94, 135-144; McWhinney, 'Canadian Federalism, and the Foreign Affairs and Treaty Making Power. The Impact of Quebec's "Quiet Revolution"', 7 *Can. Y.B. Int'l L.* (1969) 3.

12 Article I, Section 10, clause 3 of the US Constitution. See *Restatement (third) of the Foreign Relations Law of the United States* (1987) para. 302, comment f.; Rodgers, 'The Capacity of States of the Union to Conclude International Agreements: The Background and Some Recent Developments', 61 *AJIL* (1967) 1021.

13 Article 16 paras. 1-2 of the Constitution; M. Thaler, *Die Vertragsabschlußkompetenz der österreichischen Bundesländer* (1990).

14 Article 271 para. 2 of the pre-1992 Constitution.

15 Article 80. See Uibopuu, 'International Legal Personality of Union Republics of USSR', 24 *ICLQ* (1975) 811.

16 Cf. L. Henkin, *Foreign Affairs and the Constitution* (1972) 227-248; Bilder, 'The Role of States and Cities in Foreign Relations', 83 *AJIL* (1989) 821.

17 See, e.g., Agreement on Acid Precipitation between Québec and the State of New York, 26 July 1982, 21 ILM (1982) 721.

18 See, e.g., Comment of the Canadian Department of External Affairs Legal Bureau of 25 January 1979, 18 *Can. Y.B. Int'l L.* (1980) 316-317.

B. International Institutions

The picture is considerably more dynamic when it comes to international organizations. Over the last decades, States have created numerous regional and global organizations. The mere existence of a large number of these organizations does not necessarily signal a change in the structure of the international system. International organizations which are no more than an arena for the interaction of their Members merely underline the inter-State nature of the traditional system. However, States have also transferred a considerable number of functions and powers to them. To the extent that these institutions become actors in their own right and exercise some measure of authority and control they must be seen as a new dimension in the international community.

This process is more advanced in the European Community than in any other organization. The Community has assumed functions in a wide array of areas hitherto considered typical State prerogatives. These include regulation of external trade, economic policy, anti-trust regulation, social policy, regional policy and environmental protection to name just a few. These functions are exercised by way of Community legislation, administration and adjudication. The Community's power to enter into external commitments is parallel to these internal competences[19] and has found expression in numerous treaties. On the other hand, the Community is far from being a super-State. Despite progress towards the internal market, improved political cooperation in external matters and projects for economic, monetary and political union,[20] the statehood of its members is not going to vanish in the foreseeable future.[21] The most important place of European decision-making is still the Council of Ministers, which is composed of the representatives of individual governments, even though the directly elected European Parliament has made advances in some areas of legislation. The Community's budget, huge as it may seem for an international organization, is still less than two per cent of the aggregate of its Members' budgets.

On the global level, this process has been much less spectacular. Much of the activity there is simply communication and cooperation among States. The United Nations Charter provides for far-reaching functions of the Security Council in the area of peace and security, but until recently these have only been utilized to a minimal extent. Significantly, the procedures leading to such decisions deviate from the traditional concept of sovereign equality through permanent seats and the power of veto.

The General Assembly of the United Nations has become the world's clearing house for ideas and sentiments with an agenda covering practically all matters of

19 See the decision of the European Court in Case 22/70, *AETR* [1971] ECR 274.

20 See especially the Treaty on European Union, signed in Maastricht on 7 February 1992, OJ 1992 C 191/1, 31 ILM (1992) 247, in force 1 November 1993.

21 Cf. generally W. Meng, *Das Recht der Internationalen Organisationen – eine Entwicklungsstufe des Völkerrechts* (1979).

international legal concern. Although the legal authority of its resolutions is disputed, its influence on the flow of legal developments is undeniable. It may well be argued that the General Assembly is a classic example of interaction among States; that it is an arena rather than an actor. The equal voting rights of all members would tend to underline this. The behaviour of members, however, is strongly influenced by a group system which runs counter to the individualistic assumptions about an international community composed of sovereign States. The process of decision-making is not characterized by sovereign equality and consent but by a system of collective bargaining in which most States individually play a relatively subordinate role. This group dynamic has endowed the General Assembly with a role which is clearly distinguishable from the sum total of the States represented in it.

Most technical organizations would barely qualify as independent international actors at first sight. However, in some areas of their activity and in certain geographic regions, their functions go beyond mere coordination of State activity. Especially in developing countries, organizations and programmes such as the World Health Organization, the United Nations Development Programme and the United Nations Relief and Works Agency have created structures which are more reminiscent of public administration normally associated with States than of inter-governmental institutions.[22]

C. Confederate Structures

Supra-national cooperation, other than through organizations established by treaties among sovereign States, has become relatively rare. Personal unions of States under the same monarch are primarily of historical interest. The spread of republicanism and of democracy has diminished their importance. The Commonwealth (formerly the British Commonwealth), once a powerful structure, has slowly developed into a loose grouping of States with historical ties rather than any remaining authoritative structures. The Benelux Union has to a large extent been overtaken by integration in the European Community. Scandinavian States in the Nordic Council have achieved a high degree of integration, but this is more akin to cooperation among State authorities.

It remains to be seen whether, after the disintegration of the USSR, there will be substantial residual powers with a confederate body distinct from normal cooperation under international law. The Agreement Establishing the Commonwealth of Independent States, the successor to the Soviet Union, foresees not only close economic cooperation but also joint control over nuclear weapons and a joint command over a common military and strategic space.[23]

22 Cf. Buehring, 'Patterns of Authority in International Law', 27 *GYIL* (1984) 11, 17, 21.
23 Agreement of Minsk, 8 December 1991, Article 6, para. 3, 31 ILM (1992) 144.

III. A Multi-Layered Picture of International Law

The gradual diffusion of powers among different types of participants casts doubts on our traditional conception of international law. The main attraction of State-centricity is its simplicity. International law has developed techniques to ignore or interpret away alternative structures. Sub-State entities are simply projected back to the national level. Their activities, rights and obligations are attributed to the central government. International organizations are seen to derive their authority from the participating States and hence to lack status as independent actors. A differentiated picture is thereby reduced to the level of the most conspicuous and powerful participant.[24]

It is likely that the archetype of the State, as we know it, will continue to exist for some time and that it will even persist in its role as the most powerful actor. However, there is mounting evidence that the process of redistributing authoritative functions will continue and that the vertical element in a preponderantly horizontal order will continue to grow. The sovereign State is still the chief pillar of our international system, and there is no evidence that it is crumbling or is in danger of collapse. Rather, the static weight it has carried is gradually being shifted to other, for the time being, still lesser pillars. This process is gradual and irregular. It will proceed more rapidly in some regions than in others and it is likely to assume a variety of forms. The picture emerging from all this is still somewhat diffuse, but it is distinct enough to warrant a re-examination of a number of assumptions about international law to which we have become accustomed.

Rather than grope for the seat of sovereignty, we should adjust our intellectual framework to a multi-layered reality consisting of a variety of authoritative structures.[25] Under this functionalist approach what matters is not the formal status of a participant (province, state, international organization) but its actual or preferable exercise of functions.[26] For instance, it is not meaningful to attempt to isolate the point at which the European Community will be transformed from an international organization into a European State.[27] Rather, we will have to examine in detail exactly what functions and powers it has assumed from its Member States. We should get used to the idea that despite an ongoing shift of authority to the Community it will continue to exist as an international institution side by side with its Member States for a long time to come.

24 The assumptions of international lawyers about the near-exclusive role of States seem to be largely shared by international relations theory. See Abbott, 'Modern International Relations Theory: A Prospectus for International Lawyers', 14 *Yale J. Int'l L.* (1989) 335.

25 Janis, 'International Law?', 32 *Harv. Int'l L.J.* (1991) 353, 367-370.

26 Cf. Johnston, 'Functionalism in the Theory of International Law', 26 *Can. Y.B. Int'l L.* (1988) 3.

27 For a jurisprudential analysis see MacCormick, 'Beyond the Sovereign States', 56 *Modern L. Rev.* (1993) 1.

IV. The Need for Adjustment

A. The Making of International Law

1. Treaties

Classical treaty law is typical of the horizontal structure of international law and its focus on the interaction of sovereign and equal participants. It is therefore not surprising that international law has viewed the capacity of non-State actors to enter into international agreements with some reserve. Their treaty-making power is typically left to the respective sub-system, that is the national constitution in the case of sub-State entities, or the 'rules of the organization' in the case of international organizations.[28] A draft provision in the Vienna Convention on the Law of Treaties concerning the right of component States to enter into treaties if permitted by the federal constitution was deleted upon the insistence of federal States, wary of giving clues to centrifugal sentiments.[29]

Treaty-making by international organizations had become so widespread that by 1986 it was considered necessary to draft a second Vienna Convention on the Law of Treaties.[30] The outcome was a document which largely duplicates the Treaty Convention of 1969 with a few adjustments, mostly of a procedural character. The half-hearted attitude towards the admission of international organizations into the community of official treaty-makers is perhaps best illustrated by the final clauses of the 1986 Convention; the Convention is open to States and to international organizations, but only the ratifications of States count towards the number necessary for its entry into force.[31]

While the capacity of the State to enter into treaty commitments is unlimited, in principle, sub-State entities and international organizations are typically confined to the powers assigned to them either explicitly or by implication. International organizations have shown a remarkable ability to expand their treaty competences through doctrines such as implied powers.[32] Sub-State entities, on the other hand, usually remain under strict federal supervision.

The increasing scope of regulation through treaties has sometimes led to a conflict between the constitutional powers of the sub-State entities and the treaty-making

28 Cf. Article 6 in conjunction with Article 2(j) of the Vienna Convention on the Law of Treaties between States and International Organizations or between International Organizations, 21 March 1986, 25 ILM (1986) 543.

29 Draft Article 5(b) was deleted mainly upon the insistence of Canada. For detailed references see L. Wildhaber, *supra* note 8, at 265-66.

30 See *supra* note 28.

31 Articles 82(c), 84 para. 1, 85 para. 1; Cf. also Article 8 of Annex IX to the United Nations Convention on the Law of the Sea, *infra* note 38.

32 This is reflected in the 11th preambular paragraph to the 1986 Vienna Convention, *supra* note 28, which notes 'that international organizations possess the capacity to conclude treaties which is necessary for the exercise of their functions and the fulfilment of their purposes.'

monopoly of the central government.[33] Where treaty commitments undertaken by the federal government encroach upon decentralized competences, there is sometimes provision for participation by the sub-State entities in the internal decision-making process leading to the conclusion of the treaty.[34] In some instances treaties contain federal clauses making allowance for internal difficulties which may arise from the implementation of treaty provisions which fall under the jurisdiction of constituent States.[35]

The European Community has developed a different technique to deal with treaties straddling State and Community competences. These treaties are concluded in the form of 'mixed agreements' to which the Members as well as the Community are formal parties.[36] This 'double decker' method may be an interesting model for future solutions. It is quite conceivable to have different levels of authority represent the same communities in the treaty process simultaneously.[37] An increasing number of the more recent multilateral treaties are open not only to States but also to international organizations where the organizations have assumed functions in the respective areas.[38] The European Community participates in a number of general multilateral treaties which are also open to its Members. The EC signature to the Law of the Sea Convention[39] is particularly striking in view of the refusal of the United Kingdom and Germany to sign it. It is conceivable, though not likely, that this highly important treaty may one day become part of Community law while some Members persist in their refusal to ratify it.[40]

The logical outcome of these developments would be a general opening up of the treaty process for non-State actors to the extent that they have assumed the functions

33 See, e.g., the debate surrounding *Missouri v. Holland*, 252 US 416 in the United States; see also Byrnes & Charlesworth, 'Federalism and the International Legal Order: Recent Developments in Australia', 79 *AJIL* (1985) 622; Morviducci, 'The International Activities of the Italian Regions', 2 *IYIL* 1976) 201.

34 See, e.g., Article 32 para. 2 of the German Basic Law and the Lindau Agreement of 14 November 1957 between the Federal Government and the *Länder* governments; Article 10 para. 3 of the Austrian Constitution.

35 See, e.g., Article 28 of the American Convention on Human Rights, 22 November 1969, 9 ILM (1970) 673, 683.

36 See Schermers, 'International Organizations as Members of Other International Organizations', in R. Bernhardt, K. Doehring & J.A. Frowein (eds), *Festschrift für Hermann Mosler* (1983) 823, 826-831; D. O'Keefe & H.G. Schermers (eds), *Mixed Agreements* (1983).

37 The ratifications of multilateral treaties by Byelorussia (now Belarus) and the Ukraine while they were still Soviet Republics, in addition to the Soviet Union, are only of historical significance today.

38 See, e.g., Article 305 para. 1(f) of the United Nations Convention on the Law of the Sea in conjunction with its Annex IX, 21 ILM (1982) 1261, 1326, 1353; Article 14 of the Convention on Long-Range Transboundary Air Pollution, 13 November 1979, 18 ILM (1979) 1442, 1448; Articles 4(b) and 54 of the Agreement Establishing the Common Fund for Commodities, 27 June 1980, 19 ILM (1980) 896, 900, 928; Article 15 of the Treaty on Intellectual Property in Respect of Integrated Circuits, 26 May 1989, 28 ILM (1989) 1484, 1490.

39 Made on 7 December 1984; see Koers, 'Participation of the European Economic Community in a New Law of the Sea Convention', 79 *AJIL* (1979) 426.

40 The phenomenon of 'incomplete mixed agreements' is not new. For instance, by 1 January 1991 nine out of twelve EC Members, in addition to the EC itself, were parties to the Convention for the Prevention of Marine Pollution from Land-Based Sources, 4 June 1974, 13 ILM (1974) 352.

covered by the respective treaties.[41] The resulting network of treaty relations will be considerably more complicated than before. The typical horizontal treaty relationship between States is then supplemented by vertical agreements between international organizations and States[42] or even their sub-entities. An example of an existing type of vertical agreement would be a loan agreement between the World Bank and one of its Members. Diagonal relationships result where States enter into agreements with foreign sub-State entities[43] or international organizations with non-Member States.[44] The need for adjustment in our way of thinking about treaty law will be considerable.[45]

2. *Custom*

Customary law is typically associated with State practice.[46] Practice of sub-State entities is normally ascribed to the respective State if it is considered relevant at all. Whether that is a realistic assumption in areas where they act independently is another matter. Practice within international organizations may or may not be realistically characterized as State practice. Individual statements by State representatives or voting behaviour is clearly State practice. Collective practice of organs composed of State representatives is more difficult to categorize in view of the group dynamics prevailing there. Description of the practice of independent organs such as the UN Secretariat or the EC Commission as State practice is clearly a fiction.

This leads to the obvious conclusion that the international community is no longer exclusively composed of sovereign States and that hence customary international law cannot be based on State practice alone. Once it is recognized that behaviour patterns accompanied by legitimate expectations of compliance are relevant at all levels of the authoritative process of decision-making, the classification of this process as State practice is no longer entirely accurate.

41 This functional approach is reflected in Annex IX to the United Nations Convention on the Law of the Sea, *supra* note 38. Its Article 1 provides: *Use of Terms.* For the purposes of article 305 and of this Annex, 'international organization' means an intergovernmental organization constituted by States to which its member States have transferred competence over matters governed by this Convention, including the competence to enter into treaties in respect of those matters.

42 The Trusteeship Agreements were not formally concluded with the United Nations as a party but were subject to the approval of the competent UN Organ. See, e.g., Article 16 of the Trusteeship Agreement for the Pacific Islands, 2 April 1947, 8 UNTS 189, 199.

43 See, e.g., the Agreement on the Protection of Lake Constance against Pollution, 27 October 1960, between Switzerland, Austria, Bavaria and Baden-Württemberg, Austrian Federal Gazette (BGBl.) 1961/289.

44 See, e.g., Headquarters Agreement between the United Nations and Switzerland, 11 June 1946 and 1 July 1946, 1 UNTS 153.

45 Cf. also section IV. B. of this article, *infra*.

46 This is well illustrated by the definition of *jus cogens* in both Vienna Conventions on the Law of Treaties. The respective Articles 53 define a peremptory norm of general international law as a norm accepted as non-derogable by the international Community of *States* (emphasis added).

3. General Principles

General principles of law qualify as a source of international law if they are recognized by civilized nations. While the adjective 'civilized' has been disregarded as discriminatory and irrelevant, the requirement of origin in national law apparently remains. It should be obvious, however, that in federal States with distinct legal systems this cannot refer only to law at the national level. For instance, when making an assessment of the situation in the United States with respect to a purported general principle of law, it would be quite absurd to look at federal law only and to stop short of examining state law.

It is also clear that the legal principles developed by international organizations on the regional and global levels are part of this body of law. Thus, the law governing employment by the United Nations or EC competition law will yield important clues concerning general principles in these fields.

4. Decisions of International Institutions

Decisions of international institutions should be the most obvious indicator of an independent law-creating role on the international level. Attempts to press these into the Procrustean bed of the more traditional types of sources, by describing them as secondary treaty law or as highly organized State practice,[47] merely reflect the inability of the authors of these descriptions to come to terms with new decision-making processes carried out by new actors.

B. The Relationship of Different Legal Orders

1. Competing Prescriptions

The traditional question of the relationship of domestic or State law to international law becomes considerably more complex when we start to examine interrelationships in a stratified system of international legal order. Here too, we find the familiar technique of international law to relegate issues involving sub-State legal systems to constitutional law. Implementation of international law by decentralized legislative action is left to the respective constitutions.[48] In case of a conflict with international law, the law of the sub-State entity is simply regarded as part of the national law of the sovereign State to which questions of responsibility are addressed.

47 Cf. Schreuer, 'Recommendations and the Traditional Sources of International Law', 20 *GYIL* (1977) 103.

48 Article 27 of the Vienna Convention on the Law of Treaties would preclude the invocation of internal law reserving certain matters to sub-State entities as a justification for a failure to perform a treaty. Article 46 could possibly be used to claim the invalidity of a treaty which was concluded in manifest violation of a constitutional provision of fundamental importance protecting the prerogatives of sub-State entities.

The question becomes more problematic when it comes to conflicts between prescriptions of international origin. In the context of European Community law, the European Court has repeatedly affirmed the superiority of Community law over national law, but the relationship between EC law and general international law is less clear. In a 1991 decision, the European Court held that national French law prohibiting the employment of women at night was contrary to EC laws guaranteeing equal access of men and women to employment.[49] The Court did not mention the fact that France, like several other EC Members, is bound by an ILO Convention prohibiting the employment of women in night work.[50] Although the Court did not address the problem of a conflict between EC law and treaty law which bound some of the Member States,[51] the case serves as an example for the sort of competition that might arise between different international sub-systems. A reference to Article 30 of the Vienna Convention on the Law of Treaties, dealing with successive treaties relating to the same subject-matter, is no answer. Apart from the unsatisfactory nature of the solution offered there, it merely deals with overlapping rules between States. It is unable to cope with competing decision-making processes involving different law makers.

2. *Succession*

The traditional concept of State succession deals with a typically horizontal process by which States assume certain rights and duties from other States. On the other hand, when it comes to transfers of powers from one level to another, the succeeding actor may find itself confronted with legal prescriptions originally directed at a different type of actor which was its predecessor in the respective functions. Where sub-State entities are endowed with the power to enter into agreements with foreign States or their respective sub-units, they are confronted with the law of treaties as well as with existing substantive provisions of international law. When States transfer competences to international institutions,[52] these institutions are sometimes faced with parts of international law originally designed to regulate the respective functions between States.

For example, in the area of customs duties and foreign trade, the EC has taken over most of the powers previously exercised by its Members. This has raised the question of the applicability of GATT rules to the EC. The Community is not a party to the

49 Case C-345/89, *Criminal Proceedings Against Stoeckel*, [1991] ECR I-4047; see, however, Advocate General Tesauro at 4056.

50 ILO Convention (No. 89) Concerning Night Work of Women Employed in Industry, 9 July 1948, 81 UNTS 147.

51 Article 234 of the EEC Treaty preserves the rights and obligations arising from treaties concluded by Community Members before the entry into force of the EEC Treaty. See also Case 812/79, *Attorney General v. Burgoa*, [1980] ECR 2787.

52 Article 9 para. 2 of the Austrian Constitution restricts the right of Parliament to transfer powers to intergovernmental institutions to federal competences except through constitutional amendment.

Agreement. Nevertheless, the European Court has answered the question in the affirmative, holding that by stepping into the Member States' functions the Community had automatically succeeded to the rights and obligations arising from GATT.[53] Similar considerations have shaped the European Community's attitude towards obligations arising from the UN Charter. Security Council decisions imposing economic sanctions are seen to bind not only Member States, but also the Community itself.[54]

Similarly, if the Commonwealth of Independent States were to assume control over nuclear weapons, as provided by the Minsk Agreement,[55] the question would arise regarding the application to the Commonwealth of relevant rules of international law. These would include pertinent treaties in the areas of arms control and non-proliferation, and humanitarian law.

There are other situations where the adoption of functions formerly exercised by States is less obvious. The European Community has increasingly assumed powers affecting individual rights. Since Community law was initially short on express provisions concerning the protection of human rights, the European Court had to look for a legal framework outside its own black letter law. This it found not only in the civil rights provisions common to the constitutions of its Members, but also in the European Convention on Human Rights, a regional treaty concluded within the wider framework of the Council of Europe but including all Member States of the European Community. Under the European Court of Justice case-law, the substantive provisions of this treaty also bind the Community.[56]

Obvious difficulties arise when some of the States which have transferred functions to an international institution are not parties to a treaty applicable to that institution. For instance, the European Court of Justice did not rely on the European Convention on Human Rights as part of the general principles constituting part of Community law until the last EC Member State had become party to the Convention.[57] One obvious solution to partial participation is a formal accession to the treaty by the international institution itself as described above. However, this may run into technical difficulties since most multilateral treaties are only open to accession by States.[58] In addition, a treaty may contain obligations, especially of a procedural kind, which are difficult or impossible for international institutions to comply with. Thus, the strongest argument against a formal accession of the European Community to the European Convention on Human Rights is its elaborate supervision mechanism, which involves

53 Case 21-24/72, *International Fruit Company*, [1972] ECR 1219, 1227.

54 See, e.g., Council Regulation 2340/90 of 8 August 1990 concerning the prevention of Community trade with Iraq and Kuwait, OJ 1990 L 213/1.

55 *Supra* note 23.

56 Case 4/73, *Nold v. Commission*, [1974] ECR 491, 507; Case 36/75, *Rutili v. Minister of the Interior*, [1975] ECR 1219, 1232; Case 44/79, *Hauer v. Rheinland-Pfalz*, [1979] ECR 3727, 3745.

57 France, 3 May 1974.

58 See, however, *supra* note 38.

the Commission, the Committee of Ministers and the European Court of Human Rights. Formal participation by the Community would create a complicated structure involving all these bodies plus the European Court of Justice and domestic courts.[59]

A different technique to make general international law applicable in situations where international organizations have assumed powers hitherto reserved to States is the incorporation of the relevant provisions into the organization's internal law or into agreements concluded by it for specific purposes. The 'principles and spirit' of the Geneva Conventions for the Protection of War Victims of 1949 and of related treaties have been made applicable to UN peace-keeping forces by regulations issued by the Secretary General,[60] and by their incorporation into bilateral agreements with States providing armed forces.[61] A formal accession of the United Nations to the relevant treaties is regarded as problematic *inter alia* in view of the obligation of its parties to enforce their provisions through criminal jurisdiction – a power the United Nations cannot exercise at present.[62]

C. Participation

1. Admission

The traditional method of admission into the club of official international participants is recognition between States. The process is essentially bilateral and horizontal. More recently, admission of new States to international institutions has supplemented the traditional method. Both in the context of decolonization and in the recent fragmentation of Eastern European multi-ethnic States, the newly emerging States were eager to join the United Nations and regional institutions which had generous admission policies, such as the CSCE. Admittance to these multilateral arenas is seen as an official certificate of statehood. The new multilateral admission process has not replaced the traditional bilateral one, but has taken over some of its functions.[63]

Other actors have not had the benefit of institutionalized procedures for their admission to the international arena. Sub-State entities participate to the extent that other actors enter into relations with them through agreements or by other methods.

When international institutions are created, the conditions for their participation in international legal relations, as, for example, legal personality or privileges and immunities, are specifically regulated *vis-à-vis* Member States. Their status in relation to non-Members is less obvious. The ICJ has attested objective legal personality to the

59 Schermers, *supra* note 36 at 834.
60 See, e.g., para. 40 of the Regulations for the United Nations Force in Cyprus of 25 April 1964, ST/SGB/UNFICYP/1; cf. also R. Higgins, *United Nations Peace-Keeping* (1970-II) 191, 303.
61 See, e.g., Exchange of Notes between the Austrian Government and the United Nations on the Service of Austrian Contingents in the Framework of a United Nations Peace-Keeping Force in Cyprus, 21 February 1966, Austrian Federal Gazette (BGBl.) 1966/60, para. 10.
62 Memorandum of the United Nations Office of Legal Affairs, 15 June 1972, *U.N.Jur.Y.B.* (1972) 153.
63 J. Dugard, *Recognition and the United Nations* (1987).

United Nations for the purpose of pursuing claims on the international level.[64] The EC has entered into numerous treaty relations with non-Members. International organizations of lesser importance may find it more difficult to assert their official status *vis-à-vis* non-Members.[65] Ultimately, the acceptance of an international institution as an official actor also by non-Members and by other institutions will depend on its significance for the larger community and on the willingness of other accepted actors to enter into relations with it.

2. *Bilateral Relations*

Diplomatic relations among sovereign States are another typical example of the horizontal structures in the traditional system of international law. Sub-State entities have not gained admittance to this exclusive arena. Some provinces or component states have established semi-official representations abroad, often under the name of trade offices. Of course, there is agreement that these offices are not diplomatic missions. It is arguable, however, that they perform some of the functions normally connected with diplomatic relations although on a much more limited scale.

States frequently entertain permanent official representations with international organizations in which they are Members. A distinctive feature of these permanent missions is their non-reciprocal character. In some cases, we also find formal relations between organizations, and non-Member States. Among international organizations the European Community has been most conspicuous in establishing formal diplomatic ties with non-Members. There are over 130 missions accredited with the Community. The Community itself has established over 50 missions with non-Members.[66]

3. *Multilateral Cooperation*

Official international arenas like political conferences or international organizations have traditionally been closed to sub-State entities, but there are exceptions. The Ukraine and Byelorussia were original Members of the United Nations. The World

64 *Reparations for Injuries Suffered in the Service of the United Nations*, ICJ Reports (1949) 174.

65 Section 1 of the US International Organizations Immunities Act, 59 Stat. 669 (1945), 22 USCA para. 288 et seq. (1976), restricts its application to public international organizations in which the US participates. By contrast, the respective Austrian Act (BGBl. 1977/677) provides for the granting of privileges and immunities to international organizations in which Austria participates or the activities of which in Austria have been designated by the government. Both are designated as being in Austria's foreign policy interest. Cf. the Headquarters Agreement Austria-OPEC (BGBl. 1974/382).

66 An interesting new idea has been put forward in connection with the establishment of diplomatic relations between the successor States of the Soviet Union and the Member States of the European Community. Under a French proposal, joint embassies of the 12 Community Members were to be set up in the respective capitals of the new States. Under this intermediate solution, there would be individual diplomatic relations, but integrated organizational structures for their exercise. Although the idea was supported by Germany and Belgium, it seems to have been abandoned at least in relation to the larger successor States such as Russia and the Ukraine. *International Herald Tribune*, 6 February 1992, at 1.

Meteorological Organization provides for membership to territories maintaining their own meteorological service under certain circumstances with reduced membership rights.[67] However, these examples are the result of very special historical circumstances or of a specific technical orientation by the organization, and are not necessarily indicative of a general trend.

The Treaties establishing the European Community do not provide for a role of component units of Members in the decision-making process even though they have taken over some of their competences. German law provides for the inclusion of representatives of the *Länder* in national delegations to Community bodies. The German *Länder,* have also set up the office of a joint observer in Brussels which has full access to EC institutions. In addition, the German *Länder,* as well as Spanish autonomous regions, have set up individual information offices with the European Community.[68]

A different type of multilateral activity among sub-State entities involves local transfrontier cooperation. Examples are the Saar-Lorraine-Luxembourg Commission, cooperation between the regions in the European Alps or the International Commission for the Environmental Protection of Lake Constance. There is a Convention on Transfrontier Co-Operation in the framework of the Council of Europe to facilitate this process.[69]

Institutionalized cooperation among international organizations has also progressed considerably. The relationship agreements between the United Nations and the Specialized Agencies are well known. Regional organizations including the EC have been accorded observer status in the UN General Assembly.[70] At the same time, the 12 Members have sought to coordinate their positions in UN bodies, to speak with one voice and to vote jointly. Not infrequently, the Member State currently holding the Presidency in the EC Council will speak for all Twelve. At times, the representative of the Commission will also speak on the same issues on behalf of the Community.[71] As for the Security Council, there are suggestions that the United Kingdom and France as Permanent Members which are also Members of the EC should represent Community positions rather than national interests.[72] Even more radical proposals envisage a transfer of the two permanent Security Council seats to the Community. Not surprisingly, the two countries concerned have been less than enthusiastic about these ideas.

In the Specialized Agencies and in GATT, the European Community has also increasingly emerged as an independent actor. In November 1991 this process

67 Article 11 of the Constitution of WMO.

68 W. Burtscher, *EG-Beitritt und Föderalismus* (1990) 95-112; H.-J. Blanke, *Föderalismus und Integrationsgewalt* (1991); Rudolf, *supra* note 9, at 23 et seq.

69 European Outline Convention on Transfrontier Co-Operation between Territorial Communities or Authorities, 21 May 1980, *European Treaty Series* No. 106.

70 UN GA Res. 3208 (XXIX) (11 October 1974).

71 Brückner, 'The European Community and the United Nations', 1 *EJIL* (1990) 144.

72 Ibid., at 179.

culminated in the admission of the European Community to full membership of the Food and Agriculture Organization (FAO).[73] The Community had until then enjoyed observer status. However, the far-reaching competences of the Community in the areas of food and agriculture made its full participation seem appropriate. The admission of a regional economic organization to the FAO necessitated an amendment to its Constitution which had hitherto only provided for State members. The EC members continue to be members of the FAO.[74] However, membership rights will be split. The twelve votes will be cast either by the Community or by its Member States depending on the distribution of competences between the Community and its members. There are plans for an early accession of the European Community to the International Energy Agency and to the Brussels Customs Cooperation Council.

The admission of a regional international organization as a full member to a global organization is an important departure from the purely inter-governmental structure of international institutions. It could mark the starting point for a more open and flexible process of organized decision-making in the international arena in which different types of participants interact. Under this model, participation would no longer depend on the requirement of statehood but on the specific functions which have been assigned to a particular actor.

4. Adjudication

Access to international courts is also normally limited to States. The Statute of the ICJ is typical of this limitation; it grants access in contentious proceedings only to States. Participation of sub-State entities in the Court is excluded.[75] As far as international organizations are concerned, the Court's jurisdiction to give advisory opinions is sometimes used to overcome the exclusion of non-State parties. This is best illustrated by a comparison of the respective Articles 66 of the two Vienna Conventions on the Law of Treaties. The original Convention of 1969 provides for adjudication by the ICJ of disputes between States concerning peremptory rules of international law (*jus cogens*). Since this procedure is not available where an international organization is a party to the dispute, the 1986 Convention envisages advisory opinions in this situation which 'shall be accepted as decisive by all the parties'.[76] Ultimately, there is no

73 OJ 1991 C 292/8 and 10.

74 Cf. Schermers, *supra* note 36, who is against 'mixed membership'.

75 The Ukraine and Byelorussia (now Belarus) could have become parties to proceedings while they were still parts of the Soviet Union.

76 Cf. also Section 30 of the Convention on the Privileges and Immunities of the United Nations, 13 February 1946, 43 *AJIL Supp.* (1949) 1, 7; Section 2(b) of the Headquarters Agreement between the United States and the United Nations, 26 June 1947, 43 *AJIL Supp.* (1949) 8, 15. Generally, see Ago, '"Binding" Advisory Opinions of the International Court of Justice', 85 *AJIL* (1991) 439. See also Article 287 of the United Nations Convention on the Law of the Sea in conjunction with Article 7 of its Annex IX, *supra* note 38, substituting arbitration for litigation before the ICJ in disputes involving international organizations.

convincing reason why international organizations should be debarred, in principle, from contentious proceedings before the International Court.

The European Court of Justice is open to Member States and to the organs of the Community.[77] Under certain circumstances, natural or legal persons also have access to the Court.[78] This access is of vital importance for the vindication of individual rights against Community institutions. The European Court has extended the right of action by legal persons to territorial units of Member States.[79] It is therefore entirely feasible that a sub-State entity, like a German *Land*, may use this right of action to contest the legality of Community directives it has to implement under German constitutional law.

Proceedings before the European Court of Human Rights can be initiated only by States or by the Human Rights Commission.[80] Additional Protocol IX to the Convention[81] will extend this right to natural and legal persons who have brought an individual petition to the Commission. However, this new right will not be open to provinces or regions of States parties to the Convention: Article 25 explicitly limits the right of individual petition to persons, non-governmental organizations and groups of individuals.

The Convention on the Settlement of Investment Disputes Between States and Nationals of Other States[82] contains a provision explicitly opening an international procedure for adjudication to sub-State entities. Article 25 of the Convention extends the jurisdiction of the International Centre for Settlement of Investment Disputes not only to contracting States, but also to any constituent subdivision or agency of a contracting State designated to the Centre by that State.

The above examples indicate that access to international judicial arenas should not be determined by the formal status of the prospective litigants, but by the purpose of the judicial mechanism in settling disputes and in affording judicial protection. To the extent that new participants are taking over functions from States which may involve them in disputes, or which raise issues of judicial protection, it is important to open judicial procedures to these new actors, both as plaintiffs and defendants.

77 See esp. Articles 169, 170, 173, 175 and 180 of the EEC Treaty.

78 See esp. Articles 173, 175 and 179 of the EEC Treaty. In pursuance of Article 168a, added by the Single European Act, *infra* note 106 the Court of First Instance has assumed some of these powers.

79 Case 62 & 72/68, 8 March 1988, *Exécutif régional wallon and Glaverbel v. Commission*, [1988] ECR 1573.

80 Article 48 of the European Convention on Human Rights.

81 6 November 1990, *European Treaty Series* No. 140. Not yet in force.

82 18 March 1965, 575 UNTS 159.

D. Individual Rights

The protection of the rights of the individual used to follow the classical pattern of State orientation. Under traditional international law, the treatment of citizens was seen as an internal matter. Violations of rights of foreigners were regulated on the inter-State level through diplomatic protection. This situation has been transformed dramatically, not only through the development of an international law of human rights, but also through the arrival of new actors, both in their capacity as potential protectors and as potential violators of human rights.

The creation of international machineries for the supervision of human rights on the regional level, such as the European or Inter-American Conventions and on the global level in the framework of the United Nations, has given the protection of the individual a new dimension. It transcends the classical attribution of individual rights and interests to the State of nationality. However, the traditional process of diplomatic protection has also been adapted and expanded. International organizations have successfully protected their agents and employees,[83] even against the State of their nationality.[84] European Community law has given the citizens of Member States a host of substantive rights (e.g. the right of establishment) and procedures for their enforcement. A European Community citizenship has thereby been effectively created.[85] It seems only a matter of time until the Community will commence protecting its citizens *vis-à-vis* third States.

The expansion by international institutions of their range of activities has also increased the danger of a violation of individual rights by them. There have been cases of transgressions by UN Forces, in which the home countries of the victims have sought and received compensation from the United Nations.[86] In the EC, means for the protection of human rights against Community action have been developed first by the European Court of Justice[87] and later by the other Community organs.[88] At first, courts of Member States were reluctant to yield judicial protection of these rights[89] but eventually accepted that the European Court could enforce basic rights against the

83 *Reparation for Injuries Suffered in the Service of the United Nations*, ICJ Reports (1949) 174.

84 See especially the facts surrounding the *Mazilu* case, *Applicability of Article VI, Section 22, of the Convention on the Privileges and Immunities of the United Nations*, ICJ Reports (1989) 177.

85 Cf. also Arts. 8-8e of the EEC Treaty as amended by the Maastricht Treaty *supra* note 20. The new Art. 8c provides that citizens of the European Union shall be entitled to diplomatic protection against a third country by any Member State on the same conditions as the nationals of that State if their own State is not represented in the third country.

86 Exchange of Letters Constituting an Agreement between the United Nations and Belgium relating to the Settlement of Claims filed against the United Nations in the Congo by Belgian Nationals, 20 February 1965, *U.N.Jur.Y.B.* (1965) 39.

87 In addition to the cases *supra* note 56 see Case 11/70, *Internationale Handelsgesellschaft*, [1970] ECR 1125, 1135.

88 See especially the Joint Declaration on Fundamental Rights of 5 April 1977 by the Assembly, the Council and the Commission, OJ 1977 C 103/1; Declaration of Fundamental Rights and Freedoms by the European Parliament, 12 April 1989, OJ 1989 C 120/51.

89 See especially the *Solange I* decision of the German Constitutional Court, 29 May 1974, BVerfGE 37, 271.

Community institutions.[90] A future role of the European Commission of Human Rights and of the European Court of Human Rights against the European Community is feasible if the idea of accession of the Community to the European Convention on Human Rights should materialize.

E. Use of Force

International law has traditionally focused its concern with the use of armed force on inter-State relations. Efforts to contain military force by legal means through the League of Nations, the Pact of Paris or the United Nations have all concentrated on the State as the prime actor. Violence on the sub-State level is regarded with some diffidence by international law. Civil wars do not attract much interest from international lawyers until there is a foreign military intervention, or where major human rights abuses come to light. This is well illustrated by the differences in reaction by the World community to the Iraqi attack on Kuwait in 1990 and to the Serbian attacks on Croatia in 1991 and on Bosnia-Herzegowina since 1992. In the former case, there was an attack by one State on another. Therefore, the legal question seemed clear, outrage was almost unanimous and the reaction was drastic. In the latter cases, many of the factual elements were quite similar, but the description of the actors under international law was different. What we saw initially was an attack by one element of a disintegrating State on another. Even more importantly, the attacker was able to use the vestiges of the former central government, thereby gaining a semblance of legitimacy. After the recognition of the two new States and their admission to the United Nations and other international organizations, Serbia declared the withdrawal of the Federal Army and attempted to portray the ongoing hostilities as internal wars in the two countries. Despite the lack of credibility of these claims, this strategy succeeded in creating a different perspective under international law, contributing to the mix of disinterest, indecision and half-hearted action displayed by the World community.

The humanitarian law of warfare also distinguishes between inter-State hostilities and armed conflicts involving actors other than States. The four 1949 Geneva Conventions for the Protection of War Victims contained identical Articles extending some minimum protection to the victims of non-international armed conflicts.[91] By 1977, the time was ripe for a separate multilateral treaty specifically regulating the humanitarian law of hostilities below the level of sovereign States.[92]

Not surprisingly, States are reluctant to share their prerogative to use military force with other types of participants. Regional military alliances like NATO are not an

90 See especially the *Solange II* decision of the German Constitutional Court, 22 October 1986, BVerfGE 73, 339.

91 Article 3 of the four Conventions for the Protection of War Victims, 12 August 1949, 75 UNTS 31, 85, 135, 287.

92 Protocol Additional to the Geneva Conventions of 12 August 1949, and Relating to the Protection of Victims of Non-International Armed Conflicts (Protocol II), 8 June 1977, 16 ILM (1977) 1442.

exception to this phenomenon. They are organizations for the coordination of State activity in this field, rather than independent actors.

Chapter VII of the UN Charter, dealing with enforcement action by the Security Council, was an ambitious project to break the monopoly of States in the use of military force. Articles 42 to 49 provide for an elaborate balance between central action and a decentralized support system carried out by Member States. The weakness of the system lies in the dependence of the global actor (i.e. the United Nations) on the cooperation of individual States at all stages. The voting procedure in the Security Council, which is often perceived as the main obstacle to effective action, is only one aspect of this weakness. The inability to reach decisions on effective global military enforcement action masks the more fundamental problem of the Organization's lack of independent military resources. For the time being, control over military action remains on the State level. This observation is underlined by the instances in which military action was taken under the authority of the United Nations in Korea and against Iraq. In the first case, the Security Council 'recommended' that the Members furnish assistance to repel the armed attack.[93] In the second, it 'authorized' Member States to use all necessary means to implement its resolution calling for withdrawal.[94] All this is, at best, a preliminary step towards an independent role for an international institution in the military arena.

Peace-keeping operations by international organizations such as the United Nations have been considerably more effective. Their low level of military power and their purely preventive role do not make them serious competitors to States. Their strength lies not in any ability to play an independent military role, but in their usefulness to both sides of a conflict and their legal and moral authority, making attacks on them disproportionately costly in political terms.

F. Control Over Territory and Over People

Control over territory and over people is the classic and primary task of the State. In federal States, some of the functions arising therefrom are delegated or reserved to the component units. The internal allocation of these powers is left to the individual constitutional set-up and is largely ignored by international law. Some constitutions require consent by sub-State entities to a transfer of portions of their territory to other States.[95] Some provide for separate citizenship.[96] However, international law continues to look at the national government which is seen as the focal point of authority.

93 SC Res. 83 (27 June 1950).
94 SC Res. 678 (29 November 1990).
95 See, e.g., Article 3 para. 2 of the Austrian Constitution.
96 See, e.g., Article 43 of the Swiss Constitution.

In times of national crisis, identification may shift from the centre to the periphery and internal boundaries may become fracture points in disintegrating States. The demise of the Soviet Union, the collapse of Yugoslavia and the break-up of Czechoslovakia are cases in point.[97] A complete transfer of statehood to previously subordinate administrative units is no departure from the established structures, but merely an exchange of actors in the traditional roles.

The administration of territory and its inhabitants by international institutions has remained an exceptional phenomenon.[98] The mandate and trusteeship systems delegated the actual administration to States under more or less strict supervision. The outcome was a form of controlled colonialism which resulted in the declared goal of the system: self-administration in the form of independent States. A direct administration by the United Nations was established in West New Guinea for a short transitional period only.[99] In other cases, such as Jerusalem[100] and Trieste,[101] international administration was planned, but never implemented. In Namibia it was instituted but never became effective.[102] After the entry into force of the 1982 Convention on the Law of the Sea, the administration of the resources of the 'Area' by the International Sea-Bed Authority under Part XI of the Convention will be the first instance of an international institution exercising a significant measure of territorial control.

Territoriality and political identification are still very much tied up with the notion of the sovereign State. They are linked to such concepts as territorial sovereignty and nationality. Self-determination and decolonization have also largely focused on statehood as the ultimate accomplishment.[103] However, there are also pointers in the opposite direction. Decentralization and autonomy have shown their worth in diluting centralist authoritarianism and in defusing ethnic and sectional disaffection. The break-up of federal States, such as the USSR, Yugoslavia and Czechoslovakia, does not signal a failure of federalism but of communism which superimposed totalitarian structures over an ostensibly decentralized political system. Regional integration, especially in Europe, has been successful in creating wider identifications and in checking abuses of national power. To the extent that the sovereign State loses its exclusive or dominant control and is replaced by a more multi-layered political set-up, the potential for conflict inherent in territorial disputes should also diminish. National

97 In the process of the disintegration of old Yugoslavia the Security Council explicitly rejected forcible changes of the old internal administrative borders. See esp. SC Res. 713(1991) and 757(1992).

98 Cf. Buehring, *supra* note 22 at 18-19.

99 GA Res. 1752(XVII) (21 September 1962). See also *Yearbook of the United Nations* (1962) 124-127.

100 GA Res. 181(II) (29 November 1947).

101 Treaty of Peace with Italy, 10 February 1947, 49 UNTS 126.

102 GA Res. 2248(S-V) (19 May 1967).

103 See, however, the *Western Sahara* case, ICJ Reports (1975) 10 at 32, where the Court, relying mainly on GA Res. 1514(XV) and 2625(XXV), points out that decolonization and self-determination may be attained not only through emergence as a sovereign independent State but also through free association with an independent State or integration with an independent State.

independence or boundary changes are not necessarily the only or even the best form of implementation for self-determination. A combination of local autonomy or federalism with a regional system of political and economic integration, coupled with an effective international supervision of individual and minority rights, can take much of the pressure out of territorial questions. A curtailment of the predominant role of the State will also make the question of which national government has control over a particular province or locality appear less important.

The creation of a 'citizenship of the Union' as provided in the Maastricht Treaty[104] gives legal expression to broader political identifications going beyond the State of the individual's nationality. European citizenship ensures freedom of movement and residence in the entire Community, allows participation in local elections and in elections for the European Parliament irrespective of the place of residence of a candidate within the Community, and confers the right to diplomatic protection by any Member State.[105]

V. Conclusion

The examples presented here amount to no more than a loose mosaic, each element of which may be dismissed as unconvincing. However, in their entirety they do provide the contours of an emerging new picture, if only we are prepared to see it.

Many of the illustrations focus on Europe and may appear less convincing if viewed from other parts of the world. However, a theoretical framework based on uniformity must be able to accommodate all phenomena under consideration. Once a theory becomes punctuated with exceptions and inconsistencies the time has arrived to rethink it and build a new one. The fact that one important geographical area no longer fits smoothly into the traditional picture of inter-State relations should be reason enough to reconsider its theoretical assumptions. A framework based on diversity is closer to reality even if the majority of phenomena still fits into the old paradigm.

Such a framework would introduce considerable complexity. Classic international law is based on a high degree of uniformity of the participating States, although in many aspects this uniformity is a legal fiction. The new picture introduces diversity not only with regard to the different levels of organization (global, regional, national, sub-national), but also with regard to the degree to which different levels possess authority. Thus, a relatively centralist State may participate in a highly integrated regional community, whereas a State with a strongly developed federal system may be part of a regional system with only a limited degree of integration. There will be areas of the globe where State orientation persists longer than in others.

104 *Supra* note 20.

105 Articles 8-8c of the EEC Treaty as amended. See also *supra* note 85.

Yet another complicating factor is variation in the assignment of different functions to different levels of authority. International organizations will continue to specialize in economic integration, human rights or the preservation of peace and security, although there are indications that the connections between different aspects of international cooperation are close enough to make their separation impracticable. Technical cooperation, especially in Europe, has created considerable stability also in areas of high politics. The European Community has long gone beyond economic questions and has expanded into the fields of general political cooperation and even security.[106]

In the social sciences, including law, theoretical models do not just explain reality. They also influence the facts under observation. Therefore, we must be aware of the potential policy implications for the future. If the international system continues to develop in the direction outlined here, there will be advantages and disadvantages. The loss of the simplicity inherent in the inter-State system will add considerable complexity and will require an adaptation of our intellectual framework. This is not just a problem for academics and theorists who may be reluctant to adjust to new patterns of thinking. A more heterogeneous international order will also create practical difficulties resulting from confusion about the appropriate role of different actors and duplication or even multiplication of work at different levels of authority.

As against these drawbacks, there are likely to be considerable benefits arising from a modified international legal order:

1. There is likely to be more inherent stability in the system. The potential breaking points between States will be reinforced by a supporting system of contacts and relations at different levels. A laminated structure of international legal order is likely to gain in horizontal as well as in vertical strength.
2. A diffusion of power will afford a better guarantee against its abuses both internally and externally. The danger of irresponsible tyrants oppressing their peoples or starting military adventures should be drastically reduced.
3. The fading of nationalism should add rationality to international relations. The distribution of identification over several levels of political organization rather than an exclusive commitment to a fatherland, *la patrie*, or the flag will curtail the potential for irrational and dangerous mass psychology.
4. Functional specialization and decentralization should lead to an optimum allocation of official activities at different levels of government.[107] The rational distribution of tasks to sub-State, State, regional and global institutions is an extension of the federal principle to international relations.[108]

106 See esp. Article 30 of the Single European Act, 17, 28 February 1986, 25 ILM (1986) 506, 517; Title V of the Maastricht Treaty on European Union, *supra* note 20, establishing a Common Foreign and Security Policy.

107 Cf. also Kiss, Shelton, 'Systems Analysis of International Law: A Methodological Inquiry', 17 *NYIL* (1986) 45, 69; Trachtmann, 'L'Etat, C'est Nous: Sovereignty, Economic Integration and Subsidiarity', 33 *Harv. Int'l L.J.* (1992) 459.

108 The idea is reflected in the (Maastricht) Treaty on European Union, *supra* note 20, through the principle

There is no convincing reason why international relations must continue to be concentrated at the national level. Centralism is a pseudo-utilitarian concept which can be directed at all areas of public administration. Applied to external relations it is premised on a confrontational picture of international relations under which all forces need to be concentrated to counteract external threats. Such a concept of international relations is liable to be self-perpetuating. The concentration of power for the defence of national interests, widely perceived to be an appropriate reaction to international instability, is really one of the main causes for this instability.

In the process of the momentous changes in Europe in recent years, politicians have repeatedly invoked the image of the common European house. If we see our planet as the common house, we should realize that this house does not only consist of individual rooms. There are niches, apartments, floors, staircases and wings. It is the entire architecture and not the furnishing of individual rooms which provides the static stability and the overall quality of the building.

of subsidiarity as defined in the new Article 3b of the EEC Treaty and through the creation of a Committee of the Regions (new Articles 198a-198c EEC Treaty). Art. 3b defines subsidiarity as follows:

> In areas which do not fall within its exclusive competence, the Community shall take action, in accordance with the principle of subsidiarity, only if and in so far as the objectives of the proposed action cannot be sufficiently achieved by the Member States and can therefore, by reason of the scale or effects of the proposed action, be better achieved by the Community.
>
> Any action by the Community shall not go beyond what is necessary to achieve the objects of this Treaty.

The Committee of the Regions as envisaged by Art. 198a will be 'consisting of representatives of regional and local bodies'.

[11]

The Concept of Legalization

Kenneth W. Abbott, Robert O. Keohane, Andrew Moravcsik, Anne-Marie Slaughter, and Duncan Snidal

The subject of this volume is "legalization and world politics." "World politics" in this formulation needs no clarification, but "legalization"—the real focus of the volume—must be more clearly defined, if only because of its relative unfamiliarity to students of international relations. In the introduction the editors have briefly previewed the concept of legalization used throughout the volume, a concept developed collaboratively by the authors of this article. We understand legalization as a particular form of institutionalization characterized by three components: obligation, precision, and delegation. In this article, we introduce these three characteristics, explore their variability and the range of institutional forms produced by combining them, and explicate the elements of legalization in greater detail.

The Elements of Legalization

"Legalization" refers to a particular set of characteristics that institutions may (or may not) possess. These characteristics are defined along three dimensions: obligation, precision, and delegation. *Obligation* means that states or other actors are bound by a rule or commitment or by a set of rules or commitments. Specifically, it means that they are *legally* bound by a rule or commitment in the sense that their behavior thereunder is subject to scrutiny under the general rules, procedures, and discourse of international law, and often of domestic law as well. *Precision* means that rules unambiguously define the conduct they require, authorize, or proscribe. *Delegation* means that third parties have been granted authority to implement, interpret, and apply the rules; to resolve disputes; and (possibly) to make further rules.

Each of these dimensions is a matter of degree and gradation, not a rigid dichotomy, and each can vary independently. Consequently, the concept of legalization encompasses a multidimensional continuum, ranging from the "ideal type" of legalization, where all three properties are maximized; to "hard" legalization, where all three (or at least obligation and delegation) are high; through multiple forms of partial or "soft" legalization involving different combinations of attributes; and finally to the complete absence of legalization, another ideal type. None of these dimensions—far less the full spectrum of legalization—can be fully operationalized. We do, however, consider in the section entitled "The Dimensions of Legalization" a number of techniques by which actors manipulate the elements of legalization; we also suggest several corresponding indicators of the strength or weakness of legal arrangements.

Statutes or regulations in highly developed national legal systems are generally taken as prototypical of hard legalization. For example, a congressional statute setting a cap on emissions of a particular pollutant is (subject to any special exceptions) legally binding on U.S. residents (obligation), unambiguous in its requirements (precision), and subject to judicial interpretation and application as well as administrative elaboration and enforcement (delegation). But even domestic enactments vary widely in their degree of legalization, both across states—witness the vague "proclamations" and restrictions on judicial review imposed by authoritarian regimes—and across issue areas within states—compare U.S. tax law to "political questions" under the Constitution. Moreover, the degree of obligation, precision, or delegation in formal institutions can be obscured in practice by political pressure, informal norms, and other factors. International legalization exhibits similar variation; on the whole, however, international institutions are less highly legalized than institutions in democratic rule-of-law states.

Note that we have defined legalization in terms of key characteristics of rules and procedures, not in terms of effects. For instance, although our definition includes delegation of legal authority (to domestic courts or agencies as well as equivalent international bodies), it does not include the degree to which rules are actually implemented domestically or to which states comply with them. To do so would be to conflate delegation with effective action by the agent and would make it impossible to inquire whether legalization increases rule implementation or compliance. Nor does our definition extend to the substantive content of rules or their degree of stringency. We regard substantive content and legalization as distinct characteristics. A conference declaration or other international document that is explicitly not legally binding could have exactly the same substantive content as a binding treaty, or even a domestic statute, but they would be very different instruments in terms of legalization, the subject of this volume.

Our conception of legalization creates common ground for political scientists and lawyers by moving away from a narrow view of law as requiring enforcement by a coercive sovereign. This criterion has underlain much international relations thinking on the topic. Since virtually no international institution passes this standard, it has led to a widespread disregard of the importance of international law. But theoretical work in international relations has increasingly shifted attention away from the need for centralized enforcement toward other institutionalized ways of promoting cooperation.[1] In addition, the forms of legalization we observe at the turn of the millennium are flourishing in the absence of centralized coercion.

Any definition is ultimately arbitrary at the margins. Yet definitions should strive to meet certain criteria. They should be broadly consistent with ordinary language, but more precise. To achieve precision, definitions should turn on a coherent set of identifiable attributes. These should be sufficiently few that situations can be readily characterized within a small number of categories, and sufficiently important that changes in their values will influence the processes being studied. Defining legalization in terms of obligation, precision, and delegation provides us with identifiable dimensions of variation whose effects on international behavior can be empirically explored.

Our concept of legalization is a working definition, intended to frame the analytic and empirical articles that follow in this volume as well as future research. Empiricist in origin, it is tailored to the phenomena we observe in international relations. We are not proposing a definitive definition or seeking to resolve age-old debates regarding the nature of law or whether international law is "really" law. Highly legalized arrangements under our conception will typically fall within the standard international lawyer's definition of international law. But many international commitments that to a lawyer entail binding legal obligations lack significant levels of precision or delegation and are thus partial or soft under our definition.

We acknowledge a particular debt to H. L. A. Hart's *The Concept of Law*.[2] Hart defined a legal system as the conjunction of primary and secondary rules. Primary rules are rules of obligation bearing directly on individuals or entities requiring them "to do or abstain from certain actions." Secondary rules, by contrast, are "rules about rules"—that is, rules that do not "impose obligations," but instead "confer powers" to create, extinguish, modify, and apply primary rules.[3] Again, we do not seek to define "law" or to equate our conception of legalization with a definition of a legal system. Yet Hart's concepts of primary and secondary rules are useful in helping to pinpoint the distinctive characteristics of the phenomena we observe in international relations. The attributes of obligation and precision refer to international rules that regulate behavior; these closely resemble Hart's primary rules of obligation. But when we define obligation as an attribute that incorporates general rules, procedures, and discourse of international law, we are referring to features of the international system analogous to Hart's three main types of secondary rules: recognition, change, and adjudication. And the criterion of delegation necessarily implicates all three of these categories.[4]

1. See the debate between the "managerial" perspective that emphasizes centralization but not enforcement, Chayes and Chayes 1995, and the "compliance" perspective that emphasizes enforcement but sees it as decentralized, Downs, Rocke, and Barsoom 1996.

2. Hart 1961.

3. Hart 1961, 79.

4. Hart, of course, observed that in form, though not in substance, international law resembled a primitive legal system consisting only of primary rules. We sidestep that debate, noting only that the characteristics we observe in international legalization leave us comfortable in applying Hart's terms by analogy. We also observe that the international legal framework has evolved considerably in the decades since Hart

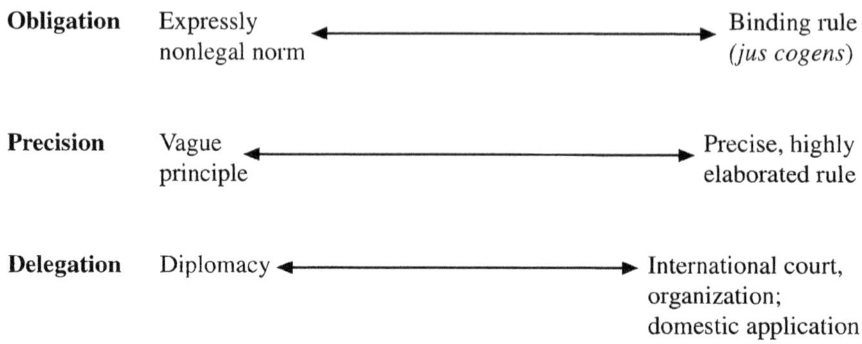

FIGURE 1. *The dimensions of legalization*

The Variability of Legalization

A central feature of our conception of legalization is the variability of each of its three dimensions, and therefore of the overall legalization of international norms, agreements, and regimes. This feature is illustrated in Figure 1. In Figure 1 each element of the definition appears as a continuum, ranging from the weakest form (the absence of legal obligation, precision, or delegation, except as provided by the background operation of the international legal system) at the left to the strongest or "hardest" form at the right.[5] Figure 1 also highlights the independence of these dimensions from each other: conceptually, at least, the authors of a legal instrument can combine any level of obligation, precision, and delegation to produce an institution exactly suited to their specific needs. (In practice, as we shall explain, certain combinations are employed more frequently than others.)

It would be inappropriate to equate the right-hand end points of these dimensions with "law" and the left-hand end points with "politics," for politics continues (albeit in different forms) even where there is law. Nor should one equate the left-hand end points with the absence of norms or institutions; as the designations in Figure 1 suggest, both norms (such as ethical principles and rules of practice) and institutions (such as diplomacy and balance of power) can exist beyond these dimensions. Figure 1 simply represents the components of legal institutions.

Using the format of Figure 1, one can plot where a particular arrangement falls on the three dimensions of legalization. For example, the Agreement on Trade-Related Aspects of Intellectual Property (TRIPs), administered by the World Trade Organization (WTO), is strong on all three elements. The 1963 Treaty Banning Nuclear Weapons Tests in the Atmosphere, in Outer Space, and Under Water is legally binding and

---

wrote. Franck reviews these changes and argues that international law has developed a general rule of recognition tied to membership in the international community. Franck 1990, 183–207.

5. On the "obligation" dimension, *jus cogens* refers to an international legal rule—generally one of customary law, though perhaps one codified in treaty form—that creates an especially strong legal obligation, such that it cannot be overridden even by explicit agreement among states.

quite precise, but it delegates almost no legal authority. And the 1975 Final Act of the Helsinki Conference on Security and Cooperation in Europe was explicitly not legally binding and delegated little authority, though it was moderately precise.

The format of Figure 1 can also be used to depict variations in the degree of legalization between portions of an international instrument (John King Gamble, Jr. has made a similar internal analysis of the UN Convention on the Law of the Sea[6]) and within a given instrument or regime over time. The Universal Declaration of Human Rights, for example, was only minimally legalized (it was explicitly aspirational, not overly precise, and weakly institutionalized), but the human rights regime has evolved into harder forms over time. The International Covenant on Civil and Political Rights imposes binding legal obligations, spells out concepts only adumbrated in the declaration, and creates (modest) implementing institutions.[7]

Table 1 further illustrates the remarkable variety of international legalization. Here, for concise presentation, we characterize obligation, precision, and delegation as either high or low. The eight possible combinations of these values are shown in Table 1; rows are arranged roughly in order of decreasing legalization, with legal obligation, a peculiarly important facet of legalization, weighted most heavily, delegation next, and precision given the least weight. A binary characterization sacrifices the continuous nature of the dimensions of legalization as shown in Figure 1 and makes it difficult to depict intermediate forms. Yet the table usefully demonstrates the range of institutional possibilities encompassed by the concept of legalization, provides a valuable shorthand for frequently used clusters of elements, and highlights the tradeoffs involved in weakening (or strengthening) particular elements.

Row I on this table corresponds to situations near the ideal type of full legalization, as in highly developed domestic legal systems. Much of European Community (EC) law belongs here. In addition, the WTO administers a remarkably detailed set of legally binding international agreements; it also operates a dispute settlement mechanism, including an appellate tribunal with significant—if still not fully proven—authority to interpret and apply those agreements in the course of resolving particular disputes.

Rows II–III represent situations in which the character of law remains quite hard, with high legal obligation and one of the other two elements coded as "high." Because the combination of relatively imprecise rules and strong delegation is a common and effective institutional response to uncertainty, even in domestic legal systems (the Sherman Antitrust Act in the United States is a prime example), many regimes in row II should be considered virtually equal in terms of legalization to those in row I. Like the Sherman Act, for example, the original European Economic Community (EEC) rules of competition law (Articles 85 and 86 of the Treaty of Rome) were for the most part quite imprecise. Over time, however, the exercise of

6. Gamble 1985.

7. The declaration has also contributed to the evolution of customary international law, which can be applied by national courts as well as international organs, and has been incorporated into a number of national constitutions.

TABLE 1. *Forms of international legalization*

Type	*Obligation*	*Precision*	*Delegation*	*Examples*
Ideal type:				
Hard law				
I	High	High	High	EC; WTO—TRIPs; European human rights convention; International Criminal Court
II	High	Low	High	EEC Antitrust, Art. 85-6; WTO—national treatment
III	High	High	Low	U.S.–Soviet arms control treaties; Montreal Protocol
IV	Low	High	High (moderate)	UN Committee on Sustainable Development (Agenda 21)
V	High	Low	Low	Vienna Ozone Convention; European Framework Convention on National Minorities
VI	Low	Low	High (moderate)	UN specialized agencies; World Bank; OSCE High Commissioner on National Minorities
VII	Low	High	Low	Helsinki Final Act; Nonbinding Forest Principles; technical standards
VIII	Low	Low	Low	Group of 7; spheres of influence; balance of power
Ideal type: Anarchy				

interpretive authority by the European courts and the promulgation of regulations by the Commission and Council produced a rich body of law. The 1987 Montreal Protocol on Substances that Deplete the Ozone Layer (row III), in contrast, created a quite precise and elaborate set of legally binding rules but did not delegate any significant degree of authority for implementing them. Because third-party interpretation and application of rules is so central to legal institutions, we consider this arrangement less highly legalized than those previously discussed.

As we move further down the table, the difficulties of dichotomizing and ordering our three dimensions become more apparent. For example, it is not instructive to say that arrangements in row IV are necessarily more legalized than those in row V; this judgment requires a more detailed specification of the forms of obligation, precision, and delegation used in each case. In some settings a strong legal obligation (such as the original Vienna Ozone Convention, row V) might be more legalized than a weaker obligation (such as Agenda 21, row IV), even if the latter were more precise and entailed stronger delegation. Furthermore, the relative significance of delegation vis-à-vis other dimensions becomes less clear at lower levels, since truly "high" delegation, including judicial or quasi-judicial authority, almost never exists together with low levels of legal obligation. The kinds of delegation typically seen in rows IV and VI are administrative or operational in nature (we describe this as "moderate" delegation in Table 1). Thus one might reasonably regard a precise but nonobligatory agreement (such as the Helsinki Final Act, row VII) as more highly legalized than an imprecise and nonobligatory agreement accompanied by modest administrative delegation (such as the High Commissioner on National Minorities of the Organization for Security and Cooperation in Europe, row VI).[8] The general point is that Table 1 should be read indicatively, not as a strict ordering.

The middle rows of Table 1 suggest a wide range of "soft" or intermediate forms of legalization. Here norms may exist, but they are difficult to apply as law in a strict sense. The 1985 Vienna Convention for the Protection of the Ozone Layer (row V), for example, imposed binding treaty obligations, but most of its substantive commitments were expressed in general, even hortatory language and were not connected to an institutional framework with independent authority. Agenda 21, adopted at the 1992 Rio Conference on Environment and Development (row IV), spells out highly elaborated norms on numerous issues but was clearly intended not to be legally binding and is implemented by relatively weak UN agencies. Arrangements like these are often used in settings where norms are contested and concerns for sovereign autonomy are strong, making higher levels of obligation, precision, or delegation unacceptable.

Rows VI and VII include situations where rules are not legally obligatory, but where states either accept precise normative formulations or delegate authority for implementing broad principles. States often delegate discretionary authority where judgments that combine concern for professional standards with implicit political criteria are required, as with the International Monetary Fund (IMF), the World Bank, and the other international organizations in row VI. Arrangements such as those in row VII are sometimes used to administer coordination standards, which actors have incentives to follow provided they expect others to do so, as well as in areas where legally obligatory actions would be politically infeasible.

Examples of rule systems entailing the very low levels of legalization in row VIII include "balances of power" and "spheres of influence." These are not legal institutions in any real sense. The balance of power was characterized by rules of practice[9] and by arrangements for diplomacy, as in the Concert of Europe. Spheres of influence during the Cold War were imprecise, obligations were partly expressed in treaties but largely tacit, and little institutional framework existed to oversee them.

Finally, at the bottom of the table, we approach the ideal type of anarchy prominent in international relations theory. "Anarchy" is an easily misunderstood term of art, since even situations taken as extreme forms of international anarchy are in fact structured by rules—most notably rules defining national sovereignty—with legal or pre-legal characteristics. Hedley Bull writes of "the anarchical society" as characterized by institutions like sovereignty and international law as well as diplomacy and

8. Interestingly, however, while the formal mandate of the OSCE High Commissioner on National Minorities related solely to conflict prevention and did not entail authority to implement legal (or nonlegal) norms, in practice the High Commissioner has actively promoted respect for both hard and soft legal norms. Ratner 2000.

9. Kaplan 1957.

the balance of power.[10] Even conceptually, moreover, there is a wide gap between the weakest forms of legalization and the complete absence of norms and institutions.

Given the range of possibilities, we do not take the position that greater legalization, or any particular form of legalization, is inherently superior.[11] As Kenneth Abbott and Duncan Snidal argue in "Hard and Soft Law in International Governance" (this volume), institutional arrangements in the middle or lower reaches of Table 1 may best accommodate the diverse interests of concerned actors. A concrete example is the argument made by Judith Goldstein and Lisa Martin in their article "Legalization, Trade Liberalization, and Domestic Politics: A Cautionary Note": more highly legalized trade rules can be problematic for liberal trade policy.

On a related set of issues—whether international legalization is increasing, or likely to increase, over time—we take no position. The comparative statics approach that informs this volume is not suitable for analyzing such dynamic phenomena. Yet the issues are important and intriguing. We undoubtedly witness increasing legalization in many issue areas. The ozone depletion regime, for example, began in 1985 with a binding but otherwise weakly legalized convention (row V). It was augmented two years later by the more precise and highly elaborated Montreal Protocol (row III). Since then, through practice and subsequent revisions, the regime has developed a "system for implementation review," with a noncompliance procedure that still falls short of third-party dispute resolution but appears to have had some impact on behavior.[12] In other issue areas, like the whaling regime described by John K. Setear, the level of legalization appears to remain largely constant over time, even as the substance of the regime changes.[13] And in still others, legalization seems to decline, as in the move from fixed to floating exchange rates. Exploration of legal dynamics would be the logical next step in the research program that this volume seeks to inaugurate.

In the remainder of this article we turn to a more detailed explication of the three dimensions of legalization. We summarize the discussion in each section with a table listing several indicators of stronger or weaker legalization along the relevant dimension, with delegation subdivided into judicial and legislative/administrative components.

The Dimensions of Legalization

Obligation

Legal rules and commitments impose a particular type of binding obligation on states and other subjects (such as international organizations). Legal obligations are different in kind from obligations resulting from coercion, comity, or morality alone. As

10. Bull 1977.
11. Compare Goldstein, Kahler, Keohane, and Slaughter, this issue.
12. Victor, Raustalia, and Skolnikoff 1998, especially chap. 4.
13. Setear 1999.

discussed earlier, legal obligations bring into play the established norms, procedures, and forms of discourse of the international legal system.[14]

The fundamental international legal principle of *pacta sunt servanda* means that the rules and commitments contained in legalized international agreements are regarded as obligatory, subject to various defenses or exceptions, and not to be disregarded as preferences change. They must be performed in good faith regardless of inconsistent provisions of domestic law. International law also provides principles for the interpretation of agreements and a variety of technical rules on such matters as formation, reservation, and amendments. Breach of a legal obligation is understood to create "legal responsibility," which does not require a showing of intent on the part of specific state organs.

The international legal system also contains accepted procedures and remedies for breaches of legal commitments. Only states injured by a breach have standing to complain; and the complaining state or its citizens must exhaust any domestic remedies within the breaching state before making an international claim. States may then pursue their claims diplomatically or through any formal dispute procedure they have accepted. International law also prescribes certain defenses, which include consent, self-defense, and necessity, as well as the broad doctrine called *rebus sic stantibus*: an agreement may lose its binding character if important conditions change materially. These doctrines automatically inject a degree of flexibility into legal commitments; by defining particular exceptions, though, they reinforce legal obligations in other circumstances.

When breach leads to injury, legal responsibility entails an obligation to make reparation, preferably through restitution. If this is not possible, the alternative in the event of material harm is a monetary indemnity; in the event of psychological harm, "satisfaction" in the form of an apology. Since achieving such remedies is often problematic, international law authorizes self-help measures, including reprisals, reciprocal measures (such as the withdrawal of equivalent concessions in the WTO), and retorsions (such as suspending foreign aid). Self-help is limited, though, by the doctrine of proportionality and other legal conditions, including restrictions on the unilateral use of force.

Finally, establishing a commitment as a legal rule invokes a particular form of discourse. Although actors may disagree about the interpretation or applicability of a set of rules, discussion of issues purely in terms of interests or power is no longer legitimate. Legalization of rules implies a discourse primarily in terms of the text, purpose, and history of the rules, their interpretation, admissible exceptions, applicability to classes of situations, and particular facts. The rhetoric of law is highly devel-

14. In linking obligation to the broader legal system, we are positing the existence of international law as itself imposing a body of accepted and thereby legitimized obligations on states. If the ultimate foundation of a legal system is its acceptance as such by its subjects, through a Kelsenian *Grundnorm* or an ultimate rule of recognition, then we are positing the existence of that acceptance by states with regard to the existing international legal system. The degree of obligation that we seek to measure refers instead to acceptance by subject states of a particular rule as a legal rule or not, that is, as binding or not binding as a matter of international law.

TABLE 2. *Indicators of obligation*

High
Unconditional obligation; language and other indicia of intent to be legally bound
Political treaty: implicit conditions on obligation
National reservations on specific obligations; contingent obligations and escape clauses
Hortatory obligations
Norms adopted without law-making authority; recommendations and guidelines
Explicit negation of intent to be legally bound
Low

oped, and the community of legal experts—whose members normally participate in legal rule-making and dispute settlement—is highly socialized to apply it. Thus the possibilities and limits of this discourse are normally part and parcel of legalized commitments.

Commitments can vary widely along the continuum of obligation, as summarized in Table 2. An example of a hard legal rule is Article 24 of the Vienna Convention on Diplomatic Relations, which reads in its entirety: "The archives and documents of the mission shall be inviolable at any time and wherever they may be." As a whole, this treaty reflects the intent of the parties to create legally binding obligations governed by international law. It uses the language of obligation; calls for the traditional legal formalities of signature, ratification, and entry into force; requires that the agreement and national ratification documents be registered with the UN; is styled a "Convention;" and states its relationship to preexisting rules of customary international law.[15] Article 24 itself imposes an unconditional obligation in formal, even "legalistic" terms.

At the other end of the spectrum are instruments that explicitly negate any intent to create legal obligations. The best-known example is the 1975 Helsinki Final Act. By specifying that this accord could not be registered with the UN, the parties signified that it was not an "agreement . . . governed by international law." Other instruments are even more explicit: witness the 1992 "Non-Legally Binding Authoritative Statement of Principles for a Global Consensus" on sustainable management of forests. Many working agreements among national government agencies are explicitly nonbinding.[16] Instruments framed as "recommendations" or "guidelines"—like the

15. Under accepted legal principles, many of which are codified in the Vienna Convention on the Law of Treaties, the intent of the parties to an agreement determines whether that instrument creates obligations that are legally binding, not merely personal or political in effect, and that are governed by international law, rather than the law of some nation. Intent is sometimes explicitly stated; otherwise it must be discerned from the overall context of an agreement, its negotiating history, the nature of its commitments, and its form. As a practical matter, however, legalization is the default position: significant agreements between states are assumed to be legally binding and governed by international law unless the parties indicate otherwise. U.S. practice on this score is summarized in the State Department's *Foreign Relations Manual*, pt. 181.

16. Zaring 1998.

OECD Guidelines on Multinational Enterprises—are normally intended not to create legally binding obligations.[17]

These contrasting legal forms have distinctive implications. Under legally binding agreements like the Vienna Convention, states may assert legal claims (under *pacta sunt servanda,* state responsibility and other doctrines of international law), engage in legal discourse, invoke legal procedures, and resort to legal remedies. Under non-binding instruments like the Forest Principles states may do none of these things, although they may make normative claims, engage in normative discourse, and resort to political remedies. Further theorizing and empirical investigation are needed to determine whether these distinctions—at least in the absence of strong delegation—lead to substantial differences in practice. The care with which states frame agreements, however, suggests a belief that they do.

Actors utilize many techniques to vary legal obligation between these two extremes, often creating surprising contrasts between form and substance. On the one hand, it is widely accepted that states expect some formally binding "political treaties" not to be observed if interests or circumstances change.[18] More frequently, provisions of legally binding agreements are worded to circumscribe their obligatory force. One common softening device is the contingent obligation: the 1994 Framework Convention on Climate Change, for example, requires parties to take various actions to limit greenhouse gas emissions, but only after considering "their specific national and regional development priorities, objectives, and circumstances."

Another widely used device is the escape clause.[19] The European Convention for the Protection of Human Rights and Fundamental Freedoms, for example, authorizes states to interfere with certain civil rights in the interest of national security and the prevention of disorder "when necessary in a democratic society," and more broadly during war "or other public emergency threatening the life of the nation."[20] Most arms control agreements include the following clause, repeated verbatim from the Limited Test Ban Treaty: "Each party shall in exercising its national sovereignty have the right to withdraw from [this agreement] if it decides that extraordinary events, related to the subject matter of [this agreement], have jeopardized the supreme interests of its country."[21] Many instruments, from the Outer Space Treaty to the Convention on the Settlement of Investment Disputes, simply allow for withdrawal after a specified notice period.

17. Although precise obligations are generally an attribute of hard legalization, these instruments use precise language to avoid legally binding character.

18. See Baxter 1980; and Schachter 1977.

19. In addition to the explicit escape clauses considered here, states are often able to escape from the strictures of particular provisions by filing reservations, declarations, and other unilateral conditions after an agreement has been negotiated.

20. These avenues of escape are quite precisely drafted and are supervised by the European Commission and Court of Human Rights, limiting the ability of states to evade their substantive obligations.

21. In contrast to the European Convention on Human Rights, this withdrawal clause is self-judging, increasing its softening effect. Nonetheless, the clause was originally inserted to impose some constraints on what might otherwise have been seen as an unconditional right to withdraw.

Other formally binding commitments are hortatory, creating at best weak legal obligations. Article IV of the IMF Articles of Agreement, for example, requires parties only to "endeavor" to adopt specified domestic economic policies and to "seek to promote" economic stability, "with due regard to [their] circumstances." The International Covenant on Economic, Social, and Cultural Rights requires parties only "to take steps . . . with a view to achieving progressively the full realization of the rights recognized in the . . . Covenant."[22]

On the other hand, a large number of instruments state seemingly unconditional obligations even though the institutions or procedures through which they were created have no direct law-creating authority! Many UN General Assembly declarations, for example, enunciate legal norms, though the assembly has no formal legislative power.[23] Instruments like the 1992 Rio Declaration on Environment and Development and the 1995 Beijing Declaration on Women's Rights are approved at UN conferences with no agreed law-making power.[24]

Instruments like these should not be troublesome in legal terms, since they do not conform to the established "rules of recognition" of international law. In fact, though, they are highly problematic. Over time, even nonbinding declarations can shape the practices of states and other actors and their expectations of appropriate conduct, leading to the emergence of customary law or the adoption of harder agreements. Soft commitments may also implicate the legal principle of good faith compliance, weakening objections to subsequent developments. In many issue areas the legal implications of soft instruments are hotly contested. Supporters argue for immediate and universal legal effect under traditional doctrines (for example, that an instrument codifies existing customary law or interprets an organizational charter) and innovative ones (for example, that an instrument reflects an international "consensus" or "instant custom"). As acts of international governance, then, soft normative instruments have a finely wrought ambiguity.[25]

Precision

A precise rule specifies clearly and unambiguously what is expected of a state or other actor (in terms of both the intended objective and the means of achieving it) in a particular set of circumstances. In other words, precision narrows the scope for reasonable interpretation.[26] In Thomas Franck's terms, such rules are

22. Some agreements authorize particular conduct rather than requiring or prohibiting it. Such provisions are usually couched as rights, using the word *may*. Gamble 1985.

23. See Chinkin 1989; and Gruchalla-Wesierski 1984.

24. This discussion also applies to instruments adopted by organizations with law-making competency but outside prescribed procedures. A significant example is the European Social Charter, adopted by all members of the EC Council except the United Kingdom. These states bypassed a unanimity requirement to avoid a U.K. veto, adopting a softer instrument to guide subsequent legislative action.

25. Palmer 1992.

26. A precise rule is not necessarily more constraining than a more general one. Its actual impact on behavior depends on many factors, including subjective interpretation by the subjects of the rule. Thus, a rule saying "drive slowly" might yield slower driving than a rule prescribing a speed limit of 55 miles per hour if the drivers in question would normally drive 50 miles per hour and understand "slowly" to mean

"determinate."[27] For a set of rules, precision implies not just that each rule in the set is unambiguous, but that the rules are related to one another in a noncontradictory way, creating a framework within which case-by-case interpretation can be coherently carried out.[28] Precise sets of rules are often, though by no means always, highly elaborated or dense, detailing conditions of application, spelling out required or proscribed behavior in numerous situations, and so on.

Precision is an important characteristic in many theories of law. It is essential to a rationalist view of law as a coordinating device, as in James D. Morrow's account of the laws of war.[29] It is also important to positivist visions of law as rules to be applied, whether through a centralized agency or through reciprocity.[30] Franck argues that precision increases the legitimacy of rules and thus their normative "compliance pull." Lon L. Fuller, like other liberals, emphasizes the social and moral virtues of certainty and predictability for individual actors.[31] In each case, clarity is essential to the force of law.

In highly developed legal systems, normative directives are often formulated as relatively precise "rules" ("do not drive faster than 50 miles per hour"), but many important directives are also formulated as relatively general "standards" ("do not drive recklessly").[32] The more "rule-like" a normative prescription, the more a community decides *ex ante* which categories of behavior are unacceptable; such decisions are typically made by legislative bodies. The more "standard-like" a prescription, the more a community makes this determination *ex post,* in relation to specific sets of facts; such decisions are usually entrusted to courts. Standards allow courts to take into account equitable factors relating to particular actors or situations, albeit at the sacrifice of some *ex ante* clarity.[33] Domestic legal systems are able to use standards like "due care" or the Sherman Act's prohibition on "conspiracies in restraint of trade" because they include well-established courts and agencies able to interpret and apply them (high delegation), developing increasingly precise bodies of precedent.

In some international regimes, the institutional context is sufficiently thick to make similar approaches feasible. In framing the EEC's common competition policy, for example, the drafters of the Treaty of Rome utilized both rules and stan-

---

10 miles per hour slower than normal. (We are indebted to Fred Schauer for both the general point and the example.) In addition, precision can be used to define limits, exceptions, and loopholes that reduce the impact of a rule. Nevertheless, for most rules requiring or prohibiting particular conduct—and in the absence of precise delegation—generality is likely to provide an opportunity for deliberate self-interested interpretation, reducing the impact, or at least the potential for enforceable impact, on behavior.

27. Franck 1990.

28. Franck labels this collective property "coherence." We use the singular notion of precision to capture both the precision of a rule in isolation and its precision within a rule system.

29. Morrow 1997 and 1998.

30. Simma and Paulus 1999.

31. Fuller 1964.

32. The standard regime definition encompasses three levels of precision: "principles," "norms," and "rules." Krasner 1983. This formulation reflects the fact that societies typically translate broad normative values into increasingly concrete formulations that decision-makers can apply in specific situations.

33. Kennedy 1976.

dards.[34] Wherethey could identify disfavored conduct in advance, they specified it for reasons of clarity and notice: Article 85, for example, prohibits agreements between firms "that . . . fix purchase or selling prices." Because they could not anticipate all problematic conduct, though, the drafters also authorized the European Court to apply a general standard, prohibiting "agreements . . . which have as their object or effect the . . . distortion of competition within the common market."

In most areas of international relations, judicial, quasi-judicial, and administrative authorities are less highly developed and infrequently used. In this thin institutional context, imprecise norms are, in practice, most often interpreted and applied by the very actors whose conduct they are intended to govern. In addition, since most international norms are created through the direct consent or practice of states, there is no centralized legislature to overturn inappropriate, self-serving interpretations. Thus, precision and elaboration are especially significant hallmarks of legalization at the international level.

Much of international law is in fact quite precise, and precision and elaboration appear to be increasing dramatically, as exemplified by the WTO trade agreements, environmental agreements like the Montreal (ozone) and Kyoto (climate change) Protocols, and the arms control treaties produced during the Strategic Arms Limitation Talks (SALT) and subsequent negotiations. Indeed, many modern treaties are explicitly designed to increase determinacy and narrow issues of interpretation through the "codification" and "progressive development" of customary law. Leading examples include the Vienna Conventions on the Law of Treaties and on Diplomatic Relations, and important aspects of the UN Convention on the Law of the Sea. Even many nonbinding instruments, like the Rio Declaration on Environment and Development and Agenda 21, are remarkably precise and dense, presumably because proponents believe that these characteristics enhance their normative and political value.

Still, many treaty commitments are vague and general, in the ways suggested by Table 3.[35] The North American Free Trade Agreement side agreement on labor, for example, requires the parties to "provide for high labor standards." Article VI of the Treaty on the Non-proliferation of Nuclear Weapons calls on the parties "to pursue negotiations in good faith on effective measures relating to cessation of the nuclear arms race . . . and to nuclear disarmament." Commercial treaties typically require states to create "favorable conditions" for investment and avoid "unreasonable" regulations. Numerous agreements call on states to "negotiate" or "consult," without specifying particular procedures. All these provisions create broad areas of discretion for the affected actors; indeed, many provisions are so general that one cannot meaningfully assess compliance, casting doubt on their legal force.[36] As Abbott and

34. Similarly, agreements administered by the WTO can, with similar legitimacy and effectiveness, specify detailed rules on the valuation of imports for customs purposes and rely on broad standards like "national treatment."

35. Operationalizing the relative precision of different formulations is difficult, except in a gross sense. Gamble, for example, purports to apply a four-point scale of "concreteness" but does not characterize these points. Gamble 1985.

36. The State Department's *Foreign Relations Manual* states that undertakings couched in vague or very general terms with no criteria for performance frequently reflect an intent not to be legally bound.

TABLE 3. *Indicators of precision*

High
Determinate rules: only narrow issues of interpretation
Substantial but limited issues of interpretation
Broad areas of discretion
"Standards": only meaningful with reference to specific situations
Impossible to determine whether conduct complies
Low

Snidal emphasize in their article,[37] such imprecision is not generally the result of a failure of legal draftsmanship, but a deliberate choice given the circumstances of domestic and international politics.

Imprecision is not synonymous with state discretion, however, when it occurs within a delegation of authority and therefore grants to an international body wider authority to determine its meaning. The charters of international organizations provide important examples. In these instruments, generality frequently produces a broader delegation of authority, although member states almost always retain many levers of influence. A recent example makes the point clearly. At the 1998 Rome conference that approved a charter for an international criminal court, the United States sought to avoid any broad delegation of authority. Its proposal accordingly emphasized the need for "clear, precise, and specific definitions of each offense" within the jurisdiction of the court.[38]

Delegation

The third dimension of legalization is the extent to which states and other actors delegate authority to designated third parties—including courts, arbitrators, and administrative organizations—to implement agreements. The characteristic forms of legal delegation are third-party dispute settlement mechanisms authorized to interpret rules and apply them to particular facts (and therefore in effect to make new rules, at least interstitially) under established doctrines of international law. Dispute settlement mechanisms are most highly legalized when the parties agree to binding third-party decisions on the basis of clear and generally applicable rules; they are least legalized when the process involves political bargaining between parties who can accept or reject proposals without legal justification.[39]

37. Abbott and Snidal, this issue.

38. U.S. Releases Proposal on Elements of Crimes at the Rome Conference on the Establishment of an International Criminal Court, statement by James P. Rubin, U.S. State Department spokesperson, 22 June 1998, <secretary.state.gov/www/briefings/statements/1998/ps980622b.html>, accessed 16 February 1999.

39. Law remains relevant even here. The UN Charter makes peaceful resolution of disputes a legal obligation, and general international law requires good faith in the conduct of negotiations. In addition, resolution of disputes by agreement can contribute to the growth of customary international law.

TABLE 4. *Indicators of delegation*

a. Dispute resolution
 High
 Courts: binding third-party decisions; general jurisdiction; direct private access; can interpret and supplement rules; domestic courts have jurisdiction
 Courts: jurisdiction, access or normative authority limited or consensual
 Binding arbitration
 Nonbinding arbitration
 Conciliation, mediation
 Institutionalized bargaining
 Pure political bargaining
 Low

b. Rule making and implementation
 High
 Binding regulations; centralized enforcement
 Binding regulations with consent or opt-out
 Binding internal policies; legitimation of decentralized enforcement
 Coordination standards
 Draft conventions; monitoring and publicity
 Recommendations; confidential monitoring
 Normative statements
 Forum for negotiations
 Low

In practice, as reflected in Table 4a, dispute-settlement mechanisms cover an extremely broad range: from no delegation (as in traditional political decision making); through institutionalized forms of bargaining, including mechanisms to facilitate agreement, such as mediation (available within the WTO) and conciliation (an option under the Law of the Sea Convention); nonbinding arbitration (essentially the mechanism of the old GATT); binding arbitration (as in the U.S.-Iran Claims Tribunal); and finally to actual adjudication (exemplified by the European Court of Justice and Court of Human Rights, and the international criminal tribunals for Rwanda and the former Yugoslavia).

Another significant variable—the extent to which individuals and private groups can initiate a legal proceeding—is explored by Robert O. Keohane, Andrew Moravcsik, and Anne-Marie Slaughter in "Legalized Dispute Resolution" (this volume). Private actors can influence governmental behavior even in settings where access is limited to states (such as the WTO and the International Court of Justice). Increasingly, though, private actors are being granted access to legalized dispute settlement mechanisms, either indirectly (through national courts, as in the EC, or a supranational body like the European Commission on Human Rights) or directly (as will shortly be the case for the European Court of Human Rights). As Keohane, Moravcsik, and Slaughter argue, private access appears to increase the expansiveness of legal institutions.

As one moves up the delegation continuum, the actions of decision-makers are increasingly governed, and legitimated, by rules. (Willingness to delegate often depends on the extent to which these rules are thought capable of constraining the delegated authority.) Thus, this form of legal delegation typically achieves the union of primary and secondary rules that Hart deemed necessary for the establishment of a legal system. Delegation to third-party adjudicators is virtually certain to be accompanied by the adoption of rules of adjudication. The adjudicative body may then find it necessary to identify or develop rules of recognition and change, as it sorts out conflicts between rules or reviews the validity of rules that are the subject of dispute.

Delegation of legal authority is not confined to dispute resolution. As Table 4b indicates, a range of institutions—from simple consultative arrangements to full-fledged international bureaucracies—helps to elaborate imprecise legal norms, implement agreed rules, and facilitate enforcement.

Like domestic administrative agencies, international organizations are often authorized to elaborate agreed norms (though almost always in softer ways than their domestic counterparts), especially where it is infeasible to draft precise rules in advance and where special expertise is required. The EU Commission drafts extensive regulations, though they usually become binding only with the assent of member states. Specialized agencies like the International Civil Aviation Organization and the Codex Alimentarius Commission promulgate technical rules—often framed as recommendations—in coordination situations. In cases like these, the grant of rule-making authority typically contains (in Hart's terms) the rule of recognition; the governing bodies or secretariats of international organizations may subsequently develop rules of change. At lower levels of delegation, bodies like the International Labor Organization and the World Intellectual Property Organization draft proposed international conventions and promulgate a variety of nonbinding rules, some for use by private actors. International organizations also support interstate negotiations.

Many operational activities serve to implement legal norms.[40] Virtually all international organizations gather and disseminate information relevant to implementation; many also generate new information. Most engage in educational activities, such as the WTO's training programs for developing country officials. Agencies like the World Health Organization, the World Bank, and the UN Environment Program have much more extensive operations. These activities implement (and thus give meaning to) the norms and goals enunciated in the agencies' charters and other agreements they administer. Although most international organizations are highly constrained by member states, the imprecision of their governing instruments frequently leaves them considerable discretion, exercised implicitly as well as through formal interpretations and operating policies. The World Bank, for example, has issued detailed policies on matters such as environmental impact assessment and treatment of indigenous peoples; these become legally binding when incorporated in loan agreements.[41] The World Bank's innovative Inspection Panel supervises compliance, often as the result of private complaints.[42]

40. Abbott and Snidal 1998.
41. Boisson de Chazournes 1998.
42. Shihata 1994.

In Austinian approaches, centralized enforcement is the sine qua non of law. Yet even domestically, many areas of law are not closely tied to enforcement; so too, much international legalization is significant in spite of a lack of centralized enforcement. And international law can draw on some centralized powers of enforcement. The UN Security Council, for example, imposed programs of inspection, weapons destruction, and compensation on Iraq for violations of international law; it also created ad hoc tribunals for Rwanda and the former Yugoslavia that have convicted national officials of genocide, crimes against humanity, and other international crimes. As in domestic legal systems, moreover, some international agencies can enforce norms through their power to confer or deny benefits: international financial institutions have the greatest leverage, but other organizations can deny technical assistance or rights of participation to violators. (These actions presuppose powers akin to rule interpretation and adjudication.) Further, international organizations from the Security Council to the WTO legitimate (and constrain) decentralized sanctioning by states. Many also monitor state behavior and disseminate information on rule observance, creating implicit sanctions for states that wish to be seen as trustworthy members of an international community.

Legalized delegation, especially in its harder forms, introduces new actors and new forms of politics into interstate relations. As other articles in this volume discuss, actors with delegated legal authority have their own interests, the pursuit of which may be more or less successfully constrained by conditions on the grant of authority and concomitant surveillance by member states. Transnational coalitions of nonstate actors also pursue their interests through influence or direct participation at the supranational level, often producing greater divergence from member state concerns. Deciding disputes, adapting or developing new rules, implementing agreed norms, and responding to rule violations all engender their own type of politics, which helps to restructure traditional interstate politics.

Conclusion

Highly legalized institutions are those in which rules are obligatory on parties through links to the established rules and principles of international law, in which rules are precise (or can be made precise through the exercise of delegated authority), and in which authority to interpret and apply the rules has been delegated to third parties acting under the constraint of rules. There is, however, no bright line dividing legalized from nonlegalized institutions. Instead, there is an identifiable continuum from hard law through varied forms of soft law, each with its individual mix of characteristics, to situations of negligible legalization.

This continuum presupposes that legalized institutions are to some degree differentiated from other types of international institutions, a differentiation that may have methodological, procedural, cultural, and informational dimensions.[43] Although me-

43. Schauer and Wise 1997.

diators may, for example, be free to broker a bargain based on the "naked preferences" of the parties,[44] legal processes involve a discourse framed in terms of reason, interpretation, technical knowledge, and argument, often followed by deliberation and judgment by impartial parties. Different actors have access to the process, and they are constrained to make arguments different from those they would make in a nonlegal context. Legal decisions, too, must be based on reasons applicable to all similarly situated litigants, not merely the parties to the immediate dispute.

On the whole, however, our conception of legalization reflects a general theme of this volume: the rejection of a rigid dichotomy between "legalization" and "world politics." Law and politics are intertwined at all levels of legalization. One result of this interrelationship, reflected in many of the articles in this volume, is considerable difficulty in identifying the causal effects of legalization. Compliance with rules occurs for many reasons other than their legal status. Concern about reciprocity, reputation, and damage to valuable state institutions, as well as other normative and material considerations, all play a role. Yet it is reasonable to assume that most of the time, legal and political considerations combine to influence behavior.

At one extreme, even "pure" political bargaining is shaped by rules of sovereignty and other background legal norms. At the other extreme, even international adjudication takes place in the "shadow of politics": interested parties help shape the agenda and initiate the proceedings; judges are typically alert to the political implications of possible decisions, seeking to anticipate the reactions of political authorities. Between these extremes, where most international legalization lies, actors combine and invoke varying degrees of obligation, precision, and delegation to create subtle blends of politics and law. In all these settings, to paraphrase Clausewitz, "law is a continuation of political intercourse, with the addition of other means."

44. Sunstein 1986.

Part III
Hard Law, Soft Law, Legalization and Norms

[12]

Hard and Soft Law in International Governance

Kenneth W. Abbott and Duncan Snidal

Contemporary international relations are legalized to an impressive extent, yet international legalization displays great variety. A few international institutions and issue-areas approach the theoretical ideal of hard legalization, but most international law is "soft" in distinctive ways. Here we explore the reasons for the widespread legalization of international governance and for this great variety in the degrees and forms of legalization.[1] We argue that international actors choose to order their relations through international law and design treaties and other legal arrangements to solve specific substantive and political problems. We further argue that international actors choose softer forms of legalized governance when those forms offer superior institutional solutions. We analyze the benefits and costs of different types of legalization and suggest hypotheses regarding the circumstances that lead actors to select specific forms. We do not purport to develop a full theory of law. Nonetheless, examining these political choices in the spare institutional context of international relations may contribute to a better understanding of the uses of law more generally.

We begin by examining the advantages of hard legalization. The term *hard law* as used in this special issue refers to legally binding obligations that are precise (or can be made precise through adjudication or the issuance of detailed regulations) and that delegate authority for interpreting and implementing the law.[2] Although hard law is not the typical international legal arrangement, a close look at this institutional form provides a baseline for understanding the benefits and costs of all types of legaliza-

For helpful comments as we developed this article, we thank participants in the conferences leading up to this special issue; our discussant Alexander Thompson and other participants at the Program on International Politics, Economics, and Security Workshop at the University of Chicago; and participants at the "half-baked lunch" discussion at Northwestern University Law School. We also thank the editors of this special issue, especially Judith Goldstein and Robert Keohane, and the editors and referees of *International Organization* for valuable comments.

1. We have profited from the insights in Keohane, Moravcsik, and Slaughter 1997, which was prepared in connection with this project.

2. For an extensive discussion of these three dimensions, which guide the articles in this issue, see Abbott, Keohane, Moravcsik, Slaughter, and Snidal, this issue.

tion. By using hard law to order their relations, international actors reduce transactions costs, strengthen the credibility of their commitments, expand their available political strategies, and resolve problems of incomplete contracting. Doing so, however, also entails significant costs: hard law restricts actors' behavior and even their sovereignty.

While we emphasize the benefits and costs of legalization from a rational perspective focused on interests, law simultaneously engages normative considerations. In addition to requiring commitment to a background set of legal norms[3]—including engagement in established legal processes and discourse—legalization provides actors with a means to instantiate normative values. Legalization has effect through normative standards and processes as well as self-interested calculation, and both interests and values are constraints on the success of law. We consider law as both "contract" and "covenant" to capture these distinct but not incompatible characteristics. Indeed, we reject vigorously the insistence of many international relations specialists that one type of understanding is antithetical to the other.[4]

The realm of "soft law" begins once legal arrangements are weakened along one or more of the dimensions of obligation, precision, and delegation. This softening can occur in varying degrees along each dimension and in different combinations across dimensions. We use the shorthand term *soft law* to distinguish this broad class of deviations from hard law—and, at the other extreme, from purely political arrangements in which legalization is largely absent. But bear in mind that soft law comes in many varieties: the choice between hard law and soft law is not a binary one.

Soft law has been widely criticized and even dismissed as a factor in international affairs. Realists, of course, focus on the absence of an independent judiciary with supporting enforcement powers to conclude that all international law is soft—and is therefore only window dressing.[5] But some international lawyers dismiss soft international law from a more normative perspective. Prosper Weil, for example, argues that increasing use of soft law "might destabilize the whole international normative system and turn it into an instrument that can no longer serve its purpose."[6] Others justify soft law only as an interim step toward harder and therefore more satisfactory

3. The international legal system has developed over several centuries. International law includes secondary norms prescribing how primary rules are to be made, interpreted, and applied, as well as institutions through which both kinds of rules are implemented. The background legal system shapes many international interactions—indeed, it helps define the very notion of an international actor.

4. To be sure, there may be irreconcilable paradigmatic differences between interest-based and normative approaches at the level of grand theory. On the ground, however, either approach can be improved by carefully incorporating the arguments made by the other, with appropriate adaptation. One can profitably employ both a hammer and a wrench without declaring one tool better for all problems and without resolving whether carpenters or plumbers are the better handymen. This is especially true when analyzing law, which inherently combines both trades.

5. This perspective is so deeply held among neorealists that they rarely discuss international law at all. Classical realists such as Hans Morgenthau recognized that states generally obeyed international law but took the lack of enforcement to mean that law did not cover the significant issues of international affairs. A modern reprise of this theme is offered by Downs and his colleagues, who critique much international cooperation for consisting of agreements that reflect what states would have done on their own and so do not change behavior. Downs, Rocke, and Barsoom 1996.

6. Weil 1983, 423.

legalization. The implication is that soft law—law that "falls short" on one or more of the three dimensions of legalization—is a failure.

We argue, in contrast, that international actors often deliberately choose softer forms of legalization as superior institutional arrangements. To be sure, soft law is sometimes designed as a way station to harder legalization, but often it is preferable on its own terms. Soft law offers many of the advantages of hard law, avoids some of the costs of hard law, and has certain independent advantages of its own.[7] Importantly, because one or more of the elements of legalization can be relaxed, softer legalization is often easier to achieve than hard legalization. This is especially true when the actors are states that are jealous of their autonomy and when the issues at hand challenge state sovereignty. Soft legalization also provides certain benefits not available under hard legalization. It offers more effective ways to deal with uncertainty, especially when it initiates processes that allow actors to learn about the impact of agreements over time.[8] In addition, soft law facilitates compromise, and thus mutually beneficial cooperation, between actors with different interests and values, different time horizons and discount rates, and different degrees of power.

The specific forms of soft law chosen reflect the particular problems actors are trying to solve. While our analysis focuses on softness in general, different forms of softness may be more acceptable or more efficacious in different circumstances. We suggest a number of variables—including transactions costs, uncertainty, implications for national sovereignty, divergence of preferences, and power differentials—that influence which forms of soft law, which combinations of obligation, precision and delegation, are likely to be selected in specific circumstances.

This article is largely an exercise in comparative statics; we ask why particular situational features lead actors to adopt specific institutional arrangements at given points in time. Soft law is frequently dynamic, however, in the sense that it initiates a process and a discourse that may involve learning and other changes over time. We incorporate these considerations in our analysis by examining how actors (imperfectly) evaluate the dynamic consequences of current soft law commitments.

For ease of exposition, and because states are essential actors in international legalization, we frame our initial discussions in terms of states and the problems they face. We recognize, however, that firms, activist organizations, and other nonstate groups operating at both the domestic and international levels are increasingly key actors in the development of international legalization, and of soft law in particular. In the final section of the article we compare alternative accounts of the role of nonstate actors to examine why such groups press for different forms of legalization. The need to deal with the competing interests and values of nonstate actors also adds to the reasons states have for pursuing soft law strategies.

We employ a range of examples, including some elaborated by other articles in this issue, to illustrate the wide variety of international legal arrangements. Although

7. For a related discussion of the benefits and costs of informal agreements, see Lipson 1991.

8. We draw on Koremenos's insightful work on how states structure treaties to enable mutual learning. Koremenos 1999.

these examples do not provide a true empirical test of our arguments, they do provide evidence for their plausibility. To characterize our examples economically along the hard law/soft law continuum, we use the notation {*O,P,D*}. The elements of each triplet refer to the level of obligation, precision, and delegation, respectively. Variations along each dimension are indicated by capital letters for high levels (for example, *O*), small letters for moderate levels (for example, *o*), and dashes for low levels (-). Thus {*O,P,D*} indicates an arrangement that is highly legalized on all three dimensions and therefore constitutes "hard law"; {*o,P,-*} indicates an issue that has a moderate level of legal obligation coupled with high precision but very limited delegation; and {*O,-,-*} indicates an issue with high legal obligation but very low precision and very limited delegation. Although this tripartite categorization remains somewhat coarse, it suggests the continuous gradations of hardness and softness that are blurred when the hard law/soft law distinction is incorrectly taken as binary.[9]

Contracts and Covenants: Rationales for Hard Law

Introduction

"Contracts" and "covenants" refer to two distinct though not incompatible understandings of international agreements. States enter into "contracts" to further interests; they enter into "covenants" to manifest normative commitments. In international legal scholarship, interest- and norm-based agreements are essentially interchangeable;[10] but international relations scholarship (like other analyses of law[11]) often seeks to distinguish between them: contracts and covenants correspond to the rationalist and constructivist perspectives, respectively, on international institutions, approaches that are usually seen as contrasting, if not mutually exclusive.[12]

In the stereotypical view, rationalists (1) see the relevant actors (usually states) as motivated largely by material interests; (2) view international agreements as "contracts" created to resolve problems of coordination, collaboration, or domestic politics; and (3) understand contracts as operating by changing incentives or other material features of interactions, such as iteration, reciprocity, information, or the influence

9. Because our examples are illustrative, we do not develop formalized coding criteria. Note that a dash (-) indicates a low level of a property, not its absence. Low delegation, for example, would include an international consultative body that facilitates political bargaining among member states. Where an international institution handles more extensive administrative functions—such as substantial information gathering, monitoring, and nonbinding arbitration—we would code delegation as *d*. Finally, where an institution includes strong adjudicative capacity or independent administrative power, we would code delegation as *D*. The dimensions of obligation and precision pose similar problems and possibilities. A more fine-grained discussion of these dimensions is contained in Abbott et al., this issue; and Abbott and Snidal 1997. The eight rows of Table 1 in Abbott et al., which reflect only high and low values of the three elements of legalization, correspond to combinations of capital letters and dashes in our notation (that is, {*O,P,D*},{*O,-,D*} . . . {*O,-,-*},{-,-,-}).

10. Some agreements with strong normative content are entitled "covenants," most notably the covenants on civil and political and on economic, social, and cultural rights. But this usage is not widespread. Many human rights agreements, for example, are simply entitled "treaty" or "convention."

11. Tyler 1990.

12. Katzenstein, Keohane, and Krasner 1998.

of particular interest groups, or through enforcement.[13] Constructivist or normative scholars, on the other hand, (1) focus on nonstate and intragovernmental actors,[14] often motivated by moral or social concerns, as the source of international norms; (2) view international agreements as "covenants" embodying shared norms and understandings; and (3) understand covenants as operating through persuasion, imitation, and internalization to modify intersubjective understandings of appropriate behavior, interests, and even identities.[15]

In studying international legalization, this sharp bifurcation is clearly misplaced. In its origins and operation, law is both an interest-based and a normative enterprise:

1. States and other actors look to law to achieve their ends whether they are pursuing interests or values. In fact, these goals are normally deeply intertwined. Business groups and states seeking rules to protect intellectual property, for example, are committed to norms of property and fairness as well as self-interest; nongovernmental organizations (NGOs) and states supporting rules to promote democracy are concerned with security and trade as well as participatory values.
2. Actors utilize both normative and interest-based strategies to create legal arrangements. Business groups and Western states supporting liberal economic rules appeal to norms of individual choice as well as economic interests; NGOs and governments seeking strong human rights rules cite material benefits—and mobilize economic leverage—along with humanitarian values.[16] Most international agreements are simultaneously contract and covenant.
3. Legal rules and institutions operate both by changing material incentives and by modifying understandings, standards of behavior, and identities. In particular, they invoke doctrines and institutions that facilitate enforcement as well as social norms of obedience to law. Concerned actors strive to bring all these effects to bear, through techniques ranging from litigation and sanctions to persuasion, normative appeals, and shaming.[17]

In the remainder of this section we explore why states seek to order their relations through hard law: institutional arrangements generally characterized as $\{O,P,D\}$ or $\{O,p,D\}$.[18] Since states most often create international legal rules and institutions by negotiation and agreement,[19] we employ contracting theory to organize our analysis,

13. Martin and Simmons 1998.
14. In this they follow modern liberal theorists. Moravcsik 1997.
15. See Finnemore 1996; Keck and Sikkink 1998. Recent years have witnessed some convergence. Rationalists increasingly recognize that interests require explanation and that institutions do much to shape them. Keohane 1988. Constructivists stress that norm entrepreneurs pursue their goals rationally, even strategically, seeking to modify the utility functions of others to accord with preferred norms. Finnemore and Sikkink 1998.
16. Klotz 1995.
17. See Klotz 1995; Keck and Sikkink 1998; and Koh 1996.
18. As noted earlier, the first and second sections of this article focus on states and the third section on nonstate actors. Even in the first and second sections, however, some arguments turn on actions by and effects on nonstate actors, often in domestic politics.
19. Our emphasis, then, is on treaties, especially multilateral regulatory treaties. Chayes and Chayes 1995. Customary law is also an important element of the international legal system, but we do not address

incorporating normative considerations as well as the interest-based factors that dominate the contracting literature.

Credible Commitments

The difficulty states have in credibly committing themselves to future behavior is widely viewed as a characteristic feature of international "anarchy" and an impediment to welfare-enhancing cooperation. In contracting theory, credible commitments are crucial when one party to an agreement must carry out its side of the bargain before other parties are required to perform, or more generally when some parties must make relation-specific investments in reliance on future performance by others.[20] In game theory, similarly, credible commitments are essential whenever some parties to a strategic interaction demand "assurance" from others, as in situations modeled by games such as Assurance, Chicken, or Prisoners' Dilemma and when parties seek to ensure that they arrive at the same coordination point.

Other assurance issues appear when one begins to disaggregate the state. For one thing, relation-specific investments can be political as well as material: a government offering economic or political concessions in return for human rights pledges, for example, would suffer domestic political costs if the other party reneged; it would therefore demand credible assurances. The government making those pledges might also wish to enhance credibility for internal purposes: to bind its successors in office or other branches of government, or to strengthen its citizens' incentives to adjust their practices and attitudes.

Legal commitments can speak to private parties abroad as well as at home. As Frederick Abbott notes in this issue, the Mexican government sought to legalize the North American Free Trade Agreement (NAFTA) in part to increase the credibility of its increasingly liberal economic policies in the eyes of foreign investors. Reversing longstanding national policy, it even accepted significant international delegation, allowing investors from NAFTA countries to take disputes to binding arbitration.

In domestic societies, legal commitments are credible because aggrieved parties can enforce them, with the power of the state if necessary. Even "hard" international law falls short of this standard: international regimes do not even attempt to establish legal obligations centrally enforceable against states.[21] Yet it is erroneous to conclude that the "formal legal status" of international agreements is therefore meaningless. Legalization is one of the principal methods by which states can increase the credibility of their commitments.[22]

---

it systematically here. Our impression, though, is that much customary law today is the result of conscious political action by states and other actors, rather than the gradual accretion of state practice. To the extent this is correct, much of our analysis will also apply to custom.

20. Williamson 1989.

21. Keohane 1984, 88–89.

22. A more extreme way to address commitment problems, analogous to the merger of firms in business relationships that raise assurance problems, is to integrate separate sovereignties into a single political unit, such as a federal state. Integration can be partial as well as complete, as the EU illustrates. Even full integration, though, cannot solve commitment and other contracting problems among the many political, economic, and other interests within and across societies.

One way legalization enhances credibility is by constraining self-serving auto-interpretation. Precision of individual commitments, coherence between individual commitments and broader legal principles, and accepted modes of legal discourse and argument all help limit such opportunistic behavior. Granting interpretive authority to courts or other legal institutions further constrains auto-interpretation.[23] Another way legalization enhances credibility is by increasing the costs of reneging. Regime scholars argue that agreements are strengthened when they are linked to a broader regime: violating an agreement that is part of a regime entails disproportionate costs, because the reputational costs of reneging apply throughout the regime. Legal commitments benefit from similar effects, but they involve international law as a whole in addition to any specific regime.

When a commitment is cast as hard law, the reputational effects of a violation can be generalized to all agreements subject to international law, that is, to most international agreements.[24] There are few alternatives to legalization when states wish to identify undertakings as reliable commitments. Alternatives like bonding and escrow are much more costly. In addition, international law provides the very foundations of statehood: principles of sovereignty, recognition, territorial competence, nonintervention, and so on. Violations weaken the international legal system and are self-defeating, at least over time.

More concretely, legalization enhances (albeit modestly) the capacity for enforcement. First, hard legal commitments, $\{O,P,D\}$ or $\{O,p,D\}$, are interpreted and applied by arbitral or judicial institutions, like those associated with the European Union (EU), the European human rights regime or the World Trade Organization (WTO). (Softer commitments may be invoked in political institutions.) Because legal review allows allegations and defenses to be tested under accepted standards and procedures, it increases reputational costs if a violation is found. The EU may currently be experiencing such aggravated costs as a result of the repeated negative legal rulings by WTO dispute settlement bodies in litigation over European restrictions on imports of hormone-treated beef (for which the EU was unable to demonstrate a legitimate scientific justification) and bananas.

Second, the law of state responsibility fixes consequences for legal violations. In particular, like some legalized regimes (such as the WTO), it authorizes proportional "countermeasures" where other remedies are unavailable. This legitimizes retaliation and clarifies its intent, reducing the costs and risks of self-help. Third, even international law can draw on some forms of centralized enforcement, through institutions like the UN Security Council and the international financial institutions.

Other interest-based costs of legal violations arise because international legal commitments often become part of domestic law. As John K. Setear points out, for ex-

23. Deconstructionists, of course, would contest these statements. In practice, however, even observers of this bent see law as constraining interpretation. Koskenniemi 1999.

24. Keohane observes that states can reduce the force of reputational effects by distinguishing the circumstances of a violation from those surrounding other agreements. Keohane 1995. In the nineteenth century, the United States sought in this way to distinguish its treaties with "savage" Indian tribes, which it frequently violated, from agreements with European countries. The effort devoted to making this distinction, however, suggests that reputational effects would otherwise have spread across all legal agreements.

ample, Congress has provided that violations of the Whaling Convention and the Convention on International Trade in Endangered Species (CITES) constitute violations of U.S. law, carrying criminal penalties.[25] Ellen L. Lutz and Kathryn Sikkink in their article in this issue further describe how international rules condemning torture and other atrocities have been characterized as customary international law and applied by U.S. courts.[26] When international commitments are incorporated into domestic law, the level of delegation associated with them rises dramatically (though it evokes weaker concern for national sovereignty): the commitments can now be applied by well-established systems of courts and administrative agencies; private actors can often initiate legal proceedings; and lawyers have incentives to invoke the rules. When supranational bodies like the European Court of Justice (ECJ) have also been granted legal authority, they can nurture "partnerships" with their domestic counterparts, strengthening both institutions.[27]

Domesticated commitments can more easily be enforced against private persons and their assets. A striking example is the recent litigation against General Pinochet, which was initiated by a Spanish magistrate enforcing international conventions banning torture and other atrocities that had become part of Spanish law. Although the British House of Lords ruled that Pinochet could not be held responsible for most of the charges against him, it did hold him answerable for acts committed after the torture convention had been incorporated into British law.

Legal commitments mobilize legally oriented interest and advocacy groups, such as the organized bar, and legitimize their participation in domestic decision making. They also expand the role of legal bureaucracies within foreign offices and other government agencies. Finally, so long as domestic actors understand legal agreements to be serious undertakings, they will modify their plans and actions in reliance on such commitments, increasing the audience costs of violations.

Legalization also increases the costs of violation through normative channels. Violation of a legal commitment entails reputational costs—again generalizable to all legal commitments—that reflect distaste for breaking the law. International law reinforces this effect through its strong emphasis on compliance (*pacta sunt servanda* and the principle of good faith).[28] To the extent that states (or certain states) see themselves as members of an international society structured by international law, reputational effects may be even broader.[29] Law observance is even more highly valued in most domestic societies; efforts to justify international violations thus create cognitive dissonance and increase domestic audience costs.

Legal obligations are widely perceived as having particular legitimacy. In Thomas Franck's words, legitimacy creates an independent "compliance pull."[30] Individuals,

25. Setear 1999.
26. Lutz and Sikkink, this issue.
27. See Burley and Mattli 1993; and Helfer and Slaughter 1997.
28. The rule of *pacta sunt servanda* is to some extent weakened by exceptions and defenses, notably the broad change-of-circumstances defense known as *rebus sic stantibus*. Yet these doctrines introduce needed flexibility; when they are found inapplicable, the normative force of the basic rule is enhanced.
29. See Wight 1977; Bull 1977; Hurrell 1993; and Buzan 1993.
30. Franck 1990.

government agencies, and other organizations internalize rules so that the advantages and disadvantages of compliance need not be recalculated each time they are invoked. Franck argues that the legitimacy of rules varies according to certain substantive qualities—determinacy and coherence, among other properties—and the procedures by which they were approved. Legal rules are often strong on these dimensions: relatively precise, internally consistent, and adopted through formalized and often elaborate procedures.

Legalization entails a specific form of discourse, requiring justification and persuasion in terms of applicable rules and pertinent facts, and emphasizing factors such as text, precedents, analogies, and practice. Legal discourse largely disqualifies arguments based solely on interests and preferences. The nature of this discourse affords legal professionals a prominent role. When authority is delegated to adjudicative institutions, proceedings can be highly formalized. Even without strong delegation, however, this discourse imposes some constraint on state action: governments will incur reputational costs within the legal community, and often beyond, if they act without a defensible position or without reasonable efforts to justify their conduct in legal terms.

Certain hypotheses regarding the independent variables that lead states to use hard law can be distilled from this analysis. First, states should use hard legal commitments as assurance devices when the benefits of cooperation are great but the potential for opportunism and its costs are high. These conditions are most likely in "contracts," such as trade or investment agreements, that include reciprocal commitments and nonsimultaneous performance. But they may also appear in "covenants"—such as environmental or labor agreements—when violations would impose significant externalities on others. Opportunism is less significant in coordination situations, where agreements are largely self-enforcing.[31] Indeed, international coordination standards are often voluntary, {-,*P*,*d*}, and are created through institutions in which private actors have a significant role. Opportunism, and thus international legalization, is also less significant in settings where national actions have few external effects.[32]

Second, states should use hard legalization to increase the credibility of commitments when noncompliance is difficult to detect, as in most arms control situations. Legal arrangements often include centralized or decentralized monitoring provisions as an aspect of delegation. Even apart from these, however, legal commitments compensate in part for the reduced likelihood of detection by increasing the costs of detected violations.

Third, states should find hard law of special value when forming "clubs" of sincerely committed states, like the EU and NATO. Here legalization functions as an *ex ante* sorting device: because hard legal commitments impose greater costs on violators, a willingness to make them identifies one as having a low propensity to defect. Conversely, hard legalization is less significant in looser groupings like the Asia-

31. Coordination agreements may not be self-enforcing when the benefits of moving the group to a new equilibrium are high. In these situations, especially when the gains to certain parties are large enough to make such attempts feasible, hard law may be useful as an assurance device.

32. Abbott and Snidal 2000.

Pacific Economic Cooperation forum (APEC), described by Miles Kahler in this issue, that are not pursuing deep cooperation and thus do not require *ex ante* evidence of a sincere commitment from members.[33]

Fourth, looking within the state, executive officials should look to hard international law to commit other domestic agencies (especially legislatures) or political groups when those officials are able to make international agreements with little interference or control, and when their preferences differ significantly from those of competing power centers. In this perspective, domestic politics and constitutional law are significant explanatory variables.

Finally, as a secondary hypothesis, legal commitments should be more credible when made by states with particular characteristics. Externally, participation in other international legal regimes should enhance credibility: it exposes states to greater reputational costs and makes them more vulnerable to countermeasures. Internally, strong domestic legal institutions and traditions should enhance credibility. Many of the special costs of violating legal commitments stem from these characteristics.

Reducing Transactions Costs

On balance, at least, hard legalization reduces the transactions costs of subsequent interactions.[34] Two types of interactions are especially relevant: one is the "managerial" process of applying and elaborating agreed rules; the other is the more adversarial process of enforcing commitments. The role of international regimes in reducing transactions costs—especially the costs of negotiating supplementary agreements—has been extensively analyzed.[35] That literature has not, however, distinguished legalization from other institutional forms.[36]

Consider the need to "manage" the application and evolution of agreements. With virtually all agreements, even those that are quite precise, provisions must be interpreted, applied to specific fact situations, and elaborated to resolve ambiguities and address new and related issues. Delegation to courts and other legal institutions is one important way states address these problems; we discuss delegation later in connection with incomplete contracts. Even where delegation is weak—for example, {*O,p,d*} or {*O,p,-*}—legalization facilitates interpretation, application, and elaboration by setting relatively clear bounds on dispute resolution and negotiation. Substantively, legalization implies that proposals for resolving disputes and for new or expanded rules must be integrated with existing norms. They should be compatible with settled rules if possible, so that bargains need not be reopened. In any case they should be compatible with the basic principles of the relevant regime, so that legal coherence is maintained.

Procedurally, hard law constrains the techniques of dispute settlement and negotiation. Even when delegation is relatively low, legalization implies that most disputes

33. Kahler, this issue.

34. As discussed later, the costs of reaching a fully legalized agreement are often relatively high, leading actors to adopt softer forms of legalization.

35. Keohane 1984.

36. Compare Abbott and Snidal 1998.

and questions of interpretation should be addressed through specialized procedures, operated primarily by legal professionals using professional modes of discourse. Even when directly negotiated solutions are permitted, the existence of legal institutions means that states will bargain "in the shadow" of anticipated legal decisions. When legal rules are in effect, moreover, unauthorized coercive behavior is generally seen as illegitimate. It is no coincidence that legalization in the WTO was explicitly tied to a requirement that member states resolve their trade disputes through the new dispute settlement procedures, not through unilateral determinations and responses—a provision aimed directly at the coercive tactics of the United States under Section 301. Even hard international law is not foolproof, of course; the principles discussed here may be ignored in practice, especially by powerful states. Nonetheless, on the whole legalization remains an effective device for organizing ongoing interactions.

Consider next the need to "enforce" commitments. The previous section examined how legalization helps states increase the credibility of their own commitments. But legalization is also significant from the perspective of the states (and other actors) that have worked to obtain commitments from others, often in the face of strong resistance. We refer to such parties as "demandeurs." Whenever there are incentives for noncompliance with international commitments, demandeurs will seek ways to forestall or respond to violations by others.

As discussed earlier, hard legalization offers a rich assortment of international and domestic institutions and procedures and normative and reputational arguments for actors in this position. Compared to alternatives like frequent renegotiation, persuasion, or coercion, it materially reduces the costs of enforcement. Other things being equal, assuming in particular that the substance of an agreement is acceptable, demandeurs should prefer hard legalization, especially in the form $\{O,P,D\}$.[37] Of course, other things being equal, states that resist agreement or desire greater flexibility should resist hard legalization, or at least strive for $\{O,p,D\}$ commitments, for these very reasons. The compromises and tradeoffs that result are discussed in the following section.

Many of the hypotheses in the previous subsection can be reformulated from the demandeur's perspective. Demandeurs should seek hard legalization (1) when the likelihood of opportunism and its costs are high, and noncompliance is difficult to detect; (2) when they wish to limit participation to those strongly committed to an agreement; and (3) when executive officials in other states have preferences compatible with those of the demandeurs, but other elites within those states have divergent preferences. Finally, demandeurs should place greatest reliance on commitments by states that participate actively in legal regimes and have strong legal institutions, professions, and traditions.

Modifying Political Strategies

As proponents of legal process theory make clear, hard legalization allows states (and other actors) to pursue different political strategies as they work to extend and

37. We consider later the specific forms of legalization preferred by powerful and weak states.

enforce (or to weaken or escape) international agreements.[38] Indeed, those strategies are often unavoidable. Both demandeurs and resisters may be as concerned with these tactical attributes as with the strategic issues of credibility and enforceability.

As defined in this issue, hard law includes specialized legal institutions. Regimes of the form {*O,P,D*} and {*O,p,D*} include judicial or arbitral organs that offer the specialized procedures and techniques of litigation as a supplement or alternative to more overtly political techniques for addressing disputes, questions of interpretation, and instances of noncompliance. Nonjudicial institutions, as in {*O,p,d*} regimes, are often authorized to interpret governing instruments, issue regulations or recommendations, draft proposed conventions, and the like. These fora combine the politics and rhetoric of law with ordinary politics.

Legal institutions often require even more subtle strategies. In some, for example, states may not even initiate proceedings. Thus, although the International Criminal Tribunal for the Former Yugoslavia (ICTY) is a valuable tool of humanitarian and interest-based politics, decisions to prosecute (or not to prosecute) are made by ICTY officials. NATO governments (and private groups) must therefore pursue such tactics as lobbying for the appointment of acceptable ICTY officials, gathering evidence, encouraging prosecutors to bring cases—as the United States did in pressing for the indictment of Slobodan Milosevic—and arranging for the arrest of potential defendants, while using the threat of prosecution to pressure the Serbian government.

Hard legal commitments are sometimes incorporated directly into the internal law of participating states; even more frequently international agreements require states to enact implementing legislation, and sometimes to establish particular implementing institutions. Domestic litigation then becomes part of the international toolkit. There may, however, be jurisdictional obstacles to litigation by state claimants. In those situations, states must engage in the subtle process of identifying, encouraging, and supporting private litigants who will advance their interests.[39] Recent scholarship analyzes the strategies that supranational judges pursue to encourage actions by private litigants and national courts that will strengthen international law.[40] National governments presumably follow parallel strategies. Karen Alter's article in this issue explores the complex strategies pursued by this range of public and private actors in the highly legalized institutions of the EU.[41]

We hypothesize broadly that states will be more likely to seek hard legalization when the political strategies it offers are advantageous to them. Mundane issues such as the availability of resources and trained personnel can be quite significant: the United States and other advanced industrial nations with large legal staffs should be more amenable to legalization than countries with few trained specialists. States

38. Koh 1997.

39. This reverses the process associated with more traditional institutions like the Iran–U.S. Claims Tribunal, where private actors encourage governments to initiate proceedings and provide support and encouragement to government litigators.

40. See Burley and Mattli 1993; Helfer and Slaughter 1997; Alter 1998b; Garrett, Kelemen, and Schulz 1998; and Mattli and Slaughter 1998b.

41. Alter, this issue.

should also favor hard legalization when they can be confident that agreements will track their preferences, for legal procedures will allow them to implement those preferences efficiently and at low political cost. This suggests that powerful states have a significant and often overlooked stake in hard legalization. And states that seek to minimize political conflict in relations with other states or in particular issue-areas should favor hard legalization, for it sublimates such conflict into legal argument.

Handling Problems of Incomplete Contracting

States sometimes attempt to write detailed agreements to constrain auto-interpretation, reduce transactions costs, and increase enforceability. But though precision has great value, it also has several problems. It may be wasteful, forcing states to plan for highly unlikely events; it may be counterproductive, introducing opaque and inconsistent provisions; it may lead to undesirable rigidity; and it may prevent agreement altogether.

In any case, writing complete contracts is extremely difficult.[42] The principal-agent literature demonstrates that asymmetric information typically makes it impossible to write an optimal contract if the agent is risk-averse. Yet even this literature assumes that one could in principle write a contract complete with respect to all possible future states of the world. In fact, given bounded rationality and the pervasive uncertainty in which states operate, they can never construct agreements that anticipate every contingency. This problem invites opportunistic behavior and discourages both relation-specific investments and value-enhancing agreements.

Delegation is often the best way to deal with incomplete contracting problems. Regimes of the form $\{O,p,D\}$ are clearly designed with this purpose in mind: they utilize administrative and judicial institutions to interpret and extend broad legal principles. The Treaty of Rome, for example, authorizes the ECJ and the European Community's legislative institutions to elaborate and apply general principles of competition law, such as "concerted practices" and "distortion of competition," through individual cases and general regulations. Even $\{O,P,D\}$ regimes grant significant powers to administrative organs and judicial or arbitral bodies. Although many provisions of the European Convention on Human Rights, for example, are quite detailed, the European Court of Human Rights must still apply general standards—such as "inhuman and degrading treatment" and "respect for . . . private and family life"—in situations that could not have been anticipated when the convention was drafted.

Softer regimes often include nonjudicial procedures for filling out incomplete contracts, though these normally require state consent. Hard legal regimes, in contrast, grant greater independence to judicial or arbitral bodies but require them to follow agreed upon principles and to act only on specific disputes and requests. This combination of attributes, along with the background rules and expectations of interna-

42. Incomplete contracting problems arise when any agreement is negotiated under conditions of incomplete or asymmetric information, risk, and uncertainty. For a recent overview, see Hart 1995.

tional law, simultaneously constrains and legitimates delegated authority. One can hypothesize that states will grant such authority when the anticipated gains from cooperation are large and there is reasonable consensus on general principles, but specific applications are difficult to anticipate.

The Advantages of Soft Legalization

Hard law facilitates international interactions in the many ways already discussed, but it has significant costs and limitations. In this section, we explore how softer forms of legalization provide alternative and often more desirable means to manage many interactions by providing some of the benefits of hard law at lower cost. We emphasize both rationalist concerns, such as contracting costs, and the special role soft legal rules and institutions play in promoting learning and normative processes.

Contracting Costs

A major advantage of softer forms of legalization is their lower contracting costs. Hard legalization reduces the post-agreement costs of managing and enforcing commitments, but adoption of a highly legalized agreement entails significant contracting costs.[43] Any agreement entails some negotiating costs—coming together, learning about the issue, bargaining, and so forth—especially when issues are unfamiliar or complex. But these costs are greater for legalized agreements. States normally exercise special care in negotiating and drafting legal agreements, since the costs of violation are higher. Legal specialists must be consulted; bureaucratic reviews are often lengthy. Different legal traditions across states complicate the exercise. Approval and ratification processes, typically involving legislative authorization, are more complex than for purely political agreements.

Two examples suggest the impact of contracting costs on forms of legalization. First, the costs and risks of national ratification procedures led the International Labor Organization (ILO) to modify its legalization strategy.[44] Throughout its history, the ILO has acted primarily by adopting draft conventions. In recent decades, however, states have been ratifying ILO conventions at a low and declining rate. Believing that this phenomenon was damaging the prestige of the organization, two successive directors-general called for the ILO to emphasize nonlegally binding instruments, such as recommendations and codes of conduct, at the expense of binding treaties in order to reduce the costs of national ratification. Although labor representatives resisted this change, the ILO has begun to adopt some new rules in softer legal form.

Second, contracting costs were used as a delaying tactic in the negotiations that led to the 1997 Organization for Economic Cooperation and Development (OECD) con-

43. The regimes literature does not always distinguish between the costs of transacting *within* regimes and the costs of *creating* regimes. In early work, regimes are seen as the legacy of hegemony, so that their creation is not directly addressed.

44. Maupain 1998.

vention restricting foreign bribery in international business transactions. In those discussions, the United States hoped to reduce the commercial disadvantage created by its Foreign Corrupt Practices Act by supporting a legally binding treaty, {*O,P,d*}, requiring all OECD members to adopt equivalent regulatory limits. As negotiations proceeded, however, the very states that had resisted any action on the issue came out in favor of a binding treaty! These nations hoped to use the high contracting costs of hard legalization to impede agreement. The United States responded by supporting a nonlegally binding OECD recommendation, {-,*P,d*}. The two sides eventually compromised by setting a short deadline for treaty negotiations and agreeing to adopt a recommendation if the deadline was not met.

The costs of hard legalization are magnified by the circumstances of international politics. States, jealous of their sovereign autonomy, are reluctant to limit it through legalized commitments. Security concerns intensify the distributional issues that accompany any agreement, especially ones of greater magnitude or involving greater uncertainty. Negotiations are often multilateral. The scope of bargaining is often not clearly delimited, since the issues themselves are ill defined (for example, is free trade in magazines an economic issue or a cultural one?). Finally, the thinness of the international institutional context (including the low prevailing level of legalization) does little to lower the costs of agreement.

Soft legalization mitigates these costs as well. For example, states can dampen security and distributional concerns by opting for escape clauses, {*o,P,d*}; imprecise commitments, {*O,p,d*}; or "political" forms of delegation that allow them to maintain future control if adverse circumstances arise, {*O,p*,-}. These institutional devices protect state sovereignty and reduce the costs and risks of agreement while providing some of the advantages of legalization. Furthermore, soft legalization offers states an opportunity to learn about the consequences of their agreement. In many cases such learning processes will lower the perceived costs of subsequent moves to harder legalization.

The international nuclear regime illustrates these advantages.[45] Although fundamental nonproliferation obligations are set out in the Nuclear Non-Proliferation Treaty and other legally binding agreements, {*O,P,d*}, many sensitive issues—such as the protection of nuclear materials—are regulated predominantly through recommendations from the International Atomic Energy Agency (IAEA), {-,*P,d*}. Recommendations deal with technical matters, such as inventory control and transportation, at a level of detail that would be intractable in treaty negotiations. They also address issues of domestic policy, such as the organization of national regulatory agencies and the supervision of private actors, that states might regard as too sensitive for treaty regulation. When a high level of consensus forms around an IAEA recommendation, member states may incorporate its provisions into a binding treaty—as occurred with rules on the management of spent nuclear fuel and radioactive waste—but even these treaties must usually be supplemented by recommendations on technical issues.

45. Kellman 1998.

The international trade regime also illustrates the advantages of soft law in costly contracting environments. The proposed charter of the International Trade Organization contemplated legally binding commitments with constraints on the right of withdrawal and significant institutionalization, {*O,P,d*}; it also covered a wide range of economic issues. Such an instrument was very difficult to negotiate and draft; its institutional strength also provoked political resistance within the United States.[46] Because of these problems, the participating states adopted the 1947 General Agreement on Tariffs and Trade (GATT) as a low-cost, interim framework for tariff reductions. Compared to the draft charter of the International Trade Organization, GATT 1947 was relatively soft: it was adopted only "provisionally," included a lenient withdrawal clause, and created only skeletal institutions, {*o,p,-*}. Over time, GATT developed into the WTO as states learned the advantages of harder legalization in governing international trade. But the history of the regime—from its earliest days through the November 1999 ministerial meeting—demonstrates clearly that achieving harder legalization is a sensitive and protracted process.

In sum, we argue that states face tradeoffs in choosing levels of legalization. Hard agreements reduce the costs of operating within a legal framework—by strengthening commitments, reducing transactions costs, and the like—but they are hard to reach. Soft agreements cannot yield all these benefits, but they lower the costs of achieving (some) legalization in the first place. Choices along this continuum of tradeoffs determine the "hardness" of legalization, both initially and over time.

In general, we hypothesize that softer forms of legalization will be more attractive to states as contracting costs increase. This proposition should be true both for relatively mechanical costs—such as those created by large numbers of actors and rigorous national ratification procedures—and for more intensely political costs like those prevailing in negotiations with potentially strong distributional effects. In the remainder of this section, we explore the hard law/soft law tradeoff in terms of several key independent variables, each of which increases the costs of international agreement. These variables include sovereignty costs, uncertainty, divergence among national preferences, differences in time horizons and discount rates, and power differentials among major actors.

Sovereignty Costs

The nature of sovereignty costs. Accepting a binding legal obligation, especially when it entails delegating authority to a supranational body, is costly to states. The costs involved can range from simple differences in outcome on particular issues, to loss of authority over decision making in an issue-area, to more fundamental encroachments on state sovereignty. While we recognize that the concept of "sovereignty" is broad and highly contested,[47] we use "sovereignty costs" as a covering term for all

46. Diebold 1952.

47. Krasner offers four meanings or categories of sovereignty: *domestic* sovereignty (the organization of authority and control within the state), *interdependence* sovereignty (the ability to control flows across borders), international *legal* sovereignty (establishing the status of a political entity in the international

three categories of costs to emphasize the high stakes states often face in accepting international agreements. The potential for inferior outcomes, loss of authority, and diminution of sovereignty makes states reluctant to accept hard legalization—especially when it includes significant levels of delegation.

Sovereignty costs are relatively low when states simply make international legal commitments that limit their behavior in particular circumstances. States typically accept these costs in order to achieve better collective outcomes—as illustrated by solutions to Prisoners' Dilemma and collective action problems that limit individual choices. Such agreements are undoubtedly exercises of legal sovereignty. Nevertheless, even they may limit the ability of states to regulate their borders (for example, by requiring them to allow goods, capital, or people to pass freely) and to implement important domestic policies (as when free trade impinges on labor, safety, or environmental regulations), thus encroaching on other aspects of sovereignty.

Greater sovereignty costs emerge when states accept external authority over significant decisions. International agreements may implicitly or explicitly insert international actors (who are neither elected nor otherwise subject to domestic scrutiny) into national decision procedures. These arrangements may limit the ability of states to govern whole classes of issues—such as social subsidies or industrial policy—or require states to change domestic laws or governance structures. Their significance is reflected in European concerns over the "democratic deficit" and complaints of American activists regarding the "faceless bureaucrats" in the WTO. Nevertheless, the impact of such arrangements is tempered by states' ability to withdraw from international agreements—although processes of enmeshment may make it increasingly costly for them to do so.

Sovereignty costs are at their highest when international arrangements impinge on the relations between a state and its citizens or territory, the traditional hallmarks of (Westphalian) sovereignty. Of course, ordinary restrictions on domestic policies can have such effects in contemporary welfare states, but these are heightened and generalized when, for example, an international human rights regime circumscribes a state's ability to regulate its citizens. Similarly, the United States has correctly been concerned that an International Criminal Court might claim jurisdiction over U.S. soldiers participating in international peacekeeping activities or other foreign endeavors. Agreements such as the Law of the Sea Convention both redefine national territory (for example, by delineating jurisdiction over a territorial sea, exclusive economic

---

system), and *Westphalian* sovereignty (preventing external actors from influencing or determining domestic authority structures). Krasner 1999. These categories overlap and do not covary in any necessary pattern.

Krasner argues that sovereignty has never been immutable, although legal sovereignty has tended to be more respected than Westphalian or other types of sovereignty. Indeed, some legal purists see sovereignty as a fundamental and inviolable legal concept relating to state supremacy in making and withdrawing from international treaties. But recent legal theorists argue that such a view is untenable given ongoing developments in international legalization; they conclude that "it is time to slowly ease the term out of polite language in international relations, surely in law." See Henkin et al. 1993, 19. We skirt these conceptual debates, focusing instead on the fact that states often perceive international legalization as infringing on their sovereignty, broadly construed.

zone, and continental shelf) and limit the capacity of states to restrict its use (for example, by establishing rights of innocent passage). Here, too, individual states retain the capacity to withdraw, but doing so may actually diminish their (legal) sovereignty, risking loss of recognition as members in good standing of the international community.

Legalization can lead to further, often unanticipated sovereignty costs over time. Even if rules are written precisely to narrow their range, or softened by including escape clauses or limiting delegation, states cannot anticipate or limit all of their possible effects.

Delegation provides the greatest source of unanticipated sovereignty costs. As Charles Lindblom points out, a grant of "authority always becomes to a degree uncontrollable."[48] The best example is the ECJ. As Karen Alter describes in this issue, ECJ rulings transformed the preliminary ruling procedure of Article 177 of the Treaty of Rome from a check on supranational power into a device through which private litigants can challenge national policies as inconsistent with European law. Similarly, while France and Canada have consistently sought to minimize the impact of expanding trade legalization on their autonomous cultural policies, they have nevertheless seen that autonomy slowly trimmed back by decisions in the WTO and NAFTA. Even nonjudicial organizations like the IMF or World Bank exert their independence in ways that go beyond the initial intentions or anticipations of the contracting states.[49]

The delegation of legal authority to independent domestic courts and agencies can create similar unexpected consequences. However, states generally feel they have ultimate control over domestic courts—they appoint the judges and control the justice departments that bring criminal actions—and so they find, in general, that domestic delegation has lower sovereignty costs.

Even the most powerful states recognize that legalization will circumscribe their autonomy. U.S. opposition to autonomous international institutions, whether the Enterprise in the Law of the Sea Convention, the International Criminal Court, or the UN more generally, reflects the special concern that delegation raises.[50] Even in NAFTA, where its political influence is paramount, the United States resisted delegating authority to supranational dispute settlement bodies for interstate disputes; only the Chapter 19 procedure for reviewing antidumping and countervailing duty rulings creates significant delegated authority. Congress also explicitly provided that the agreement would not be self-executing in domestic law, limiting delegation to national courts.[51] More recently, concern that highly legalized WTO dispute settlement institutions might expand the meaning of the Uruguay Round agreements led Con-

48. Lindblom 1977, 24.
49. Abbott and Snidal 1998.
50. Shapiro takes the extreme view that such developments are an inevitable part of the development of any legal system. Shapiro 1981. Our view is that the advantages of legalization exert a powerful pull in this direction but that sovereignty costs provide significant resistance; we should expect a mixed level of international legalization according to the characteristics of issues and states, at least in the foreseeable future.
51. F. Abbott, this issue.

gress to provide for an early review of the costs and benefits of WTO membership, including the results of legal proceedings, tied to a fast-track procedure for withdrawal from the organization. Conversely, the willingness of the United States and other countries to subscribe to more constrained institutions indicates that their benefits outweigh their sovereignty costs—at least up to a point.

The notion of sovereignty costs is more complicated when competing domestic and transnational interests affect the development of international legalization. Certain domestic groups may perceive negative sovereignty costs from international agreements that provide them with more favorable outcomes than national policy. Examples include free-trade coalitions that prefer their states' trade policies to be bound by WTO rulings rather than open to the vagaries of individual legislatures, and environmental groups that believe they can gain more from an international accord than from domestic politics. For similar reasons, although a government that anticipates staying in power may be reluctant to limit its control over an issue, a government less certain of its longevity may seek to bind its successors through international legal commitments.[52] We discuss such domestic variations in the following section.

Sovereignty costs may also be negative for external reasons, as where participation in international arrangements enhances a state's international and domestic position.[53] Key aspects of sovereignty have been codified in a variety of legal instruments, including the 1933 Montevideo Convention on the Rights and Duties of States, Article 2 of the UN Charter, and the UN General Assembly Declaration on Principles of International Law Concerning Friendly Relations Among States. Regional legal arrangements like the Organization of American States (OAS) provide much-needed support for state sovereignty. Chapter IV of the OAS Charter promotes the independence and sovereign equality of member states regardless of power differentials and protects internal sovereignty through principles of nonintervention.

Although negative sovereignty costs are an important exception, positive sovereignty costs are the more standard (and more difficult) case for international legalization. Hard legalization—especially the classic legal model with centralized judicial institutions capable of amplifying the terms of agreements in the course of resolving disputes—imposes high sovereignty costs. Thus states face tradeoffs between the benefits and sovereignty costs of different forms of legalization.

States can limit sovereignty costs through arrangements that are nonbinding or imprecise or do not delegate extensive powers. Most often, states protect themselves by adopting less precise rules and weaker legal institutions, as in the Council of Europe's framework Convention for the Protection of National Minorities, {*O,p,d*}. They frequently provide that member states must adhere to a special treaty protocol before a court or quasi-judicial body can assert jurisdiction over them, as in the

52. Colombatto and Macey offer a related view in arguing that governmental agencies seek international legalization in order to protect their administrative positions at a cost to domestic groups. Colombatto and Macey 1996.

53. In Krasner's terminology, these constitute international legal and Westphalian sovereignty, respectively.

inter-American human rights system, or that all parties to a particular dispute must consent before the case can be litigated. Still weaker forms of delegation—such as the consultation arrangements characteristic of arms control agreements, {*O,P,-*}—limit sovereignty costs even more, coupling legal obligations with political mechanisms of control and defense. Thus soft legalization offers a variety of means—none of them perfect—by which states can limit sovereignty costs.

The international money-laundering regime provides a good example.[54] Beginning in the 1980s, the United States led an effort to control the international laundering of criminal profits. Many nations resisted efforts to criminalize money laundering or to require greater scrutiny of financial transactions, fearing interference with legitimate business dealings and with the division of domestic authority between prudential regulators and prosecutors. To address these concerns, in 1989 the OECD created the Financial Action Task Force of financial experts. The task force has issued policy recommendations, administers a system of peer review, and can even impose mild sanctions. Its guidelines are not as tightly constraining as hard legal commitments and are more difficult to "enforce." Yet they provide a common basis for domestic implementation (with enough flexibility to accommodate national differences), guide behavior, and create expectations that violations will bring political costs. Task force guidelines legitimize participation in national decisions by international actors and by concerned domestic bureaucracies and NGOs. They invoke a form of legal discourse and some principles of international law. In its decade of operation, the task force has fostered a significant degree of convergence around the principles contained in its guidelines.

As this example demonstrates, soft law provides a means to lessen sovereignty costs by expanding the range of available institutional arrangements along a more extensive and finely differentiated tradeoff curve. How states evaluate these tradeoffs—and thus determine their preferences for different forms of legalization—depends on their own characteristics and the circumstances of particular issue-areas.

Sovereignty costs and issue type. Viewing constraints on national autonomy and sovereignty as costs that vary across issues, we hypothesize that states will prefer different forms of legalization in different issue-areas. At one extreme, sovereignty costs are especially high in areas related to national security. Adversaries are extremely sensitive to unanticipated risks of agreement for the standard reasons advanced by realists, including relative gains. Even allies facing common external threats are reluctant to surrender autonomy over their security affairs. Therefore it is unsurprising that even in NATO, the most institutionalized alliance ever, delegation is moderate, {*O,p,d*}, or that security arrangements have lagged behind other institutional developments in the EU. Similarly, bilateral arms control agreements like SALT can be very precise in specifying missile numbers and types and are unquestionably legally binding but are only minimally institutionalized, {*O,P,-*}.

54. Simmons 2000a.

Political economy issues display a wide range of sovereignty costs and hence of legalization. At one extreme lie technical matters on which state interests are closely aligned, such as international transportation or food standards. Here sovereignty costs are low and the incidence of legalized agreements is correspondingly high. One even sees a significant level of delegation—including to organizations in which private actors play major roles, such as the International Organization for Standardization (ISO)—where sovereignty costs are low and technical complexity makes it hard to adapt agreements rapidly without some coordinating authority. Political economy issues like investment policy, money laundering, and security-related export controls, however, remain sensitive and have not been legalized to nearly the same extent. Similarly, tax policy, which lies at the core of all state functions but increasingly requires international coordination, is characterized by many bilateral treaties but displays little overall institutionalization.

Trade issues range between these extremes—sovereignty costs are significant but are frequently outweighed by the perceived benefits of legalized agreements. This is due partly to lesser conflicts of interest among states and partly to strong domestic support from beneficiaries of legalization. Consequently, even on a given issue, sovereignty costs can vary across states and over time. For example, the sovereignty costs of agricultural agreements are typically greater for less-developed states where the sector is larger and politically central; they have gradually decreased in OECD countries along with the relative importance of agriculture.

Finally, the most highly institutionalized arrangements, such as the EU, occur where there is a strong commitment to reducing sovereignty, or where a long process of legalized cooperation has led to institutionalization even against state resistance. The history of trade institutionalization is again instructive. In many respects, the WTO today is a stronger institution than the proposed International Trade Organization. Continued success in expanding trade under GATT changed domestic political balances and lowered the costs of further legalization. Moreover, states "learned" that harder legalization (such as a stronger dispute settlement mechanism) can produce greater benefits; they may also have been reassured regarding the dangers of enmeshment. Nevertheless, vigorous continuing disputes over the future of the WTO reflect states' continued wariness of sacrificing autonomy.

Uncertainty

Many international issues are new and complex. The underlying problems may not be well understood, so states cannot anticipate all possible consequences of a legalized arrangement. One way to deal with such problems is to delegate authority to a central party (for example, a court or international organization) to implement, interpret, and adapt the agreement as circumstances unfold. This approach avoids the costs of having no agreement, or of having to (re)negotiate continuously, but it typically entails unacceptably high sovereignty costs. Soft legalization provides a number of more attractive alternatives for dealing with uncertainty.

First, states can reduce the precision of their commitments: {*O,p,d*}. Of course, if they do not know the relevant contingencies, they cannot achieve the precision of hard law even if they wish to do so, except as to better-understood aspects of the problem. Thus an arms control agreement can precisely control known technologies and can even limit research into technologies whose results can reasonably be anticipated (such as testing antiballistic missile systems). But it cannot govern technologies whose military impact cannot be foreseen. And blanket limitations on all research with potential military implications would unacceptably impair the development of beneficial civilian technologies.

But uncertainty makes precision less desirable as well as less attainable. The classic distinction between risk and uncertainty is significant here.[55] When risk is the central concern—that is, when actors cannot predict the outcome of an agreement but know the probability distribution of possible outcomes, conditional on agreement terms—precise agreements offer a way to manage and optimize risk-sharing.[56] But when circumstances are fundamentally uncertain—that is, when even the range and/or distribution of possible outcomes is unknown—a more precise agreement may not be desirable. In particular, if actors are "ambiguity-averse,"[57] they will prefer to leave agreements imprecise rather than face the possibility of being caught in unfavorable commitments. Unfamiliar environmental conditions like global warming provide good illustrations: because the nature, the severity, even the very existence of these threats—as well as the costs of responding to them—are highly uncertain, the imprecise commitments found in environmental "framework" agreements may be the optimal response.

A second way to deal with uncertainty is through arrangements that are precise but not legally binding, such as Agenda 21, the Forest Principles, and other hortatory instruments adopted at the 1992 Rio Conference on Environment and Development, {-,*P*,-}. These allow states to see the impact of rules in practice and to gain their benefits, while retaining flexibility to avoid any unpleasant surprises the rules might hold. Sometimes precision is actually used to limit the binding character of obligations, as with carefully drawn exceptions or escape clauses. These also protect the parties in case the agreement turns out to have hidden costs or unforeseen contingencies, so that states are not locked into commitments they regret.

Third, although strong delegation can aggravate the uncertainty of agreements, moderate delegation—typically involving political and administrative bodies where

55. See Knight 1921; and Ellsberg 1963.

56. More precise agreements might, for example, contain renegotiation provisions so that states can modify the agreement as events unfold. See Koremenos 1999. This case for greater precision assumes risk-averse states; risk seekers would gamble on imprecise, binding agreements. Finally, optimization of the agreement will be second-best when it is constrained by asymmetries of information exemplified in standard principal-agent models.

57. Ambiguity aversion means that actors prefer known outcomes (including the status quo) to unknown ones. When actors know the possible outcomes but do not know which of two alternative probability distributions governs them, Ellsberg characterizes ambiguity aversion as assuming that an act leads to the minimum possible expected outcome. Ellsberg 1963. In this case, agents prefer incomplete to complete contracts even at zero contracting costs. See Mukerji 1998.

states retain significant control—provides another way to manage uncertainty. UN specialized agencies and other international organizations, {-,*p*,*d*}, play restricted administrative roles across a wide variety of issues, and a small number of (mainly financial) organizations have more significant autonomy.[58] These organizations have the capacity to provide information (and thus reduce uncertainty) and some capacity to modify and adapt rules or to initiate standards.[59] In general, however, even this level of delegation appears only in areas with low sovereignty costs, such as technical coordination. More fundamental elaboration of arrangements is typically accomplished through direct political processes. Thus arms control agreements are precise and binding but limit delegation to forums that promote political bargaining, not independent third-party decision making, {*O*,*P*,-}.

Viewed dynamically, these forms of soft legalization offer strategies for individual and collective learning.[60] Consider the case where states are legally bound but in an imprecise way, as under the original Vienna Ozone Convention, {*O*,*p*,-}. These obligations offer flexibility and protection for states to work out problems over time through negotiations shaped by normative guidelines, rather than constrained by precise rules. Hortatory rules, for example, {-,*p*,*d*}, similarly provide general standards against which behavior can be assessed and support learning processes that reduce uncertainty over time. Some emerging arrangements on the rights of women and children fit this model. Agreements that are precise but nonbinding, like the Helsinki Final Act, {-,*P*,*d*}, often include institutional devices such as conferences and review sessions where states can potentially deepen their commitments as they resolve uncertainties about the issue.

Indeed, moderate delegation—including international organizations that provide support for decentralized bargaining, expertise, and capacities for collecting information—may be more appropriate than adjudicative procedures (domestic or international) for adapting rules as circumstances are better understood. Examples include the numerous international agencies that recommend (often in conjunction with private actors) international standards on a range of issues, including technology, transportation, and health. Although not binding, their recommendations provide precise and compelling coordination points to which states and private actors usually adhere. In other cases, consultative committees or formal international organizations may be empowered to make rules more precise as learning occurs. Effective institutions of this sort require a certain autonomy that states may be reluctant to grant over truly important issues.

The learning processes described here are illustrated by the joint Food and Agriculture Organization–UN Environment Program (FAO-UNEP) regime requiring prior informed consent to international transfers of hazardous chemicals and pesticides.[61]

58. Abbott and Snidal 1998.
59. Gold 1983.
60. For a rational approach to learning, see Morrow 1994; and Koremenos 1999. For a more constructivist approach, see Finnemore 1996. Our view is that both learning as acquiring information and learning as changing preferences or identity are relevant (and compatible) aspects of legalization.
61. Mekouar 1998.

The FAO adopted a "code of conduct" on the distribution and use of pesticides in 1985; UNEP adopted "guidelines" on the exchange of information on internationally traded chemicals in 1987. Because of continued concern over exports of restricted substances to developing countries, the two organizations coordinated the amendment of their respective soft law instruments in 1989 to add a requirement for prior informed consent for international transfers of hazardous substances and a procedure for handling consents. This procedure was managed by the FAO and UNEP. Both organizations sponsored extensive consultations with expert groups from government and industry and provided technical assistance. The consent system, then, involved low obligation, relatively high precision, and moderate, largely administrative and technical, delegation, {-,*P*,*d*}. At the 1992 Rio conference, supporters attempted to "harden" the consent system through a binding treaty, but this effort failed. The FAO and UNEP continued to administer the existing system, however, and a few years later the member states of both organizations authorized formal treaty negotiations. The convention approved in September 1998 tracked the FAO-UNEP system almost exactly, {*O*,*P*,*d*}.

In this section we have argued that soft legalization provides a rational adaptation to uncertainty. It allows states to capture the "easy" gains they can recognize with incomplete knowledge, without allowing differences or uncertainties about the situation to impede completion of the bargain. Soft legalization further provides a framework within which states can adapt their arrangement as circumstances change and can pursue "harder" gains through further negotiation. Soft law avoids the sovereignty costs associated with centralized adjudication or other strong delegation and is less costly than repeated renegotiation in light of new information.

Our discussion also suggests hypotheses as to when different forms of legalization are most likely to be used. Consider the four possible high/low combinations of uncertainty and sovereignty costs, two of the major independent variables in our analysis. Where both variables are low, states will be inclined toward hard legal arrangements to efficiently manage their interactions, {*O*,*P*,*D*}. When sovereignty costs are high and uncertainty is low, states will be reluctant to delegate but will remain open to precise and/or binding arrangements, {*O*,*P*,-}. Conversely, if sovereignty costs are low and uncertainty is high, states will be willing to accept binding obligations and at least moderate delegation but will resist precise rules, {*O*,*p*,*d*}. Finally, when both uncertainty and sovereignty costs are high, legalization will focus on the statement of flexible or hortatory obligations that are neither precise nor highly institutionalized, {*o*,*p*,-} or {-,*p*,-}. In all these cases, legalization provides a framework within which states can work to resolve their uncertainty, making harder legalization more attractive.

Soft Law as a Tool of Compromise

Compromise at a point in time. Soft law can ease bargaining problems among states even as it opens up opportunities for achieving mutually preferred compromises. Negotiating a hard, highly elaborated agreement among heterogeneous states is a costly and protracted process. It is often more practical to negotiate a softer agreement that establishes general goals but with less precision and perhaps with limited delegation.

Soft legalization allows states to adapt their commitments to their particular situations rather than trying to accommodate divergent national circumstances within a single text. This provides for flexibility in implementation, helping states deal with the domestic political and economic consequences of an agreement and thus increasing the efficiency with which it is carried out. Accordingly, soft law should be attractive in proportion to the degree of divergence among the preferences and capacities of states, a condition that increases almost automatically as one moves from bilateral through regional to multilateral negotiations.

Flexibility is especially important when uncertainty or one sticky problem threatens to upset a larger "package deal." Rather than hold up the overall agreement, states can incorporate hortatory or imprecise provisions to deal with the difficult issues, allowing them to proceed with the rest of the bargain. The labor and environmental side agreements to NAFTA are suggestive on this point.

Softness also accommodates states with different degrees of readiness for legalization. Those whose institutions, laws, and personnel permit them to carry out hard commitments can enter agreements of that kind; those whose weaknesses in these areas prevent them from implementing hard legal commitments can accept softer forms of agreement, perhaps through exceptions, reservations, or phase-in periods. Many treaties make such special provisions for developing countries, transitional economies, and other categories of states. States may prefer such an arrangement to either a softer agreement among all or a harder agreement with limited membership. Over time, if the soft arrangements are successful and without adverse consequences, the initially reluctant states may accept harder legalization.

The 1996 Wassenaar Arrangement for national controls on exports of conventional weapons and dual-use technologies illustrates the use of soft legalization to facilitate compromise.[62] Wassenaar is a successor to the Coordinating Committee for Multilateral Export Controls, the informal institution through which the West coordinated controls on exports to the Soviet bloc. The United States pressed for a new institution to address post–Cold War security threats like terrorism, regional conflicts, and arms buildups by rogue nations like Iraq. But it faced several barriers to agreement: nearly twice as many nations would have to take part; the "common enemy" of the Cold War no longer existed; the participating nations had very different attitudes toward particular countries and conflicts; the economic costs of export controls would fall unevenly across countries; and some states were more technically prepared than others to operate a sophisticated export control system.

The nonbinding "arrangement" overcame these barriers by incorporating substantial flexibility in all three elements of legalization, {-,*p*,-}. The core of the arrangement is the exchange of information on past exports of agreed upon products to buyers in agreed target markets. This information alerts members to suspicious acquisition patterns and focuses peer pressure against commercial undercutting. The arrange-

62. Durcht 1997.

ment operates by consensus, and member countries implement its requirements in domestic law. The United States yielded on a number of issues, such as prior approval of export sales. In return, however, it obtained inclusion of both conventional arms and dual-use goods, specific lists of controlled items, designation of some specific target nations, and a degree of transparency that allows it to respond in serious cases.

These advantages of flexibility do not come without cost. Soft law compromises make it harder to determine whether a state is living up to its commitments and therefore create opportunities to shirk. They also weaken the ability of governments to commit themselves to policies by invoking firm international commitments and therefore make it easier for domestic groups, including other branches of government, to undo the agreement. Again, states face a tradeoff between the advantages of flexibility in achieving agreement and its disadvantages in ensuring performance.

States can design different elements of an agreement with different combinations of hardness to fine-tune this tradeoff on different issues. Alternative forms of delegation can be used to limit the tendencies to shirk. In some cases, international reporting requirements may be sufficient to determine whether states are meeting their commitments. Elsewhere, requirements for domestic implementation, including domestic legalization, may empower private actors like firms or NGOs to enforce the agreement.

Compromise over time. Because even soft legal agreements commit states to characteristic forms of discourse and procedure, soft law provides a way of achieving compromise over time. Consider a patient state (low discount rate) that is seeking a concession but is unwilling to offer enough immediately (for example, in linkage to other issues) to induce an impatient state to offer the concession. The patient state may nevertheless be willing to make a (smaller) current payoff in return for a soft legal agreement that has some prospect of enmeshing the impatient state in a process that will deliver the concession down the road. Insofar as states find it progressively costly to extricate themselves from legal processes, soft law helps remedy the commitment problem that looms large in international relations.

The Helsinki process is a dramatic illustration of this form of compromise. The Soviet Union (the impatient party) had an immediate need to stabilize military and political relations with Western Europe and the United States so that economic relations could develop more rapidly. The West (the more patient party) was not prepared to recognize Soviet dominance in Eastern and Central Europe on a legally binding basis, but it was willing to do so in less precise and explicitly nonlegally binding terms—if in return the Soviets would accept a soft human rights framework that turned out to have an unexpectedly significant bite over the longer term.

The Soviets surely underestimated the long-run effects of Basket III, but their tenacious bargaining (including efforts to obscure the provisions with "nonintervention" terminology) shows that they took these concessions very seriously.[63] Thus the

63. Maresca 1985. U.S. negotiators and the American public also underestimated the long-term significance of these arrangements.

Soviet leadership addressed its pressing problems with soft commitments that deferred the costs to its successors. The subsequent inability of the Soviet regime to contain the Basket III arrangements, either domestically or internationally, illustrates the subtle strength of soft law over time.

The longer-term consequences of soft law, including processes of learning, do not mean that legal agreements have an inevitable life cycle from softer toward harder legalization. Hard law is probably more likely to evolve from soft law than from (utopian) plans to create hard law full-blown. But this does not imply that all soft legalization is a way station to hard(er) legalization, or that hard legalization is the optimal form. The contracting difficulties noted earlier may never be resolved in some issue-areas; here, the attainable soft legalization will be superior to hard law that cannot be achieved. In these cases, continuing movement toward greater legalization is neither inevitable nor necessarily desirable.

The Helsinki experience and the "backlash" against ECJ activism described by Alter in this issue suggest a further limitation on the evolution of soft law: states may learn from experience that even soft forms of legalization can have powerful effects over time. As states internalize this lesson, they will be more alert to the possibilities of enmeshment and evolutionary growth in other negotiations. It would not be surprising, for example, if the Helsinki experience were still informing China's position on (even soft) human rights commitments. Impatient states may be forced to accept soft legalization in order to obtain current payoffs, but they may demand a higher price.

Compromise between the weak and the strong. Soft legalization facilitates compromise between weak and powerful states. The traditional legal view is that law operates as a shield for the weak, whereas the traditional international relations view is that law acts as an instrument of the powerful. These seemingly contradictory views can be reconciled by understanding how (soft) law helps both types of states achieve their differing goals.

Whatever their views on soft law, traditional legal scholars generally agree that legalization aids weak states. Weil, a severe critic of soft law, writes that "it is [hard] law with its rigor that comes between the weak and the mighty to protect and deliver."[64] Michael Reisman, more favorable toward soft law, agrees that law advantages the weak.[65] These views echo analyses of constitutionalism as a movement to create a government of laws, not of men (or states), in order to constrain the powerful.[66] At the international level, rules ranging from general principles of nonintervention to agreements like the Nuclear Non-Proliferation Treaty can be seen as bounding the struggle for power.

For just these reasons, small and dependent states often seek hard legalization. To the extent it is effective, hard law offers protection and reduces uncertainty by demar-

64. Weil 1983, 442.
65. Reisman 1988, 377.
66. Lindblom 1977.

cating the likely behavior of powerful states. Lutz and Sikkink argue in this issue that Latin American states have long seen international law as providing them with exactly this type of protection from the United States.[67] Since they have less direct control over their own fates, small states also incur lower sovereignty costs from hard legalization. Indeed hard law may entail negative sovereignty costs, enhancing international standing and offering at least formal equality. Widespread African support for postcolonial boundaries, which make little sense on ethnic, political, or economic grounds, provides a striking illustration of the value of legal arrangements to weak states.

In contrast, many international relations scholars (and some critical legal scholars) hold the more skeptical view that international law is wholly beholden to international power. Powerful states have greater control over international outcomes, are less in need of protection, and face higher sovereignty costs. They have less need for legalization and more reason to resist it, even though their adherence is crucial to its success.

For these reasons, realists see international law largely as epiphenomenal, merely reflecting the distribution of power. Institutionalists also treat power (for example, hegemony and/or a capacity for decentralized retaliation) as a primary source of order and rules in the international system. Unlike realists, however, they argue that institutions have real effects, resulting in a disjuncture between the distribution of power and benefits in the system.

These perspectives can to some extent be reconciled by understanding legalization, especially soft legalization, as furthering the goals of both classes of states. Most importantly, legally binding and relatively precise rules allow strong and weak states to regularize their asymmetric relations. Because the continual, overt exercise of power is costly, powerful states gain by embodying their advantage in settled rules. Because weaker states are at a constant disadvantage in bargaining, they benefit from the certainty and credibility of legalized commitments. The result is not unlike an insurance contract, where a weaker party gladly pays a premium to a stronger one in return for the latter bearing, or in this case reducing, certain risks. In addition, both sides benefit by reducing the transactions costs of continual bargaining.

Of course, stronger states have disproportionate influence over the substance of agreed upon rules. But even the most powerful states cannot simply dictate the outcome of every negotiation because of the high costs of coercion. Instead, strong states must typically make the substantive content of legalized arrangements (just) attractive enough to encourage broad participation at an acceptable cost. Reduced bargaining costs normally provide ample room for such concessions.

Powerful states are most concerned with delegation, the major source of unanticipated sovereignty costs. As a result, forms of legalization that involve limited delegation, for example, $\{O,p,-\}$ or $\{O,p,d\}$, provide the crucial basis for cooperation between the weak and the strong. Lower levels of delegation prevent unexpected intrusions

67. Lutz and Sikkink, this issue.

into the sovereign preserves of powerful countries while allowing them significant influence over decision making. Delegation to administrative bodies rather than judicial organs allows powerful states to retain control over ongoing issue management. The structure and decision-making rules of those bodies, including formal voting procedures, provide further means of balancing members' interests.[68]

Soft legalization provides other important grounds for cooperation as well. We described earlier how legalization helps states solve commitment problems. This point becomes relevant when powerful states want small states to take actions that would leave them vulnerable. Powerful states can induce cooperation in such cases by agreeing to operate within a framework of legally binding rules and procedures, credibly constraining themselves from opportunistic behavior; with low levels of delegation, though, they can maintain predominant influence over decision making. For example, the United States ran its Gulf War operation through the UN Security Council, {*O,p,d*}, even though doing so was burdensome, because this helped it to mobilize valuable support from weaker states, including bases in Saudi Arabia and financing from Japan. Involving the Security Council also allowed the supporting states to monitor and influence the scope of U.S. activities, notwithstanding the U.S. veto.[69]

Finally, even without an external commitment problem, governments of weak states may find it domestically costly to be perceived as following the dictates of a powerful state. Organizing international arrangements in a legalized way, and delegating modest supervisory authority to international agencies, can mitigate these costs without unduly interfering with the outcomes desired by the powerful state. We have elsewhere described the role of formal international organizations as vehicles for this type of "laundering."[70]

Two examples illustrate how softness facilitates bargains between stronger and weaker states. The Law of the Sea Convention expanded the territorial sovereignty of littoral states, gave less developed countries a role in the exploitation of ocean resources, and protected such rights as military passage for powerful states. Obligation and precision are high in most parts of the agreement, but delegation is limited—

68. Where power is very asymmetric, dominant states may prefer bilateral bargaining. Thus Doremus finds that the United States pursued legalized arrangements through the patent regime for biotechnology where bargaining power was relatively equal among states, used the more political mechanism of bilateral reciprocity for semiconductors where the United States was most powerful, and used its unilateral power to enforce the copyright regime for software where its power advantage was moderate. Doremus 1996. Doremus also argues that legalization will be more likely during stages of the product cycle in which no country has a strong market advantage.

69. The legalization of the Eastern bloc during the Cold War provides another intriguing example. The Soviet Union was coercively preponderant within its sphere of influence throughout the period, but it learned early on that rule by stick was not as efficient as more balanced relations. Beginning in the mid-1950s, it transformed the Council for Mutual Economic Assistance (CMEA) from an instrument of unilateral control into an arrangement that offered Eastern European states the carrot of subsidized and secure supplies of fuel and raw materials in exchange for acquiescence to Soviet control. See Marreese 1986. The level of legalization in the CMEA was low, {*o,p,-*}, and the Soviet Union could readily have reverted to a coercive strategy, as it did in Czechoslovakia in 1968. Still, the CMEA promoted continuing cooperation among the Eastern bloc states.

70. Abbott and Snidal 1998.

although the convention creates a special tribunal it has handled very few disputes—and the operation of the Enterprise remains to be worked out in practice.

The Nuclear Non-Proliferation Treaty reflected an explicit bargain: weaker states accepted the existing nuclear oligopoly; powerful states agreed to pursue weapons restraints and technology transfer. Obligation was high, though limited by escape clauses and the twenty-five-year renegotiation clause. Precision was high in limiting the transfer of military technology, but lower with regards to commercial technology transfers. Delegation to the IAEA has been largely controlled by the major powers (who monopolize the necessary expertise).

An understanding of soft legalization helps reconcile the seemingly contradictory views of the effect of law. Viewed as a process, legalization is a form of political bargaining where powerful states are advantaged. However, the efficiency gains of legalization for the powerful—cynically, providing an efficient means to extract benefits from the weak—depend on their offering the weak sufficiently satisfactory terms to induce their participation. Viewed as an outcome, legalization appears less political, since even powerful states must accept the constraints of legal principles and discourse to take advantage of legalized arrangements. Yet powerful states have the greatest influence on the substantive legal rules, and the institutions associated with (soft) international legalization are frequently constructed to ensure them a leading voice.

The Role of Private Actors

In many issue-areas, from trade and investment to human rights and the environment, individuals and private groups are the actors most responsible for new international agreements—and for resisting new agreements in favor of the status quo. A flurry of research has documented the growing role of nonstate actors, including traditional interest groups, epistemic communities based on causal knowledge and professional disciplines,[71] and NGOs committed to normative values.[72] International conferences and organizations have become more accessible to private groups, allowing them to act internationally as well as domestically. Transnational advocacy coalitions have emerged congruent with the scope of international issues and fora.[73] At the same time, individual governmental units have increasingly engaged in transnational rule making. These trends have inspired the systematic reformulation of international relations theory from a "liberal" perspective[74] and its application to issues of international law.[75]

The same developments lead us to consider the role of nonstate actors in international legalization. Our discussion thus far, while focused on states, has been consis-

71. Haas 1992.
72. See Slaughter 1997a; Risse-Kappen 1995a; and Raustiala 1997.
73. Keck and Sikkink 1998.
74. Moravcsik 1997.
75. Slaughter 1997b and 1995a,b.

tent with the liberal assumption that government actions reflect balances of domestic interests; much of that discussion also applies to agreements among governmental units. In this section, though, we explicitly examine why nonstate actors pursue different forms of legalization. We consider three theoretical perspectives: a pluralist account in which interactions among private groups determine national preferences and international outcomes; a public choice account in which government officials pursue private rewards; and a statist account in which (partially) autonomous national governments interact with private actors.

Pluralist Interactions

In Andrew Moravcsik's pure liberal account, individuals and groups operating within (and across) states are the fundamental actors in international politics.[76] They "organize exchange and collective action" to further their interests and values. National governments merely ratify these private bargains, acting internationally—as unitary entities or through individual units—to implement the resulting national preferences.

This view implies that variations in domestic politics will produce national preferences that diverge more widely than rationalist models normally assume. For example, wide domestic variations almost certainly characterized the negotiations on Agenda 21, {-,*P*,-}, and the framework Convention on National Minorities, {*O*,*p*,-}. Divergent preferences increase transaction costs, uncertainty, and bargaining problems, making soft legalization even more valuable.

Fundamentally, however, Moravcsik's account is pluralist, viewing international outcomes as resulting directly from interactions among private individuals and groups. These interactions can be understood as political bargains between demandeur groups seeking new redistributive or normative arrangements and resister groups working to block or weaken them.

As with states, private demandeurs will normally press for hard law, other things being equal, to raise the costs of violation for other parties and to facilitate enforcement against resister groups and governments, including their own. Thus business groups in Mexico favored a legalized NAFTA and high technology firms favored a legalized WTO Agreement on Trade-Related Aspects of Intellectual Property Rights (TRIPs), while worker representatives in the ILO resisted proposals to emphasize recommendations over binding conventions. Activist groups seek international legalization to gain leverage in domestic politics, a process Margaret E. Keck and Kathryn Sikkink call the "boomerang effect."[77] Here, too, the demand for hard law should be especially strong when the risks of opportunism are high and compliance is difficult to monitor.

Hard legalization also provides new strategies for nonstate actors. First, as Robert O. Keohane, Andrew Moravcsik, and Anne-Marie Slaughter discuss in this issue, a growing number of international dispute settlement institutions are open to private

76. Moravcsik 1997.
77. Keck and Sikkink 1998, 12–13.

claimants, substantially altering political dynamics.[78] Second, when international legal rules are incorporated into national law, private actors can invoke them in national courts and agencies. Multinational firms, advocacy coalitions, and other transnational groups are best suited to pursue this strategy, at least if they have sufficient resources. Finally, legal rules present new strategies even when private litigation is restricted. Private groups can, for example, urge governments to espouse their legal claims, as foreign investors have long done; the WTO Appellate Body has recently determined that dispute settlement panels can accept friend-of-the-court briefs from NGOs.

When resister groups are able to blunt or defer demands for international action, soft legalization offers a prime instrument of compromise, just as in interstate interactions. In these situations demandeurs will seek the particular forms of legalization they are best equipped to utilize, whereas resister groups, by the same logic, oppose those elements that would be most costly for them. If demandeurs are well situated to conduct national litigation, for example, they might demand binding and precise norms (to facilitate direct applicability or incorporation into domestic legal systems) but be willing to yield on international delegation, {*O*,*P*,-}.[79]

Activist demandeurs appear to place a high priority on precise normative statements, yielding on other elements when necessary, {-,*P*,-}. This compromise often appears to suit the needs of business and other resister groups as well, since it avoids concrete legal enforcement. At the 1992 Rio conference, for example, after business interests blocked legally binding agreements on various issues, environmental groups turned their efforts to obtaining nonbinding but highly elaborated documents like the Rio Declaration, Agenda 21, and the Forest Principles.

Instruments like these are valuable tools for activists. Although they cannot be invoked as law, they support a similar normative discourse. A major technique of activist campaigns is to expose gaps between international commitments and actual government conduct.[80] Legal obligations might be more compelling, but soft undertakings can fuel "accountability politics" if they contain clear normative commitments. Instruments like the Beijing Declaration and the Helsinki Final Act also give legitimacy to issues and initiate political processes that may lead to harder law over time.

Public Choice

In the public choice account, government officials have power to affect political outcomes and act to further their own private redistributive interests. In effect, offi-

78. Participation by private actors is also crucial to the political strategies of supranational judges seeking to enhance the strength and scope of their own institutions and the bodies of law they administer. Helfer and Slaughter 1997.

79. The supporters of TRIPs did not have to make this choice: they obtained both domestic implementation and delegation to the strengthened WTO dispute settlement system.

80. Keck and Sikkink 1998, 24–25.

cials become another class of private actor negotiating political bargains. As a result, this perspective is explicitly included in Moravcsik's formulation.

From a public choice perspective, officials pursue forms of legalization that maximize their opportunities for reelection, campaign contributions, bribes, or other personal benefits. Thus, officials might support a highly legalized agreement like TRIPs as a way of making credible commitments to influential private actors in return for electoral support.

Yet soft law will often be appealing in the public choice context, especially to government officials. For one thing, soft legalization allows officials to supply present benefits to private demandeurs while retaining the possibility of extracting future rents. Legally binding rules are relatively inflexible; strong delegation introduces additional actors who may behave unpredictably. Precise but nonbinding normative commitments, {-,*P*,*d*}, may be the optimal solution.

Soft legalization also enables rent-seeking officials to minimize political losses in the face of strong private distributional conflicts. In domestic politics, officials facing such conflicts resist taking sides, hoping not to alienate either group of constituents; they use such expedients as calling for further study, supporting vague statements of principle, or passing the buck to administrative agencies. Weak obligation, precision, and delegation are the international counterparts of these actions.

Significant forms of soft law are created in "transgovernmental" institutions, such as the Basle Committee of central bankers or the International Organization of Securities Commissions. Participants do not represent states as such, but rather individual agencies within the "state."[81] Public choice theory suggests that officials concerned with advancing their influence can use these organizations to reinforce their positions or justify new regulations at home.[82] Participating agencies may be forced to rely on soft law because they lack authority to enter binding treaties. Informal arrangements may also avoid executive or legislative approval and public scrutiny. Less cynically, soft law is well suited to the loose coordination these associations normally pursue.

Statism

In a statist account—contrary to the pure public choice view—governments retain (some) autonomy, which they exercise to influence and restrict accommodations among private actors. Government preferences are determined by factors such as national self-preservation and independence, relations with other states, the nature of individual issue-areas, and prevailing ideas and norms, as well as domestic politics.

A simple statist model might assume that governments act as "transmission belts" for private bargains on most issues but intervene when those bargains would impair national autonomy. In these situations, soft legalization allows governments to respond to private demands while limiting sovereignty costs. One would expect governments in these settings to avoid legally binding commitments and to limit delega-

81. See Zaring 1998; and Slaughter 2000.
82. Colombatto and Macey 1996.

tion to competing centers of power. Again, precise but nonbinding norms with weak delegation, {-,*P*,-}, would be a frequent outcome.

Here, too, the Rio and Beijing conferences are perfect illustrations. Although environmental and women's groups are increasingly influential, at least in many countries, it is extremely unlikely that the United States or virtually any other government would have accepted the innovative and expansive Rio and Beijing declarations as legally binding obligations. Yet in soft law form, with sovereignty costs as well as economic and social costs limited, they were adopted by almost every nation in the world.

A more complex statist model might credit states with a broader range of independent preferences. Soft legalization would then function as an instrument of accommodation between the state and private actors, as well as among private actors. When the United States was considering ratification of NAFTA, for example, labor and other constituencies demanded legally binding rules on labor rights. The Clinton administration wished to respond, but it was also aware—quite apart from countervailing business pressures—of Mexico's sensitivity to interference in its internal affairs. Consequently, the administration addressed labor rights in a side agreement that was legally binding, quite precise in terms of the parties' obligation to enforce national labor laws, and with moderate delegation, {*O,P,d*}.[83] In addressing the content of national labor laws, though, U.S. negotiators accepted markedly vague rules and weaker delegation, {-,*p,d*}.

States and private actors might also have divergent discount rates. At the time of the Helsinki conference, activist groups were impatient for progress on human rights, but Western governments were more patient. The United States also hoped to retain flexibility on human rights so that it could pursue trade and security issues. In the end, U.S. negotiators accepted a nonbinding declaration.

Given independent preferences, governments might use different forms of legalization offensively as well as defensively. They could, for example, use binding agreements to forestall demands of moderately powerful domestic groups. Alternatively, they could use nonbinding or imprecise agreements to introduce potentially unpopular new rules to domestic audiences. "Framework" agreements like the Vienna Ozone Convention and the WTO services agreement change political discourse and create incentives for private actors to adjust, but leave costly regulation for the future.

Conclusion

We have analyzed the spectrum of international legalization from soft informal agreements through intermediate blends of obligation, precision, and delegation to hard legal arrangements. Although even hard international law does not approach stereotypical conceptions of law based on advanced domestic legal systems, international

83. The parallel agreement on environmental protection included an innovative provision allowing private parties to initiate reviews of compliance.

legalization nevertheless represents a distinctive form of institutionalization. Ultimately, we can only understand the inclination of actors to cast their relations in legal form, and the variety of ways in which they do so, in terms of the value those institutional forms provide for them. Put plainly, international legalization is a diverse phenomenon because it helps a diverse universe of states and other actors resolve diverse problems.

Legalization reflects a series of tradeoffs. States are typically torn between the benefits of hard legalization—for example, mitigating commitment and incomplete contracting problems—and the sovereignty costs it entails. For their part, private actors generally seek hard legal arrangements that reflect their particular interests and values, but these demands often conflict with those of other private actors or of governments. In settings like these, soft legalization helps balance competing considerations, offering techniques for compromise among states, among private actors, and between states and private actors. In addition, soft law helps actors handle the exigencies of uncertainty and accommodate power differentials.

Our analysis necessarily combines the rational incentives associated with "contracts" and the normative considerations associated with "covenants." Legalization is a strategy through which actors pursue their interests and values; it also supplies a body of norms and procedures that shape actors' behavior, interests, and identities. Thus, though we premise our analysis on the notion of actors rationally pursuing goals, we argue that they do so knowing that legalization embeds them in a partially autonomous process and discourse that constrains their behavior and may modify important understandings. The wariness with which states regard the prospect of enmeshment in such normative processes is testimony to the power of legalization—soft and hard.

More generally, the many forms of legalization remind us that international politics and international law are not alternative realms, but are deeply intertwined. Although one goal of law—as of institutions in general—is to settle key issues so that actors can regularize their interactions, the creation and development of legal arrangements is highly political. This is especially true in the international sphere, where most legal regimes are relatively new and undeveloped. Politics permeates international law and limits its autonomy.

Conversely, international politics is rooted in legal considerations. From the principles of sovereignty that define modern nation-states, through the rules of diplomacy, war, and commerce that structure their interactions, to the specific regimes they create, legalized agreements and normative processes guide and constrain the behavior of states. Without this foundation in law, neither states nor analysts could make sense of international interactions.

The deep connection of law and politics is most apparent in the area of delegation. States almost never delegate authority to independent courts of general and mandatory jurisdiction like those of advanced domestic legal systems—although more constrained judicial delegation appears to be increasing and is supplemented in many cases by the participation of national courts. More typically, even in connection with binding legal commitments, they delegate authority only to international organizations or other administrative bodies subject to direct and indirect controls. This choice of venue limits the extent to which interactions can be governed by purely legal procedures and discourse.

In forecasting the future of international legalization, we subscribe to the theories of neither Pollyanna nor Chicken Little. To be sure, the twentieth century and especially the period following World War II witnessed a remarkable expansion of international legalization. But in large part that growth merely allowed international institutions to catch up with the dramatic changes in globalization (née interdependence) that had overtaken the inherited framework. It does not follow that international legalization will continue at the same rate, or that the apparent tendency toward (somewhat) harder legalization will continue. Indeed, a central part of our argument is that states and nonstate actors can achieve many of their goals through soft legalization that is more easily attained or even preferable.

In this light, we argue vigorously against those who discount international legalization because it is so often soft. Soft law is valuable on its own, not just as a steppingstone to hard law. Soft law provides a basis for efficient international "contracts," and it helps create normative "covenants" and discourses that can reshape international politics. International legalization in all its forms must be considered one of the most significant institutional features of international relations.

[13]

Alternatives to "Legalization": Richer Views of Law and Politics

Martha Finnemore and Stephen J. Toope

The authors of "Legalization and World Politics" (special issue of *IO*, summer 2000) have done an excellent job connecting one branch of thinking about international law (rooted in the legal theory of H. L. A. Hart) to one branch of thinking about international politics (neoliberal institutionalism).[1] However, the connections between the two disciplines are broader and deeper than the volume indicates. International legal scholars have long understood that international law is more than the formal, treaty-based law on which the volume's authors focus their work. Law is a broad social phenomenon deeply embedded in the practices, beliefs, and traditions of societies, and shaped by interaction among societies.[2] Customary international law displays this richer understanding of law's operation as does the increasingly large body of what has been termed "interstitial law," that is, the implicit rules operating in and around explicit normative frameworks.[3] Similarly, legal pluralist analysis of domestic and international legal systems focuses on the interaction of overlapping state and nonstate normative systems.[4]

We show how a fuller appreciation of what international law is and how it influences behavior allows room for a wealth of intellectual connections between international legal scholarship and research in international relations—connections that are not evident from the framing of the "legalization" phenomenon in the *IO* volume we discuss here. We argue that a narrow conception of law and legalization hinders rather than helps these authors' empirical research. Narrow and stylized frameworks like this one may be useful if they provide conceptual clarity and facilitate operationalization of concepts. However, the empirical applications of

We thank Jutta Brunneé, H. P. Glenn, Rod Macdonald, René Provost, Bob Wolfe, participants in the University of Chicago Law School International Law Workshop, two anonymous reviewers, and the editors of *IO* for helpful comments on an earlier draft.

1. *International Organization* 54, 3, Summer 2000.
2. Glenn 2000.
3. Lowe 2000.
4. See Walzer 1983; and Macdonald 1998.

legalization in the volume suggest the opposite: the articles reveal that the concept of legalization as defined in the volume is peripheral, in need of revision, or generates hypotheses that are wrong. A fuller consideration of law and its role in politics might produce concepts that are more robust intellectually and more helpful for empirical research.

A Richer View of International Law

The framers of the volume are careful in defining their terms. *Legalization* refers to a specific set of characteristics that institutions may (or may not) possess: obligation, precision, and delegation.[5] Each of these characterizations may be present in varying degrees along a continuum, and each can vary independently of the others. This attention to definitions is helpful and lends coherence to the volume, but appropriating the general term *legalization* for only a few features of the law is misleading. It suggests that law *is* and can only be this limited collection of formalized and institutionalized features. The phenomenon the authors investigate might more accurately be termed *legal bureaucratization,* since it seems to involve the structural manifestations of law in public bureaucracies. We fully agree that the connections between law and public bureaucracy are important in world politics, but this connection does not exhaust law's role.[6] Under a broader view of law, the legalization of politics encompasses more than just the largely technical and formal criteria of obligation, precision, and delegation. It encompasses features and effects of legitimacy, including the need for congruence between law and underlying social practice.[7] It attends to the purposive construction of law within inherited traditions, the way participating in law's construction contributes to legitimacy and obligation, and to the continuum of legality from informal to more formal norms.[8] Indeed, without this broader view of law that causes us to pay attention to legal procedures, methodologies, institutions, and processes generating legitimacy, the authors' three components of legalization lack theoretical coherence and raise more questions than they answer, as we show.

Obviously, any analytic endeavor of this kind requires focus, and the authors are explicit about the issues they "bracket," but nowhere in the volume is there any cautionary discussion to situate the authors' very particular understanding of law's role in a larger context of the possible roles law might play.[9] Consequently, there is also no assessment of how important this specific legalization phenomenon might be among law's many influences in politics or of how this formalized legalization

5. Abbott et al. 2000, 401.
6. Barnett and Finnemore 1999.
7. Postema 1994.
8. Brunnée and Toope 2000.
9. Lutz and Sikkink display a broader sensitivity to these issues than the other articles, but they do not provide an explicit discussion of their broader view or its theoretical implications. Lutz and Sikkink 2000.

might interact with other work law does in the world. In such an extensive effort, these omissions seem surprising. Given that most *IO* readers are not lawyers, we believe that situating and more precisely specifying the authors' notion of legalization will be helpful.

The view of law presented in the volume, though important, is limited. In it, law is constructed primarily through cases and courts, or through formal treaty negotiation. The processes of law are viewed overwhelmingly as processes of dispute resolution, mostly within formal institutionalized contexts. The "international legal actions" chosen in the volume's introduction to epitomize the phenomenon of legalization are mainly examples of tribunal decisions. The secondary evidence of legalization is drawn exclusively from explicit obligations imposed by treaties.[10] Law in this view is constraint only; it has no creative or generative powers in social life. Yet law working in the world constitutes relationships as much as it delimits acceptable behavior. The very idea of state sovereignty, both a legal and a political construction, creates the context that allows for the formal articulation of treaty rules.[11] Similarly, property rights, over which political actors battle in many of the volume's articles, are themselves dynamic constructions generated by law. Oddly, given this group of authors, even the role of formal law in creating and shaping the life of institutions like the IMF, GATT, and WTO, explicitly addressed in the volume, is neglected. Theirs is an overwhelmingly liberal and positivist view of law. It is also limited to the bureaucratic formalism described by Weber and so is very "Western" in a narrow sense.[12] We are not implying that Western law, positivism, and liberalism are uninteresting theoretical frameworks, but an analysis of the role of law in world politics that is entirely constrained by these three optics, attending primarily to formal institutions, is at best partial.[13]

Despite the efforts of the framers of the volume to define terms and to expressly bracket issues, at the end of the day it is difficult to decide exactly what the authors have set out to demonstrate and what analytic work their concept of legalization is supposed to accomplish. Is legalization a dependent variable or an independent one? The framing chapters are not clear on this basic point, and the articles offer diverse, even contradictory, treatments. This diversity also begs obvious questions. If legalization is a phenomenon to be explained, what other factors might explain it, and how important are they? If legalization explains aspects of state behavior, what other independent variables should be considered in assessing legalization's role,

10. Goldstein et al. 2000, 385–86.
11. Biersteker and Weber 1996.
12. Glenn 2000.
13. For a helpful categorization of various legal theories as they relate to the question of compliance, see Kingsbury 1998. Among the competing theories of international law (and particularly of international obligation) that are not included within the volume's concept of legalization are the "world constitutive process" model of the Yale School (Lasswell and McDougal 1971; Reisman 1992), natural law approaches (Verdross and Koeck 1983), the "transnational legal process" model of Harold Koh (Koh 1997), the "interactional" framework of Brunnée and Toope (Brunnée and Toope 2000), and the rigorously rationalistic law and economics approach of Goldsmith and Posner (Goldsmith and Posner 1999).

and how might these interact with legalization?[14] Equally important for the authors, do the three defining features of legalization all have the same causes, or cause the same effects, and how would we know if they did (or did not)? In the last section of this article, we examine three applications of their concept of legalization and show that confusion about these basic issues limits the utility of their conceptualization of legalization.

Three Lacunae

Political scientists have understood for decades that formal institutions do not capture many of the most important features of politics. Indeed, the authors of this volume have a fairly broad, and by now standard, political science definition of institutions, one that focuses attention beyond their formal attributes. Institutions are "rules, norms, and decision-making procedures" that shape expectations, interests, and behavior.[15] Marrying such a broad understanding of institutions to a narrow and formal understanding of law seems both unfortunate and unnecessary. A fuller understanding of law would complement our more nuanced understanding of institutions and produce a richer joint research agenda. To illustrate, we discuss three interrelated features of international law neglected in the volume; these features are central to understanding its effects on world politics and, further, are crucial to a theoretically defensible understanding of the very specific legalization phenomenon the volume's authors employ.

Custom. The most obvious casualty of the volume's narrow framing of legalization is customary international law, with which it almost completely fails to engage. Any assessment of law's persuasive influence that neglects to treat seriously the customary law elements of such topics as state responsibility, legal personality, territory, human rights, and the use of force is bound to produce a skewed perspective. For example, customary law on the use of force stands alongside, complements, and even modifies treaty-based norms.[16] Although the UN Charter and humanitarian law treaties establish an explicit framework of norms circumscribing the use of force in international relations, no one analyzing this issue-area can afford to ignore the customary law of self-defense or the impact of the concept of *jus cogens* (peremptory norms) on the attitudes of states toward the legitimate use of force.[17] It is not surprising that the volume contains but the briefest discussion of security issues, for they simply cannot fit within a narrow judicial and treaty-based

14. See Abbott and Snidal 2000; see also Abbott et al. 2000.
15. Goldstein et al. 2000, 387.
16. *Nicaragua v. United States (Merits)* [1986] ICJ Rep. 14.
17. See Bowett 1958; and Ragazzi 1997.

perspective on law's influence in world affairs.[18] Similarly, in the area of human rights, the broadening of customary law obligations has altered the content of interstate diplomatic rhetoric and affected bilateral political relationships. Canada and Norway now engage in a trilateral "human rights dialogue" with China, for example, an engagement that could not take place in the absence of customary norms, for China has yet to ratify key human rights treaties.[19] Again, it is not surprising that the one article on human rights concludes that the legalization framework does not explain behavior particularly well.

Defining characteristics of law. A second, related, issue concerns the selection of obligation, precision, and delegation as the defining characteristics of legalization. While the volume's framers offer careful discussion of these terms, their meanings, and characteristics, they say little about why, among the universe of legal features, these three are more important than others. These three features certainly do not define law or distinguish it from other types of normativity, nor are they the source of law's power (or, if they are, that case is not made in the volume).

Precision and delegation are particularly problematic. In a number of well-established areas of international law with strong records of influence and compliance, norms are relatively imprecise. Examples include the delimitation of maritime boundaries (often accomplished on the basis of "equity"), the bases of state criminal jurisdiction (where overlapping rules are the norm), and state responsibility (including a very broad duty not to knowingly allow one's territory to be used in a manner harmful to another state). Similarly, there are wide swaths of functioning international law that do not depend in any way on extensive "delegation" of decision-making authority. Outside of the European context, the entire law of human rights operates and affects world politics without any mechanisms of compulsory adjudication. The treaty-monitoring bodies only gain jurisdiction to deal with individual cases with the consent of states, a consent only sporadically granted. For example, Human Rights Committee decisions are not enforceable. It is also rare for domestic courts to implement international human rights commitments directly within national law. A comparable pattern of influence in the absence of delegation is found in international environmental law. Many international environmental commitments continue to function on the basis of information-sharing and voluntary compliance. Where modern treaties create mechanisms to promote implementation, they are often premised on the need for positive reinforcement of obligations rather than on adjudication and sanctions for noncompliance. There is no extensive delegation of decision-making authority. Why delegation and precision should be defining fea-

18. The exception is a brief foray into ASEAN's security relationships in Kahler 2000a. The *Nicaragua* Case (1986) is discussed in Keohane, Moravcsik, and Slaughter 2000, though for purposes unrelated to an analysis of the customary law on the use of force.

19. For example, although China recently ratified the International Covenant on Economic, Social, and Cultural Rights, it has yet to ratify the International Covenant on Civil and Political Rights.

tures of legalization and what they add to the analytic power of this concept is simply not clear.

Further, the relationship among these three characteristics is unexplored, a significant lacuna since these features could contribute to contradictory developments in many circumstances. Increased precision could lead to less obligation, when prospective members of legal regimes are driven away by fears of detailed rules that are inflexible (a point actually supported by the description of the WTO offered by Judith Goldstein and Lisa Martin).[20] Delegation of decision making can also lead to less precision in rules rather than to greater clarity, as presumed by the proponents of legalization. If one considers the decisions of the International Court of Justice in boundary delimitation cases, for example, the results are clearly legal, influential, and effective in promoting compliance, but they are highly imprecise.[21] What we gain by combining, rather than disaggregating, concepts with such complex and tense interrelationships is not well explained.

Most problematic, however, is the volume's conceptualization of obligation, arguably the central preoccupation both of lawyers and of political scientists interested in how norms affect state behavior. Obligation is central to the volume's framework of legalization, yet the authors articulate no theory of obligation and seem remarkably uncurious about how a sense of obligation might be generated. In the volume's lead article, legal obligation is defined in an entirely circular fashion, with reference to its products: "Legal obligations bring into play the established norms, procedures, and forms of discourse of the international legal system."[22] We know obligation by what it achieves, but this approach does not explain how obligation creates these products. To the extent that the bases of obligation are treated at all in the framing article, the conceptualization is very thin, formal, and contractual. Obligation is created when parties enter into treaties or other express agreements. The mechanism for generating obligation is thus choice—presumably choice by utility-maximizing actors.[23] Yet both legal scholars and international

20. Goldstein and Martin 2000.

21. In the *North Sea Continental Shelf Cases* [1969] ICJ Rep. 3, the court articulated a "rule" of law that the continental shelf should be divided on the basis of "equitable delimitation taking into consideration all of the circumstances." This rule has shaped all subsequent continental shelf negotiations as well as judicial and arbitral decisions.

22. Abbott et al. 2000, 409.

23. In Abbott and Snidal's discussion of "soft law," that quintessentially fluid concept is treated as a preexisting form of institution to be chosen by states for strategic reasons. Abbott and Snidal 2000. This approach misses much of what we know from many legal analyses about how soft law works; see Chinkin 1989; Hillgenberg 1999; and Finnemore 2000. First, soft law is not simply "out there" waiting to be chosen. Part of what is "soft" about this form of law is precisely that it is in flux, in the process of becoming. How states treat it is not exogenous to soft law; it determines and shapes soft law; it is constitutive of it. Equally important, the notion that states "choose" soft law formulations is misleading. Soft law, like customary law, is not always "chosen" in a meaningful strategic sense. For example, the evolution of the "precautionary principle" or "intergenerational equity" in international environmental law is a study in normative entrepreneurship and subtle instantiation as much as in strategic choice. See Brunnée 1993; and Brunnée and Toope 1997.

relations (IR) scholars understand very well that contractual obligations alone are often insufficient to determine behavior.

More careful theorizing of these defining characteristics might have led the framers to explore some alternative features of law and develop more robust concepts. For example, one concept that is notably absent from the various analyses of obligation is legitimacy, yet legal scholars have long focused on legitimacy as an essential source of obligation and "compliance pull" in law.[24] Legitimacy in law has been argued to have a number of interrelated sources. Legitimacy is generated in part through attention to internal legal values that we seem to take for granted in the liberal democratic West but that students of repression will recognize as essential. Law is legitimate only to the extent that it produces rules that are generally applicable, exhibit clarity or determinacy, are coherent with other rules, are publicized (so that people know what they are), seek to avoid retroactivity, are relatively constant over time, are possible to perform, and are congruent with official action.[25] Law that adheres to these values is more likely to generate a sense of obligation, and corresponding behavior change, than law that ignores these values. Legal legitimacy also depends on agents in the system understanding why rules are necessary.[26] Participating in constructing law enhances agents' understanding of its necessity. Finally, adherence to specific legal rationality that all participants understand and accept helps to legitimate the collective construction of the law. Legal claims are legitimate and persuasive only if they are rooted in reasoned argument that creates analogies to past practice, demonstrate congruence with the overall systemic logic of existing law, and attend to contemporary social aspirations and the larger moral fabric of society.[27] Law that exhibits this kind of rationality—that is viewed as necessary, involves in its construction those it binds, and adheres to internal legal values—is more likely to be viewed as legitimate than law that does not have these features.

Legitimate law generates obligation, not just in a formal sense but also in a felt sense. Legitimacy thus connects obligation to behavior in important ways.[28] This is a major strain of argument in international law scholarship, one that IR scholars do read, yet the authors of the *IO* volume do not address legitimacy as part of the legalization phenomenon. They never investigate legitimacy's relationship to obligation, precision, and delegation, nor do they explore alternative hypotheses

24. See Lauterpacht 1947; Lasswell and McDougal 1971 (where legitimacy is not discussed directly but is implicit in the posited relationship between "authority" and "control"); Franck 1990; and Byers 1999.

25. See Fuller 1969; Franck 1990; and Postema 1994. These legitimating characteristics are much broader than the volume authors' concept of "precision," as indicated by Fuller's term for these values—"internal morality of law." Fuller 1969.

26. See Fuller 1969; and Postema 1994.

27. See Fuller 1969; Franck 1990; and Brunnée and Toope 2000.

28. Franck 1990.

concerning legitimacy.[29] We suspect that legitimacy is a prior variable, generating a felt sense of obligation and empowering those who delegate to do so. Variations in legitimacy almost certainly relate to variations in legalization. The spread of formal legal institutions investigated in the volume is likely to depend on the legitimacy of these formal legal processes generally and on the legitimacy of the particular configurations of these processes (the kind of delegation, the nature and content of the obligation) that these institutions embody.

Law as process. A third fundamental issue to consider is the nature of legalization itself. The authors of this volume treat law as an artifact—something created by state choice—and equate legalization with three features of the *form* of this artifact (obligation, delegation, precision). Politics thus becomes "legalized," in their view, as it displays these three features. When one thinks about what legitimates law, however, another possibility emerges. Law, and by implication legalization, may be much more about process than about form or product. Much of what legitimates law and distinguishes it from other forms of normativity are the processes by which it is created and applied—adherence to legal process values, the ability of actors to participate and feel their influence, and the use of legal forms of reasoning. A view of legalization that focused on legal relationships and processes rather than forms would be more dynamic and better suited to explaining change—which many of us, the volume's authors included, are interested in. Unlike Thomas M. Franck, we would not argue that process is the only thing that legitimates law.[30] Values suffuse legal argument and they underlie legal processes generally, so it is not sufficient to seek the power of law solely in the details of its processes of elaboration and application.[31] But it is equally suspect to craft a framework for the empirical study of legalization that ignores process in favor of an essentially structural, and product-focused, analysis.

As framed in the volume, the world's "move to law" is a move to a very particular kind of law, and not one that resonates with international lawyers who are unaccustomed to the narrow view of obligation espoused by the authors and who would doubt that precision or delegation are the hallmarks of growing normativity in international relations. A broader understanding of law would open up research connections among scholars who would not find the authors' formulation of legalization particularly engaging. Most obviously, a more culturally and sociologically attuned formulation of the role of law speaks to constructivist concerns and builds bridges between that group of IR scholars and like-minded thinkers in law. Situating law in its broader social context allows room for cultural explanations of

29. Abbott and Snidal recognize that legitimacy exists, but they do not theorize or investigate its independent causal effects on strategic choice. Abbott and Snidal 2000, 428–29. Lutz and Sikkink do explore legitimacy issues and find, as we suggest, that these are causally prior to legalization. Lutz and Sikkink 2000, 654–59.

30. Franck 1990.

31. See Hurrell 2000; and Toope 2000.

behavior and identity formation in ways that these scholars will find helpful. It also promises to reveal connections between IR theory and approaches to comparative law that address issues of identity and normative change within legal traditions.[32] Focusing on law as a set of relationships, processes, and institutions embedded in social context has the further advantage of reformulating the lively legal debate over how "soft" law "hardens" and connecting it with the rich and growing body of work on transnational norm dynamics that has occupied constructivists in recent years. Exploring the causes, nature, and effects of legal legitimacy, a task that cuts across almost all these concerns, is already receiving extensive attention in both of these disciplines.

What Difference Does Law Make?

A fuller understanding of law is not simply a pleasing accessory to the framework proposed in this volume, however. It is a necessity. The purpose of the legalization concept is presumably to facilitate empirical research. If a narrowly drawn and simplified concept generates new insights for researchers and helps them explain empirical puzzles, it may still be valuable. To assess whether legalization does this, we examine the three articles that apply the concept of legalization to different issue-areas. Our examination suggests that the concept provides little help to these researchers, not only because it contains such a narrow notion of law but also because it is inadequately theorized.

Beth Simmons, applying the concept of legalization to monetary affairs, asks why states voluntarily declare themselves bound by Article VIII rules concerning current account restrictions and unified exchange rates. She frames this as a credible commitments problem. The policy dilemma for states is to make their commitments to Article VIII rules credible to markets, thus producing desired investment flows. Law's role is to provide a "hook" or signal that makes commitments credible.[33]

The legalization concept does little work here. Simmons certainly does not need it to carry out her analysis. The only aspect of the concept Simmons treats is obligation, recasting it as "credible commitment"; precision and delegation are apparently not relevant. Conceptual equipment for credible commitment and signaling analyses have been around for a long time. Simmons could have completed essentially the same analysis without "legalization"; it is not clear how the concept helps her.

Adopting a richer view of law, as we suggest, might open this analysis to some important questions and make law more than peripheral in our understanding of these events. A focus on law's role, for example, might prompt us to ask whether or why legal commitments are credible signals to markets for all states. After all,

32. See Postema 1991; Kennedy 1997; and Glenn 2000.
33. Simmons 2000, 601.

some of the developing countries most successful at attracting investment, such as China and Indonesia, have extremely weak conceptions and applications of the rule of law. If accepting legal obligations is such an important signal to investors, as assumed here, why do investors pour so much money into countries where law is so weak?[34] If Simmons believes that domestic and international rule of law are unconnected, so that investors assume that even countries without effective rule of law domestically will be bound unproblematically in the international realm, this would certainly require some elaboration, since it cuts against prominent past work by other authors in the volume.[35]

More generally, equating law with obligation and obligation with credible commitments ignores much of what law does in monetary affairs that might be relevant to Simmons' analysis. The notion that law is merely promise-keeping ignores both the authoritative and the transformative character of law. States are not making the Article VIII decisions in a legal vacuum. The Articles of Agreement (of which Article VIII is a part) created an entire structure of law on monetary affairs, including a Weberian rational-legal bureaucracy (the International Monetary Fund) to make policy on monetary matters. Law thus created a new source of authority in monetary matters, the IMF, which generated new rules for states but also new knowledge about technical matters in economic policy that changed expectations for behavior. Throughout the period examined by Simmons, states are making their decisions about Article VIII commitments in a dynamic environment of law, rules, and economic knowledge about monetary policy, and much of this changing environment is actively promoted by the IMF. One odd feature of Simmons' analysis is that the IMF is all but absent, implying that its actions are unconnected to Article VIII decisions, even in states that have been under its tutelage. The fact that the IMF, through its technical assistance programs, is deeply involved in shaping the laws and central institutions (including central banks) of monetary politics in member states underscores this problem. Treating law's role as simply a "hook" or signal to markets ignores the fact that law, and the rational-legal bureaucracies it creates, has transformed monetary politics both internationally and domestically, enabling states to entertain this kind of commitment as a policy choice and generating the conceptual and policy equipment to make credible commitments to Article VIII desirable and possible, particularly in the developing world.

Goldstein and Martin's analysis of trade politics addresses the volume's legalization concept much more directly. They examine the effects of increasing obligation, precision, and delegation in formal trade agreements on international cooperation and compliance. They find that "more is not necessarily better" because more precision and "bindingness" in rules can mobilize protectionist groups who can now better calculate the costs of freer trade.

34. Wang's analysis of exactly this question in the case of China points squarely to the need for a broader view of how law works. Wang 2000.
35. For example, Slaughter 1995.

What work does the legalization concept do here? As in Simmons' article, Goldstein and Martin create a link between legalization and another well-known concept in political analysis, in this case, information. "Increased transparency" (better information) is added to the definition of legalization without comment in this article.[36] Information then becomes the centerpiece of the analysis. "Legalization entails a process of increasing rule precision, [ergo] a more legalized trade regime will provide more and better information about the distributional implications of commercial agreements."[37] Once we understand what legalization does to information, information does most of the heavy analytic lifting in this article, not law.

One obvious question to ask is whether increased legalization really translates into increased information and decreased uncertainty in the way the authors assume, or whether, indeed, change among the three elements of legalization correlates positively at all. This is an instance where some disaggregation of the concept might be helpful. Goldstein and Martin make a strong case that an inverse relationship exists between precision and any sense of felt obligation, since more precision tends to promote greater use of escape clauses and mobilizes interest groups for noncompliance. The inverse relationship they identify in trade can be found in other areas as well. International Court of Justice decisions on questions as diverse as formal requirements for the creation of custom or unilateral treaty commitments, the existence of regional customary law, the concept of nationality, and the legality of nuclear weapons have all been crafted to promote greater bindingness by offering less precision.

Unfortunately, however, Goldstein and Martin's findings seem not to have prompted much rethinking of the content of legalization by the volume's framers or by Miles Kahler in the conclusion.[38] Such an overall examination might have revealed additional problematic relationships among their three elements of legalization, even in the Goldstein and Martin article. For example, it is not clear that increased precision in law always increases certainty about distributional effects, as Goldstein and Martin assume. If increased precision involves delegation, uncertainty may remain high or even increase because delegation, by its nature, creates uncertainty in principal-agent relationships. Thus, members of the WTO may have more precise rules about resolving disputes than they did under the GATT, but the workings of the dispute settlement body may be sufficiently opaque or unpredictable that distributional consequences remain uncertain in many areas. Conversely, increased delegation does not guarantee more precise rules for the same principal-agent reasons, so there is no reason to think those co-vary. The overall effect of Goldstein and Martin's interesting finding about the effects of information is thus to suggest a wide array of possible relationships among legalization's core features. This, in turn, suggests that the legalization concept is itself less analytically useful

36. Goldstein and Martin 2000, 604.
37. Ibid., 604.
38. Kahler 2000b.

than its component parts, which, as we noted earlier, are not necessarily or uniquely legal.

More attention to law might lead these authors to ask some substantive questions that would bear on their findings. These authors are commendably enthusiastic about including domestic politics in their analysis yet remarkably inattentive to variations in those politics created by widely varying structures of domestic law. Law governing ratification of trade agreements, central to this analysis, differs hugely across even the democratic, industrialized countries on which these authors focus. These differences profoundly change the "logic of [domestic interest group] mobilization" in different countries, around which the analysis revolves. For example, the authors assert that it is the need for treaty ratification, with attendant public processes of debate, that gives rise to the possibility of effective protectionist backlash. Yet in Canada, the United States' largest trading partner, the treaty-making power is held by the functional equivalent of the executive branch (in practice the prime minister and cabinet), and there is no constitutional requirement for ratification by Parliament. The entire NAFTA treaty could have been concluded by the executive branch, benefiting from the legitimacy granted by an overwhelming parliamentary majority, without any opportunity for formal political debate. The limited public debate that did take place revolved around the need to involve the Canadian provinces in negotiations, for it is provincial legislatures that must transform many trade treaty obligations into domestic law. However, that debate related primarily to jurisdictional conflicts between federal and provincial authorities and did not provide significant opportunities for the protectionist concerns of particular industries or trade unions to mobilize public opposition.

These differences in legal structure are more than simply differences in the constraints or political opportunity structure surrounding strategic actors. Domestic structures of law are, themselves, mobilizing factors for a wide variety of groups involved in trade politics. Domestic law is what constitutes, empowers, and mobilizes a host of interest groups, from trade unions, to professional organizations, to business groups, to environmentalists and human rights activists. Unions have different forms and powers in different national legal contexts, as do business groups and nongovernmental organizations. Law's role in mobilizing different groups is much more profound than mere provision of information.

Attention to this broader set of legal influences might also lead the authors away from their curiously dichotomous picture of trade politics as an interaction between free-trade and protectionist interest groups. Groups may oppose trade agreements for many reasons; they may oppose some types of free trade but not others. Groups opposed to free trade can actually find inspiration for their work in specific policies and pieces of legislation passed by the same governments that now promote a free-trade agenda. Again, to take a Canadian example, anti-free-trade coalitions are mobilized by nongovernmental organizations active in the protection and promotion of indigenous culture. These coalitions are empowered by existing laws that promote Canadian content on radio and television, and in print. Such cultural and identity-oriented legal frameworks, and the legitimacy they provide for expanding anti-free-trade arguments, cannot be reduced to "economic protectionism." One can find comparable examples in French legislation and French nongovernmental organizations, especially concerning U.S. domination of the domestic market for films.

Goldstein and Martin are certainly correct that domestic politics are important in trade politics, but significant variation in domestic legal systems should provoke some caution in claiming generalized effects of domestic ratification on interest group politics. If generalizing their analysis to Canada is problematic, we suspect that generalizing to Europe and Asia, and certainly the developing world, would be even more so. More careful thought about the varied possibilities for law to shape public debates on trade—by providing information but also by constituting, empowering, and constraining different kinds of actors in different states—might yield a more defensible set of propositions.

Ellen Lutz and Kathryn Sikkink apply the legalization concept to human rights to test their hypothesis that increased legalization increases compliance with human rights law.[39] They examine three areas of human rights law—torture, disappearance, and democratic governance—and find the least compliance in the most "legalized" area, torture, and the most compliance in the least "legalized" area, democratic governance. They find stronger explanatory power for compliance in broader social variables and in the "norm cascade" that swept through Latin America in the 1970s and 1980s.

Oddly, the legalization concept seems to be most useful to these researchers who find its effects so limited. Unlike Simmons, or Goldstein and Martin, Lutz and Sikkink take us through an examination of the concept, as defined in the framing chapter, and discuss its application to their issue-area. Lutz and Sikkink do not turn legalization into some other analytic concept (like information or credible commitment) to carry out the analysis. In particular, they engage explicitly with the concept of obligation, suggesting briefly that human rights norms are often rooted in customary law. They also stress that any existing "right" to democratization can only be a social norm or a customary norm. Their findings support the understanding of obligation that we traced out earlier, an approach rooted in social processes of interaction. To be effective, obligation needs to be felt, and not simply imposed through a hierarchy of sources of law. Precision and delegation play absolutely no role in the promotion of compliance, at least with these human rights norms. Once Lutz and Sikkink find the legalization hypothesis wanting, they move into familiar conceptual turf (for Sikkink), employing the "norm cascade" concept elaborated elsewhere to explain the pattern of compliance they see.[40]

That Lutz and Sikkink focus so strongly on legalization's contribution to compliance brings us back to an important problem. As noted earlier, the framing article is not clear about analytic objectives. If the volume's purpose is primarily to

39. Lutz and Sikkink 2000.
40. Finnemore and Sikkink 1998.

describe legalization, then Lutz and Sikkink's article is beside the point. After all, the framing article does not claim that legalization will lead to greater compliance with law. Consequently, the fact that a more highly legalized area engenders less compliance than a less legalized area is neither here nor there for the framers of the volume. Yet the idea that this finding is somehow beside the point and gives no pause to the framers, as revealed by Kahler's dismissive treatment of Lutz and Sikkink's article in the conclusion, is surprising, since elsewhere the volume's authors claim to investigate the consequences of legalization that, presumably, would involve compliance.[41] More generally, if the purpose of the legalization concept is to generate hypotheses that guide research, one would expect disconfirming evidence of the type Lutz and Sikkink present to result in a rethinking of the basic concept. If the concept of legalization is both narrow theoretically, containing no theory of obligation, and weak when applied to empirical studies, parasitizing other concepts and uninterested in compliance with norms in concrete settings, then we are forced back to our central question: how much does the legalization framework deliver?

Conclusion

No analysis can do everything, but analysts must justify their choice of focus in the light of other obvious possibilities. The framers of the legalization concept are not explicit, however, about their limited view of law or about alternative views of law (or IR theory) that might yield different understandings of their cases. Further, they have not adequately theorized their definition of legalization so as to provide clear help to the empirical researchers seeking to apply the concept. We have called attention to some alternative views of law and suggested ways they can help us to address gaps in the authors' own framework that might lead researchers to examine important questions neglected in this volume. Our hope is the same as the authors'—that international law and IR scholars will begin to read each other's work more carefully and use each other's insights in analysis. Our suspicion, however, is that this process will not yield a long trail of scholarship on the concept of legalization as defined in the volume discussed here. Rather, as IR scholars read more broadly in international law, they will find rich connections between the two fields and will be able to create joint research agendas that are diverse and fruitful.

References

Abbott, Kenneth W., and Duncan Snidal. 2000. Hard and Soft Law in International Governance. *International Organization* 54 (3):421–56.

41. Goldstein et al. 2000, 386.

Abbott, Kenneth W., Robert O. Keohane, Andrew Moravcsik, Anne-Marie Slaughter, and Duncan Snidal. 2000. The Concept of Legalization. *International Organization* 54 (3):401–19.

Barnett, Michael, and Martha Finnemore. 1999. The Politics, Power, and Pathologies of International Organizations. *International Organization* 53 (4):699–732.

Biersteker, Thomas J., and Cynthia Weber, eds. 1996. *State Sovereignty as Social Construct*. Cambridge: Cambridge University Press.

Bowett, Derek W. 1958. *Self Defence in International Law*. Manchester: Manchester University Press.

Brunnée, Jutta. 1993. Toward Effective International Environmental Law: Trends and Developments. In *Law and Process in Environmental Management*, edited by Steven A. Kennett, 217–36. Calgary, Alberta: Canadian Institute of Resources Law.

Brunnée, Jutta, and Stephen J. Toope. 1997. Environmental Security and Freshwater Resources: Ecosystem Regime Building. *American Journal of International Law* 91:26–59.

———. 2000. International Law and Constructivism: Elements of an Interactional Theory of International Law. *Columbia Journal of Transnational Law* 39:19–74.

Byers, Michael. 1999. *Custom, Power, and the Power of Rules: International Relations and Customary International Law*. Cambridge: Cambridge University Press.

Chinkin, Christine M. 1989. The Challenge of Soft-Law: Development and Change in International Law. *International and Comparative Law Quarterly* 38:850–66.

Finnemore, Martha. 2000. Are Legal Norms Distinctive? *NYU Journal of International Law and Politics* 32 (3):699–705.

Finnemore, Martha, and Kathryn Sikkink. 1998. International Norm Dynamics and Political Change. *International Organization* 52 (4):887–917.

Franck, Thomas M. 1990. *The Power of Legitimacy Among Nations*. New York: Oxford University Press.

Fuller, Lon L. 1969. *The Morality of Law*. Rev. ed. New Haven, Conn.: Yale University Press.

Glenn, H. Patrick. 2000. *Legal Traditions of the World*. Oxford: Oxford University Press.

Goldsmith, J. L., and E. A. Posner. 1999. A Theory of Customary International Law. *University of Chicago Law Review* 66:1113–77.

Goldstein, Judith, and Lisa L. Martin. 2000. Legalization, Trade Liberalization, and Domestic Politics: A Cautionary Note. *International Organization* 54 (3):603–32.

Hillgenberg, H. 1999. A Fresh Look at Soft Law. *European Journal of International Law* 10:499–515.

Hurrell, Andrew. 2000. Conclusion: International Law and the Changing Constitution of International Society. In *The Role of Law in International Politics: Essays in International Relations and International Law*, edited by Michael Byers, 327–46. Oxford: Oxford University Press.

Kahler, Miles. 2000a. Legalization as Strategy: The Asia-Pacific Case. *International Organization* 54 (3):549–71.

———. 2000b. Conclusion: The Causes and Consequences of Legalization. *International Organization* 54 (3):661–83.

Kennedy, David. 1997. New Approaches to Comparative Law: Comparativism and International Governance. *Utah Law Review* 2:545–637.

Keohane, Robert O., Andrew Moravcsik, and Anne-Marie Slaughter. 2000. Legalized Dispute Resolution: Interstate and Transnational. *International Organization* 54 (3):457–88.

Kingsbury, Benedict. 1998. The Concept of Compliance as a Function of Competing Conceptions of International Law. *Michigan Journal of International Law* 19:345.

Koh, Harold. 1997. Why Do Nations Obey International Law? *Yale Law Journal* 106:2599–2659.

Lasswell, Harold D., and Myres S. McDougal. 1971. Criteria for a Theory About Law. *Southern California Law Review* 44:362.

Lauterpacht, Hersch. 1947. *Recognition in International Law*. London: Cambridge University Press.

Lowe, Vaughan. 2000. The Politics of Law-Making: Are the Method and Character of Norm Creation Changing? In *The Role of Law in International Politics: Essays in International Relations and International Law*, edited by Michael Byers, 207–26. Oxford: Oxford University Press.

Lutz, Ellen L., and Kathryn Sikkink. 2000. International Human Rights Law and Practice in Latin America. *International Organization* 54 (3):633–59.

Macdonald, Roderick A. 1998. Metaphors of Multiplicity: Civil Society, Regimes, and Legal Pluralism. *Arizona Journal of Comparative and International Law* 15:69–91.

Postema, Gerald J. 1991. On the Moral Presence of Our Past. *McGill Law Journal* 36:1153.

———. 1994. Implicit Law. *Law and Philosophy* 13:361.

Ragazzi, M. 1997. *The Concept of International Obligations Erga Omnes.* Oxford: Oxford University Press.

Reisman, Michael. 1992. The View from the New Haven School of International Law. *Proceedings of the American Society of International Law* 86:118.

Simmons, Beth A. 2000. The Legalization of International Monetary Affairs. *International Organization* 54 (3):573–602.

Slaughter, Anne-Marie. 1995. International Law in a World of Liberal States. *European Journal of International Law* 6:503–38.

Toope, Stephen J. 2000. Emerging Patterns of Governance and International Law. In *The Role of Law in International Politics: Essays in International Relations and International Law*, edited by Michael Byers, 91–108. Oxford: Oxford University Press.

Verdross, Alfred, and Heribert Franz Koeck. 1983. Natural Law: The Tradition of Universal Reason and Authority. In *The Structure and Process of International Law*, edited by R. Macdonald and D. M. Johnston, 17–50. The Hague: Martinus Nijhoff.

Walzer, Michael. 1983. *Spheres of Justice: A Defense of Pluralism and Equality.* New York: Basic Books.

Wang, Hongying. 2000. *Weak States, Strong Networks: The Institutional Dynamics of Foreign Direct Investment in China.* New York: Oxford University Press.

[14]

Legalization, Trade Liberalization, and Domestic Politics: A Cautionary Note

Judith Goldstein and Lisa L. Martin

Political scientists attempt to explain why governments adopt the policies they do. In political models, policy is the result of calculated choices made by political and economic actors. Actors' resources, and their incentives to mobilize and demand that governments attend to their interests, are the key forces explaining the policy choices we observe. When considering the impact of international legalization on political outcomes, the way in which legalization changes the interests and demands of actors provides the mechanism by which policy changes. In this article we consider how increases in the legalization of the international trade regime interact with the trade-related interests of domestic actors. Although legalization may reduce incentives for cheating by individual nations, we identify ways in which the unintended effects of legalization on the activities of domestic economic actors could interfere with the pursuit of progressive liberalization of international trade. Domestic politics cannot be treated as extraneous or as an irrational source of error that obstructs the purposes of legalization. Instead, politics operates in systematic ways and is the mechanism through which legalization exerts its effects. These effects range far beyond reducing opportunism by unitary states.

Through incremental change in the postwar years, the international trade regime has evolved away from its origins as a decentralized and relatively powerless institution and become a legal entity. The number of countries and the amount of trade covered by the rules agreed to in 1947 have expanded greatly. After 1995 and the creation of the World Trade Organization (WTO), the regime further increased its demands on members by elaborating and expanding commercial rules and procedures, including those that relate to the system of settling disputes. In practice the expansion of the regime in the post–World War II period has made trade rules more precise and binding. The result is that the implications or behavioral demands of rules have become increasingly transparent to all participants.[1]

We thank Bob Keohane, Marc Busch, Eric Anderson, James Fearon, Erica Gould, Barry Weingast, Simon Jackman, Brian Hanson, Richard Steinberg, an anonymous reviewer, and the editors of *IO* for comments on a previous version of this article.

1. Legalization refers to three aspects of international law: obligation, precision, and level of delegation to a centralized authority. Abbott et al., this issue.

We argue that this increased legalization does not necessarily augur higher levels of trade liberalization, as suggested by supporters. The weakly legalized General Agreement on Tariffs and Trade (GATT) regime was remarkably successful at liberalizing trade; it is not apparent that the benefits of further legalization will outweigh its costs. This finding derives from an analysis of domestic politics and, in particular, from the incentives facing leaders to join and then adhere to the dictates of a liberal international trade regime. We support our position through an analysis of two aspects of trade politics.

First, we examine the effect of legalization on the incentives of domestic groups to mobilize and pressure their governments to adopt policies that favor them.[2] In that legalization entails a process of increasing rule precision, a more legalized trade regime will provide more and better information about the distributional implications of commercial agreements. Information on who will gain and lose from some international action will affect the incentives of groups to mobilize for and against trade agreements. This effect on both the mobilization of groups and the balance among them will vary depending on numerous factors. In general, however, we believe that better information will empower protectionists relative to free traders on issues relating to the conclusion of new agreements and free traders relative to protectionists on issues of compliance to existing agreements.

Second, we examine the implications of a more "binding" GATT/WTO on member governments. Although GATT rules were always obligatory in a legal sense, the provisions for using escape clauses and other loopholes interacted with domestic political realities in a way that made their use increasingly rare. This fact, combined with a strengthened dispute-resolution mechanism under the WTO, has increased the extent to which governments are "obliged," in a political sense, to maintain their liberal commitments. Reducing the ability of governments to opt out of commitments has the positive effect of reducing the chances that governments will behave opportunistically by invoking phony criteria for protecting their industries. On the other hand, tightly binding, unforgiving rules can have negative effects in the uncertain environment of international trade. When considering the realities of incomplete information about future economic shocks, we suggest that legalization may not result in the "correct" balance between these two effects of binding.

In this article we develop both the theoretical reasoning and the empirical support for our cautionary note on the domestic effects of legalization. We begin by examining information and group mobilization and suggest that the predictability that comes with legalization has both positive and negative effects on the trade liberalization goal of the regime. We then investigate the "bindingness" of trade rules. Through examination of the use of safeguards and the new dispute-resolution procedure, we

2. The number and variety of groups participating in the politics of trade has grown in the last decades. Where the classic models assumed three groups with trade-related interests—consumers, import-competing groups, and exporters—other groups, whose interests span from human rights to a clean environment, have come to believe that their interests are influenced by trade negotiations. The logic of this article, explaining the interaction among international regimes, social mobilization, and domestic politics, applies to any interest that groups perceive to be influenced by international trade agreements.

argue that trade rules have become more binding, even if *pacta sunt servanda* has always applied to such rules, and that enforcement of rules is now more certain.

Given the relatively short history of the WTO, it is not possible to collect the empirical evidence that can conclusively demonstrate whether legalization has gone "too far." Instead, the theoretical reasoning about the impact of legalization on domestic politics points to trends that demand close attention. Our purpose in this article is to raise questions about the potential downside of legalization that have not received sufficient attention. Appropriately legalizing international agreements is a tricky business, as the theoretical articles in this issue attest. Governments must perform a balancing act between binding themselves tightly enough to avoid cheating and allowing the flexibility to deal with the vagaries of changing information and domestic politics. Performing this balancing act well requires a clear-headed analysis of the impact of legalization on domestic politics.

Legalization, Information, and the Mobilization of Domestic Groups

The logic of precision, delegation, obligation, and increased transparency played a large role in negotiations over transforming the GATT into the WTO. The intended effect of these modifications in the WTO was to expand the breadth of the trade regime and enhance compliance so as to increase the benefits of membership. The problem with this logic is that it neglected domestic politics. Maintenance of free trade is politically difficult and is a function of the differential mobilization of those who favor liberalization and those who oppose a further opening of the economy to foreign products. Mobilization itself is a function of a number of factors, including the cost of mobilizing and the potential gains from collective action. One consequence of legalizing the trade regime has been greater transparency and predictability about the effects of trade agreements. Increased information of this sort has mixed effects on the mobilization of domestic interests and therefore on the ability of governments to maintain support for liberal trade policies.

The Logic of Mobilization

Consider first the impact of increased precision of trade rules during the process of trade negotiations. The ability of leaders to sign an accord will depend on the groups mobilized for or against the accord. The pattern of mobilization is not always predictable; mobilizing interest groups requires overcoming collective-action problems that can be quite intense. Actors within these groups must realize first that they have a common interest in government policies. They must then come to believe that it is worthwhile to bear the costs of collective action. A number of factors can undermine mobilization. The factors most relevant to international trade include the large and diffuse nature of some economic interests, lack of information that the interests of actors are at stake in particular international negotiations, and possible calculations that the costs of influencing government policy outweigh anticipated benefits.[3]

From the perspective of encouraging the liberalization of international trade, the fact that groups who prefer economic closure might suffer from collective-action problems is a blessing. If all antitrade forces were well organized and able to exert substantial pressure on their political representatives, the prospects for liberalization would be dim. The interaction with legalization enters the analysis at this point. In that legalization entails a process of increased precision of rules and transparency of agreements, it affects the behavior of domestic groups by increasing the information available to actors about the distributional implications of trade agreements. To the extent that such knowledge enhances the mobilization of antitrade forces relative to already well-organized protrade groups, legalization could undermine liberalization. Information matters for both protectionist and proliberalization interests. However, if these groups are differentially mobilized prior to the process of legalization, information will have the larger marginal effect on the groups that are not as well organized. The structure of the multilateral trade regime, based on the principle of reciprocity, has provided strong incentives for exporters to organize throughout the post-1950 period.[4] Growing dependence on exports and the multinational character of economic interests has also led to strong and effective lobbying efforts by free-trade advocates.[5] We therefore concentrate on the likely impact of greater information on the incentives facing protectionist groups.

Oran Young, writing on this relationship between international arrangements and the collective action of groups in the context of environmental negotiations, also argues that one important aspect of international negotiations is the distributional information available about the effects of agreements.[6] He argues that if actors know precisely the distributional effects of negotiations, they will concentrate on distributive issues rather than on "integrative" bargaining that searches for arrangements that benefit all. Negotiating behind a "veil of ignorance" can have the benefit of focusing minds on the mutual advantages of international cooperation, rather than arguing about how the costs will be distributed.

Young does not bring differential patterns of domestic mobilization into his analysis. Doing so increases the force of his central argument. If antitrade groups know for certain that their interests will suffer as a result of an agreement, their expected utility of collective action increases and they should be more willing to bear the costs of political participation. Thus legalization that involves highly precise and transparent rules can have the unintended effect of encouraging the mobilization of protectionist forces that see themselves as probable losers from an agreement. To the extent that these forces can now better balance already well-organized free-trade forces, negotiations about liberalization are made more difficult.

3. Collective-action problems have been central to the literature on endogenous tariff formation. See, for example, Magee, Brock, and Young 1989; and Mayer 1984.

4. Gilligan 1997.

5. Milner 1988.

6. Young 1989.

Transparency of winners and losers also has an effect on export groups. According to Michael J. Gilligan, one explanation for the liberalization that has occurred since World War II is that the process of setting tariffs encouraged the participation of export groups.[7] Reciprocal agreements made the gains from trade more transparent to exporters, resulting in greater support for trade liberalization than had existed fifty years earlier. Just as the potential losers from a trade agreement will attempt to undercut agreements, the potential winners will have an interest in pushing their states to sign treaties. In the absence of import-competing groups, or where the relative power between the two favors exporters, we assume policy will reflect exporters' interests. To the extent that information activates protectionists, other things being equal, nations will find it harder to build a consensus around a new liberalizing agreement.

A simple model clarifies the posited relationship between information and mobilization. Define p to be the probability with which a group believes that its interests will be at stake in negotiations. This subjective probability, p, is a random variable that takes on different values as information conditions change. We begin by assuming a poor information environment, where groups know only the total number of groups affected, not which of them will be affected.

Assume that there are N groups with an interest in trade. These groups are not mobilized initially. Assume they know that n groups will be affected by negotiations but have no information about which n groups this will be. This is an extreme assumption of poor information but a useful starting point. Each group therefore estimates that it will have a stake in negotiations with probability n/N, the ratio of affected groups to all groups. Given a lack of information, this is their best guess of the probability of being affected by negotiations. Thus, in the prelegalization environment, the variable p takes on the value n/N; $p = n/N$. The value of p will change as information improves.

Given this value of p prior to legalization, does it make sense for a group to mobilize? The calculation depends on the relationship between the expected benefits and costs of mobilization. The benefits of mobilization, B, are realized only if the group is in n. If the group is not in n, it gains no benefits, but will have to bear the costs of mobilization if it chooses to mobilize. Given the pre-legalization value of p, the expected benefits from negotiations are $p*B$, or nB/N. Groups will mobilize if the expected benefits outweigh mobilization costs C; $p*B > C$. Thus each group will mobilize if $nB/N > C$ in the poor information environment. N is a large number, and the ratio n/N is typically small. Thus, unless B is extremely large or the costs of mobilization negligible, groups will not have an incentive to mobilize. Our expectation is that few groups will meet this stringent pre-legalization mobilization condition. As information improves, p increases above the n/N minimum. However, with uncertainty about the distributional implications of negotiations, p remains small and the ratio of B to C must be large to allow mobilization.

After legalization, we assume that groups know with certainty whether they will be included in negotiations; that is, their estimate of the probability p now becomes

7. Gilligan 1997.

either zero or 1, as groups know whether their interests are at stake or not. The value of the random variable p changes as information conditions change. Groups that do not have their interests at stake will not mobilize. However, the condition for groups that are affected by negotiations to mobilize is now $p^*B > C$ with $p = 1$, which is simply $B > C$. This is a much easier condition to meet, as long as collective-action costs are not prohibitive (as they may be for large, diffuse groups such as consumers). Therefore, we expect that many more groups will find it worthwhile to mobilize in the richer information environment postlegalization. Even if p does not improve to the extreme values of zero or 1, it approaches these limits, with the expected effects.

As suggested earlier, information has effects on groups that may be harmed as well as helped by negotiations. Our intention here is not to make precise predictions about the policy outcomes of relative mobilization of exporters and protectionists, but simply to draw attention to the political problems created by enhanced mobilization of antitrade groups. Clearly, information will lead both groups to mobilize, given increased certainty on how interests will fare in an agreement. However, a number of factors suggest that increased information is likely to favor proprotectionist mobilization. This position goes beyond the classic explanation, for example, Schattschneider's, that protectionist interests are concentrated and free-trade interests diffuse, which still has some force.[8]

The first factor is that the status quo favors protected groups, not potential new exporters. Since changes from the status quo require explicit affirmation—for example, ratification of a treaty—those who benefit from the status quo gain veto power. Thus typical institutional procedures that privilege the status quo will tend to favor protectionist over liberalizing interests. Another factor pointing in the same direction is the uncertain nature of gains for exporters. Exporters only know that some market will open up, not whether they will be able to capitalize on this opportunity in the face of international competition. In contrast, protectionists know precisely what protection they will be losing as a result of liberalization, enhancing their incentives to mobilize relative to exporters. Moving beyond a strictly rationalist model, we could also mention experimental evidence that actors tend to react more strongly to losses than to gains, again favoring protectionist groups in this mobilization dynamic. Finally, if we assume, as does Gilligan, that exporters are either fully or almost fully mobilized and are already participating in the political process, the increase in information should lead to a relatively greater mobilization of the less involved, that is, the antitrade groups.

The logic of precision and mobilization does not necessarily lead one to expect economic closure. When we consider the effects of more information when maintaining as opposed to creating a trade commitment, we get the opposite effect. Although information may mobilize import-competers before the conclusion of an agreement, the effect of a more legalized regime may be to mobilize exporters in cases of certain market losses, *ex post*. In this case, precision about which exporters will bear the costs of retaliation in a trade dispute works to mobilize exporting interests who would

8. Schattschneider 1935.

otherwise have no involvement in the trade dispute. Given the potential of a market loss, they will press governments to uphold trade rules. The higher the probability that the retaliatory action will hurt them, the greater their interests in expending resources to maintain liberal trade at home.

Therefore, logic suggests that increasing rule precision will have two different, and competing, effects on trade liberalization. Increased determinacy can undermine trade deals by activating import-competing groups with veto power. Conversely, precise rules regarding responses to rule breaches will result in more trade liberalization by activating export groups in the offending country. Over time, we should see not only more antitrade groups organizing but also more political activity by export groups if strategies of retaliation are appropriately designed.

Mobilizing Antitrade Groups

Empirical evidence suggests that groups affected by trade policy are often well organized and articulate. Whether the group is farmers in France, auto producers in the United States, or computer companies in Japan, those whose interests will be hurt by either continued or expanded access to foreign goods, services, and markets are articulate spokespersons for specific policies. These groups often act as veto players, and leaders who would like to negotiate the opening of world markets find that fear of competition at home undermines support for their free-trade coalition. The ability of leaders to ignore protectionist pressures rests on the willingness of proliberalization groups, those who benefit from liberalized trade, to organize and be equally active in their support. In the absence of exporters or other interested parties who articulate their free-trade positions, governments find it difficult to maintain a free-trade policy.[9]

Evidence of the effects of this problem of mobilizing and maintaining a free-trade coalition is found in all democracies and partially results from the concentrated benefits of trade barriers and their diffuse costs.[10] Rarely are those who are hurt by higher prices (consumers) present in political debate; more often, trade politics is determined by the balance between groups with specific interests in either openness or closure. In some countries, structural factors affect this balance. For example, groups may be overrepresented because of the electoral process, such as with agricultural producers in Japan, or because they have bureaucratic or corporatist support in government.

Since World War II, protectionist pressures from such groups have been mitigated through changes in the trade policymaking process, both domestic and international.[11] Reciprocal trade agreements, delegation to executive agencies, electoral re-

9. Numerous empirical studies document the importance of groups in setting trade policy. For a cross-national, cross-sectional examination of groups' involvement, see, for example, Verdier 1994.

10. On trade and interest groups, see Destler 1995; and Lohmann and O'Halloran 1994.

11. Whether it was a change in the balance of group interests or a shift in trade policymaking that explains the ability of governments to lower barriers to trade is difficult to determine in the early years of the GATT regime. Certainly, in the United States interest-group activity was muted because the costs of

form, and changing legislative voting rules help explain why countries support liberal trade policies that were difficult to defend in the pre–World War II period. The fact of liberalization and the specifics of the process are in equilibrium. The process may change either because underlying interests change or for exogenous reasons. Regardless of the particular reason for change, changes in the process have far-reaching consequences for policy. Process changes have made it more difficult for import-competing groups to find a majority to support their position while encouraging the organization of exporter interests.

The success of groups who support liberalization, however, should not be construed as evidence that policymakers no longer need to worry about veto groups undercutting trade policy. Liberalization may have changed the face of the proprotection lobby, but it has not eliminated its potential power. Even in the United States, long a proponent of the liberal trade regime, elected officials repeatedly face pressures from antitrade groups. Politicians such as Ross Perot and Pat Buchanan have mobilized voters against further trade liberalization, and authorization to join the WTO was garnered only after a significant battle in which continued participation was made contingent upon a reauthorization by Congress every five years. The potential influence of an antitrade coalition was no better evidenced than during the November 1999 ministerial meeting of the WTO in Seattle as protestors took to the streets. Even though the United States retains open markets, protrade politicians who do not strategize about the creation and maintenance of their coalitions can easily find themselves overwhelmed by protectionist demands.[12]

These social pressures have led strategic trade negotiators to bundle the gains to exporters from access to new markets with the losses to import-competing producers from new competition from abroad. Whatever the specifics of this trade-off at the negotiating table, the result must be an agreement that can garner majority support at home. If information about the distributional implication of agreements affects the propensity of groups to organize during negotiations, it may be easier to get to that "optimal bundle" in situations where some uncertainty exists about who is and who is not affected by the trade deal. Providing this information about the effects of either a potential commercial agreement, the behavior of a trading partner, or the dissolution of a trading pact is a central function of the contemporary trade regime. The WTO collects and disseminates trade data in preparation for rounds of trade talks; it monitors compliance and inventories national practices that undermine the free flow of goods and services.

---

organizing increased when the president obtained increased control of trade policymaking. Still, the shift toward openness would not have occurred without underlying social support. For an analysis of the relationship between institutional and underlying social variables, see Bailey, Goldstein, and Weingast 1997.

12. One simple metric capturing the continued involvement of proprotection groups in the United States is the number of bills entered in Congress pertaining to imports. In the 93rd–97th Congress, 1973–81, over 2,200 bills were entered; in the 98th–101st Congress, 1982–90, almost 2,300 bills were entered; and in the 102nd–105th Congress, 1991–98, over 1,600 bills were considered. Although few of these bills become law, the data suggest that liberal policy exists in the shadow of growing resistance. Numbers were obtained from Thomas Legislative Information on the Internet located at <http://thomas.loc.gov/home/thomas.html>.

Over time, the GATT/WTO regime has dramatically increased its ability to deliver this information to member countries.[13] In initial rounds of negotiations, tariff information was not systematically collected. Nations relied on data supplied by their negotiating partners, and thus the computation of offers and counteroffers for "balance" was done using often-incomplete statistics. Recognizing the need for better data, the secretariat undertook a systematic compilation of tariff and nontariff barriers following the Kennedy Round. By the time negotiators came together for the Tokyo Round, countries could utilize reports, available on computer tape, to measure the degree of reciprocity in trade deals. The information environment became even richer for the Uruguay Round. After 1985, the GATT infrastructure began to provide refined data on tariff and nontariff barriers in member countries. In 1989, the Trade Policy Review Mechanism was authorized at the Montreal midterm review of progress in the Uruguay Round. This began a process of regular country studies, providing sector and product information on practices of GATT members. The four largest trading powers—Canada, the European Union (EU), Japan, and the United States—are reviewed every two years; the sixteen member countries that are next in the value of their trade are reviewed every four years; most other members are reviewed every six years.[14] The result has been a more symmetric information environment.[15]

This increased monitoring activity in itself is not a result of "legalization" according to the definition adopted in this issue. Still, it has been tightly bound up with increased formalization and precision of commitments both at the time of and during the life of an agreement. The result is a far richer information environment than at any previous time. One aspect of WTO operations, for example, that is more public than in the past is the ministerial meeting. The November 1999 meeting was well publicized, including procedures for obtaining observer status. In response, more groups than ever before petitioned for admission to the meeting. Few of these groups were protrade, leading the secretariat to fear that the meeting would be met with pickets and protests, as it was.[16]

Along with changes in WTO policy, a key demand of antitrade groups has been less secrecy in WTO proceedings. Although some Western governments, including the United States, have defended the principle of transparency, most representatives in the WTO strenuously resist this demand.[17] Still, transparency has increased over time. Early rounds were akin to clubs. Deals were struck among a small group of like-minded representatives, behind closed doors. Later rounds eschewed this general negotiating form. Although private negotiations occurred, and were often the most productive, more time was spent in formal settings, with delegates giving pre-

13. Keesing 1998.
14. Ibid.
15. The GATT's move to the Trade Policy Review Mechanism was motivated by the perception that information was key in negotiations but that it was available only to the larger countries. Ibid.
16. More applications were received from groups asking for admission to the talks than at any previous time in the GATT/WTO's history (private correspondence). See also the *New York Times*, 13 October 1999, A12.
17. *New York Times*, 4 December 1999, A6.

pared speeches that offered few, if any, real trade concessions. Thus the demand for more transparency has been met by more open meetings and more press coverage, but the effect of these particular changes has been muted; delegates continue to worry about domestic constituencies and remain wary of saying anything that would get them into trouble at home.

Increased provision of information to delegates is not, we acknowledge, evidence of complete transparency in the trade regime. Although legalization has resulted in a movement toward transparency, we cannot claim to have reached a situation of complete and perfect information. The WTO retains many of the elements of the GATT, including its preservation of member countries' rights to secrecy. The empirical evidence does not adequately allow us to make precise estimates of the level of transparency. We can, however, identify a trend toward greater openness. When the GATT was established in the late 1940s, the confidentiality rule adopted by member countries was the strictest of any adopted by postwar international institutions.[18] The correspondence of any delegate could be claimed as privileged. If a delegate did not formally rescind a confidentiality request within three years, the information became confidential in perpetuity. Why this rule? Simply, delegates did not want information to leak back home. Offers made during negotiations could be highly sensitive, and although the final package would be made public, it came home as a "closed" deal—groups could not easily pick it apart.

The early delegates to the GATT understood that too much information would incur import-competing group pressures and undermine their ability to make trade-offs among groups. Policymakers need to be able to bundle agreements in order to procure majorities in their home countries. For politicians, the logic of membership in a multilateral trade institution is to facilitate the creation of larger bundles than are possible through bilateral bargaining.

Efforts to devise free-trade coalitions in an environment of market liberalization help explain the changing structure of trade rounds. Since the creation of the GATT, negotiators have utilized four different methods of conducting the rounds, each an attempt to finesse potential antitrade interests in member states. In the initial rounds—Geneva 1947, Annecy 1949, Torquay 1951, Geneva 1956, Dillon 1961—talks were conducted on an item-by-item basis. The form of these talks reflected the negotiating discretion of the U.S. representative. Due to the structure of U.S. trade politics, negotiators were relatively unconstrained, since they had in hand, *ex ante,* authorization to reduce tariffs, on average, by a specified amount. They could make cross-sectoral deals without fear of import-competers vetoing a final agreement. The United States abandoned its support for such a form of talks in the 1960s, partially because of efficiency concerns and what Americans perceived as an asymmetric information environment that did not favor the United States.[19] By the mid-1960s, industries were

18. Richard Blackhurst interviews.

19. Under 1951 and 1958 laws, U.S. negotiators were forced to consider data on which industries would be hurt by a trade agreement. Under peril point legislation, the U.S. Tariff Commission provided public information on the effect of tariff reductions on particular industries. This list told U.S. trading partners exactly who could and could not be included in a trade deal. This generated more information to

also demanding side payments, in both the United States and Europe, when they felt victimized in the name of other sectors' gains.[20]

Instead of negotiating item by item, participants in the Kennedy Round adopted a linear formula approach. Although advocates of this approach foresaw it as negating the power of specific groups, the formula was never a significant constraint, and the real politics of the round surrounded the balancing of members' exceptions lists. Nations came to Geneva with long lists of producers to be exempted from the linear cuts. Some nations, such as the Nordic countries, had no industries on their exception list. The United Kingdom had about 10 percent of dutiable industrial imports on its list, the United States had 18–19 percent, Japan had 20–25 percent, and the European Community had 40 percent.[21] The United States' exceptions list was compounded by its having made significant concession to textiles and having granted Article XIX relief to carpets and glass.[22] Even so, the agreements did not fare well when sent to Congress for approval.[23] Although initial authorization had elicited minimal resistance, hearings before the U.S. House Ways and Means Committee in 1968, at the close of the round, were more reminiscent of pre-1934 than post-1934 trade politics. Export groups were conspicuously absent, but import-sensitive groups appeared in large numbers and stopped passage of agreements to end the American Selling Price and reform the antidumping law concluded during the round.[24]

With a new interest in nontariff barriers and the role of the developing economies as well as a fear of import pressures, the 1973 Tokyo Round abandoned linear formulas and adopted a formula that harmonized rates. Linear formulas reduced tariffs by the same amount for all industries. Countries with peaked tariff schedules could participate in worldwide tariff reductions and not have to change the relatively high protection granted to certain products. Harmonized formulas force greater cuts on the top, producing more liberalization as well as more resistance, explaining why the formula was adopted amid much controversy. Since the United States was one of the biggest offenders of the skewed tariff schedule, U.S. negotiators had considerable difficulty finding support at home for the cuts. The final U.S. average cut of 31 percent must be considered alongside the far smaller cuts for powerful industries: 4 percent for leather; 15 percent for apparel; 16 percent for autos; and no cuts for a variety of producers, including footwear and TVs. The United States was not alone in offering a "Swiss cheese" set of offers, and agricultural groups kept cuts in their tariffs off the table all together.[25]

Although in the Uruguay Round attention was focused on nontariff barriers and GATT rules, the pattern of interest-group activity helps to explain why the round

---

groups than is even the case under the WTO. One effect, consistent with this analysis, is that access to this information explains the relatively modest tariff changes made in the 1950s. Goldstein 1993.

20. Shonfield 1976, 175.
21. Ibid., 183.
22. Goldstein 1993, 166.
23. Evans 1971, 281.
24. American Selling Price was a valuation system used for chemical imports. Ibid., 300–303.
25. Winham 1986, 17–18. A reviewer suggested the Swiss cheese metaphor, particularly applicable here since the adopted formula was Swiss.

returned to the original item-by-item approach, with deals made within, and less often across, sectors. At its core, the approach was an attempt by participants to garner support by balancing access to the home market with expanded export opportunities within sectors. All of the major nations faced stiff resistance from powerful social actors in the 1980s. The United States had used a variety of instruments, including antidumping, Section 301, and countervailing duty legislation, in response to aid requests from key sectors, such as steel, automobiles, and textiles. Even more important in both the United States and the EU was the agricultural lobby. At one point during the round the power of French farmers nearly led France to veto the Euro-American Blair House Agreement as well as the conclusion of the round itself.[26] Similarly, the textile lobby in both the United States and the EU worked to undermine the attempt to dismantle the Multi-Fiber Arrangement.[27] The power of the textile industry in the United States was no better evidenced than when a coalition of senators from the South held up the final agreement in Congress.

In all these rounds, politics was never removed from the liberalization process, although the regime's structure did affect which domestic groups were able to translate their preferences into policy. Thus, adopted formulas were never intended to be binding on parties, and national offers were rife with exceptions. Preparation for rounds involved difficult negotiations with potentially powerful veto groups, often leading to an assortment of side payments issued in the early phase of negotiations.[28] Drawing on U.S. congressional indexes, we illustrate in Table 1 one way that this phenomenon manifested. The table summarizes the rise in the number of bills that provided side payments, usually in place of a more direct policy to curb imports. During the 1975–94 period, the number of side-payment bills that made their way to the House floor is high, though fairly stable. The data for 1995–98 suggest that under the WTO even more side-payment bills were used, as our analysis predicts.

Our attention to antitrade groups derives from two related observations. First, although liberalization has been extremely successful in the postwar period, it has always occurred in the shadow of organized opposition. Second, groups respond to information about impending trade talks, which motivates them to pursue particularistic policies. The existence of continued openness should not be interpreted as an absence of proprotection group pressures. Although proprotection groups may have been more constrained, had less "voice," and been balanced by well-organized exporter groups, once organized, they have powerful effects on policy.

Has there been a rise in interest-group activity since the creation of the WTO, as suggested by our analysis? Given the WTO's brief existence, assessing the data is difficult. However, as evidenced by the significant rise in the number of groups attending the WTO's November 1999 ministerial meeting, the WTO itself has engendered

26. The three major players were all plagued by antitrade pressures during the round. In the EU, differences among member countries developed over the Common Agricultural Policy. In Japan, the issue of rice protection undercut the ruling Liberal party, and in the United States, pressure from groups polarized on fast-track legislation extension. Secchi 1997, 81.

27. Ibid., 79.

28. Goldstein 1993.

TABLE 1. *Trade bills in the U.S. House of Representatives, 1975–98*

	Number of bills	*Percentage providing side payments rather than direct protection*
1975–78	79	14
1979–82	43	28
1983–86	61	26
1987–90	61	21
1991–94	47	13
1995–98	48	38

Source: Congressional Index, various years.

more attention from a wider range of domestic groups than ever before. For a whole host of reasons, some associated with legalization, the WTO has become a focus of attention not only for labor and producer groups, the traditionally interested parties, but also for environmental, health, and safety groups. Such attention is a result of the expansion of knowledge about what the WTO is doing as well as structural changes in the scope of the regime.

The regime's effect on the mobilization of groups may also explain problems faced in initiating a new round of trade talks. The stated focus for a new WTO Millennium Round of talks is far more targeted than ever before; knowledge of who has been targeted has led to more and earlier activity than in previous rounds. The best exemplar is the agricultural sector, where good information about the locus of talks led to a cross-national campaign of producers to undercut negotiations.[29] These types of increasing pressures, generated by more information about the liberalization process, will make it more difficult to find nations willing to launch trade rounds and, for those who do make it to Geneva, more difficult to make the necessary trade-offs among producers, even if export groups stay mobilized. After the November 1999 ministerial meeting the fate of the Millennium Round remains an open question, with most observers offering pessimistic assessments.

Mobilizing Export Groups

Although the mobilization of groups circumscribes the type of new deals that are possible, it also explains the stability of signed agreements. Leaders rarely renege on a GATT trade deal, even when faced with pressure from powerful rent-seeking industries. This stability was not due to GATT sanctions against such changes. Rather, changing specific tariffs, according to the rules, was relatively easy under a number of safeguard provisions of the GATT regime. Under GATT rules, nations could change

29. Josling 1999.

TABLE 2. *Post-negotiation tariff changes by invoked article for all GATT members, 1961–90*

	Open season[a]	*Out of season*[b]	*Article 28:5*[c]
1961–66[d]	9	14	3
1967–72	8	7	15
1973–78	5	3	31[e]
1979–84	1	1	66[f]
1985–90	1	1	19
1991–93/94	4	1	5

Source: GATT Analytical Index 1994.

[a]*Open season* refers to the usage and invocation of GATT Art. XXVIII:1.

[b]*Out of season* refers to the usage and invocation of GATT Art. XXVIII:4.

[c]Before the end of a period of "firm validity," a country may reserve to modify their schedule. The numbers in this column refer not to the election of this right, but to its usage (the actual modification).

[d]The time periods correspond to two periods of "firm validity," except the last time period (1991–93/94) for which we have only three years of data. Art. XIX data are as of 1 December 1993. Art. XXVIII data are as of 30 March 1994.

[e]Of these cases, 22 are either New Zealand's or South Africa's.

[f]Of these cases, 32 are South Africa's.

tariffs every three years during the "open season," in between these times "out of season," and/or under Article 28:5, as long as the general tariff level remained the same. Keeping the overall level of tariffs stable, however, was not easy for politicians at home. The problem with giving compensation was the trade-off it created between the group pressing for aid and some other producer. This type of a trade-off is difficult for politicians.

Table 2 shows the use of these provisions for changing particular tariffs post-negotiation. What is striking is that, although the regime legally provided a substantial amount of flexibility, these provisions have only rarely been invoked. Given the thousands of products affected by cuts, only a few countries rescinded an agreement to bind their tariffs. For GATT members, these provisions were akin to a Pandora's Box. Having to change a schedule, item by item, in the absence of reciprocal benefits meant trading off one domestic sector for another. The political problems this engendered assured that few GATT countries chose to deal with import problems through these means.

Another perspective on mobilization is evident in attempts to mobilize export groups in support of free trade by strategically using threats of retaliation. States making a threat of retaliation that is intended to mobilize exporters in other countries, such as the United States in implementing Section 301, must consider how to maximize the pressure applied by exporters to the other government. Announcing threats of definite retaliation against just a few groups would not have the desired effect. These groups would certainly mobilize, but those left off the short list would not. At the other extreme, announcing a very large or vague list of possible targets of retaliation would also fail to mobilize many exporters. This tactic would create massive collective-action problems, since each exporter would be only part of a potentially universal coalition and therefore face incentives to free ride. In addition, lack of precision in the possible targets of retaliation might encourage exporters to wait and take their chances on being hit, rather than bearing the definite, immediate costs of mobilization.

With these considerations in mind, if our story about mobilization is correct, the strategic use of retaliatory threats should be quite precise. In addition, it should target a group of exporters large enough to put pressure on the government, but not so large as to exacerbate collective-action problems. Section 301 cases provide a good source of evidence on the use of retaliatory threats, since they list the potential targets of retaliation when the other government does not reach a settlement with the United States.

The case of the United States pressuring Honduras to improve its protection of intellectual property provides a clear example of the principles of targeting in action. The U.S. Trade Representative (USTR), after deciding that Honduras was not adequately protecting intellectual property rights, announced on 7 November 1997 that it would impose sanctions on certain exports from Honduras if improvement in its policy were not forthcoming.[30] The annex to this announcement listed approximately thirty groups of products that would be denied preferential tariff treatment if Honduras did not comply. The annex also specified, in case there was any question, the current duty facing these products. Comments on the list were invited from the U.S. business community and due within one month of the announcement. Public hearings were also held on the proposed list.

One noticeable aspect of the target list is its degree of precision in specifying the targets of sanctions. Rather than just citing agricultural products, for example, the list identified specific agricultural exports: "mushroom spawn," "cucumbers, including gherkins, fresh or chilled," and "pineapple juice, not concentrated, or having a degree of concentration of not more than 3.5 degrees." Tobacco exporters of all sorts were singled out, as were exporters of luggage ("trunks, suitcases, vanity cases, attaché cases, briefcases, school satchels, spectacle cases") and wood products. Another target was exporters of "statues, statuettes, and handmade flowers, valued over $2.50 each and produced by professional sculptors or directly from molds made from original models produced by professional sculptors."

By developing this degree of precision in the specification of targets, the USTR left exporters with little doubt about whether they should put pressure on the Honduran government to seek a settlement with the United States. At the same time, the list was extensive without being so comprehensive that exporters could rely on others to carry the lobbying burden for them. It would have been much simpler, for example, to announce a 25 percent across-the-board increase in duties on exports from Honduras, but this procedure would have been so encompassing that it would have exacerbated collective-action problems among exporters. One other interesting aspect of

30. See *Federal Register* 62 (7 November 1997), Docket No. 301–116 (62 FR 60299).

the list of threatened sanctions is that it identified a set of exports from which the USTR would, if sanctions were actually imposed, select a subset. Thus the list of threatened sanctions was longer than the list of actual sanctions would be, again increasing the size of the mobilized exporters' pressure group.

We find similar retaliation strategies in other trade disputes. Lists of products in trade disputes with the EU and China were, as would be expected for larger trading partners, longer than those in the case of Honduras. In 1995 the USTR launched a complaint against the EU for not offering compensation when Austria, Finland, and Sweden entered the EU and adopted the EU's common external tariff.[31] In this instance, the first product on the list of threatened sanctions was "cheese and curd," going on to list various types of cheese in excruciating detail, and clearly aiming to mobilize French farmers to pressure the EU. Perfumes and cosmetics also appeared high on the list, again suggesting a strategy of mobilizing influential French exporters. The United States has been involved in a number of disputes with China over intellectual property.[32] In these cases, textiles made up the bulk of the list, although beer and chemical exporters were also targeted. In the Chinese cases, the USTR threatened to move beyond imposing a duty to imposing quantitative restrictions on imports, limiting them to 15 percent of the previous year's level.

The threat of retaliation, if issued with an appropriate degree of precision, activates export groups. This suggests that the GATT/WTO should allow or even encourage retaliation in the face of deviation from regime rules. The GATT structure, incorporating reciprocal retaliation and/or alternative market access in response to reneging on a concession, even under safeguard clauses, may have been better than the alternative adopted by the WTO. WTO rules waive the right to both compensation and/or retaliation for the first three years of a safeguard action. Those who supported the change argued that this would encourage nations to follow the rules—when nations could defend their reasons for invoking safeguard actions as "just," they should be protected from retaliation.[33] The logic offered here suggests the opposite. Circumstantial evidence in the United States supports the argument that domestic groups organize in response to government threats that affect their market position. For example, in what was supposed to be a simple incidence of using market restrictions in a Section 301 case, the United States found it politically impossible to raise tariffs on a Japanese car, the Lexus, in large part because of resistance from Lexus dealers in the United States. Lexus dealers are not the type of group that generates great sympathy from the American people. However, during a trade dispute with Japan that came to a head in 1995, they found their interests directly at stake. In an attempt to force more opening of the Japanese market, the United States announced a list of 100 percent retaliatory tariffs on Japanese luxury goods that would go into effect on 28 June.[34] Since this list included cars with a retail value over $30,000, Lexus dealers (along

31. *Federal Register* 60 (27 October 1995), Docket No. 301–101 (60 FR 55076).

32. *Federal Register* 56 (2 December 1991), Docket No. 301–86 (56 FR 61278); see also 57 FR 38912 and 61 FR 25000.

33. Krueger 1998.

34. *New York Times*, 9 June 1995, D3.

with Infiniti and Acura dealers) found themselves directly threatened. In response they generated a large lobbying and public relations effort. In the end a midnight deal with Japan averted sanctions.

To summarize, we argue that one of the primary political effects of legalizing the trade regime will be an interaction between increased precision about the distributional implications of trade agreements and the mobilization of domestic groups, both protectionist and free trade in orientation. In this section we have surveyed evidence on trade negotiations and the use of retaliatory tariffs during trade disputes to see if mobilization does indeed respond as we expect. From a number of perspectives, we find evidence to support our claims. During negotiations, lobbying activities are conditioned on the information available to particularistic interests. Strategic politicians, who are attempting to design the negotiating process so as to increase their ability to create mutually beneficial bundles of agreements, may find it helpful to have less than complete transparency about the details of negotiations. Antitrade group pressures make negotiations more difficult, and to the extent that transparency encourages mobilization of antitrade groups it will hinder liberalization negotiations.[35] During trade disputes, politicians similarly strategize about how to reveal information so as to mobilize groups appropriately—in this instance to maximize the mobilization of exporters in the target country.

Our findings should not be interpreted as a prediction of trade closure. Rather, we make the more modest claim that attention should be paid to an underexplored effect of international legalization, that is, the mobilization of domestic groups. The analysis of the interaction of legalization, information, and domestic groups is a requisite to understanding the conditions under which legalization of the trade regime will be successful.

Tightly Binding Trade Rules

In the preceding section we argued that legalization enriches the information environment. In this section we examine a second effect of legalization linked to an increase in the obligatory nature of international rules. Legalization at its core refers to *pacta sunt servanda,* or the presumption that, once signed, nations will adhere to treaty obligations. Interpretations of this responsibility are typically rendered by lawyers using a discourse focusing on rules—their exceptions and applicability—and not on interests. Given the expanding breadth of the trade regime, we suggest that the use of legal rule interpretation has made it increasingly difficult for governments to get around obligations by invoking escape clauses and safeguards or by turning to alternative measures, such as nontariff barriers. Partly, this is a result of the increased precision of rules and the inclusion of what were extralegal trade remedies, such as voluntary export restraints, in the regime itself. But the legalization of the trade regime has also moved the nexus of both rule making and adjudicating rule violations into the center of the regime and away from member states.

35. See, for example, the history of agricultural trade in Josling 1999.

The Logic of "Bindingness"

The benefits of increased precision and "bindingness" are identified in the functionalist literature on international institutions.[36] The benefit of international institutions lies primarily in the creation of disincentives for states to behave opportunistically by reneging on trade agreements and acting unilaterally. The problem of incentives to renege on cooperative arrangements, and the role of international institutions in helping states to overcome these incentives and so reach Pareto-superior outcomes, has been central to the institutional approach to international relations.[37] The key institutional argument is that attaining cooperative outcomes is hindered by the lack of information about the intentions and behavior of others and ambiguity about international obligations that states can manipulate to their advantage. States are often caught in a "prisoners' dilemma" and find it difficult to sustain the necessary enforcement strategies to assure cooperation in the uncertain environment of international politics. The primary function of international institutions, therefore, is to provide politically relevant information and so allow states to escape from the prisoners' dilemma trap.

This argument about international institutions took shape during an era when researchers were anxious to extend their analysis beyond formal international organizations to informal institutions and regimes.[38] By focusing on legalization, the current project returns to the study of formal institutions, but the underlying logic remains the same. Making international commitments precise and explicit makes it more difficult for states to evade them without paying a cost. More precise rules allow for more effective enforcement, and legalization involves a process of increasing precision. Greater precision and transparency about the obligations and behavior of states are also created by other dimensions of legalization. Delegation of monitoring and dispute-resolution functions to centralized organizational agents, away from member states, is intended to increase the quantity and quality of information about state behavior. It therefore leads to more effective enforcement and disincentives to renege on commitments.

As we have argued, legalization has unintended effects on the mobilization of support for and against trade liberalization. Similarly, legal binding has unexpected effects on domestic politics. If agreements are impossible to breach, either because of their level of obligation or because the transparency of rules increases the likelihood of enforcement, elected officials may find that the costs of signing such agreements outweigh the benefits. The downside of increased legalization in this instance lies in the inevitable uncertainties of economic interactions between states and in the need

36. We use the term *bindingness* where the term *obligation* would seem appropriate to a political scientist. The reason is that obligation has taken on a particular legal meaning, and that meaning has been adopted in this issue. By *bindingness* we mean the political obligation created by international rules. It is a positive rather than a normative term, meaning the degree to which rules are binding, practically speaking, on governments. Rules with higher probability of enforcement, for example, are more binding (or obligatory) in this political sense.

37. Keohane 1984.

38. Krasner 1983.

for flexibility to deal with such uncertainty without undermining the trade regime as a whole. Legalization as increased bindingness could therefore constrain leaders and undermine free-trade majorities at home.

George Downs and David Rocke consider a similar question and conclude that the dynamics of domestic politics create some optimal level of "imperfection" in the application of international rules.[39] They concentrate on the uncertainty that domestic groups, particularly producers, face when they are exposed to the vagaries of the international market. They assume, reasonably, that governments are not able to perfectly anticipate negative economic shocks and the organizational capacities of groups that may be made vulnerable by trade liberalization.

The existence of uncertainty about the costs of trade agreements on the domestic level suggests that fully legalized procedures that apply high, deterministic penalties for noncompliance could backfire, leading to an unraveling of the process of liberalization.[40] Under some conditions it will be inefficient for actors to live up to the letter of the law in their commitments to one another, such as when alternative arrangements exist that increase mutual gains.[41] These alternative arrangements generally involve temporary deviations from the rules with compensation offered to the other party. The problem is to write agreements that recognize the possibility of breach but limit it to the appropriate context, such as when economic shocks occur and all will be better off by temporarily allowing deviation from rules.

At the same time, of course, writing agreements that provide the necessary flexibility creates a moral-hazard problem. If the circumstances that demand temporary deviation are not perfectly observable to other actors, parties will be tempted to cheat. Cheating in this instance would consist of a demand to stretch the rules for a while, which all would benefit from, because of an unanticipated shock, when in fact the actor is simply attempting to get out of inconvenient commitments. Such opportunistic behavior is a constant concern in strategic settings with asymmetric information. In the context of the GATT/WTO, the primary reasons that flexibility is necessary lie in the uncertainties of domestic politics. Flexibility or "imperfection" can lead to stability and success of trade agreements, but incentives also exist for states to evade commitments even when economic conditions do not justify evasion.

The enforcement structures of the GATT/WTO thus face a difficult dilemma: to allow states to deviate from commitments when doing so would be efficient but to deter abuse of this flexibility. If enforcement is too harsh, states will comply with trade rules even in the face of high economic and political costs, and general support for liberalization is likely to decline. On the other hand, if enforcement is too lax, states will cheat, leading to a different dynamic that could similarly undermine the system. Downs and Rocke, drawing on game-theoretic models, suggest that imper-

39. Downs and Rocke 1995, chap. 4.

40. Contract law recognizes the same dynamic of uncertainty requiring flexibility in contracts, under the heading of efficient breach. See Roessler, Schwartz, and Sykes 1997, 7.

41. The idea is similar to that behind the Coase theorem: efficient agreements are reached through the mechanism of one party compensating another.

fection in the enforcement mechanism is the appropriate response. Punishment for infractions of GATT commitments should be probabilistic rather than deterministic.

Changes in WTO procedures have made penalties for rule violation more certain and less probabilistic. At this point, it is difficult to say whether negotiators went too far in limiting the availability of safeguards.[42] However, we can point out one unanticipated effect of the tightening of safeguards that both ties this analysis to our earlier discussion of trade negotiations and generates predictions about future attempts to further liberalize trade. There is a direct connection between states' access to safeguard provisions and their stance during trade negotiations. Domestic interests can anticipate the effects of eliminating safeguards and so will bring more pressure to bear on governments during negotiations.[43] Those who fear the possibility of adverse economic shocks without the protection of an escape clause will be highly resistant to inclusion in liberalization. In response they will demand exclusion or, at a minimum, side payments if their sector is included in liberalizing efforts. Thus extensive tightening of safeguard provisions will lead to tougher, more disaggregated negotiations as some groups lobby strenuously for exclusion. The rise in the use of voluntary export restraints and antidumping and countervailing duty cases is almost certainly a result of this difficulty in using safeguards. It is also likely that more bindingness has led to increases in the side payments governments are forced to make to groups in order to buy their support for trade agreements. Not surprisingly, perhaps, the North American Free Trade Agreement, a highly legalized trade agreement, could only gain approval in the United States after extensive use of side payments by the government.[44]

It is also important to ask whether GATT or WTO provisions effectively deter opportunistic evasion. Mechanisms that deter evasion include domestic costs of violations, enforcement provisions, and reputational concerns. These mechanisms are identical to those identified in standard theories of international institutions, suggesting that extensive international cooperation does not always require legalization. Legal theorists studying the GATT have been surprised to find that the level of compliance was high in spite of its reliance on weakly legalized procedures. Friederich Roessler, Warren F. Schwartz, and Alan Sykes see the overall reduction in tariffs under the GATT as evidence that its procedures did in general deter opportunistic evasion.[45] Sykes also finds that reputational mechanisms in the GATT substantially constrained the United States from acting opportunistically, as does Robert Hudec.[46]

Few analysts dispute that the old trade regime was tremendously effective in reducing impediments to trade. Nevertheless, analysts and legal scholars involved in the GATT expressed dissatisfaction about many of its procedures and capacities. One

42. As we argue later, the safeguard reforms are counterintuitive for two reasons. First, they may be too difficult to invoke, undercutting their purpose. Second, since retaliation is limited, the stability evoked by activating export groups may have been undermined.

43. See also Sykes 1991, 259.

44. Hufbauer and Schott 1993.

45. Roessler, Schwartz, and Sykes 1997, 13.

46. See Sykes 1992; and Hudec 1999.

concern was that the dispute-resolution procedures seemed to have a fatal flaw, in that member states could undermine the creation of dispute-resolution panels as well as any decision that went against them. Another concern was that powerful states, particularly the United States, evaded GATT regulations when convenient. As the United States increasingly turned to unilateral remedies for perceived trade infractions, such as Section 301, other members grew increasingly concerned that the GATT was powerless in preventing unilateralism and not strong enough to provide effective enforcement.

The remedy to these problems, both in theory and in practice, was greater legalization of the GATT. As the GATT evolved into the more formal WTO, the dispute-resolution procedures were made more legal in nature and the organization gained enhanced oversight and monitoring authority. Multilateral rules of trade extended into new and difficult areas, such as intellectual property, and substituted for unilateral practices. The procedures for retaliation and compensation were made more precise and limiting. The process of negotiating the content of rules—including provisions for addressing rule breaches—led to greater precision.[47] In the next sections we evaluate these changes, asking whether or not the changes portend greater trade liberalization. Our inquiry centers on two questions. First, we ask whether the legal framework allows states to abrogate a contract when doing so would be mutually beneficial. Second, we examine the functioning of the dispute-resolution mechanism.

In sum, theoretical consideration of the problem of complying with commitments in an uncertain economic and political environment provides another angle on the function and process of legalization in the WTO. Moving toward more certain, legalized procedures constitutes a balancing act. Appropriate procedures should deter opportunism while allowing states to deviate from commitments under some circumstances. Focusing only on the problem of opportunism, which would lead us to argue consistently in favor of more legalized procedures, misses the dilemma that the institution actually faces. Given uncertainty on the domestic level, moving too far in the direction of legalizing trade could undermine the momentum toward liberalizing trade that the weakly legalized procedures of the GATT so effectively established.

Exceptions and Escape Clauses

Trade legalization has constrained states by curtailing their ability to utilize safeguards and exceptions. The issue of exceptions, their status and use, has loomed large in many of the rounds of GATT negotiations. Pressure from import-competing groups is strong everywhere, although domestic institutional arrangements vary in how well they can "buy off" or ignore this resistance. The United States, for example, has been notorious for both retaining protection on the upper part of its schedule and for making particular industry side payments before even arriving in Geneva. The United States is also responsible for the inclusion of an escape clause into the GATT's

47. On the extent of changes in the WTO, see Krueger 1998.

original design, reflecting a desire by Congress to maintain its prerogative to renege on a trade deal if necessary.[48]

Legalization of the regime has resulted in a tightening in the use of safeguard provisions, including the escape clause. Under Article XIX, a country is allowed to increase protection for a home industry if a past tariff concession does damage to it.[49] If a country backs out of an agreement or imposes some additional trade restriction, it must be applied in a nondiscriminatory way; that is, countries whose exports are not hurting your industry cannot retain a preferential position.[50] When the provision is used, other countries are allowed to retaliate by reducing an equivalent amount of concession; otherwise the country imposing Article XIX must reduce tariffs on other products, equivalent to the amount of the original concession.

Two important domestic groups are potentially affected by these limitations on the use of safeguards. If nations retaliate, exporters suffer; if the government compensates, some import-competing industry will feel increased competition. Unless offered some side payment, industries have a strong incentive to have their political representative veto their inclusion into the compensatory package. Thus both the threat of retaliation and the difficulty of reassigning tariff reductions should constrain countries from raising trade barriers as allowed under Article XIX. The logic here is consistent with that offered in the preceding section.

The data on Article XIX provide support for the argument that using this provision is difficult in practice. Table 3 shows the aggregate use of the escape clause for all GATT members. Since the 1960s, Article XIX has been invoked at a relatively consistent rate. Given increasing levels of trade, stable numbers of Article XIX invocations imply *declining* use of this mechanism. As with the safeguard measures listed in Table 2, the small number of cases, compared with the significant number of industries affected by changing tariffs, should be attributed to the difficult time countries have both with the potential for retaliation and with compensating nations through alternative tariff reductions. This difficulty explains the trend toward alternative methods of protection, such as "administered protection" in the form of subsidies and antidumping and countervailing duty provisions.[51] Nontariff barriers, though not often used in the 1950s, were, by the 1970s, used by most countries to circumvent problems with GATT rules. Licenses, quotas, and voluntary export restraints were all means to finesse the potential problems *at home* with the GATT compensatory system.

48. Goldstein 1993.

49. "Tariff concessions and unforeseen developments must have caused an absolute or relative increase in imports which in turn causes or threatens serious injury to domestic producers . . . of like or directly competitive goods." Although the invoking party is not saddled with the burden of proving that it has met these requirements, the requirements nonetheless have deterred countries from invoking the escape clause.

50. This often leads to a situation where the producers causing the problems in the first place could remain in a competitive position with the higher-cost home producer. The producers who get penalized are the middle-price traders who were not the problem. Shonfield 1976, 224.

51. Baldwin 1998.

TABLE 3. *Use of escape clause by all GATT members, 1950–94*

	Average number of cases per year	*Nontariff barrier remedies as percentage of total uses*
1950s	1.9	26
1960s	3.5	56
1970s	4.7	70
1980s	3.7	51
1990s[a]	1.2	75

Source: GATT Analytical Index 1994.
[a]Data for the 1990s run only from 1990 to 1 December 1993.

Overall, the figures in Tables 2 and 3 suggest that use of the legally available mechanisms of flexibility in the trade regime is heavily circumscribed by the interaction of the legal provisions for their use and political realities. The increasing extent to which governments are bound by the lack of realistic escape clauses is apparent when we examine the use of compensation. Although the use of safeguards has been relatively constant, compensation or retaliation in response to the invocation of a safeguard provision was more common in the earlier years—ten cases from 1950 to 1959, ten cases from 1960 to 1969, six cases in the 1970s, and three cases in the 1980s.[52]

Use of compensation and retaliation was concentrated. The United States accounted for twelve of the twenty cases between 1950 and 1970 but only one case thereafter. Australia accounted for seven of the sixteen cases between 1960 and 1980. Although American use of Article XIX did not decline until the 1980s, the kind of remedy administrators chose to use did shift over time. Compensation could occur through reducing tariff barriers elsewhere. However, this would hurt other import-competing groups, so the compensation mechanism of Article XIX is unwieldy if these groups are organized. At the same time, rescinding tariff concessions without compensation opens exporters to the threat of retaliation. For these reasons, the United States had moved toward a nontariff barrier remedy by the late 1960s. The change was rather dramatic. In the early years of the regime, between 1950 and 1969, the United States compensated for a tariff hike over 93 percent of the time.[53] Thereafter, both the use of compensation and the number of invocations declined precipitously.

Overall, the evidence on the use of safeguards and compensation suggests that strict legal provisions were not necessary to maintain openness. The pattern of use of safeguard provisions in the GATT suggests that the regime gained in politically relevant bindingness, even when in legal terms the obligatory nature of rules did not change. Still, the WTO reforms attempted to clarify and make more stringent the

52. GATT *Analytical Index,* various issues.
53. The United States invoked Article XIX fourteen times between 1950 and 1969. Of these they used nontariff barriers alone in only one case.

requirements for using safeguards. Drawing on the discussion of economic uncertainty and the need for flexibility in light of the data, we suggest that increased stringency in safeguard use may be misplaced. In fact, even the GATT provisions could be interpreted to have become too tightly binding, not allowing the necessary temporary deviations from rules that contribute to long-term stability. Escape clauses, safeguards, and the like are the legal mechanisms for dealing with a world of economic uncertainty. The provisions for their use must be heavily constrained, so as to reduce the chance that states will invoke them opportunistically. However, it appears that these constraints, interacting with domestic politics, may bind states more tightly than intended.

Our cautionary note may explain why the WTO chose to forestall retaliation for three years in cases where a safeguard provision was sanctioned. Yet the choice of this tool to deal with overbinding may be a problem. Given the logic offered in the preceding section, we suggest that nations abide by their trade agreements because the threat of retaliation mobilizes export groups to counter rent-seeking producer groups. Similarly, our analysis suggests that the mobilization of groups favored those who support openness, which, in turn, deterred states from using even legal exceptions. Given the logic of domestic politics, it is hard to know whether the benefits of this new rule in terms of flexibility will outweigh its effects on the balance between pro- and antitrade groups in WTO members.

Dispute Settlement

One of the major innovations of the WTO was to strengthen the dispute-resolution mechanism. States have lost the ability to wield a veto, which they used under the GATT to protect themselves against GATT-approved retaliation. In effect, residual rights of control have been shifted from states to the WTO, convened as the Dispute Settlement Body. According to proponents of the new system, the existence of veto power encouraged opportunism, whereas not having veto power deters such behavior. If this is the case, we should see predictable effects in the pattern of disputes brought to the WTO.

We suggest that the GATT dispute-settlement structure, by being more attentive to the realities of power and an uncertain economic environment, but also by providing publicity and possible sanctions when states blatantly disregarded regime rules, may have optimized the trade-off between constraint and flexibility that liberalization requires. As a way to examine this hypothesis, we ask whether the pattern of disputes has changed under the WTO in the manner predicted by the logic of reducing opportunism. The strong theoretical argument in favor of legalization claims that legalization is necessary to prevent opportunistic behavior. If we find that the incidence of opportunism has not changed in the face of increasing legalization, the argument in favor of legalization loses much of its force.[54]

54. We assume a goal of reducing opportunism on theoretical grounds, without claiming that all negotiators had precisely this goal in mind. Certainly the agendas of negotiators were diverse, and reducing opportunism was only one goal among many.

If the primary effect of further legalization in dispute settlement is reducing opportunism, it should appear in the data as reduced political manipulation of the regime. Eliminating the power to veto should have observable effects on the activities of states and the outcome of disputes. Political scientists are producing a burgeoning literature on GATT/WTO dispute settlement, using sophisticated statistical techniques. However, this literature, regardless of the techniques involved, cannot escape problems of selection bias, since states chose whether to bring disputes and at what stage to resolve them. Here we suggest a few simple hypotheses about how the pattern of disputes should change with legalization if its major effect is a reduction in opportunism. If the data do not support these simple hypotheses, the case for legalization is substantially weakened.

Adopting the unitary state/opportunism model, we derive propositions about how legalization should influence patterns of disputes. Assuming the problem of opportunism suggests that the loss of veto power should have two primary effects: a *deterrent* effect and a *distributive* effect. States will behave strategically both in deciding when to bring disputes and whether to comply preemptively so that others have no cause to bring a dispute. This two-sided strategic behavior could render many predictions indeterminate. To identify refutable hypotheses, we focus on expected changes in the relative behavior of developed and developing states. Since both are subject to the same incentives in deciding whether to comply with changes in GATT/WTO rules, changes in the proportions of disputes brought are likely caused by changed calculations about the chances of success in a dispute and not by changed patterns of compliance. Although developing countries have more trade restrictions than developed countries, the marginal impact of new dispute-resolution procedures on compliance decisions should be the same for both. In addition, we concentrate on just the first few years of experience under the WTO rules. Since states can change their behavior in bringing disputes more quickly than they can change their basic trade regulations, the patterns we observe should be due primarily to calculations about whether bringing disputes is worthwhile, not fundamental changes in compliance.

A deterrent effect refers to the likelihood that the existence of veto power would deter states from bringing disputes. Bringing a formal dispute is costly and time consuming, and states could calculate that doing so is not worth the trouble if the powerful will simply veto any decision that goes against them. Thus we generate a deterrence hypothesis: *the existence of veto power deters some states from bringing disputes, and with the loss of veto power these states are no longer deterred.*

In order to collect data relevant to this general hypothesis, we need to derive some observable implications from it. We do so on the assumption that the intent of legalizing dispute-resolution procedures is to reduce opportunistic behavior by powerful states such as the United States.[55] One implication is that, since powerful states can no longer veto decisions that go against them, *we should expect the proportion of complaints against developed countries to rise under the WTO* (hypothesis 1). If states were deterred from bringing complaints against the powerful because of the

55. Jackson 1998.

existence of the veto, then such complaints should have a higher probability of success as a result of the loss of the veto. Therefore, we should see more disputes brought against the powerful. This should be true even if states are, for strategic reasons, complying more fully under the WTO. Better compliance should hold for both developed and developing states; there is no reason to expect the proportion of disputes against the powerful to change as a result of changes in compliance patterns.

Second, since less powerful countries may now have a greater chance of having decisions in their favor implemented, *we should see developing countries increasingly bringing complaints* (hypothesis 2). Simply put, the deterrence hypothesis suggests that under the WTO, weak states should no longer be deterred. Like hypothesis 1, hypothesis 2 should hold even if patterns of compliance have improved, since improved compliance should hold for both developed and developing states. There is no reason to expect strategic compliance behavior to lead to a change in the proportion of disputes brought by developing countries.

Finally, a process marred by opportunism should be most evident in relations between powerful and weak states. Thus a third implication of the deterrence hypothesis is that *we should see an increase in the proportion of cases brought by developing countries against developed countries* (hypothesis 3). As the WTO depoliticizes trade and so encourages the less powerful to demand their legal rights, we should see more of these "asymmetric" disputes.

The evidence on these three hypotheses about deterrent effects is mixed.[56] Regarding hypothesis 1, of the complaints raised under the GATT through 1989, 87 percent were brought against developed states.[57] Under the WTO, this percentage has dropped, contrary to the expectation from the opportunism perspective, to 64 percent. This is likely a result of the expansion of regime rules to cover more developing-country trade. The high percentage of complaints brought under the GATT against developed states is not surprising, considering the value of their market for other states. Yet it indicates that the power to veto did not allow powerful states to deter others from bringing complaints against them. This finding suggests that the GATT, in spite of the decentralized nature of its dispute-resolution process, was able to constrain the behavior of developed countries, as Hudec also concludes.[58] Preventing opportunism does not require high levels of legalization.

Hypothesis 2 posits that developing countries will be more likely to use the WTO procedures than they were to use the GATT mechanism. If this is true, we should see the percentage of complaints brought by developing countries rising under the WTO. This prediction holds up better than the first. Under the GATT (through 1989), only 19 percent of complaints were brought by developing countries.[59] This number has risen to 33 percent in the first few years that the WTO mechanisms have been in effect. However, considering the evidence just discussed on the identity of defen-

56. For a more thorough examination of patterns of disputes in the GATT and the WTO, see Hudec 1999; and Sevilla 1998.

57. Hudec 1993, 297.

58. Hudec 1999.

59. Hudec 1993, 296.

dants, it seems likely that this increased reliance on the dispute-resolution mechanism reflects some dynamic other than a decreased ability of the powerful to deter complaints against themselves. In particular, it seems likely that increased legalization has reduced the costs of bringing suits, thus making it more frequently worth the cost of bringing a complaint for poor states, regardless of the identity of the defendant.[60] In other words, legalization has encouraged weaker states to bring more complaints, generally because doing so is easier, not because the powerful will no longer veto them.

Hypothesis 3 predicts an increase in the number of complaints brought by developing countries against developed countries under the WTO. This hypothesis fares badly, because the data show that under the GATT developing countries targeted almost solely the rich world in their disputes. Hudec's data show almost no cases of developing countries bringing complaints against one another. The exceptions are disputes between India and Pakistan. In contrast, the twenty complaints brought by developing countries so far under the WTO have been just about evenly divided between targeting the developed and developing world. Two factors might explain this finding. First, the costs of bringing disputes are now lower, so it is more often worthwhile to bring them against developing countries. Second, the Uruguay Round extended many trade rules to developing countries, so the dispute-resolution procedures can be used against them for the first time. Regardless of the particular mechanism at work, the pattern of complaints shows that the major change under the WTO procedures has been an increased willingness of developing countries to bring complaints against one another. This effect is not consistent with reduced opportunism.

If legalization reduces opportunism as intended, a second effect that should result from eliminating the veto power is enhanced equity in the outcomes of disputes. We can formalize this as a fourth hypothesis: *legalization of dispute resolution has reduced the bias toward the powerful in the settlement of disputes* (hypothesis 4). A distributive effect could be estimated by comparing the outcomes of disputes brought under the GATT versus under the WTO. Unfortunately, since few cases have yet been resolved under the WTO, we can say nothing definitive on this issue. However, we can look at dispute outcomes under the GATT to see if they tended to favor developed countries as expected. If the weakly legalized GATT mechanisms encouraged opportunism, this trend should appear as a bias toward the powerful in the outcomes of disputes under the GATT. Eric Reinhardt has provided a careful statistical study of the factors determining the distributive outcomes of GATT disputes.[61] He tests the hypothesis that powerful states tend to get a larger share of the benefits of resolved disputes. Employing a number of alternative operationalizations, Reinhardt found no evidence that asymmetries of power work in favor of the powerful. Instead, he found a bias in favor of defendants, regardless of power asymmetries.

As with the data on the choice to bring complaints, in looking at the outcomes of disputes we find little evidence that the GATT operated in an overtly politicized

60. Sevilla 1998.
61. Reinhardt 1995.

manner, with powerful states using the GATT dispute-resolution procedures to deter weaker states from bringing complaints or to force outcomes of disputes to favor the powerful. The GATT, in spite of its weak level of legalization, provided many of the benefits we expect to see from international institutions. It discouraged opportunism without a resort to highly legalized mechanisms. This finding raises further questions about the benefits that states will be able to derive from further legalization.

Improving the compliance of powerful states with their explicit obligations under the rules of international trade was one of the primary motivations behind the enhanced dispute-resolution mechanisms of the WTO. Thus moving from a politicized process to a more legalized one should have an observable impact on the behavior of powerful states. However, the evidence is weak that the WTO has made the difference intended by proponents of more legalized dispute-resolution procedures. While developing countries appear more willing to lodge formal complaints than they were previously, the complaints do not target the behavior of powerful states any more than they did before. One plausible interpretation of the evidence on the number of complaints being brought is that the GATT was in fact quite influential in constraining powerful states, leading us to ask how much value will be added by increased legalization. Considering the drawbacks of increased legalization discussed earlier, the benefits must be clear in order to justify further moves in this direction. Dispute outcomes do not show evidence of coercion by powerful states, consistent with the idea that the political sensitivity of the GATT was not as much of an impediment to liberalization as legalization proponents presumed.

Conclusion

This article was motivated by questions about the relationship between international legalization and trade. The benefits of legalization lie in the fact that the more efficiently a regime provides information, reduces transaction costs, and monitors member behavior, the harder it is for a unitary state to behave opportunistically and renege on trade agreements. However, an analysis of the domestic requisites of free trade suggests potential negative effects of legalization that must be weighed against its benefits. When we consider cooperation with the trade regime to be a function of the interests of domestic political actors, the assumption that increased legalization leads to more trade openness becomes questionable. Although we cannot demonstrate that legalization has gone so far that it threatens liberalization, we do wish to sound a cautionary note based in the impact of legalization on the mobilization of protectionist groups.

We examined three theoretical issues implicated by the legalization of the trade regime. First, we asked how greater precision at the time of negotiating treaties changes the incentives of antitrade groups to mobilize. In that legalization leads to more and better information about the distributional effects of proposed agreements, we suggested that it could actually deter the conclusion of cooperative deals. Faced with certainty of loss, the expected utility of a group's organizing increases, suggesting that negotiators could find themselves confronted by powerful veto groups, undermining their ability to construct a majority in favor of a treaty. This dynamic of information provided by a legalized regime leading to massive mobilization may help explain the level of social activism at the 1999 WTO meetings in Seattle.

Second, we applied the same logic of information and mobilization to expectations about the maintenance of agreements already in force. The logic of information here predicted a different outcome from that during negotiations. By focusing on the incentives of exporters, we argued that when exporters know that they are likely targets of retaliation, they are more motivated to organize in support of the trade regime than those subject to an imprecise threat of retaliation. Thus the prediction about the effect of changes in the information environment varies, depending upon whether we are considering the expansion of trade liberalization or compliance with enacted treaties.

Finally, we looked at the effects of a system of highly deterministic penalties on domestic actors. Here we suggested that trade regimes need to incorporate some flexibility in their enforcement procedures; too little enforcement may encourage opportunism, but too much may backfire, undermining the ability of domestic actors to find support for an open trade policy. By decreasing the ability to breach agreements, WTO negotiators may have underestimated the inherently uncertain character of the international economy and so the need to allow practical flexibility in enforcement of regime rules.

These theoretical arguments suggest the need to carefully examine the trend toward increasing legalization, weighing both its benefits and its costs. Legalization can increase social resistance to new cooperative agreements by reducing the number and type of instruments available to politicians to deal with a rise in antitrade sentiment. In addition, with less ability to finesse international rules, leaders could find themselves forced to renege on trade agreements.

Given the short history of the WTO, the empirical support for our theoretical arguments is inconclusive. Still, evidence suggests that the effects of legalization may not be as glowing as proponents argue. First, legalization may be one reason for the increased attention and activity of antitrade groups. We cannot say whether this will deter nations from further liberalization, since policy will ultimately depend on the balance of national forces between pro- and antitrade groups. Still, it is clear that those groups who are targeted for liberalization in the new round of discussions have become active proponents of particularistic policies. Second, some evidence suggests that changes in WTO rules undermine the incentive for export groups to mobilize in defense of free trade. In that the WTO makes retaliation more difficult, both because of changes in the rules on safeguard provisions and because of the process of dispute resolution, we expect exporters to mobilize less often to balance the action of rent-seeking import-competing groups.

Consideration of the effect of the more precise and binding safeguard and dispute-settlement provisions also raises questions about the turn toward legalization. Given the difficulty of their use, few countries turned to GATT safeguards, choosing instead alternative methods to deal with difficulties in compliance. Making these safeguards more difficult to use may have been both unnecessary and counterproductive—if countries found it necessary to turn to alternative mechanisms to deal with the political effects of market dislocation before, the change in rules on safeguards does little to solve the underlying problem. Similarly, our investigation of the WTO dispute-settlement mechanism gives us little reason to think that legalization in the realm of settling disputes will have significant effects on trade compliance. The GATT system was relatively effective at deterring opportunism, in spite of its political nature.

The source of stability of trade agreements is found in domestic political mechanisms. The rules of the regime influence countries by making it easier or harder to find majority support for trade openness; if the regime supports rules that are unhelpful to politicians at home, it may well undercut its own purpose. Thus the legalization of international trade could turn on itself if analysis of the benefits of legalization neglects associated political costs. Thomas Franck has argued that the greater the "determinacy" of a rule, the more legitimate it becomes.[62] Determinacy, however, may be of greater value to lawyers than to politicians, whose interests in trade liberalization will be constrained by elections. Elected officials face a dilemma. If there is too little formalism in international trade rules, politicians will be unable to commit for fear of opportunism by others; too much formalism and they lose their ability to opt out of the regime temporarily during especially intense political opposition or tough economic times. Analyses of legalization that focus on maximizing state compliance neglect complex domestic political dynamics. It is well possible that attempts to maximize compliance through legalization will have the unintended effect of mobilizing domestic groups opposed to free trade, thus undermining hard-won patterns of cooperation and the expansion of trade.

62. Franck 1995.

[15]

Sovereignty and Inequality

Benedict Kingsbury*

Abstract

Inequality within and between societies has been a neglected issue in the contemporary theory of international law. The concept of sovereignty makes this neglect possible in traditional international law, as analysis of Oppenheim's 1905 textbook demonstrates. Globalization and democratization are placing state sovereignty under strain, as international rules and institutions appear to become more intrusive, transnational civil society more active, and unitary state control less pronounced. State sovereignty as a normative concept is increasingly challenged, especially by a functional view in which the state loses its normative priority and competes with supranational, private, and local actors in the optimal allocation of regulatory authority. But discarding sovereignty in favour of a functional approach will intensify inequality, weakening restraints on coercive intervention, diminishing critical roles of the state as a locus of identity and an autonomous zone of politics, and redividing the world into zones. The traditional normative concept of sovereignty is strained and flawed, but in the absence of better means to manage inequality it remains preferable to any of the alternatives on offer.

Inequality is one of the major subjects of modern social and political inquiry, but it has received minimal consideration as a theoretical topic in the recent literature of international law. While the reluctance formally to confront inequality has many causes, it has been made possible — and encouraged — by the centrality of sovereignty as a normative foundation of international law.[1] The discipline of international law has long encompassed some disparagement of sovereignty, even

* New York University Law School. This paper owes much to the thought and generosity of Andrew Hurrell. Many thanks are also due to Laurence Boisson de Chazournes, David Caron, Donald Horowitz, Theodor Meron, Liam Murphy, Ngaire Woods, and other friends for their helpful comments on earlier drafts. It will be included in A. Hurrell and N. Woods (eds), *Inequality, Globalization, and World Politics*.

1 The sovereignty of state governments is defined in what has been perhaps the most influential and certainly the most enduring English-language treatise of the 20th century, Oppenheim's *International Law*, vol. 1 (1905), at 101, as comprising independence, and authority in the form of supremacy over territory and supremacy over persons. As 'supreme authority, an authority which is independent of any other earthly authority. ... [it] includes, therefore, independence all round, within and without the borders of the country'. (*Ibid*, at 171.) 'As comprising the power of a State to exercise supreme authority over all persons and things within its territory, sovereignty is *territorial* supremacy. As comprising the power of a State to exercise supreme authority over its citizens at home and abroad, sovereignty is *personal* supremacy.' (*Ibid.*) Although Oppenheim does not take this approach, sovereignty may also be

while simultaneously embracing it. In recent years, however, proposals to abandon the normative concept of sovereignty have acquired new vitality, drawing on contemporary perceptions that the traditional concept of sovereignty might be outmoded in a new age of globalization and democratization. These proposals are sustained by what their proponents see as an emergent global public policy animated by commitments to markets, civil society, liberal peace, the rule of law, untrammelled communication, and transnationalism. This global public policy takes modest account of equality as a style of politics and as a procedural component of democracy and the rule of law, but it is not clearly committed to the substantive reduction of global inequality. The system of sovereignty has hitherto had the effect of fragmenting and diverting demands that international law better address inequality, but if sovereignty were to be displaced as a foundational normative concept for the structure of international law, an alternative means to manage inequality would become essential. No such alternative is presently on offer. This article argues that the lack of other means to cope with inequality is a serious problem for international law that has been wrongly neglected, but that the lack of such an alternative provides a strong reason to adhere to the existing concept of sovereignty, however much it may be strained by practice and problematized by theory.

The theory of sovereignty has relieved international lawyers from the need for a general theory of the legal management of inequality in three major ways.

First, the concept of sovereignty underpins a principle of sovereign equality that has attained almost an ontological position in the structure of the international legal system. This ontological status makes enough difference in the processes of international law and politics to modestly vindicate the significance and effectiveness of the system of sovereign equality: thus very small states are procedurally on an equal footing with the largest or most powerful states in the International Court of Justice, and groups of small states have made some difference in the dynamics of multilateral bargaining on issues such as climate change. In the same spirit, legal doctrines of the special status of great powers have been in the descendant since 1945, and such matters as the structure of the Non-Proliferation Treaty or the UN Security Council are dealt with by most legal writers as anomalies, however necessary or enduring, in the scheme of sovereign equality.[2] This conceptual scheme serves, if very unevenly, as a counter to the vast inequalities that might otherwise be expected to feature in the formal structure of the legal system.

Second, the concept of state sovereignty allows questions of social and economic inequality among people to be treated in international law as a responsibility of territorial states. International law and legal institutions are able to promote market activity, for example through the World Trade Organization or the International

understood by reference to capabilities attaching uniquely to the supreme authority. The modern bureaucratic welfarist state has in many polities been understood as having unique capabilities in the organization of public power, public services, 'official' status, etc., a capability of *organizational* supremacy. See, e.g., C. Rousseau, *Droit International Public*, vol. 3 (1977), at para. 106.

2 A point made *à propos* Hans Kelsen's *The Law of the United Nations* (1950) by Danilo Zolo, 'Hans Kelsen: International Peace through International Law', 9 *EJIL* (1998) 306, at 315.

Monetary Fund, while in theory leaving largely to states the responsibility of mitigating social and economic inequalities associated with markets. Episodic attempts to address economic and social inequality directly through substantial non-market changes in the international legal order have met with little success outside the established human rights and environmental programmes.[3] Despite economic and political turbulence associated in some respects with inequality, concerns about it have remained displaced by preoccupations with reducing the role of the state in economic activity and in major market-distorting egalitarian redistribution. International institutions continue to play important roles in economic development, and political leaders in prosperous countries confronted with concerns about poverty or dislocation or maldistribution abroad increasingly hope for solutions from the World Bank and other intergovernmental agencies along with bilateral assistance and the much-vaunted voluntary sector. There is however a growing incongruence between the increasing market orientation of international law and the inability of international governance institutions or of many sovereign states to cope with problems of inequality that markets alone do not resolve. Intra-societal inequality in some countries, and unevenness in the global distribution of human flourishing whether defined in terms of well-being, capabilities, wealth or a human development index, appear to have been intensifying rather than diminishing.[4]

Third, the theory of sovereignty provides the means by which people can express, and be deemed to have expressed, consent to the application of international legal norms and to international institutional competences. Consent, whether express or tacit, plays a crucial role in legitimating international legal rules and institutional activities in situations where their legitimacy might be in doubt, as where they infringe deeply-held egalitarian principles.[5] This legitimating function is of vast importance for the international legal system. It is not clear that in the present state of heterogeneous international society, any non-consensual legitimating principle is

3 This applies to state-oriented attempts to change the terms of the international economic order, efforts to recast international law in the spirit of post-1945 European social democracy, various pre-1990s projects to build an international law of development, and ongoing efforts to develop economic and social rights. For illustrative works see K. Hossain (ed.), *Legal Aspects of the New International Economic Order* (1980); R. St.J. Macdonald (ed.), *The International Law and Policy of Human Welfare* (1978); A. Carty (ed.), *Law and Development* (1992), and M. Craven, *The International Covenant on Economic, Social, and Cultural Rights: A Perspective on its Development* (1995).

4 For illustrative works from the vast literature on unmet problems of social and economic inequality, see, e.g., United Nations Development Programme, *Human Development Report* (annual); L. Taylor and U. Pieper, *Reconciling Economic Reform and Sustainable Human Development: Social Consequences of Neo-Liberalism* (1996); Li, Squire and Zou, 'Explaining International and Intertemporal Variations in Income Inequality', 108 *Economic Journal* (1998) 26; Sen, 'Mortality as an Indicator of Economic Success and Failure', 108 *Economic Journal* (1998) 1; Chua, 'The Privatization-Nationalization Cycle: The Link Between Markets and Ethnicity in Developing Countries', 95 *Columbia Law Review* (1995) 223; M. Nussbaum and A. Sen (eds), *The Quality of Life* (1993); A. Sen, *Inequality Reexamined* (1992).

5 A great deal of jurisprudential effort has been dedicated to finding other bases of legitimacy for international law. See, e.g., H. Kelsen, *Das Problem der Souveränität und die Theorie des Völkerrechts* (1920); and the use of the concept of international community in, e.g., A. Verdross and B. Simma, *Universelles Völkerrecht*, 3rd ed. (1984).

viable; and sovereignty appears to be a relatively low-cost means to organize 'consent'.

There is thus a relationship of mutual containment between sovereignty and inequality. The system of sovereignty at least notionally precludes some forms of inequality, while helping to exclude other forms of inequality from real consideration. Conversely, inequality limits sovereignty — for example, where hierarchies are established among different political and legal units that in the traditional conception of sovereignty (now increasingly problematic) mean the subordinate units lack sovereignty. Inequality also grounds critiques of sovereignty that weaken it as a normative concept — including critiques flowing from human rights, self-determination, feminist theory, and critical theory.

Part 1 of this article will examine the relations between sovereignty and inequality in the mainstream tradition of international law, focusing on the approach charted at the beginning of the 20th century by Lassa Oppenheim and others that has endured, in its fundamentals, until the present. Although sovereignty is central to the mainstream tradition of international law, it has always been viewed with ambivalence in that tradition.[6] For mainstream writers sovereignty is at once the architecture for the present and future international legal system, an obstacle to a deepening rule of law system, a legitimation of morally dubious state conduct or social practices, a bulwark against the iniquities of dominance by powerful external forces, and a basis for identity and democratic decision-making.[7]

Globalization, democratization, privatization and the increasing self-assurance of liberal agendas have animated a shift away from this traditional ambivalence toward an outright rejection of the normative elements of universal and equal sovereignty, threatening to destabilize the established function of sovereignty as a device to contain inequality. Part 2 will consider some of these challenges, assess the extent to which

[6] Oppenheim acknowledged that the term 'is used without any well-recognized meaning except that of supreme authority', and showed some sympathy with the notion that it might usefully be eliminated from the list of necessary characteristics of statehood, and from the science of politics altogether. Oppenheim, *supra* note 1, at 108. Among contemporary writers, Louis Henkin, for example, argues: 'Sovereignty, strictly, is the locus of ultimate legitimate authority in a political society, once the Prince or "the Crown", later parliament or the people. It is an internal concept and does not have, need not have, any implications for relations between one state and another. . . . For international relations, surely for international law, it is a term largely unnecessary and better avoided.' L. Henkin, *International Law: Politics and Values* (1995), at 9–10. See also H. Laski, *A Grammar of Politics* (4th ed., 1938), at 44–45.

[7] Sketching a similar argument, David Kennedy suggests that sovereignty has been associated by members of each generation positively with its aspirations and negatively with the excessive formalism of its predecessor. In his characterization, sovereignty in 19th century international jurisprudence enabled separation of public and private, law and morals. After World War I it represented the aspirational liberalism of universality, defining familiar standardized interchangeable units, providing a basis for a strong process-based but non-substantive legal order, from which were eventually teased substantive principles such as non-intervention. Sovereignty became not a unity but a bundle of rights, 'demystified, available to be parcelled out, rearranged by law, managed by lawyers, technocrats, social engineers'. 'Some Reflections on "The Role of Sovereignty in the New International Order"', in *State Sovereignty: The Challenge of a Changing World, Proceedings of the 1992 Conference of the Canadian Council of International Law* (1992) 237, at 241.

such challenges have already led to adaptations in the traditional sovereignty-based account of international law, and note some implications for the treatment of inequality. Part 3 will consider whether the mounting critiques of the traditional concept of sovereignty might soon lead to the replacement of the present normative international law view by a functional view, and if so what the consequences might be for the management of inequality. The conclusion will return to the principal argument of this article, namely that a radical change in the international law concept of sovereignty will be hazardous without concomitant development of adequate alternative means to manage inequality.

1 Management of Inequality in Traditional Sovereignty-based Accounts of International Law

A *Equality as an Incident of Sovereignty in Traditional International Legal Doctrine*

The system of sovereign equal states represents one of the defining ideas of 20th century international relations. On it have been built the modern mainstream projects for a working system of international law. These projects have been based on status: entities of the same status enjoy comparable and reciprocal entitlements. As Oppenheim put it:

> In entering the Family of Nations a State comes as an equal to equals; it demands a certain consideration to be paid to its dignity, the retention of its independence, of its territorial and its personal supremacy. ... The equality before International Law of all member-States of the family of nations is an invariable quality derived from their International Personality.[8]

By the time of the drafting of the UN Charter, the first principle to be embedded in its architecture was an axiom: 'The Organization is based on the principle of the sovereign equality of all its Members.'

While there was widespread support for sovereign equality as a foundational principle of the international legal system, there was no agreement on its theoretical basis,[9] and unease about it persisted in practice. Neither the Concert of Europe nor the Allied and Associated Powers at Versailles operated on the basis of equality among

[8] Oppenheim, *supra* note 1, at 160–161. Of course, 'Legal equality must not be confounded with political equality.' (*Ibid*, 162.)

[9] Vattel's anthropomorphization of inter-state law has been much criticized, e.g. by Carlos Escudé, *Foreign Policy Theory in Menem's Argentina* (1997), at 30–31, but Vattel's naturalistic approach, with its remarkable analogy between equality of individuals and equality of states, has remained influential; see e.g., P. H. Kooijmans, *The Doctrine of the Legal Equality of States* (1964). It persists in assertions that the exclusion of individuals from democratic participation in local and national government is the same injustice as exclusion of large third world states from permanent membership in the Security Council. For discussion see Pinto, 'Democratization of International Relations and its Implications for Development and Application of International Law', 5 *Asian Yearbook of International Law* (1995), 111. The positivist alternative, well represented by Oppenheim, sees equality as a logical corollary of sovereignty. A third

sovereign states, yet these groupings were decisive in the formulation of major legal elements of the public order of Europe. Several prominent international lawyers recognized and endorsed special rights and responsibilities of great powers,[10] and some saw such inequalities as grounds for rejecting the theory that sovereignty entailed equality.[11] In good positivist fashion, Oppenheim treated major inequalities, such as that between the Great Powers and other powers, as political but not legal.[12] But Oppenheim, unlike the vast majority of his successors among international lawyers, regarded the balance of power as a fundamental principle of international order, and took a distinctly realist view in accepting that the use of force could be justified to maintain the balance of power. He showed no sign of believing that the inegalitarian implications of a balance of power system ought to result in its subordination to the principle of sovereign equality.

The uncertainties as to the justifications for sovereign equality and the extent to which it negated differences in power are evident also in debates of the period concerning specific international legal doctrines. Recognized sovereign states were equal for such purposes as claiming diplomatic immunity and sovereign immunity and having their laws accepted in other states' courts, but non-recognition could be used to deny the premiss for such equality, as in the case of delayed recognition of the Bolshevik government after the formation of the USSR.[13] Equality was one of the principles weighed in arms control and disarmament projects in the period between the two World Wars, but it was departed from in specific treaties that were actually adopted, such as the Washington Naval Treaty. Special problems arose in the design of international institutions. After the deadlock in negotiations at the 1907 Hague Peace Conference for a new standing international court, which found no compromise between the insistence of less powerful states that equality meant every state must be permitted to appoint a judge and the insistence of the more powerful states that such a system was unwieldy and that only great powers could expect always to have judges of their nationalities appointed, international lawyers in the US and other powerful states sought to staunch the further extension of equal rights arguments,

explanation, reciprocity, is preferred by structural realists in international relations (for whom particular configurations of power among states will largely determine the patterns of inter-state interactions), as reciprocity potentially accounts for the otherwise puzzling acceptance by states of formal equality despite disparities of power.

10 For example, T. J. Lawrence, *Essays on Some Disputed Questions in Modern International Law* (2nd ed., 1885): 'It is not merely that the stronger states have influence proportionate to their strength; but that custom has given them what can hardly be distinguished from a legal right to settle certain questions as they please, the smaller states being obliged to acquiesce in their decisions.' The same view was maintained long after the 1907 Hague Conference: see, e.g., *Idem*, *The Society of Nations: Its Past, Present and Possible Future* (1919). Identifying what he believed was a fissure that must be crossed to build an international law for the future, James Brown Scott observed: 'The "Primacy of the Great Powers" was a fixed idea with Dr. Lawrence, just as the juridical equality of nations is an obsession of the present writer.' 'In Memoriam – Thomas Joseph Lawrence 1849–1920', 13 *AJIL* (1920) 223, at 225.

11 Baker, 'The Doctrine of Legal Equality of States', 4 *BYbIL* (1923–1924) 1.

12 Oppenheim, *supra* note 1, at 161-164.

13 *Luther v. Sagor* [1921] 3 KB 532 (English Court of Appeal); *Petrogradsky Mejdunarodny Kommerchesky Bank v. National City Bank*, 253 NY 23 (New York Court of Appeals, 1930).

which they saw as an obstruction to the progressive growth of effective international legal institutions.[14] In the design of new international organizations, sovereign equality was thought to mandate membership open to all states, equality in voting power, and unanimity rules in certain binding decisions and with respect to reservations to multilateral treaties, but each phase of institutional design in fact involved compromises between sovereign equality, great power primacy and institutional efficacy.[15]

B *Racial, Religious and Cultural Diversity: To Whom Does Sovereign Equality Apply?*

Confrontation with religious, cultural and racial difference was a perennial issue in the historical development of what became the Eurocentric international legal order. An earlier tendency in the European natural law tradition to discuss international law in universal terms and by reference to a *civitas gentium maxima*,[16] albeit with important distinctions tending to favour Europeans and Christians over others, was gradually from the 18th century displaced by a view of international law as the public law of the European heartland.[17] Europe was established as the original sphere of operation of international law. There was a geographic element to this, in that many of the problems regulated by international law, and much of the relevant practice and law-making activity, arose within or between European states. But the relevant practice and interactions came more and more to involve, especially during the 19th century, extra-European states and entities; many of these states and entities accepted and applied much the same set of legal standards, although others did not. This interaction contributed to a second development, the informal doctrinal promulgation of a membership test for international society, sometimes described as the 'standard of civilization'. Extra-European entities with the attributes of statehood were admitted to the Family of Nations as their degree of civilization and intercourse with the Family of Nations warranted. The test for membership was a creation of doctrine much more than of practice, and varied among publicists. Writing in 1905, Oppenheim had no hesitation in declaring that Christianity was not a requisite of a civilized state: civilization meant simply whatever was necessary 'to enable the respective State and its subjects to understand and to act in conformity with the principles of the Law of Nations'.[18] Acceptance of the system of sovereign states, and the convenience of the strongest powers, were two elements of the test for

14 This is a major preoccupation of E. D. Dickinson, *The Equality of States in International Law* (1920).

15 L. Duguit, *Traité de droit constitutionnel* (2nd ed., 1921); J. H. Ralston, *Democracy's International Law* (1922); F. P. Walters, *History of the League of Nations* (1961); D. H. Miller, *The Drafting of the Covenant* (1928).

16 E.g. F. Suarez, *Tractatus de Legibus ac Deo Legislatore* (1612); C. Wolff, *Jus Gentium Methodo Scientifica Pertractatum* (1764/1934).

17 J. J. Moser, *Grund-Säze des Europäischen Völcker-Rechts in Kriegs-Zeiten* (1752); G. F. von Martens, *Précis du Droit des Gens Moderne de l'Europe* (3rd ed., 1821); K. G. Günther, *Europäisches Völkerrecht in Friedenszeiten* (part 1, 1787).

18 Oppenheim, *supra* note 1, at 31.

606 EJIL 9 (1998), 599–625

membership. This view conditioned a reductionist schematic of the history of international law, of which Oppenheim's account is exemplary: the international law of the Family of Nations originated amongst the Christian states of Europe, was extended with the independence of the former European colonies of the Americas and the establishment of other Christian states such as Liberia and Haiti, was extended again with the admission in 1856 of the Ottoman Empire to the advantages of the public law and Concert of Europe, and again with the acceptance of Japan as a great power after 1895.[19] In Oppenheim's view in 1905, the full members of the Family of Nations were the independent European states (including Turkey and Russia), the independent states of North, Central and South America, plus Liberia, the Congo Free State, and Japan. Egypt was half-sovereign owing to Turkish suzerainty. Tunis was half-sovereign owing to the French protectorate. Morocco and Abyssinia were regarded by Oppenheim as 'full-Sovereign States', but as members of the Family of Nations only for some purposes (for example, diplomacy and treaty-making), but not for other purposes (such as restrictions on the conduct of war). Similarly Oppenheim viewed Persia, China, Korea, Siam and Tibet as members of the Family of Nations for some purposes, but not as international legal persons with the same position as 'Christian States'.[20]

The insistence on a European model of statehood and the organization of the state, and the articulation in parochial terms of a 'standard of civilization' which was itself applied in self-serving ways, were all conducive to the structuring and promotion of a great deal of inequality. There was, in Oppenheim's view, no equality for half-civilized and similar states, states under suzerainty and under protectorate, or member states of a federal state (depending on the case). In his opinion — although this view was contested at the time — the law of nations placed no restrictions on the treatment of states or entities that are wholly outside the Family of Nations; such treatment was a matter of discretion, and frequently was 'not only contrary to Christian morality, but arbitrary and barbarous'.[21] The Eurocentric system excluded from its purview entities

[19] For a comparable, if slightly more nuanced, scheme, see J. Westlake, *International Law: Part 1, Peace* (1904), at 44–48. The practice of interactions was so much more textured as to make every element of Oppenheim's schematic summary contestable. Useful studies include G. Gong, *The Standard of 'Civilization' in International Society* (1984); H. Bull and A. Watson (eds), *The Expansion of International Society* (1984); McKinnon Wood, 'The Treaty of Paris and Turkey's Status in International Law', 37 *AJIL* (1943) 262; Yongjin Zhang, *China in the International System*, 1918–1920 (1991).

[20] Oppenheim, *supra* note 1, at 154–157. In the case of non-Christian states such as China, Korea, Siam and Persia, and the Christian state of Abyssinia: 'Their civilisation is essentially so different from that of the Christian States that international intercourse with them of the same kind as between Christian States has been hitherto impossible. ... This condition of things will, however, not last very long. It may be expected that with the progress of civilisation these States will become sooner or later International Persons in the full sense of the term' (at 148 and 149). Lorimer in 1883 offered a similar list to that of Oppenheim, although he regarded Turkey and Japan as deserving of only partial political recognition. In the case of Turkey he accepted the good qualities of the peasantry, but was unconvinced about any possibilities for progress amongst the upper classes. In the case of the Japanese, if they 'continue their present rate of progress for another twenty years' they may well become entitled to plenary political recognition. J. Lorimer, *Institutes of the Law of Nations*, vol. 1 (1883), at 101–103.

[21] Oppenheim, *supra* note 1, at 34, see also 346–347.

that powerful recognized states were not willing to treat as 'states', whether because they wished to dominate or colonize these entities, or because these did not closely resemble 'states' as the category had come to be understood, or because they showed little acceptance of the organizing ideas of the system, or because they did not seem likely to uphold international legal obligations. While a weaker entity such as Abyssinia might be excluded on grounds of difference, arguments that Meiji Japan was still too different were eclipsed by Japan's military victories, especially the 1904–1905 Russo-Japanese war. While power and interests were central to this system, they do not represent the whole explanation for the perpetuation of inequalities. The rejection of Japan's proposal for a racial equality clause in the League of Nations Covenant was evidence not just of the limited strength of Asian and African states in the Versailles diplomacy, but also of a deeper cognitive or identity-based resistance to racial equality as a global principle.[22] This was connected not only with systematic racial discrimination in independent states, but also with colonial policy in territories where the maintenance of colonial rule had come increasingly to depend on the structuring of distinctions among ethnic groups.[23]

This membership standard and the Western dominance that made it possible had the further important effect of establishing a degree of structural homology among sovereign states. The Western model of the state became established globally as a structural equilibrium or a reference point. Once established, it came to dominate the normative and ontological landscape, and helped to delegitimize the possible alternatives. Non-European forms of political organization that might have attained widespread legitimacy as alternatives to the European-style sovereign state were subordinated and delegitimized as global models, a situation which for the time being remains unlikely to be reversed, however important such non-European forms are in contemporary politics. With its global ascendancy and homologizing tendency, the Western system of international law provided some basis for the development of minimum standards on such matters as treatment of foreigners and their property, the law of the sea, recognition of governments, and perhaps even religious tolerance. Whatever its limitations and inequalities, this modest structure of international order was the foundation upon which attempts to regulate state conduct and establish legal responsibility have thereafter built.

The gatekeeping doctrines of recognition of states and membership in the Family of Nations allowed some consideration of regime type, but as between recognized member states the modest scheme described by Oppenheim in 1905 did not draw legal distinctions on the basis of regime type. The division of the world into functionally and juridically similar territorial units implied that, provided the entity was treated internationally as a state, its domestic structure and regime type did not matter.[24] This

22 Vincent, 'Racial Equality', in H. Bull and A. Watson (eds), *The Expansion of International Society* (1984), at 239.

23 See, e.g., B. Anderson, *Imagined Communities* (2nd ed., 1991).

24 For criticism, see Burley, 'Law Among Liberal States: Liberal Internationalism and the Act of State Doctrine', 92 *Columbia Law Review* (1992) 1907, at 1923–1926.

608 EJIL 9 (1998), 599–625

remained an orthodox view for most of the century, as the International Court of Justice made clear in 1986 in *Nicaragua v. USA*.[25]

Nevertheless, the characterization of the system of sovereign equality embodied in the writings of legal positivists such as Oppenheim as a 'billiard ball' approach is excessively stark. States were expected to be able to keep order, particularly to meet international obligations to foreigners. As international economic law and labour law began to develop, internal decisions of states began to be subject to external standards, as with the attempt in the early 1900s to achieve a level playing field through uniform restrictions on use of phosphorus in workplaces. There were proposals to apply viability criteria to states, although the practical application of these was limited. Oppenheim acknowledged the strength of the principle of nationality and the desirability of treating minorities within states on a basis of equality. Although the two pre-World War I editions did not contain it, the shattering effects of that conflict prompted the addition to Oppenheim's list of morals derivable from the history of international law of the proposition:

> that the progress of International Law is intimately connected with the victory everywhere of constitutional government over autocratic government, or, what is the same thing, of democracy over autocracy. Autocratic government, not being responsible to the nation it dominates, has a tendency to base the external policy of the State, just as much as its internal policy, on brute force and intrigue; whereas constitutional government cannot help basing both its external and its internal policy ultimately on the consent of the governed. And although it is not at all to be taken for granted that democracy will always and everywhere stand for international right and justice, so much is certain, that it excludes a policy of personal aggrandizement and insatiable territorial expansion, which in the past has been the cause of many wars.[26]

Judicial decisions and arbitral awards of the period also suggested awareness of the importance in international relations of the links between sovereignty and domestic structures. The arbitral tribunal in the *North Atlantic Coast Fisheries Arbitration* (1910) rejected the implication of a servitude for the USA in the territorial waters of Canada, finding that the creation of such sovereign rights for the United States would involve dividing the sovereignty over the waters. The Tribunal acknowledged that this did occur among entities with 'quasi-sovereignty', as in the Holy Roman Empire, but opined that modern states, particularly Britain, had never accepted such partitions of sovereignty, 'owing to the Constitution of a modern State requiring essential sovereignty and independence.'[27] The doctrine of international servitudes was 'little suited to the principle of sovereignty which prevails in States under a system of constitutional government such as Great Britain and the United States and to the present international relations of sovereign States.'[28] The equivocation in this statement was matched in wider political discourse. Where Woodrow Wilson sought

25 'Military and Paramilitary Activities' (*Nicaragua v. USA*) ICJ Reports (1986) 14.

26 *Oppenheim's International Law*, 4th ed., vol. 1 (A. McNair (ed.), 1928), at 100–101.

27 *Proceedings in the North Atlantic Coast Fisheries Arbitration before the Permanent Court of Arbitration at the Hague*, vol. 1 (1912), at 76.

28 *Ibid.*

to promote constitutional democracy as a general principle, E. H. Carr attacked the Wilsonian predilection for making American principles the principles of mankind, and Americans into the bearers of a higher ethic.[29]

Practice was often more nuanced than broad doctrinal assertions suggest, but it is nonetheless evident that treatment of issues of equality and inequality in the traditional conceptual structure of international law based on sovereign equality was grossly inadequate as a basis for accommodating the developments of this century; major difficulties have resulted from the simultaneous commitments to Oppenheim's basic structure and to making adequate provision for new realities.[30] Numerous devices have been honed to reconcile the system of sovereign equality and unit homogeneity with challenges posed by the facts of inequality and difference.

C *Strategies for Reconciling the Sovereign Equality System with Existing Inequalities*

Oppenheim, like many of his leading successors, was an accomplished exponent of devices to reconcile the idea of obligatory international law with the positivist conception of a legal system founded on state sovereignty, including the binding/non-binding dichotomy; the analytical separation of law and politics; and some focus on the then limited sphere of international legal process. These strategies were employed, for example, to enable adherence to the fundamental legal value of formal isonomy while limiting the range of inequalities with which the international legal system concerns itself. Thus Oppenheim, like other legal positivists, separates law from non-law so that the inequalities become social rather than legal facts. Many positivist writers emphasize consent (an analogue to the move from status to contract) as explanation for such phenomena as protectorates, oppressive rules and voting inequalities. Categories used for distinction or discrimination are defined by neutral-sounding criteria which are less likely to attract strict scrutiny; for instance, 'specially affected states' are deemed to be a relevant category in weighing competing practice to determine the existence or otherwise of a rule of customary international law,[31] but this category operates mainly (but, prudently, not exclusively) for the benefit of powerful states. The theoretical problem arising from the fact that many smaller states may not show any support (in the sense of practice) for a rule is addressed by the move from consent to consensus; this enables fixing responsibilities on states that have not

[29] *The Twenty Years' Crisis* (2nd ed., 1946), at 167.

[30] Thoughtful reviews of the evolution of international law and the tensions within it, stimulated by the publication in 1992 of the 9th edition of Oppenheim's volume on the law of peace, include Reisman, 'Lassa Oppenheim's Nine Lives', 19 *Yale Journal of International Law* (1993) 255; Grieg, 'Oppenheim Revisited: An Australian Perspective', 14 *Australian Year Book of International Law* (1993) 227; and Janis, 'The New *Oppenheim* and its Theory of International Law', 16 *Oxford Journal of Legal Studies* (1996) 329.

[31] This approach is defended in Westlake, *supra* note 19, at 16–17. It is adopted by the ICJ in the *North Sea Continental Shelf cases (Denmark v. Germany, Germany v. Netherlands)*, ICJ Reports (1969) 3.

610 EJIL 9 (1998), 599–625

in fact accepted them, and is supported by the persistent objector rule which in practice is mainly a negotiating card (or possible outlet) for the powerful.[32]

Apparent inequalities among peoples in achieving independence and statehood were addressed by separating equality of states from equality of peoples, and managing some of the more pressing demands through the principle of nationalities, the principle of self-determination, and minority rights, all formulated as universal principles but applied only selectively in practice.

Progress toward equality has been continuously anticipated in international law: in Wilsonian or Leninist versions of self-determination, in the terms of the Class A Mandates of the League of Nations, in the provisions for trusteeship and decolonization under the UN Charter, in the hopes for general and complete disarmament in UN documents. Shortcomings in the attainment of equality are explained by the relative infancy and temporary weakness of international law.[33] Enduring inequalities among equal sovereigns, such as the structural inequalities in the United Nations Charter, the Nuclear Non-Proliferation Treaty, or the voting arrangements of the International Monetary Fund, are characterized either as special functional exceptions or as temporary accommodations to the realities of power. There are debates as to how equality is most fairly expressed in representative arrangements, such as proposals for the most populous states from particular regions to become permanent members of the Security Council, but accounts of international law that would base it upon the management of inequality, for example through the principle of balance of power recognized by Oppenheim, have virtually disappeared from the literature of international law, although they are more evident in its practice.[34]

2 Challenges to the Traditional International Law System of Sovereignty and Equality

The 'traditional' account of international law as law between states uses the notion of state sovereignty as a somewhat artificial organizing device to simplify the complex world in order to manage it. 'States' represent the carving of the world into non-overlapping territorial units, now virtually exhaustive of the earth's land area, vested with the authority to regulate in their territories, the responsibility not to harm certain interests of others, and the capacity to make claims when they or their nationals are affected by illegality for which other states or international organizations are responsible. A reasonably comprehensive if decentralized effort is made to connect every individual, corporation, vessel and aircraft with at least one territorial

[32] Charney, 'The Persistent Objector Rule and the Development of Customary International Law', 56 *BYbIL* (1985) 1; Stein, 'The Approach of the Different Drummer: The Principle of the Persistent Objector in International Law', 26 *Harvard International Law Journal* (1985) 457.

[33] Cf. E. H. Carr's argument at the beginning of *The Twenty Years' Crisis* that international politics is still in its infancy — a position which indicates Carr's distance from political realists for whom basic political insights are almost timeless.

[34] Cf., however, G. Ladreit de Lacharrière, *La Politique Juridique Extérieure* (1983). For a thoughtful response see Pellet, 'Le sage, le prince et le savant', 112 *Journal de droit international* (1985) 407.

state for these purposes. Even as it was becoming entrenched in the international law framework of the world, this organizing account of the legal system among sovereign states was confronted with numerous glaring problems. Refutations of, or uncertainty about, the suitability of the 'traditional' international law concept of state sovereignty have been a feature of the international legal literature throughout the 20th century,[35] but the recent perception of a globalizing, democratizing world, no longer dominated by the politics of bipolar confrontation between nuclear alliances, has provided empirical sustenance to normative arguments against excesses of the sovereignty system that have gained ground in the West. This part will briefly consider some possible implications of contemporary phenomena for sovereignty and for alternatives to the sovereignty system.

Globalization and Changes in International Rule-making. The depth and density of rules promulgated by intergovernmental organizations is increasing, and these organizations are becoming more assertive *vis-à-vis* individual sovereign states in rule-making and in implementation. Inequality between member states has become relatively common in intergovernmental organizations: requirements of unanimity in voting, conferring a veto on all, are now rare, despite the frequent use of consensus; systems designed to reflect major interests through weighted voting or specially defined functional majorities have become more common; and a few organizations are able to make intrusive demands on member states. State dominance in rule-making organizations is slowly accommodating increased roles of non-state groups, for example private standard-setting bodies in the International Standards Organization, indigenous peoples' organizations in the Arctic Council, and the influence of industry in the operation of the Montreal Protocol stratospheric ozone regime.

The amorphous congeries of phenomena loosely denominated economic 'globalization' suggest that transnational industries and markets increasingly require forms of transnational regulation or regulatory cooperation that differ from the methods and institutions of traditional inter-state law-making. In some sectors national laws are converging around standards established in the dominant states. In others important operational norms are shaped by non-governmental groups or by market practitioners, on such matters as forest management practices, labour standards for shoe and apparel exporters, accounting standards, marine insurance terms, and interpretation of international commercial contracts. Forms of 'world law' may be emerging — whether through mimesis, or world culture, or regulatory competition — from which most states are not free to depart except at intolerable cost.[36] These emerging features of rule-making are being replicated, more slowly, in evolving systems of implementation and enforcement. National courts, administrative agencies, and perhaps even legislatures are said increasingly to function not

[35] See, e.g., Korowicz, 'Modern Doctrines of the Sovereignty of States — II', 5 *Nederlands Tijdschrift voor Internationaal Recht* (1958) 150, dividing publicists into three camps: those for whom sovereignty is 'a foundation of the whole system' of international law; those who emphasize 'the necessity of increasing limitations of State sovereignty for the benefit of the international community'; and those 'who do not consider sovereignty to be a basic criterion of the State as subject of international law'.

[36] See, e.g., G. Teubner (ed.), *Global Law without a State* (1997).

612 EJIL 9 (1998), 599–625

simply as parochial national institutions but as parts of cooperative regulatory and enforcement webs, to interact in transgovernmental networks 'with one another and with supranational tribunals in ways that would accommodate differences but acknowledge and reinforce common values.'[37] Proposals for private schemes of implementation are appearing in diverse areas, from tradable CO_2 emission permits to private contracting for enforcement of intellectual property rules.

There is some evidence of convergence of substantive legal rules across various groups of states, and of increasing cross-recognition by states of each other's national laws and institutional acts. To this body of convergent state norms must be added the norms established and applied by non-state actors *inter se*, whether with or without any state involvement — standard terms in particular industries, the UNCITRAL rules, normative practices of lawyers and other professionals in structuring capital market transactions, and the international arrangements of credit card agencies and global franchises. While these might be regarded as informal social norms, they are effective in shaping behaviour, and often constrain the regulatory possibilities effectively open to states and inter-state institutions.[38] In contemporary practice such transnational normative phenomena are important and must not be ignored simply because the sources-based conceptual apparatus of international law struggles to deal with them.[39] It is not realistic or adequate in all cases simply to reformulate such private norms on the basis of some consent or delegation by sovereign will. The net effect of such changes in the making and implementation of norms has been to shift decision-making to powerful states and non-state groups, widening the gulf between law-makers and law-takers.

Transnational Civil Society. For many proponents of the emergence of a transnational civil society, states should be seen simply as important loci of power and authority within a transnational civil society which permeates through their borders.[40] That society finds voice and political expression through states but not only through states — the interests of individuals and groups are also expressed in many other ways, and proposals abound for institutional reform to enhance such representation.[41] International law can be seen as the law of such a transnational society, regulating states but not dependent entirely on states for its existence, content, or implementation. In more ambitious versions of this theory, state sovereignty is in some respects constituted by the law of the transnational civil society, escaping the tendency within the traditional framework for international law to take sovereignty as a pre-legal social fact. Inequalities in access, participation, power and

[37] Slaughter, 'The Real New World Order', 76 *Foreign Affairs* (1997) 189.

[38] See, e.g., A. Verdross, *Völkerrecht* (5th ed., 1964); *Idem*, 'On the Concept of International Law', 43 *AJIL* (1949) 453; P. C. Jessup, *Transnational Law* (1956); Koh, 'Transnational Legal Process', 75 *Nebraska Law Review* (1996) 181.

[39] Slaughter, 'International Law in a World of Liberal States', 6 *EJIL* (1995) 503.

[40] Falk, 'The World Order between Inter-State Law and the Law of Humanity: The Role of Civil Society Institutions', in D. Archibugi and D. Held (eds), *Cosmopolitan Democracy* (1995) 163.

[41] See, e.g., T. Franck, *Fairness in International Law* (1995), on the addition of a popular assembly in the United Nations.

accountability within this emerging transnational civil society have scarcely been confronted in international law, in part because of liberal commitments to the marketplace of ideas and suspicion of attempts to regulate information.

Democratization. Democratization potentially reinforces sovereignty: democracy legitimizes state institutions, and these institutions rather than international or transnational bodies are the principal organized expression of the popular will or interests whose vindication is sought by democratic theory. Nevertheless, it is sometimes argued that the realization of true democracy in complex polities may have the consequence that the unified sovereignty of states itself disappears, undermining the assumption that unitary sovereign states are the foundation for the international legal system. Authority and power are still identifiable, but the argument is that the concentration of these in any particular location has been so thoroughly checked, balanced and dispersed that there is no traditional 'sovereignty'. The critiques of unity and centralization directed at the sovereignty model by feminist theorists, radical ecologists, advocates of democratic decentralization, and institutional cosmopolitanists all favour wide vertical dispersion of sovereignty as a means to achieve such ethical goals as peace and security, reduced oppression, global economic justice, and participation.[42] Systems of divided or dispersed sovereignty provide one possible approach to the representation problems that are central to liberal political theory. Movements toward greater power for local communities, land and government rights for indigenous peoples, autonomy for various ethnic or territorial groups, fragmentation of authority to promote identity and difference, and legal recognition of civil society organizations, all promote more pluralistic governance arrangements. Thus far, however, such arguments have been met by responses of the sort formulated by Hans Morgenthau:

> Democratic constitutions, especially those consisting of a system of checks and balances, have purposely obscured the problem of sovereignty and glossed over the need for a definite location of the sovereign power. . . . In their endeavor to make democracy 'a government of laws and not of men' they forgot that in any state, democratic or otherwise, there must be a man or group of men ultimately responsible for the exercise of political authority ... in a democracy that responsibility lies dormant in normal times. ... Yet in times of crisis and war that ultimate responsibility asserts itself, as it did under the presidencies of Lincoln, Wilson, and the two Roosevelts, and leaves to constitutional theories the arduous task of arguing it away after the event.[43]

But the reality is that crises of authority in which the pinpoint location of concentrated sovereignty must be established are sufficiently infrequent that more diffuse models are beginning to acquire some legitimacy, especially in the prosperous

[42] On the moral cosmopolitanist idea that every human being has a global stature as an ultimate unit of moral concern, see, e.g., Pogge, 'Cosmopolitanism and Sovereignty', 103 *Ethics* (1992) 48, at 49. See also T. W. Pogge, *Realizing Rawls* (1989); and C. Beitz, *Political Theory and International Relations* (1979). Pogge proposes division of sovereignty, not the creation of numerous autarkic sovereign units or Rousseau's advocacy of return to the city-state. For a more legally-oriented cosmopolitanist perspective, see Tesón, 'The Kantian Theory of International Law', 92 *Columbia Law Review* (1992) 53.

[43] Morgenthau, *Politics among Nations* (2nd ed., 1958), at 305–306.

democracies. The European Union provides the most influential archetype. Nonetheless, the state has proved remarkably enduring as a locus of authority.[44] This is true even in the European Union, the most far-reaching institutional project for divided sovereignty and multiple levels of governance. While there is clearly a possibility of the European Union evolving in ways that displace the sovereignty model of the place of the state and do not simply substitute the EU as a new sovereign,[45] states have so far managed the institutional architecture to preserve major roles for themselves in taking the crucial decisions on governance forms, and the kinds of roles played by states in international relations are still played within the EU.[46]

The cumulative pressure on the traditional international legal doctrine of sovereignty arising from these empirical and conceptual changes is considerable. Some incidents of state sovereignty — the attributes of membership in the international legal order, such as the capacities to make treaties, join the United Nations, and claim sovereign immunity in other states' courts for certain governmental acts — are deeply embedded as constitutive rules of the game in the international law system.[47] This set of arrangements, established partly on the basis of mutual interest and reciprocity, has become a structural equilibrium.[48] Each actor has incentives to be part of this membership system, both for reasons of efficacy in the conduct of international affairs and because of benefits conferred on leaders in internal politics by international recognition. No significant powerful actors have an incentive to defect from the system. It is self-enforcing, self-perpetuating, and reinforced to some degree by cognitive entrenchment. It is likely to change only

44 Applying this insight, Stephen Krasner astutely noted in 1988: 'The Soviet effort to base relations in Eastern Europe on transnational functional agencies rather than state-to-state agreements has eroded over time, despite the continued material domination of the Soviet Union.' 'Sovereignty: An Institutional Perspective', 21 *Comparative Political Studies* (1988) 66, at 89–90.

45 See, e.g., Weiler, 'The Transformation of Europe', 100 *Yale Law Journal* (1991) 2403.

46 See, e.g., A. Milward, *The European Rescue of the Nation-State* (1992); and Moravcsik, 'Preferences and Power in the European Community: A Liberal Intergovernmentalist Approach', 31 *Journal of Common Market Studies* (1993) 473. This point is emphasized in the 1993 decision of the German *Bundesverfassungsgericht* (Federal Constitutional Court) on the compatibility of the Maastricht Treaty with the German Basic Law, 33 ILM (1994) 388, 424–425. The Court held that even after the Maastricht Treaty, the FRG remains a member of an intergovernmental community, the authority of which is derived from the Member States and has binding effect in German sovereign territory only if a German order governing application of law is issued. Germany may terminate membership in the European Union by passage of an appropriate act. Germany thus maintains its status as a sovereign state in its own right as well as the sovereign equality with other states referred to in Article 2 of the UN Charter. Some subsequent German actions, including actions of German courts in the controversy concerning the EU bananas regime, substantiate the impact of this view.

47 For fuller discussion see Kingsbury, 'Judicial Determination of Foreign "Government" Status', *Law Quarterly Review* 109 (1993) 377. A sovereignty of membership is emphasized in A. Chayes and A. H. Chayes, *The New Sovereignty: Compliance with International Regulatory Agreements* (1995).

48 The issues treated here are acutely analysed by Stephen Krasner in a series of articles: 'Sovereignty: An Institutional Perspective', *supra* note 44; *Idem*, 'Westphalia and All That', in J. Goldstein and R. Keohane (eds), *Ideas and Foreign Policy* (1993), at 235; *Idem*, 'Compromising Westphalia', 20 *International Security* (1995–1996) 115; *Idem*, 'Power Politics, Institutions, and Transnational Relations', in T. Risse-Kappen (ed.), *Bringing Transnational Relations Back In: Non-State Actors, Domestic Structures and International Institutions* (1995), at 257; and in a forthcoming book on sovereignty.

incrementally unless it becomes grossly inefficient to its purposes, or suffers a crisis of legitimacy.

The position is more complex, however, in the case of other incidents of sovereignty in international law. *Independence*, in the sense of the freedom to make choices as to economic, political and social systems, domestic policy, and foreign policy, is routinely infringed. Where such infringement is non-forcible, the rules of general international law do not provide very comprehensive protection for independence, and not all of the rules bearing on this topic are upheld even by strong social pressure. Thus the prohibition of the use of force does not encompass economic coercion,[49] and economic coercion simpliciter in the conclusion of a treaty is not a ground for its nullity.[50] *Territorial supremacy* is more fully protected by international law rules, including most fundamentally the prohibition of the acquisition of territory by conquest, and the clear rules against overflight and incursions by foreign law enforcement officials. Even here, however, there are exceptions, including for example the stationing of UN guards in Northern Iraq, US air patrols over Iraq, the UN sanctions against Libya tied to the surrender of the Lockerbie bombing suspects,[51] and the relatively weak rules on remote sensing and on extraterritorial jurisdiction based on the effects doctrine. *Personal supremacy* of the state over its nationals has been eroded by human rights law, increasing acceptance of dual nationality with rights of one state of nationality against the other,[52] and increased availability to individuals and corporate bodies of a variety of national courts and international tribunals in which the action of a particular state may be challenged.[53] *Organizational sovereignty* is protected by doctrines limiting jurisdiction of other states and by the principle of non-intervention, but the burgeoning range of inter-state, mixed and private entities engaged in norm formation and governance is not closely controlled by international law; some European states found it necessary to amend constitutional monopolies on legislative power to accommodate the increasing legislative capacity of the European Community.

In sum, pressures on the traditional sovereignty-based system of international law have resulted in the weakening of the domestic/international split, percolation of

49 See also *Nicaragua v. USA* (1986) *supra* note 25, where the ICJ showed little disposition to rule against the US under general international law on the abrupt and coercive denial of sugar import quotas to Nicaragua. On non-forcible counter-measures see L. Boisson de Chazournes, *Les contre-mesures dans les relations internationales économiques* (1992).

50 The formulation in Article 52 of the 1969 Vienna Convention on the Law of Treaties provides that a treaty is void where the agreement was secured by the threat or use of force, but a proposal by a group of developing states to define force so as to include economic or political pressure was rejected. This represented, at the time, a diplomatic and legal victory for a group of Western states. For the perspective of US negotiators see Kearney and Dalton, 'The Treaty on Treaties', 64 *AJIL* (1970) 495, at 532–535.

51 For criticism of various actions of the UN Security Council on grounds of conflict with clear or contested international law principles, see Brownlie, 'International Law in the Context of a Changing World Order', in N. Jasentuliyana (ed.), *Perspectives on International Law* (1995), at 49.

52 See Franck, 'Clan and Superclan: Loyalty, Identity and Community in Law and Practice', 90 *AJIL* (1996) 359, at 376–382; and the jurisprudence of the Iran–US Claims Tribunal on claims by dual nationals.

53 Slaughter, *supra* note 39; Koh, *supra* note 38; *Idem*, 'Transnational Public Law Litigation', 100 *Yale Law Journal* (1991) 2347; L. Brilmayer, *Justifying International Acts* (1989).

commitments to formal isonomy and to some principles of substantive equality from domestic law and politics to international law, promotion internationally of forms of market equality and extra-market inequality associated with economic liberalism, gradual acceptance of international obligations toward non-state groups, the forced enlargement of the minimalist involvement of international law in human rights and in the structure of internal polities, and the clouding of the concept of international law as a pure state-privileging inter-state system. These adaptations in doctrine reflect the practical and normative inadequacies of the traditional conception of international law as the law among sovereign states that have long been recognized in international legal scholarship, but over the past century these adaptations have been accommodated by manipulation of the traditional framework rather than by construction of a widely endorsed alternative. The traditional system of sovereignty is under strain, but for the time being is continuing to creak along.[54]

3 Implications for Inequality of Discarding Traditional International Law Sovereignty

The continuing rapid changes often described as 'globalization' and 'democratization', and the new possibilities and uncertainties opened by the lifting of Cold War rigidities, have spurred intensified criticism of the traditional system of sovereign equality, and the construction of incipient alternatives.

It is all too evident that the high 20th century commitment to virtually universal formal equality of states in the sovereignty model has not resolved many of the underlying problems. In terms of their capacity to manage issues of national economic and social policy, their political ability to represent and regulate, their provision of a rule of law system and guarantees of property rights and basic civil rights, many putative states have only the trappings but not most of the effective functions of states. The activities of some state institutions appear to make human flourishing and economic activity more rather than less difficult. In some cases, they have neither monopolized the use of force nor achieved the maintenance of basic order; in other cases, there is order, but it is not provided by the institutions of the state. All of this leads to the argument that the traditional sovereignty-based system of international law has in egregious cases proved to be a travesty, in which priorities of good governance and human welfare were subordinated to a very formal commitment to ineffective structures.

One alternative to the traditional approach, deriving from Western liberal democratic theory, begins with individuals, organized into political groupings to pursue collective interests through the institutions and public politics of civil society,

[54] See the judicious discussion in Schachter, 'The Decline of the Nation-State and its Implications for International Law', 36 *Columbia Journal of Transnational Law* (1997) 7.

local, state, transnational and international institutions.[55] Institutions reflect both past decisions and the interests of particular constituencies presently wielding power. The regulatory influence of institutions characteristically reaches beyond those groups who are influential within them, but democratic principles require that all influenced by regulatory decisions have at least the possibility of a voice in the relevant institution. Regulatory competences are allocated among institutions on the basis of principles of constitutional design that vary with the architects but are seldom based purely on efficiency.[56] This approach leads to a view of state institutions not as representatives of sovereign power but simply as functional institutions competing with each other and with other actors in a market to provide cost-effective governance at the requisite standard. Responsiveness to the needs and interests of particular constituencies is a vital element of success in such a market.

What would be the effect of a general rejection of the present commitment to traditional sovereignty, and its replacement by a functionalist liberal view of market-based governance institutions? States would not disappear: they would remain the principal units of order and governance. Legal rules of mutual respect and coordination would continue to be necessary. The crucial change would be normative — the protections and status conferred by the concept of sovereignty would cease to be fundamental norms upon the maintenance of which the stability of the legal system depends, becoming instead overtly contractual, and defeasible. Just as the abolition of elaborate diplomatic orders of precedence, or of aristocratic titles, wrought a change to the normative environment without in itself redistributing material power, states would continue as loci of power and authority; but without the privilege conferred by sovereignty, some might suffer severely, and this suffering would be distributed unevenly. International law would perhaps arrive at a functional conception of sovereignty as a bargaining resource of variable quantum, similar to that described by Robert Keohane: 'Sovereignty no longer enables states to exert effective supremacy over what occurs within their territories .... What sovereignty does confer on states under conditions of complex interdependence is legal authority that can either be exercised to the detriment of other states' interests or be bargained

55 See generally Moravcsik, 'Taking Preferences Seriously: A Liberal Theory of International Politics', 51 *International Organization* (1997) 513; Keohane, 'International Liberalism Reconsidered', in J. Dunn (ed.), *The Economic Limits of Modern Politics* (1990), at 165. As Philip Allott points out, the view of democracy as a process for the expression of interests is associated especially with the United States: he contrasts this with what he regards as a distinctive post-Marxist Western European view of democracy as 'a political system for realizing the communal interest'. Allott, 'The European Community is Not the True European Community', 100 *Yale Law Journal* (1991) 2485, at 2491.

56 As Robert Boyer observes, 'asymmetry of power has definite consequences on the design of institutions, which only rarely enhance efficiency'. Boyer, 'The Convergence Hypothesis Revisited: Globalization but Still the Century of Nations', in S. Berger and R. Dore (eds), *National Diversity and Global Capitalism* (1996), at 56.

away in return for influence over others' policies and therefore greater gains from exchange.'[57]

The normative inhibitions associated with sovereignty moderate existing inequalities of power between states, and provide a shield for weak states and weak institutions. These inequalities would become more pronounced if the universal normative understandings associated with sovereignty were to be discarded, and sovereignty were to become simply a summation of the operations of the market, a bargaining resource to be traded off against other sources of value. Specific rules presently associated with sovereignty would continue to have a basis in contract and reciprocity, but the terms of these revisable bargains would reflect inequalities of power between states rather than the shared social understandings of what is inherent in statehood. Legal sovereignty would become, as the international relations aphorism has it, a variable rather than a parameter. Three more specific implications for inequality among states of a diminution in the normative power of the traditional concept of state sovereignty may be briefly noted. The question whether heightened inequalities amongst states might be justified by a reduction in inequalities and injustices among individuals and groups that an alternative system might achieve will be considered in the conclusion.

A *Diminished Restraints on Coercive Intervention*

The traditional international law concept of sovereignty constitutes an important normative inhibition to military intervention. There have been extraordinarily few cases of recolonization of former colonies once recognized as independent states.[58] Since 1945 not only has the death rate of sovereign states been remarkably low,[59] there have been few military invasions intended to terminate the independent existence of an established state. Direct large-scale unilateral military intervention without an invitation has probably been constrained somewhat by the sovereignty model and the UN Charter norms that give expression to it. Advocacy of displacing sovereignty in favour of a less state-centric, more liberal international legal order undervalues the importance of this achievement. Such advocacy is animated by international political economy and other governance issues rather than issues of

[57] Keohane, 'Hobbes's Dilemma and Institutional Change in World Politics: Sovereignty in International Society', in H.-H. Holm and G. Sorensen (eds), *Whose World Order?: Uneven Globalization and the End of the Cold War* (1995) 165, at 176–177. See also the discussion of 'operational sovereignty' in Keohane, 'Sovereignty, Interdependence, and International Institutions', in L. Miller and M. J. Smith (eds), *Ideas and Ideals: Essays on Politics in Honor of Stanley Hoffman* (1993), at 91.

[58] Strang, 'Contested Sovereignty: The Social Construction of Colonial Imperialism', in T. Biersteker and C. Weber (eds), *State Sovereignty as Social Construct* (1996) 22, at 25; Strang, 'Anomaly and Commonplace in European Political Expansion: Realist and Institutionalist Accounts', 45 *International Organization* (1991) 143.

[59] K. Waltz, *Theory of International Politics* (1979). Oppenheim reflected the experience of his times in acknowledging that every now and again the odd state would disappear and new ones appear; but while the rate of new appearances has quickened, the rate of disappearances has declined to almost zero after 1945.

military security and the use of force in inter-state wars. This emphasis is defended by proponents on the ground that the absence of international war between liberal states reduces the importance of military security in a liberal 'zone of peace'.[60] But the world is far from being a zone of peace. There is a great risk of weakening hard-won normative arguments against military intervention that have been associated, especially since 1945, with the universal system of sovereign equality.

One of the major historic arguments for intervention, used frequently in the century prior to 1945, has been the unwillingness or ineffectiveness of local authorities in discharging international obligations. This was a principal justification of, for instance, extraterritorial consular jurisdiction imposed by European powers and the US on Turkey, Japan, China, Siam, Morocco and other entities, and the collective military interventions in Mexico in 1861 (conducted primarily by France, with the support of Britain and Spain), China in 1898–1901 (the suppression of the Boxer uprising by a group of Western powers and Japan), and Venezuela in 1902 (Britain, Germany, and Italy). In Greece, Turkey, Bulgaria, Serbia, China, Argentina and several other states, one or more foreign states took control of various government revenues to ensure payment of international obligations (principally debts and reparations).[61] The tenor of Western attitudes toward such foreign administration of struggling entities may be gauged from a report on US administration of the customs house in the Dominican Republic after 1905. According to the US author of this 1907 report, in the period since the failure of the movement to annex San Domingo to the USA in 1869–70, the country had experienced 'a miserable sequence of revolution and anarchy, interrupted by ruthless and blood-stained dictatorships'. After 1899, the 'country was laid waste, the people crushed to hopelessness, the treasury left to stew in utter bankruptcy, and a host of creditors, foreign and domestic, after tightening their hold upon the future became more and more insistent in the present'. Administration of the customs house used almost 55 per cent of the net revenues to repay debts, with the remainder going to government expenditure. Once put in place 'the Dominican Republic enjoyed a civil calm and an economic well-being such as it had not known for two generations'. If continued 'we shall speedily see a West Indian people who have never had a fair chance, developing into a decent, prosperous peasantry'.[62]

The modern form of this argument holds that states deemed insufficiently democratic, or with deeply divided societies not truly represented by the state institutions, or unable or unwilling to meet the plethora of international demands for adequate regulation, institutions and policies, ought to lose their legitimacy. In particular circumstances this may culminate in forcible intervention. The normative

60 E.g., Slaughter, *supra* note 39, at 509–511.

61 Some of these episodes are discussed in Krasner, 'Compromising Westphalia', *supra* note 48, at 115.

62 Hollander, 'The Convention of 1907 between the United States and the Dominican Republic', 1 *AJIL* (1907) 287.

case for increased intervention has been made with passion and conviction,[63] but is less convincing as an argument for the uneven patterns of intervention that actually occur.[64] Force may achieve narrowly defined short-term objectives such as the delivery of food aid or the removal of a particular tyrant, but outside powers without fundamental interests directly at stake are ordinarily unwilling to commit forces on a scale or for a duration sufficient to have even a prospect of establishing long-term democracy or bringing peace to bitterly divided societies. Multilateral intervention has notable achievements, but inevitably political calculations and interests in the intervening states weigh heavily in all aspects of military operations, and in the case of conflict are likely to prevail over the liberal principles offered as justification.

B *Diminution of State Functions without Effective Alternatives*

Functionalist arguments for the delegitimation of state institutions in weak states presume that state functions are substitutable. Thus, where a state is held to have 'failed', its governance functions may be taken over by external agencies or private entrepreneurs: they may organize settlement of foreign investment disputes, repayment of debts, provision of security for diamond mines or oil pipelines, delivery of food and medical supplies, the conduct of plebiscites, and trial of alleged human rights abusers or narcotraffickers. Or outsiders may be positioned as 'trainers' or 'advisers' to judges, police forces or government ministries.

Some functions of states are not easily replicated by other institutions, however. In the traditional sovereignty system, even relatively fragile states play a potentially important function as a basis of identity and a focus of loyalty, balancing the pull of identities based on clan or ethnic group or religious solidarity or city. The representativity of the state and the performance of its institutions condition its effectiveness in these functions, but it is almost impossible for externally-based institutions to perform them. Some liberals are remarkably sanguine about this issue, proposing that the world will eventually evolve as the West is thought to have done in the account of Dan Deudney and John Ikenberry: 'As civic and capitalist identities have been strengthened, ethnic and national identity has declined. A distinctive solution to the problem of nationalism and ethnicity has evolved in the West. . . .' In their account, markets, a common civic identity, and a distinctive institutional order of international relations have produced in the West 'a complex polity spilling across the juridical borders of states and enveloping state institutions'.[65] But the West remains a region of strong and popular states. Delegitimizing the state by dispensing with its sovereignty — a process likely to be targeted on weak states outside the West

[63] F. Tesón, *Humanitarian Intervention: An Inquiry into Law and Morality* (2nd ed., 1997); M. Bettati and B. Kouchner, *Le devoir d'ingérence: peut-on les laisser mourir?* (1987). See also O. Korten and P. Klein, *Droit d'ingérence ou obligation de réaction?* (1992).

[64] Brownlie, 'Humanitarian Intervention', in J. N. Moore (ed.), *Law and Civil War in the Modern World* (1974), at 217.

[65] 'The Logic of the West', 10 *World Policy Journal* (1993–1994) 17; and a 'Response' to commentators, 11 *World Policy Journal* (1994) 122, quotations at 124.

— leaves identity and loyalty to be conditioned exclusively by other forces in ways that may disserve the liberal objectives animating this challenge to sovereignty.

Another significant function of sovereignty has been to preserve some autonomy in decision-making, and hence some space for difference, for the community within the state. The liberal functionalist argument is that such autonomy is waning because of economic globalization, that real difference is declining inexorably with cultural, economic and political convergence, and that differences protected by state sovereignty often comprise such undesirable traits as the subordination of women, the maintenance of corrupt elites, or the suppression of political dissent or religious freedom. Thus, it is argued that the economic and cultural basis of the traditional sovereignty system is disappearing and that the legal order must adjust accordingly.

The processes of colonial expansion and state formation that made the traditional sovereignty system global were themselves highly intrusive, but the system now provides a mild check on further intrusion. The formation of modern states has transformed local political forms; a return to a pre-existing 'culturally-authentic' system for the organization of power and decision-making is improbable even in countries where the modern state is least well rooted. Nevertheless, the apparent homology among state institutions for international purposes does not reflect homogenization of local political forms, let alone uniformity in the social and economic patterns to which effective political institutions must be responsive. These patterns are often inegalitarian, but the freedom to seek to exert influence in a polity still open to local concerns is an empowering attraction of the sovereignty system. Governance by outside institutions, and external intervention, may transform local politics into struggles to capture the benefits supplied from outside or to lead resistance. In the long term, state institutions may be discredited from outside without any credible alternative means to achieve particular governance functions. In weak or externally-dominated states, and in deeply divided societies or those with systemic social violence, it is not at all clear that liberal functionalist alternatives to the traditional sovereignty system are likely to be realized in practice or to effectuate enduring improvement.

C *Re-dividing the World into Zones*

The universalization of the system of formally equal sovereign states — Oppenheim's 'Family of Nations' — has been a remarkable feature of the international legal order of the past century. The quest to fulfil these universalist aspirations, to establish more substantive equality among states in their capacities to influence legal development and to pursue agendas that are not simply those of the powerful, has been a leitmotif for generations of anti-colonial *tiers-mondiste* international lawyers.[66] Emerging liberal thinking about the international legal order argues increasingly that it is

[66] See, e.g., Abi-Saab, 'International Law and the International Community: The Long Road to Universality', in R. St.J. Macdonald (ed.), *Essays in Honour of Wang Tieya* (1994) 31; and Flory, 'Mondialisation et droit international du développement', 101 *Revue générale de droit international public* (1997) 609.

possible to divide the world into zones,[67] with a liberal zone of law, constituted by liberal states practising a higher degree of legal civilization, to which other states will be admitted only when they meet the requisite standards.[68] This is in some respects a continuation of recurrent patterns in the history of Western legal thought, traceable for example in the 16th century European divisions between Christians and infidels,[69] or in James Lorimer's late 19th century division of the world into a hierarchy of civilized nations, barbarous humanity and savage humanity.[70] As in the past, this identification of zones may be defended simply as a description of existing or emerging reality,[71] but its many normative advocates see the liberal West as the vanguard of a transformed global legal order in which many of the limitations of the sovereignty-based legal system can finally be transcended. The theory of liberal and non-liberal zones proposes differential treatment where the boundaries of the liberal zone are crossed, conferring privileges based on membership in the liberal zone, and setting high barriers to entry. The new standard of civilization is defended normatively as the means to promote the advancement of the backward. It is not clear, however, why human flourishing is better promoted by the construction of an identifiable 'other', an 'us' and 'them' from amongst the myriad ways of understanding and classifying the world. The construction of the zones of law in spatial terms reflects a territorial and state-based view of the world which much of the argument from globalization and the cross-cutting constituencies of liberalism is concerned to reject. The outcome seems likely to be the maintenance of a classificatory system which is itself both an explanation and a justification for those at the margins remaining there for generations.

4 Conclusion

Proposals to move away from the traditional account of international law based on state sovereignty — the account found in Oppenheim and preponderant throughout the 20th century — have not crystallized as a single coherent alternative. Some advocate a broader view of the range of norms encompassed in the concept of 'international law': norms of interaction for individuals and groups in transnational

[67] M. Singer and A. Wildavsky, *The Real World Order: Zones of Peace/Zones of Turmoil* (1993).

[68] For critical discussion see Kingsbury, 'Whose International Law?: Sovereignty and Non-State Groups', 88 *Proceedings of the American Society of International Law* (1994) 1.

[69] Martin Wight modelled this worldview as two concentric circles, the inner one being close-knit and bound by detailed rules, the outer one being looser and subject only to rather minimal rules. See Kingsbury and Roberts, 'Introduction', in H. Bull *et al.* (eds), *Hugo Grotius and International Relations* (1990), at 14. A more nuanced analysis of views of the extra-European world in the writings of Alberico Gentili (1552–1608) is given in Kingsbury, 'Confronting Difference: The Puzzling Durability of Gentili's Combination of Pragmatic Pluralism and Normative Judgment', 92 *AJIL* (1998) 713, and B. Kingsbury, *Alberico Gentili e il Mondo Extra-europeo: gli Infedeli, gli Indiani d'America, e la sfida della differenza* (forthcoming).

[70] Lorimer, *supra* note 20, at 101.

[71] E.g., Keohane, 'Hobbes's Dilemma', *supra* note 56, at 178–180.

civil society, many of which are chosen voluntarily by contract even if they often rely on state power for enforcement; rules and decisions promulgated by state institutions in transnational dialogue with other relevant institutions; and the law controlling state action, which will be a mixture of international agreements and national law and will generally be subject to enforcement in national courts and in supranational courts of which the European Court of Justice is a prototype.[72] Others propose to move away from the requirement of explicit consent by each state as the basis for binding obligation, finding universal law in a range of normative pronouncements from intergovernmental conferences, repeated provisions in treaties, the practice of international organizations, and other evidence of a general will of a diverse international community.[73] Modern extensions of natural law approaches, including the policy science and communication approach long advocated by the New Haven School, have an enduring attraction in seeming to base international law on community policies that reflect higher purposes and not simply on the putative will of formal sovereigns.[74] These different approaches all allow greater scope for the substance of international law to be influenced by 'global public policy'. This policy spans managed trade, market liberalism, protection of intellectual property and wildlife, civil rights, public participation and a range of other values favoured in the political West. It encompasses a commitment to some basic equality among human beings, but it is not at present a strongly egalitarian policy.[75] The commitments of the various advocates differ, but the aggregate of forces pushing to shift legal thought from a normative-status view of sovereignty to a functional-contractual view are not at present accompanied by a corresponding impetus to ameliorate and manage problems of inequality.

A decline in the traditional sovereignty system weakens the relationship of mutual containment between sovereignty and inequality. The justification that sovereignty provides for the modesty of the engagement of international law with problems of inequality within national societies — the justification for the weakness of international law regimes on landlessness, unemployment, gender inequity, homelessness, basic education, mental illness — threatens to disappear at a time when inequalities in many societies are rising. Inequalities between many societies are also growing larger, while the weakening of the sovereignty paradigm would remove the segmenting buffer that has been a moral underpinning, however incoherent, for inter-societal inequalities.[76] Inequalities in the structure of transnational activities and the incidence of their legal regulation intensify these inter-societal inequalities.

[72] Slaughter, *supra* note 39, at 516–534.

[73] Charney, 'Universal International Law', 87 *AJIL* (1993) 529. Related issues are considered in Simma, 'From Bilateralism to Community Interest in International Law', 250 *RdC* (1994) 217; Grieg, 'Reflections on the Role of Consent', 12 *Australian Year Book of International Law* (1992) 125; and Pellet, 'The Normative Dilemma: Will and Consent in International Law-Making', in *ibid*, 22.

[74] H. Lasswell and M. McDougal, *Jurisprudence for a Free Society* (2 vols, 1992).

[75] Cf. Alston, 'The Myopia of the Handmaidens: International Lawyers and Globalization', 8 *EJIL* (1997) 435.

[76] See, e.g., Miller, 'The Ethical Significance of Nationality', 98 *Ethics* (1988) 647.

624 EJIL 9 (1998), 599–625

The increasing need for regulation of non-state actors, including actors in the emerging transnational civil society, and for the development of a democratic transnational law, coincides with the weakening of the prerogatives of the institutions of some states, leaving many communities dependent in practice on the regulatory efforts of the strong states or of international institutions.

People experiencing a decline in their ability to shape deleterious or unsettling changes can be expected to resist. Sovereign states open the prospect of some autonomy, the possibility for individuals and groups to make a difference in a structured political space whose institutions and community shape their conscious identities. The suspension of the OECD negotiations on the Multilateral Agreement on Investment in May 1998, which occurred not simply through the involvement of citizens' groups in the OECD but in major part through public opposition expressed in the political systems of a number of participating states, illustrates the value many individuals place on autonomous decision-making within the state in the face of the imperatives of globalization. In strong states, the US above all, there is little prospect that the autonomy inherent in the traditional sovereignty system will be compromised, and the politics of the civil society will continue to be channelled through state institutions even as the activities and concerns of the civil society gradually become more transnational. Citizenship and loyalty will continue to have a vital political meaning defined by reference to the state. The 'citizenship' of the European Union, promised but underspecified in the legal texts of the Union, seems likely to take its substance as a gloss on the enduring loyalties and citizenships of individuals attached to the Member States.

The imperative for some degree of participation and autonomy has buttressed the traditional sovereignty system. It is often argued that a new liberal global legal order, or indeed a post-modern post-sovereignty international law, will make participation and active citizenship more possible, overturning tyrannies and hierarchies and increasing freedom and community and equality. But there will not soon exist a global community which is capable of sustaining the politics and institutions necessary to realize such ambitious visions. Their realization would require not only the conceptual change which their advocates promote and have begun to achieve, but extraordinary resources which new technology and global economy do not yet provide. In their aspirational but unrealized state, such visions serve in the interim to legitimate an extraordinary range of interventionist or otherwise coercive activities in other countries that reflect struggles and dilemmas in politics in the West: removal of dictators; extraterritorial police operations against narcotics cartels allegedly protected by corrupt regimes; no-fly zones to safeguard threatened ethnic groups; the empowerment of victims of gender discrimination, religious persecution, or gun control laws; protection of the unborn, tropical forests, intellectual property, marine mammals, foreign investors, or telecommunications service providers; promotion of peace processes, free if ethnically divisive elections, and unsafe safe havens. These agendas involve, and are often responsive to, groups outside the West, but they are largely set in the West, with timing suitable to political interests in the West, and with inconsistencies and vagaries driven in many respects by dynamics in the West. To be pursued effectively they require, paradoxically, organized inequality, on a larger scale than presently exists. They require also a system for the management of inequality that international law at present lacks. The traditional sovereignty system is flawed, and will continue to be stretched and strained. But for the time being it remains a more realistic system for the management of enduring inequalities, and of other pathologies of the international system of law and politics, than any of the alternatives on offer.

[16]

Private Justice in a Global Economy: From Litigation to Arbitration

Walter Mattli

The study of private settlement of cross-border trade and investment disputes through international commercial arbitration or other mechanisms has been much neglected by scholars of international political economy and international institutions. This oversight is attributable in part to the traditional focus of international relations on intergovernmental international organizations and the lack of attention to private international institutional arrangements.[1] A further reason for the oversight is that arbitration is resolutely private, making information exceedingly difficult to obtain. Two distinguished international arbitrators, Alan Redfern and Martin Hunter, recently observed that the study of the practice of international commercial arbitration is like peering into the dark. Few arbitral awards are published and even fewer procedural decisions of arbitral tribunals come to light.[2]

Despite this difficulty, private forums for international commercial dispute resolution, of which international arbitration is an increasingly popular type, deserve much closer attention by scholars of international relations. After virtually disap-

I am grateful to Ken Abbott, Beth Yarbrough, Barbara Koremenos, Charles Lipson, Ronald Mitchell, Antonio Ortiz, and Duncan Snidal for excellent comments on earlier drafts. I also thank Debbie Davenport, Miles Kahler, Robert Keohane, Lisa Martin, Jeffrey Stacey, and the participants of the Rational Design project, the Program on International Politics, Economics, and Security (PIPES) at the University of Chicago, and a seminar at Harvard University Business School for helpful suggestions. Special thanks to Dominique Hascher, General Counsel and Deputy Secretary General of the International Court of Arbitration of the International Chamber of Commerce in Paris, for inviting me to do an internship at the court in 1998, and to Anne-Marie Whitesell for welcoming me to her legal team at the court. I benefited greatly from discussions on international commercial arbitration with Adrian Winstanley of the London Court of International Arbitration, Eva Müller of the Arbitration Institute of the Stockholm Chamber of Commerce, as well as Gerald Aksen, Lucienne Carasso Bulow, Alessandra Casella, Yves Dezalay, Bryant Garth, Thomas Heller, Christian Joerges, William Park, Susan Rose-Ackerman, Martin Shapiro, Anne-Marie Slaughter, Hans Smit, Francis Snyder, Job Taylor, and Raymund Werle.

1. Two notable exceptions are Lipson 1985; and Cutler 1995.

2. Redfern and Hunter 1991, xv. Information mainly comes from tapping the experience of the principal arbitral institutions or by looking at individual cases that come before the courts, either as a result of enforcement proceedings or because an arbitral award is challenged by the losing party.

pearing during the age of nation-state ideology in the nineteenth century, international commercial arbitration has been staging a formidable comeback in the past twenty years. Today's scene calls to memory the flourishing era of arbitration practices and institutions associated with the international trade fairs of medieval Europe. The number of arbitration forums has grown from a dozen or so in the 1970s to more than one hundred in the 1990s, and the caseload of major arbitral institutions has more than doubled during the same period.[3] Lawyers and judges agree that "there is [now] clear evidence of something of a world movement . . . towards international arbitration."[4] The Economist recently called arbitration "the Big Idea set to dominate legal-reform agendas into the next century."[5]

Even though the focus of this study is on various arbitration options, it also reflects more broadly on the market of institutions for international commercial dispute resolution for private parties. It addresses the question of why different forums for dispute resolution are selected.

In the domestic context parties who seek a binding method of resolving disputes through third-party intervention have the choice between a national public court and private arbitration. In the international context such a choice does not exist because there are no international public courts that handle international commercial disputes involving only private parties.[6] Therefore, the choice for international private parties is between recourse to a national court (that is, litigation) and recourse to private international dispute resolution, namely international commercial arbitration or so-called alternative dispute resolution (ADR) techniques, such as conciliation and mediation.[7]

Arbitration is a binding, nonjudicial, and private means of settling disputes based on an explicit agreement by the parties involved in a transaction. Such an agreement is typically embodied in the terms of a contract between the parties. Alternatively, if the contract is silent about the dispute-resolution method, the parties can select the method when the dispute arises.[8] Arbitration entrusts the settlement of a question to one or more persons who derive their powers from the private agreement.[9] Unlike judges in public courts, who must follow fixed rules of procedure and apply the laws of the land, arbitrators can dispense with legal formalities and may apply whatever procedural rules and substantive law best fit a case.

3. Brown 1993.

4. Kerr, Lord Justice of England, preface to Craig, Park, and Paulsson, 1990, xii.

5. The Economist, 18–24 July 1992, 17, survey on the legal profession. See also Wetter 1995.

6. The only exception is the European Court of Justice, which may deal with certain disputes between private parties under European Community law. Redfern and Hunter 1991, 25; Burley and Mattli 1993; Mattli and Slaughter 1995 and 1998a,b.

7. The term jurisdiction clause in an international contract is generally used to describe a forum selection that designates a public court to hear a case, while an arbitration clause refers to private international dispute resolution.

8. Even if the parties have contractually agreed to use one method, they may switch to another if they feel that the latter is more appropriate for a given dispute.

9. Mustill and Boyd 1989, 38–50.

Arbitration becomes international when the parties to a dispute reside or conduct their main business in different countries. The term commercial in international commercial arbitration is broadly conceived and covers activities such as sale of goods, distribution agreements, commercial representation of agency, leasing, consulting, transportation, construction work, joint ventures, and other forms of industrial or business cooperation.[10]

International commercial arbitration can be conducted in two ways, as ad hoc arbitration or as institutional arbitration. Ad hoc arbitration does not rely on the supervision or formal administration of an arbitration center. Institutional arbitration, in contrast, is done under the aegis of an arbitral center, usually according to the institution's own rules of arbitration.[11] The most established of these institutions are the International Court of Arbitration (ICA) of the International Chamber of Commerce (ICC), the London Court of International Arbitration (LCIA), and the Arbitration Institute of the Stockholm Chamber of Commerce (SCC Institute).[12] Many more arbitral institutions have been set up in the past decade, notably in Asia, the Middle East, and North America.[13]

I argue that the various forums of dispute resolution can be understood as indirect products of rational selection where actors select those institutions that are most effective and appropriate for given disputes. In the United States, for example, the legal counsels of major corporations have spearheaded the recent trend away from sometimes cumbersome and lengthy court proceedings toward faster and less expensive methods, such as ADR. Similarly, the surge in popularity of arbitration as a means of international commercial dispute resolution can be attributed to features of arbitration that the international business community values for a growing number of disputes, notably in the areas of technology transfer, intellectual property, engineering, and construction. These features include flexibility, technical expertise, privacy, confidentiality, and speed. In short I describe a market of dispute-resolution methods where different "suppliers" offer different venues from which the firms on the demand side can select based on their design problems. This creates an accelerated evolutionary process of forum formation (that is, accelerated by rational

10. This definition is suggested in the United Nations Commission for International Trade Law (UNCITRAL) Model Law, Art. 1 (1), fn.

11. Institutional arbitration is also referred to in the literature as "administered" or "supervised" arbitration. On institutional arbitration, see Slate 1996; Hoellering 1994; Vigrass 1993; Graving 1989; and Lowenfeld 1993.

12. Another major institution is the American Arbitration Association. Its focus is primarily on domestic arbitration; for this reason, it is omitted from the discussion in this study. (Yearly, it handles about forty thousand domestic and two hundred international arbitration cases.)

13. Due to limited space, I focus primarily on international commercial arbitration and not the more specialized arbitration as offered, for example, by the Society of Maritime Arbitration (New York), the Grain and Feed Trade Association (London), and various stock and commodity exchanges. Nevertheless, I would argue that the framework used here does shed light on some key institutional features of commodity trade and maritime arbitration. See also Mentschikoff 1961; Harris, Summerskill, and Cockerill 1993; Summerskill 1993; Covo 1993; and Johnson 1991 and 1993.

anticipation of what will sell and what will work), and the result will be very much the same as a direct rational-design effort.[14]

The key institutional dimensions along which the various methods of international dispute resolution vary are (1) procedural and adaptive flexibility, and (2) centralization of procedural safeguards and information collection. For example, flexibility is typically much lower in public court proceedings than in institutional arbitration, ad hoc arbitration, or ADR; and centralization is present in institutional arbitration but not in ad hoc arbitration or ADR.

Drawing on the analytical framework developed by Barbara Koremenos, Charles Lipson, and Duncan Snidal, I elaborate on several of the Rational Design conjectures, linking the institutional features of dispute-resolution methods to the needs or demands of private parties.[15] These conjectures can be summarized as follows: Centralization of forums to which private international parties resort to resolve their disputes increases with uncertainty about the parties' preferences or behavior (conjecture C1, CENTRALIZATION increases with UNCERTAINTY ABOUT BEHAVIOR). Such uncertainty may be low, for example, if the parties are locked in a mutually beneficial, ongoing commercial relationship; in this case, the parties' institutional demands for resolving disputes will be markedly lower than those of firms with few interactions and little knowledge of each other.

However, full information and adequate knowledge are not always sufficient to ensure compliance; enforcement problems may remain severe if the payoff from unilateral defection is significantly greater than that from mutual cooperation at the dispute-resolution stage. In this case, strong centralized procedural safeguards will be necessary to foil defection. This argument is summarized in conjecture C4, CENTRALIZATION increases with ENFORCEMENT problems.

Centralization is also likely to increase with the parties' uncertainty about the state of the world (conjecture C2, CENTRALIZATION increases with UNCERTAINTY ABOUT THE STATE OF THE WORLD)—that is, with the parties' relative lack of information, for example, about the legal environment (the laws and integrity of judges) in which arbitration takes place and about the conditions for enforceability of arbitral awards. More generally, traders with little experience in international exchange or traders from very different cultural and linguistic regions may rely more heavily on centralized support and expertise for resolving their disputes than veteran traders operating in a relatively homogenous region.

Finally, uncertainty about the state of the world may also result from the susceptibility of an issue-area to new developments or unanticipated shocks that may leave parties in uncharted legal territory. In such situations institutional flexibility may be required to resolve disputes effectively. For example, firms operating at the forefront of new production and exchange methods are likely to

14. As illustrated later, the distinction between suppliers and demanders is useful analytically, but in practice it is often blurred because methods for resolving private disputes are provided mostly by private organizations run and funded by firms themselves.

15. Koremenos, Lipson, and Snidal, this volume.

prefer a flexible form of dispute resolution that allows them to tailor rules regarding procedure, evidence, and even the substance of the case to their evolving needs. This relationship is captured by conjecture F1, FLEXIBILITY increases with UNCERTAINTY ABOUT THE STATE OF THE WORLD.

The study is organized as follows. In the first section I briefly review and critique themes in the institutional literature in international relations and economics that are relevant to this study. In the second section I discuss the key institutional differences among the various methods of international commercial dispute resolution and introduce the principal international arbitral forums. After laying this groundwork I seek to explain within the Rational Design framework why private parties select the dispute-resolution forums they do. I conclude with a discussion of ways to broaden the study.

Private Dispute Resolution and the Institutional Literature

Political scientists and economists have developed two theoretical schools, regime theory and new institutional economics (NIE), respectively, that seek to explain institutional arrangements. Unfortunately, the two schools have based their theories in part on assumptions that move the theories' reach away from the types of institutional arrangements discussed in this study.

"International regimes" are defined broadly as sets of implicit or explicit principles, norms, rules, and decision-making procedures around which actors' expectations converge in a given area of international relations.[16] In a world of rapidly growing interdependence regimes are said to help states correct "market failures" stemming from asymmetric information, moral hazard, risk, and uncertainty.[17] Regime theorists have shed important light on the nature of interstate relations, but they have overlooked the importance of nonstate actors in international relations. In particular they have failed to examine the extent to which international market players themselves can remedy "market failures" by creating private institutional arrangements. This omission has deprived the theory of the comparative institutional perspective necessary to assess the desirability of intergovernmental regimes. Only a comparative institutional analysis that weighs the costs and benefits of both private and public institutional remedies of "market failures" can provide a framework to address questions of efficiency, effectiveness, and optimal institutional design.[18] I am not implying that regime theory is flawed but rather suggesting that the theory could be strengthened by extending its focus beyond state behavior. For example, there is nothing that keeps the ICC from being viewed as a regime for its members, as I show later.

16. Krasner 1983, 2.
17. Keohane 1984, 93.
18. A related point is made in Demsetz 1969.

NIE is a rapidly growing field that has developed from the pioneering work of Oliver Williamson. It offers a rigorous conceptual framework for comparative institutional analysis.[19] NIE seeks to explain varying types of industrial organization, from straightforward market exchange to vertically integrated exchange, based on differences in transaction costs. The principal dimensions within which transactions differ are asset specificity, uncertainty, and frequency. The first is the most important; it represents the degree to which durable investments are made to support particular transactions.

NIE postulates that transaction costs are economized by assigning transactions (which differ in their attributes) to governance structures (which differ in their adaptive capacities and associated costs) in a discriminating way. Governance structures are the organizational frameworks within which the integrity of a contractual relation is decided and maintained. In particular, the higher the asset specificity, the greater the institutional complexity needed to promote efficient exchange. Examples of governance structures are economic hostages, vertical integration, unitization, and multinationalism.[20]

Nevertheless, Williamson's framework is not without shortcomings. For example, none of Williamson's governance structures would be needed if courts could resolve disputes swiftly and inexpensively. But Williamson argues that court ordering or legal centralism is inefficient. "Most studies of exchange assume that efficacious rules of law regarding contract disputes are in place and are applied by the courts in an informed, sophisticated, and low-cost way. . . . The facts, however, disclose otherwise. Most disputes, including many that under current rules could be brought to a court, are resolved by avoidance, self-help, and the like. . . . [And] because the efficacy of court ordering is problematic, contract execution falls heavily on [governance structures]."[21] This proposition is problematic. First, courts are institutions, too. A comparative institutional analysis that sets aside a large universe of institutions on the grounds of their alleged inefficiency risks being internally inconsistent. Within Williamson's framework, it is incomprehensible why inefficient institutions come into being or survive. Second, even if it established analytically (by way of ad hoc assumptions) that public courts and public law are inefficient, there remains the question of why NIE does not consider their next best substitutes, namely private courts and private law.

In short, NIE provides a sophisticated analytical framework for studying varying forms of governance. However, by overlooking the importance particularly of private courts and law, NIE may be accused of truncating the full range of variation on the dependent variable (governance forms) and thus suffering from selection bias. Williamson recognized that "a place for law [should] properly [be] provided in

19. Williamson 1975 and 1985.

20. Yarbrough and Yarbrough have recently added to this list various forms of trade liberalization. Their analysis provides a good example of how NIE can enrich the study of international institutional arrangements. See Yarbrough and Yarbrough 1992.

21. Williamson 1985, 20, 32.

any comprehensive study of contract."[22] Beth Yarbrough and Robert Yarbrough have responded to this invitation and are presently extending Williamson's framework to incorporate law and public courts in a way that is consonant with the analysis offered in this study. Courts, they argue, are not generically inefficient; rather they are not very efficacious for certain types of transactions. One type is those transactions in which asset specificity makes the historical context of a relationship critical to resolving disputes. A second type is those in which the confrontational nature of court proceedings risks damaging future relations (hence courts' historical reluctance, until recently, to become involved in many family matters). In such cases, Yarbrough and Yarbrough predict noncourt means of dispute settlement.[23]

Institutional Features of International Commercial Dispute-resolution Methods

The range of methods for resolving international commercial disputes is wide. It includes litigation in public courts, several arbitration options, and so-called ADR techniques. In this section I highlight the institutional characteristics of the various methods.

Flexibility in Dispute Resolution

A key feature of arbitration is its high degree of procedural flexibility. Arbitration provides the parties with full control over the arbitral process. The parties may decide the number of arbitrators comprising the arbitral tribunal, the appointment procedure of the arbitrators, the place of arbitration, the powers of the tribunal, and the applicable law in the dispute. In contrast, a trial before a national court must be conducted in accordance with the rules of that court. Further, public court proceedings are typically open to the public, and court decisions are published and readily available. Arbitral proceedings, however, are held in private; details about the cases, including the arbitral awards, are confidential.[24] Privacy may help firms to hide a number of facts from competitors and the public in general, such as trade secrets and know-how not guaranteed by patents or financial difficulties and other problems. Nevertheless, the parties may choose to publicize arbitral decisions either to create precedents or to provide authoritative interpretations of standard contract terms.[25]

22. Ibid., 168.
23. Beth Yarbrough, pers. comm. with the author.
24. René David, a leading French expert of international arbitration, notes that "secrecy, which is one of the reasons why arbitration is resorted to by the parties, is easily extended . . . to everything concerning arbitration." See David 1985, 31.
25. Cost is a factor, unrelated to flexibility, that is frequently said to distinguish litigation from arbitration. Arbitration centers, for example, claim that litigation is much more expensive than arbitration. This need not necessarily be true, however. First, although litigants do not pay the salary of a judge,

Flexibility characterizes not only arbitral procedures but also the actual institutions of arbitration, such as the ICA, the LCIA, and the SCC Institute. These forums can respond much more quickly to demands for new dispute-resolution rules and services than public courts. The reason is evident: Private courts are demand driven. The very same market actors who request new rules also control these courts. As noted by Alessandra Casella, these forums are shaped from the "bottom," that is, by the firms that voluntarily finance and share the "club goods" they need.[26] Thus the demanders are also the suppliers; they possess full information on how new business practices or changing market conditions affect their dispute-resolution needs. They are capable of quickly responding to new needs by creating new services and by rewriting the charters of their courts. The frequent revisions of the rules of major arbitral institutions attest to the high degree of institutional flexibility of these forums.

Many of today's arbitration practices evoke medieval Europe's private courts and the Law Merchant, a body of private commercial rules and principles that were distinct from the ordinary law of the land. The merchant courts sat in fairs, markets, seaport towns, and most other large centers of commercial activity. Merchant courts chose as judges merchants who possessed intimate knowledge of particular commercial practices and techniques. W. Mitchell, a historian of the Law Merchant, writes, "The summary nature of its jurisdiction . . . characterized the Lex Mercatoria. Its justice was prompt . . . [and] the time within which disputes [had to] be finally settled was narrowly limited."[27] Sea merchants, for example, demanded that disputes be settled "from tide to tide according to the ancient law marine and ancient customs of the sea . . . without mixing the law civil with the law maritime."[28] Another reason for using guild courts was that "under severest penalties, [the guilds] forbade members to appeal, in cases where they alone were concerned, to any court save that of the guild."[29] Merchant courts relied on sanctions such as ostracism and boycott of all future trade to ensure that traders would be held to the resolution dictated by the arbiters.[30]

Besides arbitration and litigation, there are ADR techniques. The most widely known forms of these are conciliation and mediation. Like arbitration, conciliation and mediation offer the parties great procedural flexibility. The parties pick

parties involved in arbitration must pay the fees and expenses of the arbitrators. Second, litigants are not charged for using the public facilities of the courts of law, but the parties in arbitration pay the administrative fees and expenses of an arbitral institution and these can be substantial, particularly when they are assessed by reference to the amount in dispute. In short, arbitration may or may not be less expensive than litigation; much depends on the specifics of the case and the attitudes of the parties to a dispute. Consequently, in the analytical part of the study I do not consider cost as an institutional dimension.

26. Casella 1996; see also Dezalay and Garth 1996.

27. Mitchell 1904, 12–13.

28. Ibid., 20.

29. Ibid., 42.

30. Benson 1989. See also Milgrom, North, and Weingast 1990; Greif, Milgrom, and Weingast 1994; and Cutler 1995.

conciliators or arbitrators of their choice and design procedures that best fit their cases. Typically, a mediator seeks to reduce the distance between the parties' positions and make the parties understand each other's point of view, in order that they may achieve a compromise solution. A conciliator performs a different function. After consulting all sides and evaluating the evidence, the conciliator draws up the terms of a solution that is hopefully acceptable to all parties involved in the dispute. Conciliation and mediation differ in one important respect from arbitration: they do not result in a binding or enforceable award. A mediator cannot compel the parties to reach a settlement, and a conciliator has no power to impose a compromise solution on the parties.[31]

Centralization of Forums for Resolving Disputes

International commercial arbitration can be conducted in two ways, as institutional arbitration or ad hoc arbitration. Ad hoc arbitration differs from institutional arbitration in that it does not rely on the supervision or formal administration of an arbitration center. In this sense it is the least institutional form of arbitration. In ad hoc arbitration, the parties are "on their own"; they are not bound by time limits set by arbitral institutions, and their proceedings are not monitored by any central body. The parties can leave the issuance of arbitration procedures to their arbitrators or develop their own rules and design their own arbitral management either in the initial contract or after a dispute has arisen. Alternatively, the parties may simply adopt or adapt the rules of one of the major arbitration centers but, again, without entrusting the administration of the arbitration to such centers.[32] Another increasingly popular option is to use the arbitration rules of the UN Commission on International Trade Law of 1976 (UNCITRAL arbitration rules). Reference in the parties' contract to the UNCITRAL rules will immediately incorporate a full-blown set of procedures designed specially for ad hoc arbitration.[33]

Ad hoc arbitration to resolve international commercial disputes is similar to ADR in that neither the mediator nor the conciliator is monitored by any central institution. Like the mediator and conciliator, the arbitrator in an ad hoc case depends entirely on the good will of the parties for a smooth process of dispute resolution. Ad hoc arbitration and ADR contrast sharply with institutional arbitration as offered, for example, by the ICA, where the provision of procedural safeguards and information is highly centralized. They also differ from arbitration as conducted by the LCIA, and the SCC Institute. These three institutions are

31. For this reason, ADR is sometimes combined with an adjudicatory process as a fall-back solution. For example, a contract may provide for a specific time limit to start some form of mediation or negotiation after which arbitration becomes the only method available. Park 1997b.

32. In ad hoc arbitration, parties may rely nevertheless on an "appointing authority" (for example, a court, an arbitral institution, or the chairman of a trade association) to appoint arbitrators.

33. On ad hoc arbitration, see Aksen 1991; and Arkin 1987.

TABLE 1. Institutional dimensions of methods for resolving international commercial disputes

	Litigation (public courts)	Institutional arbitration (ICA, LCIA, SCC)	Ad hoc arbitration and ADR
Flexibility	Low (typically)	High	High
Centralization			
Centralized information gathering	N.A.	High to medium	None
Centralized monitoring and other safeguards	N.A.	High to medium	None

considered in order.[34] Table 1 summarizes the key institutional dimensions along which the various methods of international commercial dispute resolution vary.

Illustration of Institutional Arbitration: Three Private Forums

International Chamber of Commerce Arbitration. The ICC is a business organization offering a wide range of services to firms engaged in international trade and investment, including commercial dispute resolution. Founded in 1919, it counts today as members over 7,000 enterprises and commercial organizations in 114 countries. Its organizational structure includes a general secretariat in Paris, employing some eighty-five persons and a secretary-general. The supreme organ is the council, which meets twice a year. Members of the council are appointed by the national committees of the ICC. Each committee may select one to three members according to its contribution to the ICC budget. The council's president is elected for a two-year term. The ICC has established several commissions and special committees to address major issues relating to international commerce, such as intellectual property, competition law, taxation, transportation, telecommunications, the environment, and bribery. Annual conferences are supplemented every three years by an ICC Congress, attended on average by some one thousand participants.[35]

A major organization within the ICC is the ICA, established in 1923.[36] The idea of such a court was conceived after World War I by businessmen wrestling with the practical difficulties of designing a dispute-resolution process acceptable to mer-

34. Most of the information about these forums comes from interviews I conducted during an internship at the ICA and visits to the LCIA and the SCC in March and April 1998.

35. Craig, Park, and Paulsson 1990, 25–27.

36. Before 15 June 1989, the court's name was Court of Arbitration of the International Chamber of Commerce.

chants of different national backgrounds.[37] It is composed of a chair, eight vice-chairs, and fifty-seven members selected by the ICC national committees and professional organizations. The members are professors, former judges, barristers, and lawyers with expertise in international commercial law and arbitration. They represent a wide range of legal traditions, including civil law, common law, and Islamic law. The ICA meets four times a month, once in plenary session and three times as comité restraint. The ICA is assisted by a secretariat located at ICC headquarters in Paris. The secretariat has a staff of thirty-eight people, including six teams of lawyers from various countries. It assumes responsibility for the day-to-day administration of ICA cases and keeps copies of all written communications and pleadings exchanged in the arbitration proceedings. It also provides assistance and information to parties, counsel, and arbitrators. The provision of centralized information is a particularly valuable service because in an international arbitration case many different national systems of law may need to be consulted, depending on where the arbitration takes place and what issues are involved. National arbitration laws may determine questions of the capacity of the parties to agree to arbitration, the validity of the arbitration agreement, the "arbitrability" of the subject matter of the dispute, and the recognition and enforcement of arbitral awards.[38]

ICC arbitration is characterized not only by a high degree of centralized information gathering but also by the extensive monitoring offered by the ICA. Arbitration proceeds in five steps:

1. The claimant submits a request for arbitration to the secretariat, and the secretariat transmits the request to the defendant, who must respond within thirty days.
2. The court appoints arbitrators and when the parties do not make their own selection chooses the place of arbitration.[39] In selecting the arbitrators, the court relies in part on recommendations from the ICC national committees. The court also fixes the arbitrators' fees and estimates the overall arbitration costs based on the amount in dispute. After receiving half of the advance on arbitration costs, the secretariat transmits the file to the arbitral tribunal. The fixing of fees by the court is intended to prevent the parties from being placed in the uncomfortable position of having to negotiate issues of remuneration with those who will be responsible for deciding their case or otherwise to avoid challenges to an arbitrator's independence.

37. Craig, Park, and Paulsson 1990, xxi. The ICA is supplemented by four other ICC bodies dealing with the settlement of international commercial disputes. They are the Commission on International Arbitration, which advises on the development of ICC Rules of Conciliation and Arbitration; the International Maritime Arbitration Organization; the International Center for Technical Expertise; and the Standing Committee on Regulation of Contractual Relations, which gives parties the possibility of referring to a neutral outsider to adjust contracts whose performance is threatened by fundamentally changed circumstances. See Craig, Park, and Paulsson 1990, 27–28.

38. Redfern and Hunter 1991, xvi. See also Gentinetta 1973.

39. ICC arbitral tribunals are composed of one or three arbitrators.

3. Within two months of receiving the file, the tribunal submits a document called the "Terms of Reference to the Court." This procedure for arriving at the terms can be compared to a prehearing conference, where the arbitrators get to know each other and become familiar with the specifics of the case. The document summarizes the parties' respective claims, states the applicable law and the place of arbitration, and specifies the procedural rules (for evidence, witness statements, and so on) The court checks the Terms of Reference for conformity with ICC rules.
4. As soon as the second half of the advance is paid, the arbitral tribunal proceeds with the case. Within six months (which the court may extend), the tribunal submits a draft award to the court.
5. The court scrutinizes the arbitral award. The court may draw the arbitrators' attention to points of substance or may suggest modifications to the form of the award.[40] Once the court is satisfied, it approves the award, and the secretariat notifies the parties.

The docket of the ICA reflects the growing popularity of ICC arbitration. The first three thousand requests for arbitration were filed between 1923 and 1977. The next three thousand were lodged between 1977 and 1987. In 1991 alone, 333 cases were filed; the yearly number of cases kept growing steadily, reaching 450 in 1997.[41] About 54 percent of the 5,666 parties involved in ICC arbitration are from Western Europe. The most frequently represented nationalities are, in order, France, United States, West Germany, Italy, United Kingdom, Switzerland, Yugoslavia, Netherlands, Belgium, Egypt, Spain, Austria, Rumania, Sweden, and Greece. A recent development is the upsurge of ICC arbitration involving parties from Eastern Europe, Latin America, and South East Asia (7.9, 11.5, and 9.5 percent, respectively, of all parties in 1996).[42]

The London Court of International Arbitration. The LCIA, another long-established arbitration institution, was inaugurated in 1892 as the London Chamber of Arbitration on the initiative of the Corporation of the City of London and the London Chamber of Commerce and Industry. In 1903 the tribunal's name was changed to the London Court of Arbitration. A joint committee, comprising representatives from the Corporation of the City of London and the London Chamber of Commerce, was formed to administer the activities of the court. In 1975 the Institute of Arbitrators (later to become the Chartered Institute of Arbitrators) joined the other two administering bodies. In 1981 the name was changed to the London Court of International Arbitration to reflect the nature of its work, which

40. The ICA returns roughly 15–20 percent of the awards to the arbitrators for revision. See Dezalay and Garth 1996, 47–48; and Smit 1994, especially 68–72.

41. See Craig, Park, and Paulsson 1990; and The ICC International Court of Arbitration Bulletin, various issues.

42. The ICC International Court of Arbitration Bulletin, various issues.

was moving steadily from domestic to international arbitration. In 1986 the LCIA was incorporated as a limited company under the control of a board of directors. It is composed of a president, who is also the chairman of the board of directors, four vice-presidents, and about twenty other members, all of whom are international arbitrators from major trading countries. The number of members drawn from the United Kingdom is restricted to no more than one quarter of the total. The court is assisted by a small London-based secretariat of about five people.

The LCIA is somewhat less involved in arbitration proceedings than the ICA. Its main function is to select arbitrators or to confirm party-nominated arbitrators. Like the ICA, the LCIA has the right to reject party-nominated arbitrators if it judges that they are not independent or that they are otherwise unsuitable. The LCIA fixes the arbitrators' fees and ensures that the arbitrators comply with the procedural timetable and respect all other rules of LCIA arbitration. Unlike the ICA, the LCIA does not require arbitrators to draft terms of reference, nor does it scrutinize arbitral awards.

Despite recent efforts to further internationalize its services, notably through the creation of four so-called users councils for Europe, North America, Asia-Pacific, and Africa, the LCIA remains an institution with a British bent.[43] This is reflected, for example, in the fact that all LCIA presidents until 1993 were British, and that 60 percent of court-selected arbitrators and 65 percent of party-nominated arbitrators are nationals from the United Kingdom. The parties most frequently involved in cases being considered by the LCIA come from the United Kingdom, United States, Australia, Canada, India, and Hong Kong.

The Arbitration Institute of the Stockholm Chamber of Commerce. A frequently named third major international arbitration institution is the SCC Institute, established in 1917 as an independent entity within the SCC. The SCC Institute is composed of a board of three members (and three deputies). The chairman of the board has to be a judge with expertise in commercial and industrial matters. Of the two other members, one has to be a practicing lawyer, the other "a person who enjoys the confidence of the business community."[44] The board is assisted by a small secretariat.

Similar to the LCIA, the SCC Institute's main role is to act as an authority to appoint arbitral tribunals. Challenges against arbitrators are handled directly by the board. The rules of the SCC Institute require that a tribunal deal with a case in an "impartial, practical, and speedy fashion," give all parties "sufficient opportunity to present [their cases]," and reach a decision "no later than one year after the case has been referred to the arbitral tribunal."[45]

43. "Users' councils" have been set up to keep the international business community apprised of the arbitration services offered by the LCIA and to identify the changing needs of business to be able to respond quickly to these needs. Membership in these councils is by invitation; members include lawyers, arbitrators, and multinational industrial, commercial, and trading organizations.

44. SCC 1988, para. 2.

45. Ibid., para. 16, 26.

The development of the SCC Institute into a major center of international commercial arbitration dates from the 1970s when the United States and the Soviet Union agreed that trade contracts between the two countries should contain a clause providing for arbitration according to the rules of the SCC Institute. The caseload of the institute grew to a yearly average of about thirty-five in the 1980s and one hundred in the 1990s. In 1997, eighty-two international cases and twenty-nine domestic cases were registered with the secretariat. The most frequently represented nationalities in recent years have been Russian, Ukrainian, and American.

Explaining Forum Selection and Institutional Variety

In this section I seek to explain why actors engaged in international trade and investment select different methods of international commercial dispute resolution. I argue that these methods respond to the varying institutional needs of different types of disputes and disputants. Such needs can be explained in terms of the uncertainty about the preferences or behavior of contractual partners, the severity of the enforcement problem, and the uncertainty about the state of the world. The empirical evidence discussed offers strong support for several Rational Design conjectures.

Uncertainty, Enforcement, and Centralization

Uncertainty about preferences and behavior varies with the relative intimacy of the relationship between parties involved in international exchange. Intimacy or closeness of a relationship, in turn, depends on the parties' homogeneity, their frequency of interaction, and their distance from each other. Robert Cooter and Janet Landa, for example, have documented how traders belonging to ethnically homogeneous commercial groups, such as the East Indians in East Africa, the Syrians in West Africa, and the Chinese in Southeast Asia, experience considerably lower levels of behavioral uncertainty when dealing with one another than when dealing with outsiders.[46] One reason is that such trading groups serve as repositories of trust, which reduces the probability of a breach of contract between insiders.

Disputes may occasionally erupt even among insiders, but they are likely to be resolved more cooperatively than conflicts among strangers.[47] Marc Galanter, a leading exponent of the law and society movement, has argued that "in order to understand the distribution of [domestic] litigation, we must go beyond the characteristics of individual parties to consider the relations between them. Are the parties strangers or intimates? Is their relationship episodic or enduring? Is it

46. See, for example, Cooter and Landa 1984; and Landa 1981. See also Greif 1992; and Curtin 1984.
47. For examples, see Auerbach 1983. See also Ellickson 1991.

single-stranded or multiplex?"[48] He finds that, generally, the more inclusive and enduring a relationship between a set of parties, the less likely disputes will be taken to official forums (public courts); instead, such parties will seek to resolve their differences in so-called embedded forums, that is, forums that are part of the social setting within which a dispute arose.[49] A classic illustration of embedded commercial interactions and dispute resolution is Stuart Macaulay's study of local business practices among firms in Wisconsin. Macaulay finds that uncertainty about contract performance is reduced by widely accepted local norms (for example, "commitments are to be honored in almost all situations—one does not welsh on a deal," and "one ought to produce a good product and stand behind it") and by close personal relationships across the boundaries of local business organizations. He notes that "salesmen often know purchasing agents well. The same two individuals occupying these roles may have dealt with each other . . . [for up to] 25 years. Each has something to give the other. . . . [T]op executives may [also] know each other. They may sit together on government or trade committees. They may know each other socially and even belong to the same country club."[50] Disputes in this business community are frequently settled without reference to the contract or potential or actual legal sanctions. "If something comes up, you get the other man on the telephone and deal with the problem. . . . One doesn't run to lawyers if [one] wants to stay in business."[51]

These examples shed light on the varying degrees of centralization of forums for resolving international commercial disputes, suggesting the following conjecture: Centralization of forums to which private international parties resort to resolve their disputes increases with the uncertainty about the parties' preferences or behavior. This conjecture is in line with Rational Design conjecture C1, CENTRALIZATION increases with UNCERTAINTY ABOUT BEHAVIOR.[52] Centralization implies a high degree of central provision of procedural safeguards and information. Such provision is characteristic of institutional arbitration; it is absent, however, in ad hoc arbitration or ADR (see Table 1).

Parties involved in an ongoing mutually beneficial relationship (possibly with dealings along many different fronts) are less likely to rely on highly institutionalized forms of dispute resolution than parties with no anticipated future relationship, that is, parties that are not repeat players or do not belong to some close-knit trading

48. Galanter 1993, 24.

49. See also Galanter 1981. For examples of embedded forums, see Doo 1973; Columbia Journal of Law and Social Problems 1970; Bernstein 1992; and Maitland 1936.

50. Macaulay 1963, 63.

51. Ibid., 61.

52. Note that I am interested in knowing not which dispute-resolution clause the parties write into a contract but which method they ultimately use. The contractual provision may differ from the actual method used. For example, parties that write an ICC arbitration clause into their contract may decide to use ad hoc arbitration when a dispute erupts. Similarly, parties may choose some form of arbitration rather than complying with a jurisdiction clause. Some contracts have no provision for resolving disputes; in these cases the parties will choose the appropriate forms when disputes erupt, provided the parties have an interest in settling their disputes. Coe 1997, 56, 161.

community. There are two reasons. First, parties in a continuing relationship can more easily control each other because the expected future gains can serve as hostage.[53] They are locked in a "win-win" situation; thus each other's behavior is quite predictable, for the parties have little to gain (but potentially much to lose) from using dilatory tactics or adopting other forms of noncooperation. They are anxious to maintain good relations and are therefore likely to be interested in reaching a quick and amicable settlement. Second, parties in a continuing relationship typically have good information about each other's past behavior, past problems, and past solutions. This knowledge may be usefully brought to bear in a new instance of conflict.

International arbitrators and lawyers whom I have interviewed have confirmed the importance of the nature of a business relationship in determining how a dispute is likely to be resolved. Typically, parties in long-term relationships have a strong preference for settling disputes through ADR or ad hoc arbitration. This finding is also supported in several writings. Bertie Vigrass, former registrar of the LCIA, summarizes the evidence as follows: "In the traditional fields of arbitration, such as maritime, construction, insurance, and commodity, it is usual for the majority of arbitrations to be 'ad hoc' in nature. This is probably because there is an on-going relationship between parties, their legal representatives, and arbitrators."[54] Four leading international arbitrators—Martin Hunter, Jan Paulsson, Nigel Rawding, and Alan Redfern—have similarly noted that "ADR provides an effective means of resolving disputes between parties who have an interest in maintaining an on-going business relationship. The parties approach the process in a spirit of negotiation and compromise, instead of adopting the adversarial positions associated with litigation."[55]

The extent of centralization of a dispute-resolution method, however, is not solely determined by the relative uncertainty about the parties' preferences or behavior. Enforcement problems may persist even in the presence of good information and knowledge about the parties if the payoff from unilateral defection is significantly greater than the payoff from mutual cooperation at the dispute-resolution stage. This implies that the more severe the enforcement problem, the greater the need for centralization (Rational Design conjecture C4, CENTRALIZATION increases with ENFORCEMENT problems).

Such enforcement problems are typical, for example, when contracts are about to expire. No long-term relationship will last forever. Construction, licensing, distributorship, joint venture, and other long-term contracts will eventually terminate, and relationships will come to an end. Logically, such changes will also affect the ways in which disputes that arise after a business relationship has ended will be resolved. Consider, for example, the case of a complex, long-term construction contract as

53. On the role of hostages in economic exchange, see Williamson 1983; and Kronman 1985.

54. Vigrass 1993, 469. See also Graving 1989, 368.

55. Hunter et al. 1993, 73. See also Perlman and Nelson 1983, 232; Coe 1997, 44–49; and Park 1997b.

described by James Myers, head of a major international construction group:[56] At the onset, the contractor, employer, and engineer are all anxious to maintain harmonious working relationships with one another. They realize that the ability of one party to perform over an extended period of time rests on the cooperation of the others. Disputes, when they arise, will be resolved swiftly, fairly, and in a friendly fashion. ADR and ad hoc arbitration are the preferred methods of resolving disputes in such settings. Parties may sometimes even refrain from presenting claims, lest the relationship be strained. Once the project is completed, however, the parties' attitudes are likely to change. A contractor who has no further business with the employer may now feel no compunction about demanding payment for additional costs accumulated during the course of the construction, and the employer will have no hesitation in dismissing such claims as baseless. Myers notes that "proceedings which occur after the completion of an [international construction] contract . . . are resolved in a distinctly adversarial atmosphere in which large sums of money are sought, with little or no 'commercial downside'—meaning that the commercial relationship has normally expired and the parties have nothing to lose by refusing to accommodate each other for the sake of continuous harmonious commercial relations."[57]

It is apparent from this example that good will, the prerequisite for successful use of ADR or ad hoc arbitration, can no longer be taken for granted after a contractual relationship has ended. In such a situation, ADR and ad hoc arbitration are doomed to failure, but institutional arbitration is in its element. Unsurprisingly, the vast majority of disputes submitted to institutional arbitration arise shortly before or after a commercial relationship has ended. The following example, a typical institutional arbitration case, explains why and illustrates how procedural safeguards and monitoring provided by arbitral institutions help to overcome the difficulties posed by defection strategies.[58]

In 1987 a large German company (the claimant) entered into an agreement with a firm in Colombia (the defendant) granting the Columbian firm the exclusive license to manufacture and distribute certain pharmaceutical and biological products in Colombia for four years. In 1991 the German company decided not to renew the license agreement, and one year later it initiated arbitration proceedings claiming that the defendant had breached certain of its surviving obligations, such as reporting inventory and sales of the licensed products and refusing to pay substantial sums. The Colombian firm refused to respond to these claims.

In this case the conflict erupted after one party decided to end a business relationship. For the Colombian firm, the termination of the contract seems to

56. Myers 1991. See also Schwartz 1995; Stipanowich 1996; and Vagts 1987.

57. Myers 1991, 316.

58. The example is based on an actual ICC arbitration case. The names of the parties have been omitted. The case captures many of the features typical of institutional arbitration, notably in licensing, distributorship, construction, and sale of goods. About 70 percent of ICC arbitration cases fall into these categories.

have triggered a change in its view about the necessity of acting cooperatively. Defection from "surviving obligations" may be seen as an attractive strategy because it brings immediate gains without imposing an obvious long-term cost. Such an uncooperative disposition typically also pervades the dispute-resolution process in this type of case. For example, the defendant could try to evade the contractual obligation to arbitrate the dispute, arguing that the matter falls under its national jurisdiction and can only be decided in a national court according to national law and procedural rules. This is precisely the strategy that the Colombian party took; it wanted the case to be tried in Colombian courts under Colombian law. If this fails, the defendant may seek to derail the arbitral proceedings by disagreeing on the choice of arbitrator(s), procedural rules, place and language of arbitration, and applicable law. It could also try to delay the proceedings by failing to appear on dates selected for hearings or by raising questions over procedural matters. If none of these dilatory tactics succeeds, the defendant still has the option of challenging the arbitral award before a national court, on the basis that the arbitral tribunal exceeded its jurisdiction or that there was a substantial miscarriage of justice in the course of the proceedings. Finally, the party may simply choose not to honor the arbitral award.

Ad hoc arbitration demands little more than simple coordination among the arbitrators, procedural rules, applicable law, and place of arbitration. The institutional demands on cases like the German-Colombian one are much more complex. Extensive monitoring and strong institutional safeguards are necessary to deprive potential bad faith and other forms of "defection" of their effects in such cases.

The ICA is an example of an organization well equipped to handle such "difficult" cases. Its rules and institutional apparatus effectively override obstacles that a noncooperative disposition by one of the parties may pose. For instance, if one of the parties refuses to participate in the arbitral proceedings, the ICA is entitled to appoint the arbitrator(s) and constitute a tribunal. The notice and summons procedure is performed by the ICC secretariat and is supervised by the court, assuring the arbitrators that the defaulting party had notice of the arbitration.[59] If one party fails to sign the Terms of Reference, the ICA may approve them and the proceedings continue. After the Terms of Reference are approved, the opportunity for a party to engage in dilatory tactics by presenting additional claims and counterclaims is minimized because such claims can only be heard on the agreement of all parties.[60]

The court closely monitors the arbitral proceedings, ensuring that time limits and due process principles are respected.[61] It replaces arbitrators who do not fulfill their functions or are behind in their work. At the end of the process, it scrutinizes the award in relation to jurisdiction and applicable law. This monitoring and checking

59. Aksen 1991, 12.

60. Ibid., 13.

61. Principles of due process include transparency of the arbitral process, the right of the parties to be called and heard, and equal treatment of the parties in the exchange of pleadings, in evidentiary matters, in resort to expertise proceedings, and in the holding of hearings.

increases the quality of the arbitral award and, in turn, reduces the chance that the losing party will challenge the award in a national court. As noted by an experienced international arbitrator, "most final awards rendered under ICC auspices are carried out voluntarily by the parties, because [of their high] quality. . . . A company that fails to carry out an [ICC award] is almost certain to lose subsequent[ly][62] and in addition runs the risk of jeopardizing its reputation in international circles."[63] Indeed, only about 6 percent of all ICC awards have been challenged by the losing party, and a minute 0.5 percent of awards rendered under the aegis of the ICC have been set aside by a national court.[64]

It is easy to see why ad hoc arbitration and ADR are ill-suited for situations represented by the German-Colombian case. If at any stage of the proceedings in ad hoc arbitration or ADR matters go unexpectedly awry and one of the parties starts acting in bad faith, there is no international supervisory institution to coerce compliance with procedural rules.[65] Furthermore, if the losing party in an ad hoc arbitration case challenges the award in a national court, the winning party will find it considerably more difficult to prove to the national court that due process rules were respected and the tribunal was impartial and objective. Not surprisingly, national courts are much more comfortable confirming commercial awards that result from a monitored arbitration process than those produced by ad hoc proceedings.[66]

Uncertainty about the state of the world and centralization. Uncertainty about the state of the world is a third variable that is useful in understanding the selection of different arbitration options. It refers to the extent to which actors involved in international exchange are knowledgeable about international commercial arbitration and possess information about the legal environment (the laws and the integrity of local judges) in which arbitration takes place and the conditions for enforceability of arbitral awards. Good information on the legal environment and enforceability is a prerequisite of successful resolution of commercial disputes. The conjecture here is straightforward: The greater the uncertainty about the present state of the world, the greater the need for centralized information on international commercial arbitration and domestic arbitration laws and practices (Rational Design conjecture C2, CENTRALIZATION increases with UNCERTAINTY ABOUT THE STATE OF THE WORLD). Such information may be particularly important in cases involving traders with little

62. In other words, when the winning party applies to a national court for recognition and enforcement of the award.

63. Aksen 1991, 22. See also David 1985, 45; and Hunter et al. 1993, 10.

64. See Craig, Park, and Paulsson 1990, 32–33; and David 1985, 50.

65. The type of problem that can arise in ad hoc arbitration is illustrated in a recent case (Intercarbon Bermuda v. Caltex Trading and Transport), where one party refused to proceed with an arbitration pursuant to an arbitration clause that provided for no institution to set the arbitration in motion. The claimant was forced to spend seven years in litigation before obtaining a federal court order compelling arbitration. Park 1995, 70. See also Coulson 1993; Aksen 1991, 8–9; and Paulsson 1993, 438.

66. David 1985, 11.

experience in international exchange or traders from very different cultural and linguistic regions. Major arbitral institutions help to provide the necessary information and procedural guidelines to enable inexperienced parties to resolve their commercial disputes in an efficient and timely fashion.

"Legal environment" encompasses domestic legislation on arbitration and court interpretations of it. The law in the location where arbitration will occur is of great importance because it may determine questions of the capacity of the parties to agree to arbitration, the validity of the arbitration agreement, the "arbitrability" of the subject matter of the dispute, and the recognition and enforcement of arbitral awards. Thus parties seeking to maximize procedural certainty may benefit from relying on centralized information on domestic arbitration laws and practices; such information will help them choose an arbitral situs where annulment of awards is not likely to be facilitated by a bribe to a local judge, where the range of nonarbitral legal questions is narrow and well defined, where the integrity of the arbitration process is ensured and any judicial meddling with an arbitrator's substantive decision is minimized, and where arbitration decisions are enforceable—if necessary, through execution against the assets of the losing party by proceedings in national courts of any state in which these assets are located.

Some countries have clear arbitration legislation, but their courts may misapply the law, for example, by adopting overelastic interpretations of "violations of public policy" as grounds for setting aside awards. Other countries may have national laws containing mandatory provisions that override explicit contractual stipulations. Two examples serve to illustrate how arbitrary and fickle domestic legal decisions regarding international arbitration may be, thus underlining the importance of centralized information on developments in national arbitration laws and practices:[67]

The Indian Supreme Court held in May 1992 that if Indian law applied to an arbitration clause, an application to set aside an award could be heard in India, even if the place of arbitration were outside India, and the Indian courts could enjoin the enforcement of the award anywhere. In other words, an acceptance of Indian law in a contract with an Indian party would ultimately lead to the Indian courts irrespective of the choice of a neutral venue.

In Singapore, in a 1988 decision, the High Court affirmed restrictions on foreign arbitration parties imposed by local practice rules. This was followed by a new Singapore Legal Profession Act, which stipulates that foreign lawyers can only appear in arbitration proceedings when the law applicable to a dispute is not Singaporean law. When Singaporean law does apply, foreign lawyers may only appear jointly with lawyers who are Singaporean nationals.

The second issue of central importance is the enforceability of arbitral awards. An award rendered in a given country may not automatically be enforceable in other countries where the losing party's assets may lie. Thus, a key function of major

67. The examples are drawn from Hunter et al. 1993. See also Park 1997a.

arbitral institutions is to collect and continuously update information on the conditions of enforceability of awards in various parts of the world. For example, by 1997 over one hundred states had acceded to the 1958 New York Convention on the Recognition and Enforcement of Arbitral Awards.[68] The majority of these states adopted the so-called reciprocity reservation. That means that their courts will enforce an award under the New York Convention only if the award has been rendered within the territory of another state that has also adhered to the New York Convention.[69] A court in a signatory country may refuse recognition and enforcement of awards only on procedural grounds, including invalidity of the arbitral agreement, denial of an opportunity to be heard, arbitrator excess of jurisdiction, arbitral procedure contrary to the parties' agreement, and annulment of the award in the country where rendered.[70] However, the interpretation by national courts of these grounds for denying enforcement of arbitral awards may vary from country to country. Therefore, major arbitral institutions also keep information on the various national interpretations.

In sum, private firms and their lawyers may often lack sufficient information about the legal state of the world to avoid expensive delays and other negative surprises. This is particularly true if the parties are inexperienced in international trade and investment or if they deal with firms from distant regions.[71] Uncertainty about the legal environment and enforceability can be reduced, at least in part, by relying on information provided by major arbitral institutions, such as the ICA or the LCIA. Such forums have the institutional capacity to monitor and record changes in domestic arbitration laws and practices around the world, especially if their memberships have a broad geographic base.

An examination of the docket of the ICA offers supporting evidence for the conjecture that firms from different regions rely more heavily on centralized support and expertise for the resolution of their disputes than firms operating in relatively homogenous regions. Table 2 lists the origin of the parties in all ICA cases since 1974. Strikingly, Western Europeans have been involved in well over half of all cases. The key finding, however, emerges from Table 3. Despite the well-known fact that Europeans (and North Americans) trade much more intraregionally than with other regions, it appears that considerably more interregional commercial

68. See UN Doc E/Conf. 26/SR., 1–25. The standard work on this treaty is Berg 1981. Besides the New York Convention, there are at least two other international enforcement conventions, the 1975 Inter-American Arbitration Convention (also called the Panama Convention) and the 1961 European Convention on International Commercial Arbitration. In addition to these conventions, many bilateral commercial and investment treaties contain enforcement provisions. For a brief historical account of the development of the various enforcement conventions, see Redfern and Hunter 1991, 60–64; see also Sanders 1996, 41–42; and Jackson 1991.

69. Hunter et al. 1993, 19. Art. III of the New York Convention provides that convention states shall recognize foreign awards as "binding and enforce them in accordance with the rules of procedure of the territory where the award is relied upon," subject to no conditions more onerous than those imposed on domestic awards.

70. Park 1995, 55–56.

71. Aksen 1991, 14.

TABLE 2. Origin of parties in ICC arbitration cases (average per period)

Region	1974–85	1986–90	1991–95	1996–97
Western Europe	59.2%	56.9%	59.7%	49.5%
Central and Eastern Europe	3.8%	3.2%	6.1%	7.1%
Middle East	8%	5.2%	4.1%	3.2%
Africa	9.2%	8.9%	5.3%	5.7%
North America (United States and Canada)	13.3%	13.8%	11.8%	13.5%
Latin America and the Caribbean	3.4%	3.6%	4.8%	11.5%
Asia	3.1%	8.4%	8.2%	9.5%

Source: ICC International Court of Arbitration Bulletin, various issues; and author's notes taken during internship at ICC International Court of Arbitration, Paris, 1998.

disputes are submitted to the ICA than disputes arising among firms from the same region, that is, Europe, North America, or any other region listed in Table 2. On average, approximately three out of four disputes brought to the ICA involve parties from different regions. This statistic contrasts sharply with the finding about the geographic distribution of ad hoc cases. According to international arbitrators interviewed in Paris, Stockholm, and New York, ad hoc cases seem to be more common among parties from relatively homogenous regions and communities.[72] However, since no institution keeps track of ad hoc arbitration cases and full information therefore does not exist, the finding about ad hoc cases must be considered tentative.

Uncertainty about the state of the world and flexibility. Uncertainty about the state of the world can also refer to the susceptibility of an issue-area to new developments or unanticipated shocks that may leave parties in uncharted legal territory. The conjecture, in this case, is as follows: The more uncertain the state of the world, the greater the desirability of a flexible method for resolving disputes (Rational Design conjecture F1, FLEXIBILITY increases with UNCERTAINTY ABOUT THE STATE OF THE WORLD), thus implying a preference of arbitration and ADR over litigation in public courts.[73]

The flexibility offered in arbitration and ADR may be valued, for example, because it gives firms operating at the forefront of new production and exchange methods the possibility of appointing experts who have the necessary technical knowledge to evaluate complex, new situations and understand the facts; an ordinary judge cannot be expected to have this specialized knowledge. Complex

72. Based on interviews at the ICA (April 1998), the SCC Institute (April 1998), and law firms in New York (October 1998).

73. On institutional flexibility and its relationship to uncertainty, see also the studies in this volume by Oatley, Richards, and Rosendorff and Milner.

TABLE 3. Regional distribution of ICC arbitration cases (average per period based on available samples)

	1974–85 (37 cases)	1986–90 (36 cases)	1991–95 (19 cases)	1996–97 (140 cases)
Intraregional disputes	30%	11%	26%	32%
Interregional disputes	70%	89%	74%	68%

Source: Author's computation based on case collections in Jarvin and Derains 1990; Jarvin, Derains, and Arnaldez 1994; Arnaldez, Derains, and Hascher 1997; and author's notes taken during internship at ICC International Court of Arbitration, Paris, 1998.

technical issues may arise in cases dealing with transfer of technology, industrial property, trademarks, technical know-how, and financial products. Brian Neill, Justice of the Court of Appeals of England and Wales, observes that "cases arise from time to time which involve questions which lie at or near the frontiers of current scientific knowledge. Can they be tried satisfactorily in the ordinary courts? There must be doubt."[74]

Flexibility also permits the expert to disregard, to some extent, the technicalities of the law in favor of a solution that accords with new business practices. An arbitral tribunal, for example, may be given powers of so-called amiable composition or, as it is sometimes put, the right to decide ex aequo et bono (in equity and good conscience); that is, the tribunal may reach a decision without applying strict legal principles, provided the decision is fair. More generally, flexibility allows the parties to tailor the rules—regarding procedure, evidence, or even the substance of the case—to their specific needs.[75]

The advantages of flexibility in dispute resolution can be illustrated with the help of a major arbitration case that involved IBM and Fujitsu, two of the world's largest computer companies. The dispute erupted over intellectual property rights to operating system software. In the early 1970s Fujitsu decided to develop and market IBM-compatible operating system software for mainframe computers.[76] A decade later, IBM confronted Fujitsu with allegations that Fujitsu's operating system programs violated IBM's intellectual property rights. After lengthy negotiations, the two companies signed two agreements in 1983; one agreement granted Fujitsu immunity and waiver of IBM claims with respect to past and future distribution of Fujitsu's programs in exchange for payments from Fujitsu to IBM; the other agreement required each party to provide the other with information relevant to

74. Neill 1988, 235. For confirming evidence of the importance of this point, see recent survey results in Bühring-Uhle 1996, 136–37.
75. Redfern and Hunter 1991, 24; see also Jones 1958, 464; and Kerr 1987.
76. This account draws on Mnookin 1994.

compatibility. These agreements, however, quickly broke down, and in 1985 IBM filed a demand for arbitration accusing Fujitsu of copying its software in violation of copyright law and IBM's rights under the 1983 agreements. Fujitsu denied violating IBM's rights and accused IBM of failing to live up to its obligations under the agreements.

The case turned out to be highly complex because of enormous legal and factual uncertainties. IBM and Fujitsu were developing software in a world of rapidly changing technology. However, no clear understanding existed of what the law of copyright was and how it applied to computer software and the particular subject matter of the dispute. One of the arbitrators involved in the case, Robert Mnookin, noted that "this was not a dispute where there was a clear and agreed understanding of the underlying law and where it was only necessary to apply clear law to particular facts. . . . There were no [prior] . . . judicial decisions. No one knew the precise scope of copyright protection."[77] Legal uncertainties were compounded by factual uncertainties. Indeed, the disputed programs involved hundreds of thousands (in some cases millions) of lines of codes, rendering fact finding exceedingly difficult.

The arbitrators overcame some of these difficulties by themselves creating the law that would bind the two parties vis-à-vis each other. First, they probed the interests of the parties to identify areas of convergence.[78] They then proceeded to develop, in close consultation with the parties' technical representatives, detailed rules to define what would and would not be permitted in compatible software development. As a result of the arbitration effort, IBM and Fujitsu agreed to set aside the 1983 agreements and execute a new agreement in 1987 that provided a successful framework for resolving all issues in dispute.

In short, arbitration enabled the parties to take a flexible approach and tailor the rules to their particular problem and underlying interests. Rather than framing the strategies in terms of penalties or exoneration for past conduct, the parties took a forward-looking strategy and actively participated in the rule-making process that eventually established clear rights and obligations between them.

Far from being an isolated case, the IBM-Fujitsu dispute is representative of a rapidly growing body of international arbitration cases dealing with intellectual property rights. This growth has been fueled by the speedy reduction of trade barriers, the proliferation of digital means of communication, and the increase of commerce via the internet. Unsurprisingly, such disputes are the fastest growing

77. Robert Mnookin at Geneva Global Arbitration Forum (21 October 1993); see Mnookin, Méan, and Robine 1994, 141–42.

78. It became clear that Fujitsu's paramount interest was to develop IBM-compatible software, but it demanded access only to external interface information, not information about internal design of IBM programs. IBM in turn was interested in ensuring that Fujitsu did not copy internal design information and that it received adequate compensation for external interface information contained in IBM programs extracted by Fujitsu.

category of cases submitted to the ICA, increasing from 8.6 percent in 1982 to an average of almost 20 percent in the past four years.[79]

The institutional characteristics, such as flexibility, that render arbitration appealing in a growing number of areas, may not, however, be necessary or even desirable in other commercial contexts, and thus the requisite dispute-resolution methods will vary. Consider, for example, the case of international loan agreements between private parties. Big companies may take out large syndicated loans to finance trade, exploit natural resources, assist take-over bids, provide working capital, construct new plants, drill rigs, buy ships, and so on. When writing international loan agreements, the lending banks will take great care in covering all contingencies that may result in losses to the banks and in seeking the best possible protection against such events. The banks will also spell out as clearly as possible what sums of money are to be paid at any particular time, how they are to be paid, and by whom.[80]

Loan agreements also contain a governing-law or choice-of-law clause that sets forth the law that determines the validity of the contractual provisions that have been inserted in the loan agreement and the effect and scope of the contractual rights and obligations expressed in the agreement.[81] As Richard Slater explains, "A bank wants to be sure that if certain events of default, which it has taken the trouble to write into its loan agreement, occur, then it is entitled to accelerate the loan[82] without having to worry about whether the event is material, whether the borrower was to blame for its occurrence, whether it was fair, or whether it was in accordance with normal practice. A bank wants as little scope as possible for debate about the meaning of the provisions in its loan agreement."[83]

It is now easy to see why bankers shun arbitration clauses and, instead, insert in almost all international loan agreements jurisdiction clauses, selecting either New York courts or the London High Court as forums (depending on whether the contract is governed by New York or British substantive law).[84] Unlike in construction, engineering, and intellectual property cases, which tend to go to arbitration, the question in international loan cases is generally quite simple: has the debt fallen due and been left unpaid, and, if so, how much is it? In most cases, establishing this fact is simple. Thus disputes under a loan agreement will

79. Based on interviews at the ICA, Paris (April 1998). One area that several interviewees identified as likely to generate heavy arbitration activity is telecommunications, the fastest growing sector of most industrialized economies. Privatization of government-owned network operators, deregulation, and the introduction of cross-border competition are fundamentally changing the industry; and many telecommunication disputes are expected to involve intellectual property issues. Interviews at the Commission of the European Union, Brussels (March 1998), and the LCIA, London (April 1998).

80. Slater 1982, 177–78.

81. Gruson 1982, 17. The vast majority of loan agreements select British or New York law, in part because of these laws' strict approach to the concepts of breach of contract and sanctity of contract.

82. "To accelerate the loan" means to terminate a lending relationship and declare all amounts outstanding under the loan agreement immediately due and payable.

83. Slater 1982, 195–96.

84. Cates and Isern-Feliu 1983, 28–29, 34.

typically relate not to matters of fact but law.[85] However, legal uncertainties or intricacies are also rare in loan cases. Legal matters under loan agreements are well covered by case precedents and statutes; thus the courts in New York and the United Kingdom possess, in most cases, the requisite information to deal expeditiously with default cases.[86] For these reasons, litigation seems a more appropriate method than arbitration for the resolution of disputes arising from international loan agreements.

Conclusion

International commercial arbitration has emerged over the past two decades as the method of choice for settling a growing number of trade and investment disputes involving private parties. Its surge in popularity can be attributed in part to the institutional attributes of arbitration, which include flexibility, technical expertise, privacy, and confidentiality. These attributes match the needs of disputants in areas such as intellectual property, transfer of technology, engineering, and construction. Arbitration options, however, are not the only methods available to private parties. The market for dispute-resolution mechanisms also includes recourse to public courts and several alternative-dispute resolution techniques.

I have argued that firms on the demand side select methods for dispute resolution according to their design problems. In other words, the various methods respond to the varying institutional needs of different types of disputes and disputants, and these needs can be explained in terms of the severity of the enforcement problem, uncertainty about the preferences or behavior of contractual partners, and uncertainty about the state of the world. More specifically, the findings are that (1) centralization of forums to which private international parties resort to resolve their disputes increases with the severity of the enforcement problem (Rational Design conjecture C4, CENTRALIZATION increases with ENFORCEMENT PROBLEMS); (2) centralization also increases with uncertainty about the parties' preferences or behavior (conjecture C1, CENTRALIZATION increases with UNCERTAINTY ABOUT BEHAVIOR); (3) the need for centralized information on international commercial arbitration and domestic arbitration laws and practices grows with greater uncertainty about the legal environment in which arbitration takes place and the conditions for enforceability of arbitral awards (conjecture C2, CENTRALIZATION increases with UNCERTAINTY ABOUT THE STATE OF THE WORLD); and (4) the desirability of a flexible method for resolving disputes increases with the susceptibility of an issue-area to new developments or unanticipated shocks that may leave the parties in uncharted legal territory (conjecture F1, FLEXIBILITY increases with UNCERTAINTY ABOUT THE STATE OF THE WORLD).

85. Wood 1980, 71–73; see also Slater 1982, 197; and Cates and Isern-Feliu 1983, 28–36.
86. Ryan 1982, 89–132.

This study thus illustrates that Koremenos, Lipson, and Snidal's analytical framework not only sheds light on institutional arrangements among states[87] but can also account for varying forms of international governance established by private parties.

My analysis, however, has only scratched the surface of a complex but fascinating area of research for scholars of international relations and other social scientists. Several issues evoked in passing merit fuller analysis. One is the study of specialized arbitration, for example, as conducted in maritime affairs or as offered by various stock and commodity exchanges. Such arbitration is typically conducted within commercial groups with strong national roots. For example, the British Coffee Trade Federation numbers over one hundred firms as members, including the leading roasters, merchants, brokers, and wharfingers in the United Kingdom. Notwithstanding its national base, the federation is linked to a wide network of transnational commodity organizations such as the Committee of European Coffee Associations, the European Federation of Coffee Roasters Associations, and the Federation of Commodity Associations. This raises the question of how this "institutional embeddedness" is likely to shape the arbitral institutions and practices of national federations.

Another question that emerges from the study of arbitration is why states have traditionally been reluctant to resort to international arbitration. Indeed, while the number of arbitration cases involving private parties has grown exponentially, instances of interstate arbitration are few. For example, after a modest beginning, recourse to the Permanent Court of Arbitration at the Hague became infrequent in the extreme. Of the twenty-five cases considered by the court, twenty-two cases were disposed of by 1935; the other three were heard in 1940, 1956, and 1970, respectively.[88]

Another example are disputes submitted to the arbitration mechanism of the International Center for the Settlement of Investment Disputes (ICSID). ICSID was created in 1966 by the so-called Washington Convention as part of the World Bank organization. ICSID's authority is limited to investment disputes where one of the parties is the host state. By 1995, only thirty investment disputes had been brought to the ICSID for arbitration, resulting in what Stephen Toope calls a "highly limited case load";[89] and Aron Broches notes similarly that "advance acceptance of [ICSID's] jurisdiction has not resulted in a large number of cases."[90]

The specific reasons for the paucity of arbitration cases involving states are varied and complex. However, one theme runs throughout history, namely the deep concern of states with maintaining sovereignty and independence combined with a perception that national autonomy and international arbitration practices are not easily compatible. Consider the following examples: In 1903 France concluded an

87. Koremenos, Lipson, and Snidal, this volume.
88. Butler 1992, 44.
89. Toope 1990, 255.
90. Broches 1979, 374; see also Gray and Kingsbury 1992.

agreement with the United Kingdom that provided for the settlement by arbitration of certain disputes that may arise between the two countries. Reference would be made to the Permanent Court of Arbitration. Tellingly, however, the signatories added a clause to the agreement stating that only those differences would qualify for submission to arbitration "that . . . do not affect the vital interests, the independence, or the honor of the two contracting states."[91] Similar provisions were inserted in other arbitration treaties of the period. Needless to say, the malleability and subjective nature of these exceptions considerably weakened the legal obligation to arbitrate disputes.[92]

Some countries considered even such watered-down arbitration clauses as too intrusive. Latin American countries, for example, rejected arbitration and insisted on so-called Calvo clauses that required foreign parties to agree to adjudication within the host state of any dispute arising out of an investment contract.[93] More recently, oil-exporting nations have manifested similar hostility to arbitration, demanding that "disputes arising between a government and operator shall fall exclusively within the jurisdiction of competent national courts."[94]

States' concern with safeguarding sovereignty is also reflected in principles of international law. One example is the distinction made between immunity from jurisdiction, also called immunity from suit, and immunity from execution, which means immunity from measures sought against the property of a state for the enforcement of an arbitral award. A waiver of immunity from jurisdiction, which follows from entering into a valid agreement to arbitrate, does not automatically entail a waiver of immunity from execution. This principle is enshrined, for example, in the ICSID Convention, which stipulates that "nothing . . . [in the ICSID Convention] shall be construed as derogating from the law in force in any Contracting State relating to immunity of that State or any foreign State from execution."[95] Similarly, the draft Convention of State Immunity that the International Law Commission published in 1991, after thirteen years of work, states that "no measures of constraint such as attachment, arrest, and execution against property of a State may be taken in connection with a proceeding before the court of another state. . . . Immunity from execution may be viewed, therefore, as the last fortress, the last bastion of state immunity."[96] Today most states have accepted doctrines of restricted immunity and waiver of immunity with respect to jurisdiction; but they continue to apply absolute immunity when it comes to actual execution.

91. Art. 1 of the agreement is quoted in Carter and Trimble 1991, 332–33.

92. On sovereignty costs in the context of regional and international legalization, see Abbott and Snidal 2000; Mattli 1999; and Mattli 2000.

93. Shea 1955.

94. 1967 OPEC resolution quoted in Craig, Park, Paulsson 1990, 647.

95. Art. 55 of Washington Convention.

96. Art. 18 of the Draft Convention of State Immunity by the International Law Commission, and Commentary on Article 18 in the Report of the International Law Commission; quoted in Sanders 1996, 73.

In practice, the shocking result can be that a party, after having put every effort into an arbitration against a state and having obtained a judgment for enforcement in its favor, finds itself unable to collect the money to which it is entitled under the award.[97] One remedy, agreeing to a waiver of immunity from execution when entering into a contract, is rarely used.[98]

In sum, traditional aversion of states to compromising over issues of national control and autonomy, as well as practical problems in enforcement that stem from the age-old principle that with sovereignty comes immunity, may take us a long way toward explaining why arbitration cases involving states have been relatively few.

97. Carter and Trimble 1991, 366.
98. Sanders 1996, 81.

Part IV
Does International Law Matter? Compliance, Legitimacy and Accountability

[17]

On compliance

Abram Chayes and
Antonia Handler Chayes

In an increasingly complex and interdependent world, negotiation, adoption, and implementation of international agreements is a major component of the foreign policy activity of every state.[1] International agreements come in a variety of shapes and sizes—formal and informal, bilateral and multiparty, universal and regional. Our concern is with contemporary agreements of relatively high political salience in fields such as security, economics, and environment, where the treaty is a central structural element in a broader international regulatory regime.[2] Some of these agreements are little more

This is an introductory chapter to a more extended study of compliance with international treaty obligations. The research has been supported by grants from the Pew Charitable Trust and the Carnegie Corporation of New York, for which we wish to express our gratitude. Earlier versions of this article were presented at seminars at the Kennedy School of Government, Harvard University, and at the University of Chicago Law School. Robert Keohane has been particularly helpful in commenting on the earlier efforts. Our thanks are also due to our many student research assistants and especially to Sean Cote, Fred Jacobs, and Jan Martinez, who labored on the references.

1. Barry E. Carter and Phillip R. Trimble, *International Law* (Boston: Little, Brown, 1991), pp. 133–252, cite a statistical study showing that of 10,189 U.S. treaties and international agreements made between 1789 and 1979, 8,955 were concluded between 1933 and 1979 (see p. 169). In the U.S. lexicon, the term "treaty" is reserved for international agreements ratified with the advice and consent of the Senate in accordance with Article 2, cl. 2 of the Constitution. Other international agreements are concluded by the President, in the great majority of cases with the authorization of Congress and less frequently on his or her own responsibility. All of these are "treaties" according to international usage, which defines a treaty as "an international agreement, concluded between states in written form and governed by international law." See Vienna Convention on the Law of Treaties (entered into force on 27 January 1980) Article 2(1)(a), in *International Legal Materials*, vol. 8 (Washington, D.C.: The American Society of International Law, July 1969), pp. 679–735 (hereafter cited as Vienna Convention on the Law of Treaties). The quotation is found on p. 701. The computer bank of the United Nations (UN) Treaty Office shows treaty growth, including multilateral and bilateral treaties and amendments, as follows: 373 treaties were entered into during the ten-year period ending in 1955; 498 in the period ending in 1965; 808 in the period ending in 1975; 461 in the period ending in 1985; and 915 in the period ending in 1991.

2. Treaty law, based on nineteenth-century practice, adopts, implicitly or explicitly, a contractual model of bilateral relationships (or, at most, agreements among a few parties), and a good deal of contemporary work in international relations reflects this same framework. Although nineteenth-century legal thought was hospitable to conceptions based on contract, they do not fit comfortably with regulatory lawmaking.

than statements of general principle, while others contain detailed prescriptions for a defined field of interaction. Still others may be umbrella agreements for consensus building in preparation for more specific regulation. Most of the agreements of concern are multilateral, except in the field of nuclear arms control, in which the cold war generated a series of bilateral negotiations and agreements between the United States and the Soviet Union.

We believe that when nations enter into an international agreement of this kind, they alter their behavior, their relationships, and their expectations of one another over time in accordance with its terms. That is, they will to some extent comply with the undertakings they have made.[3] How or why this should be so is the subject of a burgeoning literature and debate in which, for the first time in half a century, the possibility of fruitful dialogue between international lawyers and students of international relations has emerged. This article explores some basic propositions we think should frame this discussion.

First, the general level of compliance with international agreements cannot be empirically verified. That nations generally comply with their international agreements, on the one hand, and that they violate them whenever it is "in their interests to do so" are not statements of fact or even hypotheses to be tested, but assumptions. We give some reasons why we think the background assumption of a propensity to comply is plausible and useful.

Second, compliance problems often do not reflect a deliberate decision to violate an international undertaking on the basis of a calculation of interests. We propose a variety of other (and in our view more usual) reasons why states may deviate from treaty obligations and why, in particular circumstances, these reasons are accepted by the parties as justifying such departures.

Third, the treaty regime as a whole need not and should not be held to a standard of strict compliance but to a level of overall compliance that is "acceptable" in the light of the interests and concerns the treaty is designed to safeguard. We consider how the "acceptable level" is determined and adjusted.

3. We are mindful of the distinction between treaty compliance and regime effectiveness. See Oran Young, "The Effectiveness of International Institutions: Hard Cases and Critical Variables," in James N. Rosenau and Ernst-Otto Czempiel, eds., *Governance Without Government: Order and Change in World Politics* (Cambridge: Cambridge University Press, 1992), pp. 160–92; and Jesse Ausubel and David Victor, "Verification of International Environmental Agreements," *Annual Review of Energy and Environment,* vol. 17, 1992, pp. 1–43. The parties to the International Whaling Convention, for example, complied fully with the quotas set by its commission, but the whale population crashed because the quotas were too high. Nevertheless, we think the observance (or not) of treaty commitments by the parties is a subject worth studying in its own right. Moreover, treaties are ordinarily intended to induce behavior that is expected to ameliorate the problem to which they are directed, so that, if Young's warning is kept in mind, compliance may be a fair first approximation surrogate for effectiveness.

Background assumption

According to Louis Henkin, "*almost all nations observe almost all principles of international law and almost all of their obligations almost all of the time.*"[4] The observation is frequently repeated without anyone, so far as we know, supplying any empirical evidence to support it. A moment's reflection shows that it would not be easy to devise a statistical protocol that would generate such evidence. For example, how would Iraq's unbroken respect for the borders of Turkey, Jordan, and Saudi Arabia count in the reckoning against the invasions of Iran and Kuwait?

Equally, and for much the same reasons, there is no way to validate empirically the position of mainstream realist international relations theory going back to Machiavelli, that "a prudent ruler cannot keep his word, nor should he, where such fidelity would damage him, and when the reasons that made him promise are no longer relevant."[5] Contemporary realists accept that the interest in reciprocal observation of treaty norms by other parties or a more general interest in the state's reputation as a reliable contractual partner should be counted in the trade-off of costs and benefits on which a decision is based (an extension that detracts considerably from the power and elegance of the realist formula).[6] No calculus, however, will supply a rigorous, nontautological answer to the question whether a state observed a particular treaty obligation, much less its treaty obligations generally, only when it was in its interest to do so. Anecdotal evidence abounds for both the normative and the realist propositions, but neither of them, in their general form, is subject to statistical or empirical proof. The difference between the two schools is not one of fact but of the background assumption that informs their approach to the subject.

A critical question for any study of compliance, then, is which background assumption to adopt, and that question is to be resolved not on the basis of whether the assumption is "true" or "false" but whether or not it is helpful for the particular inquiry. Thus, for game-theoretic approaches that focus on the abstract structure of the relationship between states, the realist assumption of a unitary rational actor optimizing utilities distributed along smooth preference curves may have value. As Thomas Schelling said at the beginning of his classic

4. See Louis Henkin, *How Nations Behave,* 2d ed. (New York: Columbia University Press, 1979), p. 47; and p. 69 of Louis Henkin, "International Law: Politics, Values, and Functions: General Course on Public International Law," *Recueil Des Cours,* vol. 216, 1989, pp. 1–416, emphasis original.

5. Niccolò Machiavelli, *The Prince,* eds. Quentin Skinner and Russell Price (Cambridge: Cambridge University Press, 1988), pp. 61–62. For a modern instance, see Hans J. Morgenthau, *Politics Among Nations: The Struggle for Power and Peace,* 5th ed. (New York: Alfred A. Knopf, 1978), p. 560: "In my experience [states] will keep their bargains as long as it is in their interest."

6. See, for example, James A. Caporaso, "International Relations Theory and Multilateralism: The Search for Foundations," *International Organization* 46 (Summer 1992), pp. 599–632.

work, "The premise of 'rational behavior' is a potent one for the production of theory. Whether the resulting theory provides good or poor insight into actual behavior is . . . a matter for subsequent judgment."[7]

Our interest in this work is in improving the prospects for compliance with treaties, both at the drafting stage and later as the parties live and operate under them. From this perspective, the realist analysis, focusing on a narrow set of externally defined "interests"—primarily, in the classical version, the maintenance or enhancement of state military and economic power—is not very helpful. Improving compliance becomes a matter of the manipulation of burdens and benefits defined in terms of those interests, which translates into the application of military or economic sanctions. Because these are costly, difficult to mobilize, and of doubtful efficacy, they are infrequently used in practice. Meanwhile, analytic attention is diverted from a wide range of institutional and political mechanisms that in practice bear the burden of efforts to enhance treaty compliance.

For a study of the methods by which compliance can be improved, the background assumption of a general propensity of states to comply with international obligations, which is the basis on which most practitioners carry out their work, seems more illuminating.[8] We note here some of the chief considerations that lend plausibility to such an assumption. We do not suggest that these factors, singly or in combination, will lead to compliance in every case or even in any particular instance. Our claim is only that these considerations support the background assumption of a general propensity for states to comply with their treaty obligations.

Efficiency

Decisions are not a free good. Governmental resources for policy analysis and decision making are costly and in short supply. Individuals and organizations seek to conserve those resources for the most urgent and pressing matters.[9] In these circumstances, standard economic analysis argues against the continuous recalculation of costs and benefits in the absence of convincing evidence that circumstances have changed since the original decision. Efficiency dictates considerable policy continuity. In areas of activity covered by

7. Thomas C. Schelling, *The Strategy of Conflict* (Cambridge, Mass.: Harvard University Press, 1980), p. 4.

8. Oran R. Young, *Compliance and Public Authority: A Theory with International Applications* (Baltimore, Md.: Johns Hopkins University Press, 1979), pp. 31–34.

9. See George Stigler, "The Economics of Information," *Journal of Political Economy* 69 (June 1961), pp. 213–25; G. J. Stigler and G. S. Becker, "De Gustibus non Est Disputandum" (There is no disputing taste), in Karen S. Cook and Margaret Levi, eds., *The Limits of Rationality* (Chicago: University of Chicago Press, 1990), pp. 191–216; Charles E. Lindblom, *The Policy Making Process* (Englewood Cliffs, N.J.: Prentice-Hall, 1968), p. 14; and Young, *Compliance and Public Authority*, pp. 16–17.

treaty obligations, the alternative to recalculation is to follow the established rule.

Organization theory would reach the same result as economic analysis, but by a different route. In place of the continuously calculating, maximizing rational actor, it substitutes a "satisficing" model of bounded rationality that reacts to problems as they arise and searches for solutions within a familiar and accustomed repertoire.[10] In this analysis, bureaucratic organizations are viewed as functioning according to routines and standard operating procedures, often specified by authoritative rules and regulations. For Max Weber, this was the defining characteristic of bureaucracy.[11] The adoption of a treaty, like the enactment of any other law, establishes an authoritative rule system. Compliance is the normal organizational presumption.

The bureaucracy is not monolithic, of course, and it will likely contain opponents of the treaty regime as well as supporters. When there is an applicable rule in a treaty or otherwise, opposition ordinarily surfaces in the course of rule implementation and takes the form of argument over interpretation of language and definition of the exact content of the obligation. Such controversies are settled in accordance with normal bureaucratic procedures in which, again, the presumption is in favor of "following" the rule. Casuistry is admissible, though sometimes suspect. An advocate of outright violation bears a heavy burden of persuasion.

Interests

The assertion that states carry out treaty commitments only when it is in their interest to do so seems to imply that commitments are somehow unrelated to interests. In fact, the opposite is true. The most basic principle of international law is that states cannot be legally bound except with their own consent. So, in the first instance, the state need not enter into a treaty that does not conform to its interests.[12]

10. Herbert Simon, *Models of Man: Social and Rational—Mathematical Essays on Rational Human Behavior in a Social Setting* (New York: John Wiley & Sons, 1957), pp. 200–204. See also James G. March and Herbert A. Simon, *Organizations* (New York: John Wiley & Sons, 1958), p. 169. For an example of this model of organizational behavior applied to the analysis of international affairs, see Graham T. Allison, *The Essence of Decision: Explaining the Cuban Missile Crisis* (Glenview, Ill.: Scott, Foresman, 1971), chaps. 3 and 4.

11. M. Rheinstein, ed., *Max Weber on Law in Economy and Society* (New York: Simon and Schuster, 1954), p. 350: "For modern bureaucracy, the element of 'calculability of its rules' has really been of decisive significance."

12. Even in the case of peace treaties, the victor seems to attach importance to the signature of the vanquished on the document. After the Persian Gulf War, for example, the UN Security Council insisted that Iraq accept the terms of Resolution 687 establishing a cease-fire. See Sean Cote, *A Narrative of the Implementation of Section C of UN Security Council Resolution 687*, Occasional Paper, Center for Science and International Affairs, Harvard University, Cambridge, Mass., forthcoming; and Morgenthau, *Politics Among Nations*, p. 282.

More important, a treaty does not present the state with a simple binary alternative, to sign or not to sign. Treaties, like other legal arrangements, are artifacts of political choice and social existence. The process by which they are formulated and concluded is designed to ensure that the final result will represent, to some degree, an accommodation of the interests of the negotiating states. Of course, if state interests are taken to be fixed and given, the assertion that states do not conclude treaties except as they embody those interests would add little to the realist position. But modern treaty making, like legislation in a democratic polity, can be seen as a creative enterprise through which the parties not only weigh the benefits and burdens of commitment but explore, redefine, and sometimes discover their interests. It is at its best a learning process in which not only national positions but also conceptions of national interest evolve.

This process goes on both within each state and at the international level. In a state with a well-developed bureaucracy, the elaboration of national positions in preparation for treaty negotiations requires extensive interagency vetting. Different officials with different responsibilities and objectives engage in what amounts to a sustained internal negotiation. Phillip Trimble's list of the U.S. groups normally involved in arms control negotiations includes the national security staff, the Departments of State and Defense, the Arms Control and Disarmament Agency, the Joint Chiefs of Staff, the Central Intelligence Agency, and sometimes the Department of Energy or the National Aeronautics and Space Administration (NASA).[13] These organizations themselves are not unitary actors. Numerous subordinate units of the major departments have quasi-independent positions at the table. Much of the extensive literature on U.S.–Soviet arms control negotiations is devoted to analysis of the almost byzantine complexity of these internal interactions.[14]

The process is not confined to arms control but can be seen in every major U.S. international negotiation. For example, at the end of what Ambassador Richard Benedick calls "the interagency minuet" in preparation for the Vienna Convention for the Protection of the Ozone Layer, the final U.S. position "was drafted by the State Department and was formally cleared by the Departments of Commerce and Energy, The Council on Environmental Quality, EPA

13. Phillip R. Trimble, "Arms Control and International Negotiation Theory," *Stanford Journal of International Law* 25 (Spring 1989), pp. 543–74, especially p. 549.

14. See John Newhouse, *Cold Dawn: The Story of SALT* (New York: Holt, Rinehart and Winston, 1973); Gerard C. Smith, *Doubletalk: The Story of SALT I* (Lanham, Md.: University Press of America, 1985); Strobe Talbott, *Endgame: The Inside Story of SALT II* (New York: Harper & Row, 1979); Strobe Talbott, *Deadly Gambits: The Reagan Administration and the Stalemate in Nuclear Arms Control* (New York: Knopf, 1984); Raymond L. Garthoff, *Detente and Confrontation: American–Soviet Relations from Nixon to Reagan* (Washington, D.C.: Brookings Institution, 1985); and J. McNeill, "U.S.–U.S.S.R. Arms Negotiations: The Process and the Lawyer," *American Journal of International Law* 79 (January 1985), pp. 52–67. Although knowledge of the process in the former Soviet Union is less detailed, the sources cited above, among others, suggest that (making allowances for a more compartmentalized bureaucratic structure) the process was not fundamentally dissimilar.

[Environmental Protection Agency], NASA, NOAA [National Oceanographic and Atmospheric Administration], OMB [Office of Management and Budget], USTR [U.S. Trade Representative], and the Domestic Policy Council (representing all other interested agencies)."[15] In addition to this formidable alphabet soup, White House units, like the Office of Science and Technology Policy, the Office of Policy Development, and the Council of Economic Advisers, also got into the act. According to Trimble, "each agency has a distinctive perspective from which it views the process and which influences the position it advocates. . . . All these interests must be accommodated, compromised or overriden by the President before a position can even be put on the table."[16]

In the United States in recent years, increasing involvement of Congress—and with it nongovernmental organizations (NGOs) and the broader public—has introduced a new range of interests that must ultimately be reflected in the national position.[17] Similar developments seem to be occurring in other democratic countries.

In contrast to day-to-day foreign policy decision making that is oriented toward current political exigencies and imminent deadlines and is focused heavily on short-term costs and benefits, the more deliberate process employed in treaty making may serve to identify and reinforce longer range interests and values. Officials engaged in developing the negotiating position often have an additional reason to take a long-range view, since they may have operational responsibility under any agreement that is reached.[18] What they say and how they conduct themselves at the negotiating table may return to haunt them

15. Richard Elliot Benedick, *Ozone Diplomacy: New Directions in Safeguarding the Planet* (Cambridge, Mass: Harvard University Press, 1991), pp. 51–53. The Domestic Policy Council, which established a special senior-level working group to ride herd on the process, consists of nine Cabinet secretaries, the director for the OMB, and the USTR. At the time of the ozone negotiations, the council was chaired by Attorney General Edwin Meese. Other states, at least in advanced industrialized societies, exhibit similar, if perhaps not quite as baroque, internal practices in preparation for negotiations. Developing countries, with small resources to commit to bureaucratic coordination, may rely more on the judgment and inspiration of representatives on the scene.

16. Trimble, "Arms Control and International Negotiation Theory," p. 550.

17. See Benedick, *Ozone Diplomacy,* p. 57, for a description of the emphasis on Congress, industry, and environmental groups in the development of the U.S. strategy to build support for the Protocol on Substances that Deplete the Ozone Layer. For a discussion of how governments "organize themselves to cope with the flow of business generated by international organizations" in an international political system of "complex interdependence," see Robert O. Keohane and Joseph S. Nye, *Power and Interdependence,* 2d ed. (Glenview, Ill.: Scott, Foresman, 1989), p. 35.

18. Hudec uses the examples of the General Agreement on Tariffs and Trade (GATT) and the International Trade Organization (ITO): "For the better part of the first decade, GATT meetings resembled a reunion of the GATT/ITO draftsmen themselves. Failure of the code would have meant a personal failure to many of these officials, and violation of rules they had helped to write could not help being personally embarrassing." See p. 1365 of Robert E. Hudec, "GATT or GABB? The Future Design of the General Agreement of Tariffs and Trade," *Yale Law Journal* 80 (June 1971), pp. 1299–386. See also Robert E. Hudec, *The GATT Legal System and World Trade Diplomacy,* 2d ed. (Salem, N. H.: Butterworth Legal Publishers, 1990), p. 54.

once the treaty has gone into effect.[19] Moreover, they are likely to attach considerable importance to the development of governing norms that will operate predictably when applied to the behavior of the parties over time. All these convergent elements tend to influence national positions in the direction of broad-based conceptions of the national interest that, if adequately reflected in the treaty, will help to induce compliance.

The internal analysis, negotiation, and calculation of the benefits, burdens, and impacts are repeated, for contemporary regulatory treaties, at the international level.[20] In anticipation of negotiations, the issues are reviewed in international forums long before formal negotiation begins. The negotiating process itself characteristically involves intergovernmental debate often lasting years and involving not only other national governments but also international bureaucracies and NGOs. The most notable case is the UN Conference on the Law of the Sea, in which that process lasted for more than ten years, spawning innumerable committees, subcommittees, and working groups, only to be torpedoed in the end by the United States, which had sponsored the negotiations in the first place.[21] Bilateral arms control negotiations between the United States and the Soviet Union were similarly extended, and although only the two superpowers were directly involved, each felt a measure of responsibility to bring along the members of its alliance. Current environmental negotiations on ozone and on global warming follow very much the Law of the Sea pattern. The first conference on stratospheric ozone was convoked by the UN Environment Program (UNEP) in 1977, eight years before the adoption of the Vienna Convention on the Protection of the Ozone Layer.[22] The formal beginning of the climate change negotiations in February 1991 was preceded by two years of work by the Intergovernmental Panel on Climate Change, convened by the World Meteorological Organization and the UNEP to consider scientific, technological, and policy response questions.[23]

19. The Vienna Convention on the Law of Treaties permits limited recourse to the negotiating history when the treaty text is ambiguous, though the emphasis given to such history differs in various tribunals and national courts. See Vienna Convention on the Law of Treaties, Article 32. In the United States, resort to the negotiating history is much freer. See *United States v. Stuart,* 489 U.S. 353–377 (1989); and Detlev F. Vagts "Senate Materials and Treaty Interpretation: Some Research Hints for the Supreme Court," *American Journal of International Law* 83 (July 1989), pp. 546–50.

20. Robert D. Putnam, "Diplomacy and Domestic Politics: The Logic of Two-Level Games," *International Organization* 42 (Summer 1988), pp. 427–60.

21. See James K. Sebenius, *Negotiating the Law of the Sea* (Cambridge, Mass.: Harvard University Press, 1984); and William Wertenbaker, "The Law of the Sea," parts 1 and 2, *The New Yorker,* 1 August 1983, pp. 38–65, and 8 August 1983, pp. 56–83, respectively.

22. As early as 1975, the UNEP funded a World Meteorological Organization (WMO) technical conference on implications of U.S. ozone layer research. But the immediate precursor of the negotiating conference in Vienna came in March 1977, when the UNEP sponsored a policy meeting of governments and international agencies in Washington, D.C., that drafted a "World Plan of Action on the Ozone Layer." See Benedick, *Ozone Diplomacy,* p. 40.

23. The Intergovernmental Panel of Climate Change was set up by the UNEP and WMO after the passage of UN General Assembly Resolution 43/53, A/RES/43/53, 27 January 1989, "Resolution on the Protection of the Global Climate."

Much of this negotiating activity is open to some form of public scrutiny, triggering repeated rounds of national bureaucratic and political review and revision of tentative accommodations among affected interests. The treaty as finally signed and presented for ratification is therefore likely to be based on considered and well-developed conceptions of national interest that have themselves been shaped to some extent by the preparatory and negotiating process.

Treaty making is not purely consensual, of course. Negotiations are heavily affected by the structure of the international system, in which some states are much more powerful than others. As noted, the Convention of the Law of the Sea, the product of more than a decade of international negotiations, was ultimately derailed when a new U.S. administration found it unacceptable.

On the other hand, a multilateral negotiating forum provides opportunities for weaker states to form coalitions and exploit blocking positions. In the same UN Conference on the Law of the Sea, the caucus of what were known as "land-locked and geographically disadvantaged states," which included such unlikely colleagues as Hungary, Switzerland, Austria, Uganda, Nepal, and Bolivia, had a crucial strategic position. The Association of Small Island States, chaired by Vanuatu, played a similar role in the global climate negotiations. Like domestic legislation, the international treaty-making process leaves a good deal of room for accommodating divergent interests. In such a setting, not even the strongest state will be able to achieve all of its objectives, and some participants may have to settle for much less. The treaty is necessarily a compromise, "a bargain that [has] been made."[24] From the point of view of the particular interests of any state, the outcome may fall short of the ideal. But if the agreement is well-designed—sensible, comprehensible, and with a practical eye to probable patterns of conduct and interaction—compliance problems and enforcement issues are likely to be manageable. If issues of noncompliance and enforcement are endemic, the real problem is likely to be that the original bargain did not adequately reflect the interests of those that would be living under it, rather than mere disobedience.[25]

It is true that a state's incentives at the treaty-negotiating stage may be different from those it faces when the time for compliance rolls around. Parties on the giving end of the compromise, especially, might have reason to seek to escape the obligations they have undertaken. Nevertheless, the very act of making commitments embodied in an international agreement changes the

24. Susan Strange, "Cave! Hic Dragones: A Critique of Regime Analysis," in Stephen D. Krasner, ed., *International Regimes* (Ithaca, N.Y.: Cornell University Press, 1983), pp. 337–54; the quotation is on p. 353.

25. Systems in which compliance can only be achieved through extensive use of coercion are rightly regarded as authoritarian and unjust. See Michael Barkun, *Law Without Sanctions: Order in Primitive Societies and the World Community* (New Haven, Conn.: Yale University Press, 1968), p. 62.

calculus at the compliance stage, if only because it generates expectations of compliance in others that must enter into the equation.

Moreover, although states may know they can violate their treaty commitments in a crunch, they do not negotiate agreements with the idea that they can do so in routine situations. Thus, the shape of the substantive bargain will itself be affected by the parties' estimates of the costs and risks of their own compliance and expectations about the compliance of others. Essential parties may be unwilling to accept or impose stringent regulations if the prospects for compliance are doubtful. The negotiation will not necessarily collapse on that account, however. The result may be a looser, more general engagement. Such an outcome is often deprecated as a lowest-common-denominator outcome, with what is really important left on the cutting room floor. But it may be the beginning of increasingly serious and concerted attention to the problem.

Finally, the treaty that comes into force does not remain static and unchanging. Treaties that last must be able to adapt to inevitable changes in the economic, technological, social, and political setting. Treaties may be formally amended, of course, or modified by the addition of a protocol, but these methods are slow and cumbersome. Since they are subject to the same ratification process as the original treaty, they can be blocked or avoided by a dissatisfied party. As a result, treaty lawyers have devised a number of ways to deal with the problem of adaptation without seeking formal amendment. The simplest is the device of vesting the power to "interpret" the agreement in some organ established by the treaty. The U.S. Constitution, after all, has kept up with the times not primarily by the amending process but by the Supreme Court's interpretation of its broad clauses. The International Monetary Fund (IMF) Agreement gives such power to the Governing Board, and numerous key questions—including the crucial issue of "conditionality," whether drawings against the fund's resources may be conditioned on the economic performance of the drawing member—have been resolved by this means.[26]

A number of treaties establish authority to make regulations on technical matters by vote of the parties (usually by a special majority), which are then binding on all, though often with the right to opt out. The International Civil Aeronautics Organization has such power with respect to operational and safety matters in international air transport.[27] In many regulatory treaties, "technical" matters may be relegated to an annex that can be altered by vote of the parties.[28] In sum, treaties characteristically contain self-adjusting mecha-

26. Articles of Agreement of the IMF, 27 December 1945, as amended, Article 8, sec. 5, in *United Nations Treaty Series (UNTS),* vol. 2, Treaty no. 20 (New York: United Nations, 1947), p. 39. For the conditionality decision, see decision no. 102-(52/11) 13 February 1952, "Selected Decisions of the Executive Directors and Selected Documents," p. 16.

27. Convention on International Civil Aviation, 7 December 1944, Article 90, in *UNTS,* vol. 15, Treaty no. 102, 1948, p. 295.

28. Montreal Protocol on Substances that Deplete the Ozone Layer, in *International Legal Materials,* vol. 26, 1987, p. 1541, Article 2(9) (signed 16 September 1987 and entered into force 1 January 1989; hereafter cited as Montreal Protocol) as amended, London Adjustment and

nisms by which, over a significant range, they can be and in practice are commonly adapted to respond to shifting interests of the parties.

Norms

Treaties are acknowledged to be legally binding on the states that ratify them.[29] In common experience, people, whether as a result of socialization or otherwise, accept that they are obligated to obey the law.[30] So it is with states. It is often said that the fundamental norm[31] of international law is *pacta sunt servanda* (treaties are to be obeyed).[32] In the United States and many other countries, they become a part of the law of the land. Thus, a provision contained in an agreement to which a state has formally assented entails a legal obligation to obey and is presumptively a guide to action.

It seems almost superfluous to adduce evidence or authority for a proposition that is so deeply ingrained in common understanding and so often reflected in the speech of national leaders. Yet the realist argument that national actions are governed entirely by calculation of interests (including the interest in stability and predictability served by a system of rules) is essentially a denial of the operation of normative obligation in international affairs. This position has held the field for some time in mainstream international relations theory (as have closely related postulates in other positivist social science

---

Amendments to the Montreal Protocol on Substances that Deplete the Ozone Layer, in *International Legal Materials,* vol. 30, 1991, p. 537 (signed 29 June 1990 and entered into force 7 March 1991; hereafter cited as London Amendments).

29. The Vienna Convention on the Law of Treaties, signed 23 May 1969 (entered into force on 27 January 1980), Article 2(1)(a), states that " 'treaty' means an international agreement concluded between States in written form and governed by international law, whether embodied in a single instrument or in two or more related instruments and whatever its particular designation." See UN Doc. A/CONF. 39/27.

30. According to Young, " 'obligation' encompasses incentives to comply with behavioral prescriptions which stem from a general sense of duty and which do not rest on explicit calculations of costs and benefits. . . . Feelings of obligation often play a significant role in compliance choices." Moreover, "rules constitute an essential feature of bureaucracies and . . . routinized compliance with rules is a deeply ingrained norm among bureaucrats." See Young, *Compliance and Public Authority,* pp. 23 and 39. See also R. H. Fallon, "Reflections on Dworkin and the Two Faces of Law," *Notre Dame Law Review,* vol. 67, no. 3, 1992, pp. 553–85, summarizing H. L. A. Hart's concept of a law as a social rule: "From an internal point of view—that of an unalienated participant of the social life of the community—a social rule is a standard that is accepted as a guide to conduct and a basis for criticism, including self-criticism" (p. 556); Rheinstein, *Max Weber on Law in Economy and Society,* pp. 349–56; and Friedrich V. Kratochwil, *Rules, Norms, and Decisions: On the Conditions of Practical and Legal Reasoning in International Relations and Domestic Affairs* (Cambridge: Cambridge University Press, 1989), pp. 15 and 95–129.

31. We use "norm" as a generic term including principles, precepts, standards, rules, and the like. For present purposes, it is adequate to think of legal norms as norms generated by processes recognized as authoritative by a legal system. Compare H. L. A. Hart, *The Concept of Law* (Oxford: Oxford University Press, 1961).

32. The Vienna Convention on the Law of Treaties, Article 26, specifies that "every treaty in force is binding upon the parties to it and must be performed in good faith." See also chap. 30 of Arnold Duncan McNair, *The Law of Treaties* (Oxford: Clarendon Press, 1961), pp. 493–505.

disciplines).[33] But it is increasingly being challenged by a growing body of empirical study and academic analysis.

Such scholars as Elinor Ostrom and Robert Ellickson show how relatively small communities in contained circumstances generate and secure compliance with norms, even without the intervention of a supervening sovereign authority.[34] Others, like Frederick Schauer and Friedrich Kratochwil, analyze how norms operate in decision-making processes, whether as "reasons for action" or in defining the methods and terms of discourse.[35] Jon Elster, often regarded as one of the most powerful scholars of the "rational actor" school, says in his most recent book, "I have come to believe that social norms provide an important kind of motivation for action that is irreducible to rationality or indeed to any other form of optimizing mechanism."[36]

As applied to treaty obligations, this proposition seems almost self-evident. For example: in the absence of the antiballistic missile (ABM) treaty, the Soviet Union would have been legally free to build an ABM system. The exercise of this freedom would surely have posed serious military and political issues for U.S. analysts, diplomats, and intelligence officers. In due course, the United States would have responded, with either its own ABM system or some other suitable military or political move. The same act, the construction of an ABM system, would be qualitatively different, however, if it were done in violation of the specific stipulations of the ABM treaty. Transgression of such a fundamental engagement would trigger not a limited response, but a hostile reaction across the board, jeopardizing the possibility of cooperative relations between the parties for a long time to come. Outrage when solemn commitments are treated as "scraps of paper" is rooted in U.S. history.[37] It is unlikely that this kind of reaction is unique to the United States.

The strongest circumstantial evidence for the sense of an obligation to comply with treaties is the care that states take in negotiating and entering into them. It is not conceivable that foreign ministries and government leaders could devote time and energy on the scale they do to preparing, drafting,

33. William Eskridge, Jr., and G. Peller, "The New Public Law: Moderation as a Postmodern Cultural Form," *Michigan Law Review* 89 (February 1991), pp. 707–91.

34. See Elinor Ostrom, *Governing the Commons: The Evolution of Institutions for Collective Action* (Cambridge: Cambridge University Press, 1990); and Robert C. Ellickson, *Order Without Law: How Neighbors Settle Disputes* (Cambridge, Mass.: Harvard University Press, 1991).

35. See Frederick F. Schauer, *Playing by the Rules: A Philosophical Examination of Rule-based Decision-making in Law and Life* (Oxford: Clarendon Press, 1991); Kratochwil, *Rules, Norms and Decisions;* and Sally Falk Moore, *Law as Process* (London: Routledge & Kegan Paul, 1978).

36. Jon Elster, *The Cement of Society: A Study of Social Order* (Cambridge: Cambridge University Press, 1989), p. 15. See also Margaret Levi, Karen S. Cook, Jodi A. O'Brien, and Howard Fay, "Introduction: The Limits of Rationality," in Cook and Levi, *The Limits of Rationality,* pp. 1–16.

37. The quotation is from German Chancellor Theobald von Bethman-Hollweg's remark to the British ambassador about the treaty guaranteeing Belgian neutrality when Germany invaded in 1914. See *Encyclopedia Britannica,* 14th ed., s.v. Bethman-Hollweg, Theobald von. For an example of the U.S. response, see the letter of ex-President Theodore Roosevelt to British Foreign Secretary Sir Edward Grey dated 22 January 1915, quoted in Hans J. Morgenthau, *Politics Among Nations: The Struggle for Power and Peace,* 4th ed. (New York: Knopf, 1967).

negotiating, and monitoring treaty obligations unless there is an assumption that entering into a treaty commitment ought to and does constrain the state's own freedom of action and an expectation that the other parties to the agreement will feel similarly constrained. The care devoted to fashioning a treaty provision no doubt reflects the desire to limit the state's own commitment as much as to make evasion by others more difficult. In either case, the enterprise makes sense only on the assumption that, as a general rule, states acknowledge an obligation to comply with agreements they have signed.

These attitudes are not confined to foreign offices. U.S. Department of Defense testimony during the cold war repeatedly sounded the theme that arms control treaties with the Soviet Union were important in providing the stability of expectations and predictability the Pentagon needed for sound strategic planning.[38] In the United States and other Western countries, the principle that the exercise of governmental power in general is subject to law lends additional force to an ethos of national compliance with international undertakings.[39] And, of course, appeals to legal obligations are a staple of foreign policy debate and of the continuous critique and defense of foreign policy actions that account for so much of diplomatic interchange and international political commentary.

All this argues that states, like other subjects of legal rules, operate under a sense of obligation to conform their conduct to governing norms.

Varieties of noncomplying behavior

If the state's decision whether or not to comply with a treaty is the result of a calculation of costs and benefits, as the realists assert, the implication is that noncompliance is the premeditated and deliberate violation of a treaty obligation. Our background assumption does not exclude that such decisions may occur from time to time, especially when the circumstances underlying the original bargain have changed significantly.[40] Or, as in the area of international human rights, it may happen that a state will enter into an international agreement to appease a domestic or international constituency but have little

38. See, for example, the testimony of General David C. Jones, chairman of the Joint Chiefs of Staff, before the U.S. Senate Committee on Foreign Relations on the Strategic Arms Limitation Talks (SALT) II treaty, Congressional Information Service, S381-24 79, 9 July 1979.

39. It is not clear, however, that democracies are more law-abiding. See *Diggs v. Shultz,* 470 F. 2d 461 (D.C. Cir. 1972): "Under our constitutional scheme, Congress can denounce treaties if it sees fit to do so, and there is nothing the other branches of the government can do about it. We consider that is precisely what Congress has done in this case" (pp. 466–67).

40. International law recognizes a limited scope for abrogation of an agreement in such a case. See the Vienna Convention on the Law of Treaties, Article 62. Generally, however, the possibility of change is accommodated by provisions for amendment, authoritative interpretation, or even withdrawal from the agreement. See, for example, the withdrawal provision of the ABM Treaty, Article 25(2), or the Limited Test Ban Treaty, Article 4. None of these actions poses an issue of violation of legal obligations, though they may weaken the regime of which the treaty is a part.

intention of carrying it out. A passing familiarity with foreign affairs, however, suggests that only infrequently does a treaty violation fall into the category of a willful flouting of legal obligation.[41]

At the same time, general observation as well as detailed studies often reveal what appear or are alleged to be significant departures from established treaty norms. If these are not deliberate violations, what explains this behavior? We discuss three circumstances, infrequently recognized in discussions of compliance, that in our view often lie at the root of behavior that may seem prima facie to violate treaty requirements: (1) ambiguity and indeterminacy of treaty language, (2) limitations on the capacity of parties to carry out their undertakings, and (3) the temporal dimension of the social and economic changes contemplated by regulatory treaties.

These factors might be considered "causes" of noncompliance. But from a lawyer's perspective, it is illuminating to think of them as "defenses"—matters put forth to excuse or justify or extenuate a prima facie case of breach. A defense, like all other issues of compliance, is subject to the overriding obligation of good faith in the performance of treaty obligations.[42] If the plea is accepted, the conduct is not a violation, strictly speaking. Of course, in the international sphere, these charges and defenses are rarely made or determined in a judicial tribunal. However, diplomatic practice in other forums can be understood in terms of the same basic structure, reflecting, perhaps, the pervasiveness of the underlying legal framework.

Ambiguity

Treaties, like other canonical statements of legal rules, frequently do not provide determinate answers to specific disputed questions.[43] Language often is unable to capture meaning with precision. Treaty drafters do not foresee many of the possible applications—let alone their contextual settings. Issues that are foreseen often cannot be resolved at the time of treaty negotiation and are swept under the rug with a formula that can mean what each party wants it

41. Keohane surveyed two hundred years of U.S. foreign relations history and identified only forty "theoretically interesting" cases of "inconvenient" commitments in which there was a serious issue of whether or not to comply. See the chapter entitled "Commitments and Compromise," in Robert O. Keohane, "The Impact of Commitments on American Foreign Policy," manuscript, 1993, pp. 1–49.

42. See Vienna Convention on the Law of Treaties, Article 26; Lassa Oppenheim, *International Law: A Treatise,* 8th ed., ed. H. Lauterpacht (London: Longmans, 1955), p. 956; and McNair, *The Law of Treaties,* p. 465.

43. See Abram Chayes and Antonia Handler Chayes, "Living Under a Treaty Regime: Compliance, Interpretation, and Adaptation," in Antonia Handler Chayes and Paul Doty, eds., *Defending Deterrence: Managing the ABM Treaty Regime into the 21st Century* (Washington, D.C.: Pergamon-Brassey's International Defense Publishers, 1989), chap. 11. See also Young, *Compliance and Public Authority,* pp. 106–8, which discusses issues of interpretation in the context of deliberate attempts at "evasion" of obligation. We argue that alternative interpretations are frequently invoked in good faith. No doubt in practice there is often some of both.

to mean. Economic, technological, scientific, and even political circumstances change. All these inescapable incidents of the effort to formulate rules to govern future conduct frequently produce a zone of ambiguity within which it is difficult to say with precision what is permitted and what is forbidden.

Of course, treaty language, like other legal language, comes in varying degrees of specificity.[44] The broader and more general the language, the wider the ambit of permissible interpretations to which it gives rise. Yet there are frequently reasons for choosing a more general formulation of the obligation: the political consensus may not support more precision, or, as with certain provisions of the U.S. Constitution, it may be wiser to define a general direction, to try to inform a process, rather than seek to foresee in detail the circumstances in which the words will be brought to bear. If there is some confidence in those who are to apply the rules, a broader standard defining the general policy behind the law may be more effective in realizing it than a series of detailed regulations. The North Atlantic Treaty has proved remarkably durable, though its language is remarkably general: "In order more effectively to achieve the objectives of this Treaty, the Parties, separately and jointly, by means of continuous and effective self-help and mutual aid, will maintain and develop their individual and collective capacity to resist armed attack."[45]

In the arms control field, the United States has opted for increasingly detailed agreements on the ground that they reduce interpretative leeways. The 1963 Limited Test Ban Treaty (LTBT), the first bilateral arms control agreement between the United States and the Soviet Union, consisted of five articles covering two or three pages. The Strategic Arms Reduction Treaty (START) signed in 1989 is the size of a telephone book.

Detail also has its difficulties. It is vulnerable to the maxim *expressio unius est exclusio alterius* (to express one thing is to exclude the other). As in the U.S. Internal Revenue Code, precision generates loopholes, necessitating some procedure for continuous revision and authoritative interpretation. The corpus of the law may become so complex and unwieldy as to be understandable (and manipulable) by only a small coterie of experts. The complexities of the rule system may give rise to shortcuts that reduce inefficiencies when things are going well but may lead to friction when the political atmosphere darkens.

In short, more often than not there will be a considerable range within which parties may reasonably adopt differing positions as to the meaning of the obligation. In domestic legal systems, courts or other authoritative institutions are empowered to resolve such disputes about meaning as between parties in a

44. See Duncan Kennedy, "Form and Substance in Private Law Adjudication," *Harvard Law Review* 89 (June 1976), pp. 1685–788; Ronald Dworkin, "The Model of Rules," *University of Chicago Law Review* 35 (Autumn 1967), pp. 14–16; Louis Kaplow, *Rules Versus Standards: An Economic Analysis,* Discussion Paper no. 108, Program in Law and Economics, Harvard Law School, April 1992.

45. North Atlantic Treaty, Article 3, 63 stat. 2241 (signed 4 April 1949 and entered into force 24 August 1949), in *UNTS,* vol. 34, no. 541, 1949, p. 243.

particular case. The international legal system can provide tribunals to settle such questions if the parties consent. But compulsory means of authoritative dispute resolution—by adjudication or otherwise—are not generally available at the international level.[46] Moreover, the issue of interpretation may not arise in the context of an adversarial two-party dispute. In such cases, it remains open to a state, in the absence of bad faith, to maintain its position and try to convince the others.

In many such disputes, a consensus may exist or emerge among knowledgeable professionals about the legal rights and wrongs.[47] In many others, however, the issue will remain contestable. Although one party may charge another with violation and deploy legions of international lawyers in its support, a detached observer often cannot readily conclude that there is indeed a case of noncompliance, at least in the absence of "bad faith." The numerous alleged violations of arms control treaties with which the Soviet Union was annually charged were, with the exception of the radar at Krasnoyarsk in Siberia, contestable in that sense.[48] In fact, it can be argued that if there is no authoritative arbiter (and even sometimes when there is), discourse among the parties, often in the hearing of a wider public audience, is an important way of clarifying the meaning of the rules.

In the face of treaty norms that are indeterminate over a considerable range, even conscientious legal advice may not avoid issues of compliance. At the extreme, a state may consciously seek to discover the limits of its obligation by testing its treaty partners' responses. There was speculation that the pattern of Soviet deployment of Pechora-type radars prior to the construction of the phased array radar at Krasnoyarsk was an attempt to test the limits of the radar deployment provision of the ABM treaty. The Pechora sites were located as far as four hundred kilometers from the border, arguably "on the periphery of the national territory," as required by the treaty—but also arguably not.[49] The failure of the United States to react was thought by some to have contributed to the decision to site Krasnoyarsk even further from the nearest border—some seven hundred kilometers.

46. Abram Chayes and Antonia Handler Chayes, "Compliance Without Enforcement: State Behavior Under Regulatory Treaties," *Negotiation Journal* 7 (July 1991), pp. 311–31. See also Louis B. Sohn, "Peaceful Settlement of Disputes in Ocean Conflicts: Does UN Clause 3 Point the Way?" *Law and Contemporary Problems* 46 (Spring 1983), pp. 195–200. Our work-in-progress examines signs of a recent trend toward more formal dispute resolution procedures in such areas as trade, the law of the sea, and others. The current emphasis in the United States on alternative dispute resolution suggests that international judicial settlement may not be an entirely unmixed blessing, however.

47. Oscar Schachter, "The Invisible College of International Lawyers," *Northwestern University Law Review,* vol. 72, no. 2, 1977, pp. 217–26.

48. Gloria Duffy, *Compliance and the Future of Arms Control: Report of a Project Sponsored by the Center for International Security and Arms Control* (Cambridge, Mass: Ballinger, 1988), pp. 31–60.

49. See Antonia Handler Chayes and Abram Chayes, "From Law Enforcement to Dispute Settlement: A New Approach to Arms Control Verification and Compliance," *International Security* 14 (Spring 1990), pp. 147–64; and Duffy, *Compliance and the Future of Arms Control,* p. 107.

Justice Oliver Wendell Holmes said, "The very meaning of a line in the law is that you intentionally may come as close to it as you can if you do not pass it."[50] Nevertheless, deliberate testing of the kind described above might in ordinary circumstances be thought to be inconsistent with good faith observation of the treaty obligation. On the other hand, in the early years of the Interim Agreement on Limitation of Strategic Arms (SALT I) the United States played a similar game by erecting opaque environmental shelters over missile silos during modification work, despite the treaty undertaking "not to use deliberate concealment measures which impede verification by national technical means."[51] In the context of the long cold war confrontation between the United States and the Soviet Union, a certain amount of such probing seems to have been within the expectations of the parties.[52]

Perhaps a more usual way of operating in the zone of ambiguity is to design the activity to comply with the letter of the obligation, leaving others to argue about the spirit. The General Agreement on Tarrifs and Trade (GATT) prohibits a party from imposing quotas on imports. When Japanese exports of steel to the United States generated pressures from U.S. domestic producers that the Nixon administration could no longer contain, U.S. trade lawyers invented the "voluntary restraint agreement," under which private Japanese producers agreed to limit their U.S. sales.[53] The United States imposed no official quota, although the Japanese producers might well have anticipated some such action had they not "volunteered." Did the arrangement violate GATT obligations?

Questions of compliance with treaty obligations ordinarily arise as an adjunct to activity designed to achieve an objective that the actor regards as important.[54] Lawyers may be consulted or may intervene. Decisions about how the desired program is to be carried out emerge from a complex interaction of legal and policy analysis that generates its own subrules and precedents. The process is reminiscent of that in a classic U.S. bureaucracy or corporation.

50. *Superior Oil Co. v. Mississippi,* 280 U.S. 390 (1920), p. 395.

51. Interim Agreement of Limitation of Strategic Arms (SALT I), Article 5(3). See also *Compliance with SALT I Agreements,* Special Report no. 55, Bureau of Public Affairs, U.S. Department of State, July 1979, p. 4. The issue was finally resolved by Article 15(3) of the SALT II treaty, prohibiting the use over intercontinental ballistic missile silo launchers of shelters that impede verification by national technical means.

52. Unilateral assertion is a traditional way of vindicating claimed "rights" in international law. In the spring of 1986, U.S. forces engaged in two such exercises, one off the Soviet Black Sea coast in the "exercise of the right of innocent passage" (*The New York Times,* 19 March 1986, p. A1) and the other in the airspace over the Gulf of Sidra, which Libya considers its territorial waters and the United States does not. The Black Sea maneuver was concluded with nothing more than some bumping between U.S. and Soviet ships, but in the Gulf of Sidra, U.S. aircraft sank two Libyan patrol vessels that had fired antiaircraft missiles. See *Chicago Tribune,* 19 March 1986, sec. 1, p. 10; *Los Angeles Times,* 26 March 1986, p. I1; and *Los Angeles Times,* 27 March 1986, p. I1.

53. *Consumers Union v. Kissinger,* 506 F2d 136 (D.C. Cir. 1974).

54. Chayes and Chayes, "Living Under a Treaty Regime," pp. 197 and 200.

For example, the Reagan administration was bent on developing a space-based ABM system. Congress insisted that research and testing should conform to the "traditional" interpretation of the ABM treaty, which prohibited the testing of ABM "components," rather than the administration's "broad interpretation," which would have permitted full development and testing of a space-based ABM system. To ensure that it remained within the treaty constraint, the administration established a special legal unit in the Defense Department, nominally independent of the Strategic Defense Initiative (SDI) organization, to review each proposed test against an intricate set of internal rules. The unit satisfied itself that the items as tested would not be capable of performing as ABM "components," usually because of power limitations or other design characteristics known to the testers but not necessarily observable by outsiders. These rules were conscientiously applied to the testing program, and on that basis the administration maintained that it had stayed within the bounds of the traditional interpretation of the treaty.[55] No Soviet lawyer had seen or approved the rules, however (indeed, they were classified), and it is not likely that the United States would have accepted Soviet tests as compliant if the limiting design elements were not externally observable.

Even in the stark, high politics of the Cuban Missile Crisis, State Department lawyers argued that the United States could not lawfully react unilaterally, since the Soviet emplacement of missiles in Cuba did not amount to an "armed attack" sufficient to trigger the right of self-defense in Article 51 of the UN Charter. Use of force in response to the missiles would only be lawful if approved by the Organization of American States (OAS). Though it would be foolish to contend that the legal position determined President John Kennedy's decision, there is little doubt that the asserted need for advance OAS authorization for any use of force contributed to the mosaic of argumentation that led to the decision to respond initially by means of the quarantine rather than an air strike. Robert Kennedy said later, "It was the vote of the Organization of American States that gave a legal basis for the quarantine . . . and changed our position from that of an outlaw acting in violation of international law into a country acting in accordance with twenty allies legally protecting their position."[56] This was the advice he had heard from his lawyers, and it was a thoroughly defensible position. Nevertheless, many international lawyers in the United States and elsewhere disagreed because they thought the action was inconsistent with the UN Charter.[57]

55. For example, the so-called Foster box rules serve to distinguish between strategic missile reentry vehicles, which are prohibited by the ABM treaty, and tactical missile reentry vehicles, which are not, on the basis of performance characteristics such as velocity and reentry angle not mentioned anywhere in the ABM treaty. See Ashton B. Carter, "Limitations and Allowances for Space Based Weapons," in Chayes and Doty, *Defending Deterrence,* pp. 132–37.

56. Robert Kennedy, *Thirteen Days* (New York: W. M. Norton, 1971), p. 99.

57. See, for example, Quincy Wright, "The Cuban Quarantine," *American Journal of International Law* 57 (July 1963), pp. 546–65; James S. Campbell, "The Cuban Crisis and the UN Charter: An Analysis of the United States Position" *Stanford Law Review* 16 (December 1963), pp. 160–76;

Capability

According to classical international law, legal rights and obligations run between states. A treaty is an agreement among states[58] and is an undertaking by them as to their future conduct. The object of the agreement is to affect state behavior. This simple relationship between agreement and relevant behavior continues to exist for many treaties. The LTBT is such a treaty. It prohibits nuclear testing in the atmosphere, in outer space, or underwater. Only states conduct nuclear weapons tests, so only state behavior is implicated in the undertaking. The state, by governing its own actions, without more, determines whether it will comply with the undertaking or not. Moreover, there is no doubt about the state's capacity to do what it has undertaken. Every state, no matter how primitive its structure or limited its resources, can refrain from conducting atmospheric nuclear tests.

Even when only state behavior is at stake, the issue of capacity may arise when the treaty involves an affirmative obligation. In the 1980s it may have been a fair assumption that the Soviet Union had the capability to carry out its undertaking to destroy certain nuclear weapons as required by the START agreement. In the 1990s, that assumption was threatened by the emergence of a congeries of successor states in place of the Soviet Union, many of which may not have the necessary technical knowledge or material resources to do the job.[59]

The problem is pervasive in contemporary regulatory treaties. Much of the work of the International Labor Organization (ILO) from the beginning has been devoted to improving its members' domestic labor legislation and enforcement. The current spate of environmental agreements poses the difficulty in acute form. Such treaties formally are among states, and the obligations are cast as state obligations—for example, to reduce sulfur dioxide (SO_2) emissions by 30 percent against a certain baseline. Here, however, the real object of the treaty is not to affect state behavior but to regulate the behavior of nonstate actors carrying out activities that produce SO_2—generating power, driving automobiles, and the like. The ultimate impact on the relevant private behavior depends on a complex series of intermediate steps. It will normally require an implementing decree or legislation followed by detailed administrative regulations. In essence, the state will have to establish and enforce a full-blown domestic regime designed to secure the necessary reduction in emissions.

---

and William L. Standard, "The United States Quarantine of Cuba and the Rule of Law," *American Bar Association Journal* 49 (August 1963), pp. 744–48.

58. Vienna Convention on the Law of Treaties, Article 2(1)(a).

59. Kurt M. Campbell, Ashton B. Carter, Steven E. Miller, and Charles A. Zraket, *Soviet Nuclear Fission: Control of the Nuclear Arsenal in a Disintegrating Soviet Union,* CSIA Studies in International Security, no. 1, Harvard University, Cambridge, Mass., November 1991, pp. 24, 25, and 108.

The state may be "in compliance" when it has taken the formal legislative and administrative steps, and, despite the vagaries of legislative and domestic politics, it is perhaps appropriate to hold it accountable for failure to do so. Quite apart from political will, however, the construction of an effective domestic regulatory apparatus is not a simple or mechanical task. It entails choices and requires scientific and technical judgment, bureaucratic capability, and fiscal resources. Even developed Western states have not been able to construct such systems with confidence that they will achieve the desired objective.[60]

The deficit in domestic regulatory capacity is not limited to environmental agreements. The nonproliferation treaty (NPT) is supported by a side-agreement among nuclear-capable states not to export sensitive technology to nonweapons states.[61] The agreement is implemented by national export control regulations. The UN–International Atomic Energy Agency (IAEA) inspections in Iraq, however, revealed that the Iraqi nuclear weapons program was able to draw on suppliers in the United States and West Germany, among others, where governmental will and ability to control such exports are presumably at their highest.

Although there are surely differences among developing countries, the characteristic situation is a severe dearth of the requisite scientific, technical, bureaucratic, and financial wherewithal to build effective domestic enforcement systems. Four years after the Montreal Protocol was signed, only about half the member states had complied fully with the requirement of the treaty that they report annual chlorofluorocarbon (CFC) consumption.[62] The Conference of the Parties promptly established an Ad Hoc Group of Experts on Reporting, which recognized that the great majority of the nonreporting states were developing countries that for the most part were simply unable to comply without technical assistance from the treaty organization.[63]

The Montreal Protocol is the first treaty under which the parties undertake to provide significant financial assistance to defray the incremental costs of compliance for developing countries. The same issue figured on a much larger

60. Kenneth Hanf, "Domesticating International Commitments: Linking National and International Decision-making," prepared for a meeting entitled Managing Foreign Policy Issues Under Conditions of Change, Helsinki, July 1992.

61. Treaty on the Non-proliferation of Nuclear Weapons, 21 U.S.T. 483 (1970) (signed 1 July 1968 and entered into force 5 March 1970), in *International Legal Materials,* vol. 7, 1968, p. 809.

62. See Report of the Secretariat on the Reporting of Data by the Parties in Accordance with Article 7 of the Montreal Protocol, UNEP/OzL.Pro.3/5, 23 May 1991, pp. 6–12 and 22–24; and Addendum, UNEP/OzL.Pro3/5/Add.1, 19 June 1991.

63. For the establishment of the Ad Hoc Group of Experts, see Report of the Second Meeting of the Parties to the Montreal Protocol on Substances that Deplete the Ozone Layer, UNEP/OzL.Pro.2/3, Decision 2/9, 29 June 1990, p. 15. At its first meeting in December 1990, the Ad Hoc Group of Experts concluded that countries "lack knowledge and technical expertise necessary to provide or collect" the relevant data and made a detailed series of recommendations for addressing the problem. See Report of the First Meeting of the Ad Hoc Group of Experts on the Reporting of Data, UNEP/OzL.Pro/WG.2/1/4, 7 December 1990.

scale in the negotiations for a global climate change convention and in the UN Conference on Environment and Development, held in Brazil in June 1992. The last word has surely not been spoken in these forums, and the problem is not confined to environmental agreements.

The temporal dimension

The regulatory treaties that are our major concern are, characteristically, legal instruments of a regime for managing a major international problem area over time.[64] Significant changes in social or economic systems mandated by regulatory treaties take time to accomplish. Thus, a cross section at any particular moment in time may give a misleading picture of the state of compliance. Wise treaty drafters recognize at the negotiating stage that there will be a considerable time lag after the treaty is concluded before some or all of the parties can bring themselves into compliance. Thus modern treaties, from the IMF Agreement in 1945 to the Montreal Protocol in 1987, have provided for transitional arrangements and made allowances for special circumstances.[65] Nevertheless, whether or not the treaty provides for it, a period of transition will be necessary.

Similarly, if the regime is to persist over time, adaptation to changing conditions and underlying circumstances will require a shifting mix of regulatory instruments to which state and individual behavior cannot instantaneously respond. Often the original treaty is only the first in a series of agreements addressed to the issue-area. Even the START agreement to reduce nuclear arsenals contemplates a process extending over seven years, by which time it is expected that new and further reductions will have been mandated.[66]

Activists in all fields lament that the treaty process tends to settle on a least-common-denominator basis. But the drive for universality (or universal membership in the particular region of concern) may necessitate accommodation to the response capability of states with large deficits in financial, technical, or bureaucratic resources. A common solution is to start with a low obligational ante and increase the level of regulation as experience with the regime grows.

64. The now-classical definition of an international regime appears in Krasner, "Structural Causes and Regime Consequences," p. 2: "Regimes are sets of implicit or explicit principles, norms, rules, and decision-making procedures around which actors' expectations converge in a given area of international relations." Regime theorists find it hard to say the "L-word" but "principles, norms, rules, and decision-making procedures" are what international law is all about, and it is apparent from their work that formal legal norms, most often embodied in treaties, are an important structural element in most of the phenomena of interest to them.

65. See Articles of Agreement of the International Monetary Fund, Article 14, in *UNTS,* vol. 2, 1945, p. 1501; and Montreal Protocol, Article 5.

66. Under START, the agreed reductions in strategic nuclear weapons are to take place over a seven-year period divided into three phases of three, two, and two years. See U.S. Congress, Senate, *Treaty Between the United States and the Union of Soviet Socialist Republics on the Reduction and Limitation of Strategic Offensive Arms,* 102d Cong., 1st sess., 1991, S. Treaty Doc. 102-20, Article 2.

196 International Organization

The convention-protocol strategy adopted in a number of contemporary environmental regimes exemplifies this conception.

The Vienna Convention on the Protection of the Ozone Layer, signed in 1985, contained no substantive obligations but required only that the parties "in accordance with the means at their disposal and their capabilities" cooperate in research and information exchange and in harmonizing domestic policies on activities likely to have an adverse effect on the ozone layer.[67] Two years later, as scientific consensus jelled on the destructive effect of CFCs on the ozone layer, the Montreal Protocol was negotiated, providing for a 50 percent reduction from 1986 levels of CFC consumption by the year 2000.[68] By June 1990, the parties agreed to a complete phaseout by the above date and to regulate a number of other ozone-destroying chemical compounds.[69]

A similar sequence marks the Convention on Long-Range Transboundary Air Pollution (LRTAP).[70] It began with a general agreement to cooperate signed in 1979, was followed by a protocol imposing limits on SO_2 emissions in 1985,[71] and then by another imposing limits on nitrogen oxides, which was signed at Sofia in October 1988.[72] The pattern has a long pedigree, extending back to the ILO, the first of the modern international regulatory agencies, whose members agreed in 1921 only to "bring the recommendation[s] or draft

67. Vienna Convention for the Protection of the Ozone Layer (signed 22 March 1985 and entered into force 22 September 1988; hereafter cited as Vienna Ozone Convention), Article 2(2), in *International Legal Materials,* vol. 26, 1986, p. 1529.

68. Montreal Protocol, Article 2(4).

69. London Amendments, Annex 1, Articles 2A(5) and 2B(3).

70. Convention on Long-Range Transboundary Air Pollution (signed 13 November 1979 and entered into force 16 March 1983), in *International Legal Materials,* vol. 18, 1979, p. 1442.

71. Protocol to the 1979 Convention on Long-Range Transboundary Air Pollution on the Reduction of Sulphur Emissions or Their Transboundary Fluxes by at Least 30 Percent (signed 8 July 1985), UN Doc. ECE/EB.AIR/12, reproduced in *International Legal Materials,* vol. 27, May 1988, pp. 698–714; see especially p. 707.

72. Protocol to the 1979 Convention on Long-Range Transboundary Air Pollution Concerning the Control of Emissions of Nitrogen Oxides or Their Transboundary Fluxes (signed 31 October 1988 and entered into force 14 February 1991), UNEP/GC.16/Inf.4, p. 169. Additional protocols to the original convention are the Protocol to the 1979 Convention on Long-Range Transboundary Air Pollution on Long-Term Financing of the Co-operative Program for Monitoring and Evaluation of the Long-Range Transmission of Air Pollutants in Europe (signed 28 September 1984), UN Doc. EB.AIR/AC.1/4, reproduced in *International Legal Materials,* vol. 27, March 1988, pp. 698–714 (see especially p. 701); and the Protocol Concerning the Control of Emissions of Volatile Organic Compounds or Their Transboundary Fluxes (signed November 1991), reproduced in *International Legal Materials,* vol. 31, May 1992, pp. 568–611. See also the Barcelona Convention for the Protection of the Mediterranean Sea Against Pollution, in *International Legal Materials,* vol. 15, 1976, p. 290, which was accompanied by the Protocol for the Prevention of Pollution of the Mediterranean Sea by Dumping from Ships and Aircraft, UNEP/GC.16.Inf.4, p. 130, and the Protocol Concerning Co-operation in Combating Pollution of the Mediterranean Sea by Oil and Other Harmful Substances in Cases of Emergency, UNEP/GC.16/Inf.4, p. 132. The Protocol for the Protection of the Mediterranean Sea Against Pollution for Land-based Sources, UNEP/GC.16/Inf.4, p. 134, followed in 1980; the land-based sources protocol contemplates that pollution will be eliminated in accordance with "standards and timetables" to be agreed to by the parties in the future (see Article 5[2]). The Protocol Concerning Mediterranean Specially Protected Areas (UNEP/GC.16/Inf.4, p. 136) was signed at Geneva in 1982.

convention[s] [prepared by the organization] before the authority or authorities within whose competence the matter lies, for the enactment of legislation or other action."[73] The ILO then became the forum for drafting and propagating a series of specific conventions and recommendations on the rights of labor and conditions of employment for adoption by the parties.

The effort to protect human rights by international agreement may be seen as an extreme case of time lag between undertaking and performance. Although the major human rights conventions have been widely ratified, compliance leaves much to be desired. It is apparent that some states adhered without any serious intention of abiding by them. But it is also true that even parties committed to the treaties had different expectations about compliance than with most other regulatory treaties. Indeed, the Helsinki Final Act, containing important human rights provisions applicable to Eastern Europe, is by its terms not legally binding.[74]

Even so, it is a mistake to call these treaties merely "aspirational" or "hortatory." To be sure, they embody "ideals" of the international system, but like other regulatory treaties, they were designed to initiate a process that over time, perhaps a long time, would bring behavior into greater congruence with those ideals. These expectations have not been wholly disappointed. The vast amount of public and private effort devoted to enforcing these agreements—not always in vain—evinces their obligational content. Moreover, the legitimating authority of these instruments was an important catalyst of the revolutions of the 1980s against authoritarian regimes in Latin America and Eastern Europe and continues to spark demands for democratic politics elsewhere in the world.

Acceptable levels of compliance

The foregoing section identified and advanced a range of matters that might be put forward by the individual actor in defense or excuse of a particular instance of deviant conduct. From the perspective of the system as a whole, however, the central issue is different. For a simple prohibitory norm like a highway speed limit, it is in principle a simple matter to determine whether any particular driver is in compliance. Yet most communities and law enforcement organizations in the United States seem to be perfectly comfortable with a situation in which the average speed on interstate highways is perhaps ten miles above the limit. Even in individual cases, the enforcing officer is not likely to pursue a driver operating within that zone. The fundamental problem for the

73. Constitution of the International Labor Organization, 11 April 1919, Article 405, 49 stat. 2722.

74. Conference on Security and Cooperation in Europe, Final Act (1 August 1975), Article 10, in *International Legal Materials*, vol. 14, 1975, p. 1292.

system is not how to induce all drivers to obey the speed limit but how to contain deviance within acceptable levels.[75] So, too, it is for international treaty obligations.

"An acceptable level of compliance" is not an invariant standard. The matter is further complicated because many legal norms are not like the speed limit that permits an on–off judgment as to whether an actor is in compliance. As noted above, questions of compliance are often contestable and call for complex, subtle, and frequently subjective evaluation. What is an acceptable level of compliance will shift according to the type of treaty, the context, the exact behavior involved, and over time.

It would seem, for example, that the acceptable level of compliance would vary with the significance and cost of the reliance that parties place on the others' performance.[76] On this basis, treaties implicating national security would demand strict compliance because the stakes are so high, and to some extent that prediction is borne out by experience. Yet even in this area, some departures seem to be tolerable.

In the case of the NPT, indications of deviant behavior by parties have been dealt with severely. In the 1970s, U.S. pressures resulted in the termination of programs to construct reprocessing facilities in South Korea and Taiwan.[77] Recently, a menu of even more stringent pressures was mounted against North Korea, which ultimately signed an IAEA safeguard agreement and submitted to inspection.[78] The inspection and destruction requirements placed on Iraq under UN Security Council resolution 687 are, in one sense, an extreme case of this severity toward deviation by NPT parties.

Although over 130 states are parties to the NPT, the treaty is not universal, and some nonparties have acquired or are seeking nuclear weapons capability.[79] Despite these important holdouts, compliance with the NPT by the parties remains high. In fact, in recent years prominent nonparties—including Argentina, Brazil, and South Africa—have either adhered to the treaty or announced that they will comply with its norms.[80] Even the recalcitrant nonparties have not

75. Young, *Compliance and Public Authority,* p. 109.

76. Charles Lipson, "Why Are Some International Agreements Informal," *International Organization* 45 (Autumn 1991), pp. 495–538.

77. See Joseph A. Yager, "The Republic of Korea," and "Taiwan," in Joseph A. Yager, ed., *Nonproliferation and U.S. Foreign Policy* (Washington, D.C.: Brookings Institution, 1980), pp. 44–65 and 66–81, respectively.

78. See David Sanger, "North Korea Assembly Backs Atom Pact," *The New York Times,* 10 April 1992, p. A3; and David Sanger, "North Korea Reveals Nuclear Sites to Atomic Agency, *The New York Times,* 7 May 1992, p. A4. The initial U.S. response included behind-the-scenes diplomatic pressure and encouraging supportive statements by concerned states at IAEA meetings. See L. Spector, *Nuclear Ambitions: The Spread of Nuclear Weapons, 1989–1990* (Boulder, Colo.: Westview Press, 1990), pp. 127–30. Japan apparently has refused to consider economic assistance or investment in North Korea until the nuclear issue is cleared up.

79. Countries that have not ratified the NPT include Argentina, Brazil, China, France, India, Israel, and Pakistan. See Spector, *Nuclear Ambitions,* p. 430.

80. Reuters News Service, "Argentina and Brazil Sign Nuclear Accord," *The New York Times,* 14 December 1991, p. 7; "Brazil and Argentina: IAEA Safeguard Accord," U.S. Department of State

openly tested or acknowledged the possession of nuclear weapons. Thus, despite some significant departure from its norms, the NPT and the nonproliferation regime built around it have survived.

The U.S. emphasis on the importance of verification of arms control agreements seems to portend the application of a strict compliance standard.[81] However, at least since the Reagan administration, presidential reports to Congress, mandated by the Arms Control and Disarmament Act, listed a long series of alleged Soviet violations without igniting any serious move to withdraw from the applicable treaties.[82]

One of these violations, the phased array radar constructed at Krasnoyarsk, was widely regarded as a deliberate and egregious breach of the ABM treaty. Article 6 requires that early-warning radars be sited "along the periphery of [the] national territory and oriented outward." Krasnoyarsk was seven hundred kilometers from the Mongolian border and pointed northeast over Siberia. The issue was repeatedly thrashed out between the two governments over a period of years, sometimes at the highest levels. The United States linked its resolution to progress on future arms control agreements. The Soviets maintained that the installation was a space-tracking radar system and thus not subject to the prohibition, but ultimately they acknowledged the breach and agreed to eliminate the offending installation. Nevertheless, throughout this entire period the ABM treaty regime continued in full force and effect, and the U.S. administration never seriously pursued the option of withdrawal or abrogation.[83] Even in connection with its cherished SDI, the Reagan administration preferred to attempt to "reinterpret" the treaty rather than accept the more serious domestic political costs of abrogation.

Dispatch, 23 December 1991, p. 907; Reuters News Service, "South Africa Signs a Treaty Allowing Nuclear Inspection," *The New York Times,* 9 July 1991, p. A11; and "Fact Sheet: Nuclear Non-proliferation Treaty," U.S. Department of State Dispatch, 8 July 1991, p. 491.

81. The 1977 Congress enacted a requirement for "adequate verification" of arms control agreements. This was described by Carter administration officials as a "practical standard" under which the United States would be able to identify significant attempted evasions in time to respond effectively. See Chayes and Chayes, "From Law Enforcement to Dispute Settlement," pp. 147–48. It should be noted that when the Soviet Union in 1987 finally agreed to substantially unlimited on-site inspection, the United States drew back from its earlier insistence on that requirement, as it has in chemical warfare negotiations.

82. Withdrawal from all U.S.–Soviet arms control agreements is permitted on short notice if "extraordinary events related to the subject matter of the treaty jeopardize the supreme interests" of the withdrawing party. See, for example, Treaty Between the United States and the Soviet Union on the Limitation of Antiballistic Missile Systems, 26 May 1972, Article 15(2), 23 U.S.T. 3435 (1972). The law of treaties also permits the suspension of a treaty in whole or in part if the other party has committed a material breach. See the Vienna Convention on the Law of Treaties, Article 60(1),(2).

83. The closest approach to such an initiative was the mildly comic bureaucratic squabble in the closing years of the Reagan administration about whether the Krasnoyarsk radar should be denominated a material breach of the ABM treaty. See Paul Lewis, "Soviets Warn U.S. Against Abandoning ABM Pact," *The New York Times,* 2 September 1988, p. A9; and Michael R. Gordon, "Minor Violations of Arms Pact Seen," *The New York Times,* 3 December 1988, p. 5.

In the last analysis, the long list of asserted "violations" presented no threat either to the U.S. security interests that the treaties were designed to safeguard or to the basic bargain that neither side would deploy ABM systems. American political and military leaders were more than willing to tolerate nonperformance at the margin as the price of continuing constraint on a meaningful Soviet attempt to shift the strategic balance.

If national security regimes have not collapsed in the face of significant perceived violation, it should be no surprise that economic and environmental treaties can tolerate a good deal of noncompliance. Such regimes are in fact relatively forgiving of violations plausibly justified by extenuating circumstances in the foreign or domestic life of the offending state, provided the action does not threaten the survival of the regime. As noted above, a considerable amount of deviance from strict treaty norms may be anticipated from the beginning and accepted, whether in the form of transitional periods, special exemptions, limited substantive obligations, or informal expectations of the parties.

The generally disappointing performance of states in fulfilling reporting requirements is consistent with this analysis.[84] It is widely accepted that failure to file reports reflects a low domestic priority or deficient bureaucratic capacity in the reporting state. Since the reporting is not central to the treaty bargain, the lapse can be viewed as "technical." When, as in the Montreal Protocol, accurate reporting was essential to the functioning of the regime, the parties and the secretariat made strenuous efforts to overcome the deficiency, and with some success.[85]

The Convention on International Trade in Endangered Species (CITES) ordinarily displays some tolerance for noncompliance, but the alarming and widely publicized decline in the elephant population in East African habitats in the 1980s galvanized the treaty regime. The parties took a decision to list the elephant in Appendix A of the treaty (shifting it from Appendix B, where it had previously been listed), with the effect of banning all commercial trade in ivory. The treaty permits any party to enter a reservation to such an action, in which case the reserving party is not bound by it. Nevertheless, through a variety of pressures, the United States together with a group of European countries insisted on universal adherence to the ban, bringing such major traders as Japan and Hong Kong to heel.[86] The head of the Japanese Environment

84. U.S. General Accounting Office, *International Environment: International Agreements Are Not Well-Monitored,* GAO, RCED-92-43, January 1992.

85. See Report of the Secretariat on the Reporting of Data by the Parties in Accordance with Article 7 of the Montreal Protocol, UNEP/OzL.Pro.3/5, 23 May 1991, pp. 6–12 and 22–24; and Addendum, UNEP/OzL.Pro.3/5/Add.1, 19 June 1991.

86. For a report of Japan's announcement of its intention not to enter a reservation on the last day of the conference, see United Press International, "Tokyo Agrees to Join Ivory Import Ban," *Boston Globe,* 21 October 1989, p. 6. Japan stated that it was "respecting the overwhelming sentiment of the international community." As to Hong Kong, see Jane Perlez, "Ivory Ban Said to Force Factories Shut," *The New York Times,* 22 May 1990, p. A14. The Hong Kong reservation was

Agency supported the Japanese move in order "to avoid isolation in the international community."[87] It was freely suggested that Japan's offer to host the next meeting of the conference of parties, which was accepted on the last day of the conference after Japan announced its changed position, would have been rejected had it reserved on the ivory ban.

The meaning of the background assumption of general compliance is that most states will continue to comply, even in the face of considerable deviant behavior by other parties. In other words, the free-rider problem has been overestimated. The treaty will not necessarily unravel in the face of defections. As Mancur Olson recognized, if the benefits of the collective good to one or a group of parties outweigh the costs to them of providing the good, they will continue to bear the costs regardless of the defections of others.[88]

It seems plausible that treaty regimes are subject to a kind of critical-mass phenomenon, so that once defection reaches a certain level, or in the face of particularly egregious violation by a major player, the regime might collapse.[89] Thus, either the particular character of a violation or the identity of the violator may pose a threat to the regime and evoke a higher demand for compliance. This analysis would account for both the similarities and differences between the Krasnoyarsk and CITES cases. In the first case, although core security values were at stake and the violation was egregious, it did not threaten the basic treaty bargain. The United States responded with a significant enforcement effort but did not itself destroy the basic bargain by abrogating the treaty. In the second case, involving relatively peripheral national interests from the realist perspective, a reservation permitted under the treaty threatened the collapse of the regime. A concerted and energetic defense resulted.

Determining the acceptable compliance level

If, as we argue above, the "acceptable level of compliance" is subject to broad variance across regimes, times, and occasions, how is what is "acceptable" to be determined in any particular instance? The economists have a straightforward answer: invest additional resources in enforcement (or other measures to

---

not renewed after the initial six-month period. Five African producer states with effective management programs did enter reservations but agreed not to engage in trade until at least the next conference of the parties. See Michael J. Glennon, "Has International Law Failed the Elephant," *American Journal of International Law* 84 (January 1990), pp. 1–43, especially p. 17. At the 1992 meeting they ended their opposition. See "Five African Nations Abandon Effort to Resume Elephant Trade in CITES Talks," *Bureau of National Affairs Environment Daily*, electronic news service, 12 March 1992.

87. United Press International, "Tokyo Agrees to Join Ivory Import Ban," *Boston Globe*, 21 October 1989.

88. Mancur Olson, *The Logic of Collective Action* (Cambridge, Mass.: Harvard University Press, 1971), pp. 33–36.

89. For a discussion of critical-mass behavior models, see Thomas Schelling, *Micromotives and Macrobehavior* (New York: Norton, 1978), pp. 91–110.

induce compliance) up to the point at which the value of the incremental benefit from an additional unit of compliance exactly equals the cost of the last unit of additional enforcement resources.[90] Unfortunately, the usefulness of this approach is limited by the impossibility of quantifying or even approximating, let alone monetizing, any of the relevant factors in the equation—and markets are not normally available to help.

In such circumstances, as Charles Lindblom has told us, the process by which preferences are aggregated is necessarily a political one.[91] It follows that the choice whether to intensify (or slacken) the international enforcement effort is necessarily a political decision. It implicates all the same interests pro and con that were involved in the initial formulation of the treaty norm, as modified by intervening changes of circumstances. Although the balance will to some degree reflect the expectations of compliance that the parties entertained at that time, it is by no means rare, in international as in domestic politics, to find that what the lawmaker has given in the form of substantive regulation is taken away in the implementation. What is "acceptable" in terms of compliance will reflect the perspectives and interests of participants in the ongoing political process rather than some external scientific or market-validated standard.

If the treaty establishes a formal organization, that body may serve as a focus for mobilizing the political impetus for a higher level of compliance. A strong secretariat can sometimes exert compliance pressure, as in the IMF or ILO. The organization may serve as a forum for continuing negotiation among the parties about the level of compliance. An example of these possibilities is the effort of the International Maritime Consultative Organization (IMCO)—and after 1982 its successor, the International Maritime Organization (IMO)—to control pollution of the sea by tanker discharges of oil mixed with ballast water.[92] IMCO's regulatory approach was to impose performance standards limiting the amount of oil that could be discharged on any voyage. From 1954, when the first oil pollution treaty was signed, until the 1978 revisions, there was continuous dissatisfaction with the level of compliance. IMCO responded by imposing increasingly strict limits, but these produced only modest results because of the difficulty of monitoring and verifying the amount of oil discharged by tanker captains at sea. Finally, in 1978 IMO adopted a new regulatory strategy and imposed an equipment standard requiring all new

90. See Gary Becker, "Crime and Punishment: An Economic Approach," *Journal of Political Economy* 76 (March/April 1968), pp. 169–217; and Stigler, "*The Optimum Enforcement of Laws,*" p. 526. Also see Young, *Compliance and Public Authority,* pp. 7–8 and 111–27.

91. Charles E. Lindblom, *Politics and Markets* (New York: Basic Books, 1977), pp. 254–55. At the domestic level, the decision whether to intensify enforcement of the treaty implicates a similar political process, as the continuous debates in the United States over GATT enforcement testify. Our work-in-progress includes a consideration of second-level enforcement.

92. Ronald Mitchell, "Intentional Oil Pollution of the Oceans: Crises, Public Pressure, and Equipment Standards," in Peter M. Haas, Robert O. Keohane, and Mark A. Levy, eds., *Institutions for the Earth: Sources of Effective International Environmental Protection* (Cambridge, Mass.: MIT Press, forthcoming).

tankers to have separate ballast tanks that physically prevent the intermixture of oil with the discharged ballast water. The new requirement was costly to tanker operators but easily monitored by shipping authorities. Compliance with the equipment standard has been close to 100 percent, and discharge of oil from the new ships is substantially nil. The sequence reflects the changing configuration of political strength between domestic environmental and shipping constituencies in the members of IMO (and IMCO) which was originally referred to as a "shipping industry club." At the same time, the major oil companies, which in the earlier period were shipping industry allies, shifted political allegiance under environmentalist pressures.

Since the international system is horizontal rather than hierarchical, if one state or a group of states is willing to commit enforcement resources, it may be able to short-circuit cumbersome organizational procedures and pursue improved levels of compliance by its own decision. The U.S. deployment of trade sanctions under Section 301 of the Tariff Act against violators of GATT obligations reflects a unilateral political decision (1) that existing levels of compliance were not acceptable and (2) to pay the costs of additional enforcement.[93] In that case, however, gains in compliance with substantive obligations must be weighed against losses attendant on departure from the procedural norms mandating multilateral dispute settlement.[94]

Again, after a considerable period of fruitless exhortation in the International Whaling Commission, Japan finally agreed to participate in a temporary moratorium on whaling that had been proclaimed by the organization when the United States threatened trade sanctions under the Marine Mammal Protection Act.[95] The Japanese ban on ivory imports shows a mixture of economic and reputational threats. The United States hinted at trade sanctions, and the conference of the parties of CITES threatened not to schedule its next meeting in Kyoto if Japan remained out of compliance.

If there are no objective standards by which to recognize an "acceptable level of compliance," it may be possible at least to identify some general types of situations that might actuate the deployment of political power in the interest of greater compliance. First, states committed to the treaty regime may sense that a tipping point is close, so that enhanced compliance would be necessary for regime preservation. As noted above, the actions against Japan on the ivory

93. *United States Code,* Title 19, Section 2411. Section 301, however, has been widely criticized as itself a violation of GATT. See A. O. Sykes, "Constructive Unilateral Threats in International Commercial Relations: The Limited Case for Section 301," *Law and Policy in International Business* 23 (Spring 1992), pp. 263–330; and Thomas O. Bayard and Kimberly A. Elliott, "Aggressive Unilateralism and Section 301: Market Opening or Market Closing," *The World Economy* 15 (November 1992), pp. 685–706.

94. GATT, Articles 22 and 23, 30 October 1947, as amended. See "GATT Basic Instruments and Selected Documents," in *UNTS,* vol. 55, no. 814, 1950, p. 194.

95. See Steinar Andresen, "Science and Politics in the International Management of Whales," *Marine Policy,* vol. 13, no. 2, 1989, p. 99; and Patricia Birnie, *International Regulation of Whaling* (New York: Oceana, 1985).

import ban may have been of this character. After the high visibility given to the CITES moves to ban the ivory trade, there would not have been much left of the regime if Japan had been permitted to import with impunity.

Second, states committed to a level of compliance higher than that acceptable to the generality of the parties may seek to ratchet up the standard. The Netherlands often seems to play the role of "leader" in European environmental affairs both in the North Sea and Baltic Sea regimes and in LRTAP.[96] Similarly, the United States may be a "leader" for improving compliance with the NPT, where its position is far stronger than that of its allies.

Finally, campaigning to improve a compliance level that states concerned would just as soon leave alone is a characteristic activity for NGOs, especially in the fields of the environment and of human rights. NGOs increasingly have direct access to the political process both within the treaty organizations and in the societies of which they are a part. Their technical, organizational, and lobbying skills are an independent resource for enhanced compliance at both levels of the two-level game.

Conclusion

The foregoing discussion reflects a view of noncompliance as a deviant rather than an expected behavior, and as endemic rather than deliberate. This in turn leads to de-emphasis of formal enforcement measures and even, to a degree, of coercive informal sanctions, except in egregious cases. It shifts attention to sources of noncompliance that can be managed by routine international political processes. Thus, the improvement of dispute resolution procedures goes to the problem of ambiguity; technical and financial assistance may help cure the capacity deficit; and transparency will make it likelier that, over time, national policy decisions are brought increasingly into line with agreed international standards.

These approaches merge in the process of jawboning—an effort to persuade the miscreant to change its ways—that is the characteristic form of international enforcement activity. This process exploits the practical necessity for the putative offender to give reasons and justifications for suspect conduct. These reasons and justifications are reviewed and critiqued in a variety of venues, public and private, formal and informal. The tendency is to winnow out reasonably justifiable or unintended failures to fulfill commitments—those that comport with a good-faith compliance standard—and to identify and isolate the few cases of egregious and willful violation. By systematically addressing and eliminating all mitigating circumstances that might possibly be advanced,

96. See Peter M. Haas, "Protecting the Baltic and North Seas," in Haas, Keohane, and Levy, *Institutions for the Earth*.

this process can ultimately demonstrate that what may at first have seemed like ambiguous conduct is a black-and-white case of deliberate violation. The offending state is left with a stark choice between conforming to the rule as defined and applied in the particular circumstances or openly flouting its obligation. This turns out to be a very uncomfortable position for even a powerful state. The Krasnoyarsk story represents an example of this process in action. Perhaps another is the repeated Iraqi retreat in showdowns with the UN–IAEA inspection teams.[97]

Enforcement through these interacting measures of assistance and persuasion is less costly and intrusive and is certainly less dramatic than coercive sanctions, the easy and usual policy elixir for noncompliance. It has the further virtue that it is adapted to the needs and capacities of the contemporary international system.

97. For an account of the Iraqi response, see Sean Cote, *A Narrative of the Implementation of Section C of UN Security Council Resolution 687.*

[18]

How Do International Institutions Matter? The Domestic Impact of International Rules and Norms

ANDREW P. CORTELL
The University of Utah

AND

JAMES W. DAVIS, JR.
The University of Munich

Generally, scholars of international relations have attempted to show that international rules or norms influence state behavior by locating their causal significance at the level of state interactions. However, international rules and norms also affect a country's policy choice by way of the actions of domestic political actors. In particular, government officials and societal interest groups can appeal to an international rule or norm in an effort to further their objectives in the national arena. Through such appeals, international rules and norms can become incorporated into the policy debate, and, under some conditions, may ultimately affect national policy choice. The article identifies two factors that condition the extent to which an actor's appeal to an international rule or norm will influence state behavior: the domestic structural context and the domestic salience of the international rule or norm. This argument is explored through an examination of how international rules and norms have affected U.S. policy choices in both the economic and security realms. The security case examines the impact of President Bush's appeal to the norm of collective security to justify a response to the Iraqi invasion of Kuwait. The economic case covers the U.S. semiconductor industry's efforts to persuade the Reagan administration to obtain Japanese liberalization of its trade practices with regard to semiconductor devices.

Students of international relations have tried to demonstrate that international rules influence state behavior by pointing to correlations between the existence of rules and apparent rule-guided state actions (Krasner, 1983, 1991; Stein, 1983; Keohane, 1984; Donnelly, 1986; Wendt, 1987; Onuf, 1989; Martin, 1992). Yet, as several scholars have pointed out, this methodology fails to demonstrate the actual causal links between international rules and national policy choices (Kratochwil and Ruggie, 1986:763–9; Haggard and Simmons, 1987; Milner, 1988:13).[1] This article seeks to remedy this shortcoming by showing how international rules and norms can affect state behavior through the actions of domestic political actors. Our central

---

[1] On the connections between international regimes and state behavior more generally see Milner (1992).

hypothesis is that government officials and societal interest groups can appeal to international rules and norms to further their own interests in the domestic political arena. Through these appeals, international rules and norms become incorporated into domestic debates, under some conditions influencing national policy choices. Two conditions are identified as affecting the extent to which a domestic actor's appropriation of an international norm will influence state behavior: the domestic salience of the norm; and the domestic structural context within which the policy debate transpires.

A focus on the interaction between international norms and domestic actors cannot alone provide a complete account of national policy choice. To develop such an explanation requires an analysis of those factors that motivate domestic actors to appeal to international rules and norms in the first place. Our goal here is limited to opening up the black box of domestic politics in an effort to offer a better understanding of how international norms and rules affect state behavior.

The plausibility of domestic actors' appeals to international rules and norms influencing state behavior is explored through an examination of two U.S. policies, one involving economic policy and the other security policy. The economic case surveys the U.S. semiconductor industry's efforts between 1980 and 1986 to get the Reagan administration to pressure Japan to open its markets to U.S. semiconductor devices and to stop Japanese manufacturers from dumping their products in U.S. markets. The security case reviews the Bush administration's decision to seek a United Nations mandate in responding to Iraq's August 1990 invasion of Kuwait. Our analysis of these cases offers two findings. First, a similar dynamic operated in both the trade and security cases: domestic actors' appeals to international rules and norms affected the type of policy the U.S. pursued. In the trade case, private commercial interests' appropriation of international trade rules led the United States to seek another country's compliance with these rules. In the security case, the enmeshment of the collective security norm in the domestic policy debate led the United States to pursue a course of action that complied with the norm's prescriptions. Second, the evidence shows that the existence of an international regime does not necessarily imply that cooperative outcomes will result. Domestic actors can use international rules to further interests that may not be completely consistent with the original purposes the regime was meant to serve. The institutionalization of international rules into domestic political processes can, then, have both positive and negative effects for compliance.

The following section outlines the argument that international norms can become relevant domestically. Subsequently, the argument is assessed through an analysis of two U.S. policy choices. The conclusion discusses the theoretical implications of the investigation.

International Rules and the Domestic Political Process

This section has two objectives: to delineate how international rules and norms can become institutionalized in the domestic political arena; and to identify those factors that will prove most significant in determining when international rules will influence national policy choice.

Consistent with existing scholarship in international relations theory we adopt the following definitions for rules and norms. Norms represent "standards of behavior defined in terms of rights and obligations" (Krasner, 1983:2). Examples of commonly recognized international norms include sovereignty (Bull, 1979:8; Kratochwil, 1989:251), free trade (Finlayson and Zacher, 1983:282), and collective security (Ruggie, 1992:568–71). By contrast, rules constitute specific applications of norms to particular situations. In other words, "rules are specific prescriptions or proscriptions for action" (Krasner, 1983:5). For example, a number of rules have been developed under the auspices of the General Agreement on Tariffs and Trade (GATT) to regulate such practices as dumping, subsidies, quantitative restrictions, and other preferential or discriminatory practices.[2] Although there is a difference between rules and norms, the subsequent theoretical discussion does not differentiate between them. This approach is adopted because this article focuses not on norms and rules per se, but rather on the processes by which both can affect national policy.

Previous scholarship has identified two processes or pathways by which an international institution's rules or norms can become institutionalized at the domestic level. First, some have argued (Nye, 1987:400; Nadelmann, 1990:524; Duffield, 1992:838) that these rules can infuse the beliefs and values of actors within the state. As Robert McElroy (1992:42–3) notes, "[T]he conscience of a state decision maker can lead him to actually decide in favor of a particular policy action at least in part because of its moral significance." Second, it has been argued that a regime's tenets may become enmeshed in a country's domestic political processes through the standard operating procedures of bureaucratic agencies (Nye, 1987; Young, 1989:79; Duffield, 1992). Below we discuss two complementary pathways that have received less theoretical and empirical attention in the literature.

First, government officials and societal actors can invoke an international rule to further their own particularistic interests in domestic policy debates.[3] That is, a domestic actor can use the existence of an international rule to justify her own actions or to call into question the legitimacy of another's. For example, McElroy (1992:45–6) writes that "it is possible for domestic groups to mobilize around an international moral norm and thereby put pressure on a president or Congress to change American foreign policy. . . . The desire of presidents and congressional representatives for reelection and popularity creates a 'pathway' from international moral norms to norm-observant state behavior." However, this pathway can work in another fashion: governmental officials themselves may appeal to international norms to legitimate unpopular decisions. Thus, David Strang and Patricia M. Y. Chang (1993:243) note, "Reformist governments like the Spanish leftists of the 1930s and the Greek Social Democrats of the 1960s referred to International Labor Organization standards to legitimate their policies. State officials may likewise appeal to international obligations to evade constitutional restrictions." Similarly, Peter Haas's research suggests that international rules can be used to one group's advantage in national-level policy debates. Haas (1989:398, 401) concludes that "the [Mediterranean Pollution Control] regime not only provided new evidence but, more important, . . . [its] principles also empowered new domestic groups of marine scientists, who led their governments to comply more strongly with the regime and to negotiate more constructively internationally." Through this pathway international rules can serve as resources for domestic actors to use in the national arena and thus, as David Dessler (1989:467) writes, "are not concrete girders constraining action but, instead, are media through which action becomes possible."

A second way by which an international institution's rules can become institutionalized into the domestic political process is through their incorporation or embodiment in domestic laws.[4] In fact, Antonio Cassese notes that "international law cannot work without the constant help, cooperation, and support of national legal systems" (quoted in Hurrell, 1993:71). For example, much of U.S. trade law has been developed in tandem with the evolving nature of the GATT codes. Similarly, Strang and Chang (1993:242–3) report that "Sweden's 1973 Unemployment Insurance Act states that daily allowances 'will not be fixed at a lower rate than

[2] For details on these rules and their exceptions see Spero (1990:70–1).

[3] Lipson (1983:262) offers a similar claim.

[4] Robert Keohane (1994) terms this process "institutional enmeshment." Finnemore (1993) details this process.

meets the requirements of the Social Security (Minimum Standards) Convention, 1952' " of the International Labor Organization. Even more fundamentally, international rules and norms have been codified in some countries' constitutions. For example, Article 24 of the German Constitution states that "[f]or the maintenance of peace, the Federation may enter a system of mutual collective security."[5] When institutionalized in domestic legal and constitutional structures, international rules can be appropriated by domestic actors for purposes that can have reverberations in either the domestic or international sphere: to press the actor's own interests against those of other national-level actors; or to set in motion the power of the state to further the actor's interests against those of other state or transnational actors.

The foregoing argues that international rules and norms can enter national-level policy processes by two means: the actions and interests of state and/or societal actors; and the incorporation of international rules and norms into national laws. However, these pathways will not lead international rules and norms to affect a state's policies in every instance. In fact, there is likely to be some variation in the domestic impact of international rules across countries and across different issue areas within single countries.[6] This variation, it is argued below, reflects two factors: the domestic salience of the international rule or norm; and the domestic structure that prevails during a given policy debate.

Both pathways by which international rules become relevant domestically depend on the interests of state and societal actors (Müller, 1993). Even if an international rule is institutionalized in a domestic law, its activation is still contingent on the actions of government officials or societal interest groups. Yet, the preferences of government officials and of private commercial interests do not at all times translate directly into the state's policy choices. Instead, these preferences are mediated by the domestic structural conditions that prevail during the policy debate.[7] In other words, on some occasions the domestic structural context will make it difficult for domestic actors—be they state or societal—to get what they want.

As used here, domestic structure refers to the organization of decision-making authority and to the pattern of state-societal relations.[8] Each of these structural components is assumed to be issue specific; that is, they are likely to vary within a country across different issue areas. The organization of decision-making authority varies along a continuum from decentralized to centralized depending on the number of bureaucratic agencies, ministries, or other arms of the governmental apparatus that are accorded authority over an issue.[9] The state, then, is not conceived here as a rational, unitary actor; instead, the state is seen to encompass a host of actors with distinct sets of institutional biases and predispositions that will lead them to favor different foreign policy priorities on any given issue (Pastor, 1980:53).

The second structural component, the pattern of state-societal relations, captures the institutional arrangements that grant societal actors access to, and participation in, the formulation of a particular area of policy. This component also varies along a continuum, one that ranges from close to distant. State-societal relations are distant when societal actors are excluded from policy formation. By contrast, close state-societal relations result when administrative, regulatory, or legislative decision-making procedures or rules incorporate societal actors or their interests into the

[5] We thank Kurt Kissinger for bringing this example to our attention.

[6] For the possibility that the impact of international norms will vary cross-nationally see Checkel (1994).

[7] For an overview of this phenomenon across several issue areas see the essays in Ikenberry, Lake, and Mastanduno (1988); and across several different countries and time periods see Gourevitch (1986).

[8] Our conception of the domestic structural context builds on that developed in Cortell (1994). For alternative conceptualizations see Katzenstein (1985), Hall (1986), and Ikenberry (1988a).

[9] For a similar approach see Solingen (1993:280–1).

policy-making process. Such mechanisms include advisory bodies that comprise societal representatives or national laws that accord private sector actors with a legal right by which to transmit their interests to the policy process, or to elicit government action on their behalf. This structural component is likely to change over time as new rules or mechanisms are added or old ones are amended.[10]

The two structural components result in four structural configurations. These structures are depicted in Figure 1. One cautionary point should be noted: Figure 1 depicts the two structural components at the end-points of the two continuums. In reality, the two components are likely to vary in their degrees of either centralization or closeness. Consequently, the structural context that prevails during a particular policy episode may not be readily classified into the ideal-types depicted in Figure 1.

Each of the structural configurations differently affects the domestic impact of international rules and norms. In the type I and III structures, state officials serve as the primary means by which international norms and rules affect national policy choices. The primacy of state actors is expected since these two structural configurations lack institutional mechanisms that link societal actors to the policy process; as a result, societal actors' ability to use international rules and norms to their advantage in the national arena is limited.

In a type I structure, decision-making authority is restricted to relatively few government officials since decision-making authority is centralized. In this configuration, international rules will only affect national policy when and if authoritative officials are predisposed to the prescriptions and proscriptions embodied in international institutions. Thomas Risse-Kappen (1994) provides an example of how a type I structure affected the former Soviet Union's embrace of the transnational idea "common security." As Risse-Kappen (1994:209–10) writes, "Until about 1988–89, the former Soviet Union represented an extremely state-controlled domestic structure with a highly centralized decision-making apparatus. . . . Since the

Pattern of State-Societal Relations

Structure of decision-making authority	Distant	Close
Centralized	Type I	Type II
Decentralized	Type III	Type IV

Fig. 1. A typology of domestic structural contexts.

[10] On this dynamic see Goldstein (1988).

top leadership in the former Soviet Union controlled to which voices it wanted to listen . . . its worldviews needed to be predisposed toward the strategic prescriptions promoted by the transnational actors. . . . [T]he impact [of a transnational idea] depended almost entirely on the leadership's willingness to listen." Although Risse-Kappen focuses on a different international factor—transnational ideas and coalitions—his analysis nonetheless helps us to understand how a type I structure affects the capacity of international phenomena to "enter the policymaking process and become incorporated into national foreign policies" (Risse-Kappen, 1994:212).

By contrast, in a type III structure, decision-making authority is dispersed across several functionally differentiated arms of the government. Due to the fact that state-societal relations are distant in this structure, the role international rules will play in affecting state behavior is contingent on the actions and interests of government officials. If international rules do enter a policy debate, they will do so when one group of policy makers appeals to international rules in an effort to further its own preferred strategies or to block those of other officials. However, due to the pluralist nature of the policy process, the incorporation of international rules and norms into the policy debate does not guarantee that they will affect state policy.[11] Instead, the success of an appeal in a decentralized structure is conditioned by a nonstructural factor: the domestic salience of the rule or norm.

An international norm's domestic salience largely derives from the legitimacy accorded it in the domestic political context. That is, a norm's domestic strength may not correlate with the norm's international standing or institutionalization (Goertz and Diehl, 1992:646). Although difficult to measure, the norm's domestic legitimacy can be conceived of as varying along a continuum of state actions.[12] These actions consist of declaratory statements by authoritative actors as well as concrete policy choices. An examination of these actions provides an indication of the level of domestic commitment to, and legitimacy associated with, the international rule or norm.

A single declaration of support for the international rule is unlikely to make it salient domestically. However, repeated declarations by authoritative actors are indicative of the state's commitment to the rule.[13] Moreover, such affirmation symbolizes (or may come to be construed to represent) the state's association of the international rule with the advancement of the country's national interest or core values. Consequently, such commitment can create diffuse national support for the rule, or, as Gregory Caldeira and James Gibson (1995:357) explain, a "durable set of attitudes toward the legitimacy of the institution."

An international rule lacks domestic salience if the state has denied the rule's legitimacy. Such denials might take the form of the state's repeated lack of compliance with the norm's obligations, or its refusal to ratify agreements associated with the international rule. At the midpoint along the continuum, an international rule possesses a moderate degree of domestic salience. This results when a state's acceptance of the rule is limited to declaratory statements or ratifications of international agreements pertaining to the rule. Nonetheless, in adopting this strategy authoritative actors have begun to embrace the rule's prescriptions over other possible strategies, thereby enhancing the rule's legitimacy in the domestic political context. If such actions continue, the rule will attain prescriptive status: "When actors regularly refer to the norm to describe and comment on their own

[11] Evangelista (1995) makes a similar argument with regard to transnational forces.

[12] This discussion builds on Sikkink (1993:415).

[13] The appeals of nonauthoritative actors are unlikely to carry much weight. In the United States, authoritative actors are generally defined constitutionally, or through precedent. The unique authority of the president to speak on behalf of the United States on matters of foreign affairs is a function of both constitutional investiture and important Supreme Court decisions. For an extended discussion on this point see Kratochwil (1985:238–40).

behavior and that of others, the validity claims of the norm are no longer controversial, even if the actual behavior continues violating the rules" (Risse-Kappen, 1995:10). Through such action, the state now, as Harald Müller (1993:383) notes, "puts an extra burden of proof on regime opponents because in discourses about proper behavior of states and other regime actors, the regime structure serves automatically as [a] frame of reference." An international rule enjoys the greatest degree of domestic salience when the state has made concrete alterations in its policy choices, or has incorporated formal procedures into its domestic processes in an effort to be in accordance with the rule's prescriptions. In this case, the norm or rule comes to be embedded within the nation's own normative, juridical, or constitutional framework.

When decision-making authority is decentralized, a policy maker's appropriation of a salient international rule helps to empower her position in the national arena. By appealing to the salient rule or norm, the official's interests are associated with the rule's domestic legitimacy, making them difficult to challenge.[14] Strang and Chang (1993:244) note a similar dynamic. They posit that "norms are effective when they serve as resources that reinforce the purposes domestic actors are already aligned around."[15] In this way, international rules can become power resources, helping domestic actors to translate their preferences into policy.[16]

The other two structures incorporate the above dynamics, but in addition they provide societal groups with a role in the process by which international rules enter domestic policy making. In both a type II and type IV structure, state-societal relations are close. This presumes the existence of administrative, regulatory, or legislative procedures that enable societal interest groups to assume a legitimate role in the government's policy process.[17] Due to the presence of such mechanisms, societal groups possess the capacity to influence the course of policy making. In these structural contexts, a societal appeal to international rules will at the least affect the policy debate. That is, we would expect government officials to give attention to the societal group's interests. However, the extent to which a societal appeal will translate into policy, and thus affect the state's behavior, is a function of the rule's domestic salience. Accordingly, we expect a societal appeal to wield the most influence on policy choice when the societal actor utilizes a domestic procedure that sets in motion the prescriptions of an international institution. In this case, the institutional arrangements linking societal actors to the policy process serve a dual role: not only enabling societal actors to invoke the international rule, but also according them a legal right by which to elicit the government's implementation of the rule's prescriptions.

In sum, the domestic impact of an international rule or norm is expected to be a function of two factors: the domestic structure affecting the policy debate; and the domestic salience of the rule. So long as government officials possess jurisdiction over the issue, their appeals are expected to translate into policy outcomes when decision-making authority is centralized. In contrast, when decision-making authority is decentralized, the impact of government officials' appeals on the state's policy choice will depend on a nonstructural factor: the domestic salience of the international rule. Societal actors' appeals to international rules are unlikely to affect state policy when state-societal relations are distant. However, when state-societal relations are close, societal appeals are expected to influence policy making. The

[14] On how norm-governed reasoning helps to legitimate policy see Kratochwil (1989:102–4, 204–10).

[15] See also Ikenberry and Kupchan (1990:292) and Müller (1993:386).

[16] Duffield (1994:377) offers a similar observation.

[17] For the importance of such mechanisms in drawing societal actors into the policy process see Okimoto (1989:152–65).

capacity of societal actors to translate their appeals into policy choices is expected to be a function of the domestic salience of the rule.

One is tempted to limit the scope of the above argument to liberal democratic states. However, ongoing research in the field of international relations suggests that the argument developed here is applicable to both democratic and nondemocratic regimes. Daniel Thomas (1995), for example, avers that the human rights component of the Helsinki Accords empowered societal groups operating in several of the Communist regimes of Eastern Europe during the 1970s and 1980s. Jeffrey Checkel (1994) illustrates that pan-European political institutions have diffused common norms of human rights, influencing domestic debates in the Ukraine and Russia. The domestic impact of these norms, Checkel argues, was due in large part to a conducive environment created by each country's domestic structure. Similarly, Matthew Evangelista (1995) finds that variations in the Soviet Union's and Russia's domestic structural context account for differences in the impact of the Antiballistic Missile Treaty on security policy in the two countries.

The following empirical sections examine two cases in which domestic actors' appeals to international rules and norms shaped U.S. policy choices. The cases were chosen for two theoretical reasons. First, the process by which the international rules and norms enter the domestic policy debate differs in the two cases. In the trade case, societal interest groups appropriate GATT rules whereas in the security case President Bush invoked the collective security norm. This variation reflects differences in the structural context that prevailed during each policy debate, principally in the degree of closeness that characterized state-societal relations. In the trade case, the debate occurs in a structural context that resembles the type IV structure depicted in Figure 1. The security case more closely approximates a type III structure, as state officials were accorded the primary role in policy making.

Second, the domestic salience and international institutionalization of the international norms differ across the two cases. The trade case focuses on the GATT's rules and norms. These have been developed and refined through successive multilateral trade negotiations. A detailed international legal framework has emerged, large segments of which have been incorporated into American trade procedures. Consequently, if international norms do affect U.S. behavior through the pathway created by domestic actors' appeals, confirming evidence should be found in the trade arena. By contrast, the security case represents a harder test. The U.S. commitment to the collective security norm has been lodged at the declaratory level rather than in specific domestic procedures or by the way in which the country has used its armed forces. Therefore, demonstrating that domestic actors' invocation of the collective security norm guided U.S. policy options would provide strong support for the plausibility of our argument.

The two cases provide "heuristic case studies." As Alexander George (1979:51–2) writes, these offer "an opportunity to learn more about the complexity of the problem studied, to develop further the existing explanatory framework, and to refine and elaborate the initially available theory." The method of "process tracing" is employed to establish the links between the appropriation of the international norm for domestic political purposes and the impact of the norm's invocation on policy outcomes (George and McKeown, 1985). Although many have advocated (Haggard and Simmons, 1987:514; Milner, 1988:13–4) the need to reconstruct domestic decision-making processes so as to evaluate the causal significance of international norms and rules,[18] this call has not, as Etel Solingen (1994:317) notes, "been followed by an actual application." In the following empirical sections we seek to fill this void.

---

[18] On the need to focus on the links between domestic politics and international institutions more generally see Keohane (1993:295).

The U.S. Semiconductor Industry and Japanese Compliance with Free and Fair Trade

This section examines the U.S. semiconductor industry's efforts between 1982 and 1986 to persuade the Reagan administration to press Japan to remove its nontariff trade barriers and to stop Japanese semiconductor manufacturers from dumping their products in the U.S. market. In both 1982 and 1985 the American semiconductor industry appealed to the norm of free trade and other GATT rules establishing fair trade in an effort to strengthen its case in the national arena. The industry's interests did not, however, become empowered in this arena until the fall of 1985. At this time the industry activated several U.S. trade laws that enable private commercial interests to seek the enforcement of the rights accorded to them by the GATT. This section shows that the United States sought Japan's compliance with these GATT rules because the U.S. semiconductor industry had appropriated them to further its interest in the domestic policy process.

Beginning in the late 1970s Japanese semiconductor manufacturers began to erode the U.S. industry's hold on world markets. For example, by 1979 Japanese firms had captured nearly 50 percent of the American market for the best-selling, and most advanced, computer memory chip, the 16K dynamic random access memory (DRAM) ("Can Semiconductors Survive Big Business," 1979:66). By the end of 1981 Japanese firms controlled nearly 70 percent of the U.S. market for the next generation 64K DRAM (Semiconductor Industry Association, 1983:7). These were dramatic developments for U.S. semiconductor manufacturers. As recently as 1978 they had accounted for nearly 80 percent of the global DRAM market (Tyson, 1992:106).

Alarmed by the success of Japanese semiconductor firms, U.S. manufacturers turned to political activism in the early 1980s. The Semiconductor Industry Association (hereafter the SIA) publicized the industry's inability to gain greater access to the Japanese market. Even though Japan had adopted liberalization initiatives throughout the 1970s, U.S. manufacturers' share of the Japanese semiconductor market remained at its 1973 level of 10 percent in 1981 (SIA, 1985:Fig. A2; Prestowitz, 1989:Fig. 2.8). At this time, by contrast, American manufacturers accounted for over 50 percent of the U.S. and European semiconductor markets. The SIA maintained that this anomaly resulted from "unfair" Japanese trade practices. In particular, the SIA alleged that Japan used "counter-liberalization" measures that enabled Japanese semiconductor firms to operate from a protected home market. In addition, the SIA contended that Japanese companies deliberately priced their semiconductor devices below the cost of production in foreign markets to gain market share (SIA, 1981, 1983).[19] This practice constituted "dumping" and contravened not only U.S. trade laws, but also Japanese obligations under the GATT.

As the GATT is an intergovernmental agreement, private commercial interests do not have recourse to the treaty's dispute resolution mechanisms (Jackson and Davey, 1986:803). Instead, U.S. industries have access to GATT rules through Section 301 of the United States Trade and Tariffs Act of 1974. Section 301 enables private parties to petition the United States Trade Representative (USTR) to initiate an investigation "of any foreign governmental act, policy or practice that burdens or restricts U.S. commerce and either violates international obligations or is determined to be unjustifiable, unreasonable or discriminatory" (Hansen, 1987:1123). In providing U.S. private commercial interests with a mechanism by which to access GATT dispute resolution mechanisms, Section 301 seeks to ensure that other countries practice free and fair trade by the threat of potential U.S. retaliation. As

[19] On this second charge see the statement by Charles Harwood—President of Signetics Corp.—in Congress (1979:14).

Stephen Lande and Craig VanGrasstek (1986:44) explain, Section 301 "is intended to complement the formal GATT procedures rather than to replace them. The statute might best be seen as a procedural overlay to U.S. negotiating powers, through which domestic industries may formally petition their government for action in the GATT or elsewhere."

In 1982, however, unfair trade practices were vaguely defined under Section 301 (Lande and VanGrasstek, 1986:47–8; Bayard and Elliott, 1994:27–9). Consequently, the SIA did not feel confident that its petition would be successful. The industry opted instead to apply pressure on USTR and Commerce Department officials to take up the industry's case.[20] The SIA lobbied the Reagan administration "to pick up where the Tokyo Round of the Multilateral Trade Negotiations left off" (Congress, 1980:177). Specifically, U.S. manufacturers wanted the same access to Japanese markets that Japanese manufacturers enjoyed in the United States, and requested that a greater effort be made to limit the ability of Japanese manufacturers to dump their products in the U.S. market.

As a result of the semiconductor industry's lobbying efforts and calls for the enforcement of free and fair trade, a high-level United States–Japan working group was established in the spring of 1982 to discuss the general lack of reciprocity in U.S.–Japanese high technology trade.[21] But the Reagan administration did not take advantage of this working group to resolve the semiconductor industry's specific trade complaints (Prestowitz, 1989:153–5). Instead, the administration asked the Japanese government to provide all U.S. industries with greater access to the Japanese market. The agreement that emerged from the working group's discussions in November 1982 fulfilled the administration's objective: the Japanese government promised "to develop possible concrete measures to promote imports of high technology goods" (SIA, 1985:6).

Not surprisingly, this agreement did not resolve the U.S. semiconductor industry's complaints about Japan's trade practices. By the end of 1984, U.S. semiconductor manufacturers' share of the Japanese market remained at the 1973 level of 10 percent (Congress, 1985a:110, Fig. 3). Moreover, the agreement did not stop Japanese semiconductor manufacturers from dumping their devices in the American market.[22] By the beginning of 1985, Japanese manufacturers captured 92 percent of the American market for the next generation memory chip, the 256K DRAM ("Chips: The War of Tomorrow's World," 1985:69). These developments enabled Japanese manufacturers to capture the largest share of the world semiconductor market.[23]

Japan's domination of the U.S. DRAM market coincided with expressions of concern in the Congress over the then $37 billion trade deficit with Japan (Farnsworth, 1985). In March 1985 the Senate voted 92–0 in favor of a Republican-sponsored nonbinding resolution that condemned Japan's trade practices as "unfair" and called on President Reagan to retaliate by curbing imports of Japanese autos (Kilborn, 1985). In the hopes of capitalizing on the Senate action, the SIA filed a Section 301 unfair trade practices petition against the Japanese government on 14 June 1985. Later in June an additional dumping complaint was filed against Japanese manufacturers of 64K DRAMs. If the U.S. International Trade Commission (ITC) validated this complaint, antidumping duties would automatically be placed on these Japanese products by July 1986.

[20] On the SIA's strategy see Prestowitz (1989:147–52) and Gutfleish (1987:345–50).

[21] This information is derived from an interview with a former Commerce Department official.

[22] The working group agreement included a system to monitor semiconductor shipments. As it was not based on prices, however, it could not halt Japanese dumping. For more on the deficiencies of this agreement see Prestowitz (1989:154).

[23] Tyson (1992:105) reports that the Japanese share of the world market was just over 45 percent whereas the U.S. share was about 40 percent.

The SIA's decision to file a Section 301 petition marked a change from its 1982 strategy. One reason the industry appealed to international trade rules via Section 301 was that Congress had revised the wording of the statute in the Trade and Tariff Act of 1984. The statute now defined unfair trade in a manner that resonated with the industry's charges (Congress, 1985b:65). The revised Section 301 distinguished between unjustifiable and unreasonable foreign trade practices, defining the latter to include practices that resulted in "unfair and inequitable" market access (Bayard and Elliott, 1994:30–1). Robert Noyce, chairman of the Intel Corporation, the leading U.S. semiconductor manufacturer, explained that the U.S. industry sought relief under Section 301 because "Japan is simply not playing the game according to the rules that we play. We steadfastly hold on to this ideal of free trade" (Schrage, 1985). The SIA's Section 301 petition appealed directly to the international trade rules that Japan had violated:

> Japanese market barriers are inconsistent with U.S. rights under the GATT. The United States has been denied the benefit of concessions made pursuant to reciprocal rounds of tariff reductions by the Japanese government's role in the erection of a series of non-tariff barriers—initially formal quantitative restrictions, and subsequently, through liberalization countermeasures designed to perpetuate the effect of those restrictions through the establishment of a protected market structure. . . . The Japanese government's creation and continued tolerance of a market structure which acts as a barrier to foreign sales, and which adversely affects the U.S. semiconductor industry is unjustifiable, unreasonable and inconsistent with the international rights of the United States. (Wolff, Gadbaw, Howell, and Richards, 1985:vii, I)

In its Section 301 petition, the SIA called (as it had at the time of the high technology working group) on the Reagan administration: (1) to press the Japanese government to eliminate its nontariff barriers so that its domestic industries would buy more semiconductors from U.S. manufacturers; and (2) to develop along with Japan a system to monitor Japanese firms' pricing practices that would limit their capacity to dump their products (Wolff et al., 1985; Congress, 1985b, 1985c).

Section 301 enabled U.S. semiconductor manufacturers not only to transmit their preferences directly into the policy process, but also to elicit the government's action to enforce the rights granted the industry under the GATT. The government's response to a Section 301 petition is formulated by the interagency Section 301 committee. This committee includes not less than eleven executive departments. Thus, the debate surrounding the semiconductor industry's use of Section 301 occurred within a type IV domestic structural context, one characterized by close state-societal relations and a decentralized decision-making structure. In this structural context, the domestic salience of the international rule is expected to determine whether the industry's appropriation of international rules will affect U.S. policy choices. As discussed below, this factor helped to translate the industry's appeal to GATT rules into policy outcomes.

In August, the Commerce Department reported that the U.S. trade deficit had "swelled" to the unprecedented level of $135 billion ("Aides See '85 Gap," 1985:46). This figure inflamed an already protectionist Congress: at this time hundreds of trade-related bills were pending in the Congress, many of which were protectionist or targeted at Japan. To quell Congress's protectionist sentiments, President Reagan (1985) announced the formation of a cabinet strike force to "uncover unfair trading practices and to develop and execute strategies and programs to promptly counter and eliminate them."[24] The strike force's purview was intended to be limited

[24] Roberts (1985) notes that the president's speech was "plainly [intended] to blunt bipartisan Congressional efforts to impose quotas and raise tariffs to protect American jobs."

to the three Section 301 cases *"self-initiated* by the administration earlier in the month" (O'Shea, 1988:60, emphasis added).[25] Nevertheless, Commerce and USTR strike force members decided that the strike force should first resolve the SIA's Section 301 petition.

The decision to give priority to the semiconductor industry's demands appears to have resulted from three factors directly related to the industry's activation of domestic procedures that institutionalize international trade rules. First, pursuant to Section 301, the USTR had begun bilateral negotiations with its Japanese counterparts in July 1985 to seek a mutually acceptable resolution of the industry's petition. However, these talks had made little progress when the strike force was established. Second, shortly before the strike force's creation, the ITC ruled that Japanese semiconductor firms had dumped 64K DRAMs in U.S. markets, and in doing so, had injured U.S. manufacturers.[26] This finding enhanced the credibility of the industry's claims. An additional factor increased the prominence of the industry's demands in the domestic political arena. Within two weeks of the strike force's creation, three leading U.S. semiconductor firms filed additional antidumping complaints against Japan with respect to erasable programmable read only memory circuits ("Intel, AMD and National," 1985).

To resolve the SIA's Section 301 petition, Commerce and USTR strike force members proposed that the U.S. government file its own trade complaint against the Japanese firms.[27] In this manner the administration would gain leverage in dealing with the Japanese government because this action would demonstrate the seriousness with which the administration perceived the industry's trade complaint. Members of the strike force from the Departments of Treasury and State objected to this strategy. Responding to these objections, Commerce Secretary Malcolm Baldrige argued that if the Reagan administration did not resolve the industry's Section 301 complaint in a constructive manner it would give the impression that the administration was not interested in enforcing U.S. trade law and the rules of international trade that the United States had put so much energy into constructing and reinforcing. Simply put, Secretary Baldrige maintained that the Reagan administration would find itself in an awkward position if it disregarded the industry's appeal to such salient rules. The argument was persuasive. Everyone in the strike force agreed that the Reagan administration had to enforce the rules of international trade and related U.S. trade law. On that basis, the strike force authorized the Commerce Department in December 1985 to initiate an antidumping investigation of Japanese firms' pricing practices with respect to 256K DRAM memory chips (Pine, 1985).

After this initiative, the United States and Japan intensified their bilateral negotiations to resolve the semiconductor industry's Section 301 petition. By July 1986 a United States–Japan Semiconductor Trade Agreement was reached. This agreement comprised the two objectives the SIA had hoped would be attained during the earlier working group discussions: (1) a Japanese promise to "encourage" Japanese manufacturers to increase their purchases of foreign-made chips to slightly over 20 percent of the Japanese market over a five-year period; and (2) the establishment of a price monitoring system to limit the ability of Japanese semiconductor firms to dump their products in U.S. or third-country markets (Tyson,

[25] The three petitions concerned Japan's treatment of U.S. tobacco products, the U.S. insurance industry's difficulties in Korea, and Brazil's laws concerning the informatics industry.

[26] The ITC ruling concerned the June antidumping petition that Micron Technologies filed against Japanese semiconductor manufacturers with respect to 64K DRAMs (Miller, 1985:42).

[27] The information contained in this paragraph comes from an interview with a former member of the strike force and Prestowitz (1989:161).

1992:109–10).[28] In return, the United States agreed to drop all charges and possible fines against those Japanese semiconductor firms charged with dumping. However, when the monitoring system showed in early 1987 that Japanese semiconductor firms continued to dump their devices in the U.S. market, the United States imposed tariffs of 100 percent on four Japanese-made electronics products containing Japanese-made semiconductor devices. The administration did so, President Reagan declared, because it was "committed to the full enforcement of our trade agreements designed to provide American industry with free and fair trade opportunities" (Farnsworth, 1987:35).

U.S. semiconductor manufacturers asked the Reagan administration in both 1982 and 1985 to press Japan to open its market to their products and to stop Japanese manufacturers from dumping their devices in U.S. markets. Although the industry invoked the norm of free trade and fair trade rules in lobbying the Reagan administration during both policy episodes, the industry succeeded only in 1985 when it filed Section 301 and antidumping trade complaints. This case suggests that societal actors' invocation of a domestically salient international rule will be effective when they activate a set of domestic processes that are premised upon the international rule. This pathway empowered the semiconductor industry's interests as the domestic legitimacy of the industry's claim was difficult for other national actors to challenge. Ultimately, the industry's appeal led the administration to seek Japanese compliance with GATT trade rules.

Alternative Explanations

Several well-established perspectives in the international relations literature offer explanations for the differences in the strategies the Reagan administration pursued in 1982 and 1986. Each of these approaches tends, however, to focus on either the domestic or international level of analysis without investigating how international rules become intertwined with the interests and purposes of domestic actors. As a result, these perspectives cannot completely account for the Reagan administration's decision to seek Japanese compliance with international trade rules in 1986.

Realist theories, for example, would explain the differences in the two policy choices by virtue of the variation in the U.S. semiconductor industry's relative market shares (Lake, 1988a; Grieco, 1990). This perspective posits that state behavior is motivated by developments that are perceived to threaten the country's power and wealth relative to that of other countries. In particular, these theories lead us to expect that a country will respond to a decline in its semiconductor industry's relative market share since this development may affect the country's relative capabilities by putting other "firms at a competitive disadvantage, [leading] to the shrinkage of [its] industrial base, or [resulting] in the movement of high value added activity away from [its] territory" (Mastanduno, 1991:80). Accordingly, realist theories would expect the Reagan administration to try to reverse the industry's decline soon after U.S. firms' relative market share had fallen behind that of Japanese manufacturers. Thus, the Reagan administration would not be expected to act in 1982 because relative decline was not evidenced until sometime during 1985.

A realist explanation seems to account for the broad differences in the two U.S. trade policies. Nonetheless, realist theories lack a conception of the process by which systemically generated pressures get translated into policy outcomes. These theories tend to assume that a unified actor rationally calculates the national interest in

[28] The extension of this bilateral agreement to third countries challenged existing GATT practices. See Kingery (1989).

response to such pressures. This case by contrast shows that the state was far from unified with regard to the national interest. More tellingly, the country's policy choice reflected a concern for relative gains because international trade rules were enmeshed in the domestic policy process, thereby enabling the industry to use the rules to advance its particularistic concerns about its declining relative market share.

A second approach contends that an explanation for a country's policy choice can be given when societal groups and their interests or organizational characteristics are understood (Milner, 1987, 1988; Frieden, 1988). Although the 1986 Semiconductor Trade Agreement did largely reflect the industry's interests, the 1982 agreement did not. The variation in the industry's influence in the two policy debates results in part from how it appealed to international rules and norms. For example, in 1982, the industry simply invoked international rules and norms to justify its position. In 1985, by contrast, the industry filed unfair trade practices and antidumping petitions that were themselves premised on international rules and norms. In this case, the U.S. semiconductor industry had access to national laws that enable private commercial interests not only to set in motion the rights accorded to them under the GATT, but also to transmit their preferences to authoritative government officials. By virtue of this structural component, the interests of the U.S. semiconductor industry became empowered in the national policy debate. Therefore, a fuller explanation can be offered if we supplement an industry-centered focus with a nuanced understanding of the institutional conditions that affect policy making.

A third explanation focuses on the actions and interests of central decision makers (Lake, 1988b). As G. John Ikenberry (1988b:26–7) explains, this perspective "finds the state able to develop and implement autonomous preferences, even in the face of pressure from private interests. Foreign economic policy is not simply the hostage of societal groups; the state may be able to resist or blunt interest group or class demands in favor of its own set of policies." In both cases, the role of U.S. government officials looms large. During the 1982 negotiations, policy makers appear to have been responsible for the U.S. decision not to seek a solution to the semiconductor industry's complaints (Prestowitz, 1989:154). However, a focus on the interests of central decision makers cannot alone account for the Reagan administration's 1986 strategy. Instead, the evidence reveals that the U.S. semiconductor industry's appropriation of international trade rules in pursuit of its interests ultimately placed enough pressure on the Reagan administration, leading it to respond to the industry's trade complaints.

The Iraqi Invasion of Kuwait and the Norm of Collective Security

This section traces the impact of President Bush's appeal to the norm of collective security as a justification for a United States response to Iraq's August 1990 invasion of Kuwait. Both as an analytic construct and as a guide to statesmen, the norm of collective security lacks clarity and specificity, a point noted by many (Wolfers, 1962:ch. 12; Claude, 1971; Morgenthau, 1978:301–2; Kupchan and Kupchan, 1991:118; Betts, 1992). For example, Inis Claude (1971:247) writes, "Collective security has been appropriated as an honorific designation for virtually any and all multilateral activities that statesmen or scholars may regard or wish to have regarded as conducive to peace and order." At a minimum, however, the collective security norm has come to comprise the suspension of ad hoc national judgments regarding threats to the peace or breaches of the peace, and the surrender of national discretion regarding the resort to force in favor of international authorization derived from preexisting multilateral agreements or the specific stipulations of competent multilateral agencies (Claude, 1971:253).

The case shows that the United States complied with the tenets of the collective security norm in responding to the Iraqi aggression largely because the norm became enmeshed in the American domestic political debate. Specifically, President Bush repeatedly used the collective security norm to justify a response to the Iraqi invasion, providing the Congress with a tool by which it could subsequently constrain the president's capacity for unilateral action. By invoking the norm of collective security, Congress forced the president at two junctures to abandon a unilateral strategy and instead seek a U.N. mandate: first, with respect to the enforcement of trade sanctions; and second, with regard to the initiation of an offensive action to drive Iraqi forces from Kuwait. Nonetheless, once President Bush opted for a response that was consistent with the norm of collective security, Congress's power to prevent U.S. military involvement was limited.

The fact that debates over U.S. security policy were cast largely in terms of an international norm is a puzzle for students of international security, as norms are generally held to play a very limited role in security affairs (Waltz, 1979:126–30; Jervis, 1983). The collective security norm influenced the U.S. response to Iraq's invasion of Kuwait due in part to the structure of decision-making authority in the issue area. War-making authority is decentralized in the American political system; both the Congress and the president enjoy some jurisdiction over decisions affecting war and peace. This dispersion of power is set forth by the Constitution, which Corwin (1948:208) calls "an invitation to struggle for the privilege of directing American foreign policy."[29] In Article I, Section 8, the Constitution grants the Congress authority to raise and maintain armed forces and to declare war. In Article II, Section 2, the president is named as commander in chief. Further delineation of the rights, authority, and responsibilities of the executive and legislature is not provided.

Compared to other issue areas, the U.S. state is relatively insulated from societal pressures with regard to decisions over national security. Krasner (1978:86), for example, notes that "[t]he points of access for interest groups can be hundreds of times greater for a decision involving tariffs than for one about diplomatic or military action."[30] In fact, there exist few institutionalized mechanisms whereby societal interests can directly introduce their preferences into the policy process in this area. Risse-Kappen (1991:491) notes that "corporatist structures such as the military industrial complex linking business, military and political interests have only a limited impact on foreign policy decisions beyond the weapons-procurement process and demands for a certain level of defense spending." As the Gulf crisis ensued, these arrangements increased when the Congress held hearings regarding the appropriate American response. Nonetheless, the public's role in the formulation of American policy was largely consistent with what Jack Snyder (1991:288) terms "a followership model, in which an attentive public imbibes the interpretations put forward by opinion leaders."

In this structural context, the domestic impact of an international norm is expected to be a function of the actions and interests of government officials as well as the domestic salience of the particular norm. The following discussion illustrates that the decentralized decision-making structure and the salience of the collective security norm enabled the Congress to use this norm to increase its influence in the

[29] For the history of the struggle over war-making powers see Cheever and Haviland (1952), Javits and Kellerman (1973), and May (1960). There is a vast body of literature concerned with the executive-congressional rivalry for primacy in foreign policy. For the argument that presidents are paramount see Wildavsky (1966), Pious (1979), Destler, Gelb, and Lake (1984), and Koh (1990). For the converse see Ripley and Lindsay (1993).

[30] Krasner (1978:86) continues: "Decisions about the use of military force are taken in arenas, most notably the White House and State Department, that are heavily insulated from particular domestic pressure groups. Central decision-makers are not immune to the entreaties or even, as we have seen in recent years, the purses of major corporations, but they are subject to such pressures to much less a degree than, say, a Congressman from Texas voting on oil quotas."

policy debate, ultimately producing an American policy consistent with the tenets of collective security.

On August 1st, when Iraqi troops were massing on the Kuwaiti border, and again after the invasion of Kuwait, the White House called for an emergency meeting of the United Nations Security Council. On August 2nd, President Bush met with British Prime Minister Margaret Thatcher in Aspen, Colorado. The British Prime Minister was certain of the course the West should pursue vis-à-vis the Iraqi aggression:

> The Security Council acted swiftly last night under the United States' leadership . . . and rightly demanded the withdrawal of Iraqi troops. . . . The fundamental question is this: whether the nations of the world have the collective will effectively to see the Security Council resolution upheld; whether they have the collective will effectively to do anything which the Security Council further agrees, to see that Iraq withdraws and that the government of Kuwait is restored to Kuwait. None of us can do it separately. We need a collective and effective will of the nations belonging to the United Nations. (Office of the President, 1990:1182)

Following Thatcher's lead, President Bush reiterated that the norm of collective security should guide the response to the Iraqi invasion: "[W]e strongly support what Prime Minister Thatcher said about collective action and the U.N." (Office of the President, 1990:1186).

On August 5th, the president repeated the call for a collective response to the Iraqi aggression: "I view very seriously our determination to reverse this aggression. There are an awful lot of countries that are in total accord with what I've just said. We will be working with them all for collective action" (Friedman, 1990a). The president also called for U.N. sanctions under Chapter VII of the U.N. Charter. On August 6th, the Security Council voted for mandatory trade sanctions against Iraq by a vote of 13 to zero (Lewis, 1990). Throughout this period, the Bush administration's declarations stressed the collective, international nature of the U.S. response to Iraq's invasion of Kuwait (Stanfield, 1990). Through these repeated invocations, the president enhanced the salience of the collective security norm domestically, and in doing so, framed the terms of the subsequent domestic debate.[31]

The president's emphasis on collective security notwithstanding, he deployed 230,000 American troops to Saudi Arabia on August 8th. An American fleet was simultaneously assembled in the Persian Gulf. In addition, the administration announced on August 12th that the U.S. would unilaterally enforce the U.N. trade sanctions by a blockade at sea. After taking these unilateral actions, the administration, however, became the target of congressional criticism. In particular, the Congress questioned whether these steps were consistent with the basic tenets of the collective security norm. More fundamentally, the Congress sought to use its understanding of this norm to challenge the president's subsequent impulses for unilateral action. Senator Daniel Patrick Moynihan, for example, appealed to the collective security norm in questioning the president's unilateral action: "For reasons I can't understand, we haven't wanted to get U.N. sanction. Something has faltered. The Americans would be mad to go it alone" (Malcolm, 1990). Echoing Moynihan, Senator Terry Sanford warned the Bush administration against unilaterally initiating any military action: "We have accomplished our mission of

[31] It matters, then, that the president is uniquely empowered by the Constitution to speak on behalf of the United States, whereas individual members of the Congress, or of civil society, are not. For example, the Speaker of the House can announce his support for a "Two China" policy, and then reverse his position within a matter of days, as the pronouncements of the Speaker cannot commit the United States to a particular strategy, nor does the United States incur an obligation merely because the Speaker has spoken. The president, however, enjoys no such freedom of action. When the chief diplomat of the United States recognizes a foreign government, he has committed a speech act that constrains his future range of actions. Recognition cannot subsequently be withdrawn absent a "reasonable" cause.

stopping Iraq's drive to take over Saudi Arabia and the rest of the Middle East. . . . We should begin to reduce our forces in Saudi Arabia ever so slowly, and look to a more multinational force to keep the peace" (Rosenthal, 1990b). These congressional calls for adherence to a collective security framework demonstrate that after the president's initial invocation, the collective security norm was beginning to become enmeshed in the domestic political debate.

The president, however, was "eager to assert the right of the United States to act by itself" (Woodward, 1991:284). Answering a reporter's question regarding the unilateral enforcement of the U.N. trade sanctions President Bush (1990) remarked that "we have all the authority we need. And the world leaders I've talked to, particularly François Mitterrand and Margaret Thatcher agree that we have all the authority we need . . . at this juncture I'm not prepared to say whether we're going to insist on U.N. action before we go any further."

With American warships shadowing two loaded Iraqi oil tankers in Middle East waters and prepared to stop their further movement, Senator Sanford (1990) spoke for many of his colleagues when he asserted that there was an "urgent need to calm down" and to shift more responsibility to the United Nations. In response to the mounting congressional criticism of his unilateral initiative, President Bush reversed his position and began a round of urgent diplomacy to win United Nations approval of the use of military power to enforce the trade sanctions at sea (Rosenthal, 1990a). On August 25th, the United Nations Security Council authorized the enforcement of economic sanctions by halting shipping to and from Iraq. Administration officials later acknowledged that the effort to enlist United Nations support for the enforcement of the sanctions was "largely improvised and did not flow from lofty principles of international unity" (Sciolino and Pace, 1990).

One might argue that the administration's decision to seek further United Nations authority for the enforcement of the trade sanctions was motivated by a desire to maintain allied cohesion. But by August 19th, a week before the administration sought additional U.N. authority, France and Britain had already adopted the U.S. position, acknowledging that to be effective, the resolution on sanctions implied the need for "measures of verification, control and constraint" (France to Join Embargo, 1990). Without seeking additional U.N. authority, the French government ordered its fleet to enforce the trade sanctions (Goshko, 1990a). With both Britain and France on board, a senior administration official could later comment that "[o]ur strategy was that we were going to do whatever we had to on our own, and if we could bring along the U.N., fine" (Sciolino and Pace, 1990). Clearly, the administration did not view additional United Nations resolutions as being necessary for alliance cohesion. Instead it would appear that President Bush sought further U.N. authority to enforce the sanctions in response to congressional concern that the United States was abandoning its original policy of pursuing a collective response to Iraq's invasion of Kuwait. By appealing to the norm of collective security, the Congress prompted a policy reversal by the president.

The Senate opened hearings in October on the Gulf crisis and the American response. During the Senate hearings, members of Congress continued to appeal to the norm of collective security in an effort to constrain the president. For example, Claiborne Pell, the Senate Foreign Relations Committee chairman, said: "I want the record to show that I, for one, am not giving advance approval of U.S. unilateral military action." The Senator bolstered his position with an appeal to collective security under the United Nations framework: "If military action is required, the President should act under a U.N. mandate" (Goshko, 1990b). With only two of the nineteen-member Senate Foreign Relations Committee cautioning against over-reliance on the United Nations, Pell's position reflected a bipartisan consensus (Goshko, 1990b). With respect to the costs of the American buildup, Republican Senator Richard Lugar, for example, hoped the president would initiate "an international United Way Campaign" to help pay for the effort (Congress, 1990:23). The most forceful invocation of the collective security norm was made by Senator Moynihan during his questioning of Secretary of State Baker.[32] He reminded Baker that the president had premised American intervention on international norms, most importantly that of collective security. The Senator also made clear that members of Congress were intent on keeping U.S. actions consonant with this norm:

> I was struck by your written testimony and the fact that in all ten pages, at no point did you use the term "international law." At no point in your subsequent testimony have you used it. I was struck because there was no more distinct fact of President Bush's reaction to the Iraq invasion than the sudden appearance of this term in his language. On the day after the invasion, he said that what Iraq has done violates every norm of "international law." On August 20, he urged Iraq to "adhere to international law." He said international law must be enforced. . . . He would act under a treaty, under the U.N. procedures. For you to come here today and just have the subject disappear, raises the question of whether there has been a change of view or whether the President's use of this was an aberration. (Congress, 1990:119–20)

With these hearings in the background, the president faced calls for increased congressional involvement in decisions regarding the use of force in the Gulf. To a question about whether he could use force without congressional approval, the president answered that "history is replete with examples where the President has had to take action. . . . I've done this in the past and certainly would have no hesitancy at all" (Friedman, 1990b). Soon thereafter, President Bush ordered an additional 150,000 troops into the Saudi theater on November 8th in an effort to create an "adequate offensive military option" (U.S. Department of State, 1990:258). The action raised fears among many that the president was moving toward taking offensive action against Iraqi troops in Kuwait (Smith, 1992:214). Senator Bill Bradley (1990) argued that "President Bush has imperiled the international coalition he assembled so skillfully to deter Iraq's aggression in the Persian Gulf by changing to his go-it-alone offensive strategy." Senator Moynihan thought that the president "will wreck our military. He will wreck his administration, and he'll spoil a chance to get a collective security system going" (Woodward, 1991:324).

On November 13th, President Bush briefed the congressional leadership on the new buildup. Members of the Democratic leadership, largely opposed to the use of force in the Gulf, told the president that he should first receive U.N. approval for any offensive action (Feldman, 1990). Several of those present at the briefing felt that the Bush administration was looking for a way to initiate military action in Kuwait. For example, after the White House briefing, Senator Tom Harkin said: "There seems to be a fixation on provocations. I must have heard the word 'provocation' used five times" (Doherty, 1990:3882).

Administration officials later acknowledged that the November 13th meeting with congressional leaders was a turning point in their decision to seek U.N. authority to use force against Iraq (Apple, 1990; Friedman, 1990c). According to one account written at the time, "Mr. Bush, Mr. Baker and Mr. Scowcroft essentially decided after this meeting that they needed a Security Council resolution not only to keep the international coalition together, but to bring Congress along" (Friedman, 1990d). The president sent Secretary Baker to several foreign capitals to secure Security Council support for such a resolution.[33] On November 29th, the United States engineered United Nations Security Council Resolution 678 which approved

[32] But also note Republican Senator Nancy Kassebaum's similar remarks (Congress, 1990).

[33] The administration's leverage over the allies was significant. See Cooper, Higgott, and Nossal (1991). For constraints on Soviet President Mikhail Gorbachev's ability to challenge U.S. policy see Golan (1992).

the use of "all necessary means" to drive Iraqi forces from Kuwait and restore the government of the Emir.

In January 1991, President Bush, after long denying any obligation, sought a congressional resolution authorizing the use of U.S. troops, if necessary, against Iraq. In his letter to Congress requesting such authorization, President Bush underscored that any U.S. offensive action would be taken within the collective security framework of the United Nations:

> It would . . . greatly enhance the chances for peace if Congress were now to go on record supporting the position adopted by the U.N. Security Council on twelve separate occasions. Such an action would underline that the United States stands with the international community and on the side of law and decency. . . . I therefore request that the [Congress] adopt a resolution stating that Congress supports the use of all necessary means to implement United Nations Security Council Resolution 678. (Office of the President, 1991:18)

Although many members of the Democratic majority opposed the use of force, the proposed resolution's call for action under the collective security framework of the U.N. made it difficult for members to vote against the resolution. For example, in voting for the resolution, Senator Charles Robb argued that "we should commend the President for putting together a truly extraordinary coalition and for giving the United Nations a chance to play a responsible role" (*Congressional Record,* 1991b:S378). Republicans who had supported the continued use of sanctions also changed their position. One, Vermont's Republican Senator James Jeffords, explained that in voting for the use-of-force resolution, he was supporting the United Nations and the norm of collective security: "Backing away from the U.N. resolution would not serve the cause of peace, for now or for the future. This is a test, not just of how the United States responds to threats, but whether the United Nations and international diplomacy will become the primary tools for resolution of international conflicts" (*Congressional Record,* 1991b:S327). As a result of the repeated appeals to the norm of collective security by both the president and the Congress, the legitimacy of American participation in a collective response to the invasion of Kuwait could no longer be challenged.

The foregoing suggests that the multilateral character of the U.S. response to the Iraqi invasion of Kuwait resulted from the enmeshment of the norm of collective security in the U.S. policy debate. Principally, President Bush's appropriation of the collective security norm to justify a U.S. response to the Iraqi response ultimately enabled the Congress to constrain his range of responses to the Iraqi invasion. Through appeals to the same norm, Congress not only assumed a role in decisions concerning the use of U.S. forces abroad, but also fundamentally affected the nature of the U.S. response. In fact, on at least two occasions, congressional action led the president to move away from the unilateral use of force and instead to seek a collective response under the framework of the United Nations: first, with respect to the enforcement of the trade sanctions at sea; and second, with regard to the beginning of offensive actions which the evidence suggests were contemplated for November 1990. Nonetheless, the president was ultimately able to use the collective security norm as a tool to commit members of Congress to support his preference for the use of force to reverse the invasion of Kuwait.

Whether Congress constrained the president, or the president constrained the Congress, either outcome illustrates that government officials can appropriate international norms to pursue their interests in national policy debates. The impact of the international norm in this policy debate was premised on the decentralization of decision-making authority over issues of war and peace. Once the president introduced the collective security norm into the national arena, members of Congress appropriated the same norm in an effort to increase their authority in decisions over an American response to the invasion of Kuwait. Ultimately, through the actions of the Congress and the president, the United States pursued a strategy that was consistent with the tenets of the collective security norm.

Alternative Explanations

Two approaches offer compelling explanations for the sources of U.S. foreign policy: realism, and interbranch domestic politics. However, the factors stressed by these approaches do not by themselves account for the Bush administration's strategy during the Gulf crisis. A more satisfactory explanation can be generated if we supplement these models with an examination of the domestic impact of the collective security norm.

Realist theories are indeterminate with regard to the U.S. response in this case. Depending on one's interpretation of realism, a unilateral or multilateral response can be predicted. For example, a strong realist explanation for U.S. policy highlights the strategic nature of the oil-producing state of Kuwait (and Saudi Arabia) and would predict a direct American response (Waltz, 1979). This version of realism, however, leads to the expectation that the United States, as the only military superpower, would respond to the first post–Cold War crisis in a unilateral rather than a multilateral fashion.[34] What is a puzzle for some realists can be explained if we focus on the president's and the Congress's use of the collective security norm in support of their positions regarding the appropriate American response.

Another version of realism emphasizes the relative decline of the United States vis-à-vis other advanced industrial states and would accordingly predict that the country would seek allies to help defray the costs of turning back the Iraqi invasion.[35] This explanation is largely consistent with the evidence but cannot account for the U.S. decision to use the United Nations as the forum through which it would recruit allies and develop its strategy rather than rely on its long-standing defense relationships with NATO member states and Japan. The evidence suggests that this decision was not a function of hegemonic decline, but instead reflected the use of the norm of collective security by the president and Congress to further their competing interests in the domestic policy debate. Thus, an explanation for U.S. policy requires an analysis of interbranch politics.

Even if one accepts the need to examine interbranch politics to account for the U.S. policy, one might still question the significance of the norm of collective security in producing the eventual policy response. Thus, insofar as Congress is constitutionally empowered in the foreign policy sphere, it is not surprising that the Congress exercised influence over the deployment of American troops abroad. But this explanation is not compelling: the role of Congress in such decisions has historically been limited. For example, United States troops have been deployed by presidents close to 200 times, whereas Congress has declared war only five times, most recently during World War II.[36] Some argue (Auerswald and Cowhey, 1994; Lindsay, 1994) that Congress's role was enhanced with the passage of the War Powers Resolution (WPR) in 1973. Principally, the WPR requires the president to consult with the Congress "before introducing United States armed forces into hostilities or into situations where imminent involvement in hostilities is clearly

---

[34] On the multilateral character of the U.S. response, Charles Krauthammer (1990–91:25) asked, "Why the pretense?" Christopher Layne (1993) also recognizes the unilateral impulse generated by unipolarity.

[35] This hypothesis is deduced from Chapter 5 of Gilpin (1981).

[36] Congress's declarations of war have been limited to: June 18, 1812 for the War of 1812; May 13, 1846 for the Mexican War; April 25, 1898 for the Spanish-American War; April 6 and December 11, 1917 (for Germany and Austria-Hungary) for World War I; and December 8 (for Japan) and December 11 (for Germany and Italy) for World War II (*Congressional Record,* 1991a).

indicated" (United States, 1973:555). However, Congress has been less than successful in enforcing the WPR, voting to invoke the terms of the WPR only once, during the Lebanon crisis of 1983. Moreover, President Bush displayed no greater concern for the WPR than his predecessors, deploying American forces in 1989 without prior congressional consultation to oust the Noriega regime in Panama.[37] Therefore, the role Congress assumed in the Gulf crisis is relatively striking. The evidence suggests that Congress's influence was due to the domestic impact of the international norm of collective security. Specifically, the introduction of the norm into the policy process provided the Congress with a resource by which to increase its authority over the formulation of a U.S. response to the Iraqi invasion of Kuwait.

Conclusion

Whereas most previous analyses of norm compliance are cast at the level of state interaction, this article adopts a different approach. It argues that international rules and norms can affect national policy choices by operating through the domestic political process. In particular, we hypothesize that domestic actors—state or societal—can appropriate international norms and rules to further their interests in the domestic political arena. Through these appeals, an international rule or norm can enter the policy debate, under some conditions influencing the type of policy a country pursues. We identify two factors that determine whether a domestic actor's appropriation of an international norm will affect the state's policy choices: the domestic salience or legitimacy of the norm; and the domestic structural context within which the policy debate transpires. The two case studies support these postulations; they illustrate separately that U.S. compliance with the collective security norm, and enforcement of the free trade norm, were a function of the actions and interests of domestic actors.

Our focus on the domestic impact of international norms is suggestive in several ways. First, the study reinforces the utility of focusing on domestic structure as an intervening variable. In both cases, the evidence reveals that the structure of domestic political institutions plays an important role in determining whether and how an appeal to an international norm will influence policy choice.[38] In this regard, two elements of a country's domestic structure appear most significant: the relative centralization of decision-making authority and the extent to which international rules are institutionalized into domestic laws. In the security case, for example, the separation of powers divided war-making authority between the executive and legislative branches of the U.S. government. As a result, President Bush's introduction of the norm of collective security into the domestic political arena enabled congressional actors to appeal to the same norm in an effort to exercise oversight over the president's ability to make foreign policy independently. The trade case suggests that domestic interest groups' appeals to international rules will more likely affect national policy choices when these domestic groups can access domestic laws that are premised on international rules. This statement reflects not simply the fact that such laws institutionalize international rules, but more generally the fact that these laws provide private commercial interests with a legitimate means by which to introduce their preferences into the policy process.[39]

While we sought to demonstrate the domestic impact of international norms and rules, future research should examine cases in which the domestic structural context

[37] Passed over President Nixon's veto, the constitutionality of the War Powers Resolution has been denied by every president since. The history of the resolution is presented in Smyrl (1988).

[38] On the broader significance of this finding see Haggard (1991:431).

[39] Few scholars focusing on domestic institutions include trade statutes as an element of domestic structure. Two notable exceptions include Ikenberry (1988a) and Goldstein (1988).

impedes such impact. Such a research agenda would help to confirm the mediating role domestic structure plays. A similar task applies to the concept of salience. Two additional, interrelated areas for further research remain with respect to this concept. First, the processes whereby international norms become salient domestically need to be more clearly identified, and the conditions under which they obtain more systematically specified. Second, comparative research should seek to measure more precisely what level of domestic salience increases the likelihood that a norm will have an impact on policy choice.

A final implication concerns regime dynamics. The finding that international norms can shape state behavior by becoming entangled in the domestic political process suggests that regime strength and regime change are functions of such processes. This finding dovetails with one of the postulations of the emerging "constructivist" perspective in international relations theory. As Rey Koslowski and Friedrich Kratochwil (1994:227) posit, "An explanation of change . . . [requires] an understanding of rule-governed activity and the various processes by which institutions are continually reproduced and modified through the actors' practices." However, existing constructivist accounts of change tend to treat the state as a unitary actor (Dessler, 1989; Wendt, 1994, 1995). In contrast, the analysis offered here suggests the need to disaggregate the state since both government officials and societal groups can appropriate international rules, leading to their reproduction and in some cases, transformation.[40] Thus, the institutionalization of international rules into domestic politics can have both positive and negative ramifications for the functioning of the international institution itself. The cases provide examples of each dynamic.

The Gulf War provided the United Nations and the norm of collective security, for example, with enhanced legitimacy as a result of the use of the norm by President Bush and members of Congress for their own domestic political purposes. The resulting increase in the domestic salience of the United Nations and collective security may help to explain subsequent U.S. reliance on the United Nations framework for action in Iraq, Somalia, the former Yugoslavia, and Haiti. Whereas the position of the United Nations was temporarily enhanced through the appropriation of the collective security norm by government officials, the appropriation of the norm of free trade by U.S. private commercial interests led to an outcome inconsistent with the GATT.[41] Although the bilateral U.S.–Japan Semiconductor Trade Agreement did continue the trend toward greater liberalization in the international trading system, it was concluded based on a U.S. unilateral definition of "free and fair trade" and was negotiated outside existing GATT dispute settlement mechanisms. Simply put, this agreement transgressed the multilateral component of the GATT. Moreover, as several observers (Howell, Benz, and Wolff, 1986:243) note, "In the end, it was the prospect of unilateral U.S. sanctions that would reduce Japanese access to the U.S. market, and not the existence of a GATT claim, that induced the Japanese Government to enter into an agreement." Thus, the multilateral nature of the GATT may over time be superseded by bilateral agreements, or even unilateral actions, that are spurred by domestic actors who have appealed to international trade rules through such statutes as Section 301 to advance their parochial interests. In

[40] In his review of the neorealist-neoliberal debate, Robert Powell (1994:323–4) reaches the same conclusion.

[41] Opinion concerning Section 301 (and its counterpart "Super 301" which was in effect during 1989–1990) and its impact on international trade remains divided. Some observers contend (Sykes, 1991–92) that Section 301 is a legitimate market opening device since it is consistent with the GATT's fundamental goal of liberalizing trade. Nonetheless, others argue (Bhagwati, 1991) that the unilateral nature of Section 301 contradicts the GATT's multilateral norm. Hudec (1991) offers a third interpretation of the merits of Section 301. Acknowledging that the statute's use can have positive implications for GATT law and the institution's settlement of disputes, Hudec nonetheless concludes that the use of Section 301 is illegitimate since its standards of behavior do not apply to the United States.

this way, use of such domestic trade laws may in the future also erode the liberal nature of the international trade system.

References

"Aides See '85 Gap in Current Account of $135 Billion." (1985) *Wall Street Journal*, August 8, p. 46.

APPLE, R. W. (1990) "U.S. Reported Ready to Ask U.N. to Back a Gulf Assault." *New York Times*, November 16, p. A12.

AUERSWALD, D., AND P. COWHEY (1994) Ballot Box Diplomacy. Typescript. University of California, San Diego.

BAYARD, T., AND K. A. ELLIOTT (1994) *Reciprocity and Retaliation in U.S. Trade Policy*. Washington, DC: Institute for International Economics.

BETTS, R. (1992) Systems of Peace or Causes of War? Collective Security, Arms Control, and the New Europe. *International Security* **17**:5–43.

BHAGWATI, J. (1991) "Aggressive Unilateralism: An Overview." In *Aggressive Unilateralism: America's 301 Trade Policy and the World Trading System*, edited by J. Bhagwati and H. Patrick, pp. 1–45. New York: Harvester Wheatsheaf.

BRADLEY, B. (1990) "Bush Has All the Cards, So Why Bluff?" *New York Times*, November 15, p. A27.

BULL, H. (1979) *The Anarchical Society: A Study of Order in World Politics*. New York: Columbia University Press.

BUSH, G. (1990) Transcript of News Session by Bush and Two Officials on Mideast. *New York Times*, August 23, p. A16.

CALDEIRA, G., AND J. GIBSON (1995) The Legitimacy of the Court of Justice in the European Union: Models of Institutional Support. *American Political Science Review* **89**:356–376.

"Can Semiconductors Survive Big Business?" (1979) *Business Week*, December 3, p. 66.

CHECKEL, J. (1994) Institutions, Norms and Domestic Politics: Citizenship and National Identity in the New Europe. Typescript. University of Pittsburgh.

CHEEVER, D., AND H. F. HAVILAND, JR. (1952) *American Foreign Policy and the Separation of Powers*. Cambridge, MA: Harvard University Press.

"Chips: The War of Tomorrow's World." (1985) *The Economist*, August 24, p. 69.

CLAUDE, I. (1971) *Swords into Plowshares: The Problems and Progress of International Organization*, 4th ed. New York: Random House.

CONGRESS (1979) *Hearings Before the House Committee on Ways and Means: Competitive Factors Influencing World Trade in Semiconductors*. 96th Congress, 1st session. Washington, DC: Government Printing Office.

CONGRESS (1980) *Hearings Before the House Committee on Ways and Means: Trade with Japan*. 96th Congress, 2nd session. Washington, DC: Government Printing Office.

CONGRESS (1985a) *Hearings Before the Joint Economic Committee: Impact of Unfair Foreign Trade Practices*. 99th Congress, 1st session. Washington, DC: Government Printing Office.

CONGRESS (1985b) *Hearings Before the Joint Economic Committee: United States–Japan Trade: Semiconductors*. 99th Congress, 1st session. Washington, DC: Government Printing Office.

CONGRESS (1985c) *Hearings Before the Joint Economic Committee: United States–Japanese Trade in Semiconductors*. 99th Congress, 1st session. Washington, DC: Government Printing Office.

CONGRESS (1990) *Hearings Before the Senate Foreign Relations Committee: U.S. Policy in the Persian Gulf*. 101st Congress, 2nd session. Washington, DC: Government Printing Office.

Congressional Record (1991a) (10 January): S97–S182.

Congressional Record (1991b) (12 January): S323–S416.

COOPER, A., R. HIGGOTT, AND K. R. NOSSAL (1991) Bound to Follow? Leadership and Followership in the Gulf Conflict. *Political Science Quarterly* **106**:391–410.

CORTELL, A. (1994) Responding to the Challenge: International Competition and the Semiconductor Industry in the United States and Britain, 1970–1988. Ph.D. dissertation, Columbia University.

CORWIN, E. S. (1948) *The President: Office and Powers, 1787–1948*, 3rd ed. New York: New York University Press.

DESSLER, D. (1989) What's at Stake in the Agent Structure Debate? *International Organization* **43**:441–473.

DESTLER, I. M., L. GELB, AND A. LAKE (1984) *Our Own Worst Enemy: The Unmaking of American Foreign Policy*. New York: Simon and Schuster.

DOHERTY, C. (1990) Uncertain Congress Confronts President's Gulf Strategy. *Congressional Quarterly Weekly Report* **48**:3879–3882.

DONNELLY, J. (1986) International Human Rights: A Regime Analysis. *International Organization* **40**:599–642.

DUFFIELD, J. S. (1992) International Regimes and Alliance Behavior: Explaining NATO Counter Force Levels. *International Organization* **46**:819–855.

DUFFIELD, J. S. (1994) Explaining the Long Peace in Europe: The Contributions of Regional Security Regimes. *Review of International Studies* **20**:369–388.

EVANGELISTA, M. (1995) The Paradox of State Strength: Transnational Relations, Domestic Structures, and Security Policy in Russia and the Soviet Union. *International Organization* **49**:1–38.

FARNSWORTH, C. (1985) "Nation Called Unfair in Plea for Retaliation." *New York Times*, March 27, pp. D1, D15.

FARNSWORTH, C. (1987) "U.S. Retaliating with 100% Duties in Japan Dispute." *New York Times*, March 28, pp. 1, 35.

FELDMAN, L. (1990) "Capitol Hill Urges Patience in the Gulf. " *Christian Science Monitor*, November 30, p. 3.

FINLAYSON, J., AND M. ZACHER (1983) "The GATT and the Regulation of Trade Barriers: Regime Dynamics and Functions." In *International Regimes*, edited by S. Krasner, pp. 273–314. Ithaca, NY: Cornell University Press.

FINNEMORE, M. (1993) International Organizations as Teachers of Norms: The United Nations Educational, Scientific, and Cultural Organization and Science Policy. *International Organization* **47**:565–598.

"France to Join Embargo." (1990) *New York Times*, August 20, p. A7.

FRIEDEN, J. (1988) "Sectoral Conflict and U.S. Foreign Economic Policy, 1914–1940." In *The State and Foreign Economic Policy*, edited by G. J. Ikenberry, D. Lake, and M. Mastanduno, pp. 59–90. Ithaca, NY: Cornell University Press.

FRIEDMAN, T. (1990a) "Secretary Will Seek Use of Saudi Installations by American Forces." *New York Times*, August 6, p. A1.

FRIEDMAN, T. (1990b) "Bush and Baker Explicit in Threat to Use Force. " *New York Times*, October 30, p. A12.

FRIEDMAN, T. (1990c) "Lighting the Fuse?" *New York Times*, November 30, p. A11.

FRIEDMAN, T. (1990d) "How U.S. Won Support to Use Mideast Force." *New York Times*, December 2, p. A19.

GEORGE, A. (1979) "Case Studies and Theory Development: The Method of Structured, Focused Comparison." In *Diplomacy: New Approaches in History, Theory and Policy*, edited by P. Lauren, pp. 43–68. New York: Free Press.

GEORGE, A., AND T. MCKEOWN (1985) Case Studies and Theories of Organizational Decision Making. *Advances in Information Processing and Organizations* **2**:22–57.

GILPIN, R. (1981) *War and Change in World Politics*. Cambridge: Cambridge University Press.

GOERTZ, G., AND P. DIEHL (1992) Toward a Theory of International Norms: Some Conceptual and Measurement Issues. *Journal of Conflict Resolution* **36**:634–664.

GOLAN, G. (1992) Gorbachev's Difficult Time in the Gulf. *Political Science Quarterly* **107**:213–230.

GOLDSTEIN, J. (1988) "Ideas, Institutions, and American Trade Policy. " In *The State and American Foreign Economic Policy*, edited by G. J. Ikenberry, D. Lake, and M. Mastanduno, pp. 179–217. Ithaca, NY: Cornell University Press.

GOSHKO, J. (1990a) "Security Council Considers Military Action to Back Sanctions." *Washington Post*, August 21, pp. A1, A7.

GOSHKO, J. (1990b) "Baker Urged to Ask Hill Before Moving on Iraq. " *Washington Post*, October 18, p. A40.

GOUREVITCH, P. (1986) *Politics in Hard Times: Comparative Responses to International Economic Crises*. Ithaca, NY: Cornell University Press.

GRIECO, J. (1990) *Cooperation Among Nations: Europe, America and Non-Tariff Barriers to Trade*. Ithaca, NY: Cornell University Press.

GUTFLEISH, R. (1987) Why Protection? U.S. Corporate and State Responses to a Changing World Economy. Ph.D. dissertation, University of California, Berkeley.

HAAS, P. (1989) Do Regimes Matter? Epistemic Communities and Mediterranean Pollution Control. *International Organization* **43**:377–403.

HAGGARD, S. (1991) "Structuralism and Its Critics: Recent Progress in International Relations Theory." In *Progress in Postwar International Relations*, edited by E. Adler and B. Crawford, pp. 403–437. New York: Columbia University Press.

HAGGARD, S., AND B. SIMMONS (1987) Theories of International Regimes. *International Organization* **41**:491–517.

HALL, P. (1986) *Governing the Economy: The Politics of State Intervention in Britain and France*. New York: Oxford University Press.

HANSEN, P. (1987) Defining Unreasonableness in International Trade: Section 301 of the Trade Act of 1974. *Yale Law Journal* **96**:1122–1146.

HOWELL, T., S. BENZ, AND A. WOLFF (1986) International Competition in the Information Technologies: Foreign Government Intervention and the U.S. Response. *Stanford Journal of International Law* **22**:215–262.

HUDEC, R. (1991) "Thinking About the New Section 301: Beyond Good and Evil." In *Aggressive Unilateralism: America's 301 Trade Policy and the World Trading System*, edited by J. Bhagwati and H. Patrick, pp. 113–159. New York: Harvester Wheatsheaf.

HURRELL, A. (1993) "International Society and the Study of Regimes: A Reflective Approach." In *Regime Theory and International Relations*, edited by V. Rittberger, pp. 49–72. Oxford: Clarendon Press.

IKENBERRY, G. J. (1988a) "Conclusion: An Institutional Approach to American Foreign Economic Policy." In *The State and American Foreign Economic Policy*, edited by G. J. Ikenberry, D. Lake, and M. Mastanduno, pp. 210–243. Ithaca, NY: Cornell University Press.

IKENBERRY, G. J. (1988b) *Reasons of State: Oil Politics and the Capacities of American Government*. Ithaca, NY: Cornell University Press.

IKENBERRY, G. J., AND C. KUPCHAN (1990) Socialization and Hegemonic Power. *International Organization* **44**:283–315.

IKENBERRY, G. J., D. LAKE, AND M. MASTANDUNO, EDS. (1988) *The State and American Foreign Economic Policy*. Ithaca, NY: Cornell University Press.

"Intel, AMD and National File Dumping Charges Against Japan." (1985) *Electronic News*, October 7, p. 4.

JACKSON, J. H., AND W. J. DAVEY (1986) *Legal Problems in International Economic Relations: Cases, Materials and Text*, 2nd ed. St. Paul, MN: West.

JAVITS, J., AND D. KELLERMAN (1973) *Who Makes War? The President Versus Congress*. New York: William Morrow.

JERVIS, R. (1983) "Security Regimes." In *International Regimes*, edited by S. Krasner, pp. 173–194. Ithaca, NY: Cornell University Press.

KATZENSTEIN, P. (1985) *Small States in World Markets: Industrial Policy in Europe*. Ithaca, NY: Cornell University Press.

KEOHANE, R. (1984) *After Hegemony: Cooperation and Discord in the World Political Economy*. Princeton, NJ: Princeton University Press.

KEOHANE, R. (1993) "Institutional Theory and the Realist Challenge After the Cold War." In *Neorealism and Neoliberalism: The Contemporary Debate*, edited by D. Baldwin, pp. 269–300. New York: Columbia University Press.

KEOHANE, R. (1994) Contested Commitments in United States Foreign Policy, 1783–1989. Typescript. Harvard University.

KILBORN, P. (1985) "Trade Fight with Japan." *New York Times*, March 29, pp. A1, D15.

KINGERY, J. (1989) The U.S.–Japan Semiconductor Arrangement and the GATT: Operation in a Legal Vacuum. *Stanford Journal of International Law* **26**:467–497.

KOH, H. H. (1990) *The National Security Constitution: Sharing Power After the Iran-Contra Affair*. New Haven, CT: Yale University Press.

KOSLOWSKI, R., AND F. KRATOCHWIL (1994) Understanding Change in International Politics: The Soviet Empire's Demise and the International System. *International Organization* **48**:215–247.

KRASNER, S. (1978) *Defending the National Interest*. Princeton, NJ: Princeton University Press.

KRASNER, S. (1983) "Structural Causes and Regime Consequences: Regimes as Intervening Variables." In *International Regimes*, edited by S. Krasner, pp. 210–243. Ithaca, NY: Cornell University Press.

KRASNER, S. (1991) Global Communications and National Power: Life on the Pareto Frontier. *World Politics* **43**:336–366.

KRATOCHWIL, F. (1985) "The Role of Domestic Courts as Agencies of the International Legal Order." In *International Law: A Contemporary Perspective*, edited by R. Falk, F. Kratochwil, and S. Mendlovitz, pp. 236–263. Boulder, CO: Westview Press.

KRATOCHWIL, F. (1989) *Rules, Norms and Decisions: On the Conditions of Legal and Practical Reasoning in International Relations and Domestic Affairs*. Cambridge: Cambridge University Press.

KRATOCHWIL, F., AND J. G. RUGGIE (1986) International Organization: A State of the Art on an Art of the State. *International Organization* **40**:763–769.

KRAUTHAMMER, C. (1990–91) The Unipolar Moment. *Foreign Affairs* **70**:23–33.
KUPCHAN, C., AND C. KUPCHAN (1991) Concerts, Collective Security and the Future of Europe. *International Security* **16**:114–161.
LAKE, D. (1988a) *Power, Protection and Free Trade: International Sources of U.S. Commercial Strategy, 1887–1939*. Ithaca, NY: Cornell University Press.
LAKE, D. (1988b) "The State and American Trade Strategy in the Pre-Hegemonic Era." In *The State and American Foreign Economic Policy*, edited by G. J. Ikenberry, D. Lake, and M. Mastanduno, pp. 33–58. Ithaca, NY: Cornell University Press.
LANDE, S., AND C. VANGRASSTEK (1986) *The Trade and Tariff Act of 1984: Trade Policy in the Reagan Administration*. Lexington, MA: Lexington Books.
LAYNE, C. (1993) The Unipolar Illusion: Why New Great Powers Will Rise. *International Security* **17**:5–51.
LEWIS, P. (1990) "U.N. Expected to Approve Iraq and Kuwait Trade Ban." *New York Times*, August 6, p. A6.
LINDSAY, J. (1994) Congress, Foreign Policy, and the New Institutionalism. *International Studies Quarterly* **38**:281–304.
LIPSON, C. (1983) "The Transformation of International Trade: The Source and Effects of Regime Change." In *International Regimes*, edited by S. Krasner, pp. 233–271. Ithaca, NY: Cornell University Press.
MALCOLM, A. (1990) "Few from Left or Right Protest Bush's Big Stick. " *New York Times*, August 21, p. A16.
MARTIN, L. (1992) Interests, Power and Multilateralism. *International Organization* **46**:765–792.
MASTANDUNO, M. (1991) Do Relative Gains Matter? America's Response to Japanese Industrial Policy. *International Security* **16**:73–113.
MAY, E., ED. (1960) *The Ultimate Decision: The President as Commander in Chief.* New York: George Braziller.
MCELROY, R. (1992) *Morality and American Foreign Policy*. Princeton, NJ: Princeton University Press.
MILLER, M. (1985) "Big U.S. Semiconductor Makers Expected to Sue over Dumping of Japanese Chips." *Wall Street Journal*, September 30, p. 42.
MILNER, H. (1987) Resisting the Protectionist Temptation: Industry and the Making of Trade Policy in France and the United States. *International Organization* **41**:639–665.
MILNER, H. (1988) *Resisting Protectionism: Global Industries and the Politics of International Trade*. Princeton, NJ: Princeton University Press.
MILNER, H. (1992) International Theories of Cooperation Among Nations: Strengths and Weaknesses. *World Politics* **44**:466–496.
MORGENTHAU, H. (1978) *Politics Among Nations: The Struggle for Power and Peace*, 5th ed. New York: Alfred A. Knopf.
MÜLLER, H. (1993) "The Internalization of Principles, Norms and Rules by Governments: The Case of Security Regimes." In *Regime Theory and International Relations*, edited by V. Rittberger, pp. 361–388. Oxford: Clarendon Press.
NADELMANN, E. (1990) Global Prohibition Regimes: The Evolution of Norms in International Society. *International Organization* **44**:479–536.
NYE, J. (1987) Nuclear Leaning and U.S.–Soviet Security Regimes. *International Organization* **41**:371–402.
OFFICE OF THE PRESIDENT (1990) *Weekly Compilation of Presidential Documents*, August 6. Office of the Federal Register. Washington, DC: Government Printing Office.
OFFICE OF THE PRESIDENT (1991) *Weekly Compilation of Presidential Documents*, January 14. Office of the Federal Register. Washington, DC: Government Printing Office.
OKIMOTO, D. (1989) *Between MITI and the Market: Japanese Industrial Policy for High Technology*. Stanford, CA: Stanford University Press.
ONUF, N. (1989) *World of Our Making: Rules and Rule in Social Theory and International Relations*. Columbia: University of South Carolina Press.
O'SHEA, T. (1988) *The U.S.–Japan Semiconductor Problem.* Pew Foundation Cases in International Affairs, no. 139. Graduate School of Public and International Affairs, University of Pittsburgh.
PASTOR, R. (1980) *Congress and the Politics of U.S. Foreign Economic Policy*. Berkeley: University of California Press.
PINE, A. (1985) "U.S. Files Antidumping Proceedings Against Japanese Semiconductor Firms. " *Wall Street Journal*, December 9, p. 10.
PIOUS, R. (1979) *The American Presidency*. New York: Basic Books.
POWELL, R. (1994) Anarchy and International Relations Theory: The Neorealist–Neoliberal Debate. *International Organization* **48**:313–344.

Prestowitz, C. (1989) *Trading Places: How We Are Giving Our Future to Japan and How to Reclaim It*. New York: Basic Books.

Reagan, R. (1985) Speech to Business and Government Leaders. *New York Times*, September 24, p. D26.

Ripley, R., and J. Lindsay, eds. (1993) *Congress Resurgent: Foreign and Defense Policy on Capitol Hill*. Ann Arbor: University of Michigan Press.

Risse-Kappen, T. (1991) Public Opinion, Domestic Structure, and Foreign Policy in Liberal Democracies. *World Politics* **43**:479–512.

Risse-Kappen, T. (1994) Ideas Do Not Float Freely: Transnational Coalitions, Domestic Structures, and the End of the Cold War. *International Organization* **48**:185–214.

Risse-Kappen, T. (1995) Principled Ideas, International Institutions and Domestic Political Change: The Case of Human Rights. Typescript. Universität Konstanz.

Roberts, S. (1985) "Lawmakers Doubt Bills Will Be Halted." *New York Times*, September 24, p. D26.

Rosenthal, A. (1990a) "U.S. Consults U.N. on Use of Force as Navy Shadows 2 Iraqi Tankers." *New York Times*, August 20, p. A7.

Rosenthal, A. (1990b) "Confrontation in the Gulf: U.S. to Call 40,000 Reserves to Support Saudi Trooplift." *New York Times*, August 22, pp. A1, A8.

Ruggie, J. G. (1992) Multilateralism: The Anatomy of an Institution. *International Organization* **46**:568–571.

Sanford, T. (1990) Should U.S. Attack Iraq? *New York Times*, August 24, p. A29.

Schrage, M. (1985) "Semiconductor Industry Toughens Stance Against Japan." *Washington Post*, September 22, p. F2.

Sciolino, E., and E. Pace (1990) "Putting Teeth in an Embargo: How U.S. Convinced the U.N." *New York Times*, August 30, pp. A1, A15.

Semiconductor Industry Association (1981) *The International Microelectronics Challenge*. Cupertino, CA: Semiconductor Industry Association.

Semiconductor Industry Association (1983) *The Effect of Government Targeting on World Semiconductor Competition: A Case History of Japanese Industrial Strategy and Its Costs for America*. Cupertino, CA: Semiconductor Industry Association.

Semiconductor Industry Association (1985) *The Impact of Japanese Market Barriers in Microelectronics*. San Jose, CA: Semiconductor Industry Association.

Sikkink, K. (1993) Human Rights, Principled Issue-Networks, and Sovereignty in Latin America. *International Organization* **47**:411–441.

Smith, J. E. (1992) *George Bush's War*. New York: Holt.

Smyrl, M. (1988) *Conflict or Codetermination? Congress, the President, and the Power to Make War*. Cambridge, MA: Ballinger.

Snyder, J. (1991) *Myths of Empire: Domestic Politics and International Ambition*. Ithaca, NY: Cornell University Press.

Solingen, E. (1993) Macropolitical Consensus and Lateral Autonomy in Industrial Policy: The Nuclear Sector in Brazil and Argentina. *International Organization* **47**:280–281.

Solingen, E. (1994) The Domestic Sources of Regional Regimes: The Evolution of Nuclear Ambiguity in the Middle East. *International Studies Quarterly* **38**:305–337.

Spero, J. (1990) *The Politics of International Economic Relations*, 4th ed. New York: St. Martin's Press.

Stanfield, R. (1990) "Looking Beyond the Guns of August." *National Journal*, August 11, pp. 1959–1960.

Stein, A. (1983) "Coordination and Collaboration: Regimes in an Anarchic World." In *International Regimes*, edited by S. Krasner, pp. 115–140. Ithaca, NY: Cornell University Press.

Strang, D., and P. M. Y. Chang (1993) The International Labor Organization and the Welfare State: Institutional Effects on National Welfare Spending, 1960–1980. *International Organization* **47**:235–262.

Sykes, A. (1991–92) Constructive Unilateral Threats in International Commercial Relations: The Limited Case for Section 301. *Law and Policy in International Business* **23**:263–330.

Thomas, D. (1995) Between Reason and Power: The Helsinki Accords and the Decline of Communism in Eastern Europe and the Soviet Union, 1975–1989. Ph.D. dissertation, Cornell University.

Tyson, L. (1992) *Who's Bashing Whom? Trade Conflict in High Technology Industries*. Washington, DC: Institute for International Economics.

United States (1973) "War Powers Resolution." In *United States Statutes at Large*, PL 93-148. Washington, DC: Government Printing Office.

U.S. Department of State (1990) *Dispatch*, November.

Waltz, K. (1979) *Theory of International Politics*. Reading, MA: Addison-Wesley.

WENDT, A. (1987) The Agent Structure Problem in International Relations Theory. *International Organization* **41**:335–370.

WENDT, A. (1994) Collective Identity Formation and the International State. *American Political Science Review* **88**:384–396.

WENDT, A. (1995) Constructing International Politics. *International Security* **20**:71–81.

WILDAVSKY, A. (1966) The Two Presidencies. *Trans-Action* **4**:7–14.

WOLFERS, A. (1962) *Discord and Collaboration: Essays on International Politics*. Baltimore, MD: Johns Hopkins University Press.

WOLFF, A., R. M. GADBAW, T. HOWELL, AND T. RICHARDS (1985) *Japanese Market Barriers in Microelectronics: Memorandum in Support of a Petition Pursuant to Section 301 of the Trade Act of 1974, as Amended*. Washington, DC: Dewey, Ballatine, Bushby, Palmer and Wood.

WOODWARD, B. (1991) *The Commanders*. New York: Simon and Schuster.

YOUNG, O. (1989) *International Cooperation: Building Regimes for Natural Resources and the Environment*. Ithaca, NY: Cornell University Press.

[19]

THE POWER OF LEGITIMACY AND THE LEGITIMACY OF POWER: INTERNATIONAL LAW IN AN AGE OF POWER DISEQUILIBRIUM

*By Thomas M. Franck**

I. "REALISM" AND LEGITIMACY

The American Society of International Law (ASIL), incorporated by Act of Congress in 1950, was founded in 1906 "to promote the establishment and maintenance of international relations on the basis of law and justice." As we celebrate the centennial of this, the Society's principal publication, it is appropriate to examine the present and future prospects of this project. Is it still a compelling aspiration in the era of U.S. superpower-dom?

The founding of the Society and initiation of the *Journal* (*AJIL*) must be seen in the context of the then-prevalent American commitment to the idea that a world of international law and international tribunals would be a natural, even historically inevitable, extrapolation of a good American idea.[1] Speaking in 1890 to the first Pan-American Conference, President Benjamin Harrison congratulated the delegates on formulating a hemispheric arbitration agreement. "We rejoice," he said, "that you have found in the organization of our Government something suggestive and worthy of imitation."[2] At The Hague in 1907, Secretary of State Elihu Root, the founding president of the ASIL, called for the creation of an international court "which would pass upon questions between nations with the same impartial and impersonal judgment that the Supreme Court of the United States gives to questions arising between citizens of the different States."[3]

Even then, such a positive view of the potential of international law and legal institutions probably never truly reflected the view of two-thirds of the Senate nor, in all likelihood, a majority of the American public. At the end of World War II, the brief flourishing of the American-led World Peace Through World Law movement, inspired by Grenville Clark and Louis B. Sohn's book of that name,[4] again attracted the attention of law professors and internationally minded legal practitioners, but their enthusiasm was just briefly, if at all, shared by the general public and its representatives in Congress.[5]

* Of the Board of Editors.

[1] THOMAS M. FRANCK, JUDGING THE WORLD COURT 14 (1986). This founding followed by more than three decades the convening of the Institut de Droit International in 1873 at Ghent, which set as its purpose in Article 1 of its Statute, "to encourage the progress of international law in striving to become the organ of the juridical conscience of the civilized world." MARTTI KOSKENNIEMI, THE GENTLE CIVILIZER OF NATIONS: THE RISE AND FALL OF INTERNATIONAL LAW, 1870–1960, at 41 (2001) (trans. by author).

[2] *Closing the Conference*, N.Y. TIMES, Apr. 20, 1890, at 5.

[3] *Instructions to the American Delegates*, *in* 2 JAMES BROWN SCOTT, THE HAGUE PEACE CONFERENCES OF 1899 AND 1907: DOCUMENTS 191 (1909).

[4] GRENVILLE CLARK & LOUIS B. SOHN, WORLD PEACE THROUGH WORLD LAW (1958).

[5] It was not shared, either, by an influential lawyer who had migrated to the field of international relations, Prof. Hans Morgenthau. *See* HANS MORGENTHAU, IN DEFENSE OF THE NATIONAL INTEREST: A CRITICAL EXAMINATION OF AMERICAN FOREIGN POLICY (1951).

Nevertheless, for more than a century, it has been the common belief among American international lawyers and professors, as well as occupants of the White House if not the Congress, that the promotion of international law is a worthy cause, one that, over time, will triumph over narrow nationalism and, in so doing, will promote the peaceful settlement of disputes and a common, cooperative approach to the resolution of global issues.

It is thus interesting to note, on the occasion of the *AJIL*'s centenary, that this is no longer the unchallenged view among American international law professors and practitioners, let alone occupants of the White House. Emerging is a rather different approach that classifies international law as a disposable tool of diplomacy, its system of rules merely one of many considerations to be taken into account by government when deciding, transaction by transaction, what strategy is most likely to advance the national interest. Moreover, in the radically revisionist "rational choice" view of conflict adopted by some professors and practitioners, law has no greater claim than any other policy or value preference.

While this view is probably not yet held by the majority of American international lawyers, it now enjoys a wider following among American scholars than at any time in the past century, even allowing for some manifestation of isolationist sentiment in the 1930s. As for the leaders of the executive branch, it appears to be the common intuition that international law is to be seen as an anomaly, a myth propagated by weak states to prevent the strong from maximizing their power advantage.

As we celebrate our publication's centenary, this evolution in our ranks is worth considering, not so much for what it tells us about our past but for what it augurs for the future. Are we, mostly, going to come to believe that international law really is just a chimera spun by those states with little power, aided by a few Pollyannaish professors? The logic behind such a prognosis is not derisory. When a nation is the world's only superpower, why should it permit itself to be bound by norms and rules that may not always produce results that accrue to its advantage? Why should any state, in deference to law, ever forgo a realizable advantage and accept an outcome that does not maximize its national interest?

It should not and does not is the answer proffered by American advocates of "rational choice" in their theoretical writings and political practice. Increasingly, leaders of the nation and some leading theoreticians seem to have concluded that international law—even when evidenced by treaties, let alone mere custom—amounts to no more than, at most, evidence of states' temporary coincidence of self-interest. It would thus be illusory to expect law's strictures to be obeyed by powerful sovereign states when it does not serve their interest.[6]

Nevertheless, even the most dedicated contemporary American exponents of this version of "realism" are reluctant to adopt the position, so brashly flaunted by leaders and academics in Hitler's Germany, that it is the unequal distribution of power, itself, that makes classical international law, with its fastidious concern for state sovereignty and sovereign equality, so unrealistic and, hence, such a toothless factor in the choice of national-interest-maximizing strategies. Rather, they tend to the position that it is the weakness of the antiquated rules of international law—for example, in failing to distinguish between the rights of decent states and indecent ones—that makes American adherence to it irrational. Claiming that the United Nations Charter–based system has failed, they argue, in the name of realism, for sweeping it

[6] A leading, deeply historico-cultural exposition to the contrary is *Bloody Constraint: War and Chivalry in Shakespeare*, by Theodor Meron (1998), which makes a telling case based on the history of chivalrous warfare, to the effect that rules arise naturally out of societies—not necessarily ones in which the members are friendly with one another—on the basis of experience in calculating long-term mutual advantage.

aside[7] in favor of a new American (or, if possible, American-led) international order, one that America's more skeptical European friends have dubbed "legalised hegemony."[8]

To illustrate their point, American "realist" scholars point to the frequent instances in which all states—not just the United States—as a matter of rational choice still pursue their preferences by recourse to force. After examining state practice, Professor Michael Glennon finds it impossible "to avoid the conclusion that use of force among states simply is no longer subject—if it ever was subject—to the rule of law."[9] In a far more sweeping observation, Professors Jack Goldsmith and Eric Posner state that "international law does not pull states toward compliance contrary to their interests, and the possibilities for what international law can achieve are limited by the configurations of state interests and the distribution of state power."[10] These statements claim to be empirically verifiable. They assert as fact a universal tendency to disregard, or to de-emphasize, international norms when they interdict the pursuit of national self-interest.

It is not insignificant that the titles of both Glennon's recent book and the even more recent one by Goldsmith and Posner feature the "limits" of international law. Yet this effort by American international law scholars to unmask the law's fecklessness is recent and, significantly, finds virtually no echo among legal scholars outside the United States.[11]

Not surprisingly, however, the claim resonates strongly in the halls of American governance. There, deploying similar reasoning, U.S. political leaders derive impetus and justification for their recurrent recourse to force in the national interest, whether legal or not. In America we thus increasingly appear to be in the grip of a mutually reinforcing "realist" symbiosis between intellectuals and government, one in which thinkers and doers—not infrequently the same persons, moving smoothly from one bailiwick to the other—have sought to demonstrate, in thought and deed, that both law-adherent and scofflaw state behavior are more or less equivalent options in the exercise of sovereignty. In this view, law is not privileged and has no independent value. States, it is argued, do not obey the law "because they ought to" but only when it serves national policy interest. Since this is what states, in fact, do, it would be naive to pretend—or, worse, to act—otherwise. Law's power to pull states toward compliance, in this analysis, derives solely from its occasional coincidence with "real" motives, such as states' perception of the advantage to be gained from compliance, or the perceived costs of noncompliance. Accordingly, states never obey law solely because of some non-case-specific belief in the rule of law per se.

Importantly, while this sounds like a purely descriptive-empirical observation, it also has enormous prescriptive potential. If this power-realism is the prism through which law's purchase is to be understood in the future, that perception—right or wrong as a description of the present—can indeed become a self-fulfilling prophecy. In any society, but especially among states, the compliance pull of law is based on the expectation of each participant that most others, most of the time, will obey the law—all of it, not just some subsets, and not only when it

[7] Michael J. Glennon, *The New Interventionism: The Search for a Just International Law*, FOREIGN AFF., May/June 1999, at 2.

[8] GERRY SIMPSON, GREAT POWERS AND OUTLAW STATES: UNEQUAL SOVEREIGNS IN THE INTERNATIONAL LEGAL ORDER 220 (2004).

[9] MICHAEL J. GLENNON, LIMITS OF LAW, PREROGATIVES OF POWER: INTERVENTIONISM AFTER KOSOVO 84 (2001).

[10] JACK L. GOLDSMITH & ERIC A. POSNER, THE LIMITS OF INTERNATIONAL LAW 13 (2005). For a review of this book in this issue, see Edward T. Swaine, Review Essay, 100 AJIL 259 (2006).

[11] This dissonance is surveyed in Rüdiger Wolfrum, *American-European Dialogue: Different Perceptions of International Law—Introduction*, 64 ZAÖRV 255 (2004), and Hanspeter Neuhold, *Law and Force in International Relations—European and American Positions*, *id.* at 263.

is in their immediate interest to do so. That law has an inherent capacity to generate compliance is a *Grundnorm* as fundamental to the state system as it is ephemeral. It cannot be proved by reference to some antecedent norm. It is an article of faith, yet one that underpins the verifiable reality of a world in which sovereign states interact in a structured system of rules and an expectation of compliance.

That such rule-based systemic interaction exists at all among states is now being seriously debated, much to the surprise of those who had prematurely celebrated international law's arrival at a post-ontological moment.[12] Although the argument has focused on the law that purports to limit states' right to have recourse to force in their relations with peers, the discourse is increasingly implicating not only that one—for the United States—inconvenient norm, but the legitimacy of international law in general.

Both sides of the argument seem to grasp the larger stakes. Those who defend the bindingness of international law understand that law compliance is not just the consequence of strategic calculation by parties to a particular agreement—say, the one establishing the Universal Postal Union—that compliance is to their advantage. Rather, and more important, general compliance reflects most states' belief that freely incurred obligations should be met.

This belief in rule adherence is essential to the existence of an ongoing normative system of relations between sovereign states. It emanates from the value states place in law's ability to make interactions predictable. That faith in law's ability to predict state behavior is the key to its ability to pull nations toward voluntary compliance. And this is true of all law, not just the law of nations. The real power of law to secure systematic compliance does not rest, primarily, on police enforcement—not even in police states, surely not in ordinary societies, and especially not in the society of nations— but, rather, on the general belief of those to whom the law is addressed that they have a stake in the rule of law itself: that law is binding because it is the law. That, of course, is a fragile psychological belief, one, moreover, that is unverifiable. While, in every community, it constitutes an essential social construct, it is easily deconstructed. If one were able to ask the bumblebee, with its aerodynamically unviable body-to-wing ratio, how it manages to fly, it might well fall to the ground.

A grave responsibility is thus incurred by those who undermine the general belief in the independent capacity of law to affect compliant behavior, even if they direct their attack to one particularly vulnerable subset of laws. For, in essence, the debate is not merely about Article 2(4) of the UN Charter. It is not just about whether a universal treaty adhered to by 191 countries is a disposable instrument. It is about the weighing of power against legitimacy. It is a struggle for the soul of the community of nations.

That struggle will be waged with the weaponry of facts, but, more important, with that of perceptions. When a community loses faith in law's power to restrain and channel conduct, this perception propels the descent into anarchy. Of course, such a loss of faith may indeed be based, at least in part, on the perceived prevalence of unlawful behavior, on the failure of law to secure consistent compliance. But instances of noncompliance do not, in themselves, prove the inefficacy of the rules. Law is never perfectly obeyed. In cities pedestrians jaywalk, and in nations taxpayers cheat. Murders go unpunished.[13] And when intellectual and political leaders speak and act as if unlawful behavior had nullified the law, or demonstrated its "limits," they

[12] I am particularly guilty of this hubris. *See* THOMAS M. FRANCK, FAIRNESS IN INTERNATIONAL LAW AND INSTITUTIONS 4–8 (1995).

[13] Ian Brownlie has observed that, statistically, the domestic legal order of states much more frequently dissolves into revolution and civil war than the international legal order succumbs to the illegal recourse to force. IAN BROWNLIE, THE RULE OF LAW IN INTERNATIONAL AFFAIRS 14 (1998).

help create the ensuing anarchy. Nevertheless, it is the perception that law has lost its purchase, not the unlawful behavior itself, that propels the descent into social chaos.

The central role of perceptions is particularly evident in the international legal system. In the absence of a reliable international police to enforce the law, much depends upon a commonly shared belief—a prediction—that state conduct will definitely be constrained by the commitments states have accepted, either by specific consent or by virtue of their membership in a rule regime such as the United Nations. In the interstate community, the belief that *pacta sunt servanda*—that treaties, all treaties, are binding, and not just when they are convenient or advantageous—is what keeps the bumblebee of international law aloft. Belief in the law facilitates the freedom of sovereign states to act in their best interests by entering into binding arrangements. Most would agree that the freedom of states to bargain away short-term benefits in the expectation of longer-term rewards—a very useful device for realizing mutual advantage—is kept aloft by the perception that law is not merely a coincidence of self-interest: that a state on the losing end of a World Trade Organization arbitration today will comply because it can expect to win a subsequent dispute, and then justifiably expect the losing party to comply in deference to the ongoing practice of compliance. In this pattern of continuing interactions, compliance is almost always the rational choice, in every state's self-interest, because every state has a stake in actualizing the belief that the law, habitually, obligates compliance.[14]

To the "realists," this notion—that law functions to validate an expectation of compliance—is mere wishful thinking and does not comport with actual state behavior. In practice, don't states flout international law whenever it suits their interest? Well, actually, no. The real "reality" of state conduct is not that states habitually disobey the rules when they do not serve their immediate interests, but, to the contrary, that there is a demonstrable historical pattern of prevalent state compliance. This pattern, it happens, is most sorely tested in that area of international law which limits the right of states to have recourse to military force. But, even there, noncompliance is very much the exception. Unfortunately, the facts of state behavior are less important than the perceptions. It is the *perception* of habitual noncompliance that determines the toll unlawful behavior actually takes on law's capacity to maintain social order.

To illustrate: when, in a town, one murder goes unsolved and unpunished, its inhabitants would be very unlikely to conclude that they no longer lived under the rule of law. However, if a dozen murders, committed in a short time-span, similarly go unsolved, perceptions become crucial. Some citizens will demand the hiring of more police, while others may try to take advantage of the law's weakness; say, by indulging their latent talent as graffiti artists—or even as murderers. Which of these tendencies prevails—the law-reasserting or the law-deconstructing one—will be determined to a large extent by the general perception of the ability of the law to withstand its violations. The reality of the law's resilience will depend on the prevailing perception of that resilience. The "spin" put on law's capacities and prospects thus, in large part, determines its ability to survive and assert itself even against egregious or endemic violation.

This essay is intended partly to rebut the negative "spin" put on international law by a small, but growing number of American colleagues, not only in government but also in the academy.

[14] This view of the law does not argue that international lawyers should deny the effects of nonlegal factors on national behavior. On the contrary, "international lawyers would . . . benefit from a broader perspective," and a greater familiarity with the dynamics of political power "would in no way undermine the inherent stability and determinacy of international law." MICHAEL BYERS, CUSTOM, POWER AND THE POWER OF RULES 15 (1999). This is more likely to prove true if the lawyer, in familiarizing herself with power dynamics, keeps uppermost the professional commitment to the law. For an excellent summary of the argument that all states have an interest in the efficacious operation of law within the community of states, written from the perspective of moral philosophy, see ALLEN BUCHANAN, JUSTICE, LEGITIMACY, AND SELF-DETERMINATION: MORAL FOUNDATIONS FOR INTERNATIONAL LAW 289–327 (2004).

Such a response matters, because how that spin is perceived—among academics, the students they teach, and the lawyers in government they sometimes become—will largely shape future reality.

The shaping of "spin" is not to be looked down upon: it is serious business. It is about the shaping of the all-important perception of reality that determines how societies react to the challenges they face. International society, currently, is facing the familiar challenge of the scofflaw. When laws are not obeyed and violations go unpunished, it is perfectly natural for people to ask whether the imperfectly obeyed and imperfectly enforced norms have ceased to be binding on the community. One way to ask this question is: Has the imperfectly enforced rule of law lost its legitimacy? Has the law lost its compliance pull? Has law's legitimacy yielded to the naked facts of power? To address such important questions, it is necessary to examine the anatomy of compliance pull in more depth.

Sixteen years ago, in a book about legitimacy, I posed the question: Why do nations obey rules?[15] My answer was that, at least in part, they obey because they perceive the rule and its institutional penumbra to have a high degree of legitimacy. Forced, then, to answer the next question—What is legitimacy?—I argued that legitimacy is the capacity of a rule to pull those to whom it is addressed toward consensual compliance. That argument does not claim that a rule's legitimacy is the sole or, in some instances, even the primary reason a state chooses to obey the law. It does not maintain that lack of legitimacy is necessarily the sole or primary reason for any state's decision not to comply. It does claim, however, that states, in determining whether or not to obey the law, usually take into account their interest in the law as such, quite aside from whether, in any particular instance, the rules serve the national interest by validating a desired outcome. Rational choice, in other words, must take into account the important interest of a state— even a superpower—in strengthening the rule of law in interstate relations by making itself hostage to the rule, through compliance with it, even to the detriment of short-term national interests.[16]

In writing about the power of legitimacy, my primary objective was to demonstrate that rule legitimacy matters, so I focused on the elements that reinforce it: ***determinacy, symbolic validation, coherence, and adherence.*** Of these, determinacy seems the most important, being that quality of a norm that generates an ascertainable understanding of what it permits and what it prohibits. When that line becomes unascertainable, states are unlikely to defer opportunities for self-gratification. The rule's compliance pull evaporates.

Recent actions of states in Kosovo and Iraq have led to questions about the continuing compliance pull of the fundamental rule of the post–World War II legal order, the rule contained in Article 2(4) of the UN Charter that prohibits states' unilateral recourse to force except (per Article 51) in response to an armed attack. Like the "realists," I am aware that noncompliance with that law is undermining respect for it, and for international law in general. My concern is that noncompliant behavior, if tolerated, may render the content of that rule so indeterminate as to make it easy and tempting to be a scofflaw. Must we conclude that what NATO did with respect to Kosovo and what the U.S.-led states did in invading Iraq have generated a widespread perception that violations of the international law restraining states from recourse to

[15] THOMAS M. FRANCK, THE POWER OF LEGITIMACY AMONG NATIONS (1990).

[16] If a state complies with a rule that, in the short run, operates to its disadvantage, it helps to deter other states that may be tempted to violate the same, or another, legitimate law in subsequent encounters by making itself "hostage" to the rule in question. Conversely, states that violate a law to preserve a short-term interest make it easier for other states thereafter to ignore the same, or other, legal obligations. *See* THOMAS M. FRANCK & EDWARD WEISBAND, WORD POLITICS: VERBAL STRATEGY AMONG THE SUPERPOWERS 120–48 (1971).

force have dissolved the rule's element of determinacy, so that it no longer actually "binds" states?

That, it seems, is what some American commentators have concluded. Theirs is a challenge to which response must be made, for a rule that is riddled with exceptions no longer makes a clear statement and cannot be taken as a serious predictor of state conduct. As such, it invites further violations of that and other rules. Or it generates momentum for a different norm, one that accommodates the violations and makes them the basis of a new rule. For example, some are already arguing that states that harbor terrorists or violate the rights of their own people are no longer entitled to the sovereign prerogatives that underpin Article 2(4) of the UN Charter.[17]

The perception of a rule's degree of bindingness, at any particular juncture of its history, will determine its vulnerability to this sort of displacement. That all-important degree, however, is not easily measured; certainly not simply by counting the number of violations. Violations of treaties, and of universal treaties in particular, are no substitutes for legitimate amendments. Still, laws can fall into desuetude.

What follows, hereafter, is an attempt at a nuanced inquiry into the determinacy of the rule against states' unilateral recourse to force in the wake of the interventions in Kosovo in 1999 and Iraq in 2003. Has the prohibition been battered beyond recognition, forfeiting its legitimacy as nations conclude that it lacks all determinacy? Has it lost its capacity to pull states toward consensual compliance? Have we now entered an age in which anything goes?

II. Legitimacy and Determinacy

Let us begin by examining in somewhat greater detail the principal variable in determining the rule's degree of legitimacy. That variable is the rule's perceived determinacy. Has the prohibition on the unilateral recourse to force by states become meaningless through the response of states to scofflaw behavior?[18]

Determinacy is "that which makes [the rule's] message clear" or "transparent."[19] It is usually achieved by a rule text's explicit statement of a boundary between the permissible and the impermissible, or by the designation of a process for clarifying, in a contested instance, the meaning of a rule. In other words, a rule that is vague may still be seen as quite legitimate if its application in given, contested instances is open to a process that yields specificity. For example, I argued in my book *Recourse to Force* that the case-by-case interpretation by the Security Council of the prohibition on the use of force except in self-defense—in practice—has qualified the meaning of "armed attack" so as to include instances of imminent attack,[20] a view recently also taken by the high-level panel advising the UN secretary-general on Charter reform.[21] In practice, the rule evolves but remains determinate.

In instances like Kosovo and Iraq, where neither Yugoslavia nor Iraq had committed an armed attack such as to give automatic rise to a right to use force in self-defense, the Charter

[17] See discussion in SIMPSON, *supra* note 8, at 334–39.

[18] I realize that I have contributed to the confusion over this matter through the catchy title of my essay in this *Journal, Who Killed Article 2(4)?* 64 AJIL 809 (1973). The purpose of the article, of course, was not to claim that the prohibition on first use of military force was no longer binding on states but, to the contrary, to warn that, though an essential cornerstone of the postwar order, it was being progressively undermined by the conduct both of the Soviet Union and of the United States.

[19] FRANCK, *supra* note 15, at 52.

[20] THOMAS M. FRANCK, RECOURSE TO FORCE: STATE ACTION AGAINST THREATS AND ARMED ATTACKS 97–108 (2002).

[21] A More Secure World: Our Shared Responsibility, Report of the High-Level Panel on Threats, Challenges and Change, UN Doc. A/59/565, at 63, para. 188 (2004), *available at* <http://www.un.org/secureworld/report.pdf>.

designates the Security Council as the appropriate institution—the jury—for deciding, in accordance with Article 39, whether the situation has risen to the level of a "threat to the peace" that could warrant recourse to force, even in the absence of a prior armed attack. Yet, in the instance of Kosovo, NATO chose to circumvent the Council and, in the Iraqi case, the United States and Britain also chose to do so. What effect has this evasion had on the legitimacy and, thus, the compliance pull of the rules? Is there any longer a bright line between the permissible and the impermissible?

Certainly, some in the administration in Washington, and some, primarily American, scholars, have been quite vociferous in claiming that such a line between the permissible and the impermissible, whether it ever existed or not, no longer exerts any compliance pull on states.[22] They have attacked the legitimacy of the rule against recourse to force directly and, indirectly, the rule—*pacta sunt servanda*— on which all else depends in international law. They have done this in the name of humanitarian intervention and preventive measures against terrorism, both very modern issues high on almost everyone's list of concerns. These concerns, they have argued, cannot any longer be met with the old rules and processes.

Are they right?

There can be no doubt that, as a result of those recent recourses to force in Kosovo and Iraq, widespread unease can be sensed about the state of Charter-based international law applicable to war. That unease is probably even more pronounced among those of us who believe that compliance with international law is not an option but a mandate.

III. Have the Charter Rules Lost Determinacy?

The all-important question of whether the Charter rules have lost determinacy can be addressed only by reference to state practice: the conduct and opinions of a world of states. Care must be taken in defining that universe of state practice. In matters of usage and perception, the U.S. government is profoundly affected by its sense of being the world's only superpower and of the prerogatives that supposedly entails. Yet the rest of the nations, some two hundred of them, may see the rules—and act on them— quite differently. For example, the UN Security Council's persistent refusal to validate the 2003 invasion of Iraq demonstrates most states' continued reliance on the Charter rules, conduct that does not conduce to any theory of their obsolescence or delegitimation.

It also matters what we count as perceptions and usages. For example, things states do not do, or which they say they are not doing, or not saying they are doing, may be as important a gauge of the rules' efficacy as what they actually do. If rule violators are highly visible, the preponderant majority of law abiders is less so. But compliant behavior should count as much as noncompliant, in determining prevalent perceptions and usages.

The behavior of the noncompliant also requires close scrutiny. Professor H. L. A. Hart, although keenly aware of the shortcomings of international law as a system of normative obligations, nevertheless acknowledged that even in this imperfect system, nations behave as if the law were binding; not, he said, by always obeying its strictures but by acknowledging a "general pressure for conformity to the rules . . . . When the rules are disregarded, it is not on the footing that they are not binding; instead efforts are made to conceal the facts."[23]

Hart thus identified another important, but hidden, indicator of a law's legitimacy: that those who violate its strictures invariably claim not to be doing so. We tend to overlook the

[22] *E.g.*, Michael J. Glennon, *Why the Security Council Failed*, FOREIGN AFF., May/June 2003, at 16.

[23] H. L. A. HART, THE CONCEPT OF LAW 214–15 (1961).

tribute paid by scofflaws to the law they are breaching. If violators defend their actions either by distorting the law's meaning, or by lying about the facts of their violation, that strategy of denial tells us something. Perhaps it tells us that even the violators think that there is some life—some bite—left in those rules.

In most instances, states that have violated Article 2(4) of the Charter have asserted their innocence either by distorting the facts to conform to the license given by Article 51 ("self-defence"), or by interpreting that license creatively. Thus, North Korea insisted after its invasion of the South in June 1950, that it had been attacked by the South.[24] That lie might not have passed the laugh test as the Northern forces swept over Seoul toward Pusan, but the very fact that Pyongyang thought it necessary to lie attests to the North's recognition that, yes, there is a norm, one that is still universally recognized as binding and that cannot simply be disregarded with impunity. Lying about facts, it may be said, is the tribute scofflaw governments pay to international legal obligations they violate.

Equally common is the tactic of distorting what the law says. When Morocco invaded the Spanish Sahara in 1975, claiming to be "defending" Rabat's "historic title"[25] against UN efforts to implement the Saharawi people's right to self-determination, neither the International Court of Justice nor the General Assembly found that justification convincing.[26] Yet, significantly, the Moroccans at least tried to place their action within the normative framework, rather than attack its legitimacy. "Fancy lawyering" of that sort, one must suppose, is another tribute paid by scofflaw governments to the legitimacy of the international system of rules. After World War II, no government, no matter how powerful or how foolish, has thought it good tactics to say openly that the law is whatever it says it is.

Is such back-handed tribute still habitually being paid? If not, we might conclude that we are, indeed, in a world without law, where violators no longer recognize the legitimacy of the law they are violating. If the law has lost its compliance pull, we would know that, first, by the willingness of at least some states to say, as they did so often in the ages before the Charter, "La loi, c'est moi."

Of course, even if a state were to proclaim itself, openly, as above the law, that alone would not delegitimate the law, although, at some point, widespread noncompliance could have that effect. The failure of one state, even a powerful one, to obey the law raises, but does not answer, questions about the popular perception of the law's continued determinacy. To address that issue, it becomes necessary to resort to a kind of legal empiricism: to ask how many states, in how many situations of disputation, currently discredit the law pertaining to the use of force in word and deed? If the practice of these openly defiant "scofflaws" begins to overwhelm the restraint of governments that habitually comply with the law, then— but only then—it might be arguable that the rules have surely lapsed into desuetude. Or if the community of states fails to register its displeasure with the law's violation in some significant fashion, it would be arguable that the norm is being allowed to lapse into meaninglessness.

A brief examination of the history of interstatal behavior since World War II and up to the 2003 invasion of Iraq quickly demonstrates not only that states never challenged the legitimacy of the law they were violating, but, even at the risk of failing the laugh test, insisted that they were acting in full compliance with it. Vietnam averred that it had been invaded by Cambodia.[27] Moscow alleged that its occupation of Afghanistan was launched at the invitation of the legitimate

[24] *North Korean Communiques*, N.Y. TIMES, June 26, 1950, at A3.

[25] Western Sahara, Advisory Opinion, 1975 ICJ REP. 12, 130 (Oct. 16) (De Castro, J., sep. op.).

[26] *Id.*, Advisory Opinion. For the concurrent view of the General Assembly, see Question of Spanish Sahara, GA Res. 3458 (XXX) (Dec. 10, 1975).

[27] ELIZABETH BECKER, WHEN THE WAR WAS OVER 355 (1986).

Afghan government.[28] The UK government insisted that weapons of mass destruction (WMDs) were deployed in Iraq, poised to attack at forty-five minutes' notice.[29] The U.S. secretary of state unwittingly presented bogus facts to justify an invasion against Iraq's caches of prohibited WMDs.

If these avowals of fact had been true, the actions of Hanoi, Moscow, London, and Washington might well have been law-compliant. Even after the U.S. government's own 9/11 Commission concluded that there was no evidence of complicity with Al Qaeda by Saddam Hussein,[30] Vice President Dick Cheney has persisted in perpetuating that myth.[31] Why? To make the U.S. resort to force seem legally justified. Deprived of the myth, the illegality stands exposed. Even after the president's own chief weapons hunter, David Kay, reported that there were no weapons of mass destruction to be found in Iraq,[32] the Bush administration will not admit that they did not exist.[33] Why? Because to admit what is obvious to almost everyone else[34] would be to admit that the invasion of Iraq was illegal.

But why should the world's sole superpower care whether it is perceived as acting illegally? Why defend a "rational choice" in tortured legal terms? Why would some prefer to live in a bubble of false information, rather than stand exposed as facilitators of what is defined as aggression under a system of international law they revile as ineffective and contrary to rational choice? It does seem that somewhere, deep in the recesses of their reasoning process, leaders in Washington harbor a grudging awareness that the rest of the world still regards the rules, however egregiously violated by a few powerful scofflaws, as legitimate and binding. More generally, the failure of many of America's closest allies to help share the burden of invading and controlling Iraq speaks of widespread support for the "old" rules.[35]

Even a cursory examination of the post-Charter historic record makes clear that, in actual practice, almost all states, almost all the time, do abide by the strictures of Articles 2(4) and 51, refraining from resolving problems they may have with other states by recourse to force. Yes, there have been flare-ups between India and Pakistan,[36] and between India and China.[37] But during the Cold War, most scofflaw behavior was skirmishing between the superpowers. Another spate of flare-ups followed the disintegration of the Soviet empire. States in the Congo Basin, too, have exhibited instability and unlawful behavior.[38] In each instance, however, and with varying degrees of success, the UN system has been enlisted in strenuous efforts to mitigate and end those violations, applying and reinforcing precisely the rules that had been violated.[39]

[28] W. Michael Reisman & James Silk, *Which Law Applies to the Afghan Conflict?* 82 AJIL 459 (1988).

[29] "The dossier . . . suggests that Iraq could deploy chemical or biological weapons within 45 minutes of an order being given." Philip Webster, Roland Watson, & Greg Hurst, *Labour MPs Split over Iraq Dossier,* TIMES (London), Sept. 25, 2002, Home News, at 1.

[30] THE 9/11 COMMISSION REPORT: FINAL REPORT OF THE NATIONAL COMMISSION ON TERRORIST ATTACKS UPON THE UNITED STATES 334 (2004).

[31] Gloria Borger, *A Vice President Unbound,* U.S. NEWS & WORLD REP., June 28, 2004, at 34.

[32] *Ex-Inspector [David Kay] Again Says Forbidden Arms Probably Didn't Exist,* WASH. POST, Jan. 29, 2004, at A1.

[33] *Bush Stands Firmly Behind His Decision to Invade Iraq,* WASH. POST, Feb. 6, 2004, at A16.

[34] For an assertion of this obviousness, see Kofi Annan Interview (BBC News television broadcast Sept. 16, 2004), *available at* <http://news.bbc.co.uk/1/hi/world/middle_east/3661640.stm>.

[35] The Security Council has been scrupulous in its resolutions pertaining to Iraq to avoid anything that could be interpreted as a retrospective validation of the invasion.

[36] Sumathi Subbiah, Note, *Security Council Mediation and the Kashmir Dispute,* 27 B.C. INT'L & COMP. L. REV. 173 (2004).

[37] Sumit Ganguly, *India and China: Border Issues, Domestic Integration, and International Security, in* THE INDIA-CHINA RELATIONSHIP: WHAT THE UNITED STATES NEEDS TO KNOW 103 (Francine R. Frankel & Harry Harding eds., 2004).

[38] These began with the decolonization of the Belgian Congo in 1960 and the efforts of the United Nations to deal with the ensuing warfare. *Cf.* SC Res. 143 (July 14, 1960); SC Res. 169 (Nov. 24, 1961).

[39] *See* Frederic L. Kirgis, *The Security Council's First Fifty Years,* 89 AJIL 506, 532–37 (1995).

Against these highly visible instances of unlawful behavior must be set a much larger, but largely unremarked, aggregation of almost habitual compliance practice affirming the rules of the game. That so many states, so much of the time, resolve their boundary disputes by adjudication or arbitration[40] tells us the very same thing as the hapless lies of the persistent violators: that the rules against first use of force retain a high level of legitimacy in the community of states to which they are addressed.

It seems apparent to me that the normative system established by the UN Charter is not eroding. On the contrary, its legitimacy is rather consistently upheld in the rhetoric of all states and the behavior of most. The unlawful conduct of the scofflaws may be a great political problem because of the scale of the suffering it inflicts on the innocent and because of its great capacity to destabilize world order. But such aberrant behavior has not been a serious challenge to the law, because only the most extreme of its apologists openly attack the normative order or seek to replace it with any alternative set of rules. President George W. Bush's desire to make clear that the United States would act preemptively, more or less at will, whenever it thought its security threatened,[41] was not taken seriously as a legal proposition, since it was not remotely advanced as a new reciprocal right, one tenable by any nation, but, rather, in the unilateralist spirit of Thucydides' characterization of the law governing relations between Athens and little Melos during the Peloponnesian Wars: that the powerful do as they will, while the weak do as they must.[42]

Oddly, almost nothing proposed by the United States since it thus proclaimed itself the world's sole superpower has taken the form of new norms meant to govern state recourse to force, even though this is an era with complex new problems for which new rules might even be desirable. Indeed, it is remarkable that the United States, in what Andy Warhol might have called its fifteen minutes as sole superpower, has not sought to shape new rules, willfully abdicating one of the prerogatives, one would think, of superpower-dom. Instead, it has tried, even risibly, to show sometimes that it still adheres to the old rules, and at other times that it does not believe rules apply to it at all.

That does not mean, however, that no problems impinge on the continuing efficacy of norms conceived sixty years ago. They were meant to be effective in controlling the conduct of states in a world of panzer divisions. Those rules could not anticipate entirely new threats soon to be posed by weapons of mass destruction, near-instantaneous delivery systems, and substatal and transnational clashes of culture. The postwar normative order was conceived to deter established states, not shadowy transnational networks of fanatics. Thus, it is primarily obsolescence, not desuetude, that threatens the system's determinacy. If not addressed, some

[40] Boundary cases disposed of by the International Court of Justice include Frontier Dispute (Benin/Niger) (July 12, 2005); Application for Revision of the Judgment of 11 September 1992 in the Case Concerning the Land, Island and Maritime Frontier Dispute (El Salvador v. Honduras: Nicaragua intervening) (El Sal. v. Hond.) (Dec. 18, 2003); Sovereignty over Pulau Litigan and Pulau Sipadan (Indon./Malay) (Dec. 17, 2002); Land and Maritime Boundary Between Cameroon and Nigeria (Cameroon v. Nig.: Eq. Guinea intervening) (Oct. 10, 2002); Maritime Delimitation and Territorial Questions Between Qatar and Bahrain (Qatar v. Bahr.), 2001 ICJ REP. 40 (Mar. 16); Kasikili/Sedudu Island (Bots./Namib.), 1999 ICJ REP. 1045 (Dec. 13); Request for Interpretation of the Judgment of 11 June 1998 in the Case Concerning the Land and Maritime Boundary Between Cameroon and Nigeria (Cameroon v. Nigeria), Preliminary Objections (Nig. v. Cameroon), 1999 ICJ REP. 31 (Mar. 25); Territorial Dispute (Libya/Chad), 1994 ICJ REP. 6 (Feb. 13); Maritime Delimitation in the Area Between Greenland and Jan Mayen (Den. v. Nor.), 1993 ICJ REP. 38 (June 14); Land, Island and Maritime Frontier Dispute (El Sal./Hond.: Nicar. intervening), 1992 ICJ REP. 351 (Sept. 11); Arbitral Award of 31 July 1989 (Guinea-Bissau v. Sen.), 1991 ICJ REP. 53 (Nov. 12). The opinions of the Court are available at its Web site, <http://www.icj-cij.org>.

[41] THE NATIONAL SECURITY STRATEGY OF THE UNITED STATES OF AMERICA, pt. V (Sept. 17, 2002), *available at* <http://www.whitehouse.gov/nsc/nss.pdf>.

[42] THUCYDIDES, THE HISTORY OF THE PELOPONNESIAN WAR (Richard Crawley trans., Dutton 1950) (412 B.C.).

of these new problems, in time, will surely undermine the law's legitimacy. Specifically, these new challenges fall into two categories: (1) those pertaining to humanitarian intervention where the Security Council cannot respond because of the veto; and (2) those pertaining to the right of self-defense against an anticipated armed attack.

It is these problems of changing circumstance, not the actions or jurisprudential theories of a few scofflaws, that challenge the continuing legitimacy of international law pertaining to the use of force by states.

IV. HUMANITARIAN INTERVENTION

The UN Charter was written in the twilight of a great war and for the primary purpose of saving succeeding generations from another such scourge. The rules make no provision for using military force to save civilian populations from genocide or violations of human rights, let alone civil strife, starvation, or environmental degradation. Indeed, the text of Article 2(7) precludes any such "intervention" unless the situation has risen to the level of a threat to international peace and security. After all, the Charter originated in an era when, at Nuremberg, the Nazi master plan for aggressive war was the focus for prosecution of the indicted war criminals, while "crimes against humanity" received little attention from prosecutors or judges and applied only to acts that occurred after the outbreak of war.[43]

In the subsequent practice of UN organs, however, this high legal threshold has gradually been lowered and in 1999 Secretary-General Kofi Annan felt emboldened to tell the General Assembly that gross violations of human rights—rights now codified in universal treaties—could no longer be regarded as purely domestic matters, beyond the enforcement powers of the UN system. He called on states to "forge unity behind the principle that massive and systematic violations of human rights—wherever they may take place—should not be allowed to stand" and that "[s]tate sovereignty, in its most basic sense, is being redefined by the forces of globalization and international cooperation."[44] From the Congolese/Katangese wars of 1960–1962, through UN interventions in Somalia, Haiti, and Albania,[45] it has become a commonplace that the international system may lawfully intervene in situations of cataclysmic civil strife and other massive violations of human rights, with or without the consent of the government of the place where the violations are occurring.

[43] Thus, the charge of "common plan or conspiracy" was linked only to the charge of waging aggressive war, i.e., after 1939. TELFORD TAYLOR, THE ANATOMY OF THE NUREMBERG TRIALS: A PERSONAL MEMOIR 75–76 (1992); Robert H. Jackson, Statement at London Conference for the Preparation of the Trial (July 23, 1945), *quoted in* MICHAEL R. MARRUS, THE NUREMBERG WAR CRIMES TRIAL 1945–46: A DOCUMENTARY HISTORY 45–46 (1997). Although the Nuremberg Tribunal was assigned jurisdiction over "crimes against humanity," nevertheless

> the Allies were uncomfortable with the ramifications that this might have with respect to the treatment of minorities within their own countries, not to mention their colonies. For this reason, they insisted that crimes against humanity could only be committed if they were associated with one of the other crimes within the Nuremberg Tribunal's jurisdiction, that is, war crimes and crimes against peace. In effect, they had imposed a requirement of *nexus*, as it is known, between crimes against humanity and international armed conflict.

WILLIAM A. SCHABAS, AN INTRODUCTION TO THE INTERNATIONAL CRIMINAL COURT 42 (2d ed. 2004) (footnote omitted). The result was that crimes against the Jews of Germany were off limits.

[44] Secretary-General Presents His Annual Report to the General Assembly, UN Press Release SG/SM/7136, GA/9596 (Sept. 20, 1999) (text of address by Kofi Annan).

[45] SC Res. 143 & 169, *supra* note 38 (Congo); SC Res. 794 (Dec. 3, 1992) & 923 (May 31, 1994) (Somalia); SC Res. 1529 (Feb. 29, 2004) (Haiti); SC Res. 1101 (Mar. 28, 1997) (Albania).

Thus, the rules have adapted. Because they have done so quite successfully, the rules, even while evolving, have retained their determinacy. A dictator who tries to exterminate a part of his population knows that Article 2(7) cannot alone save him from intervention and punitive measures. Black-letter texts do not become less determinate when they acquire a penumbra of adaptive practice that is widely understood and preserves the rules' legitimacy in changing circumstances.

What, then, is the problem?

It is twofold.

The first problem is that efforts by the system to rescue an affected population can be stymied by the veto, or the threat of a veto, used unconscionably by any of the five permanent members. That is what happened as the paralyzed Security Council stood by during the planned extermination of eight hundred thousand Tutsi in Rwanda.[46] That is what, it is believed, would have happened in Kosovo had NATO not acted unlawfully, in the face of a threatened veto preventing forceful measures against the perpetrators.

The second problem is that threatened populations may not be saved in time because of a sort of "rescue fatigue" among the principal donors of personnel, arms, and money.

Both of these problems—the veto and rescue fatigue—are more political than legal. But the search for solutions seems to be leading toward an institutional transformation with important legal implications: a sort of regionalization of humanitarian rescue. When the Economic Community of West African States stepped in to intervene forcibly in civil wars wracking Liberia and Sierra Leone, the Security Council endorsed those actions, retroactively.[47] Is that the procedural rule evolving out of state practice? It has been argued that the Security Council, in 1999, similarly gave post hoc approval to NATO's intervention on behalf of the endangered Kosovars.[48] The new Constitutive Act of the African Union, of July 11, 2000, formally prescribes procedures for regional interventions in humanitarian crises by members of the region, whether or not that action has been approved by the United Nations.[49] But such a regional response does not strictly accord with Article 53 of the UN Charter, which requires prior approval by the Security Council before a regional organization initiates the use of force. One suggestion advanced for bridging this discrepancy might be for the General Assembly to substitute for the veto-prone Security Council in approving humanitarian interventions by regional organizations.

While the evolution of this sort of regionalism may presage a revised system of norms pertaining to humanitarian rescue, one more responsive to both the problem of the veto and rescue fatigue,[50] these problems cannot entirely be overcome by devolving more authority to the world's regions. There are several reasons for caution. Some of the most crisis-prone regions have no—or only underdeveloped and underfunded—capabilities. In other instances, the regional organization is but little trusted by minorities or governments in that part of the world.

Rather, thought needs to be given to ways to reform the veto itself, so that the rescue of endangered populations cannot be prevented at the whim of one or two Council members.

[46] An account of the futile effort in the Security Council to prevent or mitigate this crisis is in 1995 UN Y.B. 281–317, UN Sales No. E.95.I.50.

[47] SC Res. 1497 (Aug. 1, 2003) (Liberia); SC Res. 1315 (Aug. 14, 2000) (Sierra Leone).

[48] This can be inferred from Resolution 1244 (June 10, 1999), which welcomed the acceptance by the Federal Republic of Yugoslavia of the settlement imposed upon it as a consequence of NATO's recourse to force. FRANCK, *supra* note 20, at 163–71.

[49] Article 4(h) of the Constitutive Act stipulates "the right of the Union to intervene in a Member State pursuant to a decision of the Assembly in respect of grave circumstances, namely: war crimes, genocide and crimes against humanity," when such intervention is authorized by two-thirds of the members. Constitutive Act of the African Union, July 11, 2002, Art. 4(h), *available at* <http://www.africa-union.org>.

[50] *See* James E. Hickey Jr., *Challenges to Security Council Monopoly Power over the Use of Force in Regional Enforcement Actions: The Case of Regional Organizations*, 10 IUS GENTIUM 75 (2004).

This might be done by a side agreement between the five permanent members, or as many as are willing, or even by unilateral declarations by veto-wielding states, stipulating that, once the Security Council has determined that a threat to the peace exists and has set out the required remedial measures, the veto will not be used to prevent the taking of follow-up enforcement measures. One effect of such self-restraint would be to put any offender on notice that noncompliance with Security Council orders would be likely to have serious consequences.

Whether or not all, or at first only some, of the permanent members formally agree to such an updating of the practices, the rules are changing. Since Kosovo, when a large preponderance of states are convinced that a muscular rescue is necessary and urgent, they clearly will not much cavil at the taking of action by a coalition of the willing whose bona fides are demonstrable and generally acknowledged. Change may occur through negotiated agreement or by patterns of conduct that skirt the rules. Either is likely, eventually, to achieve normative reform. The International Court recognized this self-rectifying process in the *Nicaragua* case, when it pointed out:

> The significance for the Court of cases of State conduct prima facie inconsistent with the principle of non-intervention lies in the nature of the ground offered as justification. Reliance by a State on a novel right or an unprecedented exception to the principle might, if shared in principle by other States, tend towards a modification of customary international law.[51]

Law's legitimacy is not preserved by refusal to entertain rule change, and change can come about in various ways. As long as the process results in common acknowledgment of the reformed rule's universal application and of its specific content, change through practice will not undermine a rule's legitimacy.

V. Self-Defense

The same may be said with regard to situations where force is necessary to deflect an impending attack on one state by another, or by a terrorist group. The law is adapting, it is bound to adapt, and its legitimacy will be enhanced thereby.

The strict letter of the Charter (Article 51) limits the right of self-defense to situations in which an armed attack has already occurred and where the attacker is another state. Such a law might be clear, but it is nonsense in the contemporary context. Because this deficiency is widely recognized, the principal organs of the UN system have begun to improvise contextually.

Have they done so in a way that saves the determinacy, hence the legitimacy, of the rules? I believe that they have.

Article 51, by speaking of the "inherent right of self-defence," incorporates customary law notions of anticipatory self-defense spelled out in the 1837 *Caroline* memorandum of Secretary of State Daniel Webster, a right arising when the "necessity of . . . self-defence is instant, overwhelming, and leaving no choice of means, and no moment for deliberation."[52]

As determined by whom? Aye, there's the rub.

The problem does not lie with updating the right of self-defense to permit action in anticipation of an imminent attack. Rather, it lies with leaving every state free to determine whether

[51] Military and Paramilitary Activities in and Against Nicaragua (Nicar. v. U.S.), Merits, 1986 ICJ REP. 14, 109, para. 207 (June 27).

[52] Letter from Daniel Webster, U.S. secretary of state, to Henry Fox, British minister in Washington (Apr. 24, 1841), ***quoted in*** 2 JOHN BASSETT MOORE, A DIGEST OF INTERNATIONAL LAW 412 (1906), ***and in*** 29 BRIT. & FOREIGN ST. PAPERS 1840–1841, at 1138 (1857). For a discussion, see 1 OPPENHEIM'S INTERNATIONAL LAW 420–27 (Robert Jennings & Arthur Watts eds., 9th ed. 1992).

it is in such imminent danger as to be free to use anticipatory force before being attacked.[53] In legal terms, if Article 51 of the Charter is to be read as permitting state recourse to force in self-defense not just against an actual, but also against an anticipated, attack, then— unless the Article 2(4) constraint on first use is to become wholly meaningless—the decision whether such an attack is imminent cannot be left solely to each state.

Nevertheless, in the weeks before the 2003 invasion of Iraq, it was the position of the United States and the United Kingdom that they were free in law to determine for themselves whether Iraq was in material breach of prior Security Council resolutions ending the state of hostilities authorized by the Council in Resolution 678 of 1990, or whether Iraq's defiance of the regime imposed on it by Council Resolution 687 in 1991 had risen to the threshold that would justify preemptive military action under an expanded doctrine of self-defense, without any jurying of the claim of necessity. In the words of the British attorney general, even though the Security Council may "consider the matter before any action is taken," regardless of what the Council does or does not decide, "further [military] action can be taken without a new resolution of the Council."[54]

The problem, then, does not lie with formulating a norm. It lies with the process for implementing it: who, or what institution, what judge or jury, should decide whether the norm's requisites for preemptive action have been met. President Bush, in his 2004 State of the Union address to Congress, reduced the American position to the nakedly unilateral: We will never seek anyone's permission, he said, to defend the national self-interest of the United States.[55]

If that is indeed the administration's considered position, then the president will have withdrawn America from the community of states operating under international law. For that community is constituted not only by its substantive rules, but also by those institutional processes that implement the rules. The more indeterminate a norm, the more essential the process by which, in practice, the norm can be made more specific. Rules that each member of a community is free to interpret for itself, without fear of definitive contradiction, are truly rules lacking in determinacy, for they leave each member free to assert that "the rules are whatever I say they are." They then have no objective content whatsoever.

The problem that the invasion of Iraq has brought to the fore is not primarily one of defining or reforming a right to anticipatory, preemptive, or preventive self-defense in the era of WMDs, daunting as such a project may be. The problem is that, even if such a commonly acceptable right could be formulated, by treaty or by practice, it would be wholly illegitimate so long as some nations insisted on the right to interpret and apply the new rule unilaterally.

On a more practical level, it is clear that few nations would be interested in negotiating such a normative reform unless all states were committed to subordinating themselves to a credible institutional process for determining when the right is properly invoked.

Repeatedly, just before and after the invasion of Iraq, U.S. leaders asserted that the United Nations had failed because, despite Iraq's repeated defiance of the disarmament requirements imposed on it by Resolutions 687 and 1441, the Security Council had failed to pass that second

[53] The difference, in this respect, between imminent attack and latent danger was amply evident to British foreign secretary Lord Castlereagh who, in 1820, wrote: "We shall be found in our place when actual Danger menaces the System of Europe, but this Country cannot and will not act upon abstract and speculative Principles of Precaution." Castlereagh's State Paper of 1820, Minute of Cabinet (May 5, 1820), ***quoted in*** SIMPSON, ***supra*** note 8, at 348.

[54] Lord Goldsmith, Attorney General Clarifies Legal Basis for Use of Force Against Iraq, para. 11 (Mar. 18, 2003), *at* <http://www.fco.gov.uk> (statement in answer to a parliamentary question).

[55] George W. Bush, Address Before a Joint Session of the Congress on the State of the Union (Jan. 28, 2003), 39 WEEKLY COMP. PRES. DOC. 109 (Feb. 3, 2003).

resolution authorizing recourse to force.[56] But the system had not failed. Rather, two-thirds of the Council's membership had concluded, quite reasonably, that the danger of a WMD attack by, or with the connivance of, Iraq could have been prevented far better by strengthening the UN inspectors and by positioning more troops—preferably the ones already in the gulf region in preparation for an invasion—in nearby Afghanistan to deter further defiance by Saddam Hussein. At the time, this was a perfectly plausible alternative strategy for dealing with the danger posed by Iraq. In retrospect, it was clearly the better, the right, strategy, one that would have saved tens of thousands of lives and hundreds of billions of dollars while achieving the commonly desired result. It might also have enhanced the effectiveness of the UN-authorized campaign against Al Qaeda in Afghanistan.

Sadly, President Bush chose instead to take a road leading away from community and law. He said, "[W]e will not hesitate to act alone, if necessary, to exercise our right of self-defense by acting preemptively . . . ."[57] It could be replied, of course, that there is nothing really new about that claim. Arguably, as a political policy, each government has always retained, in its diplomatic arsenal, the big stick necessary to pursue its essential self-interest against any other government that is inferior to it militarily. That, however, is not necessarily the conclusion this administration wants anyone to draw. It is very unlikely that Washington is eager to have its new doctrine adopted by New Delhi and Beijing, let alone Iran and North Korea. Yet, inconveniently at such moments as this, law is all about the gander's right to the goose's sauce.

Lawyers sympathetic to the aims of the *National Security Strategy* are perfectly aware of this problem. Judge Abraham Sofaer, the legal adviser of the Department of State under President George H. W. Bush, poses the problem with characteristic clarity: "Can the concept of self-defence accommodate a role for pre-emption that satisfies the need of leaders to protect their people, without providing a ready basis for states to use pre-emption as an excuse for aggression?"[58] The answer is that there might be such a legal concept, but it certainly is not one that is on offer by the present U.S. administration.

Such a policy may seem to extract America from the rule of law's constraints, but at a high price to the national interest. This is fantasy realism, at best. It fails to take into account the opportunity costs of not acting multilaterally, that is, not acting in accordance with the rules as generally perceived. Failing to make that reckoning does significant harm to American and British interests. But it will not, thereby, have caused the multilateral system of rules to become indeterminate, or have undermined its legitimacy. It will only have made it much more difficult for Washington to protect its far-flung global interests.

As for the state of the law of self-defense, it seems to come to this: although Article 51 of the Charter literally permits a state to use force only after it has been attacked, both common sense and practice have prevented such a *reductio ad absurdum*. In the words of the high-level panel reporting to the secretary-general on UN reform in 2005, "a threatened state" may "take military action as long as the threatened attack is imminent, no other means would deflect it and the action is proportionate."[59] This view was endorsed by the secretary-general.[60] In the practice of the Organization, it has long been tacitly recognized that a nation preparing a crippling

[56] William H. Taft IV & Todd F. Buchwald, *Preemption, Iraq, and International Law*, 97 AJIL 557 (2003).

[57] THE NATIONAL SECURITY STRATEGY OF THE UNITED STATES OF AMERICA, pt. III, at 6 (Sept.17, 2002), *available at* <http://www.whitehouse.gov/nsc/nss.pdf>.

[58] Abraham D. Sofaer, *On the Necessity of Pre-emption*, 14 EUR. J. INT'L L. 209, 211 (2003).

[59] A More Secure World, *supra* note 21, at 54, para. 188.

[60] "Imminent threats are fully covered by Article 51 . . . ." In Larger Freedom: Towards Development, Security and Human Rights for All, Report of the Secretary-General, UN Doc. A/59/2005, para. 124, *available at* <http://www.un.org/largerfreedom/contents.htm>.

first strike against another may be treated as an aggressor before it has an opportunity to strike.[61] It may be dealt with in accordance with the right, expanded by the practice of states, to use force in self-defense.

However, this right to act without reference to the Security Council is limited to instances of actual or imminent attack. The right does not accrue when a state merely claims that it may eventually be the victim of a potential aggressor. Even in the era of weapons of mass destruction, such a claim to use forceful measures in preventive self-defense must still be made to the satisfaction of the Security Council, exercising its authority to sanction the use of force to prevent threats to the peace under the terms of Article 39. A state that believes itself threatened by the long-term hostile intentions of another, before resorting to preventive action, must demonstrate the actuality of that threat to the satisfaction of the appropriate international institution. Without some jurying or adjudicative process, the right of preventive action would otherwise become an unbridled license for all states to practice aggression. That would be irreconcilable with the purposes of the Charter and there is no evidence whatsoever that the community of states is ready for such a change in the norms of the system.

The high-level panel has thus rendered a real service in drawing a distinction between an imminent threat, as to which states may take proportionate preemptive action when there remains no viable alternative, and what it described as nonimminent or nonproximate threats, which may still be very serious and as to which action may, indeed, be highly desirable but must be fully justified by the claimant before the Security Council acting as a global jury.[62]

To be sure, the Security Council, let alone other institutions of the international system, is quite an imperfect analogue to the jury, although the jury is, itself, a notoriously imperfect system, one wanting except in comparison to the available alternatives. The Security Council is in need of reform, particularly in the context of its role in collective measures pertaining to humanitarian crises and anticipatory measures to preempt terrorist attacks. With respect to both, veto practices cry out for reform. If the Council is to be vested, by state practice, with performing the key jurying function in determining when states have the right to use force in anticipatory self-defense or to avert a humanitarian disaster, then the permanent members must develop a pattern of persistent self-restraint in their recourse to the veto.

The call for reform is not an instance of hollow Panglossian optimism. There are encouraging signs that the system is capable of reforming its rules to meet new crises, even if the time for reform of the veto has not yet come. An example is the Security Council's recent response to the new problem of self-defense against terrorist networks that are not states and operate across national boundaries. The Charter did not anticipate this problem. Yet, on September 12, 2001, in Resolution 1368, the Security Council made clear the responsibility and liability of those who are "sponsors of . . . terrorist attacks" or engage in "supporting or harbouring the perpetrators." Against them, the right of individual and collective self-defense was deemed to be as applicable as if they were states.[63]

Again, however, it is important to note that the right to act in self-defense against nonstatal entities and against states that were harboring aggressors although not themselves engaging in the aggression was judged to be applicable by the Security Council; it was not something simply asserted

[61] An example is Israel's attack on Egypt in 1967, after the Egyptian government unilaterally had ordered the withdrawal of the United Nations Emergency Force, which since 1956 had served as a buffer between the two enemies, and had redeployed its own forces to occupy the buffer zone in threatening posture, while declaring the closure to Israeli shipping of the Gulf of Aqaba and the Strait of Tiran. 1967 UN Y.B. 164–68.

[62] A More Secure World, *supra* note 21, at 54–55, para. 189.

[63] Resolutions 1368 (Sept. 12, 2001) and 1373 (Sept. 28, 2001), respectively, recognize the right to take individual and collective measures in the aftermath of the attack by Al Qaeda on the United States.

unilaterally by Washington. Indeed, the United States wanted this approval before resorting to force because it recognized the many benefits of multilateralizing its response in the war on terrorism.

In sum, the principal organs of the United Nations have understood the need to adapt the law pertaining to the right of self-defense in the light of changing circumstances and, to a remarkable extent, they have risen to that challenge, as their members have creatively interpreted rules that otherwise, without reform, might simply have become obsolete. What the practice has refused to accommodate, however, is the insistence of the United States and the United Kingdom that they, alone, be free to interpret the broadened rules in accordance solely with their understanding of their national interests.

This is as it must be. The Charter system consists of two strands: the substantive and the procedural. As circumstances, priorities, and even universal values change, the substantive norms must adapt. The procedures, too, from time to time need pragmatic adaptation. One aspect of the procedures, however, must not adapt. The basic procedural notion of the Charter is that every nation, before taking military action, except in self-defense against an imminent or actual armed attack, must first demonstrate to its peers that, in the terms of Charter Article 39, there exists an actual threat to the peace. If, for example, a demonstrably malevolent government is on the path to developing actual WMDs, it is well within the power of the Security Council to take action without waiting for the threat to become imminent. That determination, however, is reserved to the judgment of the Council acting as jury, and not to individual states. Without that central procedural safeguard, international relations cannot be said to have been brought within the ambit of the rule of law.

Why? Because every recourse to force, in the modern world of global interdependence, always affects the condition and well-being of many more states than merely the initiator and the object of a military action. It affects neighboring states and their populations, the environment, commerce, and, in particular, the integrity of the international system of rules and procedures in which everyone has a stake.

VI. CONCLUSION

The law pertaining to recourse to force is under stress from the confluence of two different tendencies. One tendency is to overestimate the capacity of naked power to achieve recognition of its own legitimacy by ignoring the law. The other is to underestimate the capacity of law to adapt to new circumstances while retaining the determinacy that underpins its perceived legitimacy. The conclusion, put with brevity at some cost to nuance, is that law can adapt through practice, that violations of law may be one form of practice that can have the effect of changing it, but that violations of the law, like other forms of practice, have the potential only to change the law, not to repeal it; and practice changes the law only to the extent that the change is generally approved and applied by the international community of states. Thus, violations of the law remain violations of the law until they can be described as amendments-in-practice. That the law is "amendable" in this way is not a sign of the law's weakness, but of its resilience. Had the Constitution of the United States not been capable of adaptation in this way, we would have no capacity to enter into undeclared wars or international agreements ratified by simple majorities of both houses of Congress. Whatever one might think of such adaptations, they are not a license to ignore the law.

Then why are we seeing the phenomenon of a burgeoning literature on the "limits" of international law? One aspect of this phenomenon is the tendency of growing numbers of "realists" to believe that only calculations of power and self-interest, but not much normativity, enter into states' "rational choice" in determining their actions. This notion can be shown to be wrong, both by empirically studying the prevalence of rule compliance by states even when that does not promote their preferred outcome, and also by examining the way the relatively small number of scofflaw states fervently pretend to be rule compliant.

Against the siren song of a world order created through the "rational choice" of a single superpower must be set the "rational choice" represented by adherence to the rule of law. This is not a form of moral philosophy but a hard-headed realization of the limits of power and of law's potential for serving everyone's long-term self-interest. Advocates of a "rational choice" that is law regarding can point to the self-repairing tendency of the rules to adapt and accommodate changing circumstances. They can point out that a breach of the law, if made with the approval or acquiescence of the preponderance of states, may serve not only the national interest but also that of the law itself, by effecting a needed modification. But that is quite different from the proposition that the law does not matter and neither does the *opinio juris* of other states.

Adherence to law, when seen to legitimate action, serves the national interest because it pulls states to voluntary compliance. If the Iraqi invasion had been perceived as legitimate, as was the 1991 military action to liberate Kuwait, America would not still be out there, virtually alone, bearing the brunt of the burdens, undermining its military capability, and sending its economy into turbulent danger. That, surely, should have been relevant to "rational choice."

Rational choice, for American policymakers, must mean taking international law seriously, if only because, overwhelmingly, most other states, their leaders, and scholars of international law seem tenaciously inclined to regard international law that way. It is thus rational to presume that any American endeavors undertaken to advance the national interest but requiring the cooperation of other nations—and which ones do not, these days?—should be undertaken in compliance with the basic legal rules to which most states still adhere and which the United States itself has ratified.[64]

That this view is now being challenged in America, by both our leaders and our fellow academics, should serve as a salubrious stimulant to the rest of us. Among American legal scholars, even those with contemporary experience at the higher echelons of government (during both Democratic and Republican administrations), the majority impetus is, still, to defend the importance of international law, not least as advancing the national self-interest.

In practice, the difference between the defenders and the challengers of law's empire is neither about the importance of "rational choice" nor about the primacy of the national interest in determining compliance with international law. Rather, it is between a longer view of national interest and a narrower, more immediate approach to interest gratification. Notably, both long-term and short-term approaches have an equal claim to be operating within a theory of rational choice. The former, however, takes fully into account the power of legitimacy, while the latter focuses only on the legitimacy of power.

[64] This view was best (and surprisingly) expressed recently by Prime Minister Tony Blair: "The best defence of our security lies in the spread of our values. But we cannot advance these values except within a framework that recognises their universality. If it is a global threat, it needs a global response, based on global rules." *Full Text: Tony Blair's Speech*, GUARDIAN UNLIMITED, Mar. 5, 2004, *available at* <http://politics.guardian.co.uk/iraq/story/0,12956,1162991,00.html#article_continue>.

Part V
The Laws of War and Force

[20]

THE COMPLEXITIES OF HUMANITARIAN INTERVENTION: A NEW WORLD ORDER CHALLENGE

Richard Falk[*]

I. Framing an Inquiry

The interplay between juridical support for norms of non-intervention and the actualities of interventionary diplomacy is an integral feature of a world of sovereign, yet unequal, states pursuing diverse goals. Pointing in one direction is the juridical stress on sovereignty, reinforced by spatial notions of territorial supremacy within fixed boundaries, which provides the doctrinal underpinnings of non-interventionism. Pointing in the other direction is the effort to project power and influence beyond territorial sovereignty, virtually a definition of what distinguishes a great power from an ordinary state, which creates the geopolitical pressures that result in intervention in the internal and external affairs of weaker sovereign states. This essay assesses the nature of change in interventionary diplomacy since the end of the Cold War against this conceptual background.

Part of the complexity traditionally associated with interventionary diplomacy is its confounding and varying admixtures of politics, morality, and law. These admixtures exist irrespective of whether the particular intervention is characterized as "humanitarian" — although by so describing an intervention, the moral/legal justification is given additional importance.

The political dimension is preoccupied with the decisive issues of effectiveness and acceptability: managing the means/end relationship between commitment and outcome, and assessing the acceptability of the interventionary claim in various arenas of decisionmaking and evaluation. This dimension is also crucial in determining whether the overall interest of the intervening state — including its reputation for effective and legitimate action — is promoted through the effort to influence behavior by coercive means in a foreign country and whether

---

* Albert G. Milbank Professor of International Law and Practice, Princeton University. J.S.D., Harvard University (1962); LL.B., Yale Law School (1955); B.S., University of Pennsylvania (1952).

sufficient resources can and should be brought to bear to achieve the interventionary goals within a reasonable amount of time given the level of prevailing domestic support.

The moral dimension of interventionary diplomacy focuses on vindicating the claim that the use of force is essential and proportionate: that it benefits the peoples of the target society, serves the values (and interests) of the intervening state, and contributes to the global common good.[1]

The legal dimension is concerned with invoking and establishing precedents and making legal arguments about rules and standards in support of, or in opposition to, a particular interventionary undertaking.[2]

The subject-matter of intervention evolved as an incident of the Westphalian world order. States were the only legitimate actors enjoying the rights of territorial supremacy and there existed no external legal constraints on government decisions to use force as an instrument of statecraft. While it is still true that only states possess the military capabilities and political disposition needed to fashion the sort of policy that is likely to be identified as "interventionary," recent practice over the last half-century in interventionary diplomacy has exhibited the impact of several new elements.[3]

The most significant new element impinging on interventionary diplomacy, is the role played by the United Nations and regional entities, especially in Europe. Nevertheless, the character of the United Nations' role is ambiguous both overall and from case to case. Particularly confusing is the uncertainty regarding whether a Security Council decision involves a genuinely collective and community interventionary

1. These perspectives may not point in the same direction. For instance, the 1986 United States air strike against Libya in alleged retaliation for Libya's complicity in terrorist actions against U.S. targets was and remains inconclusive from these viewpoints. It was not certain that Libya was involved in the specific terrorist incident that served as the factual basis for the interventionary claim. Neither was it clear that the targets chosen were appropriate or that the means used were proportionate. Yet the attack did not arouse any strong adverse reaction, partly because Libya had previously and blatantly acted in a provocative manner with respect to international terrorism and partly because the United States' use of limited force was widely, but not uniformly, accepted as a reasonable way to compel Libya to change its behavior (which seems to have happened in the period subsequent to the attack). For a series of skeptical assessments of the American claim, see MAD DOGS: THE U.S. RAIDS ON LIBYA (Mary Kaldor & Paul Anderson eds., 1986).

2. *See* MYRES S. MCDOUGAL & FLORENTINO P. FELICIANO, LAW AND MINIMUM WORLD PUBLIC ORDER (1961) (on the process by which claims to use force are validated in international law).

3. Russia, although no longer the global presence of the Soviet Union at the height of the Cold War, remains, since 1989, an uncontested interventionary actor in the "near abroad," the region comprised of those formally independent states that had previously been republics in the Soviet imperial system.

judgment guided predominantly by considerations of public good. Uncertainty clouds the degree to which such a decision is little more than a legitimating rationale for use of force that would otherwise be more widely viewed as "illegal" if undertaken by a state on its own or in coalition with other states. Another relatively new element is the emergence and magnitude of an array of transnational civil initiatives that seek to mitigate the suffering of people living in the target societies and participating in any warfare that results. The International Committee of the Red Cross, established in reaction to the horrific battlefield conditions of the Crimean War in the mid-nineteenth century, is suggestive of this non-governmental role that has been expanding in interventionary contexts, especially those expressly characterized as humanitarian. Also relatively novel are legal constraints on the use of force as an instrument of statecraft and formal prohibitions on all forms of coercion that possess an interventionary character.[4] A final development is the emergence of a highly articulated international law of human rights, reinforced psychologically by ideas about government and individual accountability for their gross violation. Cumulatively, heightened expectations about conformity to minimal human rights standards generate interventionary pressures, especially given the capacity of television and other innovative media to create real-time awareness of many types of inhumane behavior on a global basis.

Evaluating the effect of these normative innovations in the status of force remains controversial: are we dealing mainly with a change in discursive reality — such that what has really changed is language, not behavior — with major states still retaining, on a behavioral level, a discretionary option to use force? A middle position contends that the discursive change *alters* behavior by legitimating challenges directed at uses of force that did not previously exist. Gradually, there are moves away from reliance on force, thereby affecting in subtle ways the balance of considerations entering into the national security calculus of governments.

4. There is a long list of familiar legal authorities starting with the Pact of Paris (also known as the Kellogg-Briand Pact). Treaty Providing for the Renunciation of War as an Instrument of National Policy, Aug. 27, 1928, 46 Stat. 2343, 94 L.N.T.S. 57. The basic contemporary rule of prohibition is contained in Article 2(4) of the U.N. Charter. The prohibition of intervention by states builds on this fundamental rule. *See Declaration on the Inadmissibility of Intervention in the Domestic Affairs of States and the Protection of their Independence and Sovereignty*, G.A. Res. 2131, U.N. GAOR 1st Comm., 20th Sess., Agenda Item 107, U.N. Doc. A/RES/2131 (1966). These fundamental ideas are integrated in the *Declaration on Principles of International Law Concerning Friendly Relations and Co-operation Among States in Accordance with the Charter of the United Nations*, G.A. Res. 2625, U.N. GAOR 6th Comm., 25th Sess., Agenda Item 85, U.N. Doc. A/RES/2625 (1970).

The increased complexity of the phenomenon of intervention has had a number of contradictory effects. It has become more difficult to identify who is responsible for what. While the state continues to dominate interventionary diplomacy, it often operates indirectly, by reliance on the authorizing mandate of one or more layer of institutional authority at the regional and global levels.[5] Such indirectness of mandate dilutes and disguises the role of the state to some extent, undercuts somewhat certain anti-interventionary criticism, and shifts part of the responsibility for failure to achieve interventionary goals to the wider institutional frameworks, especially that of the United Nations. Further, norms of non-intervention in addition to prohibitions on the use of force are somewhat at odds with the contemporary view that the occasion of human rights abuse provides legal and moral grounds for disregarding the sovereign rights of states.[6]

Given this complexity, it is hardly surprising that the subject-matter of interventionary diplomacy has consistently given rise to controversy and inconclusive results. This effect has been more pervasive in constitutional democracies that claim a moral advantage and legal validation for their foreign policy initiatives, at least partly, because of the domestic accountability of their political leaders through free and periodic elections and legislative checks.[7] Discussing the reluctance of the Bush Administration to get involved on the ground during the early stages of the war in Bosnia, then-Secretary of State James Baker recalled a few years later that "the American people would not have stood for such a commitment for even three days!"[8] Such a perception of citizen skepticism about an interventionary policy operates as a definite check on a proposed intervention that is not clearly based on widely acknowledged strategic interests or national security considerations. When such lines of justification are powerfully present, then the passions of the electorate can act, on occasion, as a spur to intervene.

5. This reliance has caused rather meaningless debates as to whether the United Nations has "failed" because of the dismal outcomes in several recent peacekeeping tasks or whether the United Nations has been made a scapegoat by leading member states. *See* DAVID RIEFF, SLAUGHTERHOUSE: BOSNIA AND THE FAILURE OF THE WEST 13-23 (1995).

6. *See, e.g.*, Jarat Chopra and Thomas G. Weiss, *Sovereignty Is No Longer Sacrosanct: Codifying Humanitarian Intervention*, 6 ETHICS & INT'L AFF. 95 (1992).

7. This is not to say that the moral/legal status of an intervention is the primary ingredient of its acceptability; generally, far more relevant is the sense of interests at stake in relation to prospects for success at acceptable costs. As suggested by the experience in the Gulf War, the level of domestic support rose dramatically when a quick and easy victory resulted. Conversely, the early popularity of the Korean and Vietnam Wars dropped as the costs rose, the war dragged on, and the prospects for victory diminished.

8. Observation made during an informal meeting with the faculty of the Woodrow Wilson School, Princeton University, April 1994.

The United States seems especially susceptible to such swings of interventionary mood that can be played upon by opportunistic politicians. Such a possibility is reinforced by the American political myth of acting benevolently, rather than selfishly, on international issues, and of being a country whose actions are allegedly driven by values rather than interests. This special American need for a moral justification stems, no doubt, in part, from its own anti-colonial heritage, its recent championship of international human rights including the right of self-determination, and its tendency to disguise its selfish motivations for overseas actions.[9] This complex orientation of the United States toward intervention, inhibited by the Vietnam syndrome and encouraged by a missionary mentality, is of great world order significance at the present time because of the leadership role it has played as the sole remaining superpower.

Accompanying the changes in interventionary diplomacy has been a further stage-setting factor: the demise of the credibility of geopolitical pressures to intervene since the end of the Cold War.[10] This development reinforces the normative impact of the collapse of colonialism and the participation in global politics of leaders of ex-colonies who remain generally suspicious of *any* interventionary claim. To circumvent such resistance within the setting of the United Nations, interventionary arguments have been formulated in a manner that effectively obscures great power aspects. The rise of "humanitarian" rationalizations is an effort to reconcile the proactive impulse to intervene with the normative inhibitions on the use of force for geopolitical purposes given the present historical setting.

There is a further general observation. To the extent that intervention (aside from countries intervening in the affairs of their neighbors) is the exclusive work of great powers, its feasibility as a policy option is often shaped by the nature of the governing structure within the intervening state. If the state is authoritarian, it needs generally less public

9. Two contradictory lines of interpretation are significant. One regards the United States as a self-maximizing intervening power with little sense of moral scruple. For a powerful articulation of this view, see GABRIEL KOLKO, CENTURY OF WAR 412-51 (1994). The other sees the United States as unwilling to act coercively in foreign policy until it is first convinced of the moral correctness of its position. An influential formulation of this view is to be found in HENRY KISSINGER, DIPLOMACY (1994).

10. Geopolitical factors remain relevant in some settings. Islamic challenges in key Middle East countries may still create a new geopolitical climate favorable to intervention should the pro-Western orientation of the governments in Saudi Arabia, Turkey, and Egypt be seriously threatened. It is not difficult to imagine a number of scenarios involving a resurgent and assertive Russia, possibly aligned with China, that would raise further the geopolitical stakes in the outcome of various internal struggles for power.

support at home and is consequently less interested in mounting an elaborate justification, beyond deflecting international reactions and positing its security concerns. Such a state can also reverse its course more readily since it has not mobilized its citizenry in such a way as to be entrapped by their expectations. If the state is democratic, however, it must persuade its citizenry of the merits of an interventionary policy, especially if resistance is expected in the target society, casualties are anticipated as a distinct possibility, and there is no assurance of a rapid end to hostilities. Once persuaded, however, the termination of an intervention may be politically problematic as it could involve an acknowledgment of failure that has cost the lives of citizens. The United States has assumed much of the interventionary leadership both during the Cold War and since its conclusion, and has a particular need to rest its policy on a firm platform of public acceptance — a position that was greatly solidified during the definitive interventionary experience of this era, namely the Vietnam War.

Historical memory is also of crucial relevance, as is its most authoritative construction. It is common knowledge how governmental attitudes toward national security policy and resultant international behavior in the West were shaped after 1945 by "the lessons of Munich," and associated fears about "appeasement" and lack of military preparedness. Leaders and populations were educated about the importance of confronting early expressions of aggressive behavior, even in marginal settings, to avoid later having to deal with a more focused challenge to the established world order. Such a process of social learning was reinforced by America's lost innocence at Pearl Harbor. This realization of vulnerability to surprise attack by distant enemies was further reinforced by revolutionary technological developments associated with the means of waging war, above all by nuclear weaponry, but also by missiles, guidance and reconnaissance systems, as well as the advent of sophisticated submarines and long-range bomber aircraft.

Twenty-five years later, the Vietnam syndrome imparted a quite different message. Syllabi for social learning were updated to recognize that it is not worth the effort to address challenges in marginal arenas when the consequence is military frustration, serious division and demoralization in the core country and its allies, as well as magnified suffering and devastation in the target society. Since the Vietnam War, literally every American political leader, regardless of party or ideological orientation, has attempted to rally public support for recourse to military action in a manner that would erase the Vietnam syndrome from public consciousness once and for all, thereby removing one source of reluctance to use force in pursuit of national interests. In contrast, those opposed to interventionary diplomacy, especially those who felt harmed or betrayed by the Vietnam War have continued to regard the Vietnam syndrome as a useful cautionary inhibition upon interventionary impulses.

Such a preliminary assessment of interventionary diplomacy is lacking in historical specificity. Although interventionism has been a pervasive feature of international relations, its specific forms have varied with the times, and need to be so understood by reference to the global setting.

Interventionary diplomacy during the Cold War reflected the bipolar character of geopolitics and induced patterns of intervention that were based primarily on maintaining or disrupting ideological affiliations, especially in countries where geopolitical affinities were ambiguous and contested, and the risks of escalation seemed manageable.[11] It is revealing that the most globally dangerous instances of intervention occurred in relation to countries divided along ideological lines (Vietnam, Korea, China, and Germany) or in countries situated geographically close to one or the other superpower (Afghanistan and Cuba). Since 1989, however, the geopolitical pressures to intervene have weakened in most settings, while humanitarian pressures to intervene have strengthened.

Fundamentally, geopolitical and humanitarian pressures to intervene are of a radically different character. Both types of intervention have proved problematic given current realities about the military, economic, and political capabilities needed for an effective intervention and the extent and character of support and political will required to sustain an interventionary effort until its goals are reached. The failure of geopolitical intervention is associated mainly with its inability to overcome indigenous nationalist forces of resistance, particularly when reinforced diplomatically and militarily by counter-interventionary capabilities. The failure of humanitarian intervention, however, arises mainly because of the relatively shallow commitment on the intervening side, thereby simplifying the tactics of resistance even in the absence of counter-interventionary support.[12]

11. In essence, interventionary rivalry between the superpowers was encouraged on the periphery while avoided at the core; serious confrontations occurred in Vietnam, Korea, and Afghanistan, but not in Eastern Europe or Central America. The tense moments occurred in circumstances of uncertainty as in the Cuban Missile Crisis or with respect to access to Berlin. Governing elites in Moscow and Washington learned that testing the will of their adversary in such settings was dangerous and should be avoided.

12. To the extent that the intervention is genuinely humanitarian, in its essence, it tends to be "shallow." Shallow here means that it arises from an assessment that the mission can be completed successfully on the basis of a modest commitment of resources and without incurring serious risks of substantial loss of lives on the part of the intervening side. In

Closely related to this shift in the justifying discourse, is an apparent change in political backing. The geopolitically oriented interventions represent the outgrowth of an assessment of strategic interests by government leaders who then mobilize public support for an interventionary policy. In contradistinction, humanitarian interventions result from societal pressures, recently enhanced by a more globalized media, that finally compel a reluctant political leadership to act against its sense of the national interest, but to limit its commitments to the extent possible politically. Recent trends toward transferring formal responsibility to the United Nations can be seen as a mechanism to defuse societal pressures to act while avoiding an open-ended interventionary commitment.

Because interventionary diplomacy, especially if lacking strong geopolitical motives and sufficient capabilities, is likely to fail, the reputation of the United Nations in the field of peace and security has declined, temporarily at least. Much of this decline has been related to the perceived failures of the United Nations to respond to humanitarian emergencies in such countries as Somalia, Rwanda, Burundi, and most of all, Bosnia. This failure has been reinforced by the transfer of primary responsibility from the United Nations to NATO. This transfer is itself a complex, multi-faceted process, and can be viewed as one aspect of an approach adopted to induce the parties to agree finally, if precariously, upon a peace plan. The contrast between NATO's willingness to engage Serb resistance militarily, and the United Nations' reluctance to

contrast, an intervention that proceeds from a geopolitical rationale, even if it includes humanitarian aspects, tends to be much more open-ended with respect to the depth and breadth of the commitment. Geopolitical commitments that were characteristic of the Cold War era, exemplified by the wars in Vietnam and Afghanistan, involved massive interventions, but engendered intense nationalist forms of indigenous resistance reinforced by strong counter-interventionary responses by the superpower opposed to the success of intervention.

Another learning experience from the Cold War was that it was more hazardous to attempt a political restructuring of the target country than merely to pursue some particular objective involving a change of policy. The Gulf War is illustrative of a geopolitical intervention with humanitarian aspects. The United Nations provided the backing for the main interventionary claim, there was no prospect of significant counter-intervention, and the intervening side did not attempt the more ambitious task of political restructuring, and indeed, left Saddam Hussein as head of state despite demonizing him as the most abusive political leader since Hitler. What is relevant here is that the humanitarian aspect of the intervention was easily abandoned (that is, liberating the Iraqi people from an abusive leader and protecting the vulnerable Kurdish minority in northern Iraq and the Shi'a population in southern Iraq), especially as geopolitical calculations shifted once Iraq was removed from Kuwait and destroyed as a regional military threat. It was perceived that the main geopolitical priority was to keep Iraq united in order to contain Iran regarded as the other threat to Western interests in the region and to avoid an independent Kurdish state from further destabilizing Turkey. And, in fact, the aftermath of the Gulf War has had mainly perverse humanitarian effects as the maintenance of economic sanctions for several years has resulted in continuing casualties and hardships for the civilian population without seeming to weaken Saddam Hussein's hold over Iraq.

do so, has confirmed for many a view of United Nations ineffectiveness. Furthermore, in a crucial sense, even NATO's role was overshadowed in the peace process by the essentially unilateral character of United States diplomacy, epitomized by virtually locking up the leaders of Bosnia, Croatia, and the rump Yugoslavia in a military base in Dayton, Ohio until they finally reached an agreement. In effect, there exists now a *répertoire* of diplomatic tools and modalities for addressing humanitarian challenges, but none among them offers any strong promise of consistent success; indeed, the peace in Bosnia continues to hang precariously in the balance.

Finally, because states continue to be guided by a rather narrow conception of self-interest that does not extend to the well-being of foreign societies and their peoples, their unwillingness to intervene effectively in circumstances of great human urgency increasingly encourages independent grassroots initiatives to undertake humanitarian missions. An outstanding example of this expanding role is *Médecins sans Frontières*. More relevantly, the agents of humanitarian intervention are now often actors other than governments, especially transnational citizens associations, operating on a political logic that is shaped almost exclusively by moral considerations — largely an ethos of responsibility and solidarity — that is very different from the statist outlook that guides most governments when they are engaged in humanitarian missions. Of course, such generalizations need careful qualification. For instance, there are a series of governments of middle size, most notably those of the Scandinavian countries, Canada, and the Netherlands, that act in a more genuine humanitarian spirit, and subordinate *their* statist character to an identity shaped by the humanitarian imperative. At the same time, the capabilities and outlook of these transnational forces should not be romanticized. Some of these transnational actors are funded and otherwise dependent on one or more governments, and thus lack real independence. Also, if conflicts cross the threshold of large-scale violence, non-governmental actors generally lack the financial, diplomatic, and logistical means to address directly the core of the conflict or even to gain access to the participants.

The foregoing discussion supports the conclusion that the present status of interventionary initiatives is shaped by several realities:

- intervention in almost any foreign society is likely to entail important risks of failure for the intervening side;

- geopolitical factors may persuade leaders to take such risks, but humanitarian concerns are unlikely to do so even if backed up by strong political pressures;[13]
- defusing political pressures to alleviate human suffering without adopting a major interventionary commitment has encouraged reliance upon the United Nations;
- disillusionment with this pattern is likely to produce, at least temporarily, a reduced role for the United Nations, and greater reliance on regional actors, dominant states, and instances of an outright refusal to act;
- humanitarian concerns have also been stimulating significant transnational initiatives of a non-governmental character;
- the combination of media attention and the evolution of a human rights culture provide a coherent rationale for "humanitarian intervention" (that is, serious expectations that severe abuses of human rights, including acute economic and cultural deprivations, are matters of international concern that justify interventionary action and overcome otherwise restraining considerations associated with non-intervention commitments and attitudes); and
- this combination of developments in the last several years, especially in light of the human ordeal that has accompanied the dissolution of former Yugoslavia, has caused profound disillusionment with the capacity of the collective will in international society to protect vulnerable peoples against severe forms of abuse and suffering arising either from governmental aggression (Bosnia, Chechnya, East Timor, Tibet), acute ethnic strife (Bosnia, Rwanda, Burundi), or from governmental collapse (Somalia).

The questions raised by these realities are wide ranging. What should we learn from this dismal experience? How shall the interplay between interventionary diplomacy and international law be interpreted in light of both doctrinal formulations and the practice of states, international organizations, and transnational citizens associations? What is the legal standing of various claims of humanitarian intervention by different types of actors? How can the role of international law be strengthened without raising expectations too high? How can the constraining

13. The Gulf War discloses the relative priority of these two classes of concerns, providing an illustration of a massive geopolitical response and a minimal humanitarian response. *See supra* note 12 and accompanying text.

impact of geopolitics be acknowledged without undermining the relevance of international law?

II. Conceptual Ambiguities

Intervention is notoriously ambiguous as a legal term of art. It is used journalistically to describe all forms of influence projected primarily by governments of states (but more recently by other political actors, as well) in their interaction with one another. In general coinage, the term intervention has been reserved for situations in which a powerful state uses forcible means, characteristically including the use of military capabilities, to alter the policies or governing structures of weaker states. In geopolitical terms, intervention has been used to maintain traditional spheres of influence within the region of a powerful state, and more widely during the Cold War when the entire Third World became an arena for competitive interventionary diplomacy between the two superpowers.[14] The United States has frequently "intervened" over the course of many decades in the Caribbean and Central America to uphold its traditional control within this neighboring region — an interventionary pattern early formulated as a precept of foreign policy (The Monroe Doctrine). Nevertheless, the United States' interventionary character was somewhat disguised in each particular instance by lofty claims of protecting democracy and rescuing the people of a target society from an abusive government, and by invoking rather flimsy contentions of regional authorization. In the last several years, interventions in Grenada, Nicaragua, Panama, and Haiti have all been justified in such humanitarian terms with varying degrees of credibility.

But are each of these instances properly regarded as interventions from the perspective of international law? When a government gives its clear and uncoerced consent to the initiative of another country it removes a large part of the interventionary taint. Of course, ambiguities surround the authority to invite intervention and the genuineness of the invitation. Most recently, it is contended that when the people of the target country seek protection from their own government, their approval of interventionary action is equivalent to consent, and has the effect of removing, or at least qualifying, the interventionary taint.[15] Also, as

---

14. Regional politics is quite distinct, in many instances, from global geopolitics. Egypt's intervention in Yemen, Iran's intervention in Dhofar, and India's intervention in Bhutan and Sikkim were connected mainly with hegemonic ambitions of regional scope.

15. For influential formulations along these lines see Anthony D'Amato, *The Invasion of Panama Was a Lawful Response to Tyranny*, 84 Am. J. Int'l L. 516 (1990); W. Michael Reisman, *Coercion and Self-Determination: Construing Article 2(4)*, 78 Am. J. Int'l L. 642

in Haiti, the essentially unilateral move made by the United States to restore the elected government to power was undertaken with the blessing and collaboration of the United Nations Security Council after sustained brutality by a military regime that had usurped power from the elected civilian leadership.[16] Given the opinion of the International Court of Justice in the *Lockerbie* case[17] that there is no review of Security Council action taken within the formal scope of its authority, it would seem that any initiatives endorsed by the Security Council are effectively immunized from interventionary accusations of a legal character, at least as mounted *within* the United Nations.[18] Even the manifestly unilateral intervention by the United States in Grenada in 1983 was allegedly regionalized by reliance on the mandate of a previously unknown political actor, the Organization of Eastern Caribbean States. In a sense, such reliance on multilateral authorization is both an acknowledgment of respect for prohibitions on unilateral intervention and a dubious manipulation of this prohibition through the use of a multilateralizing figleaf. When the Soviet Union relied on similar tactics to mask its unilateralism in Eastern Europe during the Cold War, the interventionary pretexts of "invitation" or Warsaw Pact authorization were dismissed in the West as crude deceptions unworthy of rebuttal.

What, then, should be deemed to be intervention from the perspective of international law? Consent can be coerced or manufactured; public approval can be claimed, or highly contingent and unreliable. It is impossible to be too rigorous in abstract legal terms about the doctrinal contours of interventionary practice. Whenever an external agency acts coercively to alter the governing structure or orientation of a sovereign state, an interference with sovereign rights occurs, such that a challenge

---

(1984); W. Michael Reisman, *Sovereignty and Human Rights in International Law*, 84 AM. J. INT'L L. 866 (1990); but compare the strong opposing argument of Sarah A. Rumage, *Panama and the Myth of Humanitarian Intervention in U.S. Foreign Policy: Neither Legal Nor Moral, Neither Just Nor Right*, 10 ARIZ. J. INT'L & COMP. L. 1 (1993).

16. For analysis see Richard Falk, *The Haiti Intervention: A Dangerous World Order Precedent for the United Nations*, 36 HARV. INT'L L.J. 341 (1995).

17. *See* Case Concerning Questions of Interpretation and Application of the 1971 Montreal Convention Arising from the Aerial Incident at Lockerbie (Libya v. U.S.), 1992 I.C.J. 114 (Provisional Measures Order of Apr. 14), *reprinted in* 31 I.L.M. 665 (1992).

18. Obviously, it is still possible to challenge the legality of United Nations sponsored initiatives by reference to the constraining principle of "domestic jurisdiction" embodied in Article 2(7) of the U.N. Charter, but what seems unlikely is that such challenges can be successfully mounted before the International Court of Justice, given its current reluctance to review judicially the acts of the Security Council. The Court is not bound by its own precedents, and so would technically be capable of taking a different approach to contested Security Council action in the future. *See* STATUTE OF THE INTERNATIONAL COURT OF JUSTICE art. 59.

of some sort is directed at unconditional non-intervention norms. But if the governing process has collapsed or is widely perceived as engaged in massive and gross violations of human rights amounting to "crimes against humanity," especially if there is a genocidal element present, then the moral and legal requirements for intervention are surely satisfied. This is clear especially if humanitarian concerns are not intertwined with economic and strategic interests as would be the case if the target country was an important oil supplier, site of foreign investment or military base, or located in a geographically strategic place. A well-founded humanitarian claim to act can be explained either as an exception to the prohibition on non-intervention or a suspension of such a prohibition in light of the illegitimacy of the territorial government or, alternatively, the existence of anarchic conditions of brutality and chaos.

Let us consider, then, situations in which there is widespread acceptance among governments and the public that the proclaimed goal of coercive action is to alleviate suffering of the people in the target society that arises from either the breakdown of government (the so-called "failed state" problem) or by policies being pursued by governments that violate fundamental human rights of part or all of the society. In such settings, we speak generally and appropriately about "humanitarian intervention." Actually, because of the interventionary taint, especially in the ex-colonial regions, other less evocative terms of art are generally relied upon by the supporters of coercive initiatives, such as "humanitarian assistance," "humanitarian operation," and "humanitarian diplomacy." Problems of this sort cannot be dealt with properly by semantic evasion. The essence of these projects still is crossing international borders and acting within a country, allegedly to help people in a condition of acute distress. It is interventionary in this fundamental sense, and for this reason, the terminology of humanitarian intervention remains with us. Of course, underpinning the political language relied upon by participants in the discussion of policy responses to humanitarian emergencies of various sorts exist controversies that arise from different factual assessments and different perceptions regarding the mix of motives attributed to the intervening actors. As already mentioned, the range of actors participating in such an undertaking includes humanitarian non-governmental organizations, international institutions, as well as states. The range of possible motives is at least as diverse.

III. The Jurisprudential Predicament

Most of the international literature on intervention ignores geopolitical pressures and constraints. This failure has several serious consequences for our capacity to understand and act in specific situations. Part of the neglect of geopolitics is a matter of apologetics and part is a matter of wishful thinking.[19]

The apologetic part overlooks the extent to which interventionary claims are exclusively mounted by powerful states that have often in the past put forward self-serving rationalizations for their questionable uses of force to coerce weaker countries with what appear to be anti-humanitarian net effects. A recent controversial instance would be the economic coercion maintained by the United States against Cuba for several decades in the form of sanctions. It is rather strange that those international law specialists who think of themselves as realists when describing the predominance of power in international society tend still to talk as if the most powerful states in the world can be taken at face value when they purport to act as altruistic agents of change with respect to the assertion and implementation of humanitarian claims.[20] Neither international relations nor practice lends much support to such a benevolent role for great powers, nor, it should be added, does the evidence support the opposite view that geopolitically motivated action will never confer humanitarian benefits. Conclusions either way are persuasive only to the extent that their assessment is particularized by reference to the characteristics and effects of particular interventionary claims. Humanitarian factors are rarely, if ever, decisive in shaping an interventionary decision of any magnitude, although governments will often rely in public on an essentially humanitarian rationale for intervention. Such reliance is especially characteristic of intervention under the auspices of the United Nations in the years since 1989. It is partly an empirical, partly an interpretative, and partly an archival matter to assess the genuineness of such humanitarian claims, but it does not resolve the further concern as to whether intervention is legally permissible if humanitarian.

When Vietnam invaded Cambodia in 1975, presumably for security reasons, but effectively removed a genocidal regime from power, it was widely condemned. Vietnam was called upon to withdraw by the United Nations despite the danger, that by so doing, it would revive the influence of the Khmer Rouge. In fact, the successor Cambodian government, installed as a result of the Vietnamese intervention, was precluded

---

19. This distinction owes a great deal to MARTTI KOSKENNIEMI, FROM APOLOGY TO UTOPIA: THE STRUCTURE OF INTERNATIONAL LEGAL ARGUMENT (1989).

20. Compare, for instance the realist tone of THOMAS M. FRANCK, NATION AGAINST NATION (1985) with his support for an emergent norm entitling peoples to democratic forms of governance in Thomas M. Franck, *The Emerging Right to Democratic Governance*, 86 AM. J. INT'L L. 46, 63 (1992).

from representing Cambodia in the United Nations. The anti-Vietnam posture was based on geopolitical calculations in the face of the extremity of humanitarian considerations: it was deemed more important, in effect, to avoid the extension of Vietnamese influence and to placate China (then hostile to Vietnam) than to relieve the people of Cambodia from the grotesque burden imposed on their lives by the Khmer Rouge regime. Such priorities may seem extreme, but they are not anomalous when it comes to disclosing the relative impact of geopolitical and humanitarian claims on the behavior of leading states, and through their influence, of international institutions under their control.

There is another kind of geopolitical pressure operative in the years since the end of the Cold War: the *avoidance* of intervention even in the face of extreme humanitarian emergencies. The United States has been in the critical role of decisive leader with respect to the clarification of geopolitical concerns. Since its experience of encountering violent resistance in Somalia, followed by a domestic firestorm of criticism, there has existed a Mogadishu syndrome suggesting that humanitarian interventions that take the form of ground forces risk serious military confrontations. In reaction, the United States has scaled back drastically its willingness to act, directly or indirectly, to restore peace and normalcy to afflicted societies except by way of applying diplomatic muscle to hasten negotiations among adversaries as in Bosnia, the Middle East, and even Northern Ireland.[21] This reluctance by the United States has also expressed itself in terms of rigid limits on the duration of its commitment even to the implementation of the Dayton Agreement that it brokered, on an unwillingness to make open-ended financial commitments in such settings, and by a particularly notable resistance to desperate requests for even low-level United Nations operations to prevent the renewal of genocidal violence in Rwanda and its further outbreak in Burundi. Thus, in some important sense, the geopolitics of humanitarian intervention has recently worked mainly to *discourage* action at the regional or global levels premised on responses that are reflective of attitudes of collective responsibility and compassion. It is almost paradoxical that it is this anti-interventionary geopolitical mood that has been subject to as much critical commentary as the interventionism associated with geopolitics in general, and American foreign policy, in particular.[22]

21. It also lends support to preventive efforts as in Macedonia where a symbolic military presence under United Nations auspices has so far successfully sought to avoid any spillover of the warfare that could spread the conflicts in Bosnia and Croatia.

22. *See* RICHARD J. BARNET, INTERVENTION AND REVOLUTION: THE UNITED STATES ROLE IN THE THIRD WORLD (1968); *see also* KOLKO, *supra* note 9.

There is also the utopian side of the ledger in these settings, with moralists and legalists naively urging governments to do what is right without any feeling for the political constraints that surround such demands. One result is frustration and bitterness that comes with the inevitable discovery that governments will not, in general, act in a substantive manner against their material interests. This has been the unhappy fate of East Timor and Tibet, forcibly and brutally annexed against the clearly expressed will of their peoples. At the same time, agitation by transnational civil groups on such issues prevents the legitimation of oppressive arrangements that cannot be reconciled with minimal conceptions of self-determination and human rights. The basic compromise in these settings is avoidance of substantive opposition, but engagement in some sort of symbolic action that to varying degrees withholds complete legitimation. Another result of utopian thinking is terrible disappointment with the role of international law: finding it impotent to overcome the torments of peoples, and entire nations trapped in humanitarian emergencies. Both effects tend to divert attention from the constructive, if modest, roles of international law, as well as from the contributions that can be made on other avenues seeking to exert political influence.

In essence, the only way to induce action in support of such humanitarian claims is to generate enough countervailing power to overcome geopolitical inhibitions. Domestic protest in the key countries of the United Kingdom and the United States, succeeded in doing this with respect to instituting a sanctions campaign to weaken *apartheid* during the early 1980s, thereby providing the political context for an effective transnational campaign that drew upon humanitarian arguments but did not rely upon them to achieve change. In this regard, mobilized domestic and transnational pressures responsive to humanitarian emergencies can alter the geopolitical calculus to a considerable extent, especially as most political leaders are preoccupied with maintaining domestic power. A famous instance, the interpretation of which is itself a matter of continuing controversy, involved the level of United States support for the early period of Israeli statehood — prior to 1967 after which Israel became more of a strategic partner — despite the risk of weakening crucial ties with oil-rich Arab countries in the Middle East. Obviously, the impact on geopolitical calculations is greatest in a democratic country where a well-financed, deeply committed constituency imaginatively mobilizes its resources for a sharply focused campaign. The impact is particularly heightened where the same constituency has enough of a perceived connection to domestic political balances to exert pressure that will confine foreign policy within rigid parameters that make little geopolitical sense if considered purely by reference to international goals. The Cuban exile community has been remarkably effective in its efforts to maintain United States pressures on Castro's Cuba despite the undermining, since 1989, of geopolitical pretexts for a hostile relationship.

If international law, following the broad outlines of the New Haven approach associated with the work of Myres McDougal, Harold Lasswell, and more recently, Michael Reisman, is to be associated with some kind of conjointness between the authority to act and the capacity to implement, then the application of international law to the theory and practice of humanitarian intervention is highly problematic *in the current global setting.*[23] Recent experience in Somalia, Rwanda, Liberia, Burundi, Chechnya, and most of all, Bosnia and Croatia, is suggestive of both the growth of authoritative claims to act on behalf of the international community and of the absence of the capabilities to translate those claims with any consistency into outcomes that vindicate the undertaking. There is, thus, a serious gap between claim and performance with a tendency to deform the implementing policy and its agents of enactment.

Important questions ensue. Does this suggest the wisdom of a higher threshold of non-intervention despite the presence of humanitarian wrongs that need to be corrected? Does it also underscore the importance of differentiating actions by states and inter-state actors such as the United Nations and NATO from transnational civic initiatives that are carried out by independent associations of citizens?

At issue, also, is the fundamental Westphalian question of representation. It has been useful and generally reliable to treat the constituted government as the authoritative representative of the people — the "subject" of international law. Furthermore, with reason, the manipulation of counter-elites to obtain invitations and mandates to intervene, which was standard Soviet practice (as in Czechoslovakia in 1968 and Afghanistan in 1979), reinforced the view that only the legitimate, internationally recognized government has the authority to grant consent for the entry of an outside force with an interventionary mission. But this neat Westphalian view has been eroding in a variety of respects as a result of recent practice. For one thing, if the oppressed people of a country can validate interventionary force by welcoming their own

23. See Hedley Bull's important argument that international society lacks sufficient solidarity at this time to support collective ventures for the public good on a global level such as humanitarian intervention or criminal accountability of government officials. Hedley Bull, *The Grotian Conception of International Society*, *in* DIPLOMATIC INVESTIGATIONS 51 (Herbert Butterfield & Martin Wight eds., 1966).

liberation, then the voice of formal governmental authority can be cast aside rather abruptly; such is the implication of an alleged emerging right of democracy or the state-shattering practice of self-determination accompanying the break-up of the Soviet Union and former Yugoslavia.[24] Also, if there has been a collapse of government, there is no authority to grant or withhold consent, and forcible entry can be claimed, as it has been, by reference to the objective conditions of complex humanitarian emergency. But what if those empowered to represent are also the perpetrators of crimes against humanity? These leaders are simultaneously treated as negotiating partners and potential war criminals. This is the puzzle created by the 1995 Dayton Peace Agreement. It suggests that diplomacy should be less confined to its traditional governmental parameters. Instead of treating only figures such as Karadzic and Milošević as negotiating partners, there should have been discussions with "representatives" of these peoples who did not endorse or participate in crimes of state or seek to establish states along ethnically pure lines. The feasibility of such an alternative course of action is uncertain at best. Government leaders, even if associated with criminal practices, may alone possess representational capacity by having sufficient control over the sentiments and capabilities of the peoples, and it would be meaningless to deny their representational authority. Such an acknowledgment of realities has led to the acceptance of both the PLO and the IRA as necessary participants in their respective peace processes, but without the Bosnian overlay of potential indictment for previous anti-humanitarian activity.

Once that overlay exists, as is the case in relation to Bosnia, it poses a fearful dilemma: the intention to prosecute those responsible for war crimes seemingly can neither be dispensed with, nor implemented. And this indeterminacy imperils the move from war to peace, and makes the process appear vindictive to some, hypocritical to others. It is notable that even with the resumption of IRA terrorism in February 1996, there are no suggestions from responsible negotiating actors that perpetrators be treated as "war criminals" because in this instance the British government has sought to protect the population by a substantive commitment rather than abandon protection and offer those exposed to violence the symbolic solace of a future war crimes tribunal.[25]

24. This recent self-determination practice means that in situations other than decolonization peoples previously entrapped within a state have been acknowledged by the international community as entitled to engage in struggle to establish by an act of secession their own independent state. These developments are difficult to assess as they have also been the occasion for establishing "ethnic states" that are violently and cruelly "cleansed."

25. Such an observation is not to be confused with an overall endorsement of the British role; indeed, Prime Minister Major's tilt toward Unionist sentiments in Ulster for domestic

This issue of reconciling Westphalian notions of representation and legitimacy with post-Westphalian ideas of personal criminal accountability of agents of state power is at the very center of the difficulties surrounding the contemporary compromise between geopolitics and morality in the setting of "humanitarian intervention." The move to institute war crimes proceedings *in this instance* of Bosnia (and more casually, Rwanda) reflected the relative unwillingness of the great powers to use their capabilities directly, by way of the United Nations or NATO, to prevent ethnic cleansing in former Yugoslavia or genocide in Rwanda and Bosnia between 1991 and 1994. Being unwilling to act substantively when it counted most, the political pressures to act *in some manner acknowledging the humanitarian challenge* produced a variety of symbolic gestures, including the establishment of a war crimes tribunal at The Hague, an arms embargo, sanctions against Serbia, safe havens in Bosnia. These gestures had a range of effects, but overall, an ambiguous, if not a perverse, impact on the underlying wrongdoing. They shared the common feature of responding for the sake of humanitarian goals but not being committed to devoting major resources to increase prospects that the response would be effective.

The standoff between the authority to intervene and the lack of capabilities to do so effectively raises serious questions about support for the purported legality (and even morality) of given instances of humanitarian intervention. Indirectly, as well, it suggests that *at this stage of international society*, the doctrine of non-intervention provides a generally more constructive foundation for exerting the influence of international law than does an emphasis of the sort contained in Secretary-General Boutros Ghali's oft-quoted passage in *An Agenda for Peace* to the effect that sovereignty in the sense of territorial supremacy is eroding as a principle of world order. This softening of deference to the sovereignty of the territorial state is not a mere jurisprudential quibble. The policy concerns here are at least four-fold, and are not altogether internally consistent:

- upholding the sovereign rights of weak states, by stripping further the pretensions of legality away from interventionary diplomacy of an essentially geopolitical character, as was the case with the Panama intervention of 1989, that is, protecting

---

political gain in British elections may well have upset the balance within the IRA that had earlier opted for a cease-fire combined with the prospect of all-party negotiations. On the misuse by Britain of the political space during the cease-fire to pursue "the war" by other means, see the insightful article by Martin Woollacott, *Finding the Bone of Contention*, THE GUARDIAN, Feb. 17, 1996, at 22.

states against dubious interventionary claims even if backed by some humanitarian considerations;[26]

- avoiding punishing the victims and weakening tendencies toward reconciliation, by acknowledging the inability and unwillingness of leading states and international institutions (as now constituted) of an inter-governmental character to intervene effectively for predominantly humanitarian purposes in most circumstances of acute distress;[27]
- challenging the artificial line of sovereign deference that is now drawn to give Russian intervention in Chechnya or Iraqi intervention against the Kurdish regions of northern Iraq, a different, more internal legal and geopolitical status than Russian intervention in Georgia, or formerly, in the countries of Eastern Europe; and
- accepting the view that despite the unevenness of international practice, it remains beneficial to maintain maximum and flexible support for the alleviation of suffering and the establishment of peace, and thus abiding a highly selective, and inconsistent, doctrine of humanitarian intervention.

This line of analysis suggests a reconvergence of authority and effectiveness in relation to humanitarian claims as evaluated in context, thereby reinforcing not only sovereign rights and norms of non-intervention, but also endorsing a limited option of humanitarian intervention. Such an approach opens the way for humanitarian assistance in many, but not all, circumstances, and recognizes that the actors in the current phase of the Westphalian structure must often make tragic choices between diplomacies of interventionism and reconciliation. In the absence of strong strategic interests on the part of major states, or the existence of a mobilized domestic constituency that is pushing humanitarian concerns onto the foreign policy agenda in a manner that overcomes a purely geopolitical assessment of interests, only a diplomacy of reconciliation remains viable.[28]

26. *See* Rumage, *supra* note 15.

27. Humanitarian interventions might become more feasible in a wider class of instances if the United Nations or a regional actor were given the financial and peacekeeping resources to act with far greater independence of geopolitical priorities. Reconceiving geopolitics to incorporate acute humanitarian emergencies for the sake of overall global stability and investor confidence could be viewed as another *modus operandi*. The essence of this point is grasped by comparing the mobilization of resources to address the Iraqi challenge in the Gulf crisis with that occurring in response to the Serb challenge in Bosnia.

28. As argued, such pressures can work for or against intervention, and in normative terms, are a "wild card" played in specific circumstances.

In advocating such a position, it is obvious that major, and likely unfortunate, uncertainties exist in relation to the adoption of a more permissive approach to interventionary options. No one can answer the "what if" questions about various recommended interventionary initiatives alleged to support humanitarian goals. Would an early NATO action of bombing the gun emplacements around Sarajevo have lifted the siege sooner and led to a quicker, less devastating "peace"? Or would such action have led to a bloody Serbian retaliation against vulnerable United Nations forces prompting their removal or to a spread of the violence to new arenas in the Balkans?[29] Did the creation of the safe havens negligently contribute to ethnic cleansing and the containment of refugees or was it a genuine good faith effort to provide sanctuary and protection for a portion of the entrapped Muslim population of Bosnia? Clearly the inability to defend adequately several of the six safe havens contributed to the impression of United Nations impotence and responsibility, and probably suggested that had the level of Serb aggressiveness been anticipated, support for the safe haven concept would not have been forthcoming. These fundamental issues are what postmodernists (in the deconstructionist mode) are fond of calling "undecidables." The vigorous debates generated by them reveal little about the probabilities and much about the sensibilities of participants in the debate.[30]

IV. Making Humanitarian Intervention Humanitarian

My argument has been that with the end of the Cold War there has been a notable shift in interventionary diplomacy away from purely geopolitical interventionism in the direction of support for humanitarian claims to alleviate human suffering. This shift has been expressed especially strongly in United States foreign policy, both as directly

29. The retrospective claims made in light of NATO bombs bringing the Serbs to Dayton need to be tempered by the realization that their impact occurred after Milošević had abandoned maximalist Serb goals in the war and after the military buildup of Croatia and Bosnia changed the realities on the ground. Without a far more detailed analysis of causal responses at various stages of the conflict it is exceedingly difficult to draw any firm conclusions about what would have happened had bombing occurred sooner. What is clear is that the United States and other actors undertaking such earlier bombing would have had to be bureaucratically prepared in advance to cope effectively with the political fallout arising from possible failure of bombing to achieve its intended results and with possible Serb retaliatory actions.

30. To some extent the deontologically minded are drawn to positions that seem intrinsically right, acting to oppose ethnic cleansing; while the consequentially minded are drawn to positions that seem contextually sound, given likely effects of proposed actions. Some combination of perspectives is probably most likely to produce results that are both responsible and responsive; the appropriate combination is impossible to codify in any useful way.

enacted, and as channelled through the United Nations, and to some extent, NATO.

From a purely normative perspective of law and morality, this shift in interventionary practice is a welcome development. But it has foundered in key instances because it was based on a shallow commitment of resources and will, underestimating the burdens associated with carrying humanitarian diplomacy successfully to term. Earlier geopolitical interventions had also frequently failed because they engendered a combination of indigenous, nationalist resistance and counter-intervention organized by opposed geopolitical actors. Thus, interventionary success cannot be equated talismanically with money, weapons, or even ground forces.

Interventionary experience suggests a number of conclusions with respect to humanitarian emergencies. First, the best opportunity, given available levels of capability, to avoid acute suffering is normally for states to become seriously engaged in a preventive role. Such a role can include providing a symbolic presence, substantial economic relief, and making constructive diplomatic intermediary services available to the troubled states. Second, external encouragement of nationalist tendencies toward self-determination needs to be balanced effectively by adequate protection of human rights.[31] Third, once battlefield results have produced a stalemate or antagonists have reached a point of disillusionment with armed struggle, outside diplomatic moves and military forces can play a valuable catalytic role in encouraging and implementing a peace process. Fourth, during the phases of most intense humanitarian emergency, in the absence of a suitable interventionary response by states and international institutions, a maximal effort should be made to support transnational and grassroots initiatives — especially those with a non-violent, reconciling orientation — without compromising their independence. Fifth, a critical geopolitics is needed to convince those who dominate decisions over the allocation of resources, that investments in conflict-prevention, human rights (including economic, social, and cultural, as well as civil and political), and conflict-resolution are conducive to global stability and prosperity; whether such a critical geopolitics is presented as "a new realism" or as an abandonment of realism is not

31. The German recognition of Croatia and Slovenia in 1991 was in this sense anti-humanitarian even if it did support strong majoritarian claims of self-determination. Ethnically or religiously mobilized majorities pose severe human rights challenges to dissident minorities, especially as in Croatia and Bosnia, where varying interpretations of recent historical experience engendered plausible fears and established political space for opportunistic politicians to play their own minority nationalist card as Milošević did to such devastating effect in both Croatia and Bosnia.

of great importance *vis-à-vis* altering the makeup of decisions and understanding what counts for individual and collective well-being at this stage of international political life.

It is the contention of this paper that these five directions of policy have been insufficiently emphasized in the years since 1989. The consequence has been an unhealthy move from an initial unfounded enthusiasm for "humanitarian intervention" to a more recent unwarranted disillusionment. As a result, even allowing for some specific successes and mixed outcomes, the net impact of humanitarian diplomacy has been perceived to be, and in several instances has been, anti-humanitarian. The challenge now is to rededicate our energies to increase the prospect of humanitarian interventions serving humanitarian goals. Until this can be done, the failure of humanitarian intervention since 1989 will be generally interpreted as far outweighing the successes, and seem likely to continue for the foreseeable future to produce a renewal of support for the ethos of non-interventionism.

[21]

The Use of Force in International Law

Thomas M. Franck*

I. THE CHARTER AND CHANGE 7
II. INTERPRETING INTERPRETATION 11
III. THE "JURYING" FUNCTION 14

I. THE CHARTER AND CHANGE

The U.N. Charter is, at once, a freeze-frame of historically validated principles and the foundation for a dynamic political and administrative institution.

At the center of the freeze frame is what International Court of Justice Judge Sir Hersch Lauterpacht called the guiding norm of the U.N. enterprise: "there shall be no violence." The Security Council, General Assembly, and International Court are the curators of that norm. At the same time, they are also the intendants of a continually dynamic, evolving institution imbued with a spirit of relevance, one in which the emphasis is on practical problem-solving rather than formal doctrinal exegesis.

---

* Murry and Ida Becker Professor of Law, NYU School of Law; S.J.D. and LL.M., Harvard Law School; LL.D. (honorary) and L.B., University of British Columbia; President of the American Society of International Law (1998-2000); Member of the editorial board and former editor in chief of the *American Journal of International Law*; Member of the *Institute de droit international*; Member of the Council of Foreign Relations, and board member of Africa Watch.

Professor Franck has published prodigiously, with more than two dozen books on international law and relations, comparative law, and constitutional law to his credit. Several of these volumes have been awarded a Certificate of Merit by the American Society of International Law. His most recent work is RECOURSE TO FORCE: STATE ACTION AGAINST THREATS AND ARMED ATTACKS (Cambridge Univ. Press 2002).

Additionally, Professor Franck has served as legal advisor and counsel to a number of foreign governments. Presently he is a Judge *Ad Hoc* in a case before the International Court of Justice.

This implies that the meaning of the Charter does evolve as it is applied to practical situations. In particular, it suggests that the practices of U.N. organs are a reliable guide to the Organization's future directions. These principal organs deal with, and try to diminish, the incidence and consequences of humankind's seemingly incorrigible proclivity for violence. To this end, they implement the processes and procedures of the Charter and, in doing so, adapt its text to the exigencies of each crisis.

This is not unintended. In 1945, at San Francisco, it was decided by the key drafting committee that

> In the course of the operations from day to day of the various organs of the Organization, it is inevitable that each organ will interpret such parts of the Charter as are applicable to its particular functions. This process . . . will be manifested in the functioning of such a body as the General Assembly, the Security Council, or the International Court of Justice.[1]

It is significant that this statement makes the political bodies co-equal to the Court in construing Charter text. From this, Professor (Judge) Rosalyn Higgins has deduced "that the authority to decide upon disputed questions of the interpretation of the Charter belongs to the organ charged with their application."[2]

Thus, each organ acts as judge of its own competence and *modus operandi*. There is no need to amend the Charter, a formal process of great difficulty. The Charter evolves through the persistent and principled practice of its principal organs.

It need not have been that way. Greece, at San Francisco, proposed that the International Court be designated the sole arbiter of the Charter's meaning.[3] Although the proposal obtained the support of seventeen out of thirty-one votes in committee, this was not the two-thirds majority needed to amend the draft text.[4] Consequently, it may be said, with only mild overstatement, the Charter *is* what the principal organs *do*.

What they do tends to be governed, in part, by their concern for institutional effectiveness and relevance, but, perhaps even more, by the self-interest of the member states. This, then, is not the judicial process, with its formal focus on impartiality and principled consistency.

---

1. *Report of the Rapporteur of Committee IV/2, as Approved by the Committee*, Doc. 933, IV/2/42(2), 13 U.N.C.I.O. Docs. 703, 709 (1945), *reprinted in* THE UNITED NATIONS CONFERENCE ON INTERNATIONAL ORGANIZATION: SELECTED DOCUMENTS 875, 879 (U.S. Gov't Printing Office 1946).
2. ROSALYN HIGGINS, THE DEVELOPMENT OF INTERNATIONAL LAW THROUGH THE POLITICAL ORGANS OF THE UNITED NATIONS 66 (Oxford Univ. Press 1963).
3. *Id.*
4. *Id.* at 66 n.27.

Neither is it a Symposium. At San Francisco, the Netherlands proposed "an independent body of eminent men . . . known for their integrity . . . who should be available to pronounce [on] a decision of the Security Council . . . solely from the point of view of whether [it] is in keeping with . . . moral principles. . . ."[5] However high-minded, that proposal garnered almost no support.[6] Instead, the process of implementing, and thereby interpreting, the Charter has remained steadfastly political.

This is not to say, however, that the political organs' activities have had no law-making *effect*. On the contrary. How these organs have applied the Charter in actual instances is the best guide to what the text means now, and how it will evolve in the proximate future.

That the Charter is primarily interpreted by political bodies of state-representatives is also not tantamount to conceding that Charter principles are inseparable from opportunistic application of narrowly defined state interest. The diplomats representing governments at the U.N., although mostly not lawyers, nevertheless are acutely aware that what they do in fact affects the system's normative parameters. There is, thus, an incongruous tendency in the U.N.'s political organs to talk legalese, to justify actions pursued for political ends by elaborately construing what the Charter says, or ought to mean. In this way, lawyer-like diplomats seek to manage the palpable tension between what, in a specific political context, may be the sensible course of action and its potential doctrinal consequences. They realize that each action they take, or do not take, has an afterlife as, that most legal of concepts, a *precedent*.

The Secretary-General has recently addressed this tension between what needs to be done and the normative constraints on doing it. In the aftermath of the genocide in Rwanda, he asked: suppose there had been a coalition of the willing able to act preemptively, but such action had been blocked by the opposition of a permanent member.[7] Would it have been better to sacrifice the Charter rules if it were possible thereby to save a multitude?[8] Or, if there had been a choice, would it in the long run have been better to sacrifice those lives to uphold the letter of the law?[9]

---

5. Suggestions Presented by the Netherlands Government Concerning the Proposals for the Maintenance of Peace and Security Agreed on at the Four Power Conference of Dumbarton Oaks as Published on Oct. 9, 1945, 313.

6. *Id.*

7. *Report of the Secretary-General on the Work of the Organization*, U.N. GAOR, 54th Sess., 4th plen. mtg., Agenda Item 10, at 2, U.N. Doc. A/54/PV.4 (1999).

8. *See id.*

9. *See id.*

What would be the costs to the system of allowing the rules to be bent or, in Secretary Annan's words, of "setting dangerous precedents for future interventions without a clear criterion to decide who might invoke these precedents and in what circumstances?"[10]

Annan's preference, in this dilemma, is to search for new criteria that would make the rules more responsive to contemporary challenges without altogether abandoning the Charter's normative constraints on the use of force.[11] Although it has lately taken on greater urgency, this is not a new quest. In 1945, at the San Francisco Conference, France proposed an amendment to the draft Charter that would have authorized states to intervene in another nation when "the clear violation of essential liberties and of human rights constitutes in itself a threat capable of compromising peace."[12] This was rejected as too broad and vague an exception to the Lauterpachtian "no violence" principle on which the new Charter was built.[13] As an exception to that rule, it lacked clear criteria and procedures for deciding who might invoke it and in what circumstances.

The dilemma was not resolved at San Francisco and it remains largely unaddressed, although not, thanks to Secretary Annan's efforts, unrecognized.[14] Understandably, because diplomats, politicians, and civil servants are not legal philosophers, governments have been reluctant to broach the subject, recognizing it is potentially a sticky tar-baby. And yet the practical conundrum, whether in any particular crisis to enforce the strict letter of the Charter or make an exception, arises repeatedly in U.N. deliberations and is addressed often, helter-skelter, obliquely, through myriad little decisions and indecisions, actions and inactions, whenever a state asserts a right to use force for justifiable ends without obtaining the prior U.N. authorization required by the Charter.

These crises call out for practical solutions, but solutions also set precedents, especially if an otherwise appropriate action inconveniently is prohibited by the basic rules of the U.N. system. When the then-American ambassador, Dr. Madeleine Albright, defending her country's 1994 invasion of Iraq as a selfless effort to save Kurdish lives, said that: we would prefer to act together with the U.N., but if necessary, we will

10. *Id.*
11. *See id.* at 3-4.
12. Doc. 207, III/2/A/3, 12 U.N.C.I.O. Docs. 179, 191 (1945).
13. *See id.*
14. *See, e.g.*, Barbara Crossette, *Canada Tries to Define Line Between Human and National Rights*, N.Y. TIMES, Sept. 14, 2000, at A11, *available at* 2000 WL 26778140.

act without it,[15] she must have been aware that her country was setting an open-ended precedent. That, lacking clear criteria and procedures, can be distorted to permit anything, under any circumstances, by anyone and thereby undermines a Charter system based on reciprocal respect for mutually agreed universally applicable rules.

The answer to the dilemma cannot be found in the simplistic choice between either sacrificing people to preserve insensitive rules, or sacrificing the law to do the right and sensible thing. Put that way, the dilemma is too stark. Rather, nations must engage in a discursive pursuit of new principles and procedures by which the right and sensible thing can be done within an agreed, flexible, but not meaningless legal framework.

The search for agreement on such a flexible yet principled normative framework may be furthered by paying close attention to the experiential wisdom gained in fifty-five years of the practice of the principal U.N. organs. As these have interpreted and applied their jurisdiction in practice, the Charter's black-letter text has become more tensile, evolving in accordance with functional criteria and procedures in response to new and unforeseen circumstances. Out of the tangle of institutional practice has emerged some flexible yet coherent interpretation of the Charter's foundational principles.

II. INTERPRETING INTERPRETATION

The practice of principal U.N. organs has generated new criteria and procedures regarding the use of force in some circumstances not envisaged by the Charter.

(1) When faced with aggression, the Charter system has authorized "coalitions of the willing" to act in place of collective force envisaged, but never established, under article 43;

-examples include Korea (1950),[16] Kuwait (1990),[17] Somalia (1992 and 1993),[18] and Haiti (1994).[19]

15. Barbara Crossette, *U.S. Is Demanding a Quick U.N. Vote on Iraqi Pullback*, N.Y. TIMES, Oct. 15, 1994, at A1.

16. *See, e.g.*, John M. Goshko, *Beleaguered U.N. Struggles to Maintain Peacekeeping Role*, WASH. POST, Oct. 22, 1995, at A24, *available at* 1995 WL 9268378.

17. *See, e.g.*, Thomas W. Lippman & Barton Gellman, *Cheney Ends Gulf Tour on Fiery Note; 'Days Drawing Closer' for Military Solution*, WASH. POST, Dec. 24, 1990, at A01, *available at* 1990 WL 2091049.

18. *See, e.g.*, Kathy Sawyer, *U.S. Officials Estimate Cost, Length of Somalia Mission; Humanitarian Operation Seen Taking 2 to 3 Months*, WASH. POST, Dec. 7, 1992, at A27, *available at* 1992 WL 2152730.

19. *See, e.g.*, Thomas W. Lippman, *White House Seeks Talks on War Powers; Clinton Aide Calls for End of Fight Between Branches*, WASH. POST, Oct. 25, 1994, at A12, *available at* 1994 WL 2447333.

(2) When peacekeeping action has been blocked by a veto in the Security Council, the General Assembly has sometimes assumed coordinate jurisdiction to authorize similar collective measures;
-an example is the UNEF operation in Sinai (1956).[20]

(3) In some circumstances, the Charter system has condoned retaliatory action by a state against terrorists or insurgents operating from a neighboring or other state;
-examples include the Israeli action in Sinai (1956),[21] Turkey's in Iraq (1995),[22] and the action of the U.S. against Afghanistan in 2001.[23]

(4) In some circumstances, the Charter system has condoned a state's use of force to rescue its endangered citizens abroad;
-examples include Israel's Entebbe raid (1976)[24] and U.S. action against the Achille Lauro hijackers (1985).[25]

(5) In some circumstances, the Charter system has condoned a state's recourse to force to preempt an imminent attack on it;
-an example is the Israeli war against Egypt (1967).[26]

(6) In some circumstances, the Charter system has condoned a state's use of force to redress a long-standing, egregious wrong committed against itself;
-examples include the Israeli kidnapping of Adolf Eichmann (1960),[27] the Indian invasion of Goa (1961)[28] and Turkey's invasion of Cyprus (1974).[29]

---

20. *See, e.g.*, C.V. Narasimhan, Editorial, *The Problem of Palestine*, HINDU, Dec. 18, 2000, *available at* 2000 WL 30164799.

21. *See, e.g.*, Dan Burton, Commentary, *Crucial Role for the U.S.*, WASH. TIMES, Oct. 28, 1991, at E1, *available at* 1991 WL 6701165.

22. *See, e.g.*, Nicole Watts, *Panned Abroad, Turkey's Iraq Incursion Is a Hit at Home/Drive Against Kurd Rebels Winds Down*, S.F. CHRON., Apr. 26, 1995, at A8, *available at* 1995 WL 5279176.

23. *See, e.g.*, Editorial, *Long and Difficult*, WASH. POST, Oct. 28, 2001, at B06, *available at* 2001 WL 29758014.

24. *See, e.g.*, Michael Byers, *Unleashing Force*, WORLD TODAY, Dec. 1, 2001, *available at* 2001 WL 13346555.

25. *See, e.g.*, Fred Hiatt & Dale Russakoff, *Four Bunglers Shake the Global Community*, WASH. POST, Oct. 13, 1985, at A01, *available at* 1985 WL 2090440.

26. *See, e.g.*, *Key Events in Recent Palestinian History*, WASH. POST, Sept. 10, 1993, at A28, *available at* 1993 WL 2099942.

27. *See, e.g.*, Lee Hockstader, *A Holocaust Postscript; Israel to Release Eichmann's Handwritten Defense Argument*, WASH. POST, Aug. 11, 1999, at A14, *available at* 1999 WL 23297575.

28. *See, e.g.*, *The Long Road to Freedom*, TIMES (India), Dec. 17, 2001, *available at* 2001 WL 31420166.

(7) In some circumstances, the Charter system has condoned a state, or states, use of force to alleviate massive wrongs being inflicted by a government on its own people.

-examples include India's liberation of Bangladesh (1971);[30] Tanzania's ouster of Idi Amin (1978);[31] France's ouster of Emperor Bokassa of the Central African Empire (1979);[32] the British, French, and U.S. rescue of Iraqi Kurds (1991);[33] ECOMOG interventions in Liberia and Sierra Leone (1989-99);[34] and NATO action regarding Kosovo (1999).[35]

These are the seven categories of use of force in which the actual practice of the U.N. system has seemed to develop a margin of flexibility in circumstances not envisaged by the Charter. Recognition of such a margin of flexibility, however, must be cautious. The effect of U.N. practice on the law of the Charter has been gradual and is not always readily ascertained. What does emerge, however, is less a new rule than the flexible application of existing rules, in accordance with pragmatic, contextual exigencies and with narrow exceptions for situations of extreme necessity. It is also apparent from the practice of U.N. organs that a state seeking to justify its actions by reference to extreme necessity must be able credibly to demonstrate the circumstances of that necessity, the *bona fides* of its motives, the proportionality of its means, and the reasonablenesses of its objectives. This is why it made sense for the United States, in 2002, to get the Security Council unanimously to reintroduce a tough weapons-inspection regime into Iraq as a necessary exhaustion of available remedies before any resort to force.[36]

We[37] have examined seven categories of justifications offered by states for recourse to force in modalities not strictly in accordance with

29. *See, e.g.*, *World in Brief: Top Greek Diplomat Welcomed in Turkey*, WASH. POST, Oct. 4, 1999, at A18, *available at* 1999 WL 23307196.

30. *See, e.g.*, *Bangladesh: Heavens Above*, ECONOMIST, July 7, 1999, at 38, *available at* 1999 WL 7363895.

31. *See, e.g.*, Michael Kilian, *After the Fall Out-of-Work Despots Don't Always Leave a Forwarding Address when They Go into Forced Retirement*, CHI. TRIB., Sept. 30, 1994, at 1, *available at* 1994 WL 6467719.

32. *See, e.g.*, *id.*

33. *See, e.g.*, Clyde Haberman, *U.S. Military Takes Over Relief for Kurdish Refugees in Iraq*, N.Y. TIMES, Apr. 13, 1991, at A6, *available at* 1991 WL 2096357.

34. *See, e.g.*, Editorial, *A New Approach to Peacekeeping*, CHI. TRIB., July 23, 2000, at 16, *available at* 2000 WL 3688149.

35. *See, e.g.*, *id.*

36. Weapons Inspection Assessment, H.R. Res. 55, 108th Cong. (2003); United Nations Weapons Inspectors, S. Res. 28, 108th Cong. (2003).

37. The author refers to himself in the first person plural throughout this Article, however, all views expressed in this Article are the author's alone.

the Charter. In response to extreme necessity, the Charter evolves as it is applied by the principal U.N. organs. What today may be seen to be the modalities for use of force depends upon how the past is interpreted and the future apprehended.

III. THE "JURYING" FUNCTION

What can be said with some certainty is that the system, to the extent it can summon its political will to action, in future as in the past will still oppose, and raise stakes and costs of, military action taken by states that have not themselves been attacked if they do not first obtain Security Council authorization. Nevertheless, the practice of U.N. organs indicates a significant margin of flexibility in applying that general prohibition to extraordinary facts creating circumstances of extreme necessity. In many instances, the prohibition has been waived in reliance on credible evidence adduced in support of such facts, on the perceived legitimacy of the motives of those resorting to force, on the immediacy and gravity of the crisis an intervention seeks to avert, and on the proportionality and appropriateness of the measures taken.

These are contextual, textured, not absolute or simple, standards. The onus of demonstrating their applicability is on a state seeking to legitimate recourse to force by reference to them. The facts adduced must justify any relaxation of an important general principle. Thus, a state invoking anticipatory self-defense must be able to demonstrate that it faced an imminent and overwhelming attack which would have crippled its capacity to defend itself. A state claiming the right to use force to prevent an imminent human catastrophe in a neighboring state must be able to demonstrate that it has clean hands and no ulterior motives.

These modalities are essentially evidentiary rules. When absolute principles are relaxed to permit nuanced exceptions, it is evidence of the specific contextual facts that becomes crucial. Evidence for and against making an exception is usually adduced by the fact-gathering agencies of national governments and presented by their foreign ministries. The media with global reach also contribute to this important process. A significant contribution can be made by the Secretary-General and other on-the-ground U.N. agencies.[38]

38. There are several examples of the Secretary-General engaging in fact-finding on the basis of the office's independent powers under Charter article 99, or by agreement of the parties to a dispute. In 1983, in the midst of the war between Iran and Iraq, Iran alleged that Iraq had resorted to use of chemical weapons. *Iraq the Dossier—Part 3 Iraq Under Saddam Hussein*, INDEPENDENT (London), Sept. 25, 2002, at P12, *available at* 2002 WL 100759304. In his role as

These agencies' capacity to discharge the crucial fact-finding function has recently been thoroughly examined in the U.N.-sponsored "Brahimi Report,"[39] which emphasized the urgent need for "more effective collection and assessment of information at United Nations Headquarters"[40] and called for "more frequent use of fact-finding missions to areas of tension" under the auspices of the Secretary-General.[41] The problem of inadequate fact-finding, the Report concludes, goes "to the heart of the question" of peacekeeping[42] and, it may be added, of the other uses of force. The U.N. and International Atomic Energy Agency inspectors in Iraq are another example of such fact-finding.[43]

Adducing evidence is different from the process of assessing its weight and credibility: the "jurying" function. In the international system, where is the "jury of peers"?

There are essentially four forums in which such jurying occurs. One is the International Court of Justice. A second is the international political forums, the Security Council and General Assembly.

A third forum for assessing the facts is the court of public opinion, informed and guided by global television, radio and the new force of the internet. A fourth forum is the conference of states in key regional institutions. Although the Court and the media play a powerful role both in gathering and weighing evidence, it is in the collective interstatal decision-making fora of international and regional institutions that representatives of foreign ministries of states have ultimate responsibility for deciding what to make of evidence of varying credibility, probity, and significance. This is the principal locale of the jurying function. It is up to states, collectively, deliberating in agreed processes, to decide whether a case has been made for an exception to the rules intended to control

---

finder of fact and acting on his own authority, the Secretary-General dispatched several missions to the front and was able to confirm that, despite Iraqi denials, such weapons had been used. *Id.* In 1986, New Zealand and France asked the Secretary-General to render a binding opinion on the acrimonious *Rainbow Warrior* dispute. *See Ruling Pertaining to the Differences Between France and New Zealand Arising from the Rainbow Warrior Affair*, 81 AM. J. INT'L L. 325 (Jan. 1987).

39. *Comprehensive Review of the Whole Question of Peacekeeping Operations in All Their Aspects*, U.N. SCOR, 55th Sess., Item 87 of the Provisional Agenda, U.N. Doc. A/55/305-S/2000/809 (2000). This report is also known as the 'Brahimi Report' after the United Nations Peace Operations Chairman, Lakhdar Brahimi. *Id.* at iv. The entire report is currently available at the United Nation's Web page http://www.un.org.

40. *Id.* at 1, ¶ 6(d).

41. *Id.* at 54, Annex III, ¶ 1(b).

42. *Id.* at 6, ¶ 32

43. *See, e.g.*, Nadim Ladki & Irwin Arieff, *UN Tightens Vise on Iraqi Economy: Baghdad Warns of Suffering as U.S. Winds Bid to Extend Sanctions to Drugs, Boats, Trucks*, NAT'L POST, Dec. 31, 2002, at A01, *available at* 2002 WL 104088192.

and inhibit states' recourse to force. The visible manifestations of that inescapable common responsibility is now habitually exercised in large part through the U.N.'s political forums.

When the U.N. political organs are called upon to jury a claim to exemption from the general rules in reliance on a plea of extreme necessity, it can no longer be argued convincingly that the literal letter of the Charter text always controls the verdict. But conversely, it also cannot be argued, on the evidence of state behavior, that the Lauterpachtian "no violence" principle prohibiting state recourse to violence has been repealed in practice and that we are now in an institutional mode of "anything goes." States do not accept that any unilateral, unauthorized use of force in the national interest is acceptable. They do not operate in the belief that there are no rules. They do not agree that facts cannot be distinguished from lies, or humane altruism from greedy self-interest.

For a state seeking to invoke the margin of flexibility, there are hard tests, requiring sophisticated pleading backed by relevant and highly probative evidence: the sort of evidence, for example, the United States could not adduce for its claim to be rescuing its citizens from real danger in Grenada when we invaded in 1983.[44] Harder still is a state's task in marshalling this evidence effectively before the appropriate interstatal organ or organs, the "jury": the sort of thing Secretary of State Colin Powell undertook to do in the Security Council at the beginning of February 2003, in connection with Iraqi arms of mass destruction.[45]

What is evolving is a "jury" of states to decide when an instance of extreme necessity has arisen that justifies recourse to force, by a state or coalition of the willing. The great debate currently underway in this nation pits those willing to submit to such jurying against those insisting on unfettered U.S. discretion to act solely on self-perceived self-interest.

Why would the United States submit to a jury of peers? If we are, indeed, the world's only superpower then it follows that we have no peers and, thus, no reason to submit to peer review our government's judgment as to what constitutes extreme necessity warranting a waiver of the rules against recourse to force.

But are we truly the world's only superpower? Has our government not just acknowledged that, while we may be able to disarm Iraq all by

44. *See, e.g.*, Ed Magnuson, *D-Day in Grenada; The U.S. and Friends Take Over a Troubled Caribbean Isle*, TIME, Nov. 7, 1983, at 22, *available at* 1983 WL 2002316.

45. *See, e.g.*, David S. Cloud & Marc Champion, *Powell Uses Spy Photos, Tapes to Argue Iraq Is Deceiving U.N.*, WALL ST. J., Feb. 6, 2003, at A1, *available at* 2003 WL-WSJ 3958656.

ourselves, we cannot act alone to disarm North Korea?[46] What does that make the government in Pyongyang? The superpower's superpower? Is it not clear that Washington cannot prevail, alone, in almost all of those matters that matter most? It cannot alone achieve nonproliferation. Not in India, not in Pakistan, not in Israel, not in Brazil, not in North Korea. It cannot alone open societies, not even in Myanmar, let alone in China, that resist democratization. It cannot alone prevent climate change. It cannot alone control population growth. It cannot alone contain proliferating diseases. It cannot alone fight terrorism. With others, perhaps. Alone, impossible.

If these and other ends can only be pursued multilaterally, then mechanisms for multilateral action, the "jury," need to be nourished and the jurors assiduously reasoned with, not continually reminded of their power-deficit. Multilateralism is a process of doing for others the kinds of favors you want them to do for you, not reminding them, over and over, that superpowers demand favors, but do not have to bestow them. Thus, when we decide to destroy an international treaty-regime everyone else wants, be it that of a Kyoto round of environmental reforms, or the Rome Treaty establishing an International Criminal Court, we should be aware that such actions may prevail, but that they also have costs in the reciprocal withholding of support by others for initiatives that matter most to us.[47]

The call to submit to jurying our claims to use force in the face of "extreme necessity" thus is a call to modulate, to self-restrain, the so-called "only superpower's" exercise of its option to use force. But even being the only superpower does not mean never having to explain, to justify, to others.

On the contrary. The power of the monopoly superpower depends as much on the voluntary assent of other states as on its military preeminence. Preeminence, in reality, is evanescent and illusory, for our greater ability to inflict pain may be outweighed by others' greater ability to withstand it. Our Vietnam debacle should surely have taught us that. Moreover, Americans will surely sacrifice for a just cause, but that justice is hard to demonstrate to Americans if we utterly fail to demonstrate it to other nations, the "jury of peers."

---

46. *See, e.g.*, *U.S. Calls on Pyonyang to Eliminate Its Nuclear Weapons*, IR. TIMES, Dec. 28, 2002, at P11, *available at* 2002 WL 104539531.

47. *See* Glenn Kessler, *Efforts to Build Iraq Support Are Stymied by Global Resentment*, WALL ST. J. EUR., Feb. 17, 2003, at A2, *available at* 2003 WL-WSJE 3871050; Junn Sung-chull, *Feared but Not Respected*, KOREA HERALD, Apr. 8, 2003, *available at* 2003 WL 5416400.

In other words, the case for jurying is not an appeal to one-world illusion but to national self-interest. The U.N. is not our enemy. The Charter is not an obstacle to doing what needs to be done. The law is not an impediment to necessary action. Together, these are impediments only to the arrogance of power and it is that which is truly our enemy. As Emily Dickinson said, "thyself may be Thine enemy,"[48] or, in *Pogo's* reconfiguration of Admiral Perry, "We has met the enemy, and it is us."[49] It is the illusion of omniscience, the deadly temptation of those who believe they have preeminent power that, constituting hubris, leads to self-inflicted disaster.

In the community of states, as in any civilized society, there is need both for the capacity to act decisively and for institutional checks and balances that compel consideration and reconsideration of a decision to act. The international system is struggling with the need to develop both. It is in the self-interest of the United States to assist, and, surely, not to hinder, that endeavor to balance power with reason.

Adlai Stevenson may have been the one, in the early sixties, to produce the "smoking gun" that convinced the Security Council of the reasons for Washington's power-struggle with Moscow over the enforcement of nuclear missiles in Cuba.[50] But he was also the American, in another context, who cautioned his country: "Don't just do something, sit there!"[51]

The Charter system, as it has evolved, does not paralyze power. Through its system of collective security, it visualizes the deployment of great power for great causes, such as Operation Desert Storm in which many states joined to drive Iraq out of Kuwait in 1990-1991.[52] Now President Bush has said that what the *U.N.* does about Iraq will make or break the Organization. Permit me to rephrase that. What the *United States* does about Iraq, whether it acts with or without the U.N., will determine the future of the system of collective security so carefully crafted after World War II.

The U.N. Charter is not inflexible. It does not paralyze resort to force in situations of extreme necessity. But it cannot accommodate an interpretation of its constitution, the Charter, that leaves it entirely to the

48. Emily Dickinson, *No Rack Can Torture Me*, poem no. 384, stanza 4, *reprinted in* THE COMPLETE POEMS OF EMILY DICKINSON 198-99 (Little, Brown & Co., 1930).

49. Walt Kelly, *Pogo* (comic strip).

50. *See* KENNETH S. DAVIS, THE POLITICS OF HONOR: A BIOGRAPHY OF ADLAI STEVENSON 483-85 (G.P. Putnam's Sons 1967).

51. *See* THE WIT AND WISDOM OF ADLAI STEVENSON 38 (Hawthorn Books, Inc., 1965).

52. *See, e.g.*, Tim Reid & Clem Cecil, *Gulf War General Tells Bush: Don't Go It Alone*, TIMES (London), Aug. 19, 2002, at 14, *available at* 2002 WL 4235162.

discretion of one powerful state to determine whether an extreme necessity exists.

In a world of new and deadly dangers emanating from new kinds of mortal enemies, it is folly to think that America can preempt every potential threat to itself. Its military and moral preeminence can rally the nations in a system of collective security, but only if it shares the responsibility for deciding when necessity calls for action. Or we can act alone, accompanied by, at most, a few "special relationships." What we *cannot* do is *both*: both to use collective security when it suits our purposes, as in the post-conflict regimes in Afghanistan,[53] and be free to deploy unilateral force in other instances. For our repeated recourse to unilateral force would destroy the impetus for others to join in collective measures.

About this we must be clear. If we act to destroy the U.N. system because we have decided that its faults outweigh it merits, what else will take its place except lonely American imperium? There are those who do not fear that trade-off, but I am not among them.

53. *See* Samuel R. Berger, Editorial, *Building Blocks to Iraq*, WASH. POST, Aug. 1, 2002, at A27, *available at* 2002 WL 24824739; Bob Woodward, *A Struggle for the President's Heart and Mind; Powell Journeyed from Isolation to Winning the Argument on Iraq*, WASH. POST, Nov. 17, 2002, at A01, *available at* 2002 WL 102572714.

Name Index

Abbott, Frederick 262
Abbott, Kenneth W. xvi, xvii, 235–53, 257–92
Albright, Madeleine 508
Alter, Karen 268, 274, 283
Amin, Idi 141, 511
Annan, Kofi 470, 508
Anzilotti, Judge 23
Apple, R.W. 448
Arnaldez, Jean-Jacques 389
Auerswald, D. 450
Austin, J.L. 142, 144
Axelrod, Robert 203

Baker, James 448, 484
Baldrige, Malcolm 442
Bauer, Stephan xvii
Bayard, T. 440–41
Benedick, Richard 404
Benz, A. 452
Betts, R. 444
Biermann, Frank xvii
Bokassa, Emperor 511
Borchard, Edwin 38
Boutros Ghali, Boutros 499
Bradley, Bill 448
Brandeis, Justice 7
Brierly, James L. xv, 120, 173
Broches, Aron 393
Brownlie, Ian xiv, 139–46
Buchanan, Pat 316
Bull, Hedley xii, 241, 432
Bush, George H.W. 431, 444–52, 474, 484
Bush, George W. 468–9, 473–4

Caldeira, Gregory 436
Carnot, Nicolas Léonard Sadi 27
Carr, E.H. xi, 190, 349
Casella, Alessandra 374
Cassese, Antonio 433
Castro, Fidel 497
Chang, Patricia M.Y. 433, 437
Charney, Jonathan I. xiii
Charlesworth, Hilary xv
Chayes, Abram xviii, xix, 196, 399–429
Chayes, Antonia Handler xviii, xix, 196, 399–429
Checkel, Jeffrey 438
Cheney, Dick 468
Cheng, Bin 121
Chinkin, Christine xv
Clark, Grenville xi, 100, 459
Claude, Inis 444
Clausewitz, Carl von 253
Clinton, Bill 290
Coase, Ronald 150
Comte, Auguste 6, 26
Cooter, Robert 380
Coplin, William D. xv, 173–92
Corbett, Percy xv, 97, 190
Cortell, Andrew P. xix, 431–58
Corwin, E.S. 445
Cowhey, P. 450
Currie, Brainerd 101

Daniels, Joseph xix
Davey, W.J. 439
Davis, James W. Jr. xix, 431–58
Derains, Yves 389
Dessler, David 433, 452
Deudney, Dan 360
Dickinson, E.D. 40–41
Dickinson, Emily 516
Diehl, P. 436
Doherty, C. 448
Donnelly, J. xv, xvii, 431
Downs, George 201, 327
Doyle, Micheal xii
Duffield, J.S. xvii, xviii, 433
Duguit, L. 29
Dworkin, Ronald 142

Edison, Thomas 27
Ehrlich, Eugen 132
Eichmann, Adolf 510
Ellickson, Robert 410
Elliott, K.A. 440–41

Elster, Jon 410
Erich, Rafael 22
Evangelista, Matthew 438

Falk, Richard A. xiv, xx, 83–101, 481–503
Faraday, Michael 27
Farnsworth, C. 440, 443
Feldman, L. 448
Feliciano, Florentino P. 173
Finlayson, J. 432
Finnemore, Martha xv, xvii, 293–308
Fisher, Roger xv, 86
Fitzmaurice, Gerald 118, 121
Franck, Thomas M. xix–xx, xxi, 197, 199, 246–7, 264–5, 300, 338, 459–77, 505–17
Frieden, J. 444
Friedman, T. 446, 448
Friedmann, Wolfgang 85, 90, 97–8
Fuller, Lon L. 247

Gadbaw, R.M. 441
Galanter, Marc 380
Gamble, John King Jr. 239
Garrett, Geoffrey xvii
George, Alexander 438
Gibson, James 436
Gilligan, Michael J. 313–14
Glennon, Michael 461
Goertz, G. 436
Goldsmith, Jack 461
Goldstein, Judith xvii, 242, 298, 302–3, 305, 309–38
Goshko, J. 447
Gray, John Chipman 9
Grieco, J. 443
Gross, Leo xv, xvii
Grotius, Hugo xii, xiii

Haas, Peter 433
Haggard, S. 431, 438
Hansen, P. 439
Harkin, Tom 448
Harrison, Benjamin 459
Hart, H.L.A. 142–6, 237, 251, 293, 466
Hascher, Domonique 389
Hass, Ernst 98–9
Henkin, Louis xv, xviii, 401
Hertz, Heinrich 27
Heymann, Philip B. 198, 203
Higgins, Rosalyn xiii, 506
Hitler, Adolf 460
Hoffmann, Stanley xv, 98–100
Holland, Thomas Erskine 143
Holmes, Oliver Wendell 415
Howell, T. 441, 452
Huber, Judge 35
Hudec, Robert 328, 334–5
Hudson, Judge Manley O. 7, 22
Hunter, Martin 367, 382
Hurrell, A. 433
Hussein, Saddam 468

Ikenberry, G. John 360, 444

Jackson, John H. xv, 147–69, 439
Jackson, Justice 48
Jarvin, S. 389
Jeffords, James 449
Jellinek, George 9
Jenks, C. Wilfred 85, 92, 97
Jervis, R. 445
Jessup, Philip C. xiii, xv, 23, 29–54
Johnson, Lyndon B. 84, 89

Kaeckenbeeck, Georges 45
Kahler, Miles 266, 303, 306
Kant, Immanuel xi, xii, xiii
Kaplan, Morton A. 85, 99–100, 173
Karadzic, Radovan 498
Katzenbach, Nicholas deB. 85, 99, 173
Kay, David 468
Keck, Margaret E. 287
Kelsen, Hans 6–7, 29, 142
Kennan, George F. xvii, 190
Kennedy Robert 416
Keohane, Robert O. xv, xvi, 193–208, 235–53, 287, 357, 431
Kilborn, P. 440
Kingsbury, Benedict xviii, 339–65
Kirton, John J. xi–xxiii
Kokotsis, Eleonore xix
Kopelmanas, Lazare 121
Koremenos, Barbara 370, 393
Koslowski, Rey 452
Krabbe, H. 29
Krasner, S. xi, 431–2, 445
Kratochwil, Friedrich 194, 198, 410, 431–2, 452
Kupchan, C. 444
Kupchan, C. 444

Lake, D. 443–4
Landa, Janet 380

Lande, Stephen 440
Lasswell, Harold D. 95, 100, 497
Lauterpacht, Hersch xiv, 55–82, 505
Leibniz, Gottfried 27
Lerche, Charles O. 173
Lewis, P. 446
Lincoln, Abraham 353
Lindblom, Charles 426
Lindsay, J. 450
Lipson, Charles 370, 393
Lorimer, James 362
Lugar, Richard 447
Lutz, Ellen L. 264, 284, 305–6

Macaulay, Stuart 381
McDougal, Myres S. xiv, xv, 85, 94–8, 100, 103–38, 173, 497
McElroy, Robert 433
Machiavelli, Niccolò xi, 401
McKeown, T. 438
McNamara, Robert 89
McWhinney, Edward xiii
Madunic, Jelena xi–xxiii
Madariaga, Salvador de 30–31
Maine, H. 106
Malcolm, A. 446
Marconi, Guglielmo 27
Marshall, Chief Justice 36
Martin, Lisa L. xvii, 242, 298, 302–3, 305, 309–38, 431
Mastanduno, M. 443
Mattli, Walter xvii, xviii, 367–95
Maxwell, James Clerk 27
Mendlovitz, Saul 100
Milner, H. 431, 438, 444
Milošević, Slobodan 268, 498
Mitchell, W. 374
Mitrany, David 98
Mitterrand, François 447
Mnookin, Robert 390
Moravcsik, Andrew xvi, 235–53, 287, 289
Morgenthau, Hans J. xi, xiii, 3–27, 173, 190, 353, 444
Morrow, James D. 247
Moynihan, Daniel Patrick 446, 448
Müller, Harald 434, 437
Murphy, Cornelius F. xiii
Myers, James 383

Nadelmann, E. 433
Neill, Brian 389
Newton, Isaac 27
North, Douglas 150
Noyce, Robert 441
Nye, J. 433

O'Neal, John R. xii
O'Shea, T. 442
Olson, Mancur 425
Onuf, N. 431
Oppenheim, Lassa xiii, 9, 339, 342–50, 361–2
Ostrom, Elinor 410

Pace, E. 447
Palmer, Geoffrey, xv, xvii
Pareto, Vilfredo 26
Pastor, R. 434
Paulsson, Jan 382
Pell, Claiborne 447
Perot, Ross 316
Pine, A. 442
Pinochet, Augusto 264
Posner, Eric 461
Powell, Colin 514
Powell, Justice 139
Prestowitz, C. 439–40, 444
Pufendorf, Samuel von xii, 181

Rawding, Nigel 382
Reagan, Ronald 416, 423, 431–2, 439–44
Redfern, Alan 367, 382
Reinhardt, Eric 335
Reinisch, August xix
Reisman, W. Michael xiv, 103–38, 283, 497
Richards, T. 441
Risse-Kappen, Thomas 435–7, 445
Robb, Charles 449
Rocke, David 327
Rocke, Stephen 201
Roessler, Friederich 328
Roosevelt, Franklin D. 353
Roosevelt, Theodore 353
Root, Elihu 459
Rosenthal, A. 447
Ruggie, J.G. xi, 431–2
Rusk, Dean 89
Russett, Bruce M. xii

Said, Abdul A. 173
Salisbury, Lord 51
Salmond, John William 142
Sanford, Terry 446–7

Scelle, Georges 29, 96
Schattschneider, Elmer Eric 314
Schauer, Frederick 410
Schelling, Thomas 401
Schreuer, Christoph xvi, 209–33
Schwartz, Warren F. 328
Schwarzenberger, Georg xv, 36
Sciolino, E. 447
Scowcroft, Brent 448
Setear, John K. 242, 263
Sikkink, Kathryn xv, 264, 284, 287, 305–6
Simmons, Beth xv, xvii, 301–3, 305, 431, 438
Singer, J. David 95
Slater, Richard 391
Slaughter, Anne-Marie xvi, xvii, 194, 235–53, 287
Smith, Ian 141
Smith, J.E. 448
Snidal, Duncan xvi, xvii, 235–53, 257–92, 370, 393
Snyder, Jack 445
Sofaer, Abraham 474
Sohn, Louis B. xi, 100, 459
Solingen, Etel 438
Stanfield, R. 446
Stein, A. 431
Stein, Eric 85
Stevenson, Adlai 516
Stone, Julius 85, 97, 190
Story, Judge 50
Strang, David 433, 437
Suarez, Francisco xii
Sumner, William Graham 26–7
Sykes, Alan 328

Thatcher, Margaret 446–7
Thomas, Daniel 438
Thucydides 469
Toope, Stephen J. xvii, 293–308, 393
Trebilcock, Michael xvi
Trimble, Phillip 197, 199, 404–5
Tyson, L. 439, 442

Van Grasstek, Craig 440
Vattel, Emerich de xii, 181
Verdross, Alfred 50
Vigrass, Bertie 382
Visscher, Charles de 77, 173, 190
Von Furstenberg, George xix

Waldock, Humphrey 139
Waltz, K. 445, 450
Warhol, Andy 469
Weber, Cynthia 295
Weber, Max 403
Webster, Daniel 472
Weil, Prosper xvi, 258, 283
Wendt, A. 431, 452
Wild, Professor 23
Williams, John Fischer 30, 37
Williamson, Oliver 372–3
Wilson, Woodrow xi, 43, 348, 353
Wolfers, A. 444
Wolff, A. 441, 452
Woodward, B. 447–8
Wright, Quincy xv, 27
Wright, Shelley xv

Yarbrough, Beth 373
Yarbrough, Robert 373
Young, Oran xi, 312, 433

Zacher, M. 432

For Product Safety Concerns and Information please contact our EU representative GPSR@taylorandfrancis.com
Taylor & Francis Verlag GmbH, Kaufingerstraße 24, 80331 München, Germany

www.ingramcontent.com/pod-product-compliance
Ingram Content Group UK Ltd.
Pitfield, Milton Keynes, MK11 3LW, UK
UKHW050233200926
475702UK00020B/3018

* 9 7 8 1 1 3 8 3 7 8 4 2 1 *